Education for Sexuality

Concepts and Programs for Teaching

THIRD EDITION

John J. Burt

Professor and Chairman, Department of Health Education
University of Maryland

Linda Brower Meeks

Associate Professor of Health Education, School of Health,
Physical Education and Recreation
The Ohio State University

Illustrations by James C. Brower

Address orders to:
383 Madison Avenue
New York, NY 10017

Address editorial correspondence to:
West Washington Square
Philadelphia, PA 19105

This book was set in Baskerville by University Graphics
The Acquisitions Editors were Edward F. Murphy and John Butler
The Developmental Editor was Leesa K. Massey
The Project Editor was Maureen Iannuzzi
The Copyeditor was Agnes Gruliow
The Art and Design Director was Carol C. Bleistine
The Design Assistant was Virginia A. Bollard
The text design was done by William Boehm
The cover design was done by Lawrence R. Didona
The artwork was drawn by James C. Brower
The Production Manager was Tim Frelick
The Assistant Production Manager was Maureen Iannuzzi

Library of Congress Cataloging in Publication Data

Burt, John J.
    Education for sexuality.

    Bibliography: p.
    Includes index.
        1. Sex instruction.   I. Meeks, Linda Brower.
II. Title.
HQ57.3.B86   1984   612.6'007   84-10928
ISBN 0-03-063214-5

EDUCATION FOR SEXUALITY: CONCEPTS AND PROGRAMS FOR TEACHING, Third Edition   ISBN 0-03-063214-5

567   066   98765432

CBS COLLEGE PUBLISHING
Saunders College Publishing
Holt, Rinehart and Winston
The Dryden Press

For their constant reassurance that the American family is not a dying institution, I dedicate this book to my wife, Ann, and to my children, Eme, Keith, and Joe.

With love and gratitude,

John J. Burt

For their constant creative challenge and stimulation, I dedicate this book to my parents, Jim and Elsie Brower, and to our family, Larry, Sandy, William, Margaret, Billy, Meg, Beth, and Ralph.

For her love and support, I dedicate this book to my daughter, Kristen Meeks.

During the writing of the Third Edition, my secretary's daughter was sexually abused and murdered. Her tragic death inspired me to write the first grade unit "Love, Responsibility, and Making Choices," which discusses ways to protect children from persons who may harm them. I dedicate this book to the memory of Kelly Prosser and to the prevention of similar tragedies.

With love and gratitude,

Linda B. Meeks

About the Authors

John Burt has been professor and chairman of the Department of Health Education at the University of Maryland for the past fourteen years. Recognized as the Scholar of the Year in his profession in 1980, Dr. Burt is the author of three books and numerous research papers. A former president of the Association for the Advancement of Health Education, he has lectured widely throughout the country. His main interests, in addition to sex education, are philosophy and metahealth. Dr. Burt has served on the editorial board of a number of journals and has received the Honor Award of the American Alliance for Health, Physical Education, Recreation and Dance. He is a member of the national leadership honor society, Omicron Delta Kappa. Dr. Burt is married to Ann Gillett and they are the parents of three college students, Eme, Keith, and Joe. A member of the American Academy of Physical Education and a former Fellow of the American College of Sports Medicine, John Burt is an avid cyclist.

Linda Meeks is an Associate Professor of Health Education at The Ohio State University. She is noted for her expertise in teacher training and in curriculum design. Professor Meeks has taught the curriculum found in *Education for Sexuality* throughout the United States. She has used the foreign editions—Portuguese, Spanish, Japanese, French, and Italian—to train teachers overseas. Meeks is the co-author with Dr. Phil Heit of *Human Sexuality: Making Responsible Decisions,* Philadelphia: Saunders College Publishing, 1982. Meeks and Heit are also co-authors of the Charles E. Merrill *Health: Focus On You K–12* textbook series. The series includes five booklets: *Family Living* (Grades 2–4), *Strangers* (Grades 2–4), *Family Living and Human Reproduction* (Grades 5–8), *Sexually Transmitted Diseases* (Grades 5–8), and *Aging, Dying and Death,* (Grades 5–8). These materials have been integrated into the Scope and Sequence Chart found in Chapter 13. Meeks and Heit have taught the *Education for Sexuality* Scope and Sequence Chart K–12 in the United States, Greece, Jordan, and Egypt.

Preface

The Third Edition of *Education for Sexuality* adds a new dimension to the study of human sexuality. The text continues to provide updated biological information about human sexuality based on the latest scientific research findings. However, the Third Edition adds to the biological focus a special focus on the importance of responsibility in human relationships. A new Chapter 12, "Intimacy, Marriage, and Parenthood," discusses issues that need examination prior to making decisions that affect the lifestyle of oneself and others. The role of commitment in relationships is explored.

The Third Edition, like its predecessors, is a textbook for teachers. The first three sections of the book are designed to acquaint the teacher or future teacher with basic information and concepts related to sexuality. In Section Four, the *Education for Sexuality:* Scope and Sequence K–12 Curriculum is presented. A new Chapter 13, "Planning The Sex Education Curriculum," outlines the procedures for developing, implementing, and evaluating an effective sex education program. The chapter contains an *Education for Sexuality:* Scope and Sequence Chart for the K–12 curriculum. This field tested Scope and Sequence Curriculum has been duplicated and used by school systems throughout the world as a graded course of study. The remaining chapters in Section Four include detailed teaching units for the various grade levels. The teaching units in the Third Edition of *Education for Sexuality* have an added emphasis on responsibility in relationships. Teaching units on "Love, Responsibility, and Making Choices," "Friendship," "Making Responsible Decisions," and "Friendship, Dating, and Decision Making" were added at age appropriate grade levels. A new Chapter 22, "Suggested Bibliography and Films for Sex Education," provides a list of helpful resources.

Education for Sexuality was conceived, written, and designed by teachers for teachers who want to teach students responsible sexuality.

John Burt

Linda Meeks

Acknowledgments

We are most grateful to our editors, Leesa Massey and John Butler, for the many helpful suggestions that attended the preparation of the Third Edition.

A special thank you is given to Barbara Lynch for her work on the revision of this manuscript. Dr. Dennis Smith is appreciated for developing the "Suggested Bibliography and Films for Sex Education" that appears in Chapter 22.

The Third Edition of *Education for Sexuality* includes a new focus on relationships and a field tested Scope and Sequence Curriculum K–12. We are grateful to Dr. Phil Heit, co-author of *Health: Focus On You* and Associate Professor at The Ohio State University, for his curriculum contributions.

We are also grateful to our colleagues who reviewed and/or field tested materials used in our K–6 and 7–12 curriculums.

Mr. Michael Schaeffer, Prince George's County Schools, Upper Marlsboro, Maryland

Ms. Flo Ripley, Health Coordinator, Upper Arlington Schools, Upper Arlington, Ohio

Dr. Donald Hawk, Associate Professor of Health Education, The University of Cincinnati, Cincinnati, Ohio

Ms. Mary Alice Beetham, Health Education Curriculum Consultant, Columbus, Ohio

Dr. David Corbin, School of Health, Physical Education, and Recreation, University of Nebraska at Omaha

Mr. Robert Holland, former Assistant Director, Division of Elementary and Secondary Education, Ohio Department of Education, Columbus, Ohio

Mr. Braxton Tewart, Chairman for the committee that wrote the *Guidelines for Improving School Health Education K–12,* Ohio Lung Association, Columbus, Ohio

Dr. Glen Gilbert, Office of Disease Prevention, Department of Health and Human Services, Washington, D.C.

Ms. Tonee Bowsher, Elementary School Classroom Teacher, Menominee Schools, Menominee, Michigan

We are grateful to our typists, Norma Lind and Mary McKnight, for their diligent work on the completion of this manuscript. We are also thankful to the following colleagues who gave us detailed comments on the entire manuscript: Dr. James H. Price, The University of Toledo; Dr. Robert J. McDermott, Southern Illinois University at Carbondale; Dr. William L. Yarber, Purdue University; and Dr. Sherman L. Brooks, Fayetteville State University.

Contents

Section 4

Educational Aspects of Human Sexuality

SECTION 1

Introduction to Sex Education

CHAPTER 1

Sex Education as Education for Love

Love is the only satisfactory answer to the problem of human existence.

Eric Fromm
The Art of Loving

Assuming good health for yourself and others, what is the one situation that you would least like to encounter in life? Whether you are a college student or a college professor, a middle-aged adult or a retired senior citizen, a wealthy individual or a prisoner hardened to physical brutality, the answer to this question is likely to be the same: "I would dread social isolation most." Fortunately, complete social isolation is not a realistic threat for most of us, and the current population growth makes this even less likely in the future. On the other hand, each of us fights a personal battle, attempting to overcome our feelings of aloneness in the midst of a world of billions. In fact, history is a record of the human struggle with aloneness—of individuals' and entire peoples' attempts to gain recognition and appreciation, to belong, to be more than just chemical and physical processes, and to find themselves.

The time-tested antidote for a feeling of estrangement is the establishment of a sense of connectedness between one's self and the universe through deep and lasting relationships with other human beings, through ideas that are meaningful, and through a sense of purpose in life. Worthy guidelines for establishing those connections are transferred culturally from older members of the family, from religion, from schools, and even from public law. In time, a person also learns by trial and error.

The connectedness of individuals with one another is the focus of sex education. Three categories of relationships are possible: male–female relationships, male–male relationships, and female–female relationships. Each of these relationships may be maintained on a psychic basis (no physical expression) or may involve sexual expressions. When the male–female relationship includes sexual expression or desire for sexual expression, it is termed a heterosexual relationship; when male–male or female–female relationships involve sexual expression or desire for such expression, they are termed homosexual relationships. But whether the relationship is maintained on a purely psychic, heterosexual, or homosexual basis, the motivation is the same—to prevent, relieve, or counteract feelings of aloneness.

Psychiatry suggests that deep and abiding social relationships capable of counteracting aloneness must be permeated by love and that those social relationships not accompanied by love are likely to accentuate feelings of aloneness. Accordingly, love becomes the primary weapon against the major human problem of aloneness. As Dr. Erich Fromm, a world-famous psychoanalyst, expresses it:

"Love is the only satisfactory answer to the problem of human existence."[1]

Because sexual relationships are intimate forms of social relationships, we believe that the primary goal of sex education should be the integration of human love with human sexuality.

Definitions of Love

Integrating human love and human sexuality, however, is rendered difficult by the fact that definitions of love are variable and apparently ever-changing. Historically the word "love" has been used in at least four senses.[2] The first is sex or **libido.** The second, **eros,** is the drive to procreate or create; it is the urge toward higher forms of being and relationships. The third, **philia,** is friendship or "brotherly" love. The fourth love is directed toward the welfare of people—a more general type of love. The Greek word for this type of love was **agape.** All human love blends these four types of love in varying degrees. The motivations for erotic love and humanitarian love may be the same or different. Differences are highly important in terms of the effectiveness of a relationship in overcoming human estrangement. Fromm[3] points out:

> If the desire for physical union is not stimulated by love, if erotic love is not also brotherly love, it never leads to union in more than an orgiastic, transitory sense. Sexual attraction creates, for the moment, the illusion of union, yet without love this union leaves strangers as far apart as they were before—sometimes it makes them hate each other, because when the illusion has gone they feel their estrangement even more markedly than before.

When we suggest that the goal of sex education should be the integration of love and sexuality, we are talking about the universal desire for nonexploitative relationships. A complete discussion of this type of love is beyond the scope of this book, but we will briefly answer two questions:

1.   What is the nature of love?
2.   Why is love important?

What Is the Nature of Love?

Contrary to popular opinion, there is much agreement about the nature of love. Surveys of college students by us and by others reveal that the majority agree on the nature of love. Four definitions or descriptions of love approach a common theme.

---

[1]Eric Fromm, *The Art of Loving* (New York: Bantam Books, 1963), p. 6. (First published by Harper & Row, 1956.)

[2]Rollo May, *Love and Will* (New York: W. W. Norton, 1969), pp. 37–38.

[3]Eric Fromm, op. cit., p. 46.

Alexander Magoun[4] has defined love as:

> . . . the passionate and abiding desire on the part of two or more people to produce together the conditions under which each can be and spontaneously express his real self; to produce together an intellectual soil and an emotional climate in which each can flourish (that is) far superior to what either could achieve alone.

Paul Bohannan[5] notes that love is not selfless:

> Like "life" in general, love embodies what appears to be a contradiction: the satisfaction of the self through the satisfaction of the needs and desires of others.

> Far from being selfless, love provides a double satisfaction—even a triple satisfaction—to the self: once to the self because you can love and are loving; once to the self when love is reciprocated and you are loved; and once to the self because you know that, since you are loving and being loved, you must have a lovable self. When it is all there, you are well and truly "locked in." Nobody wants out.

Dr. Joseph Trainer[6] comments on the ability to love:

> The ability to love is the capacity to escape the self-containment of one's own ego and seek instead to nourish another. A person with this ability well developed is able to give love freely to someone else. In its best example it is like a floodlight. The more energy put into it, the more people it can light or warm. In turn, more light and warmth shed back on the giver, and it is characteristic of those with this ability to be as able to receive as to give. In their general relation to the world, they are giving, outgoing, friendly people, those who reach out automatically to the world around them.

About love First Corinthians states:

> Love is patient and kind; love is not jealous or boastful; it is not arrogant or rude. Love does not insist on its own way; it is not irritable or resentful. . . .

The central theme of these definitions and descriptions is that to love is to be in an active state of concern about those whom one loves; in turn, this state of concern provides a climate in which both the loved one and the lover can flourish.

Why Is Love Important?

Motivation for human behavior is a function of the entire nervous system, not of any particular portion; however, two components appear to dominate human behavior. First, there remains, as a part of evolutionary heritage, an old brain, the animal brain that appears to be concerned with the affective nature of sensory sensations such as pleasure and pain. Anatomically, it is referred to as the hypothalamus. If electrodes are implanted in certain plea-

---

[4]F. Alexander Magoun, *Love and Marriage* (New York: Harper & Row, 1948), p. 4.

[5]Paul Bohannan, *Love, Sex and Being Human* (New York: Doubleday and Co., 1970), p. 107.

[6]Joseph Trainer, *Physiologic Foundations of Marriage Counseling*, (St. Louis: C. V. Mosby, 1965), p. 10.

sure centers of the old brain in such a way that an experimental animal can stimulate its own hypothalamus ad libitum, the animal may initiate stimulation as often as 4000 times per hour, thus forfeiting opportunities for food and other distractions. Further experimentation has also located the principal centers for pain, punishment, and escape in the hypothalamus. Second, the most recently evolved brain and the factor that most differentiates humans from other animals, is the cerebral cortex. The cerebral cortex covers the hypothalamus like a skullcap; it appears to be the thinking and reasoning brain.

Most of us seem to have an almost constant struggle between the old and new brains. The old brain says, "Satisfy your needs and appetites right now and never mind the consequences to others." It is completely self-centered. But the cortex says, "If you only satisfy your own chemical and physical processes, you are not too different from a plant, a tree, or a bacterium." This description of the self is not acceptable to the cortex, which appears to be very sensitive about worthwhileness. The cortex can reason. If humans were only chemical and physical processes, there would be little need for a cerebral cortex. We sometimes refer to individuals whose cerebral cortices have been damaged as "vegetables." While this is unkind, it is nevertheless rather descriptive. It must be noted, therefore, that the cortex has a vested interest in our being worthwhile humans.

The desire to be more than just a series of chemical and physical processes or to be more worthwhile is the motivation for love. In the practice of love the lover expresses concern for the loved one:

> What does one person give to another? He gives of himself, of the most precious he has, he gives of his life. This does not necessarily mean that he sacrifices his life for the other—but that he gives him of that which is alive in him; he gives him of his joy, of his interest, of his understanding, of his knowledge, of his humor, of his sadness—of all expressions and manifestations of that which is alive in him.[7]

Love is the ability to escape self-containment and the activity of the cerebral cortex. It is not a passion of the old brain, which is completely self-contained. The decision to love is a cortical decision to do something more than just spend one's life satisfying one's chemical and physical processes. It is the decision to help others, to be worthwhile, and thereby to increase others' and one's own happiness.

Unless we escape self-containment by doing something for others, we are parasites depending on something not our own for existence or support without making a useful or adequate return. Human dignity is lost; we remain a lower animal. Loss of human dignity is traumatic to the cerebral cortex. Having become "thingified" or reduced to the animalistic functions of the old brain, the cortex may react in a defensive and immature way. It may even suggest suicide. Some examples may help to bring the problem into clear focus. A well-known and beautiful motion picture star may feel "thingified" because of the public's acceptance of her only as a sex symbol and not as a total person. Suicide may be her final decision. In like manner, if a victim of a long-term illness considers himself a parasitic burden to others and loses sight of his individual worth, he may contemplate suicide. Or a person who has exploited others for individual gain may in time come to consider himself

---

[7]Fromm, op. cit., p. 20.

repulsive. In the United States, approximately 56 people commit suicide per day. Most of these suicides are an expression by the cortex of a person's not being worthwhile. Another possible response of an offended cortex may be withdrawal into mental illness. A less drastic response may be temporary escape by means of drugs, alcohol, obsession with work, or even war.

In summary, the newly evolved cerebral cortex gives an individual the innate desire to be worthwhile, to be more than a chemical and physical process, to escape self-containment, and to be a part of something long-lasting. Thus, the need to be loved and to love has evolved.

However, love did not evolve as a selfless attribute. Too many people have the mistaken notion that to love is to be self-sacrificing, and this attitude prevents them from being loving people. To give of what is alive in one's self, to express one's talents, and to contribute freely to mankind should not be viewed as a sacrifice for others but rather as a necessity for personal sanity. To love is to reap a personal gain. It appears to be the only satisfactory answer to human existence.

Integration of Love and Sexual Behavior

As the reasoning center of the brain, the highly developed cerebral cortex provides the human being with a unique facility: the ability to profit from the compromises and mistakes of history. Thus, the sex educator can identify problematic sexual behavior with a view toward its improvement.

The history of sexual behavior reveals that the most recurrent mistake and the one most destructive of human happiness has been the failure to integrate love and sexual behavior. For example, in the 12th century love was viewed as the spiritualization and sublimation of carnal desire; consequently, a combined love and sexual relationship between man and wife was considered impossible. Marriages were arranged on an economic basis, and unfulfilled love desires were channeled into codes and causes that men pursued. In time, this concept of psychic love (without physical expression) gave way to the highly emotional love of Romanticism. Hugo G. Beigel[8] writes: "The Romanticist rebelled against the progressing dehumanization, the all-devouring materialism and rationalism, and sought escape from these dangers in the wonders of the emotions." The Romanticists reacted against the mistakes of earlier centuries and dropped love's cloak of sublimation. But the notion that love and sexuality in marriage were irreconcilable continued. Until the end of the 18th century, romantic love was carried on outside of marriage. Not until the 19th century was love considered a prerequisite to marriage. And even then, love and sex remained somewhat dissociated; that is, sex as an expression of love or for any reason other than reproduction was typically considered sinful. It was finally in the 20th century that people bravely claimed that sex was for pleasure as well as reproduction and that both aspects belonged within a relationship based on love.

The relevance of his conclusion for today's world is attested to by the observation that deviations from this concept are continually being recognized as problematic behavior (behavior that is not in the best interest of either the individual or society).

---

[8]Hugo G. Beigel, "Love: Courtly, Romantic, and Modern," *Selected Studies in Marriage and the Family,* ed. Robert F. Winch and Robert McGinnis (New York: Henry Holt, 1953), p. 350.

For example, in the middle of the 20th century, even Sweden had second thoughts about its sexual philosophy, and a conference of 200 of Sweden's most prominent physicians asked the nation to reconsider its free-and-easy sex morals. The Soviet Union has concluded that its experiences with free love were problematic. Their publication *Soviet Education* concedes the mistake in these words: "Such practices [free love] necessarily lead to a laxity and vulgarization of relationships unworthy of man, cause difficult personality problems, unhappiness and disruption of the family, making orphans of the children." Today, in fact, the Soviets condemn in other cultures sexual behavior they once defended in their own. More recently in the United States, Dr. William Masters and Virginia Johnson noted that the pendulum may have swung too far toward sex without commitment.[9] Indeed, it has come to be big business to make people believe they must be preoccupied with sex. Even psychotherapy seems to have overemphasized the role of sex.

Through society's trials and errors and reactions to previously restricting mores, however, we may have gained an understanding of the different needs and preferences for sex in the individual's life. A current finding is that people do not need or even want sex as much as they are made to think they do.[10] In a 1980 publication, Brown[11] describes a trend she calls "the new celibacy" in which other satisfactions in life may diminish or temporarily subdue sexual desire and activities. This state is seen as normal and healthy, often a byproduct in the self-actualized individual and often occurring when an individual's capabilities to love and express love are expanding in other ways.

Sex Education as Education for Love

Eric Fromm[12] has skillfully dissected love into four constituent parts:

1. Labor—meaning that one is willing to work for and give of one's self for the loved ones.

2. Responsibility—meaning that one constantly evaluates the consequences of personal behavior as it relates to others and stands prepared to help when one is needed by loved ones.

3. Respect—meaning that one refrains from exploitation of others, avoids coaction in which one benefits at the expense of the other.

4. Understanding—meaning that one tries to "stand in the shoes of another."

Sex education as education for love attempts to clarify these four constituents of love as they relate to sexual behavior.

Labor. With respect to this component, sex education has a twofold function: to point out the inconsistency in behavior of those who say they love but are unwilling to give of themselves for the person they profess to love and to expose the differences between real love and exploitative sexual love.

Responsibility. Sex education should provide the knowledge that will enable the student to evaluate and effectively handle the consequences of sexual behavior. Thus, a major portion of this book is designed to acquaint the reader

---

[9]*Newsweek* (May 14, 1973), p. 63.

[10]John Gagnon, Wm. Simon, *Sexual Conduct: The Social Sources of Human Sexuality* (Hawthorne, New York: Aldine Pub., 1973).

[11]Gabriele Brown, *The New Celibacy* (New York: Random House, 1980).

[12]Fromm, op. cit., p. 22.

with the biological, sociocultural, psychological, and physical consequences of various types of sexual behavior.

Respect. In the total realm of interpersonal relationships, probably the greatest temptation to exploit another human being is through sexual behavior. Accordingly, this book includes chapters devoted to the ethical aspects of human sexuality.

Understanding. Sex education, to be effective, should constantly remind the student that mature love must be sensitive not only to the wishes and desires of the other person but also, whenever possible, to the motivations that underlie these wishes and desires. Put another way, mature love suggests that you try to "put yourself in the shoes of the other sex" and thus gain a better understanding of sexuality as viewed from the opposite side. Such understanding is best developed through carefully planned sex education that begins with parents and is a part of the curriculum at every age or grade level. Such a program constitutes the second half of this book.

Sex Versus Sexuality

A systematic and orderly body of knowledge about the biological aspects of sex and reproduction has been available for many years; however, this body of knowledge has only slowly been accepted in the school curriculum because somehow "it didn't seem right to talk about sex as a chemical and physical process." In the past, therefore, reproductive physiology was a kind of mystery for the average student, and parents were content to keep it that way. Even medical schools only taught the basic knowledge about childbirth and contraception. Today one hears the comment that Masters and Johnson[13] were only studying chemical and physical processes (the intent of the statement being to imply that such studies do not dignify sex but are only of physiological interest). It would thus appear that if sex education is to be widely accepted, it must be more than a course in biology—it must be education for love. But since love is most effectively practiced in full view of biological consequences, sex education cannot ignore detailed biological facts. To represent this fuller context and content of sex-linked behavior, we use the word **sexuality.** As Dr. George Berry, former Dean of Harvard Medical School, writes:

> Its use . . . to connote the totality of being and the expression of maleness or femaleness, in place of the word "sex" with its implied restriction to an act, appears to be the touchstone that is freeing people to contemplate this universal characteristic of life with greater openness and composure, and in much greater depth, than has heretofore been possible."

Sexuality is a tent that encloses the biological, psychological, sociocultural, and ethical aspects of human sexual behavior. We recommend that sex education be approached in this context.

Getting Started in Sex Education

If you experience a feeling of inadequacy or apprehension as you ponder teaching your first class in sex education, don't despair—your feelings are not justified. Chances are that you already know more about sexuality than you

---

[13]William Masters and Virginia Johnson, *Human Sexual Response* (Boston: Little, Brown and Co., 1966).

do about astronomy, meteorology, electricity, or other topics that stimulate student discussion. You would not be embarrassed to look up an answer to a question related to one of these topics or to obtain a book written for the comprehension level of your class. Why not adopt the same attitude toward sexuality? Your relaxed and confident attitude will set the tone for the students in your classes.

The key to a relaxed and effective approach to sex education is confidence on the part of the teacher. There are two steps in the attainment of such confidence

Step One: Confidence Through Knowledge

Knowledge is the basic antidote for fear. Thus the first step is acquisition of biological, sociological, and psychological knowledge about sexuality. Biological knowledge takes the mystery out of human sexuality and helps you to deal with the topic as you would with other functions of the human body. Sociological data provide you with a knowledge of how people use their sexuality, and psychology attempts to explain why people behave the way they do sexually. As you study the chapters that follow, your confidence will leap upward as you increase your knowledge of sexuality, of how it is used, and of why it is used in these ways.

Step Two: Confidence Through Philosophical Assurance

Although knowledge greatly increases your confidence, it is not enough. Complete confidence can be gained only by a feeling that "what I am doing is really right." And such a feeling can come only when you have developed a sound philosophy and have related sexuality to that philosophy. This, of course, is a step that you must take for yourself, but the philosophical positions presented in this book may serve as a catalyst.

SECTION 2

The Biological Aspects of Human Sexuality

CHAPTER 2

The Biological Male

To understand the male we must dissect him not only with the scalpel of the anatomist, but also with the more blunt tools of psychology and sociology. This chapter, however, is limited to the biological aspects of maleness.

The Male Reproductive System

Very early in prenatal life special sex cells are set aside from the other cells of the body. These calls organize into a group of cells known as gonads, which develop into testes in the male.

Gonads

The testes begin to evolve about the seventh or eighth week of fetal development.

Testes

Initially, they develop in the abdominal cavity at a level just below the upper border of the hip bone. During the eighth and nine months of fetal life, the testes stimulated by their own testosterone secretion normally leave the pelvic cavity and move downward.

Early Development of the Testes

They are guided through a tunnel-like passageway in the abdominal cavity into a sac-like container outside the body cavities (Fig. 1). The tunnel is the inguinal canal; the sac is the scrotum.

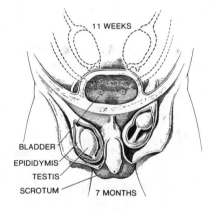

Figure 1   Descent of testes.

After the testes pass through the inguinal canal, this tunnel closes to prevent other tissues from descending into the scrotum. Thus the inguinal canal is partly or totally obliterated in 80 percent of infants over two months of age. If the inguinal canal fails to close or for some reason opens again, some of the other contents of the abdominal cavity may pass into this tunnel-like passageway. An unclosed inguinal canal can also lead to the return of one or both testes to the abdominal cavity.

The testes are found in the scrotum at birth in 96 percent of fully mature infants. For the prematurely born, the corresponding figure is 70 percent. But among those born with undescended testes, 50 percent descend normally after birth.

If the testes do not descend into the scrotum, sperm cannot be produced and the male is sterile. The medical name for the condition in which the testes do not descend is cryptorchidism, usually caused by abnormally formed testes that cannot secrete enough testosterone. In this condition, it is possible to relocate the testes by surgery and thus render the male fertile.

Cryptorchidism

Protrusion of the contents of one of the body's cavities through an abnormal opening in the cavity wall is termed herniation (Fig. 2). Hernia may occur anywhere in the body, but the male is especially susceptible to hernia through the inguinal canal.

In inguinal hernia a loop of intestine sometimes descends through the inguinal canal. Such cases are potentially hazardous because of the possibility of strangulation of the blood supply to the intestine. For this reason, hernia usually requires surgical correction.

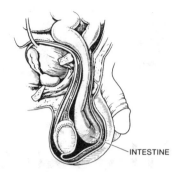

Figure 2   Hernia.

Functions of the Scrotum

The scrotum has two main functions:

1. To contain the testes.
2. To regulate temperature of the testes.

The testes are located in the scrotum because sperm cannot be effectively produced at body temperature. Sperm are most effectively produced when the temperature in the testes is 1.5 to 2°C below body temperature. Thus temperature is a critical factor for normal function of the testes.

The scrotum has two major mechanisms for regulating temperature:

Cremasteric Muscles

1. It contains many sweat glands and sweats freely.
2. It contains muscles (cremasteric muscles) that contract and bring the testes closer to the body to increase temperature and relax to lower the testes away from the body and thus reduce temperature (Fig. 3).

The two testes are approximately equal in size (2 × 1 × 1¼ inches). Usually, the left testis hangs somewhat lower than the right. The weight of the testes tends to lessen in old age.

The two major functions of the testes during the normal sequence of male growth and development are:

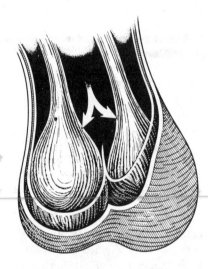

1. To produce several male sex hormones, known collectively as androgens.
2. To produce sperm.

Figure 3   Cremasteric muscles.

Both these functions remain dormant during the early years of male life. Physiologists are not sure just how the two functions of the testes are initiated, but the available evidence suggests that it happens as follows.

When the male is about ten years old, the hypothalamus releases a poorly identified hormone, which flows through a special system of blood vessels to the anterior pituitary gland.

Hormonal Stimulation

The anterior pituitary gland, in turn, sends out "gonad stimulating hormones" called gonadotropic hormones. These gonadotropic hormones pass by way of the circulatory system to the testes where they stimulate production of male sex hormones and sperm.

Hormones play an important role in human sexuality. Indeed, hormones are the direct cause of anatomical maleness and femaleness. In addition, they have

Hormones and Their Importance

medicinal uses as contraceptives, as promoters of fertility, and as therapy for the aging. However, these uses are accompanied by risks as well as benefits.

In studying the male, we shall limit our discussion to three hormones: luteinizing hormone (LH) and follicle-stimulating hormone (FSH), both produced by the pituitary gland and also known as gonadotropic hormones, and testosterone, produced by the testes.

Male Hormones

Testosterone—the primary male sex hormone—is formed by the interstitial cells (Fig. 4) of Leydig in the seminiferous tubules. Interstitial cells are numerous in the newborn infant and in the adult after puberty; at both times the testes secrete large amounts of testosterone in proportion to the amount of LH available. Testosterone is responsible for the development of the male reproductive system—the penis, scrotum, prostate gland, seminal vesicles, and genital ducts.

Testosterone

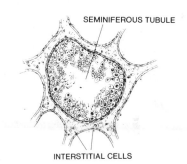

Figure 4   Seminiferous tubules and interstitial cells.

Testosterone secretion after puberty causes the penis, the scrotum, and the testes to enlarge about eight-fold until the age of 20.

When testosterone is released into the blood it is also the primary cause of secondary male sex characteristics (Fig. 5):

1. Longer and heavier bones.

2. Larger muscles.

3. Thicker and tougher skin (which during adolescence may close over the openings of sebaceous glands [oil glands], causing pimples).

4. Deep voice.

5. Distribution of body hair.

6. Development of pubic hair with a triangular border.

7. Baldness in later life.

8. Increased metabolism.

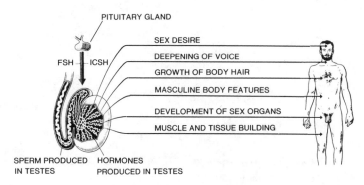

Figure 5   Male secondary sex characteristics.

Luteinizing hormone is produced by the pituitary gland. LH stimulates a special group of cells in the testes called interstitial cells, which produce testosterone. When first discovered in the male, this hormone was called interstitial cell-stimulating hormone (ICSH). Later it was found to be identical with LH in the female, and the term is now used to refer to the hormone in both sexes.

LH

The second pituitary hormone is called follicle-stimulating hormone. This hormone initiates sperm production in the male and maturation of ova in the female. In the male, FSH is responsible for the conversion of primary spermatocytes into secondary spermatocytes, but testosterone is necessary for final maturation of the spermatozoa.

FSH

The name FSH seems a bit inappropriate in referring to the male (follicles are found in ovaries). The explanation for the name is that the hormone was discovered first in the female.

Because male sex hormones may increase weight, endurance, and aggressiveness, some athletic coaches have attempted to use them to improve performance. There are two reasons this practice should be avoided:[1]

Sex Hormones and Physical Performance

1. There is no evidence that hormones actually improve performance.

2. The hormonal pills used for this purpose may cause:
   a. Shrinking of the testicles.
   b. Loss of sex drive.
   c. Dizziness.
   d. Muscle aches.
   e. Liver damage.

Sudden absence of testicular hormone causes most males to lose some of their vigor, spontaneous energy output, and sense of well-being. Also, experiments with rats clearly indicate that castration reduces spontaneous activity of these animals to a very low level.

Sperm production occurs in about 300 sections of microscopic tubes located in the testes and known as seminiferous tubules (Fig. 6). Uncoiled, this network of tubes would extend about 800 feet. These seminiferous tubules are stimulated to produce sperm by FSH, but final maturation of the immature sperm also requires testosterone.

Spermatogenesis

Spermatogenesis begins at about 12 years of age, but first ejaculation of mature sperm usually occurs at about 13 years and ten months.

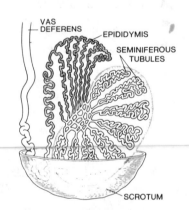

Figure 6   The testis, epididymus, and vas deferens.

The spermatogonium is the earliest form in the development of a mature spermatozoon (Fig. 7). The spermatogonium develops in the cells lining the outer wall of the seminiferous tubules. It is thought that these sustentacular cells secrete nutritional substances for the developing sperm. As these cells grow they move toward the center of the tubules. As the spermatogonium grows it moves into the first stage of sperm development: a primary spermatocyte (Fig. 7[1]). The primary spermatocyte then divides to form two sec-

The Process of Spermatogenesis

---

[1]Statement by The Joint Committee on the Medical Aspects of Sports, American Medical Association.

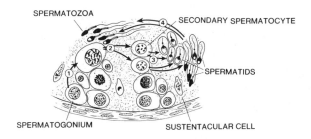

Figure 7   Sperm development.

ondary spermatocytes (Fig. 7[2]). As the secondary spermatocytes move toward the center of the seminiferous tubules, they divide into two spermatids (Fig. 7[3]). The spermatid, in turn, reorganizes its nucleus to form a compact head and becomes a mature spermatozoon (Fig. 7[4]).

In summary, spermatogenesis is a process whereby small cells contained in the lining of the seminiferous tubules are stimulated by hormonal substances to grow into mature sperm that are released into tube-like passageways. Sperm formation requires about 74 days and is not affected by sexual activity.

Factors That Affect Spermatogenesis

Numerous environmental factors affect spermatogenesis. *Stress* will reduce spermatogenesis. Studies during wartime have demonstrated that bomber crews flying six- to eight-hour strikes for 50 missions became relatively infertile.

High altitude also appears to reduce spermatogenesis: Andean miners have for many years made a trip down the mountain to regain their fertility.

Radiation may inhibit or completely block spermatogenesis.

Temperature can increase or inhibit spermatogenesis.

Immersion of the testes into very hot water may produce temporary sterility, but this seems to be a transitory effect. On the other hand, enclosing the scrotum in ice for one-half hour daily may increase the sperm count by 10 percent in some males. After a prolonged fever, sperm production may be reduced for as long as two months.

Occupations that cause the scrotum to be bound up close to the body for many continuous hours may impair sperm production—for example, long-distance truck driving. Men working near blast furnaces have a high incidence of defective spermatogenesis.

Continual compression of the testes by tight underwear (knitted briefs) or athletic supports definitely reduces the output of sperm.

Testicular Cancer[2]

Testicular cancer is diagnosed in approximately 5,300 persons each year, and although it accounts for no more than 1 percent of all cancers among males, it is one of the most frequently occurring types of cancer in adolescence and early adulthood.

Testicular cancer appears to be more frequent when the testes don't descend properly, following trauma, and after infection of the testes by the mumps

---

[2]For an excellent article for teachers see: Phillip J. Marty and Robert J. McDermott, "Teaching about Testicular Cancer and Testicular Self-Examination," *Journal of School Health,* 53 (1983), pp. 351–356.

virus. In animals it has been experimentally produced by the exposure of rats to cadmium chloride and of hamsters to zinc chloride. Despite these observations, the actual cause(s) of testicular cancer are poorly understood.

Because the testes are easily accessible, self-examination for signs of abnormalities is possible. The American Cancer Society[3] recommends the following procedure: place the index and middle fingers on the underside of the testis with the thumb on top; roll éach testis between the fingers to feel lumps or changes in size; repeat the procedure monthly. Report any lumps or changes to a physician.

Testicular Self-Examination (TSE)

Additional signs and symptoms of testicular cancer may include:

Signs and Symptoms

1. A dull ache or pain in the testes.

2. Back pain.

3. Breast enlargement with increased pigmentation of nipples.

4. Sexual indifference.

5. Decreased libido.

After their production in the testis, sperm must pass through the penis and into the female vagina in order to fertilize the ovum. The physiological mechanism by which this is accomplished is termed ejaculation.

Ejaculation

During ejaculation, sperm pass through four successive structures:

1. Epididymis.

2. Vas deferens.

3. Ejaculatory duct.

4. Urethra.

Along the way, sperm are joined or preceded by chemical contributions of five glands:

1. Seminal vesicles (right and left).

2. Prostate gland.

3. Bulbourethral glands (Cowper's glands) (right and left).

The epididymis is a coiled tube about 20 feet long, found on the posterior side of the testis (Fig. 6). The upper end of the tube, which surmounts the testis like a helmet, is called the head; the lower end is the tail.

The epididymis

After the production phase, sperm pass into the epididymis where a small quantity is stored.

Most sperm, however, are stored in the vas deferens (plural, vasa deferentia). The vas deferens emerges from the tail of the epididymis (Fig. 6). One from each testis extends for approximately 45 centimeters to enter the ejaculatory duct. The vas deferens thus functions as a passageway for sperm.

The Vas Deferens

---

[3]American Cancer Society, *How to Examine Your Testes* (New York: American Cancer Society).

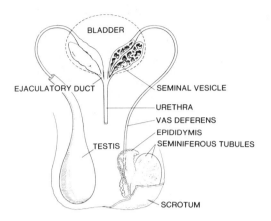

Figure 8   Seminal vesicle.

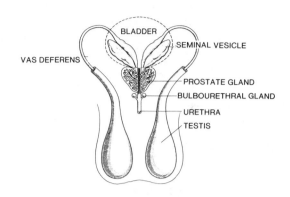

Figure 9   Prostate and bulbourethral glands.

The duct that leaves the seminal vesicles joins with the vas deferens to form one common duct known as the ejaculatory duct (Fig. 9). It is a short straight tube that passes into the prostate gland to open into the urethra.

Ejaculatory Duct

The vas deferens is joined en route by a duct from the seminal vesicles (Fig. 8). During ejaculation the seminal vesicles (one on each side of the body) add fluid secretions. The primary constituents of seminal fluid are fructose, a simple sugar that provides nutrition for sperm; prostaglandins; and fibrinogen. It may be that prostaglandins aid fertilization by making the cervical mucus more receptive to sperm and by causing reverse peristaltic contractions in the uterus and oviducts to move the sperm toward the ovaries.

Seminal Vesicles

At one time it was thought that sperm were stored in the seminal vesicles. This is not true. It has also been commonly considered that the intensity of male sex drive is related to the degree of distention of the seminal vesicles, but the currently available evidence does not appear to be sufficient to either confirm or deny this claim. However, in multiple ejaculations occurring during a short period of time—an unusual occurrence—the first ejaculation is more satisfying than subsequent climaxes.

The prostate gland is made up of glandular tissue (Fig. 9). It is pyramidal and lies just beneath the bladder. The prostate gland produces several chemical substances thought to aid sperm in their attempt to fertilize an ovum. Probably the most important role of prostatic fluid is to neutralize the acid environment of the vagina. Normally, the vagina is highly acidic, a state that is not conducive to sperm longevity or movement. Immediately after ejaculation, the semen neutralizes the acidity of the vagina.

The Prostate Gland

With aging the prostate gland tends to enlarge, and when the enlargement is pronounced urinating may be blocked. This is because the prostate anatomically surrounds the urethra. Because of its anatomical position, enlargement of the prostate may block urination (Fig. 10).

The Prostate in Disease

Also, the prostate gland is a frequent site of cancer in the male. In fact, among men over 50 years of age, cancer of the prostate is one of the leading causes of cancer death. Fewer than one man in ten survive this disease. Thus, early detection is extremely important. In the early stages of cancer of the prostate, hard lumps can be detected during rectal examination (Fig. 11). Dr. Nathaniel Shafer, a New York specialist in internal medicine, writes:

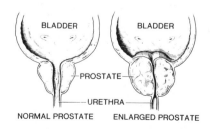

Figure 10   Prostatic hypertrophy.

> Many of these deaths are unnecessary. According to estimates, a simple five
> or ten second rectal examination would allow for over 50 per cent of the cases

to be discovered at a stage when they could be cured. However, because of social inhibitions and prudishness, a rectal examination is not performed as frequently and as routinely as it should be.

The following signs may accompany cancer of the prostate:

1. Loss in force in the urinary stream.

2. Dribbling.

3. Frequency of urination.

4. Blood in the urine.

5. Passing urine at night.

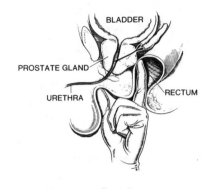

Figure 11   Rectal examination of the prostate.

Removal of the Prostate

Removal of the prostate gland may render the male sterile, but it usually does not diminish a male's sexual ability. Sterility can result for two reasons:

1. Retrograde ejaculation—meaning that in prostatic surgery the valves that regulate the passageway to the bladder are damaged and as a consequence ejaculation during the sex act is into the bladder.

2. Formerly, to prevent spread of infection, the vasa deferentia were usually cut and tied during prostatic surgery, blocking the normal passageway for sperm. This is no longer a standard procedure.

The occurrence of sterility following prostatectomy varies considerably with the surgical approach used. Newer methods of irradiation almost never render the patient sterile.

The Bulbourethral Glands

The bulbourethral glands, also called Cowper's glands, are two small glands that open by excretory ducts into the urethra (Fig. 12). They produce an alkaline fluid that lubricates the urethra and may lower the acidity in the urethra before sperm passage. The secretions of the bulbourethral glands are often referred to as precoital fluid. Although these secretions usually precede ejaculation, they may contain sperm and thus cause pregnancy.

The Penis

The penis is composed of three cylinders, each containing erectile tissue (sponge-like tissue that can fill with blood to cause erection) (Fig. 12). These three cylinders are bound together with connecting tissue, giving the outward appearance of one cylinder. This cylinder ends in a cone-like expansion called the glans penis.

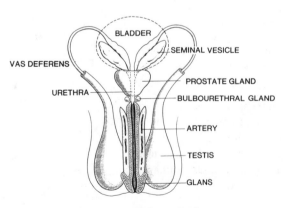

Figure 12   Bulbourethral glands and penis.

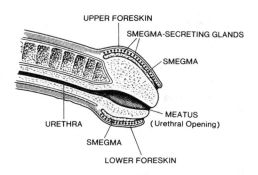

Figure 13 Smegma secretion.

A circular fold of skin called the foreskin (prepuce) covers the glans of an uncircumcised penis. A number of small glands are located in the foreskin (preputial glands) and discharge their secretions onto the glans. The accumulation of these secretions on the glans is called smegma (Fig. 13).

Circumcision,[4] or removal of the foreskin (Fig. 14), has been customary for at least 6,000 years, dating back to a time when Egyptian warriors mutilated their prisoners. Finding that amputation of arms and legs rendered their prisoners useless as slaves and that castration was associated with a high mortality rate, the Egyptians marked male slaves with circumcision. Since the Jews were largely slaves, they evolved the practice of circumcision, eventually calling it their covenant with God.[5] The practice continues, and today 80 percent of all newborn males in the United States are circumcised.[6]

The foreskin of an uncircumcised male collects, in the absence of regular cleaning, a cheesy composite of dirt and body oils called smegma, a substance thought by some to be carcinogenic.[7] Moreover, it has been observed that horse smegma causes cancer in mice.[8] Further, it has been observed that circumcised males have a lower incidence of cancer of the penis and that women married to circumcised men have a lower incidence of cancer of the cervix.

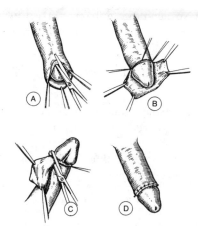

Figure 14 Circumcision.

However, some other studies have failed to establish this link between cancer and uncircumcision. This conflict between studies may be related to cleanliness, which is to say that those studies linking cancer and uncircumcision may have reflected populations in which lack of cleanliness allowed smegma to accumulate, whereas those studies finding no link may have been in countries where cleanliness prevents the accumulation of smegma.

In the presence of regular cleaning of the foreskin, there is not much evidence to recommend circumcision as a routine procedure. The American Academy of Pediatrics states:[9]

> There is no absolute medical indication for routine circumcision of the newborn. The physician should provide patients with information pertaining

---

[4]For an excellent view of this topic the future teacher should consult: R. S. McDermott, D. D. Wilson, and Phillip J. Marty, "Neonatal Circumcision," *Patient Counselling and Health Education,* 3 (1981), pp. 132–136.

[5]R. Burger and T. Guthrie, "Why Circumcision?," *Pediatrics,* 54 (1974), p. 362.

[6]D. A. Grimes, "Routine Circumcision Reconsidered," *American Journal of Nursing,* 80 (1980), p. 108.

[7]R. Burger and T. Guthrie, op. cit., p. 362.

[8]A. Plaut and A. C. Kohn-Speyer, "Carcinogenic Action of Smegma," *Science,* 104 (1949), p. 39.

[9]Report of Ad Hoc Task Force on Circumcision—Committee on Fetus and Newborn, *Pediatrics,* 56 (1975), p. 610.

to the long-term medical effects of circumcision and noncircumcision, so that they make a thoughtful decision. It is recommended that this discussion take place before the birth of the infant, so the parental consent to the surgical procedure, if given, will be truly informed. A program of education leading to continuing good personal hygiene would offer all the advantages of routine circumcision without the attendant surgical risk. Therefore, circumcision of the male neonate cannot be considered an essential component of adequate total health care.

One important argument for circumcision is that uncircumcised boys may be the object of cruel and taunting remarks by circumcised classmates, peer pressure being very important at school age. This situation is reminiscent of a time in history when women wanted to be pale because most women of their day (suffering with tuberculosis) were pale.

The point is this, circumcision is fashionable, but in the presence of regular cleaning there is little evidence to recommend it.

No significant difference in sensitivity of the penis to touch has been found between circumcised and uncircumsized males.[10]

Penis Size

Many males worry unnecessarily about the size of the penis. This worry stems from the mistaken notion that a large penis is necessary for adequate sexual function.

This worry can be eliminated by the knowledge that it is primarily the labia and clitoris that are excitable in the female, so penis size is not an important factor. Further, a penis that appears smaller when not erect tends to increase more in size during erection than an already large penis. The female vagina stretches to accommodate any size of penis.

From a statistical standpoint, the following standards for the erect penis have been reported:

	Length When Erect	Diameter
Small	3½ inches	1 inch
Average	6 inches	1½ inches
Large	More than 8 inches	2 inches

It is impossible to enlarge the size of the adult penis, either by surgery or hormonal treatment. Injection of a substance such as silicone may completely destroy the capacity for erection.

Captive Penis

Captive penis (penis trapped in the vagina) occurs in animals but not in humans. For example, there is a bone in the penis of the male dog that allows insertion into the vagina before erection. When erection occurs, the head of the penis enlarges inside the female vagina. The vagina swells and thus prevents the male dog from withdrawing until ejaculation occurs and erection of the penis subsides.

Although many humans have deep-seated fears of captive penis, there is not one authentic case on record. And only seven scientifically documented cases of bones in human penises have been reported since 1884.

---

[10]W. Masters and V. Johnson, *Human Sexual Response* (Boston: Little, Brown Co., 1966), p. 191.

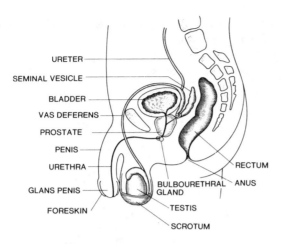

Figure 15   Male reproductive system (side view).

The urethra is a tube-like passageway extending from the bladder through the prostate gland where it is joined by the ejaculatory duct (Fig. 15). From the prostate gland the urethra passes through the penis to open to the outside. The urethra serves as the common outlet for sperm and urine.

Urethra

Prior to the passage of sperm, the acid urethra is neutralized by fluids from the bulbourethral gland.

During ejaculation, the opening from the bladder is normally closed off by a nervous reflex. If it is not closed off, as happens in disease, ejaculation is into the bladder.

The male reproductive role is two-fold:

The Male Reproductive Role

1.   Production of sperm.

2.   Transfer of these sperm to the female reproductive system.

To accomplish the latter function, the penis becomes erect, is inserted into the vagina, and sperm are ejaculated (Fig. 16). Erection occurs when the erectile tissue of the penis becomes engorged with blood (Fig. 17). The reaction of the excited nerve fibers causes the arteries of the penis to distend, allowing blood to rush into the cylinders; a simultaneous constriction of the veins prevents this blood from escaping. The erectile tissues thus fill with blood, and the penis becomes erect.

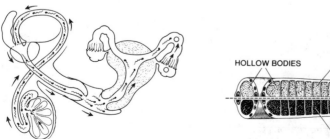

Figure 16   Fertilization.

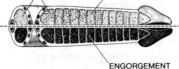

Figure 17   Erectile tissue.

Emission and ejaculation are the culmination of sexual intercourse for the male. Emission is a series of contractions (of the epididymis, vas deferens, ampulla, the muscular coat of the prostate gland, and seminal vesicles) that expel prostatic and seminal fluids and force the sperm forward. The process of ejaculation then begins as a series of rhythmic nerve impulses that increase the pressure in erectile tissue, causing ejaculation of the emission fluids from the urethra to the exterior.

Emission and Ejaculation

The male ejaculate is called semen. Semen contains:

Semen

1. Sperm.

2. Secretions from the seminal vesicles.

3. Secretions from the prostate gland.

The sperm constitute only a small portion of the semen.

Mature sperm are very small. In fact, if all the sperm responsible for producing the entire world population were brought together, their bulk would be about one half of an aspirin tablet (Fig. 18). The head of the sperm is approximately 5 microns long, the middlepiece 5 microns, and the tail 30 to 59 microns (1 micron = .001 millimeters and 1 millmeter = .04 inch). In contrast, the ovum is about 130 to 140 microns in diameter.

Sperm Size

X-bearing (female-producing) sperm are thought to have larger, oval-shaped heads, whereas Y-bearing (male-producing) sperm have smaller and longer heads.

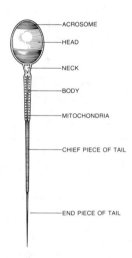

Figure 18   Structure of a sperm.

Each milliliter of semen contains approximately 120 million sperm, and the average ejaculate is 3 milliliters, containing approximately 360 million sperm. However, even in the normal male the sperm may vary from 35 to 200 million per milliliter. The following values have been established for fertility:

Sperm Number

·   At least 60,000,000/ml = normal fertility

·   40 to 60,000,000/ml = fair fertility

·   20 to 40,000,000/ml = fertility possible

·   10 to 20,000,000/ml = conception barely possible

·   Less than 10,000/ml = conception unlikely but not impossible.

If more than 25 percent of the sperm are defective, the male is likely to be sterile even though the total count is normal (Fig. 19). The reasons for diminished fertility with a low sperm count or defective sperm are not clear, but many physiologists believe that the problem has to do with preparation of the ovum for fertilization: when the ovum is expelled from the follicle of the ovary, it carries with it several layers of cells attached firmly to its surface, cells which must be removed before a sperm can reach the ovum. So in addition to the fertilizing sperm, it is thought that a very large number of assisting sperm are required to prepare the ovum. The assisting sperm are thought to release enzymes, hyaluronidase and proteinases, stored in the acrosome, and these enzymes, together with sodium bicarbonate from the fallopian tube secretions, prepare the ovum for fertilization. It is thought that the sterility associated with low sperm counts is due to a lack of these enzymes.

Sperm production seems to be quite independent of sexual activity, but the fertilizing capability of successive ejaculations is thought to decline because of the inclusion of immature sperm in the semen. However, lowered fertility may also accompany prolonged sexual rest because of the inclusion of senile spermatozoa (spermatozoa that have lost their effectiveness because of aging).

Because of the importance of sperm in human reproduction, we will examine them in more detail (Fig. 18).

After formation in the testes, sperm pass into the epididymis where they develop motility and the ability to fertilize during a period of 18 hours to ten days.

A small quantity of sperm may be stored in the epididymis, but most are stored in the vas deferens. Sperm remain fertile in storage for several months. If ejaculation does not occur during this time interval, sperm degenerate and are replaced by new ones.

Though sperm stored in the genital ducts live for many weeks, sperm that have been ejaculated into the female vagina are thought to have an effective life of about one to three days. However, sperm have been found alive in the vagina seven days after ejaculation. Their effectiveness after seven days is unknown.

Sperm frozen after ejaculation can be maintained at lowered temperatures in an effective state for a number of years (to be used for artificial insemination, Fig. 20). Recent research,[11] however, indicates that the process of freezing and thawing reduces by half the motility of spermatozoa in a specimen. Less than 20 percent of the initial motility remains after five years in storage.

After ejaculation, sperm travel at a rate of about 1 to 4 millimeters per minute, in a straight, rotating line. Their activity is greatly enhanced in neutral or slightly alkaline environments.

The migration of sperm once they have entered the female body has been difficult for scientists to study, especially in the human. Thus, neither the time interval nor the mechanism for travel is well understood.

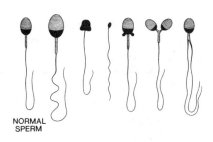

Figure 19   Abnormal sperm.

Physiology of Sperm

Life of Sperm

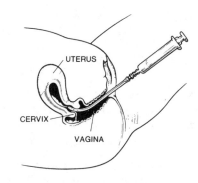

Figure 20   Artificial insemination.

Sperm Migration

---

[11]K. D. Smith and E. Steinberger, "Survival of Spermatozoa in a Human Sperm Bank," *JAMA* 223 (1973), p. 774.

Following the observation by microscope that sperm were motile, it became commonly held that sperm traveled to the oviducts by means of their own propellant activity. However, more recent observations suggest that other factors are involved. For example, nonmotile (incapable of self-movement) and motile sperm seem to move at the same rate of speed. Furthermore, sperm reach the oviducts much faster than can be explained on the basis of their propellant activity.

Rate of Travel

Observations of cows indicate that sperm pass from the cervix to the far end of the oviducts in two minutes. In a unique experiment reported by Dr. Boris B. Rubenstein and others, sperm placed in the vagina before an operation were found to "migrate through the cervix, fundus, and oviducts of women within thirty minutes after their introduction.[12] One reasonable hypothesis to explain the rapid movement of sperm suggests that the stimuli of mating or artificial insemination cause release of a hormonal substance (oxytocin) that increases uterine contractions.

Male Sterilization

Vasectomy is becoming increasingly popular as a means of birth control. There are approximately 250,000 cases per year. This is a simple surgical procedure in which the vas deferens is cut and tied off (Fig. 21).

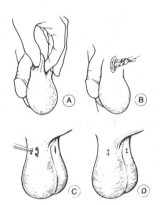

Currently there is no evidence that vasectomy interferes with sexual activity in any way. And most men return to normal sexual activity within two weeks. Approximately 98 percent of vasectomized men report the same or increased frequency of sexual intercourse. There is no evidence to support the claim that vasectomy leads to an increase in extramarital sex among men.

Vasectomy is discussed in more detail in Chapter 6 (Contraception).

Figure 21   Vasectomy.

Eunuchism

A eunuch is a man who has complete loss of testicular function owing to castration or other reasons. If this occurs prior to puberty, the secondary sex characteristics do not develop. If it occurs after puberty, the secondary sex characteristics may exhibit regression.

After castration, sexual desire decreases but is not totally diminished. Erection and ejaculation can still occur. There are cases of men participating actively in sexual intercourse 15 years after castration.

Sexual Life of the Male

The average age of first ejaculation is 13 years and 10 months. Ejaculation has been observed at eight years of age, but this is rather unusual. Indeed, only 25 percent of the male population has experienced ejaculation by age 12.

The adult has an average of three orgasms per week. The frequency of orgasm is highest between 15 and 30.

Male Climacteric

Most men have decreasing sexual function in their late 40's or 50's, but active sex life for 70 percent of the population continues past the age of 70 years. The decline has been attributed to a corresponding decrease in testosterone,

---

[12]B. B. Rubenstein, et al., "Sperm Survival in Women," *Fertility and Sterility,* 2 (1951), p. 15.

which dwindles rapidly after age 40 to about one fifth its peak at age 60. The theory connecting testosterone with sex drive is supported by the fact that sex drive decreases following castration and a variety of hormonal imbalances— hormonal imbalances which when corrected increase both testosterone levels and sex drive. Moreover, testosterone has been demonstrated to be effective in combating declining sex drive in the aging male.[13] Based upon 40 years of clinical research on this topic, Robert Greenblatt[14] concludes that although sex drive may be influenced by neurological, psychogenic, anatomical, pathological, and nutritional factors, "Libido may be spoken of as a test tube chemical equation," an equation that starts with testosterone. He further notes that testosterone is a psychotropic drug that improves well-being and lessens depression in men.

The decrease in male sexual function, called the male climacteric or **andropause,** is somewhat analogous to the menopause of the female. This may involve hot flashes, fatigue, nervousness, headache, and depression. The male climacteric, although somewhat rare, is as real[15] for some men as it is for some women. Many of these men, when given testosterone in adequate amounts, claim to experience marked improvement.

---

[13]Robert Greenblatt and Anthony Karpas, "Hormone Therapy for Sexual Dysfunction," *Postgrad Med,* 74 (1983), pp. 78–89.

[14]*Ibid.*

[15]E. L. Stearns, S. S. MacDonnell, B. J. Kaufman, et al., "Declining Testicular Function With Age: Hormonal and Clinical Correlates," *Am J Med,* 57 (1974), pp. 761–766.

C H A P T E R 3

The Biological Female

> *... hitherto woman's possibilities have been suppressed and lost to humanity, and ... it is high time she be permitted to take her chances in her own interest and in the interest of all.*
>
> Simone de Beauvoir
> *The Second Sex*

A major goal of sex education is the understanding and appreciation of femaleness by both sexes. This chapter discusses only the physiological aspects of femaleness, but a careful study of this information may eliminate some of the misconceptions, superstitions, and mysteries about female sexuality.

The Female Reproductive System

Very early in the development of an embryo, special sex cells are organized into a group of cells known as a gonad. Gonads can develop into either ovaries or testes, depending on hormonal stimulation.

Gonads

In the male, testosterone usually is secreted by the testes by the seventh to eighth week after conception, causing other male organs to develop.

In the normal female embryo, the gonads begin to evolve into two ovaries by the 10th or 11th week. The ovaries develop high in the abdomen, near the kidney. Before birth, however, they move downward to the brim of the pelvis.

Ovaries

As found in the pelvis, each ovary resembles an almond in shape (Fig. 22), about one inch wide, one and one half inches long, and one quarter of an inch thick.

Appearance

In the young woman the ovary is smooth and pink; in the older woman it is shrunken, wrinkled, and gray. Repeated discharges of ova through its surface cause the ovary to be puckered by the formation of scars.

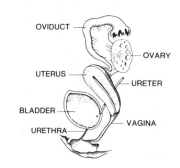

Figure 22 Female reproductive system (side view).

29

In the pelvis, the ovaries have a dual responsibility:

Function

1.   To produce ova.

2.   To secrete hormones.

At birth each ovary contains 200,000 to 250,000 small sac- or pod-like primary follicles (also called primordial follicles). The follicles contain immature ova.

Primary Follicles

It has been claimed that additional primary follicles are formed throughout the reproductive life of the female, but the consensus among scientists is that all the follicles are present at birth. Between birth and puberty, all but 10,000 of the primary follicles degenerate.

During the reproductive life of the female, approximately 375 primary follicles develop enough to expel ova. The remaining follicles degenerate; by the age of 50 most of them have disappeared.

Mature Follicles

When the female is about eight years old, the pituitary gland sends a hormonal messenger to the ovary to indicate that plans should be made to further develop the female reproductive system. Between ages 11 and 14, the pituitary gland sends increased amounts of hormones that produce the developmental period known as puberty.

Puberty

During puberty the ovaries, in response to stimulation by the pituitary gland, release the female sex hormone, estrogen, into the circulatory system. Estrogen is responsible for the development of the primary and secondary sexual characteristics of the female.

Estrogen

Under the influence of estrogen, the oviducts, uterus, and vagina (the primary sexual characteristics) all increase in size and physiological maturity (Fig. 23). The reproductive system is made ready for reproduction.

Primary Sexual Characteristics

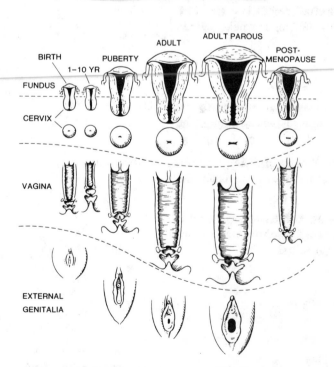

Figure 23   Growth of the female reproductive system.

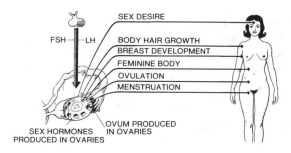

Figure 24   Female secondary sex characteristics.

The secondary sexual characteristics produced by estrogens include (Fig. 24):

Secondary Sexual Characteristics

1.   Deposition of fat in the breasts together with development of an elaborate duct system.

2.   Broadening of the pelvis and changes from a narrow funnel-like outlet to a broad oval outlet.

3.   Development of soft and smooth skin.

4.   Deposition of fat in buttocks and thighs.

5.   Development of pubic hair with a flat upper border (a triangular border is characteristic of the male).

6.   Early uniting of the growing end of long bones with the bone shaft. In the absence of estrogens females usually grow several inches taller than normal.

The Female Reproductive Role

The female reproductive system undergoes important physiological changes during puberty which initiate:

Physiological Changes During Puberty

1.   Ovulation.

2.   Menstruation.

The release of a mature ovum from the ovary is termed ovulation. Prior to ovulation, however, the primary follicles present in the ovary at birth must undergo several changes. To understand these changes, we must examine the primary follicle in more detail.

Ovulation

Each immature ovum is surrounded by a thin layer of cells usually termed follicular cells. Together, the follicular cells and the immature ovum constitute the primary follicle.

The Composition of the Primary Follicle

The primary follicles are stimulated to grow and reach maturity by two pituitary hormones: follicle stimulating hormone (FSH) and luteinizing hormone (LH). When the release of FSH or LH is inhibited by disease or by oral contraceptives, ovulation does not occur.

FSH and LH

FSH is responsible for the early growth of immature ova and the enlargement of the primary follicle. The primary follicle enlarges because of an accumulation of fluids, a process similar to the formation of a blister.

After hormonal stimulation, 15 to 20 immature follicles start to grow each month. Usually only one of these balloons outward into full maturity. The one follicle that reaches maturity is called the graafian follicle. The other follicles degenerate.

Graafian Follicle

The surface of the swelling graafian follicle has a small dot or nipple-like protrusion called the stigma. As the stigma develops, the pituitary gland increases its output of LH. LH, in turn, causes the stigma to disintegrate and the graafian follicle to rupture. The ovum thus escapes from the graafian follicle.

Stigma

The newly released ovum is a fragile structure that requires careful handling. In fact, even under optimal conditions, it can only be fertilized during the first 12 to 24 hours after it is released. So, rather than allowing the ovum "to fend for itself," the follicular cells continue to assume responsibility. The follicular cells that remain in the ovary are transformed by the action of LH into a temporary endocrine gland. This yellow glandular body is called the corpus luteum (yellow body).

A New Ovum

To prepare the female reproductive system for the reception of the ovum, the corpus luteum secretes two important hormones:

1. Estrogen.
2. Progesterone.

Before examining the effects of these hormones, however, we must review some other features of the female reproductive system.

The Fallopian tubes, named after their Italian discoverer, Gabriel Fallopius (Fig. 22), are trumpet-shaped structures lying close to the ovaries and extending to the corners of the uterus. These three- to five-inch tubes are also known as uterine tubes or oviducts.

Fallopian Tubes or Oviducts

How the ovum enters the oviduct is not completely understood. However, experiments with rabbits and monkeys and x-ray studies of women suggest that it happens in the following way.

How the Ovum Gets into the Oviducts

At the time of ovulation, the musculature of the oviduct and the ligaments by which it is suspended tend to draw the flaring end of the tube and the ovary together. Contractions of the muscular walls of the oviduct create a suction that directs the ovum into the tube. The process is further aided by a constant current created by the beating of cilia, hair-like projections found on the inner surfaces of the oviducts. Ordinarily, ova from the right ovary enter the right oviduct and those from the left enter the left tube. However, there are numerous cases on record to support the observation that crossover occurs (for example, the left tube may move over to pick up an ovum from the right ovary).

When the graafian follicle ruptures, the discharge contains more than just the ovum. The ovum is surrounded by follicular cells called cumulus cells. The cilia partially separate the ovum from the cumulus cells as the mass passes through the oviduct.

Cumulus Cells

Once inside the tube, the ovum and its cumulus are transported by the peristaltic contractions of the tube itself at a leisurely pace. The ovum arrives at the uterus three to seven days later.

Contraction of Oviducts

Fertilization of the ovum usually occurs in the upper third of the oviducts. Although this places an extra burden on the sperm in terms of travel, it is necessitated by the fact that the ovum must be fertilized during the first 12 to 24 hours or not at all.

Where Fertilization Occurs

Progesterone from the corpus luteum initiates secretion of glands in the walls of the oviduct. These secretions provide important nutrition for the ovum as it passes through the oviduct.

Nutrition

Ordinarily the female does not perceive ovulation. For some women, however, a slight discomfort may accompany ovulation. This is often referred to as mittelschmerz ("middle pain" in German). It is a transitory irritation caused by the small amount of blood and fluid released at the site of the ruptured follicle.

Mittelschmerz

The uterus, or womb, is a hollow muscular pouch located in the pelvic cavity between the bladder and the rectum. The uterus resembles a pear. It is about three inches long and two inches wide at the top, narrowing down to the cervix, or neck, where it is normally about a half to one inch in diameter.

The Uterus

The size of the uterus, however, varies with age and physiological state (Fig. 23):

1. At birth the uterus is large because of a small amount of estrogen that passes from the mother.

2. During childhood the uterus is smaller because it lacks this hormonal stimulation.

3. At puberty, estrogens signal the uterus to grow, and it reaches adult dimensions.

4. After childbearing, the uterus reaches its largest dimensions.

The uterus has three anatomical parts:

Anatomical Parts of the Uterus

1. Corpus, or body.
2. Isthmus.
3. Cervix.

The corpus, or body, is the upper muscular division of the uterus. It is dome shaped, the anterior surface being almost flat and the posterior surface being convex. The corpus is able to expand in the pregnant state because of its muscular layers.

Corpus

Below this muscular division is the constricted area of the uterus, the isthmus. The isthmus lengthens and thins out during pregnancy. It aids the corpus in causing enlargement of the womb for the growing embryo.

Isthmus

If the uterus were an upside-down milk bottle, the neck of the bottle would be the cervix. During pregnancy the cervix retains the growing embryo.

Cervix

In addition to the three anatomic parts of the uterus, there are two uterine layers:

Uterine Layers

1. Myometrium.
2. Endometrium.

The myometrium, the muscular layer of the uterus, consists of many interweaving fibers. Arteries and veins lie between the muscle fibers, giving rise during pregnancy to a spongy appearance known as stratum vasculare. After pregnancy, the arteries are kept from hemorrhaging by the constriction of these muscle fibers.

Myometrium

The endometrium, the innermost layer of the uterus, is a soft tissue richly supplied with blood vessels. It is about 3 to 4 millimeters thick.

Endometrium

This endometrium grows each month and is prepared to serve as a home for the fertilized egg. If the ovum is fertilized, it must establish a more permanent

Preparation for Implantation

connection with the mother's reproductive system in the uterus, if it is to develop into a full-term baby.

Occasionally implantation takes place in the oviduct, but because of a shortage of space at this location, such an implantation must be surgically removed (Fig. 25).

In addition to the oviducts, a fertilized egg may implant at other locations outside the uterus, including the abdominal cavity. The incidence of these nonuterine implantations, termed ectopic pregnancy, is estimated at about 1 percent. Normally, however, the fertilized ovum will implant itself in the lining of the uterus.

Ectopic Pregnancy

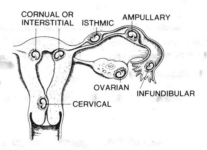

Figure 25   Ectopic implantation sites of pregnancy.

Normal Implantation

Preparation of the endometrium for reception of a fertilized egg is accomplished by estrogen and progesterone in the following way:

At the beginning of each new menstrual cycle, only a very thin layer of endometrial cells remains; the others were shed during the last menstrual flow.

Immediately after menstruation the endometrium begins a three-stage rebuilding process.

The first phase is called the proliferative phase or estrogen phase (Fig. 26). To proliferate means to grow by the rapid production of new cells, and that is exactly what happens to the lining of the uterus when it is stimulated by estrogen during the early days of the menstrual cycle. By the time of ovulation, the endometrial lining of the uterus is 2 to 3 millimeters thick.

Proliferative or Estrogen Phase

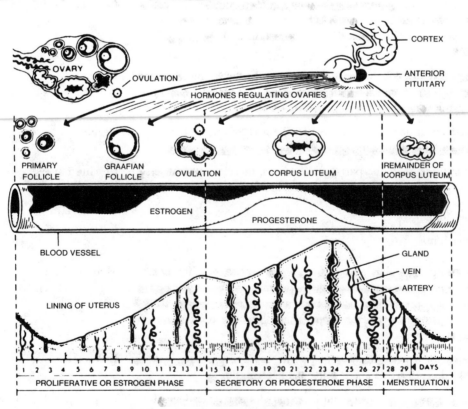

Figure 26   The menstrual cycle.

The second stage of rebuilding, the secretory or progestational phase (Fig. 26), is initiated by progesterone from the corpus luteum. The corpus luteum also secretes additional amounts of estrogens.

Acting together, these hormones:

1. Cause further growth of the cells in the endometrium.

2. Increase the blood supply in the lining of the uterus.

3. Cause the glands that have developed in the lining of the uterus to secrete endometrial fluid.

The endometrium reaches a thickness of 4 to 6 millimeters during this stage.

From the time of fertilization until implantation, the secretions of the oviducts and uterine glands provide nutrition for the ovum.

In addition to preparing the endometrium, estrogens and progesterone inhibit further release of FSH and LH so that no new primary follicles start to mature.

Progesterone inhibits the myometrium, thus preventing contraction. This is a precautionary measure to protect an implanted ovum from expulsion.

It also stimulates the development of ducts in the mother's breasts to make them ready to nourish the newborn.

In order to maintain these important functions, progesterone is at a high level during pregnancy. To do this, the corpus luteum is maintained during the early stages of pregnancy by hormones released by the developing embryo.

In the later stages of pregnancy, progesterone is secreted in large quantities by the placenta, a membrane that connects the baby to the mother. It will be discussed in connection with pregnancy in a later chapter.

If fertilization fails to take place, phase three—the menstrual phase—of the recurrent female cycle is initiated (Fig. 26), this time by a decrease in the hormones from the corpus luteum, the corpus luteum having degenerated. Thus, all these phases are under hormonal control: the proliferative or estrogen phase, responsible for the early growth of the endometrium; the secretory or progesterone phase, which completes endometrial growth and initiates secretion; and the menstrual phase, which takes off the "endometrial wall paper" so that the cycle can start again.

Immediately after ovulation, follicular cells quickly develop into a corpus luteum, which is active for 10 to 12 days. During this time it secretes estrogen and progesterone to make the endometrium receptive for a fertilized ovum.

If fertilization does not occur, the corpus luteum begins to degenerate and is replaced by connective tissue. It ends up as a tortuous white scar, the corpus albicans.

Approximately two days before the end of the normal female cycle, the secretion of estrogen and progesterone decreases sharply as the corpus luteum becomes inactive. Decreased secretion of estrogen and progesterone is thought to cause menstruation in the following way:

When hormonal stimulation of the endometrial cells stops, these cells shrink to approximately 65 percent of their previous size. Then approximately 24 hours prior to menstruation, the blood vessels to the lining of the uterus are closed off.

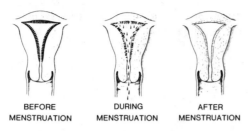

BEFORE
MENSTRUATION

DURING
MENSTRUATION

AFTER
MENSTRUATION

Figure 27   Lining of the uterus in
three stages.

In the absence of a blood supply, the lining of the uterus dies and gradually separates from the rest of the uterus. The dead tissue, together with a small quantity of blood in the uterine cavity, initiates uterine contractions. These contractions expel the contents of the uterus as the menstrual flow (Fig. 27). The menstrual flow marks the end of the three-phase female cycle.

During menstruation approximately 35 milliliters of blood, 35 milliliters of fluid, and the lining of the uterus are expelled.

The uterus develops a new lining, and bleeding stops about five days after the onset of menstruation.

Menarche is the term used to describe the first menstrual cycle; menopause marks the last cycle.

Menarche and Menopause

An abnormally large menstrual flow is termed menorrhagia. Possible causes of menorrhagia include:

Menorrhagia

1. Diseases.

2. Endocrine disorders.

3. Abnormalities of the sexual organs.

Excessive bleeding should be reported to a physician.

Amenorrhea is the absence of menstruation. If menstruation has never occurred, the condition is called *primary* amenorrhea; if it has occurred but ceases before the normal age for menopause, the condition is *secondary* amenorrhea.

Amenorrhea

Primary amenorrhea may result from:

1. Malformed or underdeveloped female organs.

2. Glandular disorders.

3. General poor health.

4. Anorexia nervosa.

5. Emotional factors.

6. Long-distance running.

Secondary amenorrhea is normal during pregnancy and while the mother is nursing. It may occur sporadically during the first and last months of a woman's childbearing years.

If amenorrhea persists, medical assistance should be sought.

At times the menstrual flow is so slight that it amounts to little more than staining. This slight staining is termed "scanty menstruation." Scanty menstruation is also caused by:

Scanty Menstruation

1. Malformed or underdeveloped female organs.
2. Glandular disorders.
3. General poor health.
4. Emotional factors.

A frequent cause of scanty menstruation is anemia, a condition in which there is a reduction in the number of red blood cells.

Scanty menstruation should be reported to one's physician.

Irregular menstrual periods may be the result of a harmless change in nature's timing. If this is the case, the irregularity will soon be corrected.

Irregularity

On the other hand, irregularity may result from a disease in some part of the body, such as the thyroid gland or ovary. Most important, irregularity can be a sign of cancer. When irregularity persists, a physician should be consulted.

It is not unusual for a woman to experience mild discomfort at the onset of her menstrual period. Because of great individual differences in response to discomfort, there is no clear demarcation between menstrual discomfort and menstrual pain. Thus, painful menstruation is largely a subjective matter.

Dysmenorrhea

However, if a woman's menstrual cramps do not yield to mild pain killers or if such cramps prevent a normal social life, a condition called dysmenorrhea is diagnosed. Dysmenorrhea is thus another term for painful menstruation.

Dysmenorrhea may be caused by:

Causes of Dysmenorrhea

1. Inflammation.
2. Constipation.
3. Psychological stress.
4. Hormone imbalance.
5. Prostaglandins.

Actually, the causes of dysmenorrhea are poorly understood by medical investigators. Two types of dysmenorrhea are related to hormonal imbalance—spasmatic dysmenorrhea and congestive dysmenorrhea.

Spasmatic dysmenorrhea is related to too much progesterone in relation to estrogen. It is most common between the ages of 15 and 25 and is less likely after pregnancy and childbirth. Hormone therapy alleviates this condition.

Congestive dysmenorrhea, or "premenstrual tension," is due to too much estrogen in relation to progesterone. The symptoms are a feeling of heaviness because of fluid retained in the breasts, ankles, and abdomen. During the week before the menstrual flow, a woman may experience irritability, tension, depression, headache, fatigue, and the urge for simple carbohydrates.

"PMS"

Prostaglandins, hormonal substances, are made by the endometrium and may be a cause of dysmenorrhea. There is a sharp increase in the amount of prostaglandins before the menstrual period, which may cause painful contractions.

In the past there was a tendency to believe that cramps were always due to some organic cause. For example, dysmenorrhea was usually attributed to the fact that the cervix was too narrow and needed to be stretched. Some believed that dysmenorrhea was caused by abnormal positioning of the uterus. Operations were often performed to correct this, but in most cases the pain was not relieved.

A popular misconception is that exercise during menstruation is attended by congestion, dysmenorrhea, and a diminution of athletic performance. A study done at the Tokyo Olympics of 66 women athletes throws an interesting light upon this topic. The study revealed that training and competition did not significantly alter the course of the menstrual cycle.

Athletics and Menstruation

The following results were obtained regarding physical performance during menses.

1. Seventy percent retained normal performance.

2. Fifteen percent did better.

3. Fifteen percent did worse.

More recently there have been a number of reports that long-distance running may produce a temporary amenorrhea.

The two products commercially produced to absorb the menstrual flow are:

Menstrual Protection

1. Sanitary pads or napkins.

2. Tampons.

The sanitary pad or napkin is made of gauze and filled with an absorbent material. It is supported in the back and front by a narrow belt, by pins, or underneath with adhesive that adheres to underpants. A disadvantage of the sanitary pad is that when soaked the pad can irritate the inside surface of the thighs.

The tampon is a roll of absorbent material about as big as your little finger. It comes in a thin cardboard or plastic tube with a string attached to the absorbent plug. The plug is placed inside the vagina. When the hymen is still intact, the tampon is placed through a small perforation in the hymen. The string is left hanging for later removal of the tampon.

Tampons

One question that usually comes to the mind of adolescent girls beginning to menstruate involves the safety of the tampon. Whereas there may be some legitimate concerns about toxic shock syndrome, many other fears and misconceptions should be abandoned.

Safety of Tampons

Because sanitary napkins chafe and become soaked and malodorous, tampons are the best protection for athletes. In the past it has been thought that athletic women, especially swimmers, should not use tampons because they would not afford complete protection. Bathtub experiments have demonstrated that tampons prevent any blood loss during swimming.

Protection During Athletics

One popular misconception is that the vagina of a woman with an intact hymen is too small to use commercial tampons. A study of 100 girls aged 12 to 19 and 174 freshmen nursing students aged 17 to 25 was conducted to determine the size of the opening at the entrance of the vagina. Of the two groups 91 percent were of sufficient diameter to use the regular size of commercially available tampons.

Size of Vaginal Opening

Since the average opening in the intact hymen is ¾ to ⅞ inch in diameter and most tampons are slightly larger than ½ inch in diameter, there is little difficulty in inserting the tampon.

There is also a distinct advantage in tampon insertion. Once the tampon is securely in place, it absorbs the menstrual flow and expands.

Thus, upon removal, the now larger tampon slightly stretches the hymenal opening. This slight stretching aids the doctor in obtaining a Pap (Papanicolaou) smear in an examination for cancer; it also makes the first coitus easier.

Tampons have other advantages. The formation of a distinctive odor of menstrual fluid occurs when the menstrual fluid is exposed to air. With the use of tampons, the flow does not come in contact with air, and hence there is no odor.

Odor

Tampons have been associated with a rare but serious disease called toxic shock syndrome (TSS), which sometimes can be fatal. TSS occurs mainly in girls and women using tampons during their period.

Toxic Shock Syndrome

Warning signs of TSS are (1) Sudden fever (usually 102°F or more) and (2) vomiting or diarrhea. If these signs occur during menstruation, the tampon should be removed at once and a doctor consulted right away.

There may be other signs such as a sudden drop in blood pressure, dizziness, or a rash that looks like a sunburn. These signs may indicate the need for emergency medical care.

The Food and Drug Administration (FDA) offers this advice:

1. The low risk of getting TSS can be almost entirely avoided by not using tampons.

2. The risk can be reduced by using tampons on and off during the period, for example, by using tampons during the day and napkins at night.

3. About one in every three girls or women who have had TSS have gotten it again and should not use tampons again until they check with a doctor.

Toxic shock syndrome is a recently identified disease caused by bacteria called *Staphylococcus aureus.* Further research is being done to find out more about this disease and why tampons have been associated with it.

Reports of this disease have been increasing. It is estimated currently that as many as 15 of every 100,000 girls and women who are menstruating will get this disease each year.

Although proportionately greater tasks are assigned to the ovaries and uterus, the vagina and external female genitalia are more than idle bystanders in female reproductive physiology.

The Vagina and External Female Genitalia

The vagina serves as

Functions of the Vagina

1. The female organ of intercourse.

2. A passageway for the arriving male sperm.

3. A canal through which the baby is born.

4. A passageway for the menstrual flow.

The vagina is a three- to four-inch muscular tube extending from the cervix of the uterus to the external genitalia. It is situated behind the bladder and in front of the rectum; its axis forms an angle of approximately 90 degrees with that of the cervix.

The vaginal tube is 6 to 7 centimeters long along its front wall and 9 centimeters long along its back wall. The vaginal wall has three layers:

1. A top mucous layer with numerous blood vessels.

2. A muscular layer (Fig. 28).

3. An elastic fibrous layer.

There are numerous folds in the vaginal canal. These folds tend to smooth out as the female bears children and ages.

The vagina can best be described as a potential space. In the normal unstimulated state, the walls of the tube are in almost direct contact with each other.

The soft "collapsed" walls open when something is forced through the vaginal tube. The tube can extend to four or five times its normal size to facilitate childbirth. The vagina also extends to adapt to the size of the penis during intercourse. The normal female vagina adapts to any size of penis. Furthermore, the inner two thirds of the vagina are practically without sensation. Thus, worry over anatomical misfits, like most sexual anxieties, is senseless.

During sexual excitement the walls of the vagina are kept moist by secretions from the uterus and by a sweating phenomenon in which the walls of the vaginal barrel pass droplets of mucoid material.

During sexual stimulation the vagina is lubricated by fluid that exudes from the walls of the vagina itself, not from special glands as once was supposed.

The hymen, or maidenhead, is a thin membrane that stretches across the opening of the vagina (Fig. 29). It varies in thickness and extent and is sometimes absent.

In the center of the hymen is a circular perforation through which the menstrual flow leaves the vagina and a tampon or internal protection can be inserted. In rare cases there is no central perforation, and the menstrual flow is blocked. This condition is referred to as imperforate hymen. Medical assistance is needed in this situation.

Contrary to popular belief, the absence of the hymen is not a sign that a girl is no longer a virgin, nor is the presence of the hymen an absolute sign of virginity. Women have come to the delivery of their first child with an intact hymen (Fig. 30). On the other hand, virginal women have been known to have a poorly developed or a broken hymen.

Vagina Size and Composition

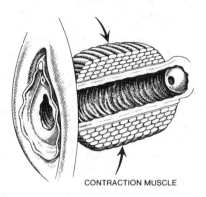

CONTRACTION MUSCLE

Figure 28   Vaginal muscles.

Adjustable Space

Vaginal Secretions

Hymen

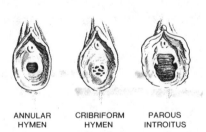

ANNULAR HYMEN   CRIBRIFORM HYMEN   PAROUS INTROITUS

Figure 29   The hymen.

Virginity

If the hymen is present it will usually rupture and tear at several points during the first coitus. The amount of bleeding accompanying the coital tearing varies. Generally there is a slight bleeding if the hymen is intact at the first coitus; however, this is not an absolute sign of virginity.

In rare cases the hymen is resistant to coital tearing and must be surgically divided before intercourse can take place. To prevent the woman's difficulty during the first sexual intercourse, the physician frequently ruptures the hymen at the time of the premarital examination.

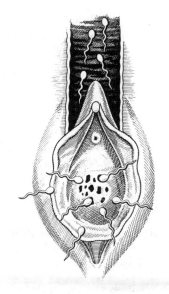

Figure 30   Virginal pregnancy.

External Female Genitalia

The term vulva, or pudendum, as generally applied includes all the female external genitalia (Fig. 31). They consist of the:

1.   Mons veneris.
2.   Labia majora.
3.   Labia minora.
4.   Clitoris.
5.   Vestibule of the vagina.
6.   Bulb of the vestibule.
7.   Greater vestibular glands.

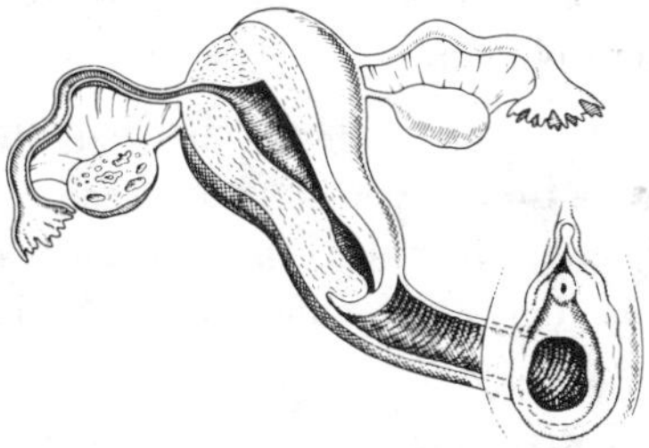

Figure 31   The female reproductive system.

Mons veneris

The fatty cushion resting over the front surface of the pubic bone is called the mons veneris. The term mons veneris is Latin for "mountain of love."

This fatty cushion protects the female reproductive organs. At puberty, hair covers the mons veneris in a triangular fashion, its base corresponding to the upper margin of the pubic bone.

Labia Majora

The labia majora are large heavy folds of skin surrounding the external opening of the vagina.

Each labium has two surfaces:

1.   An outer, pigmented surface covered with strong thick hairs.
2.   An inner, smooth surface with large sebaceous follicles.

The labia majora are richly supplied with blood vessels, which become engorged with blood during sexual excitement.

The labia minora are two smaller folds of skin situated between the labia majora. They extend from the clitoris backward for about 4 centimeters on either side of the vaginal opening.

The anterior labia minora is divided into two portions:

1. An upper portion, which forms a fold overhanging the glans of the clitoris.

2. A lower division, uniting below the clitoris to form the frenulum (an underhanging fold) of the clitoris.

Projecting between the labia minora is the small cylindrical body known as the clitoris (Fig. 32).

The clitoris is richly supplied with blood vessels, and the pudendal nerve supplies it with sensory fibers. Thus, the clitoris serves as a receptor and transmitter of sexual stimuli.

The vestibule is a space between the labia minora into which open the urethra, the vagina, and the ducts of Bartholin's glands.

The urethra opens into the floor of the vestibule, midway between the glans of the clitoris and the vaginal opening.

The bulb of the vestibule consists of two elongated masses of erectile tissue, one on either side of the vaginal opening. Each bulb is filled with a convoluted mass of veins.

The greater vestibular, or Bartholin's, glands are bean-shaped glands found behind the posterior part of each vestibular bulb. Each gland is about 5 millimeters wide at its greatest dimension. The ducts from these glands empty into the posterior part of the vestibule approximately in the middle of the labia minora.

Traditionally, vestibular glands have been presumed to provide lubrication for painless penetration of the vagina. However, on the basis of their research, Masters and Johnson[1] conclude: "Under observation . . . there never has been sufficient secretory material produced to accomplish more than minimal

Labia Minora

Clitoris

Vestibule of the Vagina

Bulb of the Vestibule

Greater Vestibular Glands (Bartholin's Glands)

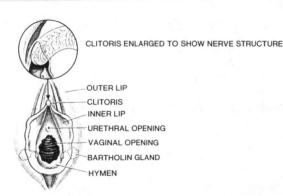

CLITORIS ENLARGED TO SHOW NERVE STRUCTURE

OUTER LIP
CLITORIS
INNER LIP
URETHRAL OPENING
VAGINAL OPENING
BARTHOLIN GLAND
HYMEN

Figure 32 Female external genitalia.

[1]William Masters and Virginia Johnson, *Human Sexual Response* (Boston: Little, Brown and Co., 1966), p. 44.

lubrication of the vaginal introitus." It is now thought that vestibular glands may create a genital scent, called a pheromone. These scents appear unimportant in humans, but among animals pheromones serve as an important means of communication. For example, a female dog in heat attracts and arouses male dogs by secretion of pheromones.

Female Climacteric

The word climacteric is Greek in origin and means "rung of the ladder"; it is used to describe the symptoms accompanying the waning production of estrogens that occurs as the woman grows older. This phase of life is also called the perimenopausal period.

The symptoms that collectively constitute the climacteric may be present for a number of years because ovarian function does not suddenly stop but gradually decreases for a variable length of time.

Signs and Symptoms of Climacteric

The oncoming climacteric is first signaled by a menstrual cycle that does not include ovulation. In this situation, progesterone is not produced, since no corpus luteum is formed.

Thus, the lining of the uterus would persist in the estrogen (proliferative) phase when it should have moved into the secretory phase.

Irregularity

As estrogen production diminishes, the menstrual cycles become irregular. Amenorrhea may occur for two or three months, followed by an excessive and prolonged menstrual flow.

In most cases menstruation does not suddenly stop without warning.

Menopause

Menopause is the term applied to the cessation of menstrual bleeding. Menopause is generally preceded by noticeable changes in the menstrual pattern. It occurs during the climacteric, but the symptoms of the climacteric both precede and follow the menopause. Most women become estrogen deficient within a year after menopause.

Menopause usually occurs between the ages of 47 and 52 years, with the average today being 50 years. This is slightly later than the figure reported in older literature. There is every reason to suggest that with good nutrition and health menopause will be further delayed.

Other Effects

Also occurring as a result of diminishing estrogen production are the following:

1. Atrophy of the primary sexual glands:
   A. The clitoris becomes smaller.
   B. The labia are reduced in size.
   C. Degenerative changes occur in the vaginal wall.

2. Changes in the secondary sex characteristics:
   A. There is a loss of pubic hair.
   B. Hair on the head becomes sparse.
   C. Hair may grow on the upper lip and chin.
   D. The breasts droop because of a loss of elasticity.
   E. The skin tends to wrinkle because it loses its elasticity.
   F. The bones become brittle.

3. Disturbances of general physiology:
   A. Hot flashes and night sweats may occur.
   B. Headaches and insomnia may become frequent.

4. Libido may be decreased or increased:
   A. Sex drive generally diminishes with aging.

B.   But some women exhibit an increased need for sexual gratification at this time of life.

5.   Psychosomatic symptoms may occur:
A.   Nervousness.
B.   Apprehension.
C.   Decrease in ability to concentrate.
D.   Irritability.
E.   Depression.

Treatment

Most healthy and well-adjusted women pass through menopause with a minimum of difficulty; only about 20 percent require medical therapy.

For those women who do have symptoms that seem to require treatment, the preferred medical approach is to use a moderate dose of oral estrogen for a month to determine whether the symptoms are caused by estrogen deficiency. Dosage can then be adjusted as appropriate.

The pros and cons of taking estrogen forever after menopause are still debated. Recent studies show that women on such estrogen therapy have a three to eight times greater risk of developing endometrial cancer; however, the validity of the research methods of these studies has been questioned. The addition of progestin to estrogen therapy seems to have benefits, including reduced risk of endometrial and breast cancers, prevention of osteoporosis (bone loss), and prevention of vaginal atrophy.

CHAPTER 4

Human Sexual Response

The moral and social values any individual applies to sexual activity derive from self, family, peers, religion, experience, and a host of other factors. The decision of whether to be sexually active, when to be active, and with whom is a personal decision. Our discussion here is from a biological point of view.

Biological sexual intercourse serves two functions: procreation and pleasurable sensation. The reproductive and pleasure functions are not physiologically dependent but may be fulfilled separately. For example, a man with a transected spinal cord could impregnate his wife but would perceive no pleasure from the act. Or a woman could experience an orgasm from stimulation of erogenous areas other than those directly associated with the reproductive system. In addition, the separation of the procreative and recreative aspects of sex has been enhanced by the development of highly effective contraceptive techniques.

Adult society is rapidly dissociating sex and procreation and emphasizing the pleasurable aspects. Nelson Foote states: "The view that sex is fun can . . . hardly be called the invention of immoralists; it is every man's discovery." People readily admit that giving or receiving pleasure is the major motivation for participation in the sex act.

In keeping with this approach to sex education, a rather progressive high school teacher began her first sex education class by "telling it like it is." She said, "Sex is for fun and reproduction and in that order." The next day she was looking for a new job. Despite this occurrence, the facts remain that 20th century American society is largely motivated by giving and receiving pleasure, and sex ranks high on the list of pleasures. It is not surprising, therefore, that more and more people are seeking help (from books, counselors, physicians, sexual partners, and others) to qualitatively enhance their sexual experiences.

A discussion of the problems that accompany sexual inadequacy is beyond the scope of this book, but an understanding of the basic human sexual response should be a part of any sex education program. In fact, such an understanding would eliminate many cases of sexual inadequacy. This chapter attempts to provide such an understanding.

Dr. Charles W. Lloyd[1] of the Worcester Foundation of Experimental Biology lists four prerequisites for normal sexual response:

1.   Functional integrity of those areas of the central nervous system that are involved.

2.   Adequate genital structures.

3.   Appropriate hormonal stimulation of the genitalia.

4.   A psychological environment that is conducive to sexual response.

Sexual activity, like most human activities, is highly dependent upon the central nervous system, which is made up of the brain and the spinal cord. The brain is subdivided into many parts. Although a knowledge of all these parts is not essential to an understanding of the human sexual response, a few basic concepts are required.

The cerebral cortex is the thinking-reasoning brain, the most highly evolved brain. Without the cortex humans function in much the same way as lower animals.

It is interesting to note, however, that decorticated animals (with the cerebral cortex removed) are capable of almost normal sexual behavior. For example, a decorticated cat given estrogen to bring her into heat exhibits:

1.   Courtship: playful rubbing and sexual crouching.

2.   Reaction after vaginal stimulation: rubbing, licking, squirming, and rolling.

Thus, sexual behavior occurs and is integrated independently of the cerebral cortex.

This does not mean that the intact cerebral cortex does not affect sexual behavior. Indeed, the cerebral cortex greatly accentuates response in the human.

Nevertheless, it would appear that sexual behavior is integrated at a level below that of the cerebral cortex. Put another way, it takes no brains to copulate!

Ruch and Patton[2] conclude that the basic elements of sexual behavior are located in the hypothalamus. This is not unexpected, since most of the "automatic" functions of the nervous system are governed by the hypothalamus.

Some sexual functions may be directed from an even lower level. For example, in the male, erection and ejaculation are regulated by the spinal cord.

In rats, rabbits, and guinea pigs, erection and ejaculation can easily be accomplished by electrical stimulation of the cord.

Also, genital stimulation can cause erection and ejaculation in the human male with a transected spinal cord. Although these men can feel no sensation, they are often capable of impregnating their wives.

---

[1]Charles W. Lloyd, "Sexual Response," *Human Reproduction and Sexual Behavior,* ed. Charles W. Lloyd (Philadelphia: Lea & Febiger, 1964), p. 455.

[2]Theodore C. Ruch and Harry D. Patton, *Physiology and Biophysics,* 20th ed. (Philadelphia: W. B. Saunders Co., 1973), p. 503.

Certain genital structures are prerequisites for normal sexual relations.

The male must have a penis, but testicles are not entirely necessary.

Cutting the vas deferens does not affect the sexual response.

In the absence of a prostate gland, the ejaculate is likely to pass into the bladder. However, this does not impair sexual sensation.

A vagina is required for normal performance of sexual intercourse. However, a vagina is not required for female orgasm. Orgasm is possible through stimulation of the clitoris and surrounding area without intercourse and also during anal intercourse. Although the clitoris is the most consistently erotic area of the female, it is not essential to sexual orgasm.

Testicular hormones are not absolutely necessary to male sexual performance. Dr. Lloyd[3] states:

> The preadolescent or hypogonadal male can engage in heterosexual activity, albeit without the intensity of satisfaction to himself or his partner that would be achieved if full androgenic stimulation had taken place.

> The sensitivity and the size of the penis and other secondary sexual tissues are enhanced by the presence of androgen.

On the other hand, the castrated male does not necessarily lose his sexual ability. Indeed, castrated males have participated in heterosexual intercourse 15 years after castration!

Estrogen is important in the development of the size and sensitivity of the erogenous structures of the female. However, orgasm sometimes occurs in the preadolescent. Once the female erogenous structures have fully developed, the removal of sex hormones seems to have little effect on the sex drive.

Both male and female sexual responses are greatly modified by the psychological environment. Indeed, it seems clear that two of the most important factors affecting female sexual response are: (1) attitude toward the partner and (2) attitude toward the self as a sexual being.

An unfavorable psychological environment is a far more frequent cause of sexual inadequacy than poorly developed genital structure, lack of hormonal stimulation, or disturbances of the nervous system.

Although the sexual experience may be modified by many factors, it is ultimately a series of physiological events. The intensity of the physiological response is attested by marked increases in heart rate, respiratory rate, and blood pressure.

Until recently, little was known about the physiological response of the reproductive system to sexual stimulation. To fill this void in our knowledge of sexuality, William Masters and Virginia Johnson published the results of several years of work in a book entitled *Human Sexual Response*.[4] The teacher is referred to this excellent book for a detailed account of the physiology of the human sexual response. Only the highlights can be included here.

Adequate Genital Structures

Male

Female

Hormonal Stimulation of Genitalia
Male

Female

Psychological Environment

Physiology of the Human Sexual Response

---

[3]Lloyd, op. cit., p. 455.

[4]William Masters and Virginia Johnson, *Human Sexual Response* (Boston: Little, Brown and Co., 1966).

The physiological responses that accompany the human sexual response appear to follow an orderly sequence. For purposes of simplicity, Dr. Masters and his colleagues have divided these responses into four phases:

A Sequence of Events

1. Excitement phase.

2. Plateau phase.

3. Orgasmic phase.

4. Resolution phase.

The excitement phase begins with the initial sexual stimulation, ranges from a few minutes to as long as several hours, and ends by passage into the plateau phase.

The Excitement Phase

In the male, the excitement phase consists of erection of the penis secondary to the engorgement of erectile tissue with blood. The testes are also elevated toward the body in this phase.

Male

Corresponding changes in the female include:

Female

1. Erection of the nipples and enlargement of the breasts.

2. Vaginal lubrication (10 to 30 seconds after stimulation).

3. Enlargement of both the length and diameter of the vaginal barrel.

4. Increase in the length and diameter of the clitoral shaft may occur.

The changes that occur during the excitement phase make heterosexual intercourse possible:

1. The erect penis can be inserted into the vagina.

2. The vagina enlarges to accommodate the penis and produces a lubricating fluid to facilitate intercourse.

During the plateau phase tension builds for the leap into orgasm.

The Plateau Phase

Further changes in the male include:

Male

1. An increase in the circumference of the penis, especially the glans.

2. Secretions of lubricating fluid from the bulbourethral glands.

3. Enlargement of the testes.

The responses in the female are:

Female

1. Further enlargement of the breasts.

2. Elevation of the uterus away from the posterior wall of the vagina.

3. Congestion of blood in the outer lengths of the vaginal barrel produces a platform within the vagina. This platform is called the orgasmic platform because it contracts during orgasm (Fig. 33).

4. Withdrawal of the clitoris into its hood.

5. Secretions from Bartholin's glands.

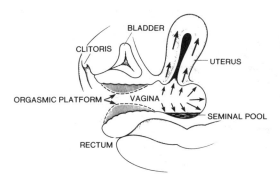

Figure 33   Orgasmic platform, seminal pool.

The orgasmic phase in both male and female consists of rapid muscular contractions that release accumulating tensions.

In the male, contractions of the full length of the shaft of the penis occur, producing ejaculation.

In the female, contraction of the orgasmic platform occurs. Muscles in the uterus and other parts of the female reproductive system may also respond.

In both males and females, the muscular contractions are approximately 0.8 second in duration.

The Orgasmic Phase

During the resolution phase, biological structures return to their pre-excitement state.

In the male, the changes observed are:

1.   Loss of erection.

2.   Decrease in size of the testes.

3.   Descent of the testes.

Changes in the female include:

1.   Loss of nipple erection.

2.   Loss of orgasmic platform (muscular contractions relieve congestion of blood).

3.   Gaping of the entrance to the cervix.

4.   Return of the clitoris from its protective hood.

5.   Immersion of the cervix into the seminal pool (Fig. 34).

The Resolution Phase

Male

Female

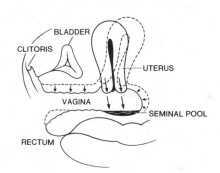

Figure 34   Immersion of cervix in seminal pool.

Because of their importance in the human sexual response, certain structures should be explained in more detail.

The clitoris is a small organ partially hidden in a prepuce or hood (Fig. 35). The prepuce resembles the foreskin of the penis, and the clitoris can retract

Special Considerations

Clitoris

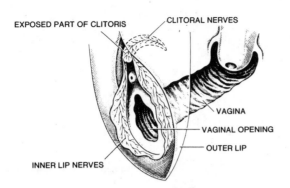

EXPOSED PART OF CLITORIS

CLITORAL NERVES

VAGINA

VAGINAL OPENING

OUTER LIP

INNER LIP NERVES

Figure 35   Nerve endings sensitive to sexual stimulation.

inside the prepuce in much the same way that the penis retracts inside the foreskin. The clitoris normally only retracts during sexual stimulation.

The clitoris has an expanded portion or glans at its distal end much like the glans at the distal end of the penis. The size of the glans of the clitoris increases during sexual stimulation secondary to congestion with blood. It does not become erect as does the penis but simply enlarges. The enlargement is rapid with direct manipulation of the clitoris but slower with breast manipulation, sexual intercourse, or fantasy.

Masters and Johnson[5] state:

1.   "The clitoris and prepuce form the most consistently erotic area of the human body."

2.   "The clitoris is . . . an organ system which is totally limited in physiologic function to initiating or elevating levels of sexual tension."

Many marriage manuals suggest that the male should locate the clitoris and remain in direct contact with it to heighten sexual tensions. Masters and Johnson level the following criticisms at this recommendation:

1.   The clitoris retracts during sexual stimulation and it is impossible for the penis to stay in direct contact with it.

2.   Direct manual contact with the clitoris may produce irritation and this technique is usually rejected during female masturbation.

Traction or pressure on the hood that protects the clitoris appears to be more desired by the female.

Masters and Johnson conclude that female orgasm occurs in the same physiological way whether it is effected through clitoral stimulation, vaginal stimulation, or other means.

Anatomical and physiological variations in the clitoris appear to play little if any role in human sexual response.

Masters and Johnson make the following observations relative to the vagina: **Vagina**

1.   In the unstimulated state it is a potential rather than an actual space; i.e., the anterior and posterior walls are essentially in direct contact.

---

[5]Masters and Johnson, op. cit., p. 45.

2. During the excitement phase the vagina enlarges to accommodate any size of penis. Owing to this facility of the vagina, sexual inadequacy is seldom a matter of anatomical misfits.

3. Within 10 to 30 seconds after sexual stimulation, lubrication of the vaginal walls occurs. The lubricating fluid comes from the walls of the vagina.

4. During the plateau phase the outer third (lengthwise) of the vagina becomes congested with blood to form an orgasmic platform.

5. The platform contracts rapidly during female orgasm.

6. Following orgasm, the platform disappears.

Aphrodisiac is the name given to any substance thought to increase the sexual drive or ability. Throughout history man has carried on a never-ending search for aphrodisiac drugs. This search has resulted in the use of extracts of trees, roots, flowers, insects, and animals, to list a few. According to Dr. Kenneth Walker,[6] an eminent British physician, aphrodisiacs are thought to exert their physiological effects in the following ways:

Drugs to Change the Human Sexual Response

1. By irritating the genital organs.

2. By stimulating the central nervous system.

3. By altering the mental state.

Spanish fly (technically known as cantharides) is an example of an irritating drug. It is obtained from a beetle found in southern Europe. When taken by mouth, this substance irritates the bladder and urethra during urination. The irritation may invoke sexual tension. Spanish fly, however, is a very dangerous drug. Dr. Walker states:

Spanish Fly

> [Spanish fly] . . . causes intense discomfort to the unfortunate patient and has been known to have fatal results.
>
> It inflames the stomach and the bowels, evokes vomiting and diarrhea and produces congestion of the kidneys.
>
> No one but a madman would take an aphrodisiac of this kind and only a criminal would prescribe it for anybody else.

Strychnine is an example of a drug that has been used to increase sexual drive by stimulating the central nervous system. There is little proof that strychnine has any real aphrodisiac power, and it is a dangerous drug that should never be used by anyone other than a physician. Its danger is suggested by the fact that it was first used to poison animals.

Strychnine

Cocaine, marijuana, LSD, amyl nitrate, and alcohol have been touted as drugs that enhance sexual drive by changing the mental state. It is possible that some of these drugs relieve inhibitions about sexual behavior, but there is no evidence that they are physiologically stimulating, with the exception of cocaine. Although little evidence is available, some suggest that cocaine produces vascular engorgement of the genital organs. Cocaine, however, is a highly dangerous drug.

Substances That Change the Mental State
Cocaine

---

[6]Kenneth Walker, "Using Drugs to Heighten Sex Desire," *Sexology* (Jul. 1967), pp. 842–845.

Marijuana

Marijuana tends to suppress psychological inhibitions; however, its disadvantage is that it may produce significant reproductive and hormonal changes. According to the National Institute on Drug Abuse, several studies have shown that marijuana can lower testosterone levels in the blood, although they remain within the normal range. Abnormal sperm movement and shapes and reduced numbers have been associated with marijuana use.

LSD

There are a few claims that, under medical supervision, LSD has proved useful in the treatment of frigidity. However, no carefully controlled studies are available.

Amyl Nitrate

Amyl nitrate has been claimed to intensify orgasm. This is probably a misconception deriving from the drug's effects of distorting one's sense of time and causing dizziness.

Alcohol

As to the effects of alcohol, Dr. Nathaniel Shafer,[7] an internist, writes:

> Most people regard alcohol as a sexual stimulant in particular; hence the great popularity of alcoholic drinks at most parties and social gatherings.
>
> In one sense it may be considered thus, in that an individual under the influence of alcohol may lose his fears, inhibitions and tensions as they pertain to the sex act.
>
> His feelings of insecurity or inadequacy may be suppressed, allowing him to perform in a satisfactory manner.
>
> However, this is not due in any way to the sexual stimulating action of the alcohol, but is an effect of its tranquilizing or calming actions.
>
> Indeed any other sedative or tranquilizer would exert a similar effect. This is especially true since so many sexual problems are of emotional origin.

But whereas small amounts of alcohol may relieve inhibitions, increasing amounts may render the male impotent.

In summary, Dr. Walker has accurately described the current dilemma that attends the use of drugs to heighten sex drive

> Throughout history, man has diligently sought far and wide for miraculous remedies, but in the end his search has always been thwarted. Either the action of the drug he has found proves erratic and uncertain or else the taking of it leads to his physical and mental degradation.
>
> In other words, man's search for an aphrodisiac has been attended with as limited success as has his search for the Philosopher's Stone and the Fountain of Youth. There is no such thing as a short-cut to Paradise.

Sexual Response and Aging

Aging does not preclude sexual functioning; however, aging men and women who experience long periods of coital abstinence may undergo premature aging of the reproductive system. In general, however, an ineffective sexual life is due less to physiological changes than to psychological aspects:

> Sexual boredom may be the greatest detriment to the effectiveness of sexual interaction between men and women in any longstanding relationship.[8]

---

[7]Nathaniel Shafer, "Alcohol and Sex," *Sexology* (Dec. 1966), pp. 351–354.

[8]William Masters and Virginia Johnson, "Sex and the Aging Process," *Medical Aspects of Human Sexuality* 16 (Jun. 1982), p. 56.

Two conditions can push a man unnecessarily toward impotence: misunderstanding the effects of aging on his sexual response and the cultural expectation that sex will end with aging. With aging, several physiological changes do begin to occur in the man's response to overt sexual stimulation:

1. It takes longer to achieve full penile engorgement and erection.

2. The expulsive pressure of ejaculation decreases.

3. The volume of seminal fluid decreases.

Psychologically, the man may participate in sexual intercourse without feeling a need to ejaculate and may even desire to have sex without ejaculation. These changes in the man may affect his partner's attitude:

1. The woman may falsely believe that she is not needed.

2. She may falsely believe that the man has another sexual interest.

3. She may falsely believe that she is not sexually attractive.

Therefore, it is important that both the man and the woman understand and be aware of these changes as they begin to occur.

Numerous physiological changes occur in the aging woman's response to overt sexual stimulation:

1. Lubrication of the vagina decreases.

2. The vaginal walls lose elasticity.

3. The facility for lengthening the vaginal barrel and increasing its diameter decreases.

4. Coital thrusting may create small fissures in the lining of the vaginal barrel.

5. Orgasmic experiences may be somewhat slowed.

6. Duration and intensity of the orgasmic episode may be reduced, but the subjective levels of sensual pleasure continue unabated.

7. The probability of painful spasms of uterine musculature during the orgasmic experience increases.

8. More precoital stimulation is required.

9. **Vaginismus** (involuntary contraction of the outer third of the vaginal barrel) occurs more frequently. (This may be an involuntary protection against painful stimuli associated with coital connection.)

After the death of a spouse, a widow or widower may experience a long period of sexual abstinence. In the aging man, this could lead to partial or complete impotence when he again engages in the sex act. Understanding by the woman is very important in this event. If not overwhelmed psychologically, the man may return to adequate sexual functioning after several attempts. Among women in their mid-50's who have lost their husbands, certain physiological changes produced by estrogen deficiency are more severe if they experience sexual abstinence of a year's duration:

1. Elasticity and involuntary vaginal expansion are reduced.

Changes in the Aging Man

Changes in the Aging Woman

Widow's and Widower's Syndromes

2.   Vaginal lubrication is reduced.

3.   The walls of the vagina become atrophic, the vaginal barrel constricts, the major and minor labia are thinned, and the vaginal outlet is constricted.

These changes, however, do not in any way prevent these women from returning to normal sexual function.

So far we have described the usual patterns of human sexual response. Sometimes these response patterns are accelerated or blocked, creating a variety of problems. A definitive discussion of these difficulties—called sexual dysfunctions—is beyond the scope of this text. However, the three most common are discussed: loss of potency and premature ejaculation by the man and failure to achieve orgasm by the woman.

Sexual Dysfunction

Although premature ejaculation is the most common of all sexual dysfunctions, the definition of premature ejaculation is not agreed upon. The range of definitions includes the following variations:

Premature Ejaculation

1.   Ejaculation before vaginal penetration.

2.   Ejaculation within ten seconds of vaginal penetration.

3.   Ejaculation within one minute after vaginal penetration.

4.   Ejaculation before a specific number of vaginal thrusts.

5.   Inability to delay ejaculation long enough for the woman to achieve orgasm 50 percent of the time.

6.   Lack of control over the ejaculatory reflex.

The last three definitions are somewhat controversial. It is somewhat arbitrary, for example, to say whether the male is responding too quickly or the female too slowly. However, if the female is normally orgasmic the responsibility for failure to continue the sex act until orgasm is reached is assigned to the male.

Almost every man will occasionally ejaculate too quickly for his partner. This is normal and should not cause concern.

The two major causes of premature ejaculation are (1) conditions that facilitate rapid ejaculation and (2) anxiety.

Causes of Premature Ejaculation

Inability to control ejaculation is probably a learned response, learned under conditions that necessitate rapid response. For example, young males often may have sexual intercourse in a parked car, when they are fearful that the police may arrive. Other instances may occur in a family residence, when the young couple is fearful of being discovered by a parent.

Learned Response

A man who feels he will be unable to satisfy his partner may have anxiety about the sex act. Focusing on this fear is likely to make him ejaculate prematurely.

Anxiety

Because premature ejaculation is usually psychological and a learned response, it can be reversed and unlearned. It is the easiest male dysfunction to treat.

Treatment of Premature Ejaculation

Two methods of treatment are typical. One is the **squeeze technique** used in Masters and Johnson therapy. The technique is a series of arousals to the point of ejaculation, with each arousal reversed by the woman's squeezing the penis around the coronal ridge. Sexual intercourse is gradually introduced in combination with the technique.

The **Semans start-stop** technique has the woman stimulate the man to the point of ejaculation several times, stopping the stimulation each time before ejaculation. Eventually, the man is capable of penile stimulation of long duration.

Impotence (erectile dysfunction) is the male's inability to produce or maintain an erection adequate for sexual intercourse in the majority of sexual contacts.

Impotence

Primary impotence is the condition of never having had the ability to maintain an erection for intercourse. **Secondary impotence** exists when a man who has succeeded at intercourse at least once cannot maintain an adequate erection.

Half of all men occasionally experience impotence. Such temporary conditions are normal and can be brought on by fatigue, emotional upset, anxiety about a decision, or intoxication by alcohol or other drugs. It is important that both the man and the woman accept these occurrences as normal and not interpret them in terms of sexual competence or changes in the personal relationship.

Occasional Impotence

The causes of impotence may be organic or psychogenic.

Causes of Impotence

About 10 percent of all cases of impotence have organic causes, for example:

Organic Impotence

- Abnormalities in genital structure
- Problems of the nervous system
- Medications
- Surgery
- Spinal cord injury
- Excessive intake of alcohol or drugs
- Vascular problems

Treatment for anatomical abnormalities usually consists of surgery to tighten the perineal muscles and to insert a penile prosthesis.

The most common cause of impotence is the male's anxiety about sexual performance. For example, one failure may lead to a preoccupation with sexual performance. The man begins to assume the role of a spectator, watching his sexual performance. As a spectator, he ceases to be a participant and this decreases his spontaneity and response, creating more anxiety and impotence. Anxiety can also be produced by an early experience in which a woman scorned him as inadequate.

Psychogenic Impotence

Masters and Johnson report that 75 percent of impotent patients can be successfully treated. Their treatment approach consists of teaching couples to remove all pressures about sexual performance, to explore their total relationship, and to experience pleasurable sensations.

Treatment

Orgasmic dysfunction (anorgasmia), the woman's inability to achieve orgasm can be primary or situational (secondary). A woman with primary orgasmic dysfunction has never achieved an orgasm (about 10 percent of all women).

Female Orgasmic Dysfunction

A woman with secondary orgasmic dysfunction has achieved orgasm at least once but cannot achieve it in coitus with any predictability. Failure to achieve orgasm was the primary complaint of 75 percent of women in a study of 260 women at the Sexual Dysfunction Clinic at Loyola University. Orgasmic dysfunction can occur even when the woman is capable of sexual arousal and of orgasm. Therefore, whether or not situational orgasmic dysfunction is a problem or not is open to interpretation. A woman may feel sexually satisfied without orgasm during coitus. A woman who finds her situation distressful, however, may wish to explore the reasons for the dysfunction and seek therapy.

Most causes of orgasmic dysfunction are psychological, but a few are physiological. For example, alcohol and other drugs can decrease the sex drive and result in orgasmic dysfunction. Congenital abnormalities such as a tight clitoral hood and surgery such as episiotomy have been associated with orgasmic dysfunction.

Causes of Orgasmic Dysfunction

Occasionally a physiological condition, such as the loss of virginity, can lead to psychological anxieties during subsequent sexual acts with the same partner.

Most often, the cause of orgasmic dysfunction is a woman's inability to identify with her partner, that is, a lack of emotional empathy. Other causes are anxieties produced by religious prohibitions, anxiety about performance, and distractions produced by other practical concerns.

Orgasmic dysfunction can be successfully treated by several methods. For example, therapies may involve having the woman first achieve orgasm by masturbation, then by clitoral stimulation by her partner, then in coitus. The Masters and Johnson program provides first a format for acting out hostilities, then for sensate focus and discovery.

Treatment

There are basically six types of sexual dysfunctions; in the male, erectile failure, premature ejaculation, and retarded ejaculation; in the female, sexual unresponsiveness, orgasmic dysfunction, and vaginismus. The three not discussed in this chapter are:

Other Dysfunctions

- **Retarded ejaculation,** which is the inability of the male to ejaculate when he desires to do so. This dysfunction is also termed **ejaculatory incompetence.**

- **Sexual unresponsiveness,** which is the inability of the female to become sexually excited and experience vaginal vasocongestion and lubrication—somewhat like erectile failure in the male.

- **Vaginismus,** which is involuntary contractions of muscles near the vaginal entrance that prevent penetration. The condition is usually psychological in origin.

CHAPTER 5

Pregnancy, Childbirth, and the Postpartum Period

Nine months after an East Coast electrical blackout, after a Midwest snowstorm, and after a flood in Italy, baby booms occurred. Such observations indicate not only that the human confined to quarters is a cuddly primate with a one-track mind, but also that pregnancy is a frequent consequence of something that occurs in such quarters.

Today many of the mysteries about pregnancy have been dispelled, and the well-informed expectant mother avails herself of the most recent scientific knowledge by arranging for medical supervision during pregnancy (prenatal care). In addition, both mother and father can profit from personally studying pregnancy and childbirth. This chapter attempts to highlight the most important details. A preliminary section presents a short and simplified discussion of the cellular basis of reproduction.

Cellular Basis of Human Reproduction

100 Trillion Cells

The human body is made up of more than 100 trillion cells, each with a specific function. For example, one type of cell permits movement, another thought, and yet another makes reproduction possible.

Parts of a Cell

Cells viewed under a microscope somewhat resemble a slice of fruit: they have an outside membrane, an object in the center similar to the pit, and a pulpy mass filling the spaces between. The outer covering is termed the cell membrane; the pulpy mass is called the cytoplasm; and the center pit (actually separated from the cytoplasm by a second membrane) is known as the nucleus.

Genes

The nucleus of a human cell contains over one million genes. These genes control the day-to-day acivities of the cell; they also provide the hereditary blueprint for reproduction.

Recently genes were chemically identified as giant molecules of a nucleic acid known as deoxyribonucleic acid (**DNA**). DNA, operating from its protected position in the nucleus, directs the activity of the cell and determines heredity.

Each human cell (excluding sperm and ova) contains 46 chromosomes. These chromosomes are composed of DNA and proteins, with proteins serving as a kind of "backbone" to support the genes.

Chromosomes

Among the 46 chromosomes found in each normal body cell, 23 are duplicate descendants of the mother (maternal chromosomes) and the remaining 23 are duplicate descendants of the father (paternal chromosomes). Thus, human chromosomes are more accurately described as 23 pairs of homologous chromosomes. Each chromosome pair carries genes that influence a specific trait, one member of the pair providing the maternal trait and the other the paternal trait.

Mitosis is the process by which a cell splits to form new cells. The first step in mitosis is replication of the chromosomes to provide the new cell with a proper control system. The first step is followed by several others, leading to complete replication of cells every 10 to 30 hours.

Mitosis

Not all human cells reproduce by mitosis. Meiosis is the cellular division by which sperm and ova (gametes) are formed. More commonly the process is referred to as spermatogenesis in the male and **oögenesis** in the female.

Meiosis

Sperm and ova, formed by meiosis, each contain 23 chromosomes and are capable of initiating the formation of a new individual by fusion with each other.

Sperm and ova contain only one half the number of chromosomes that other body cells (somatic cells) contain.

For example, consider the following distribution:

Animal	Body Cells	Gametes
Dog	56 chromosomes	28 chromosomes
Horse	60 chromosomes	30 chromosomes
Human	46 chromosomes	23 chromosomes

The human life cycle, therefore, consists of meiosis, fertilization, and mitosis.

The Human Life Cycle

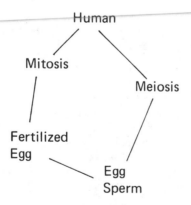

Among the 23 pairs of chromsomes found in human cells is one pair of sex chromosomes. These sex chromosomes contain the genes for development of maleness and femaleness.

The Sex Chromosomes

Depending on their shape and size, sex chromosomes are termed X chromosomes or Y chromosomes. Males have an XY pair of sex chromosomes, females an XX pair. This arrangement is true for all cells in the body except sperm and ova.

During oögenesis, eggs containing 23 chromosomes are produced. Each egg contains an X sex chromosome, never a Y. During spermatogenesis sperm containing 23 chromosomes are produced. Each sperm contains one sex chromosome—an X or a Y.

Sex Determination: X or Y

Therefore, sperm may be classified as male (having a Y chromosome) or female (having an X chromosome).

Male and Female Sperm

When the sperm fertilizes the egg, a full complement of 46 chromosomes (23 maternal and 23 paternal) is provided, including two sex chromosomes.

If a male sperm (Y chromosome) fertilizes the egg (always contains an X chromosome), the offspring will be a male (XY).

X and Y = Male

If a female sperm (X chromosome) fertilizes the egg, the offspring will be a female (XX).

X and X = Female

As we have seen, hereditary characteristics are determined by genes carried on the chromosomes. When an egg is fertilized by a sperm, the maternal and paternal genes line up so that the genes for various traits, such as hair color, are next to each other.

Dominant and Recessive Characteristics

If the maternal and paternal genes for a trait are different, then the genetic "instructions" in one set of genes override those in the other. For example, after fertilization of the ovum, paternal genes for brown eyes might line up with maternal genes for blue eyes. In this case, the genes for brown eyes are more influential, and the offspring would have brown eyes.

The more influential genes are called dominant genes, and the ones they override are called recessive. For example, brown eyes are dominant over blue, dark hair over blond, and curly hair over straight.

If the offspring inherits recessive genes (for example, blue eyes) from both the mother and the father, then the recessive trait will manifest itself.

Previously we noted that each body cell contains 23 pairs of chromosomes, including a pair of sex chromosomes. The sex chromosomes, like other chromosomes, carry genes, and the hereditary characteristics transmitted on the sex chromosomes are said to be sex-linked.

Sex-linked Characteristics

The X chromosome carries genes for a variety of human characteristics, but the Y chromosome, with the exception of its ability to direct maleness and produce "hairy ears," appears to be practically "empty" from a genetic standpoint. Therefore, when some recessive hereditary defect is carried on the maternal X chromosome, such as red-green color blindness or hemophilia, the defect will manifest itself in the male offspring (XY). This happens because the paternal Y chromosome carries no genes that could dominate the recessive defect carried on the maternal X chromosome.

In contrast, recessive defects carried on the maternal X chromosome are far less likely to manifest themselves in female offspring (XX). This is because genes carried on the paternal X chromosome may dominate the recessive defect carried on the maternal X chromosome, producing a normal offspring. If, however, both maternal and paternal X chromosomes carry recessive genes for a defect, it is sure to appear in the offspring.

Consequently, genetic defects transmitted by genes located on X chromosomes are far more likely to appear in male than in female offspring.

Occasionally, ovulation may occur more than once during a menstrual cycle; if so, and if two eggs are fertilized by two different sperm, fraternal twins result. Since fraternal twins result from two sperm and two eggs, they are no more alike genetically than any other two children by the same parents. There seems to be a hereditary tendency for fraternal twins.

Biological Basis of Twins
Fraternal and Identical Twins

Identical twins develop from one egg that divides after fertilization, and since they have inherited the same chromosomes, they are always of the same sex and very much alike.

Triplets can result from the fertilization of three separate ova, but in most cases two ova are involved. One separates and develops into identical twins.

Triplets

The approximate rates of multiple births are:

Occurrence of Multiple Births

- Twins: 1 in 80 to 90 births

- Triplets: 1 in 7000 to 8000 births

- Quadruplets: 1 in 700,000 births

In pregnancy the placenta, even in its most elementary form, produces large quantities of a hormonal substance called human chorionic gonadotropin. This substance can be detected in the blood six to eight days after fertilization of the ovum.

Pregnancy Tests
Human Chorionic Gonadotropin

Pregnancy tests are based on the fact that the urine of pregnant women contains human chorionic gonadotropin. These hormonal substances can be measured directly, but indirect tests are about 98 percent accurate.

Traditionally these indirect tests have consisted of injecting the hormonal substances into other animals (mouse, rabbit, and frog) and observing the effects. More recently, slide tests have been developed that make it possible to perform a two-minute urine test to detect pregnancy as early as 12 days after a missed menstrual period.

On the average, babies are born about 280 days after the last menstrual period. However, this is only a mathematical average, and few babies arrive exactly according to schedule. A baby may be born one to four weeks before or after this date. This date is calculated by counting back three months from the first day of the last menstrual period and adding seven days. For example, if the last period began on September 3, one would count back three months to June 3 and add seven days. The baby's due date would be June 10.

Estimating the Due Date

The moment of fertilization is termed conception. Conception normally takes place in the upper portion of the oviduct.

Conception

After fertilization, the ovum makes a three- to four-day trip through the lower portion of the oviduct to the uterus. En route, the ovum derives nutrition from secretions of the oviduct and divides by meiosis four to five days before it reaches the uterus.

The Trip to the Uterus

The ovum spends four or five days in the uterus before it becomes implanted. During this time the specially prepared uterine lining nourishes the ovum with secretions (sometimes called "uterine milk"). The ovum is developing the physiological maturity required for implantation.

Preparation for Implantation

Implantation usually occurs seven to eight days after conception. This includes approximately three days of travel through the oviduct and four to five days of development in the uterus.

Implantation

When it is ready to implant itself, the developing ovum secretes enzymes that eat into the endometrium. Then the cells of the ovum attach to the cavity formed in the endometrium. Once the ovum is implanted, the cells multiply rapidly to enlarge the connection between mother and embryo.

The Placenta

The placenta serves as lung, kidney, liver, endocrine gland, and digestive system for the developing fetus. To accomplish these functions, the placenta starts to enlarge immediately after implantation, reaching approximately three inches in length by the fourth month and eight inches by the eighth month. By time of birth it weighs about one pound.

Exchange of Substances

As the ovum grows and develops, it requires a means of obtaining nutrition and removing waste products. The placenta serves these functions.

The placenta is a physiological depot in which the transport systems of the mother and baby meet. The mother's transport system brings nutrition and oxygen to the placenta; the baby's transport system brings waste products. These substances are exchanged through small pores in the walls of the placenta.

Three Fourths of a Quart Per Minute

To ensure effective service, the mother's circulatory system sends approximately three fourths of a quart of blood through the placenta each minute. But there is no mixing of the mother's blood with the baby's blood. Rather, all substances are passed through the pores of the placenta, which separate these two transport systems. The significance of this will be discussed later in connection with Rh complications.

In addition, numerous substances may traverse the placenta and enter the fetal circulation. The following list includes a few of these well-known substances

- Some infectious organisms: e.g., viruses
- Antibodies
- Nicotine
- Alcohol
- Barbiturates
- Morphine
- Cortisone
- Penicillin
- Streptomycin
- Tetracyclines
- Tetrahydrocannabinol (active ingredient in marijuana)

Storage of Biological Materials

In addition to exchanging substances from the systems of the mother and fetus, the placenta stores various products until they are needed: calcium, iron, protein, glycogen, and other biological materials.

Hormonal Secretions of the Placenta

One of the most important tasks of the placenta is to prevent spontaneous expulsion of the growing embryo. In this connection, it is very important that the corpus luteum be maintained.

The lining and muscles of the uterus are maintained in a state suitable for pregnancy by hormonal secretions of the corpus luteum. Thus, the corpus luteum is important to normal pregnancy.

If the corpus luteum disintegrates at any time prior to the 11th week of pregnancy, expulsion of the embryo is likely. The corpus luteum is maintained by hormonal secretions from the placenta.

The hormone secreted by the placenta is called chorionic gonadotropin.

Chorionic Gonadotropin

Chorionic is an adjective derived from Greek and meaning the membrane that encloses the fetus. A portion of this membrane forms the fetal part of the placenta.

Gonad is the Greek word for seed; *tropin* is Greek for turning. Thus, gonadotropic hormones "turn" the gonads, or seeds, toward maturity. Gonadotropin, then, is a general name given to any hormone that "turns the gonads" toward maturity. These include:

1. FSH and LH from the pituitary gland.
2. Chorionic gonadotropin from the placenta.

Chorionic gonadotropin not only prevents regression of the corpus luteum but also causes it to double in size by the end of the first month of pregnancy. It also stimulates the production and release of greater amounts of estrogen and progesterone, which, in turn, maintains the uterus in a state suitable for pregnancy, thus preventing spontaneous abortion.

When the fetus is born before it is capable of surviving outside the mother's body, the event is called a miscarriage. Most miscarriages occur during the second or third month of pregnancy. More than 50 percent of miscarried embyros have deformities or biological malfunctions. Miscarriage is usually nature's way of insuring that full-term babies are healthy.

Miscarriage

Beginning at conception, the embryo moves considerably within the uterus. These movements become perceptible about midway through pregnancy.

Movement of the Fetus

At first they are detected as a gentle fluttering in the abdomen. The movements grow stronger with each day, and later in pregnancy the baby's movements may be observed.

After periods of activity the baby may remain inactive for several days. The mother should not be alarmed or worried if movements stop for a few days; this is normal.

Pregnancy is usually not suspected until three or four weeks after conception. By this time the embryo is a quarter of an inch long, has a heart beat, a two-lobed brain, and a spinal cord.

Growth of the Fetus

After two months the embryo has started to form fingers, toes, and ears, and the beginnings of eyes and facial features are present. It weighs about 1/30 of an ounce and is about 1/6 of an inch long. After eight weeks, the embryo is called a fetus and is about three inches long.

Second Month

By the end of the fourth month ears, toenails, and teeth have developed. If it were possible to see inside the uterus, the sex of the child could be determined. At the end of the fourth month the fetus is about six and one half inches long and weighs about four ounces.

Fourth Month

By the fifth month movement may be detected by the expectant mother. The physician may be able to detect a heart beat at this time, but an infant born at this time would not live.

Fifth Month

At the end of eight months the fetus weighs about five pounds and is about 18 inches long. If the baby is born during the seventh or eighth month, there is a 50 to 90 percent chance that it will survive.

Sixth to Eighth Month

Full-term (approximately nine months) girls weigh about seven pounds, whereas full-term boys average about seven and one half pounds. The range is between five and nine pounds. Full-term babies are usually 19 to 21 inches in length. A baby weighing less than five and one half pounds is said to be premature.

Full Term

The breasts become fuller and slightly tender to the touch. The nipple and dark surrounding area become darker and slightly puffy. The mother may feel a tingling, prickling sensation around the nipples in early pregnancy.

Physiological Changes in the Mother During Pregnancy

In the early stages of pregnancy, large amounts of estrogen and progesterone are secreted by the corpus luteum.

Estrogen and Progesterone Secretion During Pregnancy

Estrogen enlarges the uterus, breasts, and external genitalia.

Progesterone (1) prevents contraction of the muscles of the uterus and (2) prepares the breasts for lactation.

The average weight gain during pregnancy is 24 pounds,[1] distributed in the following manner:

Weight Gain

1.   Seven pounds is fetus.

2.   Four pounds is amniotic fluid surrounding the fetus (Fig. 36).

3.   Two pounds is the increased weight of the uterus.

4.   Two pounds are due to enlargement of the breasts.

5.   Six pounds are increased body fluids. (The mother's blood volume increases by as much as a quart.)

6.   Three pounds are increased body weight.

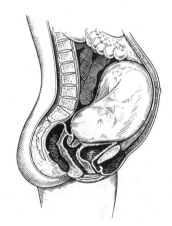

Figure 36   Amniotic sac.

By the end of the third month of pregnancy the fetus may be three inches long and weigh one ounce. As the fetus continues to grow within the uterus, the mother's abdomen must distend, causing the skin to stretch.

Body Shape

As the skin expands, pink horizontal stretch marks may appear. These marks are normal and are more pronounced in some women than in others. In general, nothing can be done about them (i.e., rubbing, cold cream, or oil will not eliminate them).

During pregnancy some food substances in the mother's blood are extracted by the placenta. This may increase the mother's appetite.

Appetite

---

[1] Arthur C. Guyton, *Textbook of Medical Physiology,* 6th ed. (Philadelphia: W. B. Saunders Co., 1981), p. 1029.

However, psychological factors may cause the woman to eat more than the body needs. Women who overeat during pregnancy may gain as much as 50 pounds.

Since the pregnant woman has different nutritional needs during pregnancy, she should seek prenatal care to assure that she obtains the extra minerals, vitamins, and proteins required.

Nutrition

During pregnancy the mother's metabolic rate increases to support the many physiological changes that take place in her body. This may result in sensations of unusual warmness. The extra weight carried during pregnancy also contributes to extra heat production.

Metabolism

During the first three months of pregnancy, the mother may experience nausea or frequent vomiting—a condition termed morning sickness.

Morning Sickness

The physiological cause of this condition is unknown, but there are two theories:

1. The placental secretions of chorionic gonadotropin in the early stages of pregnancy may be responsible for morning sickness.

According to this theory, the body develops a tolerance to chorionic gonadotropin during the later stages of pregnancy.

2. Morning sickness may be caused by chemicals released from cells that are destroyed in the lining of the uterus as the ovum implants itself in the lining.

In support of this theory, it has been observed that degeneration of other tissues produces nausea.

During pregnancy the uterus expands and exerts pressure on the bladder. Since such pressure is the normal stimulus to urinate, the expectant mother frequently feels that she shouldn't get too far from the bathroom. This is a perfectly normal occurrence during pregnancy. The increased urge to urinate is more frequent in early and late pregnancy.

Frequent Urination

One should not attempt to reduce water intake as a means of dealing with the problem because at least a quart of fluid should be ingested each day. If frequent urination becomes a major concern for the expectant mother, she should not hesitate to discuss the problem with her physician.

Because of hormonal changes, moodiness is not unusual during pregnancy. Hormonal changes may affect the emotions, and psychological ups and downs are likely. Although each woman has her unique responses to pregnancy, most women find it a happy and interesting time.

Moodiness

William Birch and Dona Meilach,[2] in *A Doctor Discusses Pregnancy,* suggest that the following conditions should be reported to the expectant mother's physician:

Danger Signals During Pregnancy

1. Any sign of bloody discharge from the vagina.

2. Persistent severe headaches.

---

[2]William Birch and Dona Meilach, *A Doctor Discusses Pregnancy* (Chicago: Budlong Press Company, 1963), pp. 27–28.

3. Severe nausea and vomiting. "Severe" means occurring several times within an hour.

4. Swelling of the ankles, feet, hands, and face, particularly if any of these puff up suddenly and finger rings feel tight. (Slight swelling during the last months in hot weather is customary.)

5. Chills and fever of over 100°F not accompanied by a common cold.

6. Continual abdominal pains that are not relieved by a bowel movement.

7. A sudden gush of water from the vagina.

8. Very frequent, burning urination.

9. An increased, unusual thirst, with reduced amounts of urine. (If you don't urinate for an entire day even though you have had normal intake of fluids, report the condition.)

Risks of Taking Drugs During Pregnancy

"The Surgeon General's report "The Health Consequences of Smoking for Women[3] states:

> Scientific studies encompassing various races and ethnic groups, cultures and countries, involving hundreds of thousands of pregnancies, have shown that cigarette smoking during pregnancy significantly affects the unborn fetus and the newborn baby. These damaging effects have been repeatedly shown to operate independently of all other factors which influence the outcome of pregnancy. The effects are increased by heavier smoking and are reduced if a woman stops smoking during pregnancy.

> Numerous toxic substances in cigarette smoke, such as nicotine and hydrogen cyanide, cross the placenta to affect the fetus directly. The carbon monoxide from cigarette smoke is transported into the fetal blood and deprives the growing baby of oxygen. Fetal growth is directly retarded. The resulting reduction in fetal weight and size has many unfortunate consequences. Women who smoke cigarettes during pregnancy have more spontaneous abortions, and a greater incidence of bleeding during pregnancy, premature and prolonged rupture of amniotic membranes, abruptio placentae and placenta previa. Women who smoke cigarettes during pregnancy have more fetal and neonatal deaths than nonsmoking pregnant women. A relation between maternal smoking and Sudden Infant Death Syndrome has now been established.

> The direct harmful effects of smoking on the fetus have long term consequences. Children of mothers who smoked during pregnancy lag measurably in physical growth; there may also be effects on behavior and cognitive development. The extent of these deficiencies increases with the number of cigarettes smoked.

> The damaging effects of maternal smoking on infants are not restricted to pregnancy. Nicotine, a known poison, is found in the breast milk of smoking mothers. Children whose parents smoke cigarettes have more respiratory infections and more hospitalizations in the first year of life.

Alcohol, like other drugs, can pass through the placenta. Excessive alcohol consumption can cause any of several defects known as fetal alcohol syn-

---

[3]The Health Consequences of Smoking for Women: a report of the Surgeon General U.S. Department of Health and Human Services, Public Health Service, Rockville, Md. (U.S. Government Printing Office: 623-877/1525) pp. iii–iv.

drome: abnormally small head, poor coordination, behavior problems, heart defects.

All drugs should be taken only with medical supervision. Tranquilizers, for example, if taken early in pregnancy may cause birth defects. Heavy use of aspirin may interfere with blood clotting in the mother and fetus.

The technical name for the entire process of birth is parturition; the common name is labor. Parturition is initiated by a combination of hormonal and mechanical factors.

Childbirth, Parturition, or Labor

Hormonal factors prevent contraction of the uterus during pregnancy but initiate contraction at the time of birth. Progesterone inhibits uterine contraction, whereas estrogen increases uterine contractility.

Hormonal Factors

The ratio of estrogen to progesterone therefore has an important effect on uterine contractility. After the seventh month of pregnancy, this ratio changes, as estrogen is secreted in proportionately greater amounts.

Currently available evidence suggests that production of a hormonal substance called oxytocin is increased at time of labor. It is thought that irritation or stretching of the cervix is the stimulus for release of oxytocin.

Oxytocin

Oxytocin is secreted by the pituitary gland, and its specific effect is to cause uterine contractions. An overdose of oxytocin during prolonged contractions can cause death of the fetus.

The following mechanical factors are thought to increase uterine contractility:

Mechanical Factors

1. Stretching of the uterine smooth muscles as pregnancy continues.

2. Intermittent stretching by movements of the fetus.

The following observations suggest that stretching or irritation increases uterine contractility:

1. Dilation of the cervix by the obstetrician frequently induces labor.

2. Rupturing of the membranes that enclose the fetus causes the head to irritate or stretch the cervix and may thus induce uterine contractions.

Before labor begins one or more of the following signs will occur:

Prelabor

1. A discharge or gush of water from the vagina indicates that the sac of amniotic fluid that has cushioned the baby during pregnancy has ruptured.

This may occur before or during labor. If it happens at home, it should be reported to the physician, since it usually means that labor is about to begin.

2. During pregnancy the mucous plug sealing the cervix is discharged and travels down through the vagina as labor is about to begin. This blood-tinged discharge is termed the "bloody show."

3. The most frequent sign is irregular contractions.

Labor is divided into three stages:

1. Contraction and dilation.

2. Delivery.

3. Afterbirth.

During the last months of pregnancy, weak rhythmic contractions begin in the uterus. These contractions become stronger as the end of pregnancy approaches. Finally, the contractions become strong enough to stretch the cervix and force the baby through the birth canal. These final and more powerful contractions are called the contractions of labor.

The first barrier to parturition is the uterine cervix. However, the cervix has become soft during the last weeks of pregnancy, so that it stretches during labor. This stretching, or dilation, of the cervix lasts until the cervix is sufficiently dilated to 8 to 10 centimeters to allow the head of the fetus to enter (Figs. 37 and 38).

The contraction and dilation stage may last 8 to 24 hours for the first pregnancy or only a few minutes for subsequent pregnancies.

Shortly after the cervix has become dilated, the baby moves into the birth canal (Fig. 39). At time of entry into the canal, 99 percent of babies are in a longitudinal position; 1 percent are in a transverse position.

In the longitudinal position, the posterior part of the top of the head usually (95 percent of cases) enters first; occasionally the brow (0.5 percent) or the face (0.5 percent) enters first. In 4 percent of longitudinal births, the buttocks, a knee, or a foot enters first; these are referred to as breech births. In the transverse position (1 in 200 births), the shoulder, arm, or hand enters the birth canal first.

After the baby has entered the birth canal, subsequent contractions of the uterus accomplish delivery (Figs. 40, 41, and 42).

The delivery stage may last up to half an hour for a first pregnancy or be as short as one minute in subsequent pregnancies.

After the baby has been expelled from the uterus, the only remaining connection with the mother is the umbilical cord, which contains the arteries and veins to the placenta (Figs. 43, 44, and 45). To accomplish final separation, the umbilical cord is tied off and cut.

Three Stages of Labor
Stage One: Contraction and Dilation

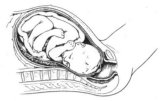

Figure 37   Childbirth sequence I.

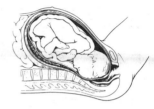

Figure 38   Childbirth sequence II.

Stage Two: Delivery

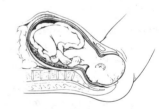

Figure 39   Childbirth sequence III.

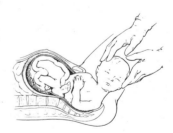

Figure 40   Childbirth sequence IV.

Figure 41   Childbirth sequence V.

Figure 42   Childbirth sequence VI.

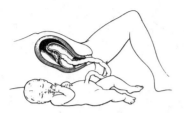

Figure 43   Childbirth sequence VII.

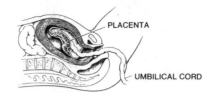

Figure 44   Childbirth sequence VIII.

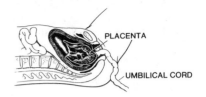

Figure 45   Childbirth sequence IX.

Shortly after delivery (10 to 45 minutes), the uterus contracts to a very small size.

Stage Three: Afterbirth

Since the placenta is unable to contract, it breaks or is sheared away from the walls of the uterus (Fig. 44). The separated placenta is expelled, together with a small amount of blood (average, 350 milliliters). Delivery of the placenta is sometimes referred to as delivery of the afterbirth (Fig. 45).

To prevent further blood loss, the uterus contracts tightly and closes off the blood vessels that went to the placenta.

About one in 50 babies must be delivered by making an incision through the abdominal wall and through the uterus. This delivery is called a cesarean birth (also cesarean section or C section) and is necessary when the pelvic area is too small, when the baby is in an abnormal position, and in certain other circumstances.

Cesarean Birth

A woman may successfully have as many as three to four cesarean deliveries. (One mother is reported to have jokingly requested that the doctor install a zipper after her sixth cesarean.)

Prepared childbirth techniques (sometimes called natural childbirth) are becoming more popular among women and couples who want to actively participate in the birth process. The techniques require training during pregnancy and usually have the added benefit of allowing the couple to share in the processes of pregnancy and birth.

Prepared Childbirth

The most widely used technique is the Lamaze method. In the Lamaze method, relaxation and controlled breathing are learned as ways of preventing tension, fear, and other uncomfortable feelings during labor and delivery.

Lamaze Technique

The LeBoyer technique focuses on the baby's experience at birth, to prevent this from being a traumatic event. The following conditions are met in the delivery room:

LeBoyer Technique

1. The newborn is placed in a tub of water at body temperature.

2. Lights are dimmed.

3. Only soft and low sounds are heard—voices and music.

4. The umbilical cord is cut *after* it ceases to pulsate.

5. The newborn has skin-to-skin contact on the mother's abdomen.

For women who do not want to give birth in a hospital setting, alternatives are more readily available today than in the past.

Birthplace Alternatives

Birthing Centers, for example, simulate the home environment. The couple, obstetrician, pediatrician, and Center staff draw up an individualized plan that meets the needs and preferences of the mother. Emergency medical equipment is available in case of need. Home births are safe if proper precautions are taken. These include proper prenatal care, screening for complications, preparation, availability of a skilled assistant, and emergency transportation. Home birth is becoming more popular as more midwives become available; however, this practice is controversial among the medical professions. Many hospitals would revoke the hospital privileges of physicians who deliver in homes.

Bonding

Bonding is the closeness and attachment established between the baby and its parents. Bonding can begin immediately after birth through soft touches, words, and physical closeness. Recent research indicates the importance of bonding by both mother and father. The early and future happiness of the baby may be influenced at this time.

Postpartum Period (after Delivery)
Normal Uterus

Within a week after delivery, the uterus decreases in weight by one half, and within four to six weeks it returns to its normal size.

Lactation

During pregnancy large quantities of estrogens are secreted by the placenta to cause physical growth of the breasts: the ductal system grows and branches, and additional fat is deposited.

Following growth of the breasts during pregnancy, progesterone causes development of secretory characteristics of special cells, in a manner rather like the effects of progesterone on the endometrium during the later half of the menstrual cycle.

Although estrogens and progesterone prepare the breasts for nursing, they actually inhibit secretion of milk.

Yet another hormone, prolactin from the mother's pituitary gland, is responsible for the secretion of milk. Prolactin increases in the mother's blood starting about the fifth week of pregnancy, but because of the inhibiting effects of large amounts of estrogens and progesterone, only small amounts of milk, called colostrum, are secreted during pregnancy.

When the placenta is delivered, the levels of estrogens and progesterone are suddenly decreased, and when the inhibiting effects of these substances are removed, milk is produced.

Release of Milk

Milk produced in the breasts is stored until the time of nursing. The mechanism for release of milk is as follows:

1. As the baby suckles, a sensation is transmitted to the mother's brain.

2. The brain, in turn, signals the pituitary gland to release the hormone oxytocin.

3. Oxytocin enters the blood and within 30 seconds causes secretion of milk.

Continued Production and Secretion of Milk

After childbirth the amount of prolactin in the mother's blood returns to its nonpregnant level within a few weeks.

However, each time the mother nurses her baby a nervous signal from the nipples causes a ten-fold increase in prolactin. Thus continued nursing causes a continued production of milk, a process that could last for several years. In the absence of the nervous signal resulting from nursing, milk production stops.

After childbirth, the uterus returns to its normal size more rapidly in lactating women than in those who have not nursed their babies. This is thought to occur because of a diminution in the amount of estrogen secreted during lactation.

Physiological factors associated with lactation may also prevent the normal menstrual cycle for the first few months after childbirth. However, the lactating woman may have normal cycles, and she is capable of becoming pregnant.

Rh is the symbol for Rhesus and stems from the discovery of an inherited protein substance first observed on the red blood cells of the Rhesus monkey.

People born with this protein substance in their red blood cells are said to be Rh-positive. Individuals without this protein are termed Rh-negative. The Rh factor is present in 85 percent of the white population and 93 percent of the black population.

The Rh factor occasionally becomes a medical problem because a woman who is Rh-negative has the capacity to develop antibodies against the Rh protein in an Rh-positive fetus. The blood of the mother and of the fetus do not usually mix, but some interchange could occur during birth. In a subsequent pregnancy, the mother's antibodies could enter the fetal blood by crossing the placenta. The antibodies would attack the fetus's red blood cells, and the result would be a stillbirth.

There is a slight chance that such a condition could occur during pregnancy. It could happen if:

1. The mother were Rh negative and the father Rh positive.

2. The baby inherited his father's Rh-positive blood.

3. The mother developed antibodies against the Rh factor.

4. These antibodies passed through the placenta and attacked the baby's blood cells.

This ordinarily does not happen during the first pregnancy because the mother has not previously been sensitized by Rh protein. However, there is a slight chance that the second pregnancy could present a problem if the baby were again Rh positive and the first pregnancy sensitized the mother to Rh factor.

Fortunately, a recent discovery makes it possible to prevent sensitization of the mother during her first pregnancy and thus to avoid the Rh problem altogether. Through proper prenatal care and an injection of Rhogam, the production of the antibodies can be prevented.

Even when the mother does become sensitized, blood transfusion both before and after childbirth is now available as effective treatment.

Sometimes there are reasons to suspect that a fetus may have inherited genetic defects. These reasons often relate to the genetic background of parents. Moreover, it has been established that women over the age of 35 are more likely to have mongoloid children. When screening tests for genetic defects reveal that the fetus has a chromosomal abnormality, the parents are provided the choice of having an abortion.

One procedure to determine chromosomal abnormality is known as amniocentesis. This procedure involves the removal of amniotic fluid—fluid that

Other Effects of Lactation

Rh Factor

Antibodies

Conditions of Risk

Prevention of Rh Sensitization

Amniocentesis

surrounds the fetus—from the mother's uterus. Amniocentesis is accomplished via a long needle inserted through the abdomen and uterus. The amniotic fluid obtained in this procedure contains fetal cells which can be analyzed for genetic defects.

In 1984 a new test for detecting genetic defects prior to birth became available in the United States. Called chorionic villi biopsy (CVB) the procedure has been used in Russia and China for a number of years.

New Test for Genetic Defects During Pregnancy

The chorion is the outer sac surrounding the fetus, and in early pregnancy it is covered with root-like projections (the villi). These projections are fetal tissue, a part of which will later differentiate into the placenta. One of these projections can easily be biopsied in early pregnancy with virtually no discomfort to the pregnant woman.

Screening tests for a variety of genetic defects can be performed on the cells obtained by chorionic villi biopsy.

CVB has a number of advantages over amniocentesis:

1.   CVB can be performed 8 to 11 weeks after the last menstrual period whereas amniocentesis is performed 17 to 20 weeks into pregnancy.

2.   Since cells are dividing so rapidly in early pregnancy, the results of CVB tests can be available within hours. Results from amniocentesis require several weeks.

3.   If a birth defect is formed and a decision to terminate pregnancy is made, abortion is easier and safer at 12 weeks than at 20 weeks.

Antibody production is essential to human health, but occasionally, as with Rh complications and tissue transplants, it can cause problems. An estimated 10 to 30 percent of female infertility may be associated with antibodies. When sperm come in contact with cervical tissue, the woman's body produces antibodies that have the ability to incapacitate sperm and thus prevent pregnancy. There is some evidence that if the male partner uses a condom for six months the level of sperm antibodies is reduced and the chances of pregnancy are increased.

Sperm Antibodies and Infertility

CHAPTER 6

Contraception

Conception is the fertilization of an ovum by a spermatozoon. The frequency with which fertilization occurs among women participating in normal sexual intercourse is termed the pregnancy rate. When no preventive measures are taken, the pregnancy rate is approximately 80 percent (that is, if 100 women were to engage in sexual intercourse for one year, approximately 80 would become pregnant).

Contraception is the prevention of pregnancy and may be accomplished by a variety of chemical, physical, or surgical means. Interception is the prevention of implantation of a fertilized egg, usually by postcoital (morning after) pills. Abortion is the early termination of pregnancy after implantation. Contraception is the earliest prevention effort; interception is a later effort; abortion is a last recourse. Contraception and interception are the subject of this chapter, and abortion is discussed in the chapter that follows.

The Effectiveness of Contraceptive Methods

The effectiveness of any contraceptive depends on several factors—theoretical effectiveness, motivation, knowledge of methods, sociological stress, availability, and acceptability—to mention a few.

Theoretical versus Use-Effectiveness

The theoretical effectiveness of a contraceptive method refers to the pregnancy rate when instructions for use are followed in careful detail. For example, the theoretical effectiveness of the contraceptive pill would be reflected by the pregnancy rate when, and only when, pills were taken exactly as prescribed.

In actual practice, the theoretical effectiveness of a contraceptive method is seldom achieved because of the high frequency of mistakes or inattention by the user. The discrepancy between theoretical effectiveness and use-effectiveness is clearly seen with the oral contraceptive: the former has a pregnancy rate of less than 1 percent, whereas the latter may have a pregnancy rate closer to 16 percent.

The student of sex education is often confused by widely conflicting reports of use-effectiveness pregnancy rates. For example, rates of 3, 11, 12, 17, and 28 percent have been reported for the condom. Which one is accurate? Unfortunately, there is no simple way to resolve the differences between various reports, but Table 1 may be useful as a general guide. The table compares theoretical effectiveness with use-effectiveness by average users.

Conflicting Reports of Use-Effectiveness

Table 1 shows that the pregnancy rate is generally higher for coital-related contraceptives (contraceptives that must be used with each coitus and that require advanced planning) such as the condom, diaphragm, spermicidal

TABLE 1:   Contraceptive Effectiveness: Theoretical and Actual Use Rates*

Method	Used Correctly and Consistently (Theoretical Effectiveness)	Average Experience in the United States (Actual Use-Effectiveness)
Hysterectomy	0.0001	0.0001
Tubal ligation	0.04	0.04
Vasectomy	0.15	0.15
Oral contraceptive (combined)	0.34	4–10
Injection of long-acting progestin	0.25	5–10
Condom + spermicidal agent	< 1	5
Low-dose oral progestin	1–1.5	5–10
IUD	1–3	5
Condom	3	10
Diaphragm (with spermicide)	3	17
Spermicidal foam	3	22
Spermicidal suppository	3	20–25
Coitus interruptus	9	20–25
Rhythm		
Calendar only	13	21
Basal body temperature only	7	20
Cervical mucus only	2	25
Lactation for 12 months	15	40
Chance (sexually active)	90	90
Douche	?	40

*Number of pregnancies during the first year of use per 100 nonsterile women initiating the method. Subjects were women who did not want to have more children.

From Robert A. Hatcher, et al., *Contraceptive Technology 1980–1981* (New York: Irvington Publishers, Inc., 1980). Reprinted with permission.

agents, and coitus interruptus. Methods less subject to patient error appear to be more effective (that is, IUD, tubal ligation, and vasectomy).

It is the role of the sex educator to present information about the theoretical effectiveness, use-effectiveness, and safety of various contraceptives. Religious and esthetic aspects of individual choice are not within the purview of sex education.

Choice of Contraceptive Method

The chapter discusses contraceptives in the following sequence: (1) oral contraceptives, (2) surgical sterilization, (3) condom, (4) IUD, (5) diaphragm, (6) spermicidal agents, (7) douche, (8) rhythm method, and (9) withdrawal.

Oral Contraceptives (OCs)

In 1937, the hormone progesterone was demonstrated to prevent ovulation in rabbits. This discovery prompted two scientific research questions:

Suppressed Ovulation

1.   Could progesterone be utilized as a human contraceptive?

2.   If so, could a readily available source of progesterone be found?

The answers to both these questions were affirmative:

Origin of the Combined Oral Contraceptive

1.   A synthetic substance (progestin) having the physiological effect of progesterone was derived from the wild Mexican yam.

2.   In 1956 progestogen and another hormonal substance (estrogen) were combined as an oral contraceptive and were found highly effective in tests conducted in San Juan, Puerto Rico.

Thus the discovery that progesterone blocked ovulation led to the production of the first oral contraceptive pill. But in addition to progestin, this pill included estrogen, added to control endometrial shedding and bleeding, thus assuring a normal menstrual flow during each cycle. Today, it is clear that estrogen in small amounts and progesterone in large amounts inhibit the production of follicle-stimulating hormone (FSH) and luteinizing hormone (LH).

Later it was found that synthetic estrogens alone prevent ovulation (natural estrogen does not consistently inhibit ovulation).

Today three major types of oral contraceptives are available:

Three Types of Oral Contraceptives

1. Combined.

2. Phasic.

3. Progestational.

Both the combined and phasic pills contain estrogen and progestin.

The combined oral contraceptive is one in which both estrogen and progestin are taken throughout the cycle. This is the most widely used of the OCs. Its popularity stems from its low pregnancy rate: when compared with combined pill users, IUD users have two times as many pregnancies; condom users, three times as many; diaphragm users, four times as many; and other contraceptive users, five times as many.

Combined OCs

More than 50 million women worldwide are now using this pill, but during the past five years there has been a 30 percent drop in sales in the United States. By contrast, sales in many Latin American countries have increased by about 50 during the same time span.

The contraceptive effect of combined OCs was initially believed to be the result of the simple blocking of ovulation. However, the observation that combined OCs have contraceptive actions in addition to the suppression of ovulation has made it necessary to revise the initial hypothesis.

How Combined OCs Work

It would now appear that at least five mechanisms may be operative:

Five Mechanisms

1. In sufficient dosage, estrogen inhibits FSH, a pituitary hormone required for ovulation.

2. In sufficient dosage, progestogen inhibits LH, a pituitary hormone required for ovulation.

3. In the user of the oral contraceptive, a thick mucus is produced in the cervix that may act as a barrier to passage of sperm.

4. Also in the user, an endometrium not suitable for implantation may be present for a greater than normal portion of the cycle.

5. Progestins may inhibit motility of sperm or decrease the viability of the fertilized egg.

The number of mechanisms operating in a given user depends on the amount of estrogen and progestin taken. This is important because the best contraceptive is the one that least affects normal physiology. Thus a pill that could be highly effective as a contraceptive and yet not block ovulation would be desirable.

Currently, however, the greater the hormonal dosage, the greater the effectiveness of the pill, and pills that block ovulation are nearly 100 percent effective when taken as directed. In the meantime, research moves toward the discovery of a pill that will not suppress ovulation or disturb the endometrium but that will be 100 percent effective.

Side Effects of Combined Oral Contraceptives

Before making a personal decision about oral contraceptives, it is important to discuss one's medical history with a physician. The following review of side effects may also be useful.

The side effects of the pill are advantageous in some cases, disadvantageous in others, and serious or even lethal for a small number of women.

The following symptoms may indicate a serious condition and should be reported to a physician at once:

Reportable Symptoms

1. Severe leg cramps.

2. Chest pain.

3. Severe headaches.

4. Blurring or loss of vision.

5. Sensations of flashing lights.

A large number of studies from several countries clearly demonstrate a higher incidence of thromboembolic (internal clotting) disorders among women who use OCs. These disorders are divisible into four types: venous thromboembolism, ischemic heart disease, cerebrovascular disease (stroke), and hypertension.

Thromboembolic Disorders

Venous thromboembolism is the formation of a clot within a vein. This happens most often in a leg vein, but clots may move from the legs to the lungs and cause serious problems (pulmonary embolism).

Venous Thromboembolism

The risk of a first episode of venous thromboembolism is considerably higher among OC users: the increased risk has ranged from 3 to 11 times higher than for those who have never used OCs.

The risk of venous thromboembolism does not appear to be associated with the length of OC use and disappears after pill use stops. With lower doses of estrogen, the risk is not as great.

Among OC users the risk of venous thromboembolism is three times higher for those with blood types A, B, or AB than for those with type O, but the reason for this is unknown.

A lack of oxygen to the heart muscle is termed ischemic heart disease, a condition frequently caused by the formation of a clot in one of the arteries that take blood to the heart. Because these arteries are called coronary arteries and because a clot is also called a thrombus, this condition is known as coronary thrombosis.

Ischemic Heart Disease

Coronary thrombosis is rare among young women (1.9 per 100,000 women ages 25 to 34), but increases rapidly with age (14.6 per 100,000 for women ages 35 to 44).

Oral contraceptives pose little risk of coronary thrombosis for young women, but the combined effects of aging and OC use greatly increase this risk. In fact, the Royal college of General Practitioners in Britain states that for women over 45, "use of oral contraceptives can be justified only in exceptional circumstances."

For women over 40 who both smoke and use OCs, the risk of ischemic heart disease may be 350 to 800 times greater than for younger women who neither smoke nor use the pill.

Obviously the safest way to use the pill is not to smoke at the same time.

There are basically two types of circulatory disorders to the brain: one in which the arteries that bring blood to the brain are blocked by a clot and a second in which an artery ruptures. The latter is usually more fatal. Both are termed stroke.

Cerebrovascular Disease

Bleeding into the space around the brain (subarachnoid space) is the most common type of stroke among women in their reproductive years, and this type of stroke appears to be increased among OC users. The death rate for pill users is approximately 9 per 100,000 women as compared with 2.3 among those who have never used OCs.

The risk of subarachnoid hemorrhage increases with duration of pill use and persists after use stops. There is some evidence that this type of stroke may be related to progestin dose.

Strokes caused by blood clots are also increased among OC users. The risk for thrombotic stroke is approximately nine times greater among women using the pill.

Higher than normal blood pressure is called hypertension, often defined as a systolic pressure above 140 mm Hg and a diastolic reading above 90 mm Hg.

Hypertension

OC users generally show a slight rise in blood pressure, 4 mm Hg systolic and 1 mm Hg diastolic. Overall, OC users are 1.5 to 3 times more likely to be hypertensive.

Blood pressure decreases in most women when OC use stops, and hypertension is no more common among former OC users than among those who have never used OCs.

Current research suggests that increases in blood pressure are associated with the progestin component of the pill.

OCs may increase circulatory disease by changes in blood coagulation, blood lipid levels, or blood pressure.

Mechanism of Thromboembolic Disorders

To date most studies have focused on the blood coagulation mechanism, and it is now known that OC use causes blood platelets to aggregate and adhere to blood vessels—a condition that favors clot formation. At the same time, OCs appear to inhibit the fibrinolytic system, a system that usually breaks down small clots. The combined effect of changes in platelet behavior and slowing down of the clot dissolving system is to increase the risk of internal clotting.

These changes in blood coagulation are thought to be related to the estrogen component of OCs.

A recent study of 50,000 women in Britain revealed that OC users under age 35 or those under 45 who did not smoke had the same death rates from circulatory disorders as women who did not use OCs.

Risk of Circulatory Disorders for Young Women

This study suggests that the risk to young women is small and that OC users ought to think carefully about their smoking habits.

Other Side Effects

It is now estimated that 1 of every 11 women in the United States will develop breast cancer at some time during her life, and any factor that might have even a slight effect on this problem is of great concern.

Breast Cancer

Research to date has generally found no significant relationship between OC use and breast cancer;[1-4] however, a recent study[5] suggests that long-term use before age 25 of OCs with high progestogen may carry a substantial risk for breast cancer. In this study, OCs with low progestogen components used before age 25 were not associated with increased rates of breast cancer.

The relationship between cervical cancer and OC use remains unclear at this time. The relationship is difficult to evaluate for the following reasons:

Cervical Cancer

1.   Women using the pill have more frequent Papanicolaou smears than those who don't. This creates a diagnostic bias in which cancer of the cervix is more likely to be detected among OC users.

2.   Sexual behavior influences cervical cancer: cervical cancer is linked to the number of sexual partners and to age at first coitus. This is significant because in the United States OC use is associated with a larger number of sexual partners.

When attempts have been made to control for sexual behavior, the results have been mixed. The majority of studies, however, have found a higher incidence of cervical cancer among OC users.

A recent comparison[6] of 6838 OC users with 3154 IUD users found a higher rate of cervical cancer among the pill users.

Benign liver tumors are greatly increased among OC users. Nonusers have an incidence rate of about 0.1 per 100,000 United States women, compared with 1 to 3 per 100,000 pill users. Moreover, benign liver tumors in OC users are more likely to rupture and cause internal bleeding.

Benign Liver Tumors

Combined oral contraceptives reduce the volume of mother's milk and the duration of lactation. The amounts of protein, fat, and calcium are also reduced.

Breast-Feeding

Women who discontinue use of the pill in order to have children do not experience an increased risk of miscarriage, birth defects, or infant death.

Future Offspring

---

[1]R. S. Pattenbarger and J. B. Kampert, "Oral Contraceptives and Breast Cancer Risk," *INSERM,* 83 (1979), pp. 93–114.

[2]M. P. Vassey, et al., "Oral Contraceptive Use and Abortion Before First Term Pregnancy in Relation to Breast Cancer," *British Journal of Cancer,* 45 (1982), pp. 327–331.

[3]M. P. Vassey, et al., "Oral Contraceptives and Breast Cancer," *British Journal of Cancer,* 47 (1984), pp. 455–462.

[4]Centers for Disease Control Cancer and Steroid Hormone Study, "Long-term Oral Contraceptive Use and the Risk of Breast Cancer," *Journal of the American Medical Association,* 249 (1983), pp. 1591–1595.

[5]M. C. Pike, et al., "Breast Cancer in Young Women and Use of Oral Contraceptives," *Lancet* (22 Oct. 1983), pp. 926–930.

[6]M. P. Vassey, et al., "Neoplasia of the Cervix and Contraception," *Lancet* (22 Oct. 1983), pp. 930–934.

The conception rate of former OC users is reduced during the first three months after stopping use of the pill, but fertility is not permanently impaired. Three months after the cessation of contraception, former OC and diaphragm users have virtually the same fertility rate.

Fecundity

Studies of the effects of the combined OCs on acne are conflicting. This undoubtedly results from the fact that one component of OCs (estrogen) suppresses the activity of sebaceous glands while progestins stimulate these glands. Thus some pill users find that their acne improves, while others find that acne is aggravated.

Acne

A number of studies point to a link between combined oral contraceptive use and gallbladder disease. It appears that the pill user is about twice as likely as the nonuser to develop gallbladder disease.

Gallbladder Disease

Research now indicates that OC users gain protection against rheumatoid arthritis. Statistical analysis reveals that pill users are half as likely to develop this condition as nonusers.

Rheumatoid Arthritis

OC users appear to have a slightly higher incidence of the fungus infection candidiasis but a lower incidence of trichomoniasis.

Vaginal Infections

Not much research has been done on the effects of OCs on toxic-shock syndrome. A few studies, however, suggest that OC users are one fourth as likely to develop the condition as women using no contraception.

Toxic-Shock Syndrome

Large doses of estrogen hasten epiphyseal closure when administered to girls prior to the growth spurt, which occurs somewhere between the 10th and 12th years in the United States. It is unlikely that OCs would be used this early, and therefore fears that pill use might limit growth are generally baseless. Moreover, there is some evidence that OCs may be useful in osteoporosis, a disease characterized by diminished bone matrix. Estrogen is known to have an osteoblast-stimulating activity, which would be useful in this disease.

Bone Growth

In a study[7] of 5151 Kaiser Health Plan subscribers, it was found that 33.5 percent had never used the pill, 27.9 percent were former users, and 38.6 percent were current users. In this study, the current users had less premenstrual moodiness and irritability than the other two groups. The dosage of progestin appeared to affect premenstrual moodiness and irritability. Within a range of 0.5 to 10.0 mg, it was found that higher doses were associated with fewer symptoms. There appeared to be no effect on users who had previous histories of depression.

Depression

Another study[8] comparing pill users and nonusers documents the occurence of depression but concludes:

> It would seem that the majority of nervousness, depression, and weight gain noted in oral contraceptive users is either coincidental or associated with the psychological impact of taking these agents, rather than with any pharmacologic effect.

---

[7]Department of Health, Education, and Welfare, *Family Planning Digest* (Washington, D.C.: Department of Health, Education and Welfare, Sept. 1973).

[8]Joseph W. Goldzieher, et al., "Nervousness and Depression Attributed to Oral Contraceptives: A Double-Blind, Placebo-Controlled Study," *American Journal of Obstetrics,* 111 (1971), p. 1013.

More than one third of women taking the pill experience negative, if slight, side effects. Reported side effects with oral contraceptive use by some women include:

1. Fluid retention, weight gain, and breast fullness or tenderness.

2. Nausea.

3. Loss of hair.

4. Worsening of acne.

5. Altered thyroid function.

6. Irritation secondary to corneal edema for wearers of contact lenses.

7. Increased body hair (hirsutism).

8. Mild headaches.

9. Spotting between periods.

10. "Mask of pregnancy," that is, darkening of skin on the upper lip, under the eyes, and on the forehead.

Beneficial Side Effects

The Food and Drug Administration's Committee on Fertility and Maternal Health now recommends that each pill package include information on the beneficial effects of combined OCs.

New Labeling

OC users often experience relief from a variety of menstrual disorders. These include premenstrual tension, irregular menses, cramps, blood loss, and in some cases anemia.

Menstrual Disorders

Women who have taken the pill for more than one year have one third the risk of PID as nonusers. It is estimated that OCs prevent two to three million cases of PID each year in the developing world.

Pelvic Inflammatory Disease (PID)

OCs may protect against PID by hindering the movement of bacteria from the vagina into the uterus. Movement of bacteria is impeded by thickening of the mucus barrier found at the entrance to the cervix and by reduced menstrual flow.

Progestins may inhibit the growth of gonococcal bacteria within the oviducts.

Implantation and growth of a fertilized ovum outside the uterus is termed ectopic pregnancy. In the United States approximately 8 in 1,000 pregnancies are ectopic. These pregnancies can cause severe pain, internal bleeding, shock, and sometimes death.

Ectopic Pregnancy

OC users experience one third the risk of ectopic pregnancy as do IUD, condom, or diaphragm users.

Ovarian cancer has a poor prognosis: the five-year survival rate is only 20 percent. In the United States the death rate for ovarian cancer is approximately 10 per 100,000 women.

Ovarian Cancer

A number of studies now suggest that OCs are protective against ovarian cancer, although the mechanism is not clear. One theory suggests that ovulation produces cysts that may be precursors of ovarian cancer. The suppression of ovulation by OC use would reduce this risk.

Oral contraceptives appear to offer some protection against endometrial cancer.[9-11] The protective effect may be related to reduced mitotic activity in the endometrium.

Endometrial Cancer

A number of studies reveal that the combined oral contraceptive affords the user protection against benign breast disease. This protection seems to depend on the progestin component of the pill.

Benign Breast Disease

Since benign breast disease is known to be associated with breast cancer, it was surprising that OC use did not also result in a reduced incidence of breast cancer. However, this was not the case, and it now seems likely that OC use protects against the type of benign breast disease that does not later develop into cancer.

Low-dose oral contraceptives, pills containing less than 50 micrograms of estrogen, are currently available and are being carefully studied. This type of pill is of considerable importance because it is associated with a lower risk of circulatory disorders.

Low-Dose Combined Orals

For most women, low-dose OCs are as effective in preventing pregnancy as are standard dose pills, but in their present form they are linked with a greater risk of menstrual disorders (breakthrough bleeding and spotting and skipped menses).

The effectiveness of low-dose OCs, however, may be reduced when they are taken in combination with a number of other drugs: antibiotics (e.g., penicillin, tetracycline, and ampicillin) and anticonvulsants (e.g., carbamazepine, phenobarbital, and phenytoin). For this reason, low-dose OCs may be contraindicated for women taking these drugs.

Biphasic and triphasic pills are designed to alter the estrogen and progesterone levels in a way that more nearly duplicates normal female physiological processes. In this approach to contraception, hormone doses are varied within each cycle. For example, with the triphasic pill the woman takes one type of pill on days 1 to 6, another on days 7 to 11, and yet another on days 12 to 22. This regimen results in a gradual rise in progesterone level throughout the cycle, with a rise and fall in estrogen level. The biphasic regimen attempts to accomplish the same thing with just two types of pills. With the conventional combined oral contraceptive, the daily hormone dose remains the same throughout the cycle.

Biphasic and Triphasic Pills

The biphasic and triphasic pills appear to be about as effective as the traditional pill, and they have two advantages: a lower total monthly dose of hormones and less breakthrough bleeding and spotting.

In 1972 the Food and Drug Administration (FDA) approved for use in the United States an oral contraceptive containing only a progestational agent.

Progestational Pills

This pill is known as the minipill; it represents an attempt to avoid many of the side effects associated with the combined estrogen-progestin pill.

---

[9]D. W. Kaufman, et. al., "Decreased Risk of Endometrial Cancer Among Oral Contraceptive Users," *New England Journal of Medicine*, 303 (1981), pp. 1045–1048..

[10]Centers for Disease Control Cancer and Steroid Hormone Study, "Oral Contraceptive Use and the Risk of Endometrial Cancer, "*Journal of the American Medical Association*, 249 (1983), pp. 1600–1604.

[11]B. E. Henderson, et. al., "The Epidemiology of Endometrial Cnacer in Young Women," *British Journal of Cancer*, 47 (1983), pp. 749–756.

Side effects such as headache, nausea, vomiting, breast tenderness, and back and abdominal pain are decreased with the minipill.

Although the minipill may produce fewer side effects, it has a higher dropout rate for medical reasons than the combination oral contraceptive.

Two major drawbacks are:

1. A significant incidence of unpredictable bleeding.

2. A pregnancy rate of about 3 percent.

Also, the FDA noted that about 8 percent of the degradation products of norethindrone (a synthetic progestogen commonly used in oral contraceptives) become biologically active estrogens.

Research with the minipill has further confirmed the antifertility mechanism of progestogen:

1. Synthetic progestin suppresses the release of LH and prevents ovulation and the formation of corpus luteum in approximately one third of cycles.

2. Progestin may alter the endometrium to make it unsuitable to receive a fertilized egg.

3. Progestin may produce thick mucus in the cervix, which may adversely affect sperm viability or motility.

Nonoral Hormonal Contraceptives

A low-dose long-acting injectable progesterone (medroxyprogesterone acetate, or Depo Provera) is now available. For this contraceptive regimen, injections are required every three months.

Medroxyprogesterone acetate (DMPA) inhibits LH, thereby preventing ovulation. Its theoretical effectiveness is a 0.3 to 0.5 percent rate of pregnancies.

Women taking DMPA must sign a consent form that instructs them about side effects. Potential side effects include excessive bleeding, cessation of menses, decreased libido, headaches, dizziness, and weight gain.

Vaginal Ring

An experimental approach to the use of nonoral progestin involves a vaginal rubber ring (Fig. 46) about the size of a diaphragm; it releases small amounts of progestin that are absorbed by the body.

The woman inserts the ring herself at the end of her regular cycle. It is left in place for three weeks and then removed and thrown away. Menstruation follows removal of the device.

Progestin Implants

Progestin enclosed in a Silastic capsule may also be implanted under the skin (Fig. 47) for long-term contraceptive use. Limited tests of progestin implants have yielded good results.

Postcoital Contraception or Interception

Recent research indicates that diethylstilbestrol (DES), a synthetic estrogen, is an effective postcoital contraceptive. It is known as the morning-after pill. Actually, it is taken for five days.

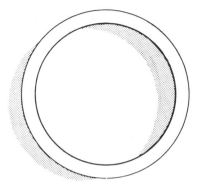

Figure 46   Vaginal ring for progestin administration.

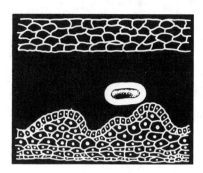

Figure 47   Progestin implant.

In a report[12] of over 9,000 midcycle exposures treated with estrogens, only 29 pregnancies occurred. Dr. Richard P. Blye[13] notes:

> Sufficient evidence has accrued to indicate that daily administration of 50 mg of diethylstilbestrol, 30 mg of conjugated equine estrogen, or 5 mg of ethinyl estradiol for 5 consecutive days is probably effective in preventing pregnancy if instituted within 72 hours of unprotected midcycle coital exposure.

However, the FDA has urged that DES "be considered as an emergency treatment only and that it . . . not be considered as a method of birth control with continuous and frequently repeated therapy."[14] The FDA has further proposed that labels be issued to warn persons who might use DES of the association of estrogen with blood clots and other side effects. DES has been associated with cancer of the vagina in young women whose mothers used the drug during pregnancy for reasons other than contraception.

At present, the mechanism whereby postcoital estrogen prevents pregnancy is unknown.

How Postcoital Pills Work

Dr. Blye has suggested six possibilities:

1. Alteration of tubal transport.

2. Prevention of embryonic viability.

3. Prevention of sperm transport.

4. Loss of sperm viability.

5. Luteolysis (chemical breakdown of corpus luteum).

6. Asynchronism of uterine endometrium.

---

[12] J. M. Morris and G. van Wagenen, "Interception: The Use of Postovulatory Estrogens to Prevent Implantation," *American Journal of Obstetrics and Gynecology*, 115 (1973), p. 101.

[13] Richard P. Blye, "The Use of Estrogens as Postcoital Contraceptive Agents," *American Journal of Obstetrics and Gynecology*, 116 (1973), p. 1044.

[14] Department of Health, Education and Welfare, *Family Planning Digest* (Washington, D.C.: Department of Health, Education and Welfare, May 1973).

Among these theories, alteration of tubal transport is one of the most popular.

Normally a newly fertilized egg spends three or four days in the oviduct and another three or four in the uterus before it begins the process of implantation. If the fertilized egg arrives too early, the endometrium is inadequately developed, and the egg will degenerate.

Estrogens are known to increase the rate of secretion of tubal fluid, to stimulate ciliary activity of the upper portion of the tube, and to increase peristaltic activity of the tubal muscles. In view of these effects, postcoital estrogens may prevent pregnancy by altering the time sequence between fertilization and implantation.

Alteration of Tubal Transport

Based on recommendations by the International Planned Parenthood Federation, research is now underway to evaluate the use of OCs as one-time postcoital contraceptives or morning-after pills.

Postcoital Use of OCs

Studies completed suggest that two pills taken as soon as possible after coitus and two more taken 12 hours later but within 72 hours after coitus reduce the chances of pregnancy fivefold.

This approach to postcoital contraception appears to be as effective as the traditional method (use of estrogen alone), and it has the added advantage of being less likely to cause nausea and vomiting, symptoms that often stop women from taking the full seven-day course of estrogen. However, if pregnancy is not terminated by these pills, the embryo is much more likely to be deformed and abortion would be recommended.

Surgical Sterilization

Vasectomy is a simple surgical procedure that involves cutting and tying of the vas deferens to prevent the passage of sperm (Fig. 21). The procedure can be done with a local anesthetic in a physician's office. Vasectomy does not interfere with ejaculation, since the sperm constitute only a very small portion of the semen.

Vasectomy

Vasectomy is nearly 100 percent effective, the failure rate being only 0.15 percent. Failure may occur for one of three reasons:

Effectiveness

1. The vas deferens reconnects after surgery.

2. The surgery is done incorrectly.

3. Sperm were present during the first three months after surgery and no backup method was used.

After vasectomy the male is generally considered sterile when two consecutive semen examinations are found to be negative and when three months have passed. Until then, a backup method for contraception should be used because viable sperm may have been present at the time of surgery.

Irrigation of the distal end of the vas deferens with sterile water immediately after vasectomy reduces the problem somewhat, but not entirely. Table 2 summarizes the results of studies of 125 men having vasectomy without irrigation and 111 having vasectomy followed by irrigation with 20 milliliters of sterile water.

TABLE 2:   **Percentage of Males with Positive Sperm**
Counts After Vasectomy*

	12 Weeks	15 Weeks	30 Weeks
Nonirrigated	33.6	25.5	5.6
Irrigated	16.2	6.3	0.0

*Adapted from Ian Craft and John McQueen, "Effect of Irrigation of the Vas on Postvasectomy Semen-Counts," *Lancet,* (1972), p. 515.

Relatively little research exists on the side effects of vasectomy because changes are difficult to measure in the living male. The available evidence, however, suggests that side effects are minimal.

Side Effects

About 50 percent of men having vasectomies develop antibodies to their sperm. These antibodies aid in processing the dying cells and do not seem to have any negative effect. In these cases, reversible vasectomy may not restore fertility.

One study[15] of vasectomized monkeys reported that these monkeys developed atherosclerotic plaques in their arteries at a greater rate than nonvasectomized monkeys. However, study of human vasectomy patients has found no relationship with atherosclerotic changes.

The most likely side effects would be excessive bleeding, blood clots, infection, or epididymitis. No major long-term side effects have complicated vasectomy, and reports of death are extremely rare.

The endocrine system is not affected by vasectomy:

> Evidence that the endocrine status remains the same after vasectomy is supported by the fact that the plasma testosterone and seminal fructose levels are unaltered and there are no microscopic changes in the interstitial cells of the testis. Postvasectomy testicular biopsy shows normal spermatogenesis.[16]

Surveys of men having vasectomies indicate that:

Sexual Relations

1.   Approximately 60 percent report the same frequency of sexual relations.

2.   An increase was reported by 38 percent.

3.   Only 2 percent reported a decrease.

The few studies available indicate that vasectomy does not lead to greater promiscuity among men.

The male requesting a vasectomy is usually informed about the procedure and the low probability of reversibility and is provided a period of time to consider the matter.

Decision about Vasectomy

[15]N. J. Alexander and T. B. Clarkson, "Vasectomy Increases the Severity of Diet-Induced Atherosclerosis in Macacca Fasculars," *Science,* 201 (1978), p. 538.

[16]Robert E. Hackett and Keith Waterhouse, "Vasectomy—Reviewed," *American Journal of Obstetrics and Gynecology,* 116 (1973), p. 438.

Some physicians use specific criteria to determine eligibility for vasectomy— for example, 30 years of age and having at least two children. Others believe that vasectomy should be available to any adult upon request.

Currently approximately 250,000 vasectomies are performed in the United States each year.

Vasovasostomy

Although the chances of restoring fertility after a vasectomy have improved in recent years, this cannot be counted on; hence, the decision to undergo vasectomy should be considered definitive.

A vasovasostomy is an operation to reverse a vasectomy. Early studies reported the chances of successfully reversing a vasectomy to be approximately 20 percent. More recently, microsurgical techniques have increased the chances to 70 to 90 percent in some cases. Improved success of vasovasostomies is related to the techniques of the vasectomy: the length of the section removed, the location of the surgery, the use of electrical coagulation techniques, the type of ligation, and the amount of time that has passed since the vasectomy.[17]

Tubal Ligation

Female sterilization by tubal ligation (Fig. 48) involves cutting the oviducts, removing a small section of the tubes, and tying off the cut ends. Tying off the tubes prevents the egg from passing to the uterus. Instead, the egg harmlessly disintegrates in the oviduct. The failure rate of tubal sterilization is only 0.04 percent, owing to the occasional cases in which tubes grow back together.

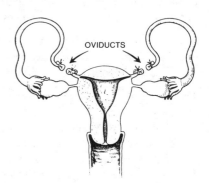

OVIDUCTS

Figure 48   Female sterilization.

Laparotomy

If the incision to locate the oviducts is made through the abdomen, the procedure is termed a laparotomy.

Colpotomy

Colpotomy is a technique of tying the oviducts by making an incision in the vagina rather than in the abdomen. The technique dates back to the early 19th century and has recently attracted new interest after extensive use in India.

According to proponents of this procedure, it offers the following advantages:[18]

1.   It can be done on an outpatient basis.

2.   Only 5 to 15 minutes are normally required for the operation.

3.   Local anesthesia is sufficient.

4.   There is less postoperative pain than with other techniques.

---

[17]R. A. Hatcher, et al., *Contraceptive Technology 1982–83,* 11th ed. (New York: Irving Publishers, 1982), pp. 191–192.

[18]Department of Medical and Public Affairs, The George Washington University Medical Center, "Sterilization," *Population Report, Series C,* 3 (June 1973).

5. There is no visible scar.

6. Instruments are simple, inexpensive, and usually available wherever gynecological services are offered.

7. Major complication and morbidity rates (in developing countries) are low.

8. The failure rate is only about 1 percent.

9. It is possible to combine the procedure with early pregnancy termination or other gynecological procedures.

The disadvantages of the vaginal approach compared with the abdominal approach is that the complications of infection and hemorrhage are twice as common.

Cauterization (Endoscopy)

Sterilization may also be accomplished by cauterizing (burning) the oviducts rather than tying them. A laparoscope (an instrument to visualize the abdominal area through a small incision) is inserted through the abdomen (laparoscopy), through the vagina (culdoscopy), or through the vagina and uterus (uteroscopy), and the oviducts are cauterized with an electric current.

The procedure may be performed on an outpatient basis using only local anesthesia. The woman is told to expect three seconds of sharp pain as each tube is cauterized.

The procedure appears to be effective, convenient, and relatively inexpensive. Only about 1 percent of such patients experience complications requiring additional abdominal surgery.

Some procedures require two incisions, but a more advanced laparoscope makes it possible to complete the entire procedure through a single small incision.

Reversing Female Sterilization

At present, female sterilization should be viewed as a permanent method of birth control. The odds against reversing this procedure are not good—approximately 20 percent. The reversal success rate, however, will probably improve in the near future. In fact, some surgeons are now reporting a 60 percent success rate with microsurgery. Unfortunately, ectopic pregnancy following reversal is about ten times higher than normal.

Clips and rings are now being used to occlude the oviducts and prevent pregnancy. Because these procedures cause less tubal damage, it is anticipated that the reversal rate will be much higher.

The Condom

The condom is a sheath worn over the penis to prevent sperm from entering the vagina. These are usually made of latex rubber and shaped like the finger of a glove (Fig. 49). Condoms may have a plain end or a small reservoir to contain the ejaculated semen.

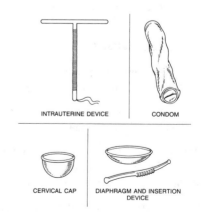

INTRAUTERINE DEVICE | CONDOM

CERVICAL CAP | DIAPHRAGM AND INSERTION DEVICE

Figure 49 Mechanical contraception.

In their early history, condoms were often referred to as "skins" because they were made from sheep intestines. Today "skins" have been largely replaced with thin, strong latex condoms.

Condoms do not require fitting by a physician, are harmless, and are very easy to use. They are the third most widely used contraceptive method in the United States.

Since 1938, condoms sold or shipped in interstate commerce have been subject to control by the Food and Drug Administration and their quality has improved. Nevertheless, quality does vary. Condoms sold by mail order and from vending machines tend to be less reliable than those purchased in drugstores. Inferior material, exposures to heat, and age (more than two years) can cause the condom to deteriorate and tear during intercourse.

Quality

The theoretical effectiveness of the condom is 97 percent; however, use effectiveness is only 80 to 85 percent.

Maximizing Protection

Rupture is a cause of failure with the condom. In case of rupture, the female should immediately apply a contraceptive jelly.

When the condom is unrolled, care should be taken to prevent formation of an air pocket in the tip. This could cause rupture.

A lubricant helps to prevent tearing and may be applied after the condom is in place. Prelubricated condoms are also available. Vaseline should not be used because it can decompose the rubber.

The condom should be worn throughout sexual intercourse; otherwise, an unexpected ejaculation might cause pregnancy.

The penis should be withdrawn soon after ejaculation. During withdrawal of the penis, the rim of the condom should be held to prevent spillage of semen.

Condoms carried in wallets may deteriorate because of heat.

Some women produce antibodies against sperm, resulting in infertility. In such cases, condoms may be used for 6 to 12 months to reduce the woman's antibody titre. Subsequent conception may become possible when the condom is not used.

Special Use of Condoms

Sex therapists often recommend condoms for men who have premature ejaculation because condoms tend to dull sensation and may delay ejaculation.

The condom is also useful in preventing the spread of venereal disease.

Diaphragm

The diaphragm is a shallow rubber cup with a reinforced circular perimeter that is flexible. Its diameter ranges in size from 55 to 100 millimeters.

The diaphragm was developed about 90 years ago by a German physician, Wilhelm P. J. Mensinga.

For contraceptive use the diaphragm fits between the walls of the vagina and covers the cervix (Fig. 50). Before the diaphragm is inserted, spermicidal agents are applied to the inside of the diaphragm and around the rim.

It has been shown that the diaphragm is moved about during coitus; hence, it is only partly effective as a mechanical barrier to sperm. Its main contraceptive function is to hold the spermicidal agent near the cervical os.

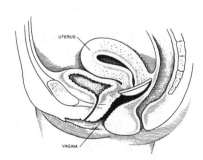

Figure 50   Diaphragm.

The theoretical effectiveness of the diaphragm is 97 to 98 percent, but use-effectiveness is only 75 to 80 percent.

Maximizing Effectiveness

The diaphragm must be fitted by a physician or other trained professional, and the female user must be trained to insert it properly. Since the vagina expands in the sexually responding female, the largest size of diaphragm that can be worn without discomfort should be selected.

The diaphragm should be inserted not more than 2 hours before intercourse and should be removed 8 to 16 hours after coitus. After use, the diaphragm should be washed with soap and water, dried, and may be coated with corn-starch (but not a perfumed powder or talcum powder).

Since the vagina may be stretched, the diaphragm should be rechecked for size after childbirth. Also, the diaphragm should be checked regularly for tears and stored away from heat.

One research study[19] has demonstrated a lower incidence of cervical cancer among diaphragm users.

Diaphragm and Cervical Cancer

The same points apply to use of the cervical cap, which differs from the diaphragm in that it fits onto the cervix rather than lying diagonally across the vaginal tube.

Cervical Cap

Spermicidal agents used alone are not a highly effective method of contraception; the use effectiveness rate is 78 percent. However, spermicides do increase the effectiveness of both the condom and the diaphragm.

Intrauterine Devices (IUDs)

Although intrauterine devices have only recently come into the limelight in the United States, the basic concept of inserting something into the uterus to prevent pregnancy has been used for more than 2,000 years. In the 19th century, intrauterine devices (stem pessaries) were used for the correction of uterine displacement as well as for contraception.

An Old Method

In the early 1900's, Grafenberg, a German scientist, developed a silver ring for insertion into the uterus. After studying the effectiveness of the ring, he reported in 1930 that the pregnancy rate was only 1.6 percent. Nevertheless, Grafenberg's ring was poorly received. Placing something in the uterus just did not seem like a good idea to medical scientists. Thus, Grafenberg joined the list of scientists who will be remembered as being ahead of their times.

Grafenberg

Resurgence of interest in the IUD was prompted by the report of Japanese workers regarding the use of plastic material for intrauterine contraceptive devices (Fig. 51).

Plastic IUD

Use of plastic IUDs made insertion possible through the cervical canal without dilating the cervix (Fig. 52).

Through the Cervical Canal

This is accomplished by compressing the IUD into a small tube, inserting the tube through the cervical canal, and then discharging the IUD from the tube, allowing the IUD to expand to its normal shape and size.

---

[19]N. H. Wright, et al., "Neoplasia and Dysplasia of the Cervix Uteri and Contraception: A Possible Protective Effect of the Diaphragm," *British Journal of Cancer,* 38 (1978), pp. 273–279.

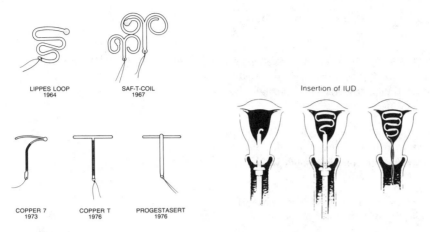

Figure 51   Intrauterine devices (IUD's).

Figure 52   Insertion of IUD.

The devices currently approved by the Food and Drug Administration are:

1. Lippes loop.

2. Saf-T-Coil.

3. Copper T (Cu-T).

4. Copper 7 (Cu-7).

5. Progestasert T.

Biologic Effect

The mechanism whereby the IUD prevents pregnancy is poorly understood because human experimentation is difficult, and the IUD has different effects with different species of animals.

In chicken and sheep, the IUD inhibits transport of spermatozoa. In the rabbit, sow, cow, and ewe, the function of the corpus luteum is impaired. However, in humans, the IUD does not prevent ovulation or menstruation.

TABLE 3:   **Physical Characteristics of IUDs IUD Strings, and IUD Insertion Mechanisms**

Type IUD	Length (mm)	Width (mm)	Inserter Barrel Widest Diameter (mm)	Color of Strings	Number of Strings	Other String Characteristics
Loop A	33.0	22.5	5.26	Blue	1 or 2	1 thick; 2 thin
Loop B	34.0	28.0	5.30	Black	1 or 2	1 thick; 2 thin
Loop C	35.0	30.0	5.30	Yellow	1 or 2	1 thick; 2 thin
Loop D	36.0	30.0	5.33	White	1 or 2	1 thick; 2 thin
Small Saf-T-Coil	21.5	25.5	3.76	Green	2	Thin strings
Medium Saf-T-Coil	32.0	30.0	4.50	Green	2	Thin strings
Large Saf-T-Coil	33.0	38.0	4.50	Green	2	Thin strings
Copper-7	36.0	27.0	3.07	Black	1	Thin string
Copper-T	36.0	31.5	5.96	Light Blue (variable)	2	Thin strings
Progestasert-T	36.0	32.0	6.0	Translucent	2	Thin strings (one precut at 9 cm)

From Robert A. Hatcher, et al., *Contraceptive Technology 1980–81* (New York: Irvington Publishers, Inc., 1980). Reprinted with permission.

Currently the favored theory about how IUDs prevent pregnancy is that changes in the internal milieu of the uterus prevent pregnancy by rendering the walls of the uterus chemically unsuitable. Apparently, IUDs produce local inflammatory responses that interfere with the normal development of the uterine lining or that make it toxic to either sperm or fertilized eggs.

The Advisory Committee on Obstetrics and Gynecology of the Food and Drug Administration states:

> Studies have shown rather uniformly that there are alterations in the endometrium. These studies, based on the examination of endometrial biopsies and hysterectomy specimens, show grossly a thickening of the endometrium with edema and pressure effects. Indeed, in many instances, an impression of the device may be seen on the endometrium with edema and pressure effects. Microscopic examination shows that the endometrium directly adjacent to the device is thin and ulcerated.

Contraception from the IUD is considered reversible; however, some concern exists that the higher rates of pelvic inflammation associated with IUDs and with partial or full obstruction of the oviducts will eventually result in a higher than normal infertility rate for IUD users.

Effectiveness of IUDs

The theoretical effectiveness of IUDs is 95 to 99 percent, and their use-effectiveness is 94 percent. The effectiveness can be maximized by use of condoms or foam on days 10 to 18 of the menstrual cycle.

Although the presence of copper or progestin in an IUD is designed to increase the effectiveness, the Saf-T-Coil has the highest effectiveness rate, followed by copper IUDs, then by Progestasert.[20]

IUD Expulsion

Occasionally, the IUD is expelled by the body, usually during menstruation. Therefore, the user should check for the string attached to the device after each menstrual period.

Use of the IUD

Accurate figures as to the number of people using the IUD in the United States are not available, but it is estimated that approximately 10 percent of the married women under 30 years of age use IUDs, and 60 million women throughout the world use them.

The relatively low price of the IUD makes it highly suitable for countries with nationwide family planning programs. The following countries have extensively used the IUD:

1. India.
2. Pakistan.
3. South Korea.
4. Taiwan.

Complications from Uterine Perforation by IUDs

If an IUD is not properly inserted, uterine perforation may occur. The subsequent bleeding and infection can be serious; thus, only a well-trained clinician should insert the IUD.

---

[20]Hatcher, op. cit., p. 57.

If pregnancy occurs with an IUD in place, the IUD should be removed for two reasons. First, if pregnancy occurs and the IUD is left in place, the chance of abortion is 50 percent. Second, most IUD users who abort show signs of infection. If retrieval of the IUD (by traction on the string) is not possible, a therapeutic abortion should be considered. The IUD and pregnancy are a potentially dangerous combination.

IUD and Pregnancy

The most serious complication related to use of IUDs is pelvic inflammatory disease (PID), that is, infections of internal reproductive organs or other pelvic areas. The percentage of women developing PID within the first year of IUD use may be as high as 25 percent.[21] Immediate treatment is essential or PID may lead to infertility, hospitalization, and even death. In this connection, a number of studies—directly contradicting early studies—now suggest that tailless IUDs are less likely to produce PID.

Pelvic Inflammatory Disease

The symptoms of PID include abdominal, back, pelvic, and leg pain; fever or chills; vomiting; vaginal discharge at end of menstrual flow; prolonged or difficult menstrual bleeding; bleeding after intercourse; painful intercourse; and painful urination.

For a few months after insertion of an IUD, 10 to 20 percent of women experience heavier menstrual bleeding, irregular bleeding, cramping, or abdominal pain.

Menstrual Bleeding and Cramping

Chances of a tubal pregnancy are increased with IUD use. Because infection is a high risk if a tube ruptures, an IUD user should see her physician whenever she misses her period.

Ectopic Pregnancy

Spermicidal Agents

Spermicidal contraceptives consist of an inert base substance to hold the preparation in the vagina and against the cervix. In addition, they include spermicidal chemicals, usually nonylphenoxypolyethoxy ethanol, that kill the sperm.

A variety of spermicidal preparations are available without prescription. These include:

1. Contraceptive cream.
2. Contraceptive jelly.
3. Vaginal foam.
4. Foaming tablets.
5. Suppositories.

Foams are generally more effective than creams or jellies.

Maximizing Effectiveness

Spermicidal preparations should not be applied more than 30 minutes before sexual relations, and they should not be removed for six to eight hours. Spermicidal preparations should be reapplied if intercourse occurs again within eight hours of the original application.

A new spermicidal suppository, Encare or Encare Oval, has been available in the United States since 1977. It is deposited high on the vagina ten minutes

Suppository

---

[21]Hatcher, op. cit., p. 74.

before intercourse. It effervesces into a thick barrier that is effective for an hour. The manufacturers of Encare claim a 99 percent use-effectiveness rate in studies, but others believe more studies should be made to establish the rate.

The contraceptive sponge is a soft, white, round polyurethane sponge containing spermicide. It is designed to be held in place by the muscles of the upper vagina. The sponge traps and absorbs sperm, killing them on contact. The safety of the contraceptive sponge has not been confirmed. Concerns about its relationship to toxic shock syndrome exist.

Contraceptive Sponge

Douche

The douche is a contraceptive technique in which the vagina is washed out with water or other substances. The objective is to remove semen before sperm can enter the uterus. Of the contraceptive techniques discussed, douching is the least effective (a 40 percent failure rate). Sperm can be found in the opening of the cervix within 90 seconds after intercourse. This means that the douche usually would not be performed in time to be of any value. Even when performed quickly, the douche is very unreliable as a contraceptive technique, although it is usually better than doing nothing.

The Rhythm Method

Normally a woman releases only one egg during each menstrual cycle, and this egg must be fertilized within 12 to 24 hours or not at all.

The objective of the rhythm method is to schedule sexual intercourse in such a way as to avoid the presence of sperm during the life span of the egg. Sperm remain viable up to 72 hours, and it is now believed that sperm can survive for up to five days in the female reproductive tract under optimal conditions.

Thus, the effective practice of rhythm requires some basic knowledge of physiology.

The three types of rhythm are the calendar method, the basal body temperature method, and the mucus method. Their use-effectiveness rates are only 75 to 80 percent.

Effectiveness

One way of practicing rhythm is termed the calendar method because it involves keeping records on a calendar. The method is ineffective and is described here only as a matter of general information. Failure rates as high as 40 percent have been reported.

The Calendar Method

Women tend to ovulate about midway through their menstrual cycles. Thus, if the length of the cycle were known, it would be possible to predict with some degree of accuracy the approximate time of ovulation.

How the Calendar Method Works

Although the length of the menstrual cycle is no more predictable than the time of ovulation, the menstrual cycle can be objectively measured (i.e., the menstrual flow is an outward sign that the cycle has ended, whereas the time of ovulation has no outward sign).

The calendar method is based on the concepts that the length of past cycles is a clue to the future and that ovulation occurs on day 14 plus or minus 2 days of the menstrual cycle. To use this method, the woman keeps a record of the length of each menstrual cycle for a year. Day one of the cycle is the first day of menstrual bleeding. This provides her with some indication of the variability that can be expected in the length of her cycles.

The longest and shortest cycles represent the greatest variability. In practice, 18 is subtracted from the number of days in the shortest cycle. This determines the first day on which intercourse is likely to result in pregnancy. For example, if the shortest cycle were 24 days, then 24 minus 18 equals 6. Thus day 6 would be the first fertile day, and abstinence from sexual intercourse should begin on this day.

To determine the last fertile day, 11 is subtracted from the number of days in the longest cycle. For example, if the longest cycle were 28 days, one would substract 11 days from 28 to determine that the last fertile day would be day 17.

Thus, in this example, days 6 through 17 would be unsafe for sexual intercourse.

Because the length of last year's cycles may not be an accurate index of the length of this year's cycles, this method is not recommended.

Basal Body Temperature Method

The basal body temperature method is somewhat more reliable than the calendar method. The method is based on a physiological clue that ovulation has occurred.

It happens this way:

1. After ovulation the follicle from which the egg was discharged develops into a corpus luteum.

2. This newly formed structure secretes progesterone into the blood.

3. Progesterone increases metabolism and thus increases body temperature.

The slight increase in body temperature that accompanies the secretion of progesterone is an outward clue that ovulation has occurred. Although the increase in body temperature is very small, it is a reliable clue if the temperature is properly taken and if no infection is present. Careful attention must be given to the details of this method.

One problem of the method is that an infection or any factor that might produce a fever could constitute a false clue that ovulation has occurred. Fortunately, most infections have other apparent symptoms.

Another source of concern is the fact that the body's metabolism and temperature increases with such factors as eating food, excitement, physical exercise, irregular sleep, and use of an electric blanket. To avoid the influence of some of these factors, only the basal body temperature is used.

Basal temperature refers to the temperature when the body is at complete rest. It is best determined before getting out of bed in the morning.

It may be taken orally or rectally, but rectal temperatures tend to be more accurate.

Temperature is best determined through use of a basal body thermometer, which may be obtained at any drugstore. This thermometer has a range of only a few degrees, from 96°F to 100°F, with tenth-of-a-degree graduations to make it easier to determine small changes in temperature.

Period of Increased Temperature

Immediately before ovulation, the basal body temperature decreases by 0.2°F (0.11°C). Twenty-four to 72 hours after ovulation has begun, the basal body temperature rises by 0.4° to 0.8°F (0.22 to 0.44°C) above normal. The observed rise continues until a day or two before menstruation.

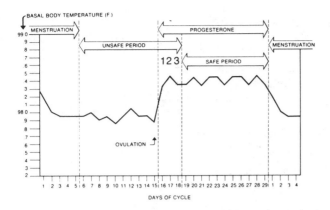

Figure 53   Rhythm method by basal body temperature.

As progesterone disappears, the temperature returns to its former low level during the first day or two of menstruation.

If pregnancy occurs, the temperature remains high because progesterone is formed during pregnancy. Pregnancy is the likely cause if the basal body temperature remains high for more than 18 days.

Sexual relations may safely begin after the temperature rise has been observed for 3 consecutive mornings.

The Safe Period

If the rise in temperature is due to progesterone (not infection), conception is highly unlikely during the remainder of the cycle.

If sexual relations are limited to this part of the cycle, the rhythm method is as effective as use of the IUD, condom, or diaphragm. However, this method does not assure safety for the days of the cycle before ovulation occurs.

Changes in a woman's mucus secretions occurs just before ovulation. After menstrual bleeding the vagina discharges a white cloudy mucus. As midcycle approaches, the amount of mucus increases and the mucus becomes clearer. On one or two peak days the mucus is clear, slippery, and stringy, and the vagina feels wet. Ovulation usually occurs within 24 hours of the last peak day. Four days after ovulation the mucus is once again cloudy and white. To avoid pregnancy, a woman should abstain from sexual intercourse from the first day of the mucus discharge until four days after the last peak day.

The Mucus Method

Before using this method, a woman should be carefully trained by a professional to accurately identify the mucus. It can be confused with spermicides, semen secretion from sexual intercourse, and vaginal infections.

Withdrawal (Coitus Interruptus)

In the withdrawal technique the male withdraws the penis from the vagina just before ejaculation. This method has been found unsatisfactory for the following reasons:

1.   It is generally not satisfying from either a physiological or a psychological standpoint.

2.   The possibility of pregnancy is great because depositing even a few drops of semen in the vagina may cause pregnancy. Moreover, pre-ejaculatory fluid may contain sperm. Its use-effectiveness rate is only 75 to 80 percent.

Considerations in Selecting a Contraceptive Method

The following observations reported by the Alan Guttmacher Institute[22] are worthy of consideration by those wishing to make an informed decision about contraception:

1. Approximately 10 percent of women who rely on their husband's use of condoms get pregnant during the first year of marriage.

2. Approximately 18 percent of women who rely on diaphragms get pregnant during the first year of marriage.

3. During the first year of marriage 2.4 percent of the women who rely on the pill, 4.6 percent who rely on IUDs, 17.9 percent who rely on spermicides, and 23.7 percent who rely on rhythm become pregnant.

4. Unplanned pregnancies (more than half of all pregnancies in the United States) are a greater threat to women's health than contraception.

5. If health were the only consideration, "a woman's safest course would be to start with the pill ... for four years to get the maximum protection against ovarian cancer, have the number of children she desired by the mid-20's and then persuade her husband to have a vasectomy."

6. Childbirth is a greater risk to health than use of the pill, except for women who are over 40 or for women who use the pill and smoke when they are over 35 years old.

7. "Women under 25 get maximum benefits from the pill and are at minimum risk."

8. The pill "prevents more illness than it causes." The 500 deaths attributed to the pill each year are offset statistically by an estimated 850 ovarian cancer deaths prevented by pill use.

---

[22]Victor Cohn, *Washington Post* (29 Sept. 1983).

CHAPTER 7

Abortion

Abortion. It is, without question, the most emotional issue of politics and morality that faces the nation today. The language of the debate is so passionate and polemical, and the conflicting, irreconcilable values so deeply felt, that the issue could well test the foundations of a pluralistic system designed to accommodate deep-rooted moral differences.

Time, April 6, 1981

In January 1973 the United States Supreme Court ruled (Doe v. Bolton and Roe v. Wade) that a state does not have the right to interfere with the decision of a woman and her physician to effect an abortion during the first trimester of pregnancy. The court further ruled that during the second trimester the state could impose only those regulations relating to the pregnant woman's health and safety and that abortion could be prohibited during the third trimester only if such prohibition posed no threat to the woman's life or health. In striking down the abortion laws of Texas and Georgia, the Court in effect rejected the "right to life" theory that the fetus is a person with legal rights. This decision, coupled with the advances in medicine that render early abortion several times safer than childbirth, means that a woman has the right to decide this intensely personal matter—the legal blocks have been removed. It is now a social, psychological, philosophical, or theological question for the individual woman.

In the ten years that have elapsed since the Supreme Court ruling, it has been bitterly attacked by "pro-life" advocates and some legal scholars, but the decision remains the law of the land.

Definitions of Terms

The following definitions of terms will facilitate our discussion of abortion.

Spontaneous abortion is abortion occurring without outside intervention.

Spontaneous Abortion

Induced abortion is brought on intentionally by use of drugs, instruments, radiation, or other means.

Induced Abortion

Threatened abortion is the appearance of the signs and symptoms of a possible abortion. Signs include vaginal bleeding with or without intermittent pain. If the attachment to the uterus is not interrupted, pregnancy may continue.

Threatened Abortion

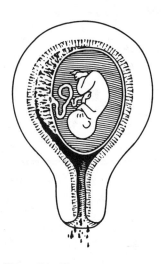

Figure 54   Threatened abortion.

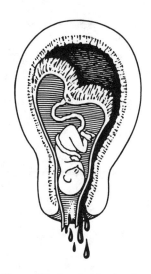

Figure 55   Inevitable abortion.

Imminent abortion is a condition characterized by bleeding and progressively increasing pain. If hemorrhage is slight, the condition may be reversed, but only with hospital facilities. If hemorrhage is severe, the uterus must be medically emptied.

Imminent Abortion

Inevitable abortion is a condition in which bleeding and severe abdominal cramps progressively increase. Excessive blood loss may occur. The condition demands immediate curettage (scraping of the uterus) and sometimes blood transfusions.

Inevitable Abortion

Incomplete abortion is an abortion with continuous uterine bleeding caused by retention of the products of conception. Surgical emptying of the uterus is required.

Incomplete Abortion

Complete abortion is an abortion in which all the products of conception are expelled.

Complete Abortion

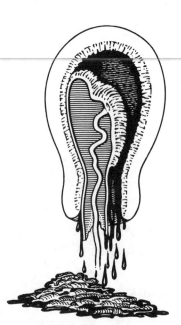

Figure 56   Incomplete abortion.

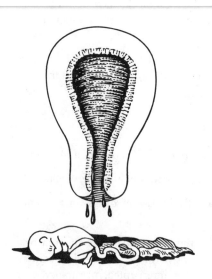

Figure 57   Complete abortion.

Missed abortion is a condition in which a dead fetus is retained in the uterus. Usually spontaneous expulsion occurs, but abdominal surgery may be necessary in rare cases.

Missed Abortion

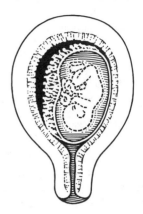

Figure 58   Missed abortion.

Septic abortion is a condition in which there is an infection of the products of conception, usually resulting from an attempted interference during early pregnancy. Antibiotic treatment and curettage are necesary.

Septic Abortion

Habitual abortion is a condition in which the woman spontaneously aborts fetuses three or more consecutive times, without apparent cause.

Habitual Abortion

Therapeutic abortion is the termination of a pregnancy in the interest of the woman's health.

Therapeutic Abortion

Criminal abortion, formerly defined as an abortion deliberately produced for nonmedical reasons, is currently defined as an abortion that does not accord with public law.

Criminal Abortion

Embryonic abortion is an abortion that occurs before the fifth week of pregnancy.

Embryonic Abortion

Fetal abortion is an abortion that occurs after the fifth week of pregnancy.

Fetal Abortion

During the first eight weeks of pregnancy, the ovum is relatively poorly protected and nourished. It is not surprising, therefore, that between 10 and 15 percent of all pregnancies end in spontaneous abortion. About 75 percent occur before the 16th week, and the great majority occur before the 8th week.

Spontaneous Abortion (Miscarriage)

Between the 8th and 12th weeks, the incidence of spontaneous abortion decreases because of improved fetal attachment. Therefore, there is a tendency to retain some of the products of conception when an abortion occurs at this time.

Improved Fetal Attachment

After the first trimester of pregnancy, the placenta is firmly established and spontaneous abortion is far less likely.

Spontaneous abortion is often nature's way of preventing a deformed fetus from developing to full-term pregnancy; more than half of aborted fetuses are clearly defective. In other cases miscarriage may be caused by maternal abnormalities—for example, infectious diseases, hormonal abnormalities, or malnutrition. The cause of many spontaneous abortions remains unknown.

Nature's Way

Miscarriage is usually signaled by vaginal bleeding (spotting) and subsequent cramps. At the first sign of a possible miscarriage, the woman should go to bed and notify her physician at once.

Vaginal Bleeding and Cramps

After an abortion, it is sometimes necessary to scrape the uterus to remove any remaining materials. To help the physician determine the necessity for this procedure, any products of conception that are expelled should be retained for examination.

One spontaneous abortion does not mean that difficulty should be expected in subsequent pregnancies. Three or more spontaneous abortions without apparent cause indicates the need for special tests and sometimes for bed rest during pregnancy. But even then, normal pregnancy is often possible.

Subsequent Pregnancy

The tendency to experience spontaneous abortion during the second trimester appears to be exacerbated by a previously induced abortion in which the cervix was dilated. In a study[1] by British physicians, a tenfold increase was observed in the incidence of miscarriage among women who had had an induced abortion. For this study, postabortive women were compared with women who had undergone childbirth or a spontaneous abortion without cervical dilation.

The authors subscribe to the view[2] that abortion is "at best, a failure of contraception or, at worst, a failure of the healing and teaching professions to educate Americans effectively about contraception, and of society to make birth control services readily available to all who want them." We do not view abortion as human failure. On the other hand, we clearly recognize that an abortion always represents a crisis in a woman's life. Hence, the following discussion is an attempt to answer the question of what a woman needs to know in order to make an intelligent decision about whether or not to have an abortion.

Induced Abortion

The National Center for Health Statistics compiled the incidence rates of different types of abortions. The results are presented in Table 4.

Frequency of Different Types of Abortions

As shown in Table 4, most induced abortions (approximately 70 percent) are by vacuum curettage. This procedure continues to increase in popularity, and it is estimated that by the late 1980's more than 90 percent of all abortions will be by uterine aspiration. The simplicity of the procedure makes it highly suitable during the early stages of pregnancy.

---

[1]C. S. W. Wright, S. Campbell, and J. Beazley, "Second-Trimester Abortion After Vaginal Termination of Pregnancy," *Lancet,* 1 (1972), p. 1278.

[2]Bonnie Douber, et al., "Abortion Counseling and Behavioral Change," *Family Planning Perspectives* (Apr. 1972), pp. 23–27.

TABLE 4: **Percent Distribution of Induced Terminations of Pregnancy in the United States By Type of Procedure, According to Period of Gestation**

Type of Procedure	All Periods of Gestation	Period of Gestation*		
		UNDER 13 WEEKS	13–15 WEEKS	16 WEEKS OR MORE
All procedures	100.0	100.0	100.0	100.0
Suction curettage	92.8	97.1	70.9	23.5
Sharp curettage	1.5	1.5	0.9	0.7
Saline instillation	3.4	0.5	16.8	52.0
Prostaglandin instillation	1.2	0.2	7.1	18.9
Hysterotomy	0.0	0.0	0.2	0.2
Hysterectomy	0.0	0.0	0.1	0.1
Other	1.0	0.7	4.1	4.6

*Percent distribution. From U.S. Public Health Service, National Center for Health Statistics, "Monthly Vital Statistics Report" (25 Oct. 1982).

Vacuum curettage is a relatively simple medical procedure that takes five to ten minutes. A hollow tube (vacurette) is inserted into the uterus. When the tube contacts the amniotic sac, vacuum pressure is turned on, and in less than one minute the physician observes the products of conception pass through a transparent tube and into a collecting bottle.

Vacuum Curettage (Suction)

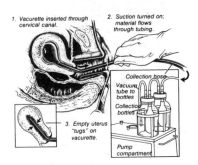

Figure 59   Vacuum curettage.

Cervical Dilation

Preparation for vacuum curettage and follow-up care are considerably more involved.

The cervix guards the entrance and outlet to the uterus and must be dilated to accommodate the size of an object that would pass through it. Dilation precedes uterine aspiration.

To prevent pain during mechanical dilation of the cervix, a local anesthetic is injected to numb the uterine area. For paracervical blocking, Xylocaine, Carbocaine, or a similar agent is injected in the posterior vagina behind the cervix. When the cervix is dilated to about the width of a finger, the physican inserts the vacurette.

After vacuum curettage is completed, as an added precaution the physician scrapes away any material that adheres to the lining of the uterus.

After vacuum curettage, recuperation is almost immediate, and in a few hours the woman may resume her normal life, though intercourse should be avoided for three weeks.

Menstrual-like bleeding usually persists for up to one week and spotting for another two weeks. Sanitary napkins may be used. Tampons should be avoided because they increase the likelihood of infection. Any fever, pain, or excessive bleeding after an abortion should be reported to one's physician immediately.

Physicians Only

Although vacuum curettage is a relatively safe and simple procedure under the supervision of a physician, it can be extremely dangerous when attempted by the lay person. For example, a vacuum cleaner connected to the uterus may extract the uterus from the pelvic cavity and be immediately fatal.

Menstrual Extraction

A menstrual extraction is possible after a missed period. The procedure is similar to vacuum curettage but does not require dilation. The woman feels only a mild cramp.

Technically, menstrual extraction is not an abortion since pregnancy cannot be determined at this time. However, if a fertilized egg is present in the uterus, it is removed by the procedure, and pregnancy can be determined after the fact; hence, the procedure has been termed by some persons as "the perfect pregnancy test for women who didn't want to be pregnant."

Dilation and Curettage

Dilation and curettage (D&C) is the name given to the medical procedure in which the cervix is stretched open (dilated), and the lining of the uterus is scraped (curettage). In a D&C, a curette (an object shaped like a small spoon

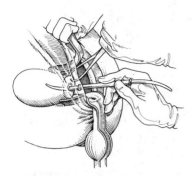

Figure 60   Dilatation of cervix.

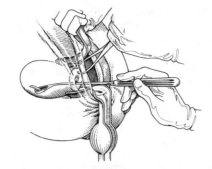

Figure 61   Curettage.

with a long handle) is inserted into the uterus for purposes of scraping (Fig. 60).

The loosened products of conception are then removed from the uterus with forceps. The procedure requires approximately 15 minutes.

Although a D&C may be used to terminate pregnancy of 8 to 15 weeks, its most frequent use is to cope with abnormal bleeding, for example, during the menstrual period, between periods, or after menopause.

Vacuum curettage has largely replaced the D&C as the most popular method for abortion. D&C requires hospitalization and general anesthesia.

Saline Procedure

Vacuum curettage and D&Cs are not generally recommended after the 14th week of pregnancy. As may be seen in Table 4, none were performed after the 16th week. Between the 14th and 25th weeks, the saline procedure is the method most often used.

The saline procedure is based on two physiological principles: (1) a strong saline solution kills the fetus, and (2) death of the fetus diminishes the secretion of placental hormones that sustain pregnancy.

In the saline procedure, a needle is inserted through the abdominal and uterine walls, and part of the amniotic fluid is removed. This fluid is replaced with a strong saline solution. During the subsequent 24 to 48 hours, the woman goes into labor and delivers the products of conception. The process is often physically painful and emotionally distressing.

Hysterotomy

A hysterotomy is a surgical technique in which an incision is made through the abdominal and uterine walls, and the fetus and placenta are removed. In recent years, the saline procedure has tended to replace the hysterotomy, which has the greatest number of complications and highest mortality rates of all abortion methods.

Prostaglandins and Abortion

In 1935 a class of biologically active substances was discovered in human seminal fluid. This class of long-chain fatty acids was labeled prostaglandins since they were thought to come from the prostate gland. However, it is now known that the richest source of prostaglandins is the seminal vesicles.

Today it is known that the prostaglandins are found in nearly all human tissues and that they have a wide range of physiological effects. These effects include uterine contractions and increased muscular activity in the oviducts.

Working from these observations, medical scientists have successfuly used prostaglandins to induce labor, menses, and abortion. Additional research suggests that the prostaglandins may have contraceptive value when used postcoitally to interrupt ovum transport or to inhibit progesterone formation by the corpus luteum.

Several problems remain, however, before the pharmacological application of the prostaglandins can be realized.

First, there is a high incidence of side effects.

Second, the prostaglandins are not potent by the oral route of administration, and the intravenous route can only be utilized in a hospital or clinical situation. More recently, however, intravaginal administration has been demonstrated to be effective.

Third, it appears that the success rate for inducing labor, menses, or abortion is considerably less than 100 percent. This is also the case for postcoital interruption of ovum transport or inhibition of progesterone formation.

The complications accompanying induced abortions are related to the time during pregnancy when the abortion occurs. During the first trimester of pregnancy, abortion is a safe procedure.

Postabortal Complications

Approximately 1 percent of postabortal women have serious complications. Some common complications are perforation of the uterus, hemorrhage, pelvic infection, damage to the cervix, and fever.

The Joint Program for the Study of Abortion[3] reported no deaths among more than 30,000 women undergoing abortion during the first trimester. The overall mortality for abortions performed in New York City was 5 per 100,000 (7.7 for residents and 3.5 for nonresidents) The mortality was nine times higher for abortions at 13 or more weeks than for those done at 12 or fewer weeks.

In 1976 the Abortion Surveillance Report by the Center for Disease Control showed that the number of deaths was 116 from nearly 4 million legal abortions performed from 1972 to 1976, giving a rate of 3 deaths per 100,000 abortions.

Mortality rates by method of abortion are summarized in the following table:

Method	Deaths per 100,000 Abortions
Vacuum Curettage	1.7
Saline	15.5
Hysterotomy/Hysterectomy	42.4

The most common causes of death are infection, hemorrhage, embolism, and reaction to anesthesia.

After an induced abortion, contraception should be resumed or initiated at once.

Ovulation after Induced Abortion

Ovulation may occur as early as 10 days after abortion.[4] The average time for resumption is approximately 22 days.

[3]Bonnie Douber, et al., "Abortion Counseling and Behavioral Change," *Family Planning Perspectives* (Apr. 1972), pp. 23–27.

[4]E. F. Boyd and E. G. Holmstrom, "Ovulation Following Therapeutic Abortion," *American Journal of Obstetrics and Gynecology*, 113 (1972), p. 469.

A recent study by the National Center for Health Statistics covering 13 states revealed:

Abortion Facts

· The peak age for induced abortion was 18 years for white women and 21 for black women.

· Approximately six out of ten women having induced abortion had had no previous live births.

· The median gestational duration for women having abortions was 9.2 weeks.

· Suction curettage accounted for 93 percent of all abortions.

· Complications were reported for less than 1 percent of all women having abortions.

· For white women there were 344 abortions per 1,000 live births compared with 599 for black women.

· The median age for married women (27.5 years) having abortions was nearly 6 years older than that for unmarried women (22.0).

· Women having abortions had the same educational level as women carrying their pregnancies to term.

· The frequency of abortions per 1,000 live births was greater for residents of metropolitan areas than for residents of nonmetropolitan areas.

TABLE 5: Abortion Rate per 1,000 Women Ages 15–44

U.S.S.R.	180.0
Rumania	88.1
Cuba	52.1
United States	30.2
Japan	23.1
Sweden	20.9
Italy	15.8
England	12.0
Canada	11.6
West Germany	6.2

From Population Council, "Induced Abortion: A World Wide Review, 1981" (Dr. Christoper Tietze).

In a study of repeat abortions in New York City, Dr. Edwin F. Daily and his co-workers[5] found that only 2.5 percent of induced abortions involved women who had had abortions previously.

Repeat Abortions

A number of psychosociological and spiritual considerations also enter into the decision-making process. These, of course, are different for each individual woman, depending on the principles and presuppositions operative in her personal life. Hence, it is difficult to advise another person about induced abortion. It is the hope of the authors that responsible sexual behavior, including the use of contraceptives and/or abstinence, will preclude the necessity for a decision about abortion.

Abortion—An Examination of Personal Responsibility

[5]Edwin F. Daily, et al., "Repeat Abortions in New York: 1970–72," *Family Planning Perspectives* (Spring 1973).

CHAPTER 8

Sexually Transmitted Diseases (STDs)

In the traditional classification of human diseases, a category known as venereal diseases (VD) included syphilis, gonorrhea, chancroid, granuloma inguinale, and lymphogranuloma venereum. Today, health scientists prefer the term sexually transmitted diseases (STDs) because it avoids some of the stigma associated with the term VD while simultaneously emphasizing the fact that a wide range of diseases may be transmitted by sexual contact. In addition to the usual five venereal diseases, STDs include a long list of diseases, including such well known ones as herpes genitalis, venereal warts, acquired immune deficiency syndrome (AIDS), trichomoniasis, candidiasis, and nongonococcal urethritis. Since granuloma inguinale, lymphogranuloma venereum, and chancroid are not very widespread, they are omitted from this chapter.

Many authorities in sex education are of the opinion that STDs should be considered only in connection with infectious diseases and not as part of the sex education curriculum. They feel that a discussion of STDs detracts from the "beauty" of sexuality. Inadvertently, this attitude promulgates the notion that "nice" people don't get and should not talk about STDs. But an examination of health statistics indicates that thousands of nice people contract STDs in the same way. Indeed, STDs are almost as dependent upon the sex act as pregnancy; the fact that disease is an undesirable consequence is not a justification for separating it from other aspects of sex education. To do so would be analogous to discussing the beneficial effects of a drug while postponing a discussion of any dangerous side effect. In fact, the major reason that STDs continue to exist and spread is that they are so "undiscussable." Medical science has identified the causes of STDs and the ways they are transmitted; it has also developed effective cures for many of the diseases.

Furthermore, STDs are not out of place in a discussion of love. A major component of love is responsibility, which includes not transmitting STDs to another person. Responsibility thus requires a knowledge of STDs and how they are transmitted, which is the subject of this chapter.

For convenience of study, diseases have been grouped into broad categories. Three of these categories provide a perspective for the present chapter:

1. Hereditary diseases.

2. Congenital diseases.

3. Infectious diseases.

Hereditary diseases are acquired at conception, whereas congenital diseases are acquired between conception and birth.

Infectious agents invade the body to produce the category known as infectious diseases.

Some STDs are congenital, all are infectious, but none are hereditary.

More than 20 human diseases can be transmitted in a sexual way. The most common STDs are discussed in this chapter. These diseases and their causative agents are listed in Table 6 in the order in which they are discussed.

TABLE 6:   **STDs and Their Causes**

Disease	Organism	Agent
Gonorrhea	*Neisseria gonorrhoeae*	Bacterium
Syphilis	*Treponema pallidum*	Bacterium
Herpes genitalis	Herpesvirus (type 2)	Virus
Acquired immune deficiency syndrome (AIDS)	Unknown	Unknown
Venereal warts	*Condylomata acuminata*	Virus
Nongonococcal urethritis	*Chlamydia trachomatis*	Bacterium
Trichomoniasis	*Trichomonas vaginalis*	Protozoan
Monila	*Candida albicans*	Fungi
Pediculosis	*Phthirus pubis*	Parasite

Gonorrhea

Gonorrhea is an old disease. Some medical historians believe that it was known to the Jews in Old Testament times; it is described in the Book of Leviticus.

The word "gonorrhea" means "flow of seed" and was used by Galen in 130 A.D. to describe the signs of the disease that occur in males. A common slang term for the disease is "clap."

In the early history of the disease, it was thought that gonorrhea was a symptom of syphilis. This mistaken notion probably resulted from observations of patients with both diseases. Indeed, the early medical scientist John Hunter inoculated himself with the pus formed in a patient with gonorrhea and contracted both gonorrhea and syphilis. Not realizing that he had both diseases, Hunter concluded and taught that gonorrhea was the first stage of syphilis—a misconception that is still prevalent today.

Gonorrhea Today

Among the infectious diseases reportable to public health authorities in the United States, gonorrhea currently ranks as number one (Table 7).

TABLE 7:   **Rank Order for the Frequency of STDs (Estimated New Cases per Year)**

1. Gonorrhea	1 million
2. Herpes	300,000 to 1 million
3. Syphilis	30,000

TABLE 8: **Geographical Distribution of Cases of Gonorrhea**

Population Size	Incidence per 100,000
Small towns and rural areas	84
50,000 to 200,000	290
200,000 and over	610

Gonorrhea is chiefly found in large metropolitan areas (Table 8).

Geographical Factors

The incidence is three times higher among males, primarily because the majority of infected females are asymptomatic. The age range 20 to 24 years has the highest rate, followed by teenagers (15 to 19 years).

The gonorrhea epidemic appears to be worldwide and has been increasing since the mid-1950's. The World Health Organization reports an increase from 60 million cases in 1969 to 200 million in 1977. The Centers for Disease Control estimated over a million cases in the United States currently.

World Picture

Numerous interwoven factors appear to be responsible for the increased incidence of gonorrhea. Some of these include the following.

1. Asymptomatic infections appear to have increased among males. This means that a smaller number of males are being effectively treated, a factor that contributes to the spread of gonorrhea.

2. Certain strains of the gonococcus are definitely less sensitive to antibiotics, and the recommended dosage of penicillin has now reached the full capacity that the buttocks can tolerate.

3. Increased population mobility has rendered contact tracing almost impossible.

4. Indiscriminate heterosexual and homosexual intercourse appears to have increased.

5. Oral contraceptives increase female susceptibility to gonorrhea. A woman taking the pill has an 80 percent chance of contracting gonorrhea from a sexual partner who has the disease, whereas a woman not on the pill has only a 30 percent chance. It appears that the pill increases pH in the area of the cervix and alters mucous secretions. Both conditions are thought to favor the growth of the bacteria.

6. The condom has decreased in popularity in recent years. This undoubtedly favors spread of gonorrhea.

7. Although no statistical data are available, many are of the opinion that oral and anal sexual practices have increased. At any rate, more cases of rectal and pharyngeal gonorrhea are currently being reported. This increased reporting, however, may be the result of an increased awareness among physicians.

In 1879, A. Neisser identified the bacterium that causes gonorrhea and named it the gonococcus. These bacteria are bean- or kidney-shaped and are found in pairs. In smears containing pus, the gonococci are seen inside white cells.

The Gonococcus

To survive, the bacteria require:

1. A pH of 7.2 to 7.6; they are killed by even weak acids.

2. A temperature of 35° to 36°C; they cannot survive a 3° change.

3. A moist environment; they die immediately on drying.

4. Columnar or transitional epithelium; they cannot attack the labia or vagina (stratified epithelium).

When the gonococcus dies, it releases an irritant (endotoxin).

It is now clear that detectable antibodies are produced in gonorrhea—an observation that has led to the development of a number of blood tests for gonorrhea. To date, however, none of these is reliable enough for general use.

Blood Tests for Gonorrhea

Despite the production of a small number of antibodies, an attack of gonorrhea confers no lasting immunity.

No Immunity

Among adults, gonorrhea is spread almost exclusively by sexual intercourse.

Transmission

In children, infection by contaminated materials or pus is possible but not frequent. The gonorrhea bacteria are ingested but not killed by white blood cells; thus pus is infectious. The organism dies quickly with drying, but repeated use of bath water could be a means of transmission in young children.

Gonococcal conjunctivitis (infection of the eyes) may occur from passage through the birth canal of an infected mother. If infected, the baby's eyes may be destroyed within a few days. This condition was at one time the most frequent cause of blindness in infancy. Today most states require that the eyes of all newborn children be treated with silver nitrate or some other substance (tetracycline or erythromycin) to kill the gonococcus (Fig. 62). Also, most states require reporting of any inflammation of the eyes of a newborn to the health department.

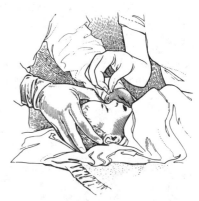

Figure 62   Application of silver nitrate at birth.

Not all persons exposed to gonorrhea contract the disease. Although the true transmission rate is unknown, it is thought to be less than 50 percent.

Transmission Rate

The reason for this seeming immunity is unknown. Recent evidence, however, suggests that the answer may be that other bacteria are known to prevent the spread of gonorrhea. In studies of men, researchers have isolated 60 different bacteria that inhibit gonorrhea.

This finding could lead to medical application whereby physicians may attempt to modify the genital flora to decrease susceptibility to gonorrhea.

The short incubation period of gonorrhea infections means that a person can become infectious in just a few days, making it possible for gonorrhea to be spread more rapidly than contacts can be traced.

The Course of Gonorrhea

In the male the gonococcus attacks the mucous membrane lining the urethra (Fig. 63).

Gonorrhea in the Male

The results of this attack are:

1. Swelling and irritation of the urethral tissue.

2. A painful burning sensation with urination.

3. A yellowish discharge from the penis.

The pain is usually distressing enough to induce the male to see his physician. In other cases, however, there may be no pain.

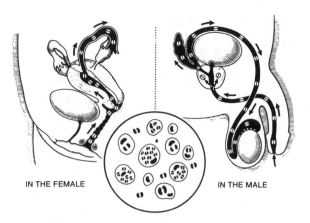

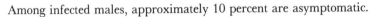

IN THE FEMALE   IN THE MALE

Figure 63   Gonorrhea.

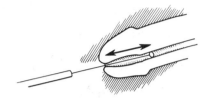

Figure 64   Urethral culture.

Among infected males, approximately 10 percent are asymptomatic.

To detect gonorrhea, the physician obtains a urethral culture (Fig. 64).

If gonorrhea is diagnosed, treatment with penicillin can have dramatic results. The urethral discharges may stop within 24 hours, and the disease may be completely abated in a short time.

However, some gonococcal bacteria are resistant to penicillin. Although other antibiotics are effective against gonorrhea, their effects are not so dramatic as those of penicillin.

Treatment

For uncomplicated cases of gonorrhea the most widely used drugs are penicillin and tetracycline.

Aqueous procaine penicillin can be administered intramuscularly in one visit. Probenecid, a drug that slows the elimination of penicillin from the body, is taken prior to this treatment.

Some physicians think that uncomplicated cases of gonorrhea should be treated with tetracycline, with penicillin being held in reserve for more serious cases. This recommendation comes from the fear that extensive use of penicillin may result in development of gonococcal bacteria capable of producing penicillinase, a substance that allows them to resist treatment with penicillin. These types of bacteria are thought to have developed in the Far East, and armed forces personnel and travelers have transmitted them to contacts in the United States. More than 500 such cases have been reported in the United States, but because of prompt contact tracing, they have not spread. These penicillin-resistant bacteria are treatable with spectinomycin.

Despite concern over this problem, many physicians prefer the penicillin approach to treatment, pointing out that such a treatment is also effective in aborting incubating syphilis.

Untreated Gonorrhea in the Male

Untreated gonorrhea, like other infections, spreads to adjacent parts of the body. In the male, it may spread to the posterior portion of the urethra, the prostate, the seminal vesicles, or the bulbourethral glands.

In advanced stages it may cause sterility or break through the walls that separate the reproductive system from other parts of the body, and eventually cause arthritis or heart disease.

Resistance

Great individual variation in resistance to gonorrhea has been observed. If large numbers of gonococci are placed directly into the urethral canal, less than half the inoculated males will contract gonorrhea.

The condom prevents contamination of the urethra and is undoubtedly the most effective measure for prevention of the spread of gonorrhea by sexual intercourse.

Prevention

In the female, gonorrhea passes through three stages (Fig. 63):

Gonorrhea and the Female

1. Infection of the urethra or cervix, which is often so mild as to go unnoticed.

2. Pelvic invasion by the disease.

3. A stage of residual and often chronic infection.

Approximately 90 percent of infected women are asymptomatic. Thus the female becomes a chronic reservoir for the disease. Even the most advanced technique of smear and culture examinations yields a 20 percent incidence of false negative results. This difficulty in diagnosis of female gonorrhea is a major problem in controlling the disease.

Hidden Disease

Complications of gonorrhea are more serious in the female because the disease may affect any of the pelvic organs or may even break through to attack other parts of the body. The adult vagina is not susceptible to the bacteria, but the urethra, cervix, uterus, and oviducts may be attacked.

Later Complications

As the disease advances, the female may experience fever, nausea, vomiting, and lower abdominal pain. Lower abdominal pain usually occurs when the infection has spread to the oviducts.

Treatment is essentially the same as for males.

Treatment

All patients treated for gonorrhea should have follow-up tests to be sure that the disease has been arrested. These tests consist of repeated cultures that are free of the bacteria.

Follow-up

The male is considered cured if a month passes without urethral discharge and if pus cells and bacteria are absent in the urine.

The female is considered cured when multiple successive examinations of the urethra and cervical canal indicate an absence of gonococcal bacteria.

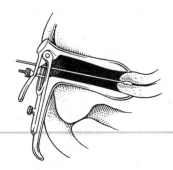

Figure 65   Endocervical culture.

In addition to urethral and cervical infections, pharyngeal, rectal, and ophthalmic gonorrhea are of increasing concern.

Additional Sites of Infection

At one time it was thought that the mucosa of the pharynx was unable to support growth of gonococci. More recently, however, it has become clear that this was a misconception. Indeed, pharyngeal gonorrhea has been reported[1] in 22 percent of patients who were named as gonorrhea contacts and who also practiced fellatio. And in 13 percent of this group, the pharynx was the only site of positive culture. It has also been demonstrated that pharyngeal gonorrhea can spread to other parts of the body. In general it is asymptomatic.

Pharyngeal Gonorrhea

[1]Henry Pariser, "Asymptomatic Gonorrhea," *Medical Clinics of North America,* 56 (Sept. 1972), pp. 1127–1132.

Rectal gonorrhea is generally asymptomatic. In one study[2] routine swabs of both the cervix and rectum were taken of 307 women in the Norfolk Venereal Disease Clinic. Forty percent of the women diagnosed as infected also had positive rectal cultures, and 20 percent had positive rectal test results but negative cervical test results.

Rectal Gonorrhea

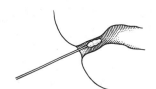

Figure 66   Anal culture.

The gonococcus may be transmitted by fingers or moist towels to the eyes. Failure to recognize and treat this type of infection may result in impaired vision.

Ophthalmic Gonorrhea

In recent years a number of strains of gonococci have become resistant to antibiotics. This resistance may constitute a major problem in the control of gonorrhea in the future.

Resistance of Gonococci to Antibiotics

Dr. Frederick Sparling has summarized the problem to date:[3]

> Antibiotic resistance among gonococci has gradually increased in many areas of the world, including the United States, for over a decade. Resistance is often multiple in that strains relatively resistant to penicillin usually exhibit decreased sensitivity to tetracycline, erythromycin, chloramphenicol, and many other drugs, including streptomycin. Preliminary evidence suggests that there may be a common basis for resistance to several of these drugs. If this is substantiated, it is unlikely that use of combinations of these drugs would forestall development of resistance, nor would switch to generalized use of any one (tetracycline) lead to disappearance of resistance to the others (penicillin). Exceptions to this are sulfa drugs (sensitivity has increased at the same time it has decreased to the others) and spectinomycin. The latter holds promise as an injectable drug for patients infected with gonococci which do not respond to penicillin or tetracycline. Resistance to all drugs except streptomycin is relative; presently available schedules of penicillin or tetracycline are still effective. Limited epidemiological data suggest that very intensive and perhaps more prolonged therapy may help prevent selection of still more resistant strains.

Syphilis

Syphilis is caused by spirochetes. These organisms can only be seen against a dark background (in the same way that stars are only seen at night). But when seen through a microscope against a dark field, the spirochete appears as a pale, turning thread. Because of this appearance, its discoverers called it *Treponema pallidum* (trepein [Greek]—turn + nema [Greek]—thread, pallidum [Latin]—pale). The bacterium is a member of the order of Spirochaetales and of the family Treponemataceae, and consequently the disease is sometimes referred to as a spirochetal infection.

A Spirochete Infection

Treponema pallidum is a living cell that requires special environmental conditions.

Characteristics of *Treponema pallidum*

---

[2]Henry Pariser and A. F. Marino, "Gonorrhea—Frequently Unrecognized Reservoirs," *Southern Medical Journal,* 63 (1970), p. 198.

[3]P. Frederick Sparling, "Antibiotic Resistance in *Neisseria Gonorrhoeae*," *Medical Clinics of North America,* 56 (1972), pp. 1133–1144.

It is very susceptible to drying and dies in about 30 seconds on a doorknob or toilet seat.

It is very susceptible to high temperatures—above body temperature. Elevating the body temperature to 106°F for only a few hours causes destruction of a large percentage of active syphilitic organisms; this method was once used in treatment.

T. pallidum is killed by mild antiseptics, even soap and water.

The spirochete divides asexually approximately every 30 to 33 hours.

Transmission

Syphilis is transmitted to another person in the following way: *T. pallidum* from the lesion of an infectious person passes through the intact mucous membranes or abraded skin of a second person. Moisture is essential to transmission, a condition met by sexual intercourse and intimate kissing in the presence of infectious lesions. Dentists and throat surgeons have accidentally contracted syphilis from treating infected patients. In a very unusual case syphilis was transferred by dual use of lipstick (this required that both women have a break in the skin of the lips).

Syphilis is thus not transmitted by doorknobs, dishes, or toilet seats.

Having entered the body, spirochetes are carried by the blood to every organ of the body. If the infected person happens to be a pregnant woman, spirochetes may be passed into the fetal circulation, causing serious consequences or death of the fetus. (Congenital syphilis is discussed in more detail in a later part of this chapter.)

Spirochetes may also be found in menstrual blood, but they do not survive in the vaginal tract in the absence of a lesion.

Stages of Syphilis

Untreated syphilis passes through the following stages (Fig. 67).

1. Incubation period.
2. Primary stage.
3. Secondary stage.
4. Latent stage.
5. Late (tertiary) stage.

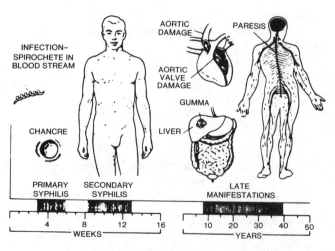

Figure 67   The stages of syphilis.

The incubation period consists of the time interval between the entrance of an infectious agent and the beginning of the signs and symptoms of the disease. The incubation period ranges from 10 to 60 days with an average of 3 weeks.

Incubation Period

Assume that 1,000 bacteria entered the body by moist transfer. (Syphilis has been produced by as few as ten spirochetes.) These spirochetes start to spread through the body and to multiply every 30 to 33 hours. By the end of three weeks, 10 billion spirochetes have accumulated, passed through the circulatory system, and been deposited around the blood vessels of tissues throughout the body.

Spread of Bacteria Through the Body

It is doubtful that the spirochetes multiply in the blood, but when they are deposited in the tissues they resume multiplication.

Spirochetes cannot be detected in the blood during the incubation period. This is because blood tests for syphilis detect antibodies against syphilis rather than the presence of *T. pallidum*. Thus, blood tests remain negative until antibodies have developed (approximately four to six weeks after infection).

Spirochetes multiply and spread through the body during the incubation period and later cause lesions of the skin or mucous membranes during subsequent stages of syphilis.

The primary stage of syphilis is signaled by the appearance of a lesion at the site of entry of the spirochete. This stage may last one to five weeks.

Primary Syphilis

The lesion that appears at this time is called a chancre (Fig. 68). It is usually one quarter to one half inch in diameter and is formed by white cells that pack into the invasion area. The chancre usually begins as a red elevated area that breaks down to form a painless ulcer.

Chancre

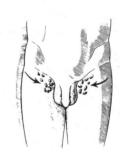

Figure 68   Chancroid.

The chancre is usually hard but can be soft. It generally feels hard and button-like.

It is ordinarily not tender to touch. It doesn't hurt. It doesn't itch.

Multiple chancres may develop.

In approximately 95 percent of cases, the chancre appears on or in the genital organs. In women it commonly appears on the cervix, where it is often missed on examination.

In unusual cases the chancre may appear anywhere:

1.   In the mouth or around the anus.

2.   One man is reported to have developed a chancre on his arm where his wife bit him.

The chancre usually disappears in about two weeks. (In unusual cases it may last as long as three months.)

Disappearance of Chancre

Thus the individual who recognizes a new lesion and says, "I will wait awhile and see if it goes away before I see my doctor," makes a dangerous mistake. The chancre is the only outward sign of primary syphilis, and the individual who fails to report this to his physician passes untreated into the stage of secondary syphilis.

Dr. Lewis M. Drustin[4] has made the important observation that antibiotics given for another illness during this period may obscure the chancre without adequately treating syphilis.

In addition to the chancre, lymph glands usually swell during primary syphilis. These enlarged nodes (known as satellite bubo) are found in the site of the regional lymph drainage three to four days after the appearance of the chancre. The nodes are round and rubbery, without redness of the overlying skin. They are usually firm, freely movable, and nontender.

Lymph Node Enlargement

Because the chancre that is symptomatic of primary syphilis resembles lesions caused by other factors, it is impossible to make an absolute diagnosis from the appearance of the lesion.

Diagnosis of Primary Syphilis

Absolute diagnosis can only be established by demonstration of *T. pallidum* in the local lesion. Blood test results do not become positive until the fourth to sixth week of syphilis because the incubation period averages three weeks and the primary stage of syphilis lasts one to five weeks. Therefore, it is possible for the patient to pass through the primary stage of syphilis with a negative blood test result. A blood test result is likely to be negative at the time the chancre appears.

Primary syphilis is completely curable if properly treated. The preferred treatment for primary syphilis is penicillin administration. When penicillin sensitivity prevents use of this drug, other antibiotics, such as erythromycin and tetracycline, may be used. It should be noted that there are different types of penicillin and what is suitable for the treatment of one STD may not be suitable for another.

Treatment

The secondary stage of syphilis begins about nine weeks (range, six weeks to six months) after initial infection. This stage represents the time during which lesions are present and the disease is infectious. This time span may range from three months to several years, with an average of two years.

Secondary Syphilis

When *T. pallidum* enters the body, it passes via the blood to all parts of the body. During this stage, the spirochetes that have been spreading produce secondary lesions, especially in mucous membranes and in the skin (Fig. 67). The skin lesions appear as a flattened, slightly raised red rash.

Lesions covered with skin are not infectious. However, such lesions contain many spirochetes, and if their outer covering is eroded spirochetes may escape and pass to another person.

Moist lesions frequently occur in the anogenital region and in the mouth. The outer covering of these moist lesions is easily eroded, making them highly infectious. Thus the disease is spread by sexual contact for a purely biological reason—by means of the moist lesion—not from any malevolent design to punish those who engage in sex.

Secondary syphilis is far more infectious than primary syphilis because the secondary lesions are numerous, whereas there may be only one lesion during primary syphilis.

During secondary syphilis the body develops antibodies against syphilis. Thus results of blood tests for syphilis are positive during this time.

Diagnosis and Treatment

When developed, these antibodies hold the spirochetes in check and bring an

---

[4]Lewis M. Drusin, "The Diagnosis and Treatment of Infections and Latent Syphilis," *Medical Clinics of North America*, 56 (Sept. 1972), pp. 116–174.

end to the lesions. When this occurs, the individual passes out of the secondary stage of infection.

Secondary syphilis is readily curable. The treatment of secondary syphilis is the same as that for primary syphilis.

Latent Syphilis

"Latent" means hidden. Accordingly, there are no observable manifestations during the latent stage of syphilis. This stage of syphilis may last 5 to 50 years, more commonly 10 to 20 years.

Because surface lesions are not present, the person with latent syphilis cannot transmit the infection, except congenitally.

There is one danger, however: the antibodies holding the spirochetes in check may lose control and allow the individual to revert to secondary syphilis. This is most likely to occur during the first year of latent syphilis.

Diagnosis and Treatment

Latent syphilis can only be diagnosed by blood tests. It is curable at this stage by antibiotic therapy.

Late (Tertiary) Syphilis

Late syphilis is the most serious stage for the infected individual. This stage is often referred to as "symptomatic syphilis" because of the serious symptoms that occur. The spirochetes that were held in check during the latent stage now begin to multiply again and attack body organs. Late syphilis may cause grave damage to any organs of the body, but the most frequently involved structures are (Fig. 67):

1. Heart and blood vessels.

2. Brain, spinal cord, and their coverings.

3. Eyes.

If the primary and secondary stages of syphilis go undetected, the first sign of syphilis may be a very serious consequence of the disease process. Late syphilis cripples, blinds, and kills many people every year.

Late syphilis is treatable in that antibiotics will kill the spirochetes that cause the symptoms, but the damage itself is not reversible.

The Natural Course of Untreated Syphilis

If a large group of people with syphilis go untreated, what would happen to them? The answer to this question comes from a study completed in Oslo, Norway.

Being firmly convinced that the recommended treatment for syphilis was inadequate, Professor Boeck[5] withheld treatment from 1,978 patients between 1891 and 1910. To protect the community, these patients were hospitalized until they had passed through the secondary stage. When they were no longer infectious, they were released.

A follow-up study of 1,404 of these patients was completed in August 1951. The results of this study represent the best information available about the natural course of untreated syphilis:

1. If syphilis is not treated, the patient may relapse from the latent stage to the infectious secondary stage. In the Oslo study 23.6 percent of the patients had a relapse; of those patients, 85 percent had lesions in the

---

[5]E. Gurney Clark and Niels Denbolt, "The Oslo Study of the Natural Course of Untreated Syphilis," *Medical Clinics of North America,* 48 (May 1964), p. 3.

mouth, throat, or anogenital region where they could be easily eroded and thus become infectious.

2.   About one third of untreated patients with syphilis develop late destructive lesions of syphilis.

3.   Approximately 23 percent can be expected to die as a result of syphilis.

4.   Two thirds of all untreated patients can be expected to go through life with minimal or no physical inconvenience.

Serous material taken from a moist lesion of primary or secondary syphilis may be examined under a dark-field microscope to confirm or deny the presence of syphilis. It is estimated, however, that 70 percent of syphilis is diagnosed on the basis of blood tests.

Tests for Syphilis

There are two types of blood tests for syphilis—reagin and treponemal. Both types are based upon antibody response to infection. When spirochetes invade the human body, two types of antibodies develop—nonspecific antibodies (reagins) and treponemal antibodies.

Blood Tests for Syphilis

Reagins develop in response to tissue-treponemal reactions. With proper treatment and disappearance of treponema, the reagin titer returns to a low level. Hence, reagin tests are useful both in diagnosis and as treatment criteria.

Reagin Tests

The most widely used reagin test is the relatively simple Venereal Disease Research Laboratory (VDRL) test. Its value is limited to screening, since reagins are nonspecific and may increase in such conditions as infectious mononucleosis, heroin addiction, leprosy, and malaria, to mention a few.

The VDRL test is based on the observation that animal tissue extracts (from the heart and liver) cause reagins to aggregate. These extracts are easily obtained, and the VDRL test can be used conveniently in any laboratory situation.

If the result of the VDRL test is positive, a treponemal test is usually required to guard against the possibility that the increased numbers of reagins may have been due to factors unrelated to syphilis.

Treponemal Tests

Currently the Fluorescent Treponemal Antibody Absorption test (FTA-ABS test) is the most widely used treponemal test. It is more difficult and expensive to perform and is usually a follow-up to positive VDRL tests.

In the FTA-ABS test, treponemal antigens are added to test blood samples. If the sample contains specific antibodies, the treponemal antigens absorb them. The process can be observed under a microscope.

Regarding the current status of knowledge about tests for syphilis, Dr. Sidney Olansky states:[6]

Current Status of Blood Test for Syphilis

> For many years syphilologists have strived to produce a single reproducible serologic test for syphilis which would serve as a standard test and a reliable specific test to eliminate biologic false-positive reactions. We have essentially accomplished both aims in the VDRL slide test for the former and the FTA-ABS test for the latter. With these two procedures essentially all problems in serodiagnosis can be resolved.

---

[6]Sidney Olansky, "Serodiagnosis of Syphilis," *Medical Clinics of North America,* 56 (Sept. 1972), pp. 1145–1150.

After adequate treatment of syphilis, serological (blood) tests have the following patterns:

1.   If treatment is given before the chancre develops, this first lesion will probably not appear and serological tests will remain negative.

2.   When treatment occurs during the primary stage but before blood test results become positive, serological test results usually remain negative, and the chancre rapidly disappears.

3.   If treatment is received during the primary stage but after blood test results become positive, about 12 months must elapse before test results become negative again.

4.   If treatment is delayed until the secondary stage, about 18 months are required for blood test results to become negative again. Ninety to 95 percent of patients do have a negative reaction for syphilis after an 18-month period.

5.   Individuals infected for two years or more before treatment may remain serologically positive for the remainder of their lives. This is true even though they are cured of the disease.

Congenital syphilis is transmitted to the fetus through the placenta. This seldom occurs before the fourth month of pregnancy. It is hypothesized that the placenta contains a barrier to the bacteria (Langhans' layer of the chorion) until the 16th week.

Congenital Syphilis

Thus treatment of the mother prior to the fourth month of pregnancy will prevent prenatal syphilis. After this date, bacteria pass through the placenta to infect the fetus.

Approximately 25 percent of infected fetuses die before birth. Another 25 to 30 percent die shortly after birth. Of untreated children who survive, 40 percent develop symptomatic syphilis.

Herpes

Herpes is the name of a family of more than 50 viruses, 5 of which affect humans. Viruses of this family have an affinity for the nervous system and usually move along nerve pathways until they reach the skin, where they cause blisters and sores. One well-known disease caused by this virus is herpes varicella (chickenpox).

The two major types of herpes infections are:

Types of Herpes

1.   Oral herpes simplex (Type I).

2.   Genital herpes simplex (Type II).

The incubation periods for both types range from 2 to 20 days, with an average of 6 days.

Oral herpes is often seen in children under five years old. The symptoms are cold sores or fever blisters. The skin eruptions clear up on their own and do not produce scars. A severe case may be accompanied by fever, loss of appetite, bad breath, and swollen neck glands.

Oral Herpes

Oral herpes is usually limited to the upper half of the body but may affect the genital area. It may be transferred from the mouth to the genitals during oral–genital sex.

Recurrent oral herpes is a possibility once a person has been infected. The virus retreats into the facial nerve and hibernates until its next attack. The virus is with a person for life, and symptoms recur during times of stress: in the presence of other infections, injury, or emotional stress.

Oral herpes is not the same as canker sores, which are unrelated. Canker sores are grayish-white with red rims and occur inside the lips and cheeks or on the gums or tongue. They are not contagious.

Genital Herpes

Genital herpes is probably the most common STD after gonorrhea, and its incidence is increasing. The Centers for Disease Control estimate between 300,000 to 1 million new cases each year.

Symptoms

Although the symptoms of genital and oral herpes are similar, the two viruses are different in many biochemical and biological aspects. In genital herpes, painful external sores or groups of sores, measuring one or more millimeters in diameter, appear in the genital area. Women develop clusters of small, painful blisters in the vaginal, cervical, urethal, and anal areas. They experience tingling, itching, and burning during urination. Men get similar sores on the shaft of the penis and sometimes on the buttocks. In both men and women, the infection may be accompanied by fever, headache, loss of appetite, and general malaise. Regional swelling of lymph nodes is common, with the nodes being very tender.

Treatment

Genital herpes cannot be cured completely, although eventually the sores become crusty and heal without scarring. Treatment is limited to control of symptoms, including pain, itching, and burning sensations. Compresses are mainstays in treatment. Silver nitrate, potassium permanganate, benzalkonium, and boric acid are frequent remedies. More recently, the new antiviral drug isoprinosine has shown great promise in treatment.

Recurrence

The genital herpes virus withdraws to the spinal cord where it can become reactivated later. Recurrence is associated with other infections, emotional upsets, and menstruation. Recurring episodes are less severe than the initial one.

Pregnancy and the Newborn

A pregnant woman with active herpes has a 50 percent chance of infecting the infant at birth. Such infections are thought to be transmitted in the birth canal, and obstetricians recommend cesarean section for women who have symptoms of herpes within several weeks of delivery. The child is thought to be safe if the disease has run its course three or four weeks before delivery. However, it is suspected that the virus can also pass through the placenta, and spontaneous abortion associated with infection has been reported. Half of infected infants die, and of the survivors, half suffer severe brain or eye damage.

Herpes Keratitis

Herpes keratitis, an eye inflammation, is a leading cause of infection-related blindness. It is contracted simply by touching an active herpes sore somewhere on the body and then rubbing the eye.

Cervical Cancer

There is substantial evidence that the herpes virus is related to cancer of the cervix, although this is not unequivocally established. Women with this infection have cervical cancer rates seven times higher than have women of the same age but without genital herpes.

Acquired Immune Deficiency Syndrome (AIDS)

A New STD

In 1981 a new disease that diminishes the body's immunity against invading agents was discovered. This new disease, called acquired immune deficiency syndrome, is a very serious condition in which victims become susceptible to diseases that would normally be resisted. AIDS appears to be transmittable by sexual contact.

AIDS is a very unusual disease in that its danger to human health is not through direct damage to tissues and organs but by a crippling of the body's immunity.

A Public Health Priority

Obviously any disease that compromises the body's capacity to resist organisms and toxins is of grave concern, and the United States Public Health Service has declared AIDS a top priority. Currently 6 of the 11 research components at the National Institutes of Health are involved in multidisciplinary studies of AIDS

To better understand AIDS, let us begin with a brief description of immunity.

Immunity

White blood cells called lymphocytes constitute the body's main defense against infection. Lymphocytes are derived from special cells in the embryo and are constantly being produced by the bone marrow. After "preprocessing," the lymphocytes come to be located in lymph nodes and in special lymphoid tissues that are advantageously located throughout the body to intercept invading agents.

Lymphocytes

One group of lymphocytes is preprocessed by the thymus gland to operate as attack cells. Called T-lymphocytes, these cells attach to foreign agents and attempt to render them harmless.

T-lymphocytes

A second group of lymphocytes is preprocessed to produce antibodies. It is not clear where in the body this preprocessing takes place, but since this group of lymphocytes was first discovered in birds in which the preprocessing occurs in the bursa of Fabricius, they are called B-lymphocytes. B-cells make possible the process of vaccination.

B-lymphocytes

Working together, antibodies and T-cells protect the body against most organisms and toxins. However, a weakening of this defense system opens the body to a variety of diseases. Indeed, in persons with a genetic lack of lymphoid tissue the possibility of survival is slight.

Immune Deficiency

In AIDS the body's defense system is weakened primarily by an alteration in the normal functioning of T-cells.

It is not clear what causes this change in T-lymphocytes, but there is strong evidence to suggest that it may be a virus. Research teams in the United States and France now think that they have discovered a variant form of a human T-cell leukemia virus (HTLV) that is the cause of AIDS. The virus, called HTLV-III, has been identified in patients with pre-AIDS, and blood samples from 88 percent of patients diagnosed as having AIDS showed antibody reactions to the newly discovered virus.

Research into the origin of AIDS is difficult because AIDS weakens immunity instead of causing direct damage. Hence, it is difficult to determine whether viruses found in the body of victims actually caused AIDS or whether these viruses entered the body after its defenses were weakened. Moreover, it is possible that a virus could enter the body, modify its T-cells, and disappear before the signs and symptoms of AIDS actually occur. In two cases T-cell viruses were found early in AIDS victims but disappeared within six weeks. The incubation period for AIDS appears to be between 4 and 30 months, meaning that a virus could easily cause a weakening of the body's defense system and disappear prior to the onset of the diseases.

The symptoms of AIDS are not consistent but may include: **Symptoms**

- Fever.

- Night sweats.

- Enlarged lymph nodes.

- Unexplained weight loss.

- Yeast infections.

- Diarrhea.

- Persistent Coughs.

- Fatigue.

- Loss of appetite.

AIDs is a devastating disease for which there is no known cure. Treatment   **Prognosis**
consists of trying, in the absence of a healthy immune system, to hold other
diseases in check. Over time the prognosis is grim. The two diseases most
commonly found in AIDS patients are *Pneumocystis carinii* pneumonia, a
parasitic lung disease, and Kaposi's sarcoma, a type of cancer. Against the
latter disease, interferon—a virus-fighting protein produced by the body—
has been of limited value.

Since its discovery in 1981, more than 4,087 cases and 1,758 AIDS-related   **The Spread of AIDS**
deaths have been reported in the United States. AIDS has also been reported
in 17 other countries. Over three dozen children in the United States have
been found to have AIDS, and two dozen of them have died from the
disease.[7,8]

To date, most AIDS cases have occurred in people belonging to one of four
groups:

1. Sexually active homosexual and bisexual men.

2. Persons with hemophilia.

3. Present or past abusers of intravenous drugs.

4. Haitian immigrants coming to the United States.

The Public Health Service has recommended that the following steps be taken   **Prevention**
to prevent the spread of AIDS:

1. Sexual contact should be avoided with persons known or suspected
of having AIDS.

2. Having multiple sexual partners and sexual contact with those who
do should be avoided.

3. Members of high-risk groups should refrain from donating blood.

4. Physicians should order blood transfusions for patients only when
medically necessary.

---

[7]Arthur J. Ammann, "Is There an Acquired Immune Deficiency in Infants and Children?"
Pediatrics, 72 (1983), pp. 430–432.

[8]A. Rubinstein, "Acquired Immune Deficiency Syndrome in Infants," *American Journal of
Diseases of Children,* 137 (1983), pp. 825–827.

AIDS does not appear to be transmitted by casual or even close daily contact with AIDS patients. It is a disease that appears to be transmitted primarily by sexual contact or by the transfer of body fluids from one person to another. Observations to date indicate that AIDS is not a disease that is transmitted through the air.

At present there is great hope that a blood test for AIDS will soon be available. If the disease is definitely proven to be caused by a virus, then it may be possible to develop an effective blood test and even a protective vaccine. Meanwhile, AIDS can only be diagnosed by the onset of signs and symptoms that signal weakened immunity.

Venereal Warts

Venereal warts are caused by a virus and usually appear one to three months following exposure to an infected person. In the male the warts are most common on the penis, especially the glans. However, they may appear on any part of the genitalia. In the female warts are more common on the vaginal outlet, but the labia, vaginal walls, and cervix may all be involved.

Warts are treated by the application of podophyllum ointment, which causes them to dry up. If the warts are massive, surgery may be required.

Nongonococcal Urethritis

Urethritis is an inflammation of the urethra. It may be caused by several factors, only one of which is gonorrhea.

When urethritis is not caused by gonorrhea, it is usually referred to as "nongonococcal" or "nonspecific" urethritis.

Two categories of nongonococcal urethritis are recognized:

1. Those that spread in a venereal way.

2. Those that spread in a nonvenereal way.

The causes of nongonococcal urethritis are unclear. Some inflammations appear to be caused by viruses. Others are thought to be associated with mycoplasmas (members of a genus of bacteria). For others there is no detectable cause.

Trichomonal Infections (Trichomoniasis)

The parasite *Trichomonas vaginalis* was described by Donne in 1836. The parasite is a flagellate protozoon.

Trichomonas vaginalis infection is estimated to afflict up to 25 percent of women and can be found in 12 to 15 percent of men with urethritis. The parasite is usually transmitted sexually, producing vaginitis in women and urethritis in men. Because the parasite can survive for several hours on moist objects at room temperature, trichomoniasis can be contacted by a woman who uses a moist washcloth or towel that was recently used by an infected woman. However, this kind of contact is thought to be highly unlikely.

The incubation period for this disease is 4 to 28 days.

In women the disease ranges from symptomless to very painful. Frequently there is a greenish-yellow vaginal discharge and soreness and itching of the vulva and the skin on the inside of the thighs. In some cases the woman is miserable, and even walking is painful.

Dyspareunia (painful intercourse) may occur.

Men are often symptomless carriers of the organism.   **Men**

Sometimes there is a urethral discharge akin to that of gonorrhea. Discomfort on urination is common.

Sometimes erections are painful and intercourse impossible.

Complications in women include urethritis, cystitis, bartholinitis (inflamma-   **Complications**
tin of Bartholin's gland), and infection of Skene's ducts.

Complications in men include prostatitis, cystitis, epididymitis, and urethral stricture.

Treatment of trichomoniasis with oral doses of metronidazole is effective.   **Treatment**
Sexual partners must be treated simultaneously to prevent passing the disease back and forth indefinitely.

Moniliasis (Monila)

A yeast-like organism known as *Candida albicans* is part of the normal vaginal flora. Occasionally its growth increases to cause a condition known as moniliasis. Such increases are often secondary to diabetes, pregnancy, long-term antibiotic therapy, and oral contraceptive use.

Candida albicans thrives on menstrual blood and often becomes troublesome just before and after menstruation.

The infection produces inflammation of the vaginal wall and causes white patches, resembling thrush, of the vagina and cervix.

The patient complains of severe itching and creamy-white discharges containing lumps.

In rare cases, the organism enters the bloodstream. *Candida albicans* may be detected in a small percentage of males having nongonococcal urethritis. The extent to which fungi are causative in this condition is unclear.

Mycostatin vaginal tablets or creams are used for treatment.

Pediculosis Pubis

Phthirus pubis is the scientific name for a crab louse that infests the hairs of the anogenital region and feeds on the blood of the host.

The ova of this organism attach to the skin at the base of pubic hairs and hatch within seven to nine days.

Phthirus pubis causes an itching type of dermatosis. Other symptoms may include redness of the skin, blood in the urine, and frequent urination in small amounts.

Cure is usually rapid with application of parasiticides in powder or lotion or gamma benzene hexachloride or shampoo or lotion and laundering of clothing and bed linens.

Protection Against STDs

Use of condoms is probably the best protection against STDs available to the sexually active person. One of the best demonstrations of this fact was a French Study[9] in which the sexual partners of over 700 women known to be infected with gonorrhea or trichomoniasis were investigated. This investigation revealed that less than 1 percent of 302 men who claimed to have used a condom contracted gonorrhea, and only 2 percent contracted trichomoniasis. Among those who did not use a condom, 97 percent contracted gonorrhea and 33 percent, trichomoniasis. A study of 2,017 American women in a family planning clinic showed that those who used a diaphragm or whose partners used condoms had cervical gonorrhea about 20 percent as often as pill and IUD users.[10] A study of sexually active United States college students revealed that 43 percent of men who did not use condoms were infected with an organism thought to cause nongonoccal urethritis, compared with a 14 percent infection rate among those who reported regular use of condoms.[11]

The question has been raised whether an agent as small as a herpes virus may be able to pass through a condom. This does not appear to be likely: a condom is watertight and airtight, and water and air molecules are thought to be about 1,000 times smaller than a herpes virus (Fig. 69). Moreover, studies in which herpes viruses were placed in a condom revealed that they did not pass through the pores of the condom membrane. This was also true when the condom was placed under stress that simulated coital movement.[12,13]

Some theorists have suggested that if 25 percent of individuals at risk used even a 50 percent effective prophylactic, the incidence of gonorrhea would drop by 80 percent in the first year and be almost eliminated in four years. A major problem, however, is a core of about 20 percent who refuse to use condoms. This group contributes disproportionately to the spread of gonorrhea.

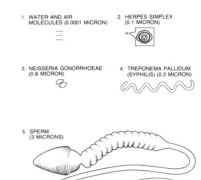

Figure 69 Comparison of the size of some agents restrained by a condom (diameter size reported in microns, a unit equal to one thousandth of a millimeter).

[9]A. Siboulet, "Maladies Sexuelles transmissibles: intérêt des traitements prophylactiques," *Prophylaxie Sanitaire et Morale,* 44 (Nov.–Dec. 1972), pp. 155–159.

[10]L. Keith, G. S. Berer, and W. Moss, "Cervical Gonorrhea in Women Using Different Methods of Contraception," *Journal of the American Venereal Disease Association* 3 (Sept. 1976), pp. 17–19.

[11]W. M. McCormack, Y. H. Lee, and S. H. Zinner, "Sexual Experience and Urethral Colonization with Genital Mycoplasma: A Study of Normal Men," *Annals of Internal Medicine,* 78 (May 1973), pp. 696–698.

[12]L. Smith, et al., "Efficacy of Condoms as Barriers to HSU-2 and Gonorrhea: An In Vitro Model [Abstract]," Presented at the First STDs World Congress, San Juan, Puerto Rico, November 15–21, 1981.

[13]L. Corey, "Genital Herpes: An Overview and Update." *Helper* 4 (Mar. 1982), pp. 1–2.

Philosophical, Psychological, and Social Aspects of Human Sexuality

CHAPTER 9

Intelligent Choice of a Sexual Life-Style

Carefully consider the types of behavior listed in Table 9, and then decide which types are acceptable or unacceptable according to your personal set of values.

Now think about your responses and try to identify the criteria that you used in making your decisions.

A Moral Principle

Our own observation is that the most widespread contemporary principle individuals use for deciding issues of right and wrong is that an individual should be free to act, provided his or her actions adversely affect no one else. This is not a new moral principle for the governance of human conduct, and those who subscribe to it find an old friend in the writings of John Stuart Mill, who described the principle clearly and succinctly in his essay *On Liberty:*

> . . . the sole end for which mankind are warranted, individually or collectively, in interfering with the liberty of action of any of their number is self-protection. That the only purpose for which power can be rightfully exercised over any member of a civilized community, against his will, is to prevent harm to others. His own good, either physical or moral, is not a sufficient warrant. He cannot rightfully be compelled to do or forbear because it will be better for him to do so, because it will make him happier, because, in the opinion of others, to do so would be wise or even right. These are good reasons for remonstrating with him, or reasoning with him, or persuading him, or entreating him, but not for compelling him or visiting him with any evil in case he do otherwise. To justify that, the conduct from which it is desired to deter him must be calculated to produce evil to someone else. The only part of the conduct of anyone for which he is amenable to society is that which concerns others. In the part which merely concerns himself, his independence is, of right, absolute. Over himself, over his own body and mind, the individual is sovereign.

Although Mill's principle is widely accepted today, like any principle, it provides no guidelines for interpretation in the context of specific behavior. In matters of sexual behavior, which actions adversely affect others? In case of disagreement, who shall make the binding decision, the individual or society?

TABLE 9: **Values and Human Sexuality**

Type of Behavior	Value Choice	
	Right	*Wrong*
Premarital sex	____	____
Abortion	____	____
Homosexuality	____	____
Masturbation	____	____
Oral-genital sex	____	____
Sodomy	____	____
Rape	____	____
Extramarital sex	____	____

Today's world is permeated by value conflicts over sexual behavior. For example, many states have returned the right to engage in homosexual behavior to the individual, but some states, in the words of Mill, "visit evil" on the homosexual. Likewise, the states do not agree in their laws regarding premarital sex, oral-genital sex, and sodomy. And although the United States Supreme Court has ruled that a state does not have the right to interfere with the decision of a woman and her physician to effect an abortion during the first trimester of pregnancy, most states have not changed their laws prohibiting abortion. Application of Mill's principle is no less difficult today than when he first asserted it in 1859.

Choosing a Sexual Life-Style

Within a relatively short time span, ethical positions in the United States have changed from a prescribed morality to acceptance of Mill's principle that what you do is your own business as long as it doesn't adversely affect others.

A Time of Rapid Change

Nevertheless, accepted sexual life-styles have been vigorously and persistently assailed. Cultural expectations for women's sexual experience have changed from "nonorgasmic response" to "multi-orgasmic response" and back to "non-goal-oriented sexual behavior," all within one decade. Trends away from "premarital chastity" toward "sex with affection," "communal sex," "wife-swapping," and then back to "sex with love" have been observed.

Currently, it appears that with the exception of rape most of the legal sanctions against different modes of sexual behavior are headed for repeal. Hence, the intelligent selection of one's own sexual life-style constitutes a major contemporary concern.

Future Trends

With a view toward self-actualized sexual behavior, we have discussed the following questions with thousands of people of all ages during the last decade:

Self-Actualized Sexual Behavior

How does one intelligently decide among such alternatives as:

- permissiveness vs. committedness?

- masturbation vs. restraint in auto-eroticism?

- premarital chastity vs. premarital sex?

- heterosexuality vs. homosexuality?

- oral sex vs. forbearance of oral sex?

- marriage vs. singleness?

- children v. childlessness?

- marital fidelity vs. extramarital sex?

Discussion and research into these varieties of behavior have led us to the conclusion that no single alternative or set of alternatives holds a monopoly on happiness. Hence, alternatives must be decided on an individual basis: there are no absolutes.

But the fact that societal prescriptions have been lifted and alternatives are now primarily a matter of choice does not mean that sexual happiness is more easily obtained. In fact, coping with sexual freedom is a more difficult task for most people than being told what to do. In this regard, Ayn Rand asserts:[1]

> Neither life nor happiness can be achieved by the pursuit of irrational whims. Just as a man is free to attempt to survive by any random means, as a parasite, a moocher or a looter, but not free to succeed at it beyond the range of the moment—so he is free to seek happiness in any irrational fraud, any whim, any delusion, any mindless escape from reality, but not free to succeed at it beyond the range of the moment nor to escape the consequences.

Self-actualizing people select their sexual life-styles on the basis of careful thinking, not by the pursuit of irrational whims or the persuasions of others.

Rational Selection of a Sexual Life-Style

Intelligent decision making presupposes a basis for deciding—a criterion or set of criteria. At present, the most popular criterion appears to be: if it makes you happy, then it's right, as long as it doesn't hurt anyone else. In general this appears to be an excellent criterion, with one exception: it is a retrospective ethic that legitimizes any type of behavior with the excuse, "I thought it would make me happy, and I didn't have any idea it would hurt anyone."

A Modified Criterion

Because of this important exception, we recommend the following modified criterion: a selected life-style component should be tested when, and only when, the probability of hurting one's self or others is small (that is, one has the duty to consider the effects on one's self and on others). This criterion presupposes that an individual does not have the right to be destructive of self or others. It also implies a moral obligation to carefully study the possibility that an action may be destructive.

Sexual Life-Style as a Noncontradictory Joy

The ultimate goal is to promote sexual behavior to the level of a noncontradictory joy. In her book, *Atlas Shrugged,* Ayn Rand noted:

> Happiness is a state of noncontradictory joy—a joy without penalty of guilt, a joy that does not clash with any of your values and does not work for your own destruction.

Accordingly, the major question behind the selection of a sexual life-style becomes: What are the conditions necessary to render one's sexual life style a noncontradictory joy?

---

[1]Ayn Rand, *The Virtues of Selfishness* (New York: New American Library, 1961).

In our opinion, the most enlightened answer to this question appears to be:

One's sexual life-style has the highest probability of contributing to a state of noncontradictory joy when it occurs within the framework of an interpersonal relationship that is permeated by love, accompanied by open communication, and guided by a knowledge of human sexuality.

Previous chapters have dicussed love (Chapter 1) and biological knowledge of sexuality (Chapters 2 through 8); before proceeding, let's discuss open communication.

There appears to be a categorical imperative in the realm of human sexual behavior: thou shalt not discuss your likes and dislikes with others. This attitude appears to be widespread among people of all socioeconomic backgrounds, educational levels, religious affiliations, and liberal or conservative positions. And it is this same attitude that is at the root of many cases of sexual inadequacy.

Open Communication

At least two beliefs block open communication about sexuality:

1. Sexual behavior is intended primarily for procreation and only secondarily for pleasure; open discussion of the pleasure aspects perverts one's total approach to sexuality.

2. Sexual behavior should be a natural joy. If it is not, there is something wrong—with one's biological or psychological self or perhaps with one's partner. In either case it is too sensitive to discuss because it reflects inherent weaknesses or insincere interpersonal relationships.

But love demands that these sensitive communication blocks be removed. Love demands open discussion regarding penalties of guilt, clashes of values, and general likes and dislikes. Love demands that each partner work to promote sexual behavior to the level of a noncontradictory joy.

Approaches to the Permissiveness-Committedness Continuum

Although teachers and parents have taken countless approaches to the permissiveness-committedness continuum, most approaches can be assigned to one of these four categories:

1. The "mute" approach in which no attempt is made to address the problem.

2. The "comfortable pew" approach in which adult society refuses to buck what it views as a widespread trend toward sexual freedom, choosing instead to limit its advice to methods of preventing pregnancy and veneral diseases.

3. The "indoctrination" approach in which the "goodness" of some specific code of behavior is expounded and reinforced.

4. The "interpersonal relationship" approach suggested by Kirkendall[2] and other contemporary writers, which recommends a sexual ethic based on mutually satisfying interpersonal relationships.

---

[2]Lester Kirkendall, *Premarital Intercourse and Interpersonal Relationships* (New York: Julian Press, 1961).

Findings themselves unable to select and adhere to a code of sexual behavior, many parents and teachers elect not to discuss the question at all with younger persons. If this approach were made explicit, it could be stated this way: "We as adults refuse to give you the results of our experiences with sexual behavior or our interpretations of the accumulated experiences of the generations before us. You must decide your code of sexual behavior on the basis of trial and error or any bits of information that you can find." Stated this way, most will agree, this is not a reasonable or effective approach.

The Mute Approach

Pierre Berton in his critical analysis of the Anglican Church of Canada contends that the church in its attempts to remain popular has refused to speak out on issues of great importance and in so doing has turned its back on its first principles. He says it this way in his book, *The Comfortable Pew:*

The Comfortable Pew Approach

> In the great issues of our time, the voice of the Church, when it has been heard at all, has been weak, tardy, equivocal, and irrelevant. In those basic conflicts that ought to be tormenting every Christian conscience—questions of war and peace, of racial brotherhood, of justice versus revenge, to name three—the Church has trailed far behind the atheists, the agnostics, the free thinkers, the journalists, the scientists, the social workers, and even, on occasion, the politicians. It has, for instance, virtually ignored the whole contemporary question of business morals, the tensions within industry and labour, the sexual revolution that has changed the attitudes of the Western world.

The comfortable pew approach as applied to sex education is one in which popular trends go unopposed. The attitude is one of: "Well, I guess it is all right if that's what everyone wants."

If adult society could agree on a specific code of sexual conduct, and if young people were bits of clay that could be shaped, reinforced, and maintained in whatever way society had decided, then sexual ethics would be a matter of little concern. But even a superficial examination of adult sexual codes, in theory or practice, yields little agreement as to a single code of conduct. Attempts to shape or indoctrinate others to fit an arbitrary mold not only are doomed to failure in an enlightened society but are themselves immoral. Abraham H. Maslow,[3] writing on the topic, states:

The Indoctrination Approach

> I believe this is the model of education which we all have tucked away in the back of our heads and which we don't often make explicit. In this model the teacher is the active one who teaches a passive person who gets shaped and taught and who is given something which he then accumulates and which he may then lose or retain, depending upon the efficiency of the initial indoctrination process and of his own accumulation-of-fact process. I would maintain that a good 90% of "learning theory" deals with learnings that have nothing to do with the intrinsic self that I've been talking about, nothing to do with its specieshood and biological idiosyncrasy. This kind of learning too easily reflects the goals of the teacher and ignores the values and ends of the learner himself. It is also fair, therefore, to call such learning amoral.

Lester Kirkendall and Roger Libby[4] state: "A sexual relationship is an interpersonal relationship, and as such is subject to the same principles of interaction as are other relationships." This concept is so basic that its full mean-

The Interpersonal Relationship Approach

---

[3]Abraham H. Maslow, "Some Educational Implications of the Humanistic Psychologies," *Harvard Educational Review* (Fall 1968).

[4]Lester A. Kirkendall and Roger W. Libby, "Interpersonal Relationships—Crux of the Sexual Renaissance," *The Journal of Social Issues* (Apr. 1966).

ing is frequently missed. Clearly translated, it means that sexual behavior must be evaluated in terms of its effects upon human relationships. Thus one can ask about a certain type of sexual behavior—does it improve or degrade the relationship (that is, does it help or hurt yourself and the other person)? When viewed in this context, there is a criterion whereby sexual behavior can be evaluated. One can say more than "Oh, that's definitely wrong" or "That kind of behavior is all right." Rather, one can state, "That type of behavior degrades or improves human relationships." This latter approach facilitates communication, since it replaces such essentially meaningless terms as "right" and "wrong" with more exacting terms that explain why certain behavior is considered right or wrong.

As an example, nearly everyone would agree that rape represents a kind of sexual behavior that makes it difficult for people to get along well together— it renders interpersonal relationships unpleasant, undignified, stressful, unhealthy, and unsafe. On the other hand, most people would agree that the ideal kind of interpersonal relationships are those that are mutually advantageous. Such relationships produce a climate in which each person can flourish, a climate that is far superior to what either can achieve alone.

A Fifth Approach

We suggest a fifth approach to the problem of locating one's sexual life-style on the permissiveness-committedness continuum. We suggest a modification of Mill's moral principle that an individual should be free to act, provided his actions adversely affect no one else. A selected life-style component should be tested when and only when the probability of hurting one's self or others is very small. This modification assumes that an individual does not have the right to be destructive of self or others and that before acting an individual has a moral obligation to study carefully the probability of the destructiveness of the action. Finally, based on study of the sexual encounter among heterosexuals, we recommend five criteria designed to promote sexual behavior to the level of a noncontradictory joy (that is, joy that is nondestructive).

Commitment: Conditions Accompanying Sexual Behavior

The remainder of this chapter is a discussion of permissiveness versus committedness in heterosexual relationships. The discussion includes criteria for sexual relationships, marriage, nonmarriage contracts, and the Playboy philosophy. Other alternatives in sexual life-style (for example, homosexuality, masturbation, number of children) are discussed in subsequent chapters.

In attempting to render participation in the sex act a noncontradictory joy, how does one decide between the alternatives of permissiveness and committedness? Which has the higher probability of producing noncontradictory joy?

Our opinion is that one's sexual life-style has the highest probability of contributing to a state of noncontradictory joy when it occurs within the framework of an interpersonal relationship permeated by love. Note the probability sense of this opinion. We do not contend that permissiveness is wrong or that it ought to be punished; we contend that committedness has a greater capacity for achieving a state of noncontradictory joy than does permissiveness.

Even when there is general agreement about the need for committedness, the more troubling question appears to be: How much commitment should accompany the different types of sexual behavior?

For example, contemporary youth have vigorously and persistently claimed that a marriage certificate does not render sexuality a noncontradictory joy.

And many would go a step further and suggest that marriage doesn't even increase the probability of promoting sex to the level of a noncontradictory joy. A high divorce rate, widespread sexual inadequacy among the married, extramarital sex, and poor mental health among many married partners add validity to this claim.

But clearly some degree of commitment should be reached before participating in the sex act. If not marriage, then what?

In some countries, it is possible to negotiate a two- or three-day contract in which the two parties agree upon how to deal with any troublesome consequences of their sexual behavior. Whatever else the contracts might represent, they at least include an element of responsible behavior. Such contracts clearly attempt to render sex more of a noncontradictory joy.

But in our opinion, these contracts omit some important factors. Therefore, we suggest that agreement to the following conditions be obtained before participation in heterosexual intercourse. We believe these conditions will promote heterosexuality to the level of a noncontradictory joy.

Condition 1

Both partners in sexual intercourse must be certain that they are not infected with a venereal disease. The best way to achieve this certainty is through regular medical examinations, including blood tests.

In view of the facts that venereal diseases are widespread and some are incurable, it is in the best interest of both parties involved and any offspring that might result to have precautionary tests for venereal diseases.

Anyone refusing to have such a test shows little concern for others. The degree of risk that one is willing to take with a second person is directly proportional to a lack of concern about that person. Open agreement to tests for venereal diseases represents a test of the maturity of the interpersonal relationship that exists between the two persons involved.

Condition 2

Prior to participating in sexual intercourse, both partners should agree upon the desirability or undesirability of having children. If children are not wanted, a mutually acceptable and effective form of contraception should be planned.

Condition 3

Prior to participating in sexual intercourse, both partners must recognize their responsibility to love and care for any offspring that may result or carefully evaluate the effect of an abortion.

An unloved, unwanted child begins life without the human dignity that should be everyone's birthright. That person is, in a sense, degraded from birth. To disregard this responsibility violates an elementary principle of human conduct: one must accept the consequences of one's actions as they affect both one's self and others.

Consider the three statements that follow. Which represents the most desirable interpersonal relationship?

1. The pill is 100 percent effective so we are not concerned about pregnancy.

2. The pill involves a slight chance of pregnancy if not properly taken so we agree to love any offspring that occurs or to be supportive of each other before and after abortion.

3. We are not ready or desirous of having children, but if pregnancy occurs we are prepared mentally and financially to love and take care of any offspring or to undergo abortion.

You should know that unwanted pregnancies are not infrequent even among persons who are well informed about contraception. One large Midwestern university health service estimates a rate of 40 unwanted pregnancies per week among unmarried college girls. Moreover, half of all pregnancies in the United States today are reported to be unintended.

Agreement to condition 3 is not at all unreasonable. As with the first condition, open agreement to love any offspring or to be supportive before and after abortion is a test of the maturity of the interpersonal relationship that exists between the two persons involved.

Condition 4

Prior to participating in sexual intercourse the two people involved should have some notion of their direction and goals in life and be able to answer the question: How does participation in sexual intercourse fit into the goals that I have set for myself and the goals of my partner?

Put another way, sexual intercourse is an activity for mature persons—for persons who are mature emotionally and psychologically, as well as physically.

A sexual relationship may be novel but it is not the way to find one's self. The results of a study of unwed mothers by the Community Council of Greater New York will help to explain this concept.

The majority of unwed mothers in this study:

1. Did not belong to clubs or other groups.

2. Did not enjoy visiting with other people.

3. Did not like sports and games.

4. Were attempting to find themselves through intimate sexual experience.

Condition 5

One person must not exploit another. To counter exploitation it must be agreed that sexual intercourse is for the mutual improvement of both people involved.

Here are some motivations for sexual intercourse that tend to exploit the other person:

1. For self-gratification.

2. A way of gaining independence from parents.

3. A way of getting back at someone.

4. A way of trapping a husband.

5. A way of holding on to a boy or girl friend.

6. A way to become "popular."

7. A way to demonstrate manhood.

8. A way of relieving personal anxiety.

The notion that today's young person is more promiscuous than previous generations is a myth. For example, today's youth are far less likely to visit a prostitute than the youth of previous generations. And they do not tolerate exploitation when they are able to discern it.

In a five-year survey of over 500 students per year, we found that contemporary youth consistently preferred or approved of sexual intercourse with a person one loves or for whom one has deep affection.

Changes in attitude in either a more or a less permissive direction were usually a consequence of "how they were treated in the interpersonal relationship." As a consequence of being hurt, college women tended to become either more puritanical or more permissive. Men tended to respond to opportunity or to love.

These findings suggest that the major problem in achieving noncontradictory joy in heterosexual behavior is not the ethic one subscribes to but the factors that cause one to deviate from that ethic.

Humans have a highly developed capacity for sincere self-deception, and in highly emotional situations they often agree to things to which they ordinarily would not agree; that is, they compromise themselves.

Furthermore, the history of sexual relationships abounds with cases in which human beings have insincerely agreed to any or all proposals in order to gain the opportunity they wanted. Opportunity and insincerity have constituted and probably always will constitute major problems in sexual encounters.

Forms of Sexual Life-Style

Unfortunately, there is no satisfactory way to be sure that individuals will follow through on what they say they will do—that is, that they are sincere in their statements. Marriage offers some advantages but no guarantee.

In our experience, most young people agree that these five conditions are reasonable. Many, however, do not feel that their private agreement to these conditions necessitates marriage.

Marriage

Marriage appears to offer the following four advantages to those interested in sexuality as a joy without penalty of guilt.

> 1.   Public agreement to a life-time commitment constitutes marriage. It prevents a considerable amount of misunderstanding socially and legally and insulates the couple from many social threats to their relationship.

> 2.   Marriage offers a major psychological advantage for both persons. It helps to prevent the feeling: "I am just on trial." It also provides the self-confidence that accompanies the feeling: "I am accepted and loved as a total person—not just as a sexual partner."

Nena and George O'Neill make an interesting observation on this point in their book *Open Marriage:*

> Theoretically, marriage should not be necessary to have a full one-to-one relationship. You should not even need marriage to legitimize a child, for that matter. In a world of true human understanding, a child should be legitimate just because he is born. All the requirements for succoring the young— maternal care, assuring interdependency and cooperation with others, as well as psychological intimacy—can theoretically be met without legal marriage. The love and companionship existing between a couple does not need a piece of paper, a marriage document, to make it work, to assure its existence or its perpetuation. Or does it?

> Commitment to another cannot be legislated. True commitment comes from within, not from outside a relationship. The signing of a contract cannot guarantee you another's commitment in the emotional sense; why should the absence of such a contract mean a lack of commitment? It shouldn't, of

course. But unfortunately, it often does, often enough to make even those who are sure of their partner's commitment think twice. We would not need the marriage contract in actuality if all of us had reached a stage of human development that assured mutual responsibility and trust between all people. Unfortunately, this utopian brotherhood is far short of achievement. In our all too real world, the ultimate step in the establishment of trust between man and woman is still the marriage contract. With this final step each says to the other: here's my deck of cards, the full deck, all of them open on the table, nothing held back.

3.   Marriage offers the security needed to openly communicate one's problems, hang-ups, likes, and dislikes. This includes sexual inadequacies.

In recent years, increasing assertiveness by women appears to have brought to light some problems experienced by men.

4.   Marriage affords a stable framework within which one can more easily cope with value clashes related to contraception, pregnancy, and abortion.

The main argument for a trial marriage goes like this:

The Trial Marriage

To get to know someone, you must live with him or her. You have to see how the other person reacts to the minor upsets and major crises of daily living.

This argument implies that if you don't like the trial marriage partner when you "really" get to know the other person, you can at that point terminate the relationship and avoid further unhappiness.

And at first glance, trial marriages appear to have some value. But when we dissect away the "outer coat," one frequently exposes other motivations for trial marriages, especially as they are propounded in the United States.

The major motivation for trial marriages stems from the popular misconception that most divorces result from sexual incompatibility rather than from poor interpersonal relationships in general. Therefore, most American trial marriages are prompted by the desire for a sexual tryout under conditions that are "more relaxed or more respectable than just premarital sex." Is there value in this motive?

From a biological standpoint, the vagina is adjustable to any size of penis, and the size of the penis has little effect on the woman's satisfaction. Thus one doesn't have to be concerned about "anatomical misfits." Rather, the two best indicators of sexual adequacy in the future are:

1.   Feelings toward the partner.

2.   Attitude toward sexuality.

The one best predictor is one's feelings toward the partner, but even when two people love each other very much, attitudes toward sex can be poor.

Such attitudes may reflect early training and value development and have little to do with feelings for the husband, wife, or partner. But even the most irrational attitudes are learned, and with patience, understanding, and love, there is a good chance that they can be unlearned.

The best criteria by which one can predict future sexual satisfaction are the same criteria that forecast good interpersonal relationships.

Although the Playboy philosophy is generally recognized for the exploitative philosophy that it really turns out to be, it does deserve discussion.

The Playboy Life-Style

Harvey Cox, in his book *The Secular City,* makes these thought-provoking statements about the Playboy philosophy and *Playboy* magazine:

1.   Playboy and its less successful imitators are not "sex magazines" at all. They are basically antisexual.

They dilute and dissipate authentic sexuality by reducing it to an accessory, by keeping it at a safe distance.

2.   . . . Sex becomes one of the items of leisure activity that the knowledgeable consumer of leisure handles with his characteristic skill and detachment. . . .

The girl becomes a desirable—indeed an indispensable—"Playboy accessory."

3.   . . . The infallible answer from the oracle never varies: sex must be contained, at all cost, within the entertainment-recreation area. Don't let her get "serious."

4.   . . . For the insecure young man with newly acquired free time and money who still feels uncertain about his consumer skills, Playboy supplies a comprehensive and authoritative guidebook to the forbidding new world to which he now has access. . . .

It tells him not only who to be; it tells him how to be it, and even provides consolation outlets for those who secretly feel they have not quite made it.

5.   . . . Playboy really feeds on the existence of a repressed fear of involvement with women, which for various reasons is still present in many otherwise adult Americans.

So Playboy's version of sexuality grows increasingly irrelevant as authentic sexual maturity is achieved.

The exploitative philosophy of *Playboy* has contributed to bringing sex out into the open in the United States.

Dr. William Masters, coauthor of *Human Sexual Response,* says this of his interview with *Playboy:*

We hope that something like this interview—appearing in the magazine I regard as the best available medium of sex education in America today—will help do it [it referring to the need for healthy objectivity about sexuality].

But Virginia Johnson, the other coauthor of *Human Sexual Response,* says in the same interview:

What I'm about to say may not go over well with some Playboy readers, but the fact is that for the first time in many decades, the girl is running the sexual show.

She is not a victim; she doesn't have to put up or shut up. Although this issue is still in limbo, we're on the right road toward placing value on sexual activity within a human relationship as opposed to simple emphasis on natural drives. . . .

CHAPTER 10

Masturbation

In view of the extremely widespread occurrence of autogenital stimulation throughout the class Mammalia it seems illogical to classify human masturbation as abnormal or perverted.

This form of sexual expression appears to have its evolutionary roots in the perfectly normal and adaptive biological tendency to examine, to manipulate, to clean, and incidentally to stimulate the external sexual organs.

The human capacity for symbolic behavior has permitted marked increase in the sexual significance of masturbation by linking it with fantasy and imagination.

But the basic potentialities are a part of the biological inheritance of the species.

We believe that the relative infrequency of self stimulation among mature people in most societies is a consequence of social conditioning.

Clellan S. Ford and Frank A. Beach
Patterns of Sexual Behavior

For purposes of this chapter, masturbation will be defined as the deliberate manipulation of some part of the reproductive system in anticipation of an erotic reward.

What Is Masturbation?

Different individuals masturbate in a variety of ways, and one individual may utilize several methods. Some of the more common methods will be described.

Methods of Masturbation

Probably the most frequent method of female masturbation is manipulation of the clitoral area. Masters and Johnson report that very few women masturbate by applying direct pressure to the sensitive glans of the clitoris. Rather, they manipulate the shaft of the clitoris or the mons area surrounding it. Manipulation of the mons area appears to be just as effective after the clitoris is removed (clitoridectomy).

Female Masturbation

Another method of female masturbation involves thigh rubbing. Squeezing the thighs applies pressure to the labia and indirectly to the clitoris.

Other methods include:

1. Fingering or inserting something in the vagina.

2. Inserting something in the urethra.

3. Pulling clothing between the legs.

4. Stimulating the breasts.

5. Fingering the rectum.

The male usually masturbates by manipulation of the penis with the hand.   **Male Methods**

Other methods involve coital movements against a variety of objects.

Fingering of the rectum is a seldom used method.

Dual masturbation is masturbation in the presence of another person who is   **Dual Masturbation**
also masturbating. This type is most frequently observed among young boys.

Mutual masturbation refers to two individuals who practice manual mastur-   **Mutual Masturbation**
bation on each other.

Studies of the incidence of masturbation are not in complete agreement, but   **Incidence of Masturbation**
the following conclusions seem justified:

1. Almost all males masturbate at some time in their life.

2. The percentage of women who have masturbated ranges between 40
and 70.

Whereas frequent masturbation may modify one's self-concept, it appears to   **Excessive Masturbation**
have no long-term biological effect. For example, Dr. Jan Raboch of the Sex-
ological Institute of Charles University in Prague writes:[1]

> One of the most interesting patients that I have ever had was a 27-year-old
> Jew who came to our clinic shortly after World War II. He had spent a
> number of years in Nazi concentration camps. He stated that, in 1943 and
> 1944, the Nazis had grouped in a camp in Poland about twenty young and
> healthy men and fed them comparatively well.
>
> During twenty-one months they were forced, under inspection, to masturbate
> regularly every three hours, night and day. . . .

Despite this ordeal, Dr. Raboch reported:

> We were unable, however, in spite of a most careful examination, to discover
> in him signs of any disturbance of the function of his genital organs. His
> fertility was found normal. When he married later, his potency was good.

The Sex Information and Education Council of the United States has defined   **Philosophical Positions**
four philosophical positions on masturbation:

> A. The traditional view, which regards masturbation as always gravely
> sinful and as harmful to health—with some modification of its severity
> and rigidity in light of new scientific knowledge;
>
> B. The view of many religionists, which sees masturbation often as an
> imperfect egocentric eroticism that deflects the individual from the Chris-
> tian concept of sexuality as being ideally an essential relation with
> another;
>
> C. An attitude of neutrality, which accepts masturbation, recognizes
> that further study of its various patterns is required, but is not prepared
> to encourage it as something positively good;

[1] Jan Raboch, "Men's Most Common Sex Problems," *Sexology* (Nov. 1969), pp. 60–63.

D. And a more radical position, which views masturbation as not only harmless, but positively good and healthy, and therefore encourages it among young people as an aid to more mature psychosexual growth.

In many respects, development of a personal philosophy toward masturbation seems unimportant. Since it is a harmless act, what difference does it make?

Developing Your Own Philosophical Position

One student has likened it to "picking your nose"—as long as you do it in private it really doesn't make any difference. But many people experience considerable guilt about masturbation, and philosophical clarification is important.

A careful study of the four positions described above may assist you with personal value clarification. In addition to the conduct of your own sexual life style, it is especially important that you consider how you might deal with the masturbatory habits and attitudes of your children.

In preparation for the guidance of children, it might be useful to study the opinions of several medical experts. After reviewing their work, try to formulate your own philosophy toward masturbation.

Masturbation Among Children

Dr. Harrison S. Evans, a California psychiatrist, states:[2]

Masturbation in children is accepted by medical and psychiatric authorities as an essentially normal phenomenon, and it constitutes a phase in most children's development when they are exploring and becoming acquainted with their body.

A Normal Phenomenon

Masturbation is not believed to be a source of damage to the child, either physically or mentally. It does not have a weakening effect on the body or mind. It does not draw out any of the child's vital energy, as old wives' tales would tend to suggest.

Not a Source of Damage

There are two basic things for you to understand as you come to deal with your child's masturbatory activity.

What It Means to the Child

First, as a parent, you should try to clarify what this activity means to the child. If the child is socially healthy, interested in his playmates and in his surroundings, and engages in masturbation as part of his curiosity and passing pleasure, then masturbation will probably subside as further maturation and social development take place.

Is He Socially Healthy?

You can be quite sure that other things will come to absorb the child's attention and provide pleasurable outlets, and as a consequence there will be fewer occasions when the child will need to turn to autoeroticism (masturbation for pleasure and satisfaction).

Masturbation as a phase of experience can actually have a beneficial effect on the child's emotional development because it helps to establish the genitals securely within the body scheme so that at a later appropriate time they can become readily activated and used in a normal heterosexual manner as a part of a normal marriage.

A Beneficial Effect

However, not all masturbatory activity is normal and healthy. If your child is shy, sensitive, and withdrawn, and if it appears that he has become too dependent on masturbation as a source of satisfaction and relief of tension, then in this instance masturbation might be considered a pathological reaction.

Not Always Healthy

---

[2]Harrison S. Evans, "What Do You Tell Parents Who Are Concerned About Their Children's Masturbation?" *Medical Aspects of Human Sexuality*. 1 (Nov. 1967), p. 3.

In a situation such as this masturbation is probably not a phase in normal development, but rather a symptom of psychological disturbances that need attention by a specialist, usually a child psychiatrist.

The second thing of importance for you to understand is that as a parent you should clarify your own feelings about masturbation and your child's interest in sex and in his genitals.

Your Own Feelings

In many instances it is the parents' feelings that constitutes the real problem rather than the child's transitory sexual curiosity and exploration.

Some parents, for various reasons, may see masturbation as something that is shameful, dirty, wicked, and an early sign of depravity rather than what it actually is, namely, a developmental phase.

Not Dirty and Wicked

If parents have these feelings, then they may very well overreact to the child's essentially normal behavior.

The parent may inappropriately threaten or punish the child, thus arousing guilts and repressions which later on in life may impair the child's adjustment.

It is my opinion that for you as a parent the appropriate reaction is to accept this behavior as essentially normal, handle it casually, guide and lead the child to interests outside of himself, provide a happy relationship of affection and security, and give answers that are simple and to the point when sexual questions arise in connection with masturbation and the dawning awareness of sexuality in general.

How to React

If there is evidence that masturbation is excessive or compulsive, and if the child has a poor social and psychological adjustment, do not threaten or punish but seek out help to understand the child's basic problem and work toward correcting this rather than focusing primarily on the masturbation itself, which in this instance is a symptom of underlying personality difficulty whose solution will also solve the masturbation problem.

Dr. Saul Harrison, professor of psychiatry at the University of Michigan, writes:[3]

Some children invest most of their attention and energy in compulsive masturbation. This may cause justifiable parental concern, not because of the myth about masturbation sapping one's reserve of energy, but because compulsive masturbation is a symptom of an emotional problem which also renders the child afraid or unable to engage in other age-appropriate activities. Such excessive masturbation serves as a means of consolation or as a substitute for relationships with other people.

Dr. Herbert A. Holden, president of the California Academy of General Practice, states.[4]

Masturbation occurs most frequently when the child is unhappy and bored. In older children, similar organization of the life pattern to fill the day with activity and interest is important.

Dr. Harry Bakwin, professor of clinical pediatrics at New York University School of Medicine, suggests:[5]

---

[3]Saul Harrison, "Viewpoints," *Medical Aspects of Human Sexuality,* 1 (1967), p. 21.
[4]Herbert A. Holden, "Viewpoints," *Medical Aspects of Human Sexuality,* 1 (1967), p. 13.
[5]Harry Bakwin, "Viewpoints," *Medical Aspects of Human Sexuality,* 1 (1967), pp. 16–17.

. . . A child who is unhappy or bored is more likely to resort to masturbation than one whose life is satisfying. However, the parents should not be made to feel that they are responsible for the child's practice. The intensity of the erotic urge varies widely, and masturbation is often practiced to excess even under the best of home surroundings.

Discussion with the adolescent consists first of all of a clarification of the nature of the habit. False ideas about the dire effects of masturbation are corrected. The universality of the practice is pointed out. In this way feelings of guilt, unworthiness, isolation, and shame are relieved.

This is not to say that the habit is to be condoned, much less encouraged. Its uselessness and misdirection of energy are pointed out. . . .

The home and school situation is reviewed and sources of unhappiness probed. It is helpful to be aware of the common reasons for concern in the adolescent—unpopularity, failure to live up to scholastic aspirations, failure in athletics, concern about the home situation, physical illness, short stature in the boy, tallness in the girl, and so on.

In addition to the foregoing discussion, the opinions of several medical experts regarding the general topic of masturbation are presented.

Dr. Lawrence Kolb[6] comments about parental attitude:

Masturbation, commonly practiced by children, requires treatment only if the parental or adult attitudes toward the act have instilled in the child anxieties and fears that affect his personality development adversely. More frequently the problems of masturbation in a child involve clarifying misconceptions of ill-effects of the procedure in the minds of the parents and preventing radical efforts to prevent the act.

The other varieties of body manipulation . . . are relatively of little importance.

Nelson's *Textbook of Pediatrics*[7] describes methods of masturbation, notes that although it is a normal activity it is inadvisable to encourage masturbation, and suggests that the most helpful treatment is to remedy the environmental situation:

Masturbation may be performed by manipulation of the genitals, by movement of the thighs or contraction of the perineal musculature, by copulatory movements sometimes with an object such as a pillow between the legs; or an equivalent sensation may be derived from tight clothing or activities such as horseback riding, straddling rails and climbing trees. In the younger child who is not aware of the cultural taboo against masturbation, the parents may observe the activity or the associated signs of intense concentration and excitement. Most children sense parental disapproval, however, and the activity is carrried out in privacy. Rarely, the child may masturbate openly, an act which suggests poor awareness of social reality by the child or lack of censorship by the parents. Some well-meaning parents who know that masturbation is a normal activity may inadvisedly encourage it.

Within certain limits masturbation is normal. In the young child it represents a self-gratification analogous to thumb-sucking. In the older child,

---

[6]Lawrence C. Kolb, *Noyes' Clinical Psychiatry,* 7th ed. (Philadelphia: W. B. Saunders Co., 1968).

[7]Calvin F. Settlage, in *Textbook of Pediatrics,* ed. Waldo E. Nelson, 8th ed. (Philadelphia: W. B. Saunders Co., 1969).

particularly the adolescent, it serves the purpose of exploring and experimenting with newly developing sexual capacities and feelings and may aid in gaining control over the sexual urges and becoming less afraid of them.

Masturbation occurs most commonly at bedtime when anxiety is increased owing to separation or fear of loss of control over sexual and aggressive impulses. For the same reasons the child is most likely to masturbate when he is alone and lonely. This fact leads to the logical, but usually mistaken, assumption that the urge to masturbate is the motive for rather than the consequence of being alone. Masturbation may also be performed, sometimes repetitiously and compulsively, as a reassurance against fear of injury to the private parts. Excessive masturbation suggests some problem or deficiency in object relationships. In some instances it is a symptom of a neurotic or more severe disorder.

It is appropriate for the parent to censor open masturbation and to be concerned about excessive masturbation, but to forbid it absolutely, to shame the child, to threaten punishment or to suggest injury to the genitals not only is ineffective, but also tends to create guilt and additional anxiety which may even increase the activity. The most helpful treatment is to remedy any environmental situation which is interfering with gratification of the child's needs or is causing tension and anxiety. It is important that the child be reassured that masturbation does not cause physical or mental deterioration. The adolescent should be given an explanation of ejaculation, orgasm and menstruation, so that he or she can understand them as normal body functions.

Ian Gregory[8] traces the evolution of attitudes toward masturbation:

Masturbation is sexual pleasure obtained by manipulation of the genitals or other erogenous parts of the body. Individual masturbation is widely practiced by the higher animals and by all races of mankind, particularly by immature males who have not yet established an adult heterosexual relationship, and by adults of both sexes who have been deprived of a normal heterosexual outlet. The use of artificial genitalia resembling those of the opposite sex has been reported in literature since the time of Aristophanes . . . and mutual masturbation may be practiced by males or females with members of the same or opposite sex. During the middle ages, the Church condemned all forms of sexual indulgence other than genital intercourse between husband and wife with the express purpose of having children. Masturbation became regarded as evil and perverse, and was frequently referred to as 'self-abuse.' Even in the present century it was thought by many physicians and other educated people to lead to insanity or other tragic consequences, and masturbation in girls sometimes led to surgical removal of the clitoris. More recently it has become regarded as a normal part of sexual activity and the accumulative experience reported in the Kinsey studies amounted to 93 per cent in males (decreasing from adolescence onwards) and 62 percent in females (increasing to middle age). It is therefore regarded as abnormal only if practiced in public, or at the exclusion by choice of heterosexual genital union, as frequently occurs following certain of the deviant acts. . . .

---

[8]Ian Gregory, *Fundamentals of Psychiatry,* 2nd ed. (Philadelphia: W. B. Saunders Co., 1968).

CHAPTER 11

Homosexuality

On December 15, 1973, I was instantly cured of mental illness together with millions of my gay brothers and sisters.

> Gay statement to the press occasioned by the American Psychiatric Association's decision to remove homosexuality from its list of mental disorders.

Homosexual behavior refers to sexual relations, either overt or psychic, between individuals of the same sex. The word homosexual is derived from the Greek root *homo,* which means sameness. Homosexual behavior among females is often termed "lesbianism" after the female homosexual relations that were immortalized in the poetry of Sappho of the Greek isle of Lesbos. Despite use of this special term for the female homosexual it should be noted that such behavior is equivalent to sexual relations between males. Other synonyms for homosexuality include homogenic love, contrasexuality, homoeroticism, similisexualism, uranism, and sapphism (lesbianism).

History tells us that homosexual behavior is not of recent origin. For example, Dr. Frank S. Caprio[1] in his book *Variations in Sexual Behavior,* states:

> Sodomy (usually refers to anal intercourse) is derived from the name of the town, Sodom, where the inhabitants, during Biblical times, incurred the wrath of God by wishing to consort sexually with the angels who had descended from Heaven. The town was therefore destroyed.

> Pederasty (anal intercourse often with young boys) . . . was widely practiced in ancient times in Asia, the Orient and more specifically, in Greece. . . . It is interesting to note also that pederasty in Rome was known as "Greek love."

Dr. Panos Bardis[2] reports in a study of "Sex Life in Ancient Greece":

> . . . many of Greece's gods and heroes were often described as homosexuals: Poseidon, the god of the sea; Apollo, the god of the sun; Heracles (Hercules), the greatest hero in Greek mythology; Ganymede, the cup-bearer of Zeus; and numerous others.

> Among Greece's mortals, some of the most famous men were also homosexuals. Solon, the great Athenian lawgiver and elegiac poet, one of the Seven Sages of ancient times, was homosexual.

---

[1]Frank S. Caprio, *Variations in Sexual Behavior* (New York: Grove Press, Inc., 1955), p. 85.

[2]Panos Bardis, "Sex Life in Ancient Greece," *Sexology* (Oct. 1965), pp. 156–159.

The intrepid conqueror, Alexander, when he marched against Asia, was accompanied by his young male lover, Hephaestion. Later, during a magnificent and spectacular festival at Ecbatana, Hepaestion fell ill and, after 7 days, died.

Alexander was so heartbroken and inconsolable that he fasted for 3 days; crucified Hephaestion's physicians; ordered the entire empire to go into mourning; had chapels erected to his beloved friend in many cities; and, in May 323 B.C., buried him in Babylon. The funeral, with a 200-foot-high pyre and other extravagances, was one of the most ostentatious, theatrical, and sumptuous ceremonies of all times.

Regarding other famous persons who were homosexual, Dr. Caprio[3] states:

According to Moll, Octavius was supposed to have had sexual intercourse with Caesar, Tiberius was notorious for his cruelty and subjected boys to immoral sexual practices . . . Nero was another who indulged in sexual activity with young boys. . . .

Michaelangelo, Shakespeare, Oscar Wilde, Byron, Walt Whitman, Tchaikowsky and numerous other famous men are said to have had homosexual tendencies. Wilde, in fact, was tried, sentenced and found guilty of homosexuality.

Other literary figures said to be homosexual include Noel Coward, Somerset Maugham, Marcel Proust, André Gide, and Jean Cocteau.

Homosexuality has a long history, and many of the current problems that relate to homosexual behavior are not really new. With this in view, the material that follows in this chapter describes homosexuality, discusses its causes, and attempts to present some of the human problems that accompany it.

Varieties of Sexual Behavior

Human sexual behavior may be divided into four major categories: autosexual, heterosexual, katasexual, and homosexual.

In autosexual behavior, the individual focuses upon himself. Masturbation is the usual form of autosexual behavior. A variety of techniques and inanimate objects may be utilized in masturbatory behavior.

Autosexual Behavior

In heterosexual behavior, the individual prefers a sexual partner of the opposite sex.

Heterosexual Behavior

Heterosexual behavior includes:

1. Sexual intercourse, in which the male penis is inserted in the female vagina.

2. Mutual masturbation, in which one or both partners masturbate the other.

3. Anal intercourse, in which the male penis is inserted in the anal canal of the female.

4. Cunnilingus, in which oral stimulation of the female genitals is provided.

---

[3]Caprio, op. cit.

5. Fellatio, in which the penis is inserted into the mouth of the female partner.

6. Soixante-neuf (French for 69) in which fellatio and cunnilingus are performed at the same time.

It should be noted that none of these six kinds of sexual behavior is considered homosexual when it takes place between partners of opposite sexes.

A third type of sexual behavior is katasexual behavior, in which the individual selects a nonhuman partner. Bestiality is another name given to human-animal relationships.

Katasexual Behavior (Bestiality)

A fourth type of sexual behavior, the subject of this chapter, is homosexual behavior. In homosexual behavior the individual has sexual relations with or emotional attachments to a partner of the same sex.

Homosexual Behavior

Overt homosexual behavior includes:

1. Mutual masturbation by two individuals of the same sex.

2. Sodomy—refers to any illegal sex act but most often is used to describe anal intercourse between two males. Pederasty is another term for anal intercourse, usually between an adult and minors.

3. Cunnilingus—oral stimulation of the female genitals by another female.

4. Fellatio—oral stimulation of the penis by another male.

5. Mutual cunnilingus (two females).

6. Mutual fellatio (two males).

In attempting to differentiate between heterosexuality and homosexuality, it is important to know that it is not one's behavior but rather one's attitude that is most important. Heterosexuality is an affectional preference for a person of the opposite sex; homosexuality is an affectional preference for someone of the same sex. Thus sexual behavior alone cannot stand as a criteria by which to determine heterosexuality and homosexuality. For example, a heterosexual may under certain conditions engage in homosexual behavior; a homosexual may under certain conditions engage in heterosexual behavior; or both heterosexuals and homosexuals may remain entirely celibate.

Heterosexuals and Homosexuals

This distinction is a critical one: a number of homosexuals have lost their jobs simply because they made their affectional preference public, while remaining entirely celibate.

What is it like to realize that you are homosexual? In their book *Lesbian Woman*,[4] Del Martin and Phyllis Lyon answer:

Realizing Homosexuality

It doesn't just happen to you. It isn't as if you wake up suddenly one morning and say to yourself, "I am a Lesbian." Or that you make a conscious decision—"that is what I'm going to be from now on"—as if it were an acceptable goal in life.

Though many Lesbians believe they were born that way, we tend to feel that persons are born sexual: not heterosexual or homosexual, just sexual. And the

---

[4]Del Martin and Phyllis Lyon, *Lesbian Woman* (San Francisco: Glide Publications, 1972), p. 26.

direction a girl's sexuality may take depends upon her individual circumstances and life experiences, and how she reacts to them. It's rather like a slowly emerging awareness of herself as someone who is different, who is responding in ways that are apparently not usual to others, and yet seem very natural to her.

Sometimes this awareness begins very early in life. While a child of five doesn't know anything about the sex act and couldn't care less, she can experience a strange attraction to other little girls, or perhaps just one girl singled out of the group. She may play with boys and feel a certain camaraderie and affection for them, but the emotional attachment she feels for girls may be entirely different.

Realization of male homosexuality appears to be somewhat similar.

Currently, the etiology of homosexuality is unknown. Although a number of theories have been advanced, the evidence presently available fails to substantiate any of them.

Etiology of Homosexuality

Homosexuality is not simply a matter of:

1. What one's mother or one's father did or did not do.

2. Genetic or hormonal factors.

3. Early seduction by other homosexuals.

4. Arrested psychosexual development.

5. Mental illness.

Like heterosexuality, the etiology remains unclear.

This does not mean that the cause or causes will not be discovered in the future. One large-scale[5] study of identical twins revealed that the twin pairs were all of the same sexual orientation. Nonetheless, the evidence currently available is not sufficient to indicate a biological cause of homosexuality. Chromosome and endocrine studies have revealed no significant differences between homosexuals and heterosexuals. The psychological literature related to causes of homosexuality is also very ambiguous.

Although the cause or causes of homosexuality are unknown, most homosexuals are very sensitive about questions relating to the etiology of their sexual orientation. This probably stems from the fact that most heterosexuals asked the question in a sense that means—"What went wrong to make you different from the rest of us?"

A Sensitive Question

In a discussion of homosexuality in a sex education class, a visiting homosexual speaker was asked, "What caused you to be a homosexual?"

Addressing himself to the men in the class, he answered with a series of revealing questions:

· Did you ever search the depths of your soul attempting to discover what makes you like women?
· Did you ever wonder what your mother did or your father didn't do to make you a heterosexual?

---

[5]F. J. Kallmann, "A Comparative Twin Study of the Genetic Aspects of Male Homosexuality," *Journal of Nervous and Mental Diseases*, 115 (1952), pp. 283–298.

* Have you ever considered consulting a psychiatrist with a view toward correcting your problem of liking women?
* Thinking back carefully, were you ever molested by a female when you were a child?
* Could it be that your problem relates to the fact that most of your elementary school teachers were women?
* Does your like for women stem from a hate for men?
* Did some series of events arrest your psychosexual growth?
* Is there a history of mental illness in your family?

Most of you have never thought about the cause of your heterosexuality, and you probably aren't very concerned about it now.

Similarly, I do not know the cause of my homosexuality, and I am concerned about it only because the homosexual life style has been historically, and is currently, attended by a pervasive type of negativism that we (homosexuals) are trying to change.

But we don't want to be "changed to heterosexuals" anymore than you want to be "changed to homosexuals."

These comments do not tell us very much about the cause or causes of homosexuality, but they do provide an important perspective. Researchers should investigate the etiology of heterosexuality and homosexuality with equal vigor and objectivity.

An Important Perspective

This is an important perspective because heretofore most of the work in this area has focused on theories to explain "what went wrong to make homosexuals different from heterosexuals."

Perhaps its would have been wiser to start with the question: What causes heterosexuality?

At any rate, the etiology of both homosexuality and heterosexuality remains obscure, or as George Weinberg aptly states it:[6]

The fact is that the combination of physiological readiness and social experience resulting in the development of any erotic preference—homosexual or heterosexual—is so intricate that science has not been able to fathom it as yet. No group of experts in any field can predict who will be homosexual. . . .

Although very little is known about the cause or causes of homosexuality, four rather well-defined attitudes toward homosexuality have developed. Each of these attitudes deserves careful consideration, and although we appear to live in a time of freedom of thought and discussion, it might be suitable to preface these opinions with a thought from John Stuart Mill:

Attitudes Toward Homosexuality

. . . Were an opinion a personal possession of no value except to the owner, if to be obstructed in the enjoyment of it were simply a private injury, it would make some difference whether the injury was inflicted only on a few persons or on many. But the peculiar evil of silencing the expression of an opinion is that it is robbing the human race, posterity as well as the existing generation—those who dissent from the opinion, still more than those who hold it. If the opinion is right, they are deprived of the opportunity of exchanging error for truth; if wrong, they lose, what is almost as great a

[6]George Weinberg, *Society and the Healthy Homosexual* (New York: St. Martin's Press, 1972).

benefit, the clearer perception and livelier impression of truth produced by its collision with error.

The four attitudes are:

1. The homosexual is a "dirty pervert" who belongs in jail. That this is a common opinion of heterosexuals is evidenced by the fact that homosexual acts are often against the law.

"Dirty Perverts"

2. Homosexuals should be tolerated if they don't touch or try to indoctrinate minors.

On the other hand, people of this persuasion will not allow homosexuals to teach in their schools or to hold high-level government positions.

Heterosexual Tolerance

3. Homosexuality is an illness that requires treatment.

An Illness

Although most professional groups have reversed their positions on the issue, the view that homosexuality is an illness continues to be widespread. This view persists, in part, because of statements in the psychological literature of the 1960's. For example, Dr. Warren Walker[7] writes:

> Most psychiatrists consider this condition definitely pathological, and believe that we are all biologically programmed to be heterosexual.
>
> It is also believed by most psychiatrists that this condition is neither hereditary nor congenital nor constitutional, rather that early life experiences and relationships may in some way present barriers to the realization of the native biological programming.

Also in support of this view, Dr. Daniel Cappon[8] writes:

> There is no evidence whatsoever of a hereditary, constitutional, hormonal, somatic or organic basis for homosexuality.
>
> It is an exclusively psychogenic condition.
>
> Moreover, it is never basic or primary but the end result of a number of overdetermined, layered psychopathologic factors.

Dr. George Kriegman,[9] clinical professor of psychiatry at the Medical College of Virginia, writes:

> . . . let me make one thing clear: homosexuality as an enduring sexual pattern is an illness, no different than other illness, and is a symptom of deep-seated emotional difficulty.
>
> Despite propaganda to the contrary, there is no such thing as a well-adjusted, happy homosexual.
>
> Homosexuality is a psychoneurotic disorder.

Dr. Frank S. Caprio,[10] a world-known psychiatrist, states in his book, *Variations in Sexual Behavior:*

---

[7]Warren H. Walker, "Homosexuality—Current Concepts and Attitudes," *Rocky Mountain Medical Journal,* 66 (1969), pp. 42–43.

[8]Daniel Cappon, "Understanding Homosexuality," *Postgraduate Medicine,* 42, (1967), pp. A131–136.

[9]George Kriegman, "Homosexuality and the Educator," *The Journal of School Health,* (May 1969), pp. 305–311.

[10]Caprio, op. cit.

Female homosexuality at best is a form of cooperative or mutual masturbation—a symptomatic expression of a neurotic personality; a disturbance in the infantile psychosexual development; a regression to narcissism. . . .

Because of their socially disapproved modus vivendi, female inverts suffer from a pervading sense of loneliness and as a consequence are unhappy.

I personally am convinced that lesbians would not be healthy persons even if they lived in a society where sexuality with one's own sex was socially acceptable. There is seldom any permanence to a lesbian alliance. Lesbians become dissatisfied, jealous and change partners frequently.

In the foreword to his book, *Homosexuality,* Dr. Edmond Bergler[11] writes:

1.   The homosexual of either sex believes that his only trouble stems from the 'unreasonable attitude' of the environment.

2.   If he were left to his own devices, he claims, and no longer needed to fear the law or to dread social ostracism, extortion, exposure (all leading to constant secrecy and concealment), he could be just as "happy" as his opposite number, the heterosexual.

3.   This, of course, is a self-consoling illusion. Homosexuality is not the 'way of life' these sick people gratuitously assume it to be, but a neurotic distortion of the total personality.

4.   It is granted that heterosexuality per se does not guarantee emotional health; there are innumerable neurotics among heterosexuals, too.

5.   But there also exist healthy heterosexuals, and there are no healthy homosexuals.

6.   The entire personality structure of the homosexual is pervaded by the unconscious wish to suffer; this wish is gratified by self-created trouble-making. This "injustice-collecting" (technically called psychic masochism) is conveniently deposited in the external difficulties confronting the homosexual.

7.   If they [fears] were to be removed—and in some circles in large cities they have been virtually removed—the homosexual would still be an emotionally sick person.

A fourth attitude holds that:

A Different Sexual Orientation

1.   Homosexuals are healthy and as capable of happiness as heterosexuals.

2.   Homosexual relationships have as much power as antidotes for human loneliness as do heterosexual ones.

3.   It is arrogant to view persons as perverted or ill simply because their sexual orientation is different from your own.

4.   One should be sensitive and loving toward homosexuals, treating any sexual advances as compliments rather than as causes for rejection.

5.   Interpersonal relationships should not be influenced by a knowledge of another person's sexual orientation; that is, homosexuals and heterosexuals should be viewed and treated as human beings rather than as products of different sexual orientations.

---

[11]Edmond Bergler, *Homosexuality* (New York: P. F. Collier, Inc., 1962).

In support of this view, Dr. Franklin E. Kameny writes:[12]

Gay Is Good

. . . to those of my fellow homosexuals who may read this, I say that it is time to open the closet door and let in the fresh air and the sunshine; it is time to doff and to discard the secrecy, the disguise, and the camouflage; it is time to hold up your heads and to look the world squarely in the eye as the homosexuals that you are, confident of your equality, confident in the knowledge that as objects of prejudice and victims of discrimination you are right and they are wrong, and confident of the rightness of what you are and of the goodness of what you do; it is time to live your homosexuality fully, joyously, openly, and proudly, assured that morally, socially, physically, psychologically, emotionally, and in every other way: Gay is good. It is.

Based on their sociological studies, Drs. William Simon and John Gagnon state:[13]

Life-Style Management

. . . most homosexuals manage fairly well when we consider the stigmatized and, in fact, criminal nature of their sexual interest. In a group of homosexuals with extensive histories of homosexuality, we found about 80 per cent reported no trouble with the police, and an additional 10 per cent had had minor contacts but were not arrested. Only 20 per cent reported problems of managing relations with their parental families, and about 10 per cent or less reported difficulties in school work. Of those who had had military experience, only one fifth reported difficulties.

Commenting on the American Psychiatric Association's decision to remove homosexuality from their list of mental disorders, Dr. Robert L. Spitzer stated:[14]

We decided a medical disorder either has to be associated with subjective distress, pain or general impairment in social functioning. Homosexuality is not regularly associated with either.

In his book *The Lord Is My Shepherd and He Knows I'm Gay,* Reverend Troy Perry, founder and pastor of the first church for homosexuals, describes his aspirations:[15]

Religion

. . . I dream of that time when all people who are gay, all who are hiding it, will step forth freely into the light of truth, total acceptance and understanding. I fervently dream and pray for that time when there is an end to hiding, an end to fear, an end to being victimized. I dream that we can all come out of hiding, that we can all stand tall and walk with our heads held high, because we are gay and we are proud. We will throw our arms around each other's shoulders without any shame. We will laugh together, weep together, share together, and march together. There will be an end to fear! We will stand together! We will unite! We will all know that we are God's own creatures, that he loves us, that He created us, that He blesses us, that He's proud of us, that He cares for us!

---

[12]Franklin E. Kameny, "Gay Is Good," *The Same Sex* (Philadelphia: Pilgrim Press, 1969), p. 145.

[13]William Simon and John Gagnon, "Homosexuality: The Formulation of a Sociological Perspective," *The Same Sex* (Philadelphia: Pilgrim Press, 1969), p. 17.

[14]*Washington Post* (Dec. 16, 1973).

[15]Troy Perry, *The Lord Is My Shepherd and He Knows I'm Gay* (Los Angeles: Nash Publishing, 1972), pp. 227–228.

George Weinberg[16] has coined the term homophobia to describe an "unreasonable fear of homosexuals," and Kenneth Smith[17] has developed a "homophobic scale."

To determine your homophobic rating, answer the following nine questions yes or no.

1. Homosexuals should be locked up to protect society.

2. It would be upsetting for me to find out I was alone with a homosexual.

3. Homosexuals should be allowed to hold government positions.

4. I would not want to be a member of an organization that had any homosexuals in its membership.

5. I find the thought of homosexual acts disgusting.

6. If laws against homosexuality were eliminated, the proportion of homosexuals in the population would remain about the same.

7. A homosexual could be a good President of the United States.

8. I would be afraid for a child of mine to have a teacher who was homosexual.

9. If a homosexual sat next to me on a bus I would get nervous.

"No" to 3, 6, and 7 and yes to the others is indicative of homophobia.

How does one differentiate knowledge from speculation as they relate to homosexuality? In the absence of quality research, how does one filter the list of opinions to arrive at a personal view of homosexuality?

A struggle with these questions appears to bring only more questions:

Can homosexuality contribute to a state of noncontradictory joy? If not, why not?

How are these two questions influenced by the social arrogance of heterosexuals?

Can the sexual orientation of the homosexual be changed? Should it be changed?

These are confusing questions without clear answers.

On the other hand, good questions are the first step toward enlightened answers, and if this chapter does nothing more than render clear the major questions regarding homosexuality, it will have served a major purpose.

Putting the homosexual in jail is not an enlightened approach to matters of individual difference. Hence, several attempts at legal reform have been initiated in this and other countries.

The Wolfenden Report[18] in England is now a classic example of successful

---

[16]George Weinberg, *Society and the Healthy Homosexual* (New York: St. Martin's Press, 1972).

[17]Kenneth Smith, "Homophobic Scale," cited by George Weinberg, *Society and the Healthy Homosexual* (New York: St. Martin's Press, 1972).

[18]*Report of the Committee on Homosexual Offences and Prostitution* (London: H. M. Stationery Office (Cmmd. 247), 1957).

reform. In 1954, the House of Lords appointed a committee to study the problem of homosexual offenses and prostitution. Under the leadership of Sir John Wolfenden, the committee submitted its report in 1957.

Legal reform came almost exactly ten years after publication of that report. The conclusions of this committee and the thinking that led to these conclusions were reviewed for the American Psychiatric Association by Sir John Wolfenden[19] in 1968.

In part, he stated:

> We came to the view that the function of the criminal law in this area of behavior is to safeguard public order and decency and to protect those who for whatever reason are properly regarded as the weak and therefore deserving society's protection.

> We conclude that in this area the private behavior of an adult individual, male or female, is no concern of the criminal law. I stress "an adult individual" because we were as deeply concerned as any other collection of 15 citizens to protect children, the mentally weak, and the officially subordinate.

> But I suggest that if this guideline is followed a coherent and logical pattern emerges. Let me be more explicit.

> It is no concern of the criminal law if two adult consenting males indulge in homosexual behavior in private.

> It may be a form of behavior of which you and I disapprove; we may be disgusted by it; we may, on all sorts of moral grounds, find it repugnant.

> But none of those subjective reactions of ours have anything to do with criminality. Every day I come across forms of behavior to which all these descriptions apply; but that fact does not entitle me to demand that those who behave in this way should be sent to prison.

> I disapprove of adultery; and so do a good many other people. We do so because we think this sort of behavior is immoral, or wrong, or "not right."

> But I do not demand that adulterers and adulteresses should be subject to the criminal law.

> If men and women, or men and men, or women and women, indulge in sexual acts in public, I not only disapprove, I think the law ought to do something about it.

> And I think this because I think the law's business is to protect me and my wife and children from affronts against decency.

> I do not think this because I think such behavior immoral. I do not think the law has a right to enter, as it were, anybody's bedroom.

> Sexual behavior is nobody's business except that of those immediately concerned, unless their behavior offends against public order and decency.

> This is the basis in logic for the two halves of our recommendations, that homosexual behavior between consenting males in private should be no concern of the criminal law and that solicitation by prostitutes in public places should render them liable to prosecution.

In the United States, the American Law Institute in its *Model Code* came to the same conclusion as the Wolfenden Committee.

---

[19]Sir John Wolfenden, "Evolution of British Attitudes Toward Homosexuality," *American Journal of Psychiatry*, 125 (1968), pp. 792–797.

Regarding this conclusion, Dr. Ralph Slovenko,[20] professor of law at the University of Kansas, writes:

> The Wolfenden Committee in England and the American Law Institute in its *Model Code* have recommended that sexual relations of a homosexual nature between consenting adults should no longer be subject to law, provided they take place in private.
>
> The reasons given are the lack of harm to the secular community, the unenforceability of the penal law, the unsuitability of imprisonment for offenders, the undue interference in personal affairs, the strain placed by the law on limited police resources, and the opportunities created for blackmail.

Dr. Don Harper Mills,[21] associate clinical professor of forensic medicine and pathology at the University of Southern California, appears to speak for an increasing number of people when he states:

> Though discreet, consensual homosexuality is not a threat to public safety and decency, I do not pass on the issue of its effect on morality.
>
> However, I question the propriety of using the vehicle of criminal law to enforce any particular pattern of moral behavior, so long as it does not directly affect fundamental societal interests.
>
> Finally, is it not reasonable to conclude that restricting one's freedom of choice in areas of private morality by means of criminal law is itself morally improper?
>
> If homosexual behavior per se is morally wrong, its deterrence should be the responsibility of religious, social, and medical health bodies, not of the state.

---

[20]Ralph Slovenko, "Homosexuality and the Law," *Medical Aspects of Human Sexuality,* 1 (1967), pp. 35–38.

[21]Don H. Mills, "Viewpoints," *Medical Aspects of Human Sexuality,* 1 (1967), pp. 51–52.

CHAPTER 12

Intimacy, Marriage, and Parenthood

Intimate relationships generally fall within a continuum that ranges from "destructive" through "satisfactory" to "high quality" (Fig. 70).

Figure 70

Most people want high-quality intimate relationships. They desire high quality intimate relationships with their marriage partners and their children. High quality intimate relationships require a great deal of work and self-knowledge. They require the development of certain skills while dating to prepare for an intimate high-quality marriage. They require the development of certain skills to prepare for high quality intimate parenthood. Not all relationships attain this desired status. On the other hand, satisfactory relationships are so much better than aloneness that many people are content to achieve this status. In fact, some people even find destructive relationships better than aloneness. Thus, there is a full continuum of intimate relationships. The discussion in this chapter focuses on promoting destructive and satisfactory relationships to the level of high quality.

Human Intimacy

What is an intimate relationship? Intimate is defined as (1) belonging to one's deepest nature, (2) offering informal warmth or privacy, or (3) having a very private or personal nature. Hence an intimate relationship is one in which you share your personal and private nature with another individual.

This sharing may be in many directions, but we will focus on four types of intimate relationships: philosophical intimacy, psychological intimacy, creative intimacy, and physical intimacy. In turn, a relationship that involves all four types of intimacy shall be defined by us as total intimacy.

Although total intimacy appears to be an ideal relationship for marriage partners, parents, and their children, few actually achieve it. More realistically, it represents a goal toward which one might work. But total intimacy is so powerful and so significant that it is very important to understand its nature. An important first step is the understanding of each of the four individual components of total intimacy.

Philosophical Intimacy

Philosophical intimacy is a sharing of your philosophy of life and your life principle(s). It is the sharing of "what's important in your world." To achieve philosophical intimacy, you must have clarified your philosophy of life. When a person has a philosophy of life, (s)he has a life principle.

A life principle is a generalized, accepted intention of purpose that is applied to specific choices and circumstances. This life principle runs through the fabric of our choices like the dominant theme in a piece of music: it keeps recurring and is heard in different settings. Having a life principle is a matter of psychological economy. It diminishes the wear and tear of having to make all decisions from the ground up.[1]

A philosophy of life and a life principle identify your framework for living. They tell others what is important to you. They tell others how you make decisions. They tell others your reasons for living. They clarify how your religious values affect your choices and behavior. Philosophical intimacy helps others know who you are and the values that you hold.

Psychological intimacy is the sharing of your needs, drives, weaknesses, strengths, intentions, emotional feelings, and deepest problems. Having psychological intimacy with another individual usually occurs gradually. A healthy person usually does not share his or her deepest thoughts and feelings with a stranger. The sharing evolves after a level of trust is developed. The greater the level of trust, the greater the likelihood of psychological intimacy.

Psychological Intimacy

Another factor also affects the ability to achieve psychological intimacy. You are more likely to have psychological intimacy when you are able to communicate feelings. The most effective way to communicate feelings is to use "I-messages."

I-messages are statements about the self, revelations of inner feelings and needs, information not processed by others. An I-message has three parts:[2]

1. The first component involves the identification of a specific behavior.

2. The second component pins down the tangible or concrete effect of the specific behavior described in the message's first part.

3. The third states the feelings generated by the effect.

Clearly stated, an I-message contains a behavior, an effect, and a feeling. An I-message enables partners to communicate openly. An I-message is quite different than a "you-message." A you-message is a shaming and blaming message that blocks psychological intimacy.

I- versus You-Messages in Psychological Intimacy

• I-Message—When you didn't call (behavior), I wondered why (effect) and I worried (feeling).
• You-Message—You were thoughtless and selfish to forget to call.

An I-message keeps communication open and allows a partner the opportunity to respond without feeling threatened. A you-message puts another person on the defensive. It blocks the sharing needed for psychological intimacy.

In summary, psychological intimacy is more likely to be achieved when partners (1) trust one another and (2) communicate openly. When you have psychological intimacy, you feel accepted. This component of intimacy enables you to "be yourself."

---

[1] John Powell, *Unconditional Love* (Niles, Iowa: Argus Communications (1969).
[2] Thomas Gordon, *Parent Effectiveness Training* (New York: New American Library, 1970).

Creative Intimacy

Creative intimacy is sharing in the work or development of a project, task, or creation of something new. It may be associated with a single co-creative act (e.g., building a house, having and rearing a child, writing a book, producing a play, or completing any single project). On the other hand, creative intimacy may be a way of life for those involved.

Creative intimacy is different from philosophical and psychological intimacy in that the medium of sharing goes beyond discussion and emotional response. In creative intimacy, you reveal yourself "while working." Your talents or lack of talents become apparent without discussion as you make contributions to the collective effort.

For example, partners may select a project to complete as a team. They may redecorate their home, painting and wallpapering. Each of their skills is utilized to complete the project. Nonverbally they affirm one another during their efforts.

Of course, the opposite may also occur in a relationship. While engaged in creative efforts, partners may nonverbally or verbally disapprove of one another. This destroys the willingness to participate in creative intimacy, injures self-concept, and interferes with the relationship.

Creative intimacy is needed for a relationship to grow. To achieve creative intimacy, there must be "quantity" and "quality" time. There must be a time set aside to engage in creative efforts with a partner. This time must be quality time—time in which both partners and the relationship are affirmed.

Physical Intimacy

Physical intimacy is the sharing of physical expressions and affection. Physical intimacy includes a range of behaviors that express warmth and closeness. Marriage partners show physical expression when touching, caressing, holding hands, and kissing. Foreplay and sexual intercourse are more intimate forms of physical expression.

Nonmarried partners or dating partners must make decisions about behaviors and expressions of physical intimacy. These decisions must be consistent with philosophical values. Most persons agree that junior and senior high school students are not ready to include sexual intercourse in their expression of physical intimacy. It is important to note that the warmth and closeness of the relationship is a better gauge of physical intimacy than is the act of sexual intercourse.

Total Intimacy

As stated previously, total intimacy encompasses philosophical, psychological, creative, and physical intimacy. Total intimacy is difficult to achieve, yet it affords the greatest chance for a high-quality relationship. An important question is, "How can education for sexuality promote destructive and satisfactory relationships to the level of intimate high quality?"

Dating: Assessing the Four Components of Total Intimacy

Dating is the sharing of social activities and time spent with a person of the opposite sex. Dating affords the opportunity to examine the four components of intimacy within the framework of a relationship. Dating provides a chance to gain self-knowledge and knowledge of a potential partner.

The Burt-Meeks Total Intimacy Checklist can be used to assess your level of intimacy in a relationship. It can be used to assess the level of intimacy of your partner. Most important, it can be used to initiate a discussion about your relationship and its quality.

A Relationship Projection

Your levels of intimacy with a partner are a key factor in predicting the success of marriage to that partner. There are other factors that also contribute to the likelihood of success in marriage.

Meeks and Heit in their book *Human Sexuality: Making Responsible Decisions* discuss the seriousness of a marriage:[3]

> Before you form a long-term committed partnership, you need to gather certain information. For example, when forming a business partnership most men and women carefully gather information regarding (1) goals, (2) definition of roles, (3) assets, (4) liabilities, (5) budget, (6) investments, (7) expansion, (8) competition, and (9) growth. These nine projections make it easier for you to decide whether or not the partnership will be a success. To build a successful marriage, you would be wise to gather information based on these nine components—a relationship projection.

A relationship projection would include the following information:

1. A statement of the *goals* of each partner and of the marriage.

2. A statement of the *role* each partner will play in the married relationship.

3. A statement describing the *assets* that each partner contributes to the relationship.

4. A statement describing the *liabilities* or weaknesses of each partner and of the relationship and a plan to deal with each.

5. A carefully planned *budget* or schedule adjusting expenses during a certain period to the estimated or fixed income for that period.

6. A statement describing *investments* to be made.

7. A plan for *expansion*, enlarging the size of the family, or maintaining a partnership of two with no children.

8. A statement describing the agreement of partners about *competition* and a pledge for fidelity that is mutually agreed upon.

9. A commitment to *growth* that describes new directions for the relationship.

Burt-Meeks

Total Intimacy Checklist

DIRECTIONS: Complete the checklist first for yourself. Answer yes or no to each question. Then substitute "my partner" for "I." Ask your dating partner to complete the checklist for himself/herself and then for you. Discuss the checklist.

   I. PHILOSOPHICAL INTIMACY: The sharing of your philosophy of life and your life principle with your partner.
   ____ 1. I have a clearly stated philosophy of life and am able to express it.
   ____ 2. I know what I value.
   ____ 3. My behavior is consistent with my philosophy of life and that which I value.

   II. PSYCHOLOGICAL INTIMACY: The sharing of your needs, drives, weaknesses, strengths, intentions, emotional feelings, and deepest problems with your partner.

---

[3]Linda Meeks and Phil Heit, *Human Sexuality: Making Responsible Decisions* (Philadelphia: Saunders College Publishing, 1982).

_____ 4. I am able to identify and express my needs, drives, weaknesses, strengths, intentions, emotional feelings, and deepest problems.

_____ 5. I demonstrate effective communication skills, I-messages, and listening.

_____ 6. I trust myself and others.

III. CREATIVE INTIMACY: The sharing in the work or development of a project, task, or creation of something new with your partner.

_____ 7. I have identified a variety of projects and tasks upon which to work with a partner.

_____ 8. I plan a time to participate in these projects and tasks.

_____ 9. I am able to affirm another and to be affirmed while working on mutual projects.

IV. PHYSICAL INTIMACY: The sharing of physical expression and affection with a partner. This does *not* imply that potential partners should have sexual intercourse to measure their level of physical intimacy. Expressions of warmth and closeness are a more accurate gauge.

_____ 10. I am able to express affection.

_____ 11. I am able to receive affection from a partner.

_____ 12. My expression of physical intimacy is consistent with my values.

DIRECTIONS: After completing the checklist, discuss your relationship and its quality with your partner. Then examine questions 13 through 15 of the checklist.

V. TOTAL INTIMACY: A relationship that includes philosophical, psychological, creative, and physical intimacy.

_____ 13. My partner and I have identified the strengths and weaknesses in our relationship.

_____ 14. My partner and I have a plan to achieve greater levels of intimacy in our relationship.

_____ 15. The relationship has the potential to include all four components of intimacy.

The Marriage Contract

Partners have a greater likelihood of succeeding at marriage when they are willing and able to discuss intimacy and to make a relationship projection. The marriage contract has more meaning. Rather than an "I do" at a public ceremony, the "I do" becomes a personal pledge that affirms a desire to achieve and maintain intimacy and to continually grow in the relationship.

Growth in a Marriage

Renewed growth is an important component in the framework of an intimate high-quality relationship. Partners are continually changing; thus, marital relationships continually change. For example, each of the following changes in one of the components of intimacy might affect the level of total intimacy in the relationship:

· A partner becomes more active in the church and wants the other partner to share this interest to achieve a higher level of philosophical intimacy.

· A partner fails to reach an important occupational goal and needs extra support to maintain psychological intimacy.

· A partner becomes involved in a new sport and wants the other partner to share this interest for renewed creative intimacy.

· A partner's sexual drive increases and there is a need for more physical intimacy.

Marriage partners need to be sensitive to these changes to maintain each of the four components of total intimacy. When a marriage appears to be in trouble, partners might examine each of these four components to assess what might be causing the breakdown in the relationship: Why is the relationship satisfactory rather than high-quality? How might the relationship be destructive? Answers to these questions may provide some ways in which the partners can renew and revitalize the relationship.

Divorce and Dissolution

Sometimes marriage partners cannot renew and revitalize levels of intimacy in the relationship. The relationship becomes destructive, and the partners want to terminate the marriage contract. Divorce and dissolution are two legal ways to terminate marriage. In a divorce, the court determines the conditions for the termination of the marriage contract, including the division of property and custody and visitation arrangements for children. In a dissolution, partners mutually agree to stated terms, there is a waiting period, and the court approves the terms. Laws regarding divorce and dissolution vary from state to state.

The Parent-Child Relationship

Thus far our discussion has focused on assessing levels of intimacy during dating and on maintaining and heightening levels of intimacy in marriage. Now we will discuss the parent-child relationship, the four components needed for total intimacy, and high-quality parent-child relationships.

Parenthood Option

Several years ago a number of persons grouped together to form the National Alliance for Optional Parenthood (NAOP). It is the purpose of this group to make persons aware that parenthood is optional. There are at least three options or choices[4] from which you can choose:

1.   You can remain childless.

2.   You can become a parent by either having children or adopting children.

3.   You can remain childless but select an alternative to parenthood such as writing children's books, becoming a teacher, and so forth.

We suggest that if you are thinking about the second option—becoming a parent—you should first examine the role of intimacy in the parent-child relationship. Parent-child relationships also generally fall within a continuum that ranges from "destructive" through "satisfactory" to "high-quality" (Figure 71).

Figure 71

High quality parent-child relationships are best achieved by parents who work towards developing the four types of total intimacy—philosophical, psychological, creative, and physical—with their child or children. Let's examine the role each type of intimacy plays in developing a high quality parent-child relationship. We can also examine how the learning a child experiences at an early age affects his or her ability to become intimate with others.

Philosophical Intimacy

Parents provide their children with their first attitudes about philosophical intimacy and its importance. Parents who desire high-quality relationships make serious efforts to instill their values in their children. They share their philosophy of life and their life principle. They discuss the importance of philosophy in making responsible decisions. The child learns a frame of ref-

[4]For more information, the NAOP offers a number of leaflets, including "Am I Parent Material?" and "Children, Why Not?" Write to: National Alliance for Optional Parenthood, 2010 Massachusetts Avenue NW, Washington, D. C. 20036.

erence. When the child exhibits behaviors that vary from this frame of reference, the parents discuss these differences.

Parents who have clear values and who are able to communicate these values to their children provide a meaningful experience in philosophical intimacy. A parent-child relationship without philosophical intimacy is confusing: the child does not know what parents value and does not have a frame of reference to internalize. Children who do not have this experience will have to learn about philosophical intimacy elsewhere if they are to achieve it in an adult relationship.

Parents also provide their children with their first experience in psychological intimacy. They can create an atmosphere of trust and open communication in which their children feel accepted and are willing to share weaknesses, strengths, needs, emotional feelings, and problems.

Psychological Intimacy

Some parent-child relationships lack psychological intimacy. These children may not learn to be trusting. These children may fear psychological intimacy. They may be unable to share their innermost feelings in important relationships. These children must gain other experiences and/or counseling to prepare them for psychological intimacy in adult relationships.

Parents can give their children their first feelings of teamwork within the family. The family setting can provide a medium for creative intimacy. Family members can work together and enjoy leisure-time activities. Creative intimacy becomes a way of life.

Creative Intimacy

In some families, creative intimacy is lacking. Family members may not have mutual projects or they may not affirm one another while engaged in creative efforts. Without early experiences in creative intimacy, children must learn this teamwork in another setting.

The parent-child relationship begins soon after birth. Children who receive soft touches, are spoken to, held, and looked at frequently by the mother and father in the first few days of life cry less and smile and laugh more.[5] These children learn that physical intimacy is pleasurable and they feel secure giving and receiving affection. Without early experiences in giving and receiving affection, it is more difficult to achieve physical intimacy in adulthood.

Physical Intimacy

The four components of total intimacy—philosophical, psychological, creative, and physical—play a vital role in promoting destructive and satisfactory parent-child relationships to the level of high quality.

There are other things that parents can do to create high quality relationships with their children. These are described in the Parent Pledge to Achieve A High Quality Relationship with Children.

Other Factors in High-Quality Parent-Child Relationships

One of the statements, number 7, needs further discussion. Parents who want to have intimate, high quality relationships with children must examine ways to develop self-control and self-discipline in their children. Discipline is training that develops self-control and self-discipline. Some people think discipline and punishment are synonymous, but they are not. Punishment is one way to teach discipline and self-control, and some research indicates that it may be one of the least effective ways.

Disciplinary Techniques

Preventive discipline involves discussing behaviors with children. The goals of preventive discipline are to help children repeat desirable behaviors and to

Preventive Discipline

---

[5]M. Klaus and J. Kennel, *Maternal Infant Bonding* (St. Louis: C. V. Mosby, 1976).

Parent Pledge to Achieve a High-Quality Relationship with Children

1.   I will set aside a quantity of time as well as quality time to spend with my children.

2.   I will learn about the age-appropriate development of children so that I can set realistic expectations for my children.

3.   I will teach my children rules to insure their health and safety.

4.   I will give my children love and affection.

5.   I will teach my children with a positive attitude, avoiding condemnation and criticism.

6.   I will teach my children moral and ethical values.

7.   I will teach my children self-discipline and self-control by example and by using effective disciplinary techniques rather than child abuse.

8.   I will provide economic security for my children.

9.   I will recognize that my children have rights, and I will respect these rights.

10.   I will raise my children in a stable, secure family that is free of substance abuse. (Free from the abuse of alcohol, marijuana, amphetamines, etc.).

change undesirable behaviors. I-messages are the most effective messages for accomplishing these goals. A parent might say, "When you leave your bike outside it may get stolen, and I am angry." The parent avoids you-messages such as "You never take care of the things that belong to you."

Behavior Modification

Behavior modification is a disciplinary technique in which parents use positive rewards to encourage children to repeat desirable behaviors and negative rewards to stop undesirable behaviors. The parent would praise the child for remembering to put his or her bicycle away. The parent might plan a special reward. On the other hand, the parent wants to modify undesirable behaviors. A child who leaves the bicycle in an unsafe place may not be permitted to ride the bike for three days.

Logical-Consequences Discipline

Logical-consequences discipline allows the child the opportunity to experience the results of undesirable behavior so that (s)he will want to change the behavior. The child who frequently forgets the lunch that was packed for school gets no lunch as a substitute. The child learns to remember to take the lunch to school.

Physical Punishment

Physical punishment is a form of discipline in which an act such as spanking is used to teach a child not to repeat undesirable behavior. Spanking only appears to facilitate the disciplinary process in two instances. First, when a child is small a parent may slap the child's hand to prevent a behavior that might harm the child. For example, the parent might stop the child's hand if (s)he tries to put a fork in an electrical outlet. Second, a parent might use a slap on the young child's buttocks or hand to get the child's attention. The slap should not hurt the child.

Through research much has been learned about the effects of spanking. Research indicates that spanking is relatively ineffective in teaching long-range self-discipline and self-control. In fact, it often creates feelings of hostility between parent and child that interfere with intimate high-quality relationships.

What kinds of parents are most effective in teaching their children self-discipline and self-control? Research describes such parents as those who (1) set limits for their children, (2) are consistent in their actions, (3) are neither too strict nor too easy, (4) discuss behavior with their children, and (5) listen to their children and to their feelings.

Effective Discipline

Unfortunately not all parent-child relationships are high-quality and include the four components needed for total intimacy. Some parent-child relationships are destructive. Maltreatment of children, or child abuse, usually falls into one of four general areas:

Child Abuse

- physical abuse.

- neglect.

- emotional maltreatment.

- sexual abuse.

Some forms of maltreatment, abuse, and neglect are more difficult to detect than others, but there are usually signs or indicators to suggest that a child may be in need of help. These indicators basically are of three types:[6]

Indicators of Child Abuse

- Physical indicators, such as the child's appearance (including apparent physical injury).

- Behavioral indicators, such as behavior that the child exhibits as the result of maltreatment.

- Environmental or circumstantial indicators, including social, cultural, or familial factors that are known to correlate with various kinds of abuse and neglect.

These three indicators are identified and described for each of the four types of child abuse listed on pages 166 to 172, under Clues to Recognizing Child Abuse and Neglect.

In many cases, destructive and abusive parent-child relationships can be prevented by identifying parents to be who are more likely to be abusive and providing these future parents with help. A potentially abusive parent may show several of these characteristics:[7]

Identifying the Abusive Parent

- The mother denies the pregnancy, refuses to talk about it, has made no plans whatsoever.

- The mother is very depressed over the pregnancy.

- The mother is not willing to gain weight during the pregnancy.

- The mother is alone and frightened, especially of the prospect of the delivery.

- The mother lacks support from the father or her family.

- The parent is overly concerned with what the sex of the baby will be.

---

[6]"Clues to Recognizing Child Abuse and Neglect," *Prevention and Reporting Kit* (Ohio Department of Public Welfare, Children's Protective Services, 30 East Broad Street, 30th Floor, Columbus, Ohio 43215).

[7]"Warning Signals: Can We Recognize a Potentially Abusive Parent Before a Child is Born?" *Prevention and Reporting Kit* (Ohio Department of Public Welfare, Children's Protective Services, 30 East Broad Street, 30th Floor, Columbus, Ohio 43215).

- The parent is overly concerned with how the baby will perform, whether it will measure up to standards.

- The parent feels that the child is going to be "one too many children."

- The parent wanted an abortion but did not go through with it or waited until it was too late.

- The parents considered giving up the child but changed their minds.

- The parents are isolated, do not have relatives or friends.

- After delivery of the baby, the parent shows no active interest in it, doesn't want to touch or hold it, seems hostile toward it, and is disappointed over its sex.

- After the baby comes home, the parent is very bothered about the baby's crying; sees the baby as too demanding, yet frequently ignores the baby's needs, not comforting it when it cries; and finds changing diapers distasteful.

- The parent doesn't have fun with the baby, doesn't talk to the baby, and says mostly negative things about it.

- One parent resents the time the other spends with the baby and is jealous of any affection shown toward the baby.

The presence of these characteristics does not mean that abuse or neglect will occur. At times parents who are experiencing anxiety may exhibit one or more of these characteristics. However, if several of these characteristics persist for a continued period of time, the parents should seek help.

The parent-child relationship needs continual examination. An important question is, "How can education for sexuality promote destructive and satisfactory parent-child relationships to a level of high quality?" There are at least three answers to this question:

Preparing for High Quality Parent-Child Relationships

1. Teach potential parents about the four components of total intimacy.

2. Ask potential parents to agree to each of the ten conditions listed in the Parent Pledge to Achieve A High Quality Relationship with Children.

3. Include a required course of child rearing, growth, and development in high schools.

Clues to Recognizing Child Abuse and Neglect[8]

I. Physical Abuse

Some of the more common physical indicators are:

Physical Indicators

- Bruises
  occurring on the posterior side of the body.
  occurring in unusual patterns.

---

[8]Used with permission from *Prevention and Reporting Kit* (Ohio Department of Public Welfare, Children's Protective Services, 30 East Broad Street, 30th Floor, Columbus, Ohio 43215).

occurring in clusters.

occurring on an infant, especially on the face in various stages of healing.

- Burns

immersion burns, such as "stocking burns" or doughnut-shaped burns on the buttocks.

cigarette-type burns, especially on the palms of hands, soles of feet, or genitals.

rope burns, possibly related to confinement.

dry burns, such as those caused by an iron.

- Lacerations and Abrasions

on lips, eyes, or any portion of an infant's face.

of gum tissue, caused by forced feeding.

on external genitals.

- Missing or loosened teeth

- Skeletal injuries

metaphyseal or corner fractures of long bones; caused by twisting and pulling.

epiphyseal separation—separation of the growth center at the end of the bone from the rest of the shaft; caused by twisting or pulling.

periosteal elevation—detachment of periosteum from shaft of bone with associated hemorrhaging periosteum and shaft.

spinal fractures.

stiff, swollen, enlarged joints.

- Head injuries

absence of hair.

hemorrhaging beneath scalp, caused by pulling hair.

subdural hematomas, caused by hitting or shaking.

retinal hemorrhages or detachment, caused by shaking.

nasal or jaw fracture.

- Internal injuries

duodenal or jejunal hematoma, caused by hitting or kicking.

rupture of inferior vena cava.

peritonitis, which can be caused by hitting or kicking.

Behavioral Indicators

These and other physical indicators should be considered in light of their consistency with the child's medical history, the developmental ability of the child to inflict self-injury and any other indicators, such as behavioral or environmental indicators.

The behavioral indicators of physical abuse are varied and are influenced by the severity and frequency of the abuse, the age of the child at onset of abuse, the nature of the child's relationship to the abuser, the availability of supportive persons, and the child's genetic endowment for coping.

A child who is abused frequently and severely at an early age is likely to exhibit these low-profile behavioral characteristics:

- unusually neat in eating habits.

- overly compliant to avoid confrontation.

- lacking in curiosity.

- fearful of physical contact.

- excessively self-controlled.

- lacking in development because all efforts are being directed at self-protection.

- cries little.

- enjoys little or nothing.

- can perform motor skills but does not want to.

- may appear autistic.

A child who is less severely and less often abused and who is a little older at onset is likely to exhibit some of these behavioral characteristics:

- timid, easily frightened.

- has psychosomatic complaints, such as enuresis and vomiting.

- craves affection.

- continues to affirm love for abusing parent.

- experiences delay in language acquisition.

- has difficulty with school in spite of normal ability (energy is misdirected).

- exhibits sporadic temper tantrums.

- assumes the role of parent in the parent-child relationship or is extremely immature in parent-child interactions.

- shows indiscriminate attachment to strangers.

A child who is mildly, infrequently, or inconsistently abused at an older age is likely to exhibit these characteristics:

- hurts other children.

- may try to "make happen" what (s)he expects in order to gain a feeling of control.

- shows extreme aggressiveness.

- has raging temper tantrums.

- is hyperactive.

- has a short attention span.

- is demanding.

- shows lag in development.

- may seem accident-prone or clumsy.

These indicators should prompt careful watchfulness for physical injuries. Children are often embarrassed by abuse and as fearful as their parents are of the possible consequences of discovery. The known—no matter how bad— is often less frightening than the unknown, especially to young children. These children will often wear inappropriate clothing, such as long sleeves in hot weather, to hide injuries, or they may refuse to change clothes for gym at school.

In addition to the physical and behavioral indicators of physical abuse, there are environmental indicators, those social, cultural, and familial circumstances that increase the likelihood of abuse. Some of these factors are:

- family crises of unemployment, death, desertion, or ill health.

- severe personal problems, such as drug addiction, alcoholism, or mental illness.

- geographic and/or social isolation of the family.

- perception of the child as different or difficult.

- parents' unawareness of appropriate behavior for child at given age.

- parental characteristics stemming from own childhood abuse.

Although most persons are capable of abuse under conditions of excessive stress, this last factor bears special comment in that many seriously abusive parents share characteristics common to persons who have been abused or poorly parented themselves as children. In fact, most such parents have been victims of abuse. The personal characteristics of abusive parents are:

- poor self-concept.

- passive marital relationship or marital difficulty.

- fear of authority.

- lack of skills to meet one's own emotional needs.

- belief of necessity for harsh physical discipline.

- undue fear of spoiling the child.

- rigidity or compulsiveness.

- hostility and aggressiveness.

- acceptance of violence as a means of communication.

- poor emotional control, impulsiveness.

- emotional dependency of the nonabusive spouse to the point that (s)he will not intervene and will protect the abusive spouse.

- unreasonable expectations of the child.

II. Neglect

Neglect is essentially inadequate or dangerous child-rearing practices. It may not produce visible signs, and it usually occurs over a period of time.

The general physical indicators of neglect are:

- abandonment.

- lack of adequate supervision.

- lack of adequate clothing for the weather.

- lack of good hygiene.

- lack of necessary medical or dental care.

- lack of adequate nutrition.

- lack of safe, warm, sanitary shelter.

The child who is neglected, like the child who is abused, will exhibit one or more behavioral indicators. These commonly are:

Behavioral Indicators

- failure to thrive among infants.
- falling asleep in school.
- poor learning.
- poor school attendance or chronic lateness.
- chronic hunger or tiredness.
- begging or collecting leftovers or stealing other children's lunches.
- coming to school early and staying late.
- dull, apathetic appearance.
- squinting.
- use of drugs or alcohol.
- engaging in vandalism.
- engaging in sexual misconduct.

The neglected child is often, although not always, living in an environment characterized by one or more of the following elements:

Environmental Indicators

- a large family with marital disruption.
- poverty.
- long-term parental illness.
- indifferent parental attitude.
- situational stress, such as unemployment.
- lack of material resources.
- parental characteristics stemming from neglect.

As with abusive parents, neglectful parents frequently have been victims of the same type of parenting that they provide for their children. The following are personal characteristics or behaviors of neglectful parents:

Parents' Personal Characteristics

- apathy.
- craving for excitement or change.
- desire to be rid of the demands of the child.
- lack of interest in the child's activities.
- low acceptance of the child's dependency needs.
- lack of skill as parents.
- little planning or organization.
- frequent unkemptness.

III. Emotional Maltreatment

Emotional maltreatment, or mental injury, is usually related to a constellation of interactions and is cumulative in effect. Like physical abuse, emotional abuse can be thought of as ranging from mild, infrequent, or isolated acts mixed with support, to a pervasive, psychologically destructive pattern of parenting.

Behavioral indicators are the best indicators of emotional abuse. Among these are:

Behavioral Indicators

- hyperactivity or withdrawal.
- overeating.
- fire-setting.
- nervous skin disorders.
- psychosomatic complaints.
- autism or failure to thrive.
- suicide attempts.
- truancy or other disciplinary problems.
- delinquency or aggressiveness.
- hypochondriasis.
- over-submissiveness.
- behavior that is either too adult or too infantile.
- stuttering.
- enuresis.

The environmental indicators frequently related to emotional maltreatment are:

Environmental Indicators

- continuous emotional friction in the home.
- mentally ill or immature parents.
- excessive drinking or drug addiction.
- criminal involvement.
- inappropriate discipline.
- home values in conflict with society's values.
- frequent marriages or broken homes.
- no recreation provided or permitted.
- promiscuity or prostitution.
- rejecting parents who withhold love.
- discriminatory treatment among children in the family.

IV. Sexual Abuse

Sexual abuse is relatively difficult to detect outside the clinical setting for several fairly obvious reasons. The physical trauma is not exposed. The victim is usually reluctant to reveal the abuse. There is a general lack of awareness of the prevalence of child sexual abuse and lack of confidence in detecting it.

The physical indicators of sexual abuse include:

- bruises of or bleeding from external genitalia, vagina, or anal regions.

- swollen or red cervix, vulva, or perineum.

- presence of semen, pregnancy, tests positive for gonococcus or other sexually transmitted diseases.

- torn, stained, or bloody underclothes.

- pain or itching in the genital area.

- hymen stretched at a very young age.

Behavioral indicators are frequently the best or only signs you may have. The sexually abused child usually exhibits one or more of these characteristics or behaviors:

- poor peer relationships.

- regression (may appear mentally retarded).

- sexual promiscuity.

- aggressiveness or delinquency.

- prostitution.

- truancy from home.

- drug usage.

- difficulty walking or sitting.

- seductive behavior.

- reluctance to participate in recreational activity.

- preoccupation, in young children, with sexual organs of self, parents, or other children.

- confiding in a friend or teacher.

- reporting to authorities.

Usually when a child says (s)he has been abused, it is true. If a young girl states that anything has been placed in her vagina, believe it. She has no frame of reference for this unless it has happened.

What are the environmental indicators associated with sexual abuse? Some common elements tend to distinguish such cases. These are:

- prolonged absence of one parent.

- overcrowding.

- alcoholism.

- social and/or geographic isolation.

- intergenerational pattern of incest.

- parental characteristics indicative of sexual abuse, such as extreme protectiveness of the child, jealousy of the child, frequent refusal to allow the child any social contact, distrust of the child, and accusing the child of sexual promiscuity.

SECTION 4

Educational Aspects of Human Sexuality

CHAPTER 13

Planning the Sex Education Curriculum

There is an important saying in community health that is highly applicable to the sex education curriculum: "Planning without action is futile and action without planning is fatal."[1] The sex education curriculum should be carefully planned to assure its success. Several steps are involved in this process:

1. Developing a philosophy of sex education.

2. Forming an advisory committee.

3. Designing the education for sexuality curriculum: scope and sequence K–12.

4. Implementing the sex education curriculum.

5. Evaluating the sex education curriculum.

Developing a Philosophy of Sex Education

An important first step in preparation for implementing a sex education curriculum is the formulation of a philosophical position paper that justifies why this curriculum is needed in the schools.

There are many different reasons for teaching sex education. Some people believe that sex education is a panacea for many existing social problems. They might offer some of the following reasons for the inclusion of sex education in the curriculum.

Sex Education and Social Problems

- to reduce unwanted pregnancy.

- to reduce the divorce rate.

- to eradicate venereal disease or STD.

- to thwart promiscuous sexual behavior.

[1]Mary E. Hawthorne and J. Warren Perry, *Community Colleges and Primary Health Care: SAHE Report* (Washington, D.C.: American Association of Community and Junior Colleges, 1974).

They build a case for sex education by listing many facts and statistics related to the prevalence of social problems that might be eradicated with education. This is one approach to the justification of the sex education curriculum.

Another approach emphasizes the promotion of optimal health and the promotion of a healthy, happy, balanced life-style. This approach does not rely on the prevalance of social problems as justification for the sex education curriculum. It is not a crisis-oriented approach.

Promotion of Optimal Health and Life-style

This approach may be more meaningful and impactful because it views the sex education curriculum as a normal outgrowth of the goals of education.

The authors support the view that sex education is necessary for a student to develop a healthy, happy, balanced life-style.

The philosopher Immanuel Kant wrote, "The three grand essentials to happiness in this life are something to do, someone to love, and something to hope for."

Three Essentials to Happiness

The school has a role in promoting each of these essential ingredients to happiness:

The School's Role

1. The school prepares students to have *something to do*. It prepares young people for a vocation.

2. The school prepares students to form satisfying interpersonal relationships—to have *someone to love*.

3. The school assists students in developing a code of ethics that values other persons and provides a reason to value their future—*something to hope for*.

Each of these essential ingredients to happiness provides justification for sex education.[2]

As students look for something to do, each is accompanied by a sexual self. No matter what a person does, (s)he is male or female. Acceptance of one's sexuality and that of others influences what one does—one's life work. Work and working relationships are more likely to promote happiness when a person accepts his or her sexuality and that of others.

Something To Do

The next essential ingredient of happiness, someone to love, is more directly related to the need for a sex education curriculum. If loving someone is one of the three essentials of happiness, then the study of loving relationships is quite important.

Someone to Love

Erich Fromm, author of *The Art of Loving*,[3] says that a person learns the ability, or art, of loving. This is an important justification for education about sexuality.

To fulfill this essential ingredient of happiness, the authors believe students need to learn:

1. To integrate love and sexual behavior.

2. To develop a responsible and caring attitude toward sexuality.

3. To form loving relationships.

---

[2]The "Something to Do, Someone to Love, Something to Hope For" rationale for sex education is taken from Linda Meeks and Phil Heit, *Human Sexuality: Making Responsible Decisions* (Philadelphia: Saunders College Publishing, 1982).

[3]Erich Fromm, *The Art of Loving* (New York: Bantam Books, Inc., 1963), p. 46.

4. To make responsible decisions.

5. To communicate effectively with others.

To this end, students need to have information about sexuality. The authors have provided twelve content areas as a framework for the sex education curriculum.

·   Education for Love.

·   The Biological Male.

·   The Biological Female.

·   Human Sexual Response.

·   Pregnancy, Childbirth, and Postpartum Period.

·   Contraception.

·   Abortion.

·   Sexually Transmitted Diseases.

·   Intelligent Choice of a Sexual Life-Style.

·   Masturbation.

·   Homosexuality.

·   Intimacy, Marriage, and Parenthood.

The final essential ingredient of happiness identified by Immanuel Kant is something to hope for. A person who has a philosophy of life that identifies a reason for living has the greatest chance of attaining happiness. When a person has a philosophy of life, (s)he develops a life principle.

Something to Hope For

> A life principle is a generalized, accepted intention of purpose that is applied to specific choices and circumstances. This life principle runs through the fabric of our choices like the dominant theme in a piece of music: it keeps recurring and is heard in different settings. Having a life principle is a matter of psychological economy. It diminishes the wear and tear of having to make all decisions from the ground up.[4]

When a person has a life principle, (s)he has a framework to use when making decisions about sexuality that promote happiness.

What framework or life principle should be woven throughout the sex education curriculum? The authors suggest that responsible decisions about sex are accompanied by the question "What is the loving action to take?"

A loving action involves the four ingredients or aspects of love that Erich Fromm mentions in his book *The Art of Loving*. These are:[5]

The Goal: Loving Actions

1. *Respect:* to respect others means that you think they are worthwhile. You listen to their ideas even when they are different from yours.

2. *Responsibility:* to be responsible means that others can depend on you. If you love others, they should be able to count on you and your wise behavior.

---

[4]John Powell, *Unconditional Love* (Niles, Iowa: Argus Communications, 1969).
[5]The definitions are adapted from a discussion in Linda Meeks and Phil Heit, *Family Living and Human Reproduction* (Columbus: Charles Merrill, 1982), pp. 4–5.

3. *Understanding:* to be understanding means that you care how others feel and how your behavior might affect them.

4. *Labor:* to labor means to work hard, to share work to demonstrate that you care. To labor also means to demonstrate self-discipline to adhere to your values.

The sex education curriculum the authors propose is not lacking in ethics. Loving actions form the framework that is woven through the curriculum as a basis for making responsible decisions.

Parental Support for Sex Education

Most surveys show that 80 percent of Americans think that public schools should provide some sort of sex education.[6]

Only 3 percent of those surveyed object to sex education. Those who object to sex education generally are concerned about sex education curricula that are void of values upheld by the community. They have strong objections to students making up their own minds.[7] They do not want their youngsters to be given facts and then left with "Now what will you do?"

A Framework that Handles Ethical Decisions

The authors empathize with these concerns. This is the authors' reason for designing a curriculum with an ethical framework, one based on *loving actions that are evidenced by respect, responsibility, understanding, and labor.*

When the authors have worked with administrators, teachers, parents, and clergy, this ethical framework has alleviated the concerns that these persons have.

For example, a parent might ask "Does your curriculum suggest that my child can set his or her own time to come home from a date?" The answer is no. Loving actions are accompanied by *respect* for parents and for their guidelines.

Another question might be, "Does your curriculum support the family as being important?" The answer is yes. Loving actions are accompanied by *labor,* working to keep family relationships stable.

And one of the most pertinent questions raised is, "In your curriculum, do you take a neutral position on young people having premarital sexual intercourse?" The authors' answer is no. We do not avoid this topic or take a neutral position. We support the view of most parents:[8]

> Persons who want to form loving relationships place a value on sexual intercourse. This close relationship has meaning. They are willing to wait until they are older and more mature before having sexual intercourse. Making a responsible decision to wait to have sexual intercourse requires self-discipline. When you make responsible decisions about sex, you will respect yourself and others will respect you.

The authors believe that young people need information about their sexuality and that this information must be examined within an ethical framework upon which decisions can be based. In the curriculum provided in *Education for Sexuality,* all decisions are not labeled "acceptable." All decisions are not left to the whims and desires of students. Instead, students are taught that decisions are acceptable only when they are responsible and accompanied by loving actions.

---

[6]Constance Horner, "Is the New Sex Education Going Too Far?" *The New York Times* (7 Dec., 1980).

[7]Constance Horner, op. cit.

[8]Linda Meeks and Phil Heit, *Family Living and Human Reproduction* (Columbus: Charles Merrill Publishing Co., 1984), p. 12.

Thus, a key element in the philosophy of this program is the commitment to teach the student the difference between responsible and irresponsible decision making. The authors have utilized the guidelines for making responsible decisions that permeate *The Health: Focus on You* K–12 health education textbook series.*

These guidelines define a responsible decision as a decision that is

1. healthful.
2. safe.
3. legal.
4. respects you and others.
5. follows parents' guidelines.

The guidelines in *Health: Focus on You* make it easier for young people to make a responsible decision. Here are examples:

1.   A girl learns how to examine her breasts in her health class. She decides to examine her breasts monthly. A boy learns to examine his testes. He decides to regularly perform testicular self-examination. Each makes a responsible decision to choose behaviors that are *healthful.*

2.   A girl is riding in a car with her boyfriend. He begins to drive very fast. She asks him to drive at the speed limit or to take her to the next store where she can call someone to take her home. She makes a responsible decision that *promotes safety.*

3.   A boy is offered a marijuana cigarette on a date. Smoking marijuana is against the law. He says "no," choosing behavior that is *legal.*

4.   A boy gossips about a girl at school. Another boy asks him to stop. The second boy shows *respect for others.*

5.   A girl's parents have a guideline that she cannot go to a drive-in movie with a boy. A boy asks her to a drive-in. She says "no," making a responsible decision that follows her *parents' guidelines.*

6.   A family does not believe in premarital sex because of their religious convictions. A girl is pressured to have sex by her boyfriend. She says "no," making a responsible decision to follow her *parents' guidelines.*.

Parents and educators welcome the guidelines for responsible decision making identified in the *Health: Focus on You Program.* When there are carefully chosen guidelines for decisions, parents support a sex education curriculum.

A large number of national groups have gone on record as being supportive of sex education. A list of these groups include:[9]

Professional Support for Sex Education

- The Association for the Advancement of Health Education.

- The American College of Obstetricians and Gynecologists.

- The American Medical Association.

- The American Public Health Association.

---

*Available from Charles E. Merrill Publishing Co., 1300 Alum Creek Drive, Columbus, Ohio 43216.

[9]Clint E. Bruess and Jerrold S. Greenberg, *Sex Education: Theory and Practice* (Belmont, California: Wadsworth, Inc. 1981), p. 58.

- The American School Health Association.

- The National Association for Independent Schools.

- The National Congress for Parents and Teachers (PTO).

- The National Council of Churches.

- The National Education Association (NEA).

- The National School Boards Association and the American Association of School Administrators (joint committee).

- The Synagogue Council of America.

- The United States Catholic Conference.

- The United States Department of Health, Education, and Welfare (now separated into the Department of Health and Human Services and the Department of Education).

Forming an Advisory Committee

After the school system has prepared a statement of its needs and philosophical position, the next step is to appoint persons to the advisory committee that will develop a sex education curriculum to meet the needs of the community.

The advisory committee should include a variety of persons with varied expertise. Some of these persons might include:

1. School administrators.

2. Elementary school teachers.

3. Middle school teachers.

4. Secondary school teachers.

5. School nurses.

6. School psychologists.

7. Parents in the community.

8. Clergy in the community.

9. Physicians in the community.

10. Persons from various health agencies in the community.

Some school districts also select students to become members of the advisory committee. The persons who make up the advisory committee review the existing sex education curricula that are available. In addition, they examine (1) the needs of the community, (2) the concerns of parents, (3) the concerns of teachers, and (4) the needs and concerns of students.

The advisory committee establishes a set of guidelines for teaching human sexuality. An example of such guidelines appears below.

Guidelines for Teaching Human Sexuality*

Since the very basis of life itself is the ability of an organism to reproduce itself, it is of fundamental importance that young people gain a knowledge in

---

*Adapted from the 1973 Columbus Public Schools Guidelines for Teaching Human Sexuality, Columbus, Ohio.

a systematic, factual manner of the processes involved. However, because human reproduction is related to the family unit, religion, morality, sexuality, emotions, attitudes, physical health, economic considerations, and the mores of our society, teaching in this area must be approached in a careful, studied manner.

The following are presented as guiding concepts:

1. The values of the family in our society should be emphasized—its attractions and benefits, as well as the responsibilities involved in starting a family. We believe in the dignity and value of each human being in the family structure.

2. The importance of moral living and high ethical standards of personal conduct are recognized in the teaching of human sexuality. When teaching about human sexuality, it is better for teachers to center discussion on factual information and traditional mores rather than to express opinions without substantiation.

3. Because of the various interpretations of the term, the word "sex" needs to be well defined, since the word refers to a quality of the person, not merely to the genitals or to reproduction. Sexuality is a way of being and relating to the world.

4. Appropriate, accepted terms should be used when discussing sex and reproduction as educational topics.

5. The best setting for sex education is found when the topic presents itself in a natural kind of situation. Health, biology, social studies, English, home economics, and other classes often afford this kind of opportunity.

6. Education about sex and human reproduction is but one phase of health education and should be kept in perspective within the total course.

7. Questions need straightforward answers—sometimes in class, sometimes in private. However, there are some matters, such as birth control methods, that may not be appropriate for certain classes or occasions. At times the teacher should explain that a parent, physician, or minister is more qualified on this matter or should be consulted about a particular question.

8. If there is parental objection to a student being in the sex education phase of a health course, alternative arrangements will be made for the student during the time the subject is under discussion.

Designing the Sex Education Curriculum: Scope and Sequence K–12

The advisory committee adapts existing curricula and designs a curriculum to meet the needs of the community. The authors provide two Scope and Sequence Charts for this purpose.

The Burt-Meeks *Education for Sexuality: Concepts and Programs for Teaching Scope and Sequence Chart K–6* includes a grade level designation of units. Each unit is based on concepts that are appropriate and important for that

Scope and Sequence K–6

age group. The units also consider the developmental tasks of middle childhood—about 6 to 12 years of age:[10]

1. Learning physical skills necessary for ordinary games.

2. Building wholesome attitudes toward oneself as a growing organism.

3. Learning to get along with peers.

4. Learning to appreciate masculine or feminine social roles.

5. Developing fundamental skills in reading, writing, and calculating.

6. Developing concepts necessary for everyday living.

7. Developing conscience, morality, and a scale of values.

8. Achieving personal independence.

9. Developing attitudes toward social groups and institutions.

The units in the Scope and Sequence Chart K–6 are included in detail in Chapters 14 to 20. Elementary and middle school teachers usually request materials that are written in detail. They want to know exactly what to say to students to reinforce and teach the appropriate concepts. The authors have successfully field-tested these units at the suggested grade levels. However, school systems may vary in their needs. An advisory committee can examine these units and decide which ones to teach and at which grade levels.

Burt-Meeks Education for Sexuality: Concepts and Programs for Teaching Scope and Sequence Chart K–6

Grade Level	Unit Title	Concepts
Kindergarten	Our Body Parts	1. There are many people and places that help with health at school. 2. There are many body parts. 3. A boy's body and a girl's body are different.
	All About Me Books	1. There are many changes as we grow. 2. All people are alike in some ways. 3. All people are different in some ways. 4. Some people have handicaps. 5. Everyone has many kinds of feelings. 6. Each person is special.
	Animal Families	1. Life comes from life. 2. Life comes from the same kind of life. 3. All animal babies have a father and a mother in the beginning. 4. There are two kinds of life—male and female. 5. All animal babies grow up to be adults.
First grade	Love, Responsibility, and Making Choices*	1. Love is a special feeling you have for yourself and others. 2. Love is a way of acting. 3. There are many ways to share love. 4. Some choices show love more than others. 5. Parents who are loving have rules for health and safety. 6. Some persons may harm you. 7. There are ways to protect yourself from strangers and persons who may harm you.
	Families†	1. A family is a group of people who belong together.

[10]Robert J. Havighurst, *Developmental Tasks of Education* (New York: David McKay Co., Inc.), pp. 19–33.

Grade Level	Unit Title	Concepts
First grade	Families (cont.)	2. All mothers have children, but mothers may be different in other ways.
		3. All fathers have children, but fathers may be different in other ways.
		4. Some family members live together in the same house.
		5. Some family members may not live together all the time.
		6. Some parents get a divorce.
		7. Some children have stepparents, stepbrothers, or stepsisters.
		8. Some children are adopted.
		9. Some family members have special needs—the aging or the handicapped.
		10. Families share love, work, and play.
Second grade	The Seed Experiment	1. There are many kinds of seeds from which life begins.
		2. The seeds or eggs in a plant are found in the ovary.
		3. These seeds need care to grow.
		4. Each seed grows into the kind of plant it came from.
		5. The bringing about of the birth of the plant of the same kind is called reproduction.
	Living Things That Come from Eggs	1. Different kinds of eggs grow into different kinds of animals.
		2. Living things need only parents to make them.
		3. All babies are made by joining a sperm and an egg.
		4. Eggs must be fertilized before they can grow.
		5. Mammal eggs grow in the mother's uterus.
Third grade	Growth of a Chick	1. When fertilization occurs, an egg cell from the mother is joined by a sperm cell from the father.
		2. An egg cell must be fertilized to grow into a living thing.
		3. An animal is an embryo in the earliest stages of development.
		4. Often preparation is needed for the birth of a new living thing.
		5. A new living thing needs care.
	Friendship	1. Self-concept is the feeling a person has about himself or herself.
		2. Each person needs time alone to develop a positive self-concept.
		3. Each person needs to have friends.
		4. Friends should be chosen carefully.
		5. There are many friendship skills.
		6. Sometimes friends disagree.
		7. Family members (parents) have friends, too.
Fourth grade	Where Babies Come From	1. The human body is made of many parts called cells.
		2. The cell is governed by DNA.
		3. Half of the DNA in each cell comes from the mother and half from the father.
		4. All of the body's cells develop because of orders sent out by the DNA in the very first cell.
		5. Half of the first cell comes from the mother, and half of the first cell comes from the father.
		6. It takes an egg cell from the mother and a sperm cell from the father to make a baby.

Grade Level	Unit Title	Concepts
Fourth grade	Where Babies Come From (cont.)	7. The father puts his penis inside the mother's vagina so that the sperm that carry his half of the DNA can fertilize an egg cell from the mother.
		8. A man and woman should love one another and agree to love and take care of children before having them.
		9. A man and woman should marry before having children.
	Heredity	1. Heredity is the passing of characteristics from a mother and a father to an offspring.
		2. A baby inherits 23 chromosomes from the mother and 23 chromosomes from the father.
		3. The sex of the baby is determined by the pairing of an X chromosome from the mother and an X or a Y chromosome from the father.
		4. A gene for a particular trait from the mother and a gene from the father are located at the same point on matching chromosomes.
		5. Genes determine what a person will look like and how a person will develop.
		6. A pair of genes, one from the mother and one from the father, may be alike or different.
		7. When members of a pair of genes are not the same, one of the genes (dominant gene) will influence heredity more than the other gene (recessive gene).
Fifth grade	Discovering Yourself	1. The parts of the body that are involved in producing offspring make up the reproductive system.
		2. Puberty is the period when hormones cause secondary sex characteristics to develop in boys and girls.
		3. The parts of the male reproductive system include the scrotum, testes, seminiferous tubules, epididymis, vas deferens, seminal vesicles, ejaculatory duct, prostate gland, Cowper's glands, urethra, and penis.
		4. The organs in the male reproductive system are necessary for the production, movement, and nourishment of sperm.
		5. Semen is a mixture of fluids and sperm.
		6. Ejaculation is the discharge of semen from the male urethra.
		7. If a male ejaculates while he is sleeping, it is called a wet dream or nocturnal emission.
		8. The parts of the female reproductive system include the ovaries, uterus, oviducts, vagina, mons veneris, labia, and clitoris.
		9. The hymen is a thin membrane that covers the vaginal opening.
		10. The menstrual cycle includes the maturing of an ovum, ovulation, thickening of the wall of the uterus, and menstruation.
		11. During the menstrual flow a girl has to use some protection—tampon or feminine pads—to absorb the blood.
		12. Tampon use under some circumstances has been linked to a rare disease called toxic-shock syndrome.
		13. Health habits such as maintaining a balanced diet and regular exercise are needed for a healthy menstrual cycle.

Grade Level	Unit Title	Concepts
Fifth grade	Making Responsible Decisions‡	1. A decision is a choice that you make. 2. For every decision, there are at least two choices. 3. For every decision, there are results. 4. For every decision, there are risks. 5. Decision making is deciding which of two or more choices you will make. 6. Facts, peer pressure, and your family are some of the things that influence your decisions. 7. Making a decision requires that you consider the following steps: identify the problem, list the choices you could make, list the risks for each choice, think about the results, and evaluate your choice. 8. A responsible decision is a decision that is (1) healthful, (2) safe, (3) legal, (4) respects you and others, and (5) follows parents' guidelines.
Sixth grade	The Family as the Basic Unit of Society	1. The pituitary gland secretes FSH, which causes other hormones to initiate puberty in the male and the female. 2. The secondary sex characteristics are the changes in the male and female bodies that result from hormonal influences at puberty. 3. The parts of the male reproductive system include the scrotum, testes, seminiferous tubules, epididymis, vas deferens, seminal vesicles, ejaculatory duct, prostate gland, Cowper's glands, urethra, and penis (review). 4. The parts of the female reproductive system include the ovaries, uterus, oviducts, vagina, mons veneris, labia, and clitoris (review). 5. Before fertilization or the coming together of the sperm and the egg, there must be a coming together of the father and the mother. 6. Intercourse is a special way that married husbands and wives express their love for one another. 7. During intercourse, the man places his erect penis inside the woman's vagina and moves it back and forth, causing semen to be released into the vagina. 8. The union of the sperm and egg is called fertilization. 9. A design for a new baby is laid out when the chromosomes and genes from the sperm are joined with the chromosomes and genes from the egg. 10. During the growth period in the uterus, the embryo uses the placenta to obtain food and oxygen and to remove wastes. 11. The pregnant woman's health habits—nutrition, drug use, diseases—affect the health of the growing baby. 12. At the eighth week of development, the embryo begins to resemble a human being and is called a fetus. 13. Many changes occur in the month-by-month development of the fetus from fertilization to birth. 14. There are three stages in the birth process: the baby's head appears in the birth canal, the baby is born, and the afterbirth is expelled.

Grade Level	Unit Title	Concepts
Sixth grade	The Family as the Basic Unit of Society (cont.)	15. Each family member has a responsibility to the helpless new baby to care for it and love it so that it may grow up happily and healthfully.
	Adolescence§	1. Adolescence is the time when the body of a boy or a girl changes from that of a child to an adult.
		2. Hormones control and regulate growth and development during adolescence.
		3. There are many physical changes during adolescence.
		4. Girls usually show physical changes (ages 11–13) before boys (ages 12–14).
		5. There may be many rapid changes in emotions during adolescence.
		6. Social growth has to do with the progress you make in relating to other people.
		7. Parents, other adults, and community social services assist adolescents in emotional and social growth.
		8. Stress is the body's reaction to any demand made upon it.
		9. Stress may be healthful or harmful.
		10. Adolescents can learn to make a plan to deal with harmful stress.
	Friendship, Dating, and Decision Making‖	1. Feeling good about yourself helps you to express love to others.
		2. Four skills that will help you become a loving person are labor or work, responsibility, respect, and understanding.
		3. There are many kinds of loving relationships.
		4. A friend is someone you know well and like.
		5. Certain skills are helpful in forming and maintaining friendships.
		6. Friends of the opposite sex are important.
		7. Dating is sharing social activities and time with someone of the opposite sex.
		8. Parents help establish guidelines for dating behavior.
		9. A value is a decision about how much people or things mean to you.
		10. It is important to have the self-discipline to behave in ways that show others what you value.

*The concepts in the unit on Love, Responsibility, and Making Choices are used with permission from Meeks-Heit *Strangers* (Columbus, Ohio: Charles Merrill Publishing, 1984.) This booklet is written for grades 2, 3 and 4. It can be purchased from Charles Merrill Publishing, 1300 Alum Creek Drive, Columbus, Ohio 43216.

†The concepts in the unit on Families are used with permission from Meeks-Heit *Family Living* (Columbus, Ohio: Charles Merrill Publishing, 1984.) This booklet is written for grades 2, 3, and 4. It can be purchased from Charles Merrill Publishing, 1300 Alum Creek Drive, Columbus, Ohio 43216.

‡The concepts in the unit on Making Responsible Decisions are adapted from Meeks-Heit *Health: Focus on You—Grades 4, 5, and 6* (Columbus, Ohio: Charles Merrill Publishing Co., 1984). This K–12 health education textbook series is used in school districts throughout the United States and in several foreign countries. For more information write Charles Merrill Publishing Co., 1300 Alum Creek Drive, Columbus, Ohio 43216.

§The concepts in the unit on Adolescence are used with permission from Meeks-Heit *Health: Focus on You—Grade 6* (Columbus, Ohio: Charles Merrill Publishing Co., 1984).

‖The concepts in the unit on Friendship, Dating, and Decision Making are used with permission from *Family Living and Human Reproduction* (Columbus: Charles Merrill Publishing Co., 1984). This booklet is written for students in grades 5, 6, 7, and 8. It can be purchased from Charles Merrill Publishing Co., 1300 Alum Creek Drive, Columbus, Ohio 43216.

The Burt-Meeks *Education for Sexuality: Concepts and Programs for Teaching Scope and Sequence Chart 7–12* is divided into 12 content area units. For each unit, there are a number of objectives for the teacher to use for classroom instruction.

Scope and Sequence 7–12

The 12 units correspond to the outline of content in Chapters 1 through 12 of this book. In Chapter 21, the authors suggest teaching strategies that help the student reach the objectives.

The content and learning strategies also take into consideration the developmental tasks of adolescence—about 12 to 18 years of age:[11]

1. Achieving new and more mature relations with peers of both sexes.

2. Achieving a masculine or feminine social role.

3. Accepting one's physique and using the body effectively.

4. Achieving emotional independence from parents and other adults.

5. Achieving assurance of economic independence.

6. Selecting and preparing for an occupation.

7. Preparing for marriage and family life.

8. Developing intellectual skills and concepts necessary for civic competence.

9. Desiring and achieving socially responsible behavior.

Burt-Meeks Education for Sexuality: Concepts and Programs for Teaching Scope and Sequence Chart 7–12

Grade Level	Unit Title	Objectives
7–12	Sex Education as Education for Love	The student will be able to: 1. define love. 2. describe the human need for love. 3. describe the integration of love and sexual behavior. 4. list and explain the four skills practiced by a loving person. 5. differentiate between the terms "sex" and "sexuality."
	The Biological Male	The student will be able to: 1. describe the structure and function of the following organs: scrotum, testes, seminiferous tubules, epididymis, vas deferens, seminal vesicles, ejaculatory duct, prostate gland, bulbourethral glands, urethra and penis. 2. describe how the scrotum controls the temperature of the testes. 3. explain the development of an inguinal hernia. 4. describe the causes and treatment for cryptorchidism. 5. describe the onset of puberty in the male. 6. identify the secondary sex

[11]Robert J. Havighurst, *Developmental Tasks and Education,* 3rd ed. (New York: Longman Co., Inc., 1981), pp. 43–82.

Grade Level	Unit Title	Objectives
7–12	The Biological Male (cont.)	characteristics produced by testosterone.
		7. describe how a man examines his testes for cancer.
		8. identify six characteristics of mature sperm.
		9. identify factors that may affect the production of sperm.
		10. list five signs that may indicate an enlarged prostate and perhaps cancer.
		11. define circumcision and list the advantages and disadvantages of this procedure.
		12. discuss three facts about penis size.
		13. describe the physiological mechanisms that produce an erection.
		14 discuss the sequence of events that occur during ejaculation.
		15. define noctural emissions or wet dreams.
	The Biological Female	The student will be able to:
		1. describe the structure and function of the following organs and structures: the mons veneris, the labia majora, the labia minora, the clitoris, the vestibule, the urethral opening, the introitus, the hymen, the uterus, the oviducts, and the ovaries.
		2. identify four functions of the vagina.
		3. describe the hymen and virginity.
		4. describe the onset of puberty in the female.
		5. identify the secondary sex characteristics produced by estrogen.
		6. define vaginitis and ways to avoid this condition.
		7. discuss the relationship between DES and vaginal cancer.
		8. describe the female breast self-examination.
		9. identify characteristics that increase a woman's risk of breast cancer.
		10. describe the three phases of the menstrual cycle: proliferative phase, secretory or progestational phase, and menstrual phase.
		11. discuss products available to absorb the menstrual flow.
		12. explain toxic-shock syndrome.
		13. describe the following menstrual conditions: menarche, amenorrhea, spasmodic dysmenorrhea, congestive dysmenorrhea, menorrhagia.
		14. discuss the cause, symptoms, and treatment of symptoms of menopause.
		15. describe the female pelvic examination.

Grade Level	Unit Title	Objectives
7–12	Human Sexual Response	The student will be able to:

1. identify four prerequisites for normal heterosexual response.
2. discuss the role of the nervous system in sexual response.
3. identify the genital structures needed for sexual response.
4. describe the causes of erection.
5. identify changes that occur to the male genitalia during the excitement phase.
6. describe the changes that occur to the female external and internal genitalia during the excitement phase.
7. describe the changes that occur to the female breasts during sexual response.
8. describe changes that occur to the male and female during the plateau phase of sexual response.
9. differentiate between male and female orgasm.
10. differentiate between male and female response during resolution.
11. discuss penis size and female sexual response.
12. describe the effects of drugs on sexual response—aphrodisiacs, anaphrodisiacs, alcohol, LSD, marijuana, and cocaine.
13. discuss necking, petting, and sexual response.
*14. discuss with parents limits, self-discipline, and guidelines for sexual behavior.
15. discuss the differences in excitement response in males and females.
16. discuss male and female sexual response in relation to aging.
17. discuss sexual dysfunction including premature ejaculation, impotence, and orgasmic dysfunction.

Pregnancy, Childbirth, and Postpartum Period

The student will be able to:
1. discuss the cellular basis of human reproduction.
2. discuss the pairing of chromocomes and heredity.
3. describe how the sex of a child is determined.
4. differentiate between dominant and recessive genes.
5. explain the basis for identical and fraternal twins and triplets.
6. describe the processes of conception, implantation, and pregnancy.
7. discuss the physiological changes in a woman during pregnancy.
8. describe month-by-month development of the fetus.

Grade Level	Unit Title	Objectives
7–12	Pregnancy, Childbirth, and Postpartum Period (cont.)	9. identify and describe the stages of labor. 10. discuss cesarean birth. 11. discuss the role of RH factor in pregnancy. 12. evaluate the benefits of breast-feeding and bottle-feeding. 13. discuss the effects of diet and drug abuse by the mother of the unborn, including fetal alcohol syndrome. 14. discuss the health risks that accompany teenage pregnancy. 15. evaluate the different childbirth techniques and birth-place alternatives, including Lamaze and LeBoyer techniques. 16. discuss sperm antibodies and infertility.

	Contraception	The student will be able to:
		1. differentiate between theoretical and use-effectiveness of contraceptive alternatives.
		2. describe each of the following birth control methods and explain (a) how each works, (b) instructions for effective use, (c) effectiveness, (d) benefits, (e) side effects, (f) contraindications, and (g) cost:
		    abstinence
		    oral contraceptives
		    surgical sterilization
		    condom
		    IUD
		    diaphragm
		    spermicidal agents
		    rhythm
		    douche
		    withdrawal
		    sponge
		3. discuss sexual behavior, responsibility, and use of contraception by males and females.
		*4. discuss contraceptive use and sexual behavior guidelines with parents.

	Abortion	The student will be able to:
		1. define each of the following terms that describe abortion:
		    spontaneous missed
		    induced septic
		    threatened habitual
		    imminent therapeutic
		    inevitable criminal
		    incomplete embryonic
		    complete fetal
		2. describe induced abortion procedures, health care and health care facilities, and risk factors in:
		    uterine aspiration
		    dilation and curretage
		    saline and prostaglandin use

Grade Level	Unit Title	Objectives
7–12	Abortion (cont.)	hysterotomy menstrual extraction 3. explain the current federal and state abortion laws. 4. explain the position on abortion held by right-to-life and pro-choice (right-to-choose) groups. *5. discuss abortion ethics and values with parents.

	Veneral Diseases—Sexually Transmitted Diseases	The student will be able to:
		1. differentiate between diseases that are hereditary, congenital, and infectious.
		2. define veneral or sexually transmitted disease.
		3. identify the modes of transmission, symptoms, diagnosis, treatment, and complications of the following sexually transmitted diseases:
		    gonorrhea
		    syphilis
		    chancroid
		    nongonococcal urethritis
		    herpes genitalis
		    trichomoniasis
		    monila
		    pediculosis pubis
		4. describe eight ways in which sexually transmitted diseases can be prevented.

	Intelligent Choice of Sexual Life-Style	The student will be able to: 1. define noncontradictory joy. 2. discuss factors in open communication. 3. differentiate between permissiveness and committedness. 4. identify five criteria for participation in responsible sexual behavior. 5. identify the advantages of waiting until marriage to have sexual intercourse. 6. discuss the limits, risks, advantages, and disadvantages of trial marriage and cohabitation. 7. discuss ways to set limits on sexual behavior in relationships. 8. discuss ways to say "No" when pressured to have sexual relations. *9. discuss decision making and limits for sexual behavior with parents. 10. discuss ways to protect against rape and other forms of sexual abuse.
	Masturbation	The student will be able to: 1. define masturbation. 2. describe myths about masturbation. 3. list four philosophical positions on masturbation. *4. discuss masturbation with parents.

Grade Level	Unit Title	Objectives
7–12	Homosexuality	The student will be able to: 1. define homosexuality. 2. identify biological, psychoanalytical, environmental, and behavioral theories related to homosexuality. 3. discuss five prevalent societal attitudes that exist toward homosexuality. 4. describe traits common to the homosexual life-style. 5. identify common assumptions about homosexuality. 6. discuss homophobia. 7. discuss legal aspects of homosexuality. *8. discuss homosexuality with parents.
	Intimacy, Marriage, and Parenthood	The student will be able to: 1. define intimacy. 2. identify and describe four types of intimacy—philosophical, psychological, creative, and physical. 3. differentiate between a high-quality relationship, a satisfactory relationship, and a destructive relationship. 4. identify the three components in a I-message. 5. identify and describe nine factors that can be used to make a relationship projection for a successful marriage. 6. discuss renewed growth in relationships and marriage. 7. define and describe divorce and dissolution. 8. identify and describe three options to parenthood. 9. discuss the four types of intimacy—philosophical, psychological, creative, and physical—in the parent-child relationship. 10. list ten things parents can do to achieve high-quality relationships with their children. 11. discuss the effectiveness of each of these disciplinary techniques—preventive discipline, behavior modification, logical-consequences discipline, and physical punishment. 12. identify and describe three types of indicators for each of the four types of child abuse. 13. identify the characteristics of a potentially abusive parent.

Many audiovisual and reading materials can be used to reinforce the concepts for grades K–6 and the performance objectives for grades 7–12. These audiovisual and reading materials should be carefully reviewed by the advisory committee. Some suggested materials are listed in Chapter 22, Suggested Bibliography and Films for Sex Education.

Suggested Bibliography and Films for Sex Education

Implementing the Sex Education Curriculum

Implementing the sex education curriculum begins with (1) teacher training and (2) parent in-service workshops. There are a number of opportunities for teachers to be trained. Many universities have teacher training courses for which teachers can receive graduate credit. These courses may be taught at a university or as a workshop in the field. In addition to courses, the teachers may be trained during an in-service day. A curriculum consultant can train the teachers.

Parents might be sent a notice about the sex education curriculum with an invitation to attend an orientation meeting. At a large gathering, a speaker can acquaint the parents with the scope and sequence of the entire K–12 curriculum. It is important for parents to observe the spiral of learning by grade level.

After the overview, the parents can visit their children's classrooms. The classroom teacher can discuss the specifics of the sex education curriculum with parents:

· When the units will be taught.

· What audiovisual materials and instructional handouts will be used.

· What books the students will read.

· What assignments will be made.

· How the parents will be involved in the learning process.

Parents need reinforcement that they have the primary responsibility for the sex education of their children. The school is assisting by providing age-appropriate learning experiences. The school will emphasize responsible decision making.

Very few, if any, parents will object to their children having this instruction. However, many school districts want to be certain that they have parental approval. They send a notice similar to the one in Figure 72 to parents.

Evaluating the Sex Education Curriculum

When the *Education for Sexuality* Curriculum is implemented in a school district, the advisory committee should plan for a review and evaluation of the program. The review and evaluation should consider each of the ten areas found on the checklist below.

Education for Sexuality Evaluation Checklist

_____   1.   Our parents felt adequately informed and involved in the sex education of their children.

_____   2.   Our teachers felt confident and adequately prepared to teach the units that were assigned to them for their grade levels.

TROY CITY SCHOOLS

_____
(Building)

_____
(Date)

Dear Parents,

During the next several weeks your child's health class will be studying the topic of Human Sexuality. The goal of Troy Schools' program encompasses all of sexuality: feelings about being male or female, attitudes toward family and other interpersonal relationships and the responsibilities associated with these relationships. Just teaching students how their bodies work does not help them deal with their sexuality or with social pressures from peers. Please call_____if you have any questions or concerns. We will be glad to clarify any questions you may have.

If for some reason you feel your child should not participate in these classes, please sign this form and return it to your child's teacher. Your child will be required to participate in all of the activities if the form is not returned.

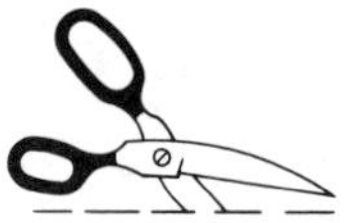

✂ — — — — — — — — — — — — — — — — — —

I have read the notice concerning Human Sexuality and do not want

_____participating in these classes. I understand
(student's name)

that alternate activities have been planned for him/her during this time.

_____
(Parents' signature)

_____
(date)

Figure 72

_____ 3. The units taught at each grade level were age-appropriate for our school district.

_____ 4. The films used reinforced the concepts and objectives identified for the units.

_____ 5. The bibliography of reading materials used reinforced the concepts and objectives identified for the units.

_____ 6. The theme of responsible decision making was evident throughout the instruction of the program.

_____ 7. The students were tested for each concept (K–6) and for performance objectives (7–12) at the completion of each unit.

_____ 8. The students responded favorably to the outcomes of instruction.

_____ 9. The community responded favorably to the outcomes of instruction.

_____ 10. A list of suggested changes for future instruction was prepared.

CHAPTER 14

Sex Education of the Kindergarten Child

The development of certain basic concepts selected to serve as a foundation for sex education throughout the elementary years is an important and interesting objective for the kindergarten teacher. The units that follow are designed to help kindergarten teachers develop a program specifically designed to meet this objective. The three units for kindergarten are: (1) Our Body Parts, (2) All About Me Book, and (3) Animal Families.

Our Body Parts

An Overview of Unit One

During kindergarten, students are quite conscious of the differences between the male and female body parts, but often they are uncomfortable in discussing them. The unit "Our Body Parts" is designed to help them overcome any self-conscious attitudes or hidden curiosity they have concerning the male and female body parts. As a part of this unit, kindergarten students are taken on a bathroom tour to casually but deliberately mention the difference between boys and girls—the penis and the vagina. After returning to the classroom, a review with the naming of all of the body parts is scheduled. The genitals are reviewed with the other body parts. Important concepts developed in this unit are: (1) there are many people and places that help with health at school; (2) there are many body parts; and (3) a boy's body and a girl's body are different.

All About Me

An Overview of Unit Two

Two of the developmental tasks for this age group are: (1) building wholesome attitudes toward one's self as a growing organism and (2) learning to get along with peers. In this unit, the children make a book that illustrates their growth patterns from birth. They examine ways in which their growth patterns are similar or different from those of their peers. They talk about their peer relationships. Important concepts developed in this unit are: (1) there are many changes as we grow; (2) all people are alike in some ways;

(3) all people are different in some ways; (4) some people have handicaps; (5) everyone has many kinds of feelings; and (6) each person is special.

Animal Families

An Overview of Unit Three

Young children are especially interested in animals and their pets. The thoughtful teacher can channel this natural enthusiasm into a pupil-centered learning situation. The students begin the unit "Animal Families" by discussing their own pets and are led into a discussion of animal life in general. As the children play games with animal cutouts they learn the following concepts: (1) life comes from life; (2) life comes from the same kind of life; (3) all animal babies have a father and a mother in the beginning; (4) there are two kinds of life—male and female; and (5) all animal babies grow up to be adults. The kindergarten teacher should be careful to inculcate those concepts that will lay the foundation for future study of reproduction. However, the teacher can be somewhat flexible to allow the children to enjoy their exploration of animals in areas other than life structure. Flexibility will add to class enthusiasm and interest in the unit.

Unit 1:

Our Body Parts

As children enter kindergarten, the teacher should familiarize them with the school building. A building tour can be used to satisfy this need. The children should visit the principal's office, the nurse's office, the gymnasium, the school library, the auditorium, and the art room.

Building Tour[1]

During this tour a teacher can plan stops at both the girls' and boys' restrooms. At this time, the teacher can explain the differences between the boys' and girls' bathrooms—the urinal. The teacher can point out the anatomical differences between boys and girls, explaining that little girls don't use urinals because they have a vagina instead of a penis.

Bathroom Tour

After returning to the classroom the teacher can show the class diagrams of male and female bodies. The children can name the body parts:

Naming Body Parts

head	fingers	vagina
eye	thumbs	buttocks
nose	fingernails	thighs
ear	shoulders	legs
mouth	chest	knees
lips	abdomen	ankles
necks	pelvis	feet
arms	scrotum	toes
elbows	penis	toenails
hands	anus	navel

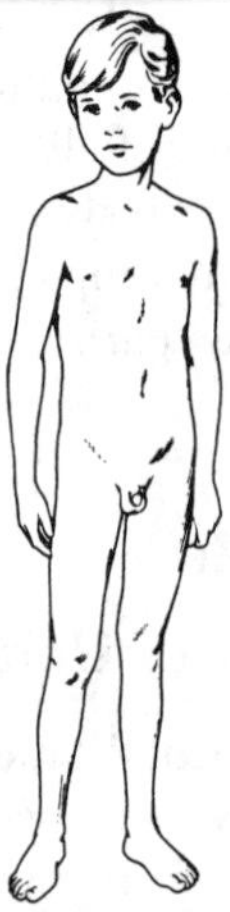

Figure 73
Male child.

Figure 74
Female child.

[1]This activity was taken from "Growth Patterns and Sex Education," *The Journal of School Health*, XXXVII (May 1967), published by the American School Health Association.

Unit 2:

All About Me Book

In this unit, the children will learn about themselves and others by making an "All About Me" booklet. Before beginning the unit, send a letter home to parents. Ask the parents to send in information about their child when the child was small. How many pounds did the child weigh at birth? How many inches long was the child? What was the child's hair color? If possible, have the children bring in a baby picture. Then the children will have information to use in completing the "All About Me Book."

Teacher Directions

The following materials are also needed:

scissors	yardstick
yarn	tape
glue	colored construction paper
staples	

Today we are going to learn about someone who is very special. You know this person very well. You are with this person all the time. This person is *YOU*.

Introduction to All About Me Book

You are going to make a book about yourself. The book will be called the "All About Me Book." You will make the cover for your book first. Make a large picture of your face on the paper I am giving you.

(Display the baby pictures around the room.) Many of you brought pictures of yourself when you were a baby. Let's walk around the room and look at these pictures. How are you just like you were when you were a baby?

Growth

How have you changed? You have changed because you have gotten bigger. You have grown. There are many ways you change as you grow.

You grow taller. How many inches long were you when you were a baby? How tall are you now? (Cut a piece of yarn the length the child was as a baby. Cut a piece of yarn the length the child is now. Attach these two pieces of yarn to a sheet of paper for a page in the book. On the sheet write "I was _____ inches when I was born. Now I am _____ inches tall.)

You have also gained weight. How much did you weigh when you were born? How much do you weigh now? (On the same page write "I weighed _____ pounds when I was born. Now I weigh _____.")

(Use a tape measure to measure the waist and neck, the length of a leg, and the length of an arm. Cut string to these lengths. Attach these to another page. Write "my waist, my neck, my arm, my leg.")

There are still other ways that you have grown. Your hands are larger. Your feet have grown. (Make a page for the book by tracing a hand. Label it "my hands." Make another page with the child's footprint. Label it "my foot.")

Handprints, Footprints

All people grow and change. This is one way you are like others. In what other ways are you like others? Draw a picture that shows one way you are like others.

In Some Ways You Are Like Others

No one is just like you. Mary has freckles. Raymond runs faster than all the other boys his age. Can you tell me one way that you are different from others? (Have the children draw another picture for their book.)

In Some Ways You Are Different

Some people are different because they have a handicap. Persons who have a handicap have something different about their mind or body. A boy without a leg may use a cane to walk. He has a handicap. A girl who cannot hear is deaf. She may have a hearing aid. This boy and this girl have handicaps. Their bodies are different. But they are like you in many other ways.

Handicaps

Some children and grownups learn very slowly. They have a handicap. They are different because they do not learn as easily as others. But they are like you in many other ways.

Do you know anyone with a handicap? What things do you like to do together? How is this person like you?

(Show the class pictures of children's faces that are happy, sad, angry, etc.)

Your Feelings

What can you tell from looking at this child's face? You can tell how this child feels. Everyone has feelings. Sometimes you feel happy. Sometimes you feel sad. Sometimes you feel angry. Draw a picture of yourself being happy. (This picture will be a page in the booklet.)

Draw a picture of yourself sad or angry. Sometimes you may not like the way you feel. A boy your age had a puppy. The puppy was hit by a car. The boy was very sad. He talked about his sad feelings with his mom and dad. You can talk about your feelings with your parents. You can talk with other grownups too.

Now you are going to draw the last picture for your book. I want you to think of something you like about yourself. I like to teach. I think I'm a good teacher. I'll draw a picture of me teaching. What will you draw? What do you like about yourself?

You Are Special

(Staple the All About Me Book together.) Your parents think you are very special. Take your book home and share it with them. (The All About Me Book can be used for a PTA meeting or a Valentine gift for parents.)

Sharing with Parents

Use the following questions for review:

Review Questions

1. What changes occur as you grow?

2. How are you like others?

3. How are you different from others?

4. What is a handicap?

5. What are feelings?

6. What are some feelings you have had?

7. How are you special?

Unit 3:

Animal Families

Lesson 1

For presentation of this unit the teacher may use a large feltboard and felt cutouts of nine different animal families: dog, cat, duck, bear, horse, lion, rabbit, cow, and human. At the end of this unit are simple pictures of these animal families. The teacher may cut these out and use them as patterns.

An alternate way to present this unit might involve a bulletin board with thumb tacks to attach the animals.

As the unit is presented, the different animal families will be placed on the feltboard. Allow the children to place the animals on the animal family board. After each lesson the children will make cutouts for their own animal family board.

Demonstration Guidelines

Today I thought we might talk about our animal friends and their babies.

Our Animal Friends and Their Babies

Some of our animal friends live right at home with us while others live in the zoo.

Our animal friends who live at home with us are called pets; many of you have baby animals for pets.

Our Pets Who Live with Us

How many of you have a pet at home? What kind of pet do you have? *Mary? Sue? Pedro?* (Call on several children to talk about their pets to gain their attention.)

It's fun to talk about our pet animals, isn't it?

Today I brought some pictures of our zoo and some pet animal friends, and we are going to learn about them.

Our animal friends have families just as you and I do. We are going to make an animal family board together to learn about their animal families.

An Animal Family Board

On our board we are going to put the animals in each of the different animal families together.

Before presenting the following unit on animal families have each of the children make a feltboard in miniature. For their feltboards each child will need an empty cigar box, a small amount of contact paper, rubber cement, a roll of colorful binding tape, and a piece of felt no larger than the size of the box cover.

Feltboard in Miniature

Have each child cover the sides and cover of the box top with the contact paper. Next, have each cover the inner face of the box cover with felt. Rubber cement may be used to attach the felt to box cover. Colorful binding tape is used to edge each side and the top of the box. This binding provides extra reinforcement.[2]

Let's begin by talking about a family we all know; in this family is a familiar animal many of us have for pets.

The Dog Family

See if you can guess which animal this is.

---

[2]From Robert Olson, "Feltboard in Miniature," *Grade Teacher,* LXXIX (Oct. 1961), p. 47.

This animal is known as man's and woman's best friend; it barks when a stranger comes near and wags its tail when it sees a friend.

Who knows what this animal is? (*A dog.*)

A dog belongs to a family just as you and I do; a dog belongs to the dog family.

Dogs Belong to a Family

(Show the picture of the puppy.) What do we call a dog when it is a baby? (*A baby dog is called a puppy.*)

How many of you have a puppy?

Listen to this funny story one man wrote about puppies; it might remind you of a puppy you know.

A Story About Puppies

> **I Had a Dog and a Cat**
> by Karl Capek
>
> All puppies are alike; they are all born with the same habits and grow according to the same rules of the game.
>
> They crawl into places where they have no business; make seventy-seven puddles a day; tear people's socks; eat what they ought not to, for instance chairs, strings, soaps, carpets, and fingers; sleep in the basket on the clean washing; cry for help every five minutes; learn to bark; and are quiet only when they are causing some . . . damage.
>
> All this is a . . . law of Nature, valid for all of the puppies in the world.

If you have a puppy, the puppy probably chews your slipper and makes puddles on your rug just as the man in the story said.

Don't be too angry, though. Remember that all puppies are alike in these mischievous ways.

Puppies are alike in another way too; every puppy has a mother and a father. (Place the mother and the father dog on the animal family board.)

All Puppies Have a Mother and a Father

The puppy's mother and father are called parents; all puppies have parents.

All Puppies Have Parents

The mother, the father, and the baby belong to each other. We call them a family.

Would someone like to put the baby puppy alongside the parents on our family board, since they all belong to each other?

Have the children make their own dog family for their animal feltboard in miniature. You can make several patterns for them to use from the picture provided at the end of this unit. While the children are working on their dog families you can ask them questions individually:

Unit Activity: Feltboard in Miniature

- Does a dog belong to a family?
- What is a dog called when it is a baby?
- What mischievous things do dogs do?
- How are all puppies alike?
- What are a puppy's mother and father called?
- What do we call a mother, father, and baby who belong to each other?

Lesson 2

All baby animals belong to a family with a mother and a father.

This probably doesn't seem strange to you, since most children belong to a family with a mother and a father, too.

Let's learn about some other baby animals and their families.

Who knows of a family that has a baby that purrs and plays with yarn? *(The cat family.)*

Come pick out the members of this family. (Allow one of the children to choose the mother, father, and baby animal belonging to the cat family.)

(Holding up the picture of the kitten.) What do we call the baby in this animal family? *(A kitten.)*

A baby kitten's mother is called a tabbycat. (Hold up the picture of the mother cat.)

The baby kitten's father is called a tomcat. (Hold up the picture of the tomcat.)

The mother tabbycat and father tomcat have a baby, so we call them parents.

All mothers and fathers who have a baby are called parents. We will put Mr. Tomcat, Mrs. Tabbycat, and baby kitten close to each other on our animal family board because they are a family and belong together.

Who would like to do this for me?

We will have to put them close together because there will be many families to place on our animal family board.

We already know about two families, and we still have all of these animals and their families left. (Refer to the animal cutouts still not on the animal board.)

There are many, many animal families in the world; let's learn about another animal family.

I will tell you about the family, and let's see if you can guess the name of the family without seeing the picture of the animal.

This family lives in the water. The animals in this family go "quack, quack." They are the . . . (point to a child to guess) *(duck family).*

(Pick a child.) Come show us the mother, the father, and the baby who belong to the duck family. (Place the animals the child has chosen on the animal family board.)

(Ask the class if the child has picked the right animals for the duck family.)

But I wonder how we can be sure that we have picked the right mother and father and baby to belong to each other?

(Ask the child who volunteered to find the family.) Why did you pick this mother, this father, and this baby to belong together as the duck family?

All Animals Belong to a Family with a Mother and a Father

The Cat Family

A Mother and a Father Who Have a Baby Are Called Parents

The Duck Family

Yes, you are right. We know that they are a family because they are so much alike.

Family Members Are Alike

Families are always alike. A mother and a father will always have a baby who is just like them.

A Mother and a Father Have a Baby Like Them

The baby kitten was very much like her mother tabbycat and father tomcat. (Point to them on the animal family board.)

The baby duckling is very much like its parents too. (Refer to them on the animal family board.)

It's very much like its mother duck and very much like its father duck.

How do we know which animals belong to a family? (*Family members are alike.*)

Have each child make a cat and a duck family for the animal feltboard in miniature. You can make several patterns for them to use from the pictures provided at the end of this unit. As the children are working on their cat and duck families you can ask them questions individually:

Unit Activity: Feltboard in Miniature

· What is a cat called when it is a baby?

· What do we call all mothers and fathers who have a baby?

· How can we be sure that we have picked the right mother and father and baby to belong to each other?

Lesson 3

Now that we know that family members are very much alike, it will be easy for us to identify many other families.

Family Members Are All Alike

Let's take the bear family next.

The Bear Family

When a bear is a baby, it is called a cub.

Who can pick out the baby cub for me and show it to the class? (Allow a child to do this.)

Who can pick out the mother bear and the father bear? (Place them on the animal family board.)

How do we know that this one is the cub (point to the picture the child has chosen) and not this one? (Point to the father or mother bear.)

(Allow the children to guess.) You are right. Although the cub looks like its parents we can pick it out easily because it is so much smaller.

A Baby Animal Is Much Smaller than Its Parents

When a cub is born it is so small that it is only the size of its mother's paw; it weighs only one half pound.

Imagine how tiny the cub looks next to the parents. Each of the parents weighs over 600 pounds!

But the cub will weigh 600 pounds when it grows up too.

All babies grow up, and as they grow up they become bigger, just like their parents. (Point to the cub and then to its parents.)

All Babies Grow Up

When they grow bigger and have had many birthdays, they are no longer babies; they are grownups.

Another word for "grownup" is adult; when babies grow up they are adults.

When Babies Grow Up They Are Adults

Your mother was once a baby girl, but she grew up and is an adult now.

Your father was once a baby boy, but he grew up and is an adult now.

This cute little baby cub will grow up too. What will we call the baby cub when it grows up? *(Adult.)*

If you have a pet you probably already know how fast baby animals grow up to be adults.

It seems that whenever we get a kitten or a puppy for a pet in a short time it is grown up.

All animals grow up to be adults. Who can come up to our animal family board and show us an adult animal?

(Allow several children to come and point to the adults. As the child points to an adult animal you will say:) Yes, the tomcat is an adult. He was a kitten when he was a baby, but he grew up.

Have each child make a bear family for the animal feltboard in miniature. You can make several patterns for them to use from the pictures provided at the end of this unit. As the children work on their bear family you can ask them questions individually:

Unit Activity: Feltboard in Miniature

· What is a bear called when it is a baby?

· How big is a cub when it is born?

· Will a cub ever be as big as the parents?

· What is another word for grownup?

· What is a baby cub called after it grows up?

Lesson 4

We know that all baby animals grow up to be adults. Let's meet the horse family and see how its babies grow up to be adults.

The Horse Family

A baby horse is called a foal.

The horse parents, the father stallion (show him) and the mother mare (show her) have two baby foals.

Have one of the children put the mare and the stallion on the family board.

One of their baby foals is a filly (girl) and the other baby is a colt (boy).

When animal babies are born they are either girls or boys.

When a Baby Is Born It Is Either a Boy or a Girl

If the animal baby is a boy we call him a male.

A Boy Baby Is a Male

What is another name for a baby colt? *(Male.)*

What is another name for a baby boy cub? *(Male)*

What is another name for the baby boy kitten? *(Male.)*

A boy is always a male—when he is born, when he is growing, and even when he grows up to be an adult.

Boys Are Always Males

Fathers were born as boy babies; fathers are males too.	**Fathers Are Males Too**
Let's put the baby colt by his father; they are both males. (Pick a child to do this.)	
If a baby animal is a girl she is a female; the baby filly is a female.	**A Girl Baby Is a Female**
What do we call the baby girl kitten? (*Female.*)	
What do we call the baby girl cub? (*Female.*)	
A girl is always a female—when she is born, when she is growing, and even when she grows up to be an adult.	**Girls Are Always Females**
Mothers were born as girl babies; mothers are females too.	**Mothers Are Females Too**
Let's put the baby filly by her mother; they are both females. (Pick a child to do this.)	
In our class we have many boys and girls; this means that there are many males and many females in our class.	
Ask different children whether they are males or females.	
Have each child make a horse family for the animal feltboard in miniature. You can make several patterns for them to use from the pictures provided at the end of this unit:	**Unit Activity: Feltboard in Miniature**
As the children are working on their horse family you can ask them questions individually:	

- What is a horse called when it is a baby?

- What is another name for an animal baby that is a boy?

- What is another name for an animal baby that is a girl?

- Is a mother a male or a female?

- Is a father a male or a female?

Lesson 5

How lucky we are to have males and females, fathers and mothers, girl babies and boy babies, and families for them to belong to.	**The Remaining Families**
Speaking of families we still have all of these families left. (Point to the animals not yet on the animal family board.)	
We will want all of them to be together with their families on our animal family boards.	
Let's put the rest of the animals with their families.	
Who would like to put the deer family together on our animal family board?	**The Deer Family**
Who would like to put the lion family together on our animal family board?	**The Lion Family**
Who would like to put the rabbit family together on our animal family board?	**The Rabbit Family**
Who would like to put the cow family together on our animal family board?	**The Cow Family**

Now that we have learned so much about families, you may have been wondering why it is that animal families are so much like your own.

The Human Animal Family

The truth is that you are an animal too; your family is the human animal family. You have a mother and a father. They are your parents.

We Are Animals Too

(Teaching note: You may want to mention that all children do not live with their mother and father. Some children may not know one or both of their parents.)

Your father and mother are called human beings, and human beings have human babies who grow up to be just like you.

Who would like to put the human animal family on the animal family board?

Now we have all of our animal friends with their families; let's see how much we can remember about animal families.

Activities for Review

To develop the concept that all animals have a family with a mother and a father have the children go through the alphabet and name an animal family for each letter, i.e., antelope family, bear family, cat family, dog family, elephant family.

Animal Family Alphabet

One child is the conductor. (S)he stands behind the chair of the first child in the group. The teacher shows a card with a word or a picture, depending on reading level. If the conductor says the word first (s)he continues to be conductor and moves to the next child. If a child who is seated says the word first, (s)he becomes the conductor.

Streetcar Game[3]

The words to be printed on cards for use in this game are:

animal	parents	horse
friend	cat	colt
pet	kitten	girl
baby	duck	boy
family	bear	male
dog	cub	female
puppy	grownup	lion
mother	adult	rabbit
father	human	cow

Divide the class into two teams. Keep score on the blackboard. Ask them the review questions. You will find these questions at the end of this unit.

A Quiz with Teams

You may use the two-page coloring activity, "Animal Families," to review the concepts the child has learned in this unit. (This two-page coloring activity is included at the end of this unit and may be duplicated for distribution.) Pass the sheets out to the class. You will then read the directions with the child. For example, begin by saying "Color the baby." Point to the three

A Color Reviewing Activity

---

[3]The source for the framework of the streetcar game is: Mary Jackson Ellis and Mayon Atherton, *The First Grade Log,* Vol. I (Minneapolis: T. S. Denison and Co., 1956).

choices. Have the children color the baby. Then read the next set of directions, "Color the parents." You will want to read the directions with the children to make sure that you are testing family concepts and not reading ability. When the children are finished, collect the color drawings and check to see that the children have grasped the concepts. You will want to clear up any mistakes the children have made. After you have started them on the following activity the children will be busy working by themselves. During this time you might pass back their drawings and individually help the children who have made mistakes.

Have the children make cutouts of different animal families for their felt-boards in miniature. Encourage them to make cutouts of animals other than those that have been used already in class. When they have finished, have them show the class their cutouts and tell about the animal family they have made.

Unit Activity: Feltboard in Miniature

It was fun to talk about the cat family, the bear family, the dog family, and all of these other families; it is great fun to talk about our own families too.

A Drawing Activity

I'm going to give each of you a sheet of paper to draw your family. When you have finished, you can tell us about your family.

Reviewing the Unit

1. What are our animal friends who live at home with us called?

Questions for Review

2. What are our animal friends who belong to each other called?

3. In what ways are all puppies alike?

4. What are a baby animal's father and mother called?

5. What do we call all mothers and fathers who have a baby?

6.   How can we be sure that we have picked the right mother, father, and baby to belong to each other?

7. What will a mother and father's baby look like?

8. What do we call a baby when it grows up?

9. How can we tell which animals belong to a family?

10. How can we tell which is the baby animal in a family?

11. When a mother and a father have a baby, what are they called?

12. What do we call a baby when it grows up?

13. When a baby is born it can be either a boy or a ——— ?

14. What can we call a baby animal if it is a boy?

15. Is a boy always a male, even when he grows up?

16. What is another name for a baby animal that is a girl?

17. Is a girl a female when she is growing up?

18. Is a mother bear a female?

19. Do you belong to an animal family?

20. What is the name of the family we all belong to?

Animal Families

COLOR THE BABY

COLOR THE PARENTS

COLOR THE MOTHERS

Figure 75

Figure 76

The Bear Family

Animals can be arranged
on feltboard like this

Figure 77

The Deer Family

Animals can be arranged
on feltboard like this

Figure 78

The Cat Family

Figure 79

The Dog Family

Figure 80

The Rabbit Family

Figure 81

The Duck Family

Figure 82

The Horse Family

Animals can be arranged
on feltboard like this

Figure 83

The Lion Family

Animals can be arranged on feltboard like this

Figure 84

The Cow Family

Animals can be arranged
on feltboard like this

Figure 85

The Human Family

Figures can be arranged
on feltboard like this

Figure 86

CHAPTER 15

Sex Education of the First Grade Child

Children learn basic concepts about love, responsibility, and making choices from their families. It is important that the children recognize what they have learned. They must also realize that all families are not alike. The two first grade units are: (1) Love, Responsibility, and Making Choices and (2) Families.

Love, Responsibility, and Making Choices.

An Overview of Unit One

One of the purposes woven throughout the framework of the K–12 curriculum is to promote loving actions. This unit examines the relationship between love and responsible behavior. The children learn the following concepts: (1) love is a special feeling you have for yourself and others; (2) love is a way of acting; (3) there are many ways to share love; (4) some choices show love more than others; (5) parents who are loving have rules for health and safety; (6) some persons may harm you; and (7) there are ways to protect yourself from strangers and persons who may harm you.

Families

An Overview of Unit Two

Important to the successful development of the child's future interpersonal relationships are the quality of his or her relationships within the family. The first grade teacher helps the child explore the family and family relationships through careful discussions and through developing a family album. These activities help the child learn the following concepts: (1) a family is a group of people who belong together; (2) all mothers have children, but mothers may be different in other ways; (3) all fathers have children, but fathers may be different in other ways; (4) some family members live together in the same house; (5) some family members may not live together all the time; (6) some parents get a divorce; (7) some children have stepparents, stepbrothers, and stepsisters; (8) some children are adopted; (9) some family members have special needs—the aging and the handicapped; (10) family members share love, work, and play.

Unit 1:

Love, Responsibility, and Making Choices

(Show the class a picture of a parent and child hugging. Also show a picture of a grandparent and a child doing something together. Then show a picture of a child playing with a pet. Have the children discuss the pictures.)

What Is Love

Each of these pictures shows love. What is love? (Wait for answers.) Love is a special feeling you have for others. Love is a special feeling you have for yourself.

Love is also something you do. You show love by the way you act. How does the boy show that he loves his dog? He hugs his dog. He feeds his dog. He takes his dog for a walk. He takes care of his dog.

Love and Actions

How do your parents show love for you? Your parents may hug you. Your parents may make dinner for you. Your parents help you keep your clothes clean. Your parents do things because they love you.

What things do you do at home to show your parents you love them? Do you have a pet? How do you show love for your pet? Do you have grandparents? There are ways to show others you love them. You can tell them. You could write your grandmother or grandfather a letter. You could set the table for your parents. You can keep your room clean.

Love is a special feeling you have for yourself. There are things to do to show that you care about yourself. You can take care of your body. You can get plenty of sleep. You can eat healthful foods. You can brush your teeth. What do you do to take care of yourself?

Loving Yourself

Your parents help you take care of yourself. Your parents have rules. A rule is something that tells you how to act. Your parents make rules because they love you.

Parents Have Rules

Your parents may not let you play in the street. This is a rule. It tells you what to do. It keeps you safe.

Your parents may have a set time when you must go to bed. This is a rule. You follow your parents' rule. You get enough sleep. Then you are healthy.

All parents who love their children have rules. Love is a way you feel about others. It is a way you feel about yourself. But love is a way that you act too.

Unfortunately not all people are loving. Some people do not care about others. Some people even hurt others. They may even hurt children.

Some People Are Not Loving

Your parents want you to be safe. They want you to stay away from persons who might harm you. But how do you know who might harm you? Most of the people you know well will not harm you. These are the people in your family and the people your family knows well.

Other people are strangers. A *stranger* is someone you do not know well. Because you do not know a stranger, you do not know if the stranger is nice or cruel. This is why your parents tell you to stay away from strangers.

Your parents make many rules to keep you healthy and safe. They do not want you to be afraid. But they want you to be careful so no one will harm you.

(The following information (pages 219–222) is taken from *Caution Without Fear: A Personal Safety Program.*[1])

Rules to Follow when You Are Away from Home

Children should be made aware that some people might abuse them and even kill them. Explain that these people have sick minds, but they look normal and are often very friendly. Give the children examples of how strangers might approach them; offering candy, toys, or money, having a cute puppy to pet, asking for directions, saying your mother sent them to pick you up, etc. Stress that children should not stop or answer strangers. A stranger could grab a child and quickly put her in the car and drive off. Children should not be out at night and should go with a "buddy" or a group of children even in the daytime. Suggest the children wear a high-powered whistle around their necks on a "break-away" chain that will not choke. Explain that the whistle should be blown loudly if they are threatened with a dangerous situation. Be sure they know how to report anything suspicious about a stranger to the principal, teacher, and parents. The next child the stranger stops may not be wise enough to avoid danger. Discuss with the children the importance of going right home after school. Never go to a friend's house if no adult will be there. Have the children discuss the rules to follow when they are away from home.

Rules to Follow when You Are Away from Home

1. Never go with strangers.

2. Do not go near a stranger's car, even if (s)he is just asking a question.

3. Do not go out after dark unless you are with an adult.

4. Walk to school or other places with a friend or a group of friends.

5. If you are bothered by or see other children bothered by strangers, tell your parents, teachers, principal, and the police.

6. Always have a quarter with you in case you need to call home or the police.

7. Learn to be observant. Be able to describe peculiar people and unusual events.

8. If someone you don't know says your mother sent them to get you, ask them what the "magic word" is. If they don't know, don't go with them; tell an adult.

9. If a motorist drives up and makes remarks, turn and go in the opposite direction. (S)he won't want to make a U-turn and call attention to himself.

10. If your area has Block Parents, find where their homes are where you live.

11. If a stranger bothers you, make lots of noise. Go to the nearest

---

[1]*Caution Without Fear: A Personal Safety Program* (Columbus, Ohio: The Central Ohio Council of Camp Fire, Inc., 1920 Northwest Boulevard, 1982).

house and go in as though you lived there. Tell the people that live there what happened.

Play the Secret Code Game. With younger children a large drawing of the Secret Code Wheel on poster board and the whole group working the message out on a blackboard or a large sheet of paper works well. Older children could work the code out individually.

Secret Code Game

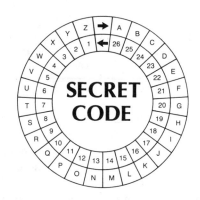

Figure 87

When You Are Away from Home

· 13–22–5–22–9   9–18–23–22   4–18–7–19

· 8–7–9–26–13–20–22–9–8.   23–12   13–12–7

· 20–12   13–22–26–9   26

· 8–7–9–26–13–20–22–9–8   24–26–9.

· 4–26–15–16   4–18–7–19   26   20–9–12–6–11

· 12–21   21–9–18–22–13–23–8.

Discuss the following rules with the children:

Rules to Follow when You Are at Home Alone

1. Lock all doors and windows.

2. Do not open the door for anyone, even a police officer or repairperson. Open the door only for a member of your family.

3. Turn on an outside light.

4. Let neighbors know that you are home alone so they can watch for anything unusual.

5. Know how to use the telephone and follow the Telephone Rules.

6. Play music or television quietly.

7. Occupy yourself. Keep busy.

8. Make sure that the police telephone number and other emergency numbers are in sight, near the phone.

9. If you can't find a telephone number for the police, dial 0 for operator. The operator will get the police for you.

10. If you hear or see something, call a neighbor or the police.

11. Relax. You are safely locked inside. There is no reason to be afraid.

Telephone Rules

1. Answer promptly and politely. Say "Hello." Don't give your name or your family's name.

2. Speak clearly and directly into the telephone mouthpiece.

3. Talk at a moderate rate and volume.

4. Do not tell anyone your parents are not at home. Say "They can't come to the phone right now, may I take a message?"

5. Do not give your address to anyone.

6. Do not talk to others in the room while you are on the phone.

7. Do not stay on the phone longer than necessary. Someone else may be trying to call you.

8. If someone gives you trouble, just hang up. If they are abusive, report the call to your parents and to the police.

9. When asked "What number is this?" reply "What number are you calling?" Never give your phone number over the phone.

10. Never answer personal questions over the telephone.

11. If someone tries to sell you something over the phone, just say "No thank you" and hang up.

12. When you make an emergency call—in case of fire, to the police, etc.—do not hang up until the person you have called has hung up.

13. Never let a stranger into your home to make a phone call, even if (s)he says it's an emergency.

Directions for Emergency Cards

1. Give each child one colored sheet of poster board measuring approximately 5 × 8 inches and 12 popsicle sticks (available at craft shops).

2. Use marking pens and self-adhesive labels to list the Fire, Police, Emergency Squad, Doctor, Mom/Dad work number, Poison Control Center, close neighbor or family member number, I live at _____, and home phone number. (In a real emergency, the child might forget the home address or phone number.) Each label is attached to a popsicle stick.

3. Write in telephone numbers. The children will have to fill in the doctor's, neighbor's, and parents' work numbers at home.

4. Leaving room at the top for a decal or some kind of decoration, glue the sticks to the card.

5. Use a paper punch to make a hole in the top of the card. String the card with bright yarn so it can be hung up.

"What Would You Do If?" Questions

Safety Review Questions

• If you are home alone and a police officer or repairperson comes to your door?

• If a "nice-seeming" stranger stops his or her car and offers you a ride?

• If you are shopping with your mother and you get lost?

• If you see someone trying to get into your home?

• If a stranger says your mother sent him/her to get you, what question do you ask?

• If someone started calling you bad names and tried to pick a fight?

• If you were home alone and a stranger came to the door?

• If you were home alone and you got a phone call that scared you?

• If there was a big dog in your neighborhood who barked at you and scared you?

• If you have to take a test next week and you are scared?

- If you are camping in the woods and you get lost?

- If your little sister or brother eats something that you think is poison?

- If your friend dares you to do something dangerous?

- If a stranger wants you to come over to the car to see something?

- If you are home alone and you hear noises?

- If a stranger says (s)he will give you a nice gift if you ride with him or her?

Safety Problem Solving

(Describe the situation to the class. Discuss the temptation. Discuss the safest way to act. Remember, safe actions follow the rules the children have just learned.)

Situation	Temptation	Safe Action
1. "Magic word": Your mother has told you that your babysitter or another driver will pick you up. She has told you and the babysitter that you'll use a "magic word" technique. The technique works like this. *Before* you get into the car, the driver has to know the magic word. For today, the magic word is _____. If the driver doesn't know the magic word, you don't get into the car.*	No temptation.	*Listen for* the "magic word" before you get in.
2. New toys: You're in the park and a stranger has an interesting-looking toy. The stranger asks you to take a walk to see some more toys and to meet her kids.	New toys. New Friends.	Always play with a buddy. Say "No" to the stranger. Discussion: why would you always play with a buddy or a group, especially when away from home?
3. Telephone: Your mother has gone to the store and the telephone rings. A friendly sounding stranger asks if any adults are home. What do you say?	Chance to talk on the phone.	"My mother can't come to the phone now. Can I take your name and number and have her call you back?" Discussion: Why don't you say, "She's not home?" Why don't you identify yourself or give your address?
4. Following: You're walking to the store and a car slows down. A person asks if you want a ride. Of course you say "No," but (s)he keeps following you. What do you do?	No temptation.	Run to the nearest store or other public place. If none is available, yell for help, turn, and run back the other way, staying out in the open.

Unit 2:

Families

A family is a group of people that belongs together. Each of you belongs to a family. Your family is like other families in some ways. We will talk about the ways your family may be like other families.

Introduction

Your family may be different from other families in some ways too. We will talk about the ways families are different from each other. Then you will know more about your family and about other families.

How many people are in your family? Do all family members live with you? (Respect children's right to privacy if they do not volunteer answers.)

Family Members

One way that families are different is by the number of people in them. A family may have many family members. Here are some names of family members. Have you heard these names?

mother	stepfather
father	stepmother
brother	stepbrother
sister	stepsister

Sometimes your parents are not married anymore. One of your parents may have died. Your parents may have gotten a divorce. A divorce is a legal way to end a marriage. Parents get divorced for many reasons. (Read the children a book about divorce.)

Death and Divorce and the Family

One or both of the parents may get married again to someone else. Then a child may have a stepparent. A *stepmother* is a woman who marries a person's father. A *stepfather* is a man who marries a person's mother. A stepmother or a stepfather may have children. Then a child may have a *stepbrother* or a *stepsister*.

Sometimes a family may adopt a child. To adopt means to take a child of other parents into the family. Sometimes children are adopted when they are born. Other children are adopted when they are older. (Read the children a book about being adopted.)

Adopted Family Members

Draw a picture of all the members of your family.

The children will make a family album with this unit. The materials needed are leather for the cover, yarn to bind the cover, and manila filler paper. Have the children design the cover and title the album "Our Family." The first insert in the album will be the picture the child has drawn of the family.

Unit Activity: Family Album

Some people in your family may have special needs. Maybe you have an older family member living with you. Your grandmother or grandfather may live with you. Or they may live close by. They could also live in a special home for older people.

Older Family Members

Older persons may have special needs. Some older persons walk with a cane. Some may be in a wheelchair. Some may not hear as well as you. You may talk more loudly than usual so they can hear you.

Older family members have many of the same needs as you do. They need someone with whom they can talk. They need other family members to listen. They need to do things and to be helpful. How can you spend time with an older family member?

Draw a picture for your family album of an older family member with you.

Unit Activity: Family Album

Someone in your family may have a handicap. A handicap is when the body or mind works in a different way. A family member may not have a leg. This is a handicap. A family member may not learn as fast

Having a Handicap

as others. This is a handicap. (Give examples of handicaps.) In other ways, these family members are like you. Someone with a handicap needs love too. This family member needs to feel close to you. You can share fun times. What things can you do with one another?

Read the following poem to the class:[2]

Our Home

Our House
by Dorothy Brown Thompson

Our house is small—The lawn and all

Can scarcely hold the flowers;

Yet every bit, the whole of it,

Is precious for it's ours!

From door to door, From roof to floor,

From wall to wall we love it;

We wouldn't change for something strange

One shabby corner of it!

The space complete in cubic feet

From cellar floor to rafter

Just measure right, and not too tight

For us, and friends and laughter!

(Have the children discuss their homes.) A home is where the family lives. A family may live in a house or in a condominium. A family may live in an apartment. Sometimes two families live together. They share a home.

Some children have two homes. They may live with one parent and a family sometimes. Then they may live with the other parent or visit the other parent.

Draw a picture of your home for the family album. You may want to draw two pictures.

Unit Activity: Family Album

A father is a man who has a child. There are many different things that fathers do. They may work to earn money for the family. They may do housework to make the home a nice place in which to live. They may play games with their children. They may help with the housework.

My Father(s)

Draw a picture of your father and/or stepfather for the family album. (Children without a father can draw a male adult friend.)

Unit Activity: Family Album

Have the children give examples of times that mother has scolded them for breaking a rule. Bring out the concept that mothers forgive and love their children all the time. Read the following poem:[3]

My Mother(s)

A Boy's Mother
by James Whitcomb Riley

My mother she's so good to me,

If I was good as I could be,

---

[2]Wilma McFarland, *For a Child* (Philadelphia: Westminister Press, 1947).
[3]James Whitcomb Riley, *Joyful Poems for Children* (New York: Bobbs-Merrill Co., 1946).

I couldn't be as good—no sir!—

Can't any boy be good as her!

She loves me when I'm glad er sad;

She loves me when I'm good er bad

An'; what's a funniest thing, she says

She loves me when she punishes.

I don't like her to punish me—

That don't hurt—but it hurts to see

Her cryin'!—"Nen I Cry; An' nen

We both cry an' be good again.

She loves me when she cuts an' sews

My little cloak an' Sund'y clothes;

An'; when my Pa comes home to tea,

She loves him 'most as much as me.

She laughs an' tells him all I said,

An' grabs me up an' pats my head;

An' I hug her, an' hug my Pa

An' I love him purt' nigh as much as Ma.

A mother is a woman who has a child. There are many different things that mothers do. Mothers may work outside the home to earn money for the family and to have a satisfying career. Mothers may do housework to make the home a nice place in which to live. They may play games with their children. They may help with housework.

Draw a picture of your mother and/or stepmother for the family album. (Children without a mother can draw a female adult friend.)   **Unit Activity: Family Album**

Have the children discuss the following questions about their brothers (stepbrothers):   **My Brother (Stepbrother)**

- Do you have a brother or a stepbrother?

- Is he bigger or smaller than you?

- What kinds of things does he like to do?

- What have you learned from your big brother or stepbrother?

- Have you ever helped your little brother or stepbrother to learn to do new things?

- What do you like best about your brother or stepbrother?

Have the class draw a picture for the family album entitled "My Brother and I" ("My Stepbrother and I").   **Unit Activity: Family Album**

Have the children discuss the following questions about their sisters (stepsisters):   **My Sister (Stepsister)**

- Do you have a sister or a stepsister?

- Is she bigger or smaller than you?

- What kinds of things does she like to do?

- What have you learned from your big sister or stepsister?

- Have you ever helped your little sister or stepsister to do new things?

- What do you like best about your sister or stepsister?

Have the children draw a picture for the family album entitled "My Sister and I" ("My Stepsister and I").

Unit Activity: Family Album

For the discussion of a new family member, bring a baby doll to class. Other materials that are necessary include: diapers, safety pins, powder, wash cloth, towel, small tub, soap, and baby bottle. As you discuss helping parents with the baby, you can show the children how to bathe the baby, how to give the baby a bottle, and how to change the diapers. Emphasis should be placed on helping the new family member.

A New Family Member

Discussion questions for "A New Family Member":

- Do any of you have a baby in your family?

- Is the baby a boy or a girl?

- What "special" things do mothers and fathers have to do for babies?

- Do mothers and fathers sometimes have to spend a lot of time with the baby? Why?

- What things do you like to do for the baby?

- Why does a baby need older brothers and sisters?

Have the class draw a picture for the family album entitled "Baby and I." Those children who do not have a baby in the family can draw a picture of what they think they were like when they were a baby.

Unit Activity: Family Album

Discuss ways that the family works together: cleaning the house, raking leaves, doing dishes, and so forth. Discuss why it is important for everyone to be helpful.

Our Family Works Together

Have the children draw a picture for the family album of the family working together with the title "Being Helpful." Have them copy the following poem for their album:[4]

Unit Activity: Family Album

Being Helpful

I love to help my mother.

Mother loves to help me too.

So now we help each other

To get the work all thru.

I love to help my daddy.

He likes to help me, too.

So I found out that helping

Is the best thing to do.

---

[4]Mary Jackson Ellis, Pearl Esko, and Robert Kane, *The First Grade Log,* Vol. II (Minneapolis: T. S. Denison and Co., 1962).

Preceding the discussion of this topic, the children have discussed sharing work with the family. To introduce the topic of "Family Relationships," begin with the idea that there are many, many things to share with the family other than work. Ask the children what other things they can share with their families.

I am going to give you some examples of things that could happen in any family. Then I would like to have you tell me what you would do to help.

If you have trouble deciding, pretend that you are another member of the family and try to think what kind of help you would like.

Baby brother has knocked over your favorite toy. It is lying on the floor, broken into many pieces. Baby brother starts to cry. What would you do?

Last night father promised that he would take you to the movies tonight. Father comes home tonight looking very tired and weary. Father had a very hard day at work. What would you do?

Younger sister and you have had a very bad fight. Both of you were wrong. Younger sister says, "I'm sorry." What would you do?

Older sister has a chance to go to the lake, but she cannot go unless the dishes are done. She only has a few minutes to get ready and many, many dishes to dry. What would you do?

Older brother has come home with very good grades in school. He tells you about his good grades. What would you do?

Has something special, good or bad, ever happened to you that you wanted to share with your family? How did your family help you?

Have the children draw a picture of their family sharing something special, good or bad, together.

To review the role of different family members have the children make paper-bag puppets of mothers, fathers, sisters, brothers, and babies. Divide the children into groups to give the following puppet shows:

· "The Way Sisters Are"

· "The Way Brothers Are"

· "The Way Mothers Are"

· "The Way Fathers Are"

· "The Way Babies Are"

Ask the children whether there are any other pictures they want to color to include in their album. The children might have some good suggestions for the class. Allow time for them to complete the pictures that were their own ideas.

Family Relationships

Unit Activity: Family Album

Puppet Show

Completing the Family Album

CHAPTER 16

Sex Education of the Second Grade Child

Second grade children are interested in the growth of all living things. They are curious about the origin of life, how new life grows and develops, and how new life is reproduced. Their interest focuses on life itself, not necessarily on reproduction in sexual terms. The second grade teacher's main objective is to give the children an overview of the origin and development of the living things in their surroundings. The two units that follow are designed to accomplish that end.

Seed Experiment

An Overview of Unit One

Second grade children are interested in exploring and manipulating the environment on their own. The second grade unit "The Seed Experiment" allows the children to study the growth and development of different seeds through their own experiments. Art projects and nature walks are added to allow the children to express creativity in their learning. The basic concepts to be developed in this unit are: (1) there are many kinds of seeds from which life begins; (2) the seeds or eggs in a plant are found in the ovary; (3) these seeds need care to grow; (4) each seed grows into the kind of plant from which it came; (5) the bringing about of the birth of a plant of the same kind is called reproduction. This unit is a deliberate effort to present the groundwork for the study of human and animal reproduction.

Living Things That Come from Eggs

As Overview of Unit Two

Upon completion of the seed experiment the children will have developed their first basic concepts of fertilization and will be ready to proceed to a more complex study of reproduction. The unit "Living Things That Come from Eggs" provides a stepping stone from reproduction in animals to reproduction in humans. The teacher uses classroom demonstrations to explain animal reproduction. The following concepts are developed: (1) different kinds of eggs grow into different kinds of animals; (2) living things need only parents

229

to make them; (3) all babies are made by joining a sperm and an egg; (4) eggs must be fertilized before they can grow; and (5) mammal eggs grow in the mother's uterus. The unit capitalizes on the safety of the uterus as a nest for the growth of an egg. The children have a corner in the classroom with the nests of different animals to show the contrast. Thus, reproduction in higher animals is distinguished from reproduction in the lower animals.

Unit 1:

The Seed Experiment

Here is a seed. (Show the children a seed.)   **What Is a Seed?**

A seed is a little plant.

A seed is a little plant that has not yet started to grow.

A seed will grow, though.

We want to find some seeds and watch them grow.

Before we go looking for seeds let's look at some of the seeds we have here on our seed chart.

Let's read the seed story on the seed chart together.

The following poem should be reprinted in large letters on a chart. Beside   **The Seed Story**
each line would be a picture of a seed to show as an example. Also have each of the following seeds to pass around to the children for them to see.

> Seeds are funny things.
>
> Some have stickers; (cottonwood seeds)
>
> Some have wings; (maple seed)
>
> Some are big; (peach seed)
>
> Some are small; (flower seed)
>
> Some are round and flat; (lima bean)
>
> Some are like a ball; (acorn seed)
>
> Some are hidden inside of fruits; (orange seed)
>
> Some are in pods; (sweetpeas)
>
> Some are in roots under the ground; (radish)
>
> Some seeds are food and good to eat; (pumpkin seed)
>
> Corn and beans and fruit for a treat.[1]

Seeds are everywhere!   **Seeds Are Everywhere**

Have the following poem printed on a chart and read it with the children.[2]

> Some little seeds have parachutes
>
> To carry them around.
>
> The winds blow them

---

[1] Mary Jackson Ellis and Mayon Atherton, *The First Grade Log*, Vol. I (Minneapolis: T. S. Denison and Co., 1962).

[2] Ellis, et al., op. cit., Vol. II.

Swish, swish, swish

Then gently lays them on the ground.

Arrange for the class to go on a nature walk. If you cannot arrange for the walk, ask the children to take a walk with their mothers or fathers to look for seeds.

We are going on a walk to look for seeds that lie on the ground.

If we look carefully, we will find many, many seeds outdoors.

There are many seeds indoors too; ask your mother or father to help you find some seeds in the kitchen and bring them to school.

Tomorrow we will plant the seeds that we find.

Allow the children to show the seeds they have brought. Ask them what kinds of seeds they have. If they don't know, tell them. If you don't know, tell the child that you will try to find out what kind of seed it is. Give the child one of your seeds so that (s)he will know what kind of seed (s)he has. The children must know the names of the seeds they plant.

We have many, many kinds of seeds.

Each one of our seeds will grow into the kind of plant it came from.

If we know the kind of plant the seed came from, we will always know what the seed will grow into.

Here is a bean seed; the bean seed will grow into a bean plant.

Here is a grapefruit seed; the grapefruit seed will grow into a grapefruit plant.

Play a game. Each child will stand and say "I have a _____ seed. What will grow from my _____ seed?" The class will guess.

Before we plant our seeds we are going to draw a picture of the kind of plant that it will grow into.

I have a grapefruit seed; I am going to draw a picture of a grapefruit. See Figure 88.

After we finish our pictures we are going to tape the picture to a stick and put the stick in the soil by our seed.

Then we will know for sure what kind of plant is growing.

Pass out paper to the class for their drawings. The paper should be about 4 by 4 inches. Use popsicle or pushup sticks or pencils to support the pictures.

Now we are ready to plant our seeds.[3]

Make a hole with your finger in the soil of your (eggshell, tin can, old cup, flowerpot).

Put your seed into the hole and cover it with soil.

Sprinkle the soil with water and put the seed in the sunlight.

Finding Seeds

What Kinds of Seeds Do We Have?

Activities to Develop the Concept That Life Comes from the Same Kind of Life

Figure 88

_____

[3]Adapted from Millicent Selsam, *Seeds and More Seeds* (New York: Harper & Row, Publishers, 1959).

The sun will shine down into the soil and the water will soak into the seeds; the seeds will grow.

Plan for a "caring" period each day. The children will water their seeds and watch for their growth. Wait until the plants have sprouted through the soil before going on.

We planted many, many kinds of seeds.

Each of our seeds grew into the kind of plant it came from.

Let's make a bulletin board to show what we have learned about seeds.

On the top of our bulletin board we will print, "Every seed grows into the kind of plant it came from."

There are so many different kinds of seeds that each of us will have a job to do.

Decide how much room you will have on your bulletin board for posters. Divide the class into that number of groups. Each group mounts a seed in the upper left-hand corner of their poster. They print the name of the seed under the mounting. In the middle of the poster paper they draw the plant the seed comes from, e.g., grapefruit, lemon, maple tree. In the lower right-hand corner they mount one of the leaves from the plant. They will print the name of the plant under the leaf. See Figure 89.

Seeds Grow into the Kind of Plant They Came from

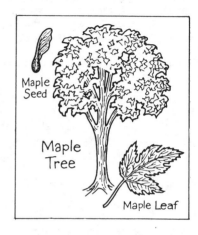

Figure 89

We know that every seed grows into the kind of plant it came from, but where is the seed when it is inside the plant?

Let's see if we can find out where seeds come from.

You will need a flower and a magnifying glass for this teaching activity. (The teacher can use Figure 90 on the overhead projector also.)

Let's look at a flower.

In the flower, just above the point where the flowers join the stem, there is a special place called the *ovary*.

If you want to see the ovary you can pull the petals off the flower.

The ovary is the green thing in the center of the flower.

Inside the ovary are tiny little *eggs*.

If you want to see the eggs you can pull apart the ovary very carefully.

The eggs grow until they become seeds.[4]

Then they stop growing; before they can start growing again they must be placed in the ground.

Sometimes we speak of the ground as mother earth.

The earth is the great mother in the body of which seeds begin to grow to be plants—flowers, vegetables, trees and grain.

Where Do Seeds Come from?

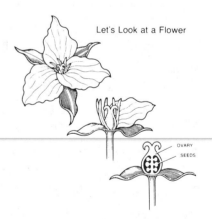

Figure 90

Eggs Grow into Seeds

----

[4]Karl DeSchweinitz, *Growing Up* (New York: The Macmillan Co., 1947).

This bringing about of the birth of a new plant of the same kind is called reproduction.

Reproduction

When a mother plant dies she leaves new seeds.

These seeds grow into more plants.

How lucky we are to have seeds!

Have each child plant a flower seed in a flowerpot for his mother. The children can fingerpaint the flowerpots. Then have each one write a story to his mother about the flower. Have the class work together on the story. You can help them by printing the story on the blackboard. You will want the story to include these concepts:

Review Activity

1. The seed comes from the ovary of the plant.

2. The seed assures us that there will be more of the same kind of plants.

3. The seed will grow to be a plant in the ground.

The explanations the children have for the story will indicate to you whether they are ready for the next unit on eggs, where they come from, and where they grow.

Preparing for the Next Unit

Unit 2:

Living Things That Come from Eggs

Lesson 1

As the lesson is introduced, the teacher holds up pictures of a variety of eggs.

Many, Many Eggs

Eggs, eggs, eggs! White eggs, speckled eggs, tremendous eggs, tiny eggs. Eggs with hard shells and with soft coverings.

How different they are from each other. And no wonder! Because different kinds of eggs grow into different kinds of animals.[5]

Same Kind of Life

You see, life begins in the same way for all these living things. (Show pictures of plant, fish, turtle, frog, bird, dog, cat, human baby).

Life Comes from Life

All these living things began life as an egg—a very tiny egg at that!

Have your class make different kinds of eggs from colored paper or clay. You might allow the children to color some hard-boiled eggs. Put your egg display beneath a bulletin board on a table. Title the bulletin board "Living Things That Come from Eggs." Have the children draw living creatures that come from eggs to put on the board.

Bulletin Board Suggestion

Have you ever copied anything? A picture? A poem? Some words? (Allow for responses.)

An Egg Copies

Everywhere around us we see things that are copies.

Sometimes it takes many, many people to make a copy of something.

---

[5]Millicent Selsam, *All About Eggs* (New York: William R. Scott, Inc., 1952).

Many people and machines are needed to copy nonliving things. (Show pictures of car, truck, house, school.)

Complicated nonliving things are sometimes made in factories. (Have a picture of an assembly line in a factory.)

Stop here for a discussion of the many things made in factories. You might want to have a picture of an automobile factory and a model of a toy car. You can discuss the many complicated parts of a car. Then discuss the number of men and machines that are needed to make cars.

Many, many people are needed to copy a complicated nonliving thing.

A car is not living; many men and machines are needed to make a car.

A truck is not living; many men and machines are needed to make a truck.

A house is not living; many men and machines work together to make a house.

Turtles, cats, dogs, ponies, kittens are living; they have many complicated parts. Who makes them?

Living things only need parents to make them; parents make everything that is necessary for new life to begin.

Father and mother bear make everything that is necessary to make baby bear.

Father and mother cat make everything that is necessary to make baby kitten.

Father and mother dog make everything that is necessary to make baby puppy.

Parents have body parts to make what is necessary to have a baby that is just like them.

(Using a felt board or a blackboard make two column headings, "Mother" and "Father.")

The mother has a body part that makes eggs.

(Put the word "eggs" under the Mother heading.)

You might have already guessed the name of the body part that makes eggs. It is called . . . the ovary.

Put the word "ovary" under the Mother column.

The father has a body part that makes seeds. (Put the word "seeds" under the Father heading.)

The father's body part for making seeds is called the testis. (Put the word "testis" under the Father heading. Have the children repeat the word.)

The father's seeds are called sperms. (Put the word "sperms" under the father heading in place of the word "seeds." Have the children repeat the word "sperm.")

Now we know the names of the two important body parts in parents.

Many Needed to Copy Nonliving Things

Parents Needed to Copy Living Things

Parents' Body Parts

The Ovary

The Testes

Two Important Body Parts

1. What is the mother's body part called? *The ovary* (point to the word on the board).

2. What is the father's body part called? *The testis* (point to the word on the board).

We also know that these body parts make two parts that are necessary to make a baby.   **All Necessary Parts Are Made**

1. What does the mother's ovary make? *(Eggs.)*

2. What does the father's testis make? *(Sperms.)*

Now we can ask, "How is a baby made?"   **Body Parts Must Be Put Together**

First, let us see how factories make things.

In a car factory there are many parts—windows, doors, seats. Can anyone think of any more parts?

All these parts are put together and we have a car. (Allow children to help put a toy car model together.)   **A Car Is Made**

Let us suppose we are in a book factory. What parts do you suppose we'd find there? Pages, cover, pictures. (Have these materials available plus tape and glue.)   **A Book Is Made**

Who can make a book from these parts? (Allow children to construct the book from the parts.)

We would put the pages and pictures together, and we'd have a book.

Now we know how a car and a book are made:

1. To make a car we put together all the necessary parts that are made in a car factory.

2. To make a book we put together all the necessary parts that are made in a book factory.

How do you suppose we make a baby?   **A Baby Is Made**

A baby is made the same way that a book, a car, a doll, and a toy are made; all the necessary parts are put together.

One thing is different though: the only parts that are necessary to make a baby are the egg from the mother and the sperm from the father.   **Only Two Parts**

All babies are made by joining an egg and a sperm.   **The Egg and the Sperm Join**

When an egg from a mother bear and a sperm from a father bear come together, a baby bear is made.

What is made when an egg from a mother cat joins a sperm from a father cat? *(Kitten.)*

What is made when an egg from a mother duck joins a sperm from a father duck? *(Duckling.)*

How is a puppy made? An egg from a mother dog joins with a sperm from a father dog.

Now we know how all living things are made: a sperm joins with an egg.

When you make the following statement, write the words "sperm" and "egg" on the board and then join them to show fertilization. It will look like this:

When a sperm joins an egg, we say that the egg has been fertilized.   **Fertilization**

This is just another way of saying that all the necessary parts are together and that the baby can now start to grow.

Review: This is a good place to end the lesson to review the concepts before   **Review Questions**
going on. Use the review questions and suggestions below.

1. Does life begin the same way for all living things?

2. How do all living things begin life?

3. What will a frog egg grow into?

4. What will a fish egg grow into?

5. Who makes a car?

6. Who makes a truck?

7. Who makes living things?

8. Who makes a puppy?

9. Who makes a kitten?

10. What body part does a mother have in her body?

11. What body part does a father have in his body?

12. How is a car made?

13. How is a book made?

14. How are all babies made?

15. How is a baby bear made?

16. How is a baby fish made?

17. What do we call the egg when the sperm joins together with it?

18. What do we mean when we say the egg is fertilized?

Give each of the children a card with one of the words below written on it.   **Mailman Game**
Tell the children not to show anyone their cards. Have each of the words
below printed on another set of cards. Place the cards in a line across the
chalk tray. Choose a mail deliverer. Each child will come up to ask the mail
deliverer if (s)he has any mail for him/her. Instead of asking for mail with a
name on it (s)he will ask for the word printed on his/her own card. The mail
deliverer must find the card the other child asks for. If (s)he can find the right
card (s)he remains the mail deliverer. If not, the other child becomes the mail
deliverer. Keep playing the game until every child has had a chance to ask

for a word. Also, make sure that several children have a chance to be the mail deliverer. The words to use for the cards:

testis	living
sperm	father
seeds	mother
eggs	ovary
parents	fertilization

Lesson 2

We learned yesterday that a sperm must be joined with an egg in order for a baby to begin.

All living things begin new life in this way.

But for different living things the sperm from the father meets the egg from the mother in different ways.

The way the sperm and egg meet determines where the fertilized egg will grow into new life.

Sometimes the sperm from the father and the eggs from the mother meet in the water; this is where the eggs of most fish have their homes or nests.

Let's see how the father's sperm and the mother's eggs meet.

As you explain the lesson outlined below on fish fertilization to the children, you should demonstrate. For your demonstration you will need a fishbowl with sand and rocks in the bottom. You will also need two clay models of fish. When you are modeling the clay fish, make a small opening under the mother fish's body and a small opening under the father fish's tail. (See Figure 91). Allow your models to harden so that they can be placed in water. Model some very tiny eggs and fill the hole of the mother fish with them. Mold some very tiny sperm and fill the father fish with them. Use different colors of clay for the egg and the sperm so the children can tell the difference between them. You will want to mold the eggs and sperm just prior to the demonstration so that they are soft and pliable. When you are finished cover the holes with invisible scotch tape to keep the eggs and sperm inside the fish. Now you are ready to demonstrate.

(As you present the lesson, begin by demonstrating how fish make nests for their eggs. For this you will need a fishbowl, water, sand, and rocks. To make the nest, place sand in the bottom of the fishbowl. Cover half of the sand with rocks. Fill the fishbowl with water.)

When the nest is complete, you can put the mother fish over the nest; pull the tape off the opening and the mother's eggs will fall in the nest. The mother fish swims away. Now put the father over the nest; pull off the tape and the sperms will fall over the eggs. With your fingers join the sperms and the eggs (illustrating fertilization).

Point out to the children that the fish have left their eggs. Now put models of other sea creatures into the fishbowl. Allow them to attack the eggs, allowing only a few to survive. This illustrates the idea that many fish eggs must be laid to insure the birth of a few new fish because of the low level of protection afforded them.

Sperm Joins Egg

Sperm and Egg Join in Different Ways

Fish Eggs

Demonstration Guidelines

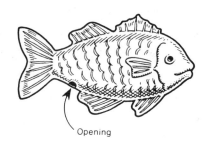

Opening

Figure 91

The mother fish is like all other mothers; she has two ovaries in her body.   **Mother Fish Has Ovaries**

She has many eggs in each ovary waiting to be laid; before she lays them, a nest is made.   **A Nest for the Fish Eggs**

Sometimes the father fish digs a nest for these eggs on the bottom of the pond.

Scoop, scoop, scoop. He scoops up the sand with his tail.

Sometimes the mother fish cleans off a rock or a stone for the nest.

Brush, brush, brush. Mother fish clears a space on a rock or stone for her eggs.

Mother fish releases her eggs into the nest through an opening under her body.   **Mother Fish's Task**

Her job is complete; the eggs are in a nest ready to be met by the sperms.

The eggs must be met by the father's sperms so that they will be fertilized.

When eggs are fertilized they can grow.

As soon as mother fish has laid her eggs, father fish gets ready for his half of the job.   **Father Fish's Task**

Father fish swims over to the nest. He pours his sperms out through an opening under his body near his tail.

His sperms cover the eggs.

When one of the sperms joins one of the eggs, the egg is fertilized.   **Fertilization**

A fertilized egg can grow into a baby fish.

You might think that many, many new fish babies would begin to grow since there were so many sperms and eggs.

Actually, very few new fish babies develop.

You see, the eggs that are fertilized (met by sperm) are not in a very safe nest.   **An Unsafe Nest**

There is not much protection for the eggs while they are growing in the nest in the water.

Many fish and other animals who are very hungry are swimming around looking for something to eat.   **The Hungry Enemies**

They see the eggs. Gobble, gobble, gobble. They are a tasty meal.

Poor fish eggs—some of them never get to grow up to be fish.

The water is not a very safe nest for eggs to grow in.

The eggs of most frogs have their homes in the water too.   **Frog's Eggs**

Let's see how the frog's sperms and eggs meet.

We remember that all mothers have ovaries. Mother frogs have ovaries too.   **Mother Frogs Have Ovaries**

She has many, many eggs in her ovaries. Here is the way she releases the eggs.

Father frog sits on mother frog's back.

He presses his large thumbs against the mother frog's sides. (See Figure 92).

This causes several thousand—that is many, many eggs!—to come out of mother frog.

As the eggs come out of mother frog, father frog pours his sperms over them.

An Unusual Meeting

Figure 92

If one of father frog's sperms reaches and enters one of mother frog's eggs, the egg will be fertilized and begin to grow.

But where will the eggs begin to grow into a frog? Father and mother frog didn't make a nest for the eggs.

The fertilized eggs have no nest in which to grow. They just float around in the water. (See Figure 93).

Some of them grab onto weeds or twigs in the water and grow there. Others begin to grow as they float in the water.

We know that many, many frog eggs begin to grow. Do you think many of the frog eggs grow into frogs?

You are right. Frog eggs aren't any luckier than fish eggs.

Fertilization

Eggs Without a Nest

Figure 93   Fertilized frog eggs.

Many fish and other animals who are very hungry are swimming around looking for something to eat.

They see the frog eggs. Gobble, gobble, gobble. They are a tasty meal.

Poor frog eggs—some of them never get to grow up to be frogs.

The water is not a very safe nest for many kinds of eggs to grow in.

The Hungry Enemy

The Vicious Sea

Activities for Review

Allow children to make a bulletin board with the caption. "The Sea Is a Dangerous Home for Eggs." Cover the bulletin board with blue paper. Select different children to make the following out of construction paper: mother fish, father fish, eggs, sperms, rock nests, sand nests, and hungry enemies. Place these on the bulletin board. Pin light blue plastic over the bulletin board.

Bulletin Board

The nest and its safety is the theme used in this lesson and in the lessons to come. You will want to have an ongoing activity in the classroom where the children can draw conclusions and make comparisons. Shoe box nests for each lesson will suffice to keep this ongoing project.

Shoe Box Nest

Have the children make a display of the sea and the nest for the fish eggs in a shoe box. Choose a corner in the room for the display. As the following lessons are presented, other shoe box displays are put in the corner.

Lesson 3

The following lesson is presented as the teacher demonstrates. You will need a bird's nest, a clay model of a mother bird, a clay model of a father bird, clay sperms and eggs, and a straw 1 inch long.

Demonstration Guidelines

In this lesson it is difficult to show the clay birds actually mating, but you can show the children where the openings in the mother's and father's bodies are. You also will be able to show the tube in the mother bird that leads to the outside of the body. When you are modeling the mother bird, make her opening round enough and long enough so that you can slip the straw into the hole. Also make sure that you make the mother bird's eggs small enough to pass through the straw.

After you have told the children how the sperm meets the egg, you can pull the straw out of the mother bird and show it to the children. You can show them the fertilized egg passing down the tube.

Birds and chickens grow from eggs like the fish and the plants but instead of growing in the water or in the ground, they grow in a nest.[6]   **A New Nest**

The mother hen makes a special nest for her eggs. She gathers straw from the farmyard.   **Mother Hen Makes a Special Nest**

The mother hen then goes looking for little chips of wood and twigs.

She gathers the straw, the wood chips, and the twigs and piles them in a safe place.

The mother hen goes about building a nest.

Twist, turn. Twist, turn. She uses her beak to weave all the pieces together.

At last the nest is done; the mother hen is ready to lay her eggs.   **The Nest Is Done**

Father rooster is close at hand; he knows that the nest is finished.

He begins to make circles around the hen; it's a strange sight!

Squawk! Squawk! Squawk! Father rooster makes a lot of noise.

Finally father rooster jumps on mother hen's back.

He presses his tail feathers very close to the mother hen's tail feathers.

He presses very closely at one spot; this is the spot where the father rooster has a very small hole in his body.   **Two Important Openings**

The hen has a very small hole by her tail feathers too.

The father rooster tries to get his tiny hole right next to the tiny hole in the mother hen.

When the father rooster gets the two holes next to each other, he sends his sperms from a place inside his body through his tiny hole into the hen's tiny hole and to a place inside her body.   **Father's Sperms Pour into the Mother's Body**

---

[6]DeSchweinitz, op. cit.

The mother hen's tiny hole leads to a place where she keeps her eggs.

The sperms from the father rooster meet the eggs.

When one of father rooster's sperms gets inside one of the mother hen's eggs, the egg is fertilized.

Joining of the Sperm and the Egg

The fertilized egg can begin to grow into a baby chick.

The Beginning of a Chick

A hard shell forms over the egg. Lucky egg! The shell will help to keep the egg safe.

A Shell for Protection

After the hard shell covers the egg, the mother hen lays the egg.

The egg goes from the place where eggs are stored in the hen down a little tube which looks like a straw, and drops into the nest. (Use models to demonstrate.)

The Egg Journey

The nest is a safe place for the egg to grow; the baby chick grows inside the egg.

A Safe Nest

The mother hen helps the egg grow by sitting on it to keep it warm.

The baby chick keeps growing, growing, growing.

One day the baby chick is ready to be born. The baby chick breaks the shell with his beak.

A Chick Is Born

The baby chick is born.

Lucky chick eggs—most of them get to grow up to be chickens.

They are much safer in their nest than the fish eggs or the frog eggs.

Figure 94

Activity for Review

Rather than having a committee make a shoe box nest for the display, each child will make a bird's nest this time. You can have them bring twigs and straw and mud to work with. If you have clay available, you can have them model a bird and eggs. If not, the children can use construction paper to do this. As they are working on their nests you can mingle among the children, asking them questions individually to make sure that they have understood the lesson. When their shoe box displays are done, you can put the following poem on the board. The children can copy it. Then they can take their shoe-box nests and poem home to their parents.

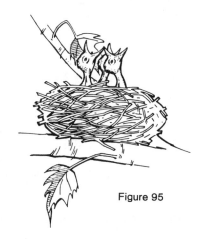

Figure 95

What Robin Told
by George Cooper[7]

How do robins build their nests?

Robin Redbreast told me—

First a wisp of yellow hay

In a pretty round they lay;

Then some shreds of downy floss,

Feathers too, and bits of moss.

Woven with a sweet, sweet song;

This way, that way, and across;

---

[7]Wilma McFarland, *For a Child* (Philadelphia: Westminster Press, 1947).

That's what Robin told me.

Where do robins hide their nests?

Robin Redbreast told me—

Up among the leaves so deep,

Where the sunbeams rarely creep.

Long before the winds are cold,

Long before the leaves are gold,

Bright eyed stars will peep and see

Baby robins—one, two, three;

That's what Robin told me.

Lesson 4

So many different kinds of eggs. Eggs in water, eggs in the sand, rough eggs, smooth eggs, big eggs, and little.

Many Kinds of Eggs

Then outside of the mother's body they break open their shells or coverings; and out come . . . frogs . . . chickens . . . baby robins.

Other animals have babies too. But you never see their eggs at all. Where are they?[8]

The Case of the Missing Eggs

The dog, the elephant, the mouse, and the four-legged animals grow from eggs but they do not grow in the ground or in the water.

They grow up in the nest but the nest is not in the trees or bushes or in the grass.[9]

Let's see if we can find the nest where dog eggs change into puppies.

For the following lesson use pictures of male and female dogs for demonstration. As you present the lesson, point out the different anatomical features. The picture of the male dog should clearly show the penis. The picture of the female dog should clearly show the vaginal opening.

Demonstration Guidelines

Figure 96   Male dog.

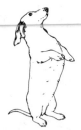

Figure 97   Female dog.

We know where the mother dog keeps her eggs, don't we? Who can tell us? . . . (The mother dog keeps her eggs in the ovary.)

Eggs in the Ovary

If we could see inside the mother dog, we would find a tiny tube leaving the ovary.

A Tube Passageway

---

[8]Selsam, op. cit.
[9]DeSchweinitz, op. cit.

The mother dog's eggs are waiting in the tiny tube for the father dog's sperms.

The mother dog has an opening outside her body that leads inside her body to where she stores her eggs.

Mother Dog's Important Openings

This opening is right by mother's tail. It is called the vagina.

(Have the children repeat the word. Point to the vaginal opening of the female dog in the picture.)

This opening called the vagina is where the father dog's sperms can get inside mother dog to meet with her eggs.

Vagina Leads to Eggs

Do you remember where the father dog's sperms are made? . . . (*The sperms are made in father dog's testes.*)

The father dog's sperms have a long trip to make to meet the mother dog's eggs.

A Long Journey

The father dog has a special part of his body called the penis to help his sperms make this trip.

The Fingerlike Penis Helps

You may have seen the penis of a father dog.

The penis looks like a large finger. It is between the father dog's hind legs. (Point to the penis of the father dog on the drawing.)

When father dog wants his sperms to enter the mother dog, he climbs upon her back.

He puts his penis into mother dog's opening (vagina) and sends many, many, many sperms into her body. This is called mating.

Mating

The sperms have little tails; sperms beat their tails back and forth so they can swim.

The sperms swim to meet the mother dog's eggs. When one of father dog's sperms enters into one of mother dog's eggs, the egg is fertilized.

The Beginning of a Puppy

But instead of the fertilized egg's dropping out of mother dog's body into a soft nest as a mother bird's eggs do, the egg begins growing in a nest inside the mother.

A Nest Inside the Mother

(Show the picture of the puppies growing in the uterus of the mother dog.)

The nest inside the mother dog is a warm, safe place for the egg to grow in. It looks something like a small sac.

It is called the uterus. (Have the children repeat.)

The uterus is the nest where the fertilized egg grows to be a puppy.

When the egg has grown into a puppy, the puppy leaves the mother through an opening by her tail. (*Vagina.*)

Figure 98   Pregnant dog.

The puppy is born. Puppies are lucky!

A Puppy Is Born

The Safest Nest of All

> What better place could there be in which to grow? The eggs which fish lay in nests under the water can be washed away and hurt by storms, and sometimes bird's eggs are broken by being blown out of nests.[10]

---

[10]DeSchweinitz, op. cit.

But nothing like this can happen to an egg that grows up to be a baby inside its mother's uterus.

Here are some pictures of other babies growing inside the uterus of their mother. (Show the pictures of the other baby animals growing in the uterus. Use the animal flashcards at the end of this unit.)

Show the children the picture of the baby calf growing in the cow's uterus. Use Figure 99 with the overhead projector. Have the children work as a class on a story to tell what has happened.

After the children have finished their story they can draw a baby calf beside its mother. The children can read the following poem together.

Review

Figure 99   Pregnant cow.

The New Baby Calf
by Edith Newlin[11]

Buttercup, the cow, had a new baby calf,

a fine baby calf,

a strong baby calf,

Not strong like his mother

But strong for a calf

For this baby calf was so new!

Buttercup licked him with her strong warm tongue,

Buttercup washed him with her strong warm tongue,

Buttercup brushed him with her strong warm tongue.

And the new baby calf liked that.

The new baby calf took a very little walk,

a tiny little walk,

a teeny little walk,

But his long legs wobbled

When he took a little walk,

And the new baby calf fell down.

Buttercup told him with a low soft 'Moo-oo!'

That he was doing very well for one so very new

And she talked very gently, as mother cows do

And the new baby calf liked that!

The new baby calf took another little walk

a little longer walk,

a little stronger walk,

He walked around his mother and he found the place to drink

And the new baby calf liked that!

Buttercup told him with another low moo

That drinking milk from mother was a fine thing to do.

---

[11]May Hill Arbuthnot, *Time for Poetry* (Glenview, Illinois: Scott, Foresman and Co, 1959).

That she had lots of milk for him and for the farmer too.

And the new baby calf liked that!

The new baby calf drank milk every day,

His legs grew so strong that he could run and play,

He learned to eat grass and then grain and hay,

And the big baby calf grew fat!

Lesson 5

We have seen how the eggs of different animals are fertilized and grow into baby animals. (While you are reviewing, show pictures of the following eggs and their nests. You can also have the children refer to their shoe box displays.)	**Many Nests**
The eggs of the fish are fertilized in the water and grow into baby fish in nests of sand or rocks.	**Fish Nest**
The eggs of frogs are fertilized in the water and grow into baby frogs while they hang on twigs in the water.	**Frog Nest**
The eggs of birds are fertilized inside the mother bird and then laid into a nest of twigs and mud to grow into baby birds.	**Bird Nest**
The eggs of dogs are fertilized inside the mother and grow into puppies in a little sac inside the mother called the uterus.	**Dog Nest**
The eggs of horses are fertilized inside the mother and grow into foals in a little sac inside the mother called the uterus.	**Horse Nest**
The eggs of cows are fertilized inside the mother and grow into calves in a little sac inside the mother called the uterus.	**Cow Nest**
Human eggs are fertilized and grow in the same way that dogs', horses', and cows' eggs do.	**Human Nest**
Human eggs are made inside the mother. They are made in the ovary. There are two ovaries inside every woman. In one of these ovaries, a very tiny egg forms.	**Human Eggs**
This egg moves from the ovary into a tube. The egg moves slowly through the tube waiting for the father's sperm to meet it.	
Do you remember where sperm are made in the father?	**Human Sperm**
Yes, the sperm are made in the father's testis. There are two testes in a sac between the father's legs.	
When a mother and a father who love each other decide to have a baby, the father must send his sperm inside the mother to meet the egg.	**Human Mating**
The father has a penis to help his sperm get inside the mother.	
Father puts his penis inside an opening between mother's legs called the vagina. The father's sperm swim out of the penis into the vagina.	
The sperm swims, swims, and swims to meet the egg. Sometimes the sperm do not meet the egg. When a sperm meets an egg, the egg is fertilized.	**Fertilization**

Then all the necessary parts are joined together for a human baby to grow.

The fertilized egg moves all the way through the tube and drops into a special muscle, which is like a nest inside the mother.

Human Nest

Do you know the name of the nest inside the human mother where the egg grows to be a baby? *(Uterus.)*

The fertilized egg grows inside the uterus until the baby is ready to be born.

Birth

When the baby is ready to be born, it passes out of the uterus and through the vagina.

The baby is born. The nest inside a human mother is the safest nest of all.

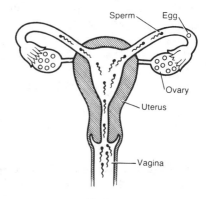

Figure 100

Activities for Review

To review "Living Things That Come From Eggs" that the children have learned, play the animal nest flashcard game using the pictures of mother animals and of fertilized eggs growing into baby animals. (See Figures 101 through 104.) Cut out each of these animals separately, and glue each to a cardboard flashcard. Place all the flashcards showing animal mothers together. Place all the flashcards showing fertilized eggs growing into babies together. Have the children match the cards properly. As they match the mother with the fertilized egg, ask them which father animal fertilized the egg and where the egg will grow into a baby animal.

Animal Nest Game

Example:

- Flashcard? *(Mother cow.)*

- Who fertilized the egg? *(Father cow.)*

- Where is the nest for the egg to grow? *(Inside the mother.)*

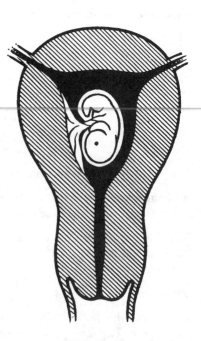

Figure 101

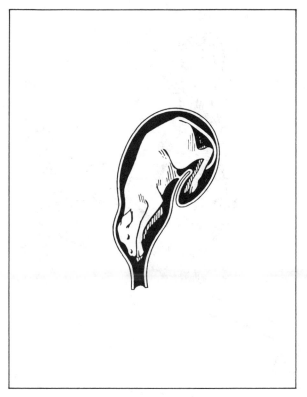

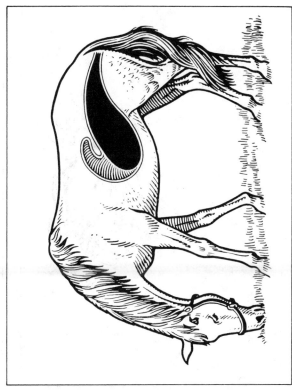

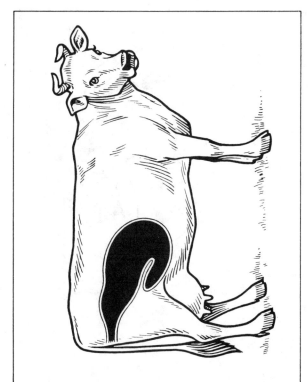

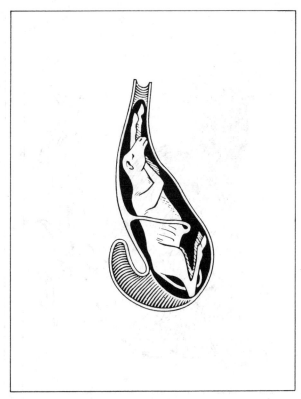

Figure 102

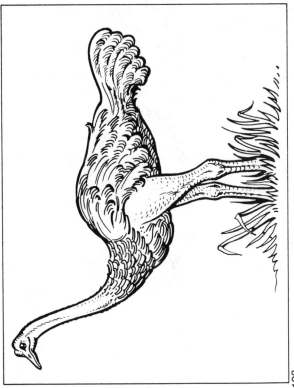

Figure 103

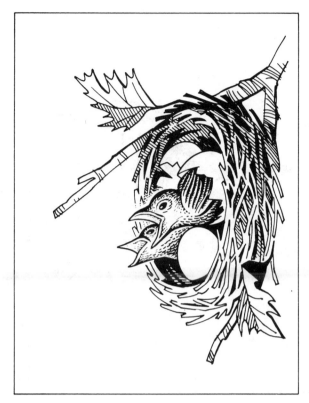

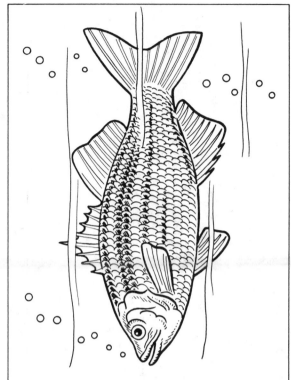

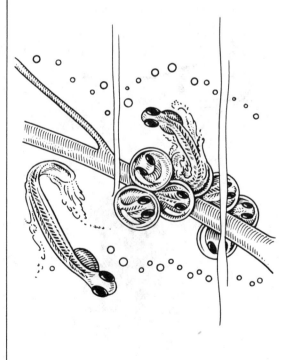

Figure 104

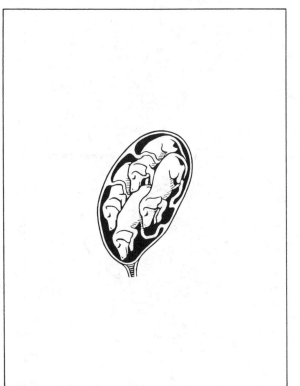

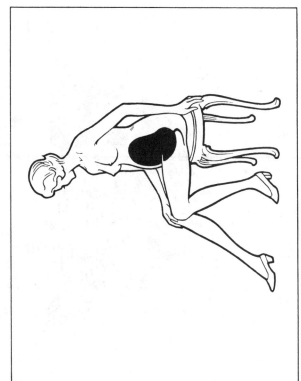

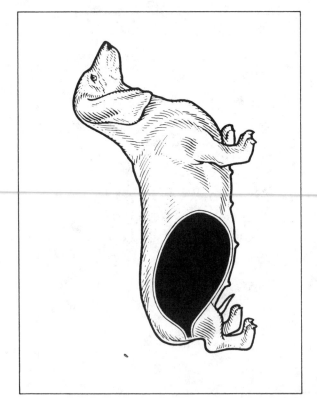

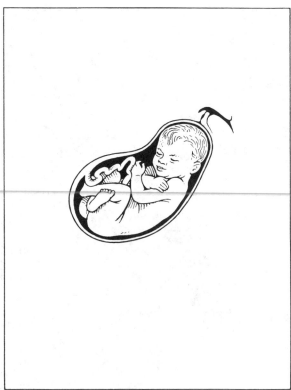

Figure 105

CHAPTER 17

Sex Education of the Third Grade Child

The third grade child is fascinated with the surrounding environment and may spend days, often weeks, in examining and exploring special interests in detail. These interests, coupled with a newly formed attention to interactions with others, provide the third grade teacher with a favorable setting for the development of concepts of sex education. The objectives of the third grade teacher are to explore in depth the development of new life and to assist the third grade child in developing and evaluating interpersonal relationships. In view of this, two units have been planned: (1) Growth of a Chick and (2) Friendship.

Growth of a Chick

An Overview of Unit One

The teacher who plans carefully can develop a unit that encompasses many areas of the curriculum. Reading, art, writing, and mathematics may be carefully woven into the daily curriculum to study the growth of a chick. The teacher can capitalize on this integrated approach, allowing ample time to spend on a 21-day classroom project. The classroom suspense and curiosity in the breeding of baby chicks will afford the third grade teacher numerous opportunities to explain the following concepts: (1) when fertilization occurs, an egg cell from the mother is joined by a sperm cell from the father; (2) an egg cell must be fertilized to grow into a living thing; (3) an animal is an embryo in the earliest stages of development; (4) often preparation is needed for the birth of a new living thing; and (5) a new living thing needs care.

Friendship

An Overview of Unit Two

A child develops successful interpersonal relationships from experiences in a variety of situations, including those experiences with family, with friends, and within the classroom. The third grade unit on friendship recognizes the experiences that can be deliberately planned by the third grade teacher to enhance pupil interaction. Children learn that they must make a concentrated effort to develop qualities and activities that will enhance their interactions with others. They also explore their own abilities and evaluate their success in being a friend to themselves. This unit develops the following attitudes, values, and concepts: (1) self-concept is the feeling a person has about himself/herself; (2) each person needs time alone to develop a positive self-concept; (3) each person needs to have friends; (4) friends should be chosen carefully; (5) there are many friendship skills; (6) sometimes friends disagree; (7) family members (parents) have friends, too.

Unit 1:
Growth of a Chick
Teacher Orientation

The following unit on the fertilization of a hen's egg and its growth to a chicken provides a valuable background for the child on growth and reproduction. The children will be better able to grasp the life concepts involved if their attention is kept by allowing them maximum involvement. For this purpose this unit is organized into several activities that cover a time-span of a short lesson each day for four weeks. A calendar accompanies this unit to allow the teacher to effectively plan the necessary activities.

Introduction to the Teacher

The teacher should arrange ahead of time to purchase fertilized eggs for the classroom experiment. Plan to have them delivered to your classroom on a Wednesday morning.

Purchase of Fertilized Eggs

Construct a homemade incubator for the fertilized eggs. You will need a tub filled with straw, a thermometer, and an infrared light. Place the infrared light beside the fertilized egg or eggs to keep them warm. The thermometer should also be placed beside the eggs so that one can easily see whether the temperature in the tub is being maintained at 100° F.

Constructing a Homemade Incubator

The lessons that follow are coordinated with the 21-day incubation period of the chick egg. The objective of the lessons is for the child to understand how the egg became fertilized and how the egg grew into a chick. In order to have the child grasp the scope of this project (s)he should keep a diary for this 21-day period. The contents of the diary are outlined day by day for the teacher (weekends are not included); see the accompanying "A Calendar of Events: Birth of a Chick."

Classroom Activity: a Diary of Events

Day 1: Introduction to Growth and Reproduction

Place fertilized eggs in an incubator in the classroom. Make sure that you choose an area that is visible to as many of the children as possible.

Demonstration Preparation

Class, we are going to have a special project for the next 21 days. We are going to watch this egg grow into a chick.

Introduction to Classroom Project

You have probably seen eggs that look like this one before. You may have eaten them for breakfast or used them to bake a cake.

But those eggs are not the same as the eggs we have here.

Although both kinds of eggs were laid by a mother hen, there is still a very important difference.

Two Kinds of Eggs

The eggs you buy at a grocery store have not been joined by the father's sperm cells.

Grocery Store Eggs

A Calendar of Events: Birth of a Chick

Monday	Tuesday	Wednesday	Thursday	Friday	Saturday	Sunday
		1 Day 1 diary, eggs in incubator	**2** Day 2 diary, review	**3** Day 3 diary	**4** —	**5** —
6 Day 6 diary, candling the eggs	**7** Day 7 diary	**8** Library reading, film study, bulletin board	**9** Library reading, film study, bulletin board	**10** Library reading, film study, bulletin board	**11**	**12**
13 Day 13 diary	**14** Homemade brooder, feed trough, chick waterer	**15** Homemade brooder, feed trough, chick waterer	**16** Day 16 diary	**17** Poems for diary	**18**	**19**
20 Day 20 diary	**21** Birth diary, naming and caring announcements	**22** Review				

That is why you cannot hatch a chick from an egg that you eat for breakfast or an egg you use to bake a cake.

We know that for new life to begin to grow, an egg cell from the mother must be joined with a sperm cell from the father.

Here is a picture of the mother hen. (Show Figure 106 on an overhead projector.) **Look at the opening under her tail feathers.**

You will see a long tube inside the mother hen. This tube is called the oviduct.

No Sperm—No Chicks

New Life—an Egg, a Sperm

The Mother

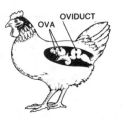

Figure 106   The chicken's egg-laying system.

The oviduct is a long tube inside the mother hen that leads to the mother hen's ova or eggs.

Almost every day in a mother hen's life one of her eggs gathers a lot of food around it and enters the oviduct.

The food that an egg gathers around it is a yellow color. It is called yolk.

Have you ever seen the yolk of an egg? (Crack an egg and show the children the yolk.)

See the little white cloudy spot on the egg yolk? This is called the germspot.

The germspot is a special place on the yolk for a sperm cell.

If no sperm cell from the father rooster is in the germspot, no chick can grow.

The egg will be laid by the mother hen. You will use it to bake a cake or to eat for breakfast.

But we already know that! Let's find out how an egg grows into a chick.

Here is a picture of some sperms from a father rooster. (Show Figure 107 on an overhead projector.) **Sperms are made inside the father rooster.**

The father rooster wants his sperms to get inside the mother hen so her egg will grow into a chick and will not be a breakfast egg.

The Long Oviduct

An Egg in the Oviduct

Gathering Food for the Trip

The Yolk of an Egg

Germspot—a Cloudy Spot

A Special Place for Sperm

Father Rooster's Sperm

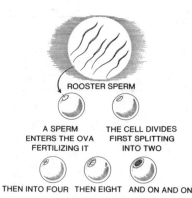

Figure 107   How fertilization begins.

[1]Figures 106 and 107 adapted from Louis Darling, *Chickens and How to Raise Them* (New York: William Morrow & Co., 1955).

Father rooster has a hole beneath his tail feathers too.

Beneath the Tail Feathers

He makes a lot of squawking noises and circles around mother hen to get her attention.

The father rooster then presses the opening beneath his tail feathers against the opening beneath the mother hen's tail feathers.

The Two Openings Meet

When the two openings are touching, the father rooster sends many, many sperms into the mother hen.

Father Rooster Sends Sperm into the Hen

The sperms are now in the oviduct. They will swim toward the egg.

Sperms Swim toward Egg

One of the sperms will meet with the egg. Do you remember where the sperm will meet the egg? (*The germspot.*)

Now the germspot on the egg can start growing into a chick.

Germspot Starts to Grow

The hen makes a very comfortable nest for the egg to grow into a chick. The nest is made of straw and twigs.

A Nest for the Egg

When the nest is done, the mother hen will lay the egg. It will pass down the oviduct and come out of the hole beneath the hen's tail feathers.

As the egg comes down the oviduct, it is surrounded by egg white. You have probably seen the white of an egg. (Use Figure 108 on an overhead projector.)

Egg White Surrounds the Egg

Then two sacs form a cover around the egg. At last a hard shell covers the egg.

Two Sacs and a Shell

The egg is well protected when it comes out of the hole beneath the mother hen's tail feathers and is laid into the nest.

A Well Protected Egg

The egg will have a lot of growing to do before it can become a chick. It will grow for 21 days.

21 Days of Growing

Have each of the children make a calendar. They can decorate their calendars by drawing a chick at the top.

Calendar Activity

Explain to the children that the class is going to carefully observe the growth of the chick. Each student is going to keep a record of happenings in a diary called "Egg to Chick."

Class Activity: a Diary of Events

Give each child materials to make a diary: leather and yarn for a cover, construction paper for inserts. Have them design a cover carefully.

For the first day in the diary have the children draw a picture of the mother hen showing her oviduct and some eggs. Then have the children draw a picture of the sperms, which come from the father rooster. Last, in the classroom, have the children draw a picture of the nest that has the egg in it.

Diary of Events: Day 1 Contents

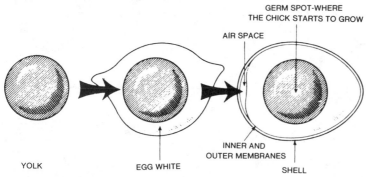

Figure 108　Development of an egg.

A magic change begins in the egg when it is kept warm. Most of the time an egg is kept warm by the mother hen.

The mother hen sits on the eggs to keep them warm. Our eggs are warm too.

We are keeping our eggs in an incubator. An incubator is a warm nest that is a substitute for the mother hen.

We don't need the mother hen to keep our eggs warm because they are in the incubator.

Lesson for Day 1

A Warm Substitute

Figure 109   Classroom incubator.

When the eggs are kept warm, the germspot starts to grow. It will take the form of a baby chick in a day or two. (Use Figure 110).

The Germspot Grows

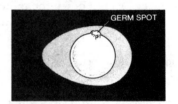

Figure 110   Growth of a chick—Day 1.

Have the children make a page for their diary numbered "day 1." The diary recording should include:

Recording the Events in the Diary

1. An explanation of how an egg is fertilized.

2. An explanation of the protective coatings the egg gathers.

3. An explanation of how an egg is laid.

4. An explanation of the beginning of growth in the egg.

Lesson for Day 2

List the following sentences on the board. Have the children put these sentences in the right order.

Reviewing the Lesson for Day 1

1. The rooster sends his sperm into the hen.

2. The egg is kept warm.

3. The egg begins to grow into a chick.

4. The hen makes an egg.

5. A yolk covers the egg.

6. A shell covers the egg.

7.   The hen lays the egg.

8.   White covers the yolk of the egg.

Let's learn what is happening in our egg today. (Put Figure 111 of the sac forming around the yolk on the overhead projector.)

When the egg has been growing for two days, a sac-like skin grows around the yolk.

This sac is attached to the stomach of the chick. This is how the chick gets its food.

Lesson for Day 2

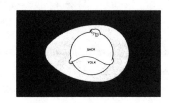

Figure 111   Growth of a chick—Day 2.

Have the children make a page for their diary numbered "day 2." The diary recording should include:

1.   An explanation of the formation of a sac-like structure.

2.   An illustration of the diagram projected for the class.

Recording the Events in the Diary

Lesson for Day 3

Have the children subtract today's date from the date that the chickens will hatch to find out how many days remain.

Who can tell the class how many days the chick has been growing in the egg? *(Three days.)*

Let's take a look to see how our chick is coming along. (Show overhead Figure 112 for day 3.)

Now that the egg has been growing for three days, we can notice many changes.

Calendar Activity

Lesson for Day 3

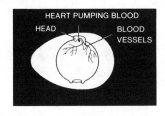

Figure 112   Growth of a chick—Day 3.

Look at the sac we talked about yesterday. The sac completely surrounds the yolk today.

Look at all the red tubes that are going from the yolk to the chick. Do you know what these red tubes are? You have them in your body. *(Blood vessels.)*

Yes, they are blood vessels. The blood vessels carry blood with food from the yolk to the growing chick.

We said that the yolk and the white were going to help the egg grow into a chick. Do you know how?

The yolk and the white are the food the growing chick is using.

The chick needs a lot of food. It's beginning to take shape and look more like a chick.

We call the chick an embryo when it begins to take shape.

Sac Surrounds the Yolk

Red Tubes Bring Food

Embryo—Chick Takes Shape

Look carefully at the chick embryo, and you will see that a head is starting to form.

At the end of three days the chick has a head, it has many blood vessels, and it has a heart.

Have the children make a page for their diary numbered "day 3." The diary recording should include:

1. A picture of the embryo after three days.

2. A description of the embryo after three days.

Lesson for Day 6

Have the children subtract today's date from the date that the chickens will hatch to find out how many days remain.

Now our egg has been growing for six days. It needs more and more food.

That is why there are so many more blood vessels. These extra blood vessels covering the yolk are bringing more food to the growing chick. (Show Figure 113 for day 6 on the overhead projector.)

The chick has grown a great deal. What can we see now?

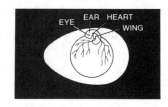

Figure 113   Growth of a chick—Day 4.

1. A wing.

2. An ear.

3. The heart.

4. An eye.

On the sixth day your class should examine the egg or eggs to see whether the chicks are developing. The process for examining the chick is called "candling." (Use Figure 114 in the overhead projector.)

To see what is going on inside the egg, candle it. Cut an oval hole a little smaller than the egg in a piece of black paper or cardboard. Hold the cardboard over a strong light. Place the egg in the hole. You will find that you can see the shape of the growing chick quite well.

There will be a small dark spot in the center of the egg with a network of fine lines radiating from it. The dark spot is the beginning of a chick, and the lines in the network are blood vessels, which are bringing food from the yolk to it so that it can grow. If the egg is not good, there will be no definite lines or shapes in it, and it should be thrown away. When you are candling eggs, do not keep them away from the hen too long or let them become chilled.[2]

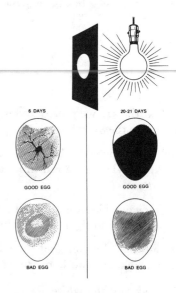

Figure 114   Candling an egg.

---

[2]From Darling, op. cit.

Have the children make a page for their diary numbered "day 6." The diary recording should include:

Recording the Events in the Diary

1. A picture of the embryo after six days.

2. A description of the embryo after six days.

3. An explanation of candling.

Lesson for Day 7

The embryo has been growing for one week now. At last it has begun to take the shape of a baby bird.

Lesson for Day 7

If we look closely at the chick embryo (show Figure 115 for day 7 on the overhead projector)**, we can see that it has all its body parts.**

Name the parts of the chick that you see:

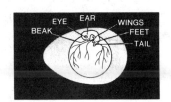

Figure 115   Growth of a chick—Day 7.

Tail	Ear
Beak	Eye
Wings	Feet

Have the children make a page for their diary numbered "day 7." The diary recording should include:

Recording the Events in the Diary

1. A picture of the embryo after seven days.

2. A description of the embryo after seven days.

Have the children subtract today's date from the date that the chickens will hatch to find out how many days remain.

Calendar Activity

Lessons for Day 8, 9, and 10

During the next three-day period the children will be exposed to outside materials and activities related to their project. Below are some suggested activities. Perhaps your students will have some additional ideas of their own.

Teacher Orientation

Assemble a collection of library books for the children to read. There are many books available on eggs and chickens for this purpose. These books are listed in the Suggested Bibliography and Films for Sex Education. In addition to books on eggs and chickens, gather books on the development of eggs in other animals. Allow the children to read during class.

Library Reading

Perhaps you would like to show one of the many films listed under Suggested Audiovisuals for Sex Education. This serves as a useful review for the children.

Film Study

Have the children plan a bulletin board for the classroom. Allow the children to decide what they would like to have on this bulletin board. Have the class decide how they are going to divide the responsibilities so that each child will have a job to do.

Bulletin Board

Have the children make pages in their diary numbered "day 8," "day 9," and "day 10," The children will have participated in different learning experiences on these three days. They should record in their diary what they have learned from the outside material they consulted.

Recording the Events in the Diary

Lesson for Day 13

After 13 days have passed the unborn chick is quite well formed. (Show Figure 116, the 13-day-old embryo, on the overhead projector.)

The chick has been growing and growing and using up its supply of food.

The growing chick embryo has used almost all the white of the egg.

Some of the white still remains. It is still enclosed in a sac connected to the stomach of the chick.

This yolk will be used by the chick in the final growing days. Let's find out how many growing days are left.

Have the children subtract today's date from the date that the chickens will hatch to find out how many days remain.

Have the children make a page for their diary numbered "day 13." The diary recording should include:

1.   An illustration of the embryo after 13 days.

2.   A description of the food that remains after this 13-day growing period.

Lesson for Day 13

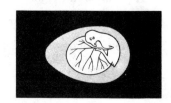

Figure 116   Growth of a chick—Day 13.

Calendar Activity

Recording the Events in the Diary

Lessons for Days 14 and 15: Preparation for the Birth of the Chickens

Young chicks are hard to raise and require a great deal of care. Explain to the children that the class will need to prepare for the birth of the chickens. The class should prepare a comfortable home for the chicks to replace the nest. (See Figure 117.)

> The younger chicks are hard to raise and require a great deal of care. They must be kept warm with artifical heat from 4–6 weeks. A heater for this purpose, called a brooder, can be made from two big cardboard boxes and an electric light. Infrared bulbs, which are especially good for brooders, can be bought at most hardware stores and from mail order houses. The bulb should be big enough to keep the temperature at about 90° F.[3]

Homemade Brooder

The homemade brooder should be placed in a large crate with litter covering the floor. The litter can be bought at a feed store. Litter can also be made from dried grass, clippings, dry leaves, chopped hay, shavings, or sawdust. You will also want to place a chick waterer and feed trough in the crate. Below are diagrams showing how to make them. Allow the children to make them.

A Home for the Chicks

Many different kinds of feed are sold to persons planning to raise chickens. Feed is available at feed stores and at your local market. You will need two kinds of feed—scratch and mash.

Purchasing Feed for the Chicks[4]

Mash is a combination of cod liver oil; meat scraps; alfalfa; fish; and ground corn, wheat, and oats. Three types of mash can be purchased: starting, growing, and laying mash. Purchase starting mash for the chicks for the first five to six weeks; then switch to growing mash until they are four months old.

---

[3]Figures 118, 119, and 120 and accompanying text adapted from Darling, op. cit.
[4]Adapted from Darling, op. cit.

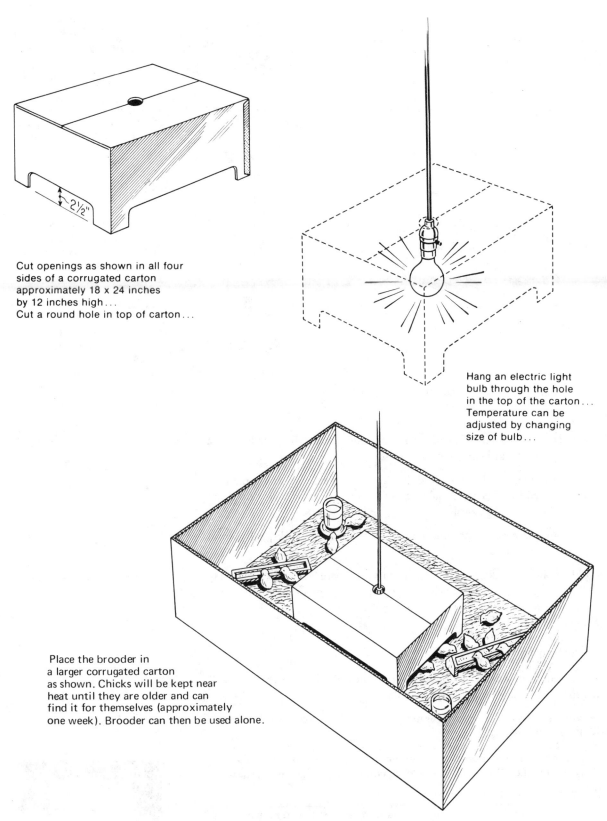

Cut openings as shown in all four
sides of a corrugated carton
approximately 18 x 24 inches
by 12 inches high...
Cut a round hole in top of carton...

Hang an electric light
bulb through the hole
in the top of the carton...
Temperature can be
adjusted by changing
size of bulb...

Place the brooder in
a larger corrugated carton
as shown. Chicks will be kept near
heat until they are older and can
find it for themselves (approximately
one week). Brooder can then be used alone.

Figure 117   A brooder for chicks.

Cut hole in metal jar lid . . .

Attach short lengths of wood
to lid as shown . . .

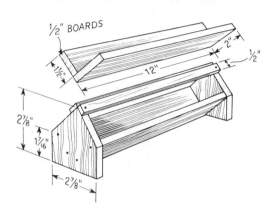

½" BOARDS

2"

½"

12"

1½"

2⅞"

1⁷⁄₁₆"

2⅞"

Figure 118 Chick feed trough.

Fill jar with water
and screw on lid.
Hold small pie pan or dish,
upside down, against wood . . .
Turn over quickly.

Figure 119 Chick waterer.

Scratch feed is a combination of corn, oats, and wheat. Intermediate size scratch is fed to the growing chicks.

In addition to mash and scratch feed, purchase some calcium and some grit. Calcium is used by the hen to make eggshells, and grit is used to help grind the food in the chicks' gizzards.

If you should need additional information on feeding the chicks, call a local feed store or veterinarian.

Have the children make pages for their diary numbered "day 14" and "day 15." The diary record should include a description of the preparations being made for the birth of the chicks.

Recording the Events in the Diary

Lesson for Day 16

Have the children subtract today's date from the date that the chickens will hatch to find out how many days remain.

Calendar Activity

The chick embryo has been growing 16 days. There are only five more days before the egg hatches.

Lesson for Day 16

You can see that as the chick embryo grows, more and more of the yolk is used. (Show Figure 120, the 16-day-old embryo, on the overhead projector.)

The chick has really taken shape. See how nicely its feathers are growing.

Figure 120 Growth of a chick—Day 16.

Have the children make a page in their diary numbered "day 16." They diary recording should include:

Recording the Events in the Diary

1. An illustration of the 16-day-old embryo.

2. A description of the embryo after 16 days of growing.

Lesson for Day 17

Have the children write stories and poems about chickens for their diaries. Some of these stories and poems can be placed on a bulletin board in the classroom.

Poems for the Diary

Lesson for Day 20

Have the children subtract today's date from the date that the chickens will hatch to find out how many days remain.

Calendar Activity

Only one day is left until our chicken will pop out of the egg to come out into the world.

Lesson for Day 20

The growing chick is making its last-minute preparations. Do you remember when we said earlier that the special sac was so important for food?

Now the sac begins to pull the remaining yolk into the chick's stomach. (Show the illustration of the 20-day-old embryo; Figure 122.)

This will fill up the chick's stomach so that the chick will have enough food in its stomach for two days after it is born.

The chick is starting to breathe now. Air comes through very small holes in the shell of the egg.

Have the children make a page in their diary numbered "day 20." The diary recording should include:

Recording the Events in the Diary

1. An illustration of the 20-day-old embryo.

2. A description of the embryo after 20 days of growing.

Lesson for Day 21: the Birth of the Chicks

Have the children subtract today's date from the date that the chickens will hatch to find out how many days remain.

Calendar Activity

The 21 days that the chick grows inside the shell are over. We have to keep a close watch on the nest now.

Lesson for Day 21

Figure 121   Growth of a chick—Day 19.

Figure 122   Growth of a chick—Day 20.

The first sign that the chick is ready to be hatched is a tapping sound coming from the egg.

Birth of the Chick

The little chicks have a tiny, hard point right on the end of the bill.

The Egg Tooth

This tiny, hard point is called an egg tooth. The chick uses the egg tooth to tap against the shell.

Tap, tap, tap. The chicken pecks at the shell. (Show the illustration of the 21-day-old chick breaking the shell, Figure 123.)

The chicken taps for a while and then rests a while. By tapping the inside of the eggshell the chick can break it.

Figure 123   Growth of a chick—Day 21.

It takes about four hours for the chick to break the eggshell. Then at last the chick comes out of the egg slowly.

Four-Hour Birth

The chick is very weak from all its tapping. The chick is also very wet from being inside the egg.

After three hours the chick dries out and is a fluffy yellow chick, which needs a lot of care.

For the first week of its life a chick must be kept very warm. Usually the chicks stay under the mother hen just as you curl under your soft blanket on a cold night.

Keeping the Chick Warm

We made a brooder for our chicks. The brooder is a warm place for the chicks to crawl into.

The Warm Brooder

The chicks will soon need food. Chicks eat mash. Mash looks like the cereal you eat for breakfast.

Mash Is Like Cereal

If we keep our chicks well fed and warm, they will grow up.

Chicks Grow Up

Some of the chickens will grow up to be father roosters. Other chickens will grow up to be mother hens.

More Roosters—More Hens

Then a father rooster and mother hen can get together and have more chicks.

More Chicks!

Have the children make a page in their diaries called "The Chick's Birthday." The diary recording should include:

Recording the Events in the Diary

1. A description of the birth of the chick.

2. A drawing of the newborn chick.

Have the class decide upon a name for the chick or chicks. Then have the class decide how they would like to divide the responsibility of caring for the chicks.

Naming and Caring for the Chick

Have the children make birth announcements, announcing the birth of the chicks and inviting the rest of the school to see the chicks. These can be sent to the principal, nurse, librarian, and other classrooms.

Announcing the Chick's Birth

Reviewing the Unit

1. How does all animal life begin?
2. Where does an egg come from?
3. What is the oviduct?

Questions for Review

4. What is the name of the yellow food that gathers around the egg?
5. What is the germspot?
6. What is the difference between a breakfast egg and an egg that will grow into a chick?
7. How do the father rooster's sperms get into the mother hen?
8. What part of the egg starts to grow into a chick?
9. What protective coverings does the egg gather as it comes down the oviduct?
10. How long does it take for an egg to grow into a chick?
11. What are two ways of keeping the eggs warm?
12. When the egg has been growing for two days, what grows around the yolk?
13. Why does the chick have red tubes coming to it from the yolk?
14. What do we call a chick when it begins to take shape?
15. How do you candle an egg?
16. What happens to the yolk the day before a chicken is hatched?
17. How does the chicken get air to breathe before it is hatched?
18. What is the first sign that a chick is ready to hatch?
19. What part of the chick helps it to break the eggshell?
20. How long does it take the chick to break the eggshell?
21. What does the chick look like when it finally comes out of the eggshell?
22. How does a chick stay warm when it is first born?
23. What do baby chicks eat?
24. When the chicks grow up what will they be?
25. If there are more hens and more roosters there will be more _____.

Unit 2:

Friendship

Let's pretend that all of you are coming to my house for dinner tonight. I don't know what to serve for dinner, so I'm going to make a list on the board of what you would like to eat.

My, we have a long list, don't we? If I serve all these different foods I can make each one of you happy.

When you make someone else happy, you are usually happy yourself. That is why it is so important to make others happy—both of you will benefit.

Let's make another list. This time we'll pretend that you are going to someone's house after school.

You may choose any play activity you want with your friend. What would you choose?

(List the activities on the board. Make a long list with many varieties of activities.)

Now let's review our list. We know that to make others happy we like to share play activities of their choosing.

I'll read down the list of activities, and you can mark down a point for yourself each time I name an activity you like to do and know how to do.

Introduction

Making Others Happy

You can look at your number of marks and evaluate the number of interests you share with your classmates. How many of your classmates could you share something with?

One of the best ways to make new friends is to share common interests with them. Expressing a sincere interest in the activities of others lets them know that we would like to have them as our friends.

(Have each child bring to class the necessary equipment or toys (s)he needs to demonstrate an activity (s)he enjoys. Divide the class into groups, allowing each child to get a "taste" of some activities with which (s)he is not already familiar.)

A "Tasting" Party

We have learned many new activities to share with our friends. As we grow we will keep learning and improving ourselves until we have many interests and abilities.

Solitary Activities

Boys and girls who have many interests and abilities, numerous likes and few dislikes, will have many friends to choose from. They will certainly have many good times.

There are times, though, when friends aren't around. It's really important to know how to be a friend to yourself.

Stop and think of the last time you were alone. Did you find many interests to occupy your time?

(Discuss hobbies: What are they: What are different types of hobbies? Why are hobbies important? Have the children tell about their hobbies and plan new hobbies for the year.)

Class Discussion

We have been learning about the interests and activities of our friends. We learned that boys and girls who have many interests and abilities, numerous likes, and few dislikes will have many friends from which to choose.

But interests and abilities are not the only characteristics of good friends. There are many personal characteristics that people have that make them better friends.

Personal Friendship Qualities

I like a friend to whom I can tell a secret and who will never tell anyone else. What kind of a friend do you like?

(Have the children name several personal characteristics involved in forming friendships.)

Class Discussion

There is an old saying, "To have a friend you must be a friend."

We have named many important qualities that good friends have. To be a good friend we must work very hard to have all the qualities we mentioned.

Let's write a list of friendship qualities and keep it in our desk drawer. Each day before we go home from school we'll look at our list and ask ourselves how hard we are trying to be a friend to others.

Class Activity

Of course you'll want to keep your list to yourself because it is very personal, but if you are working hard to be a good friend, others will certainly know it.

Sometimes friends have a difference in how they think or how they feel. This difference is called a disagreement. All friends have disagreements from time to time.

Disagreeing with Friends

When you have a disagreement with a friend, try to think of ways to work it out. Talk with your friend. Tell your friend exactly how you feel. Listen to your friend's feelings.

Let's discuss a disagreement. Kristen and Meg are friends. They play after school. They often go to Kristen's house to play school. Kristen is usually the teacher. One day Meg does not go over to Kristen's house. Kristen calls her. Meg says, "I *always* come to your house. And you are always the teacher. I'd rather roller-skate or play at my house." Meg sounds angry. Kristen is hurt. What can these friends do?

Friends and Your Family

Everyone needs friends. If you have brothers and sisters, they have friends. Your parents have friends too.

Sometimes you want to be alone with your friends. You may play in the basement or bedroom and shut the door. Other family members need to be alone at times also. Your parents may want to talk alone with a friend.

Your parents may want to talk to a friend on the telephone. When they do, they need to listen to their friend. They cannot listen to you at the same time. Wait until they are off the phone until you talk with them.

Your Parents and Your Friends

Sometimes your parents like some of your friends more than others. They like friends that have good manners. They like friends that follow rules to be healthy. They like friends that follow rules to be safe. They want you to choose friends carefully.

Here is a list of children with whom you could play. Which ones would your parents like you to have as friends?

1. Miguél follows his parents' rules. He does not play in a field in which your parents have told you not to play.

2. Tyrone is fun. He is a good baseball player. He uses dirty words that you are not allowed to use.

3. Jessica talks back to her parents and to other adults.

4. Susan has good manners. She shares her games with you.

CHAPTER 18

Sex Education of the Fourth Grade Child

In the fourth grade the attention of the normally inquisitive and curious child is transferred from the living things around the child to the child itself. Children in this age group are fascinated by the human body, its many parts, and their functions. The fourth grade teacher's main objective is to help the child learn more specific details about the body and about male and female roles in reproduction and heredity. Two units are suggested for fourth grade: (1) Where Babies Come From and (2) Heredity.

Where Babies Come From

An Overview of Unit One

Fourth grade children vary immensely in their ability to grasp and retain new concepts. This often presents the fourth grade teacher with a problem in introducing a new unit. The authors have inserted the story "Where Babies Come From" to alleviate the teacher's difficulty. The authors grant permission to the classroom teacher to reproduce this story and the pictures by mimeograph or photocopy for each student. The pictures accompanying the story are included in the atlas. Thus, an alternate method of having the class learn the material is for the teacher to read the story slowly, showing the illustrations at the appropriate time on the overhead projector. From the story the children learn at their own speed of mastery that: (1) the human body is made of many small parts called cells; (2) the cell is governed by DNA; (3) half of the DNA in each cell comes from the mother and half from the father; (4) all of the body's cells develop because of orders sent out by the DNA in the very first cell; (5) half of the first cell comes from the mother and half from the father; (6) it takes an egg cell from a woman and a sperm cell from a man to make a baby; (7) the man puts his penis inside the woman's vagina so that the sperm that carry his half of the DNA can fertilize an egg cell from the mother; (8) a man and woman should love one another and agree to love and take care of children before having them; and (9) a man and woman should marry before having children.

Heredity

An Overview of Unit Two

An effective teacher will organize learning in such a manner that new concepts will build upon concepts previously mastered. The unit "Heredity" is developed as an expansion of the concepts mastered in "Where Babies Come From." The children are aided in their organized sequential learning situation by visible demonstration models of the hereditary process. Demonstration techniques are included for assistance in the mastery of the following subject matter: (1) heredity is the passing of characteristics from a mother and a father to their offspring; (2) a baby inherits 23 chromosomes from the mother and 23 chromosomes from the father; (3) the sex of the baby is determined by the pairing of an X chromosome from the mother and an X or a Y chromosome from the father; (4) a gene for a particular trait from the mother and a gene from the father are located at the same point on matching chromosomes; (5) genes determine what a person will look like and how a person will develop; (6) a pair of genes, one from the mother and one from the father, may be alike or different; and (7) when a pair of genes are not the same, one of the genes (dominant gene) will influence heredity more than the other gene (recessive gene).

Unit 1:

Where Babies Come From

Foreword

Dear Boys and Girls:

We are writing this book to answer a question that you have frequently asked: Where do babies come from?

When you have finished reading this book, your parents or teacher will help you with any other questions that you might want to ask.

The human body is made up of many small parts called cells. The cells are like the bricks in a house: it takes many bricks to make a house and it takes many cells to make a boy or a girl.

Some of your cells make it possible for you to move; these are called muscle cells. Other cells produce tears to wash your eyes. Some cells help you to fight disease and to get well when you are sick. The cells that allow you to think are called brain cells. The food that you eat is

Figure 124   The parts of a house.

Figure 125   The parts of a muscle.

taken to your muscles through tunnels that have walls made of cells. Thus, cells make up all parts of your body.

A car, like a person, is made of many parts. It has tires, an engine, windows, seats, and other parts. But a car needs a driver to make it go. The driver decides how fast it will go and in what direction it will move.

Figure 126   The parts of a car.

A train also has many parts but it needs an engineer to make it go. The engineer determines how fast and in what direction the train will move.

Each of the cells in your body has its own driver or engineer. His name is Mr. DNA. He is not a real man, just a long string of chemicals. But scientists refer to him as the boss of the cell, and we shall call him Mr. DNA.

Figure 127   A cell.

Mr. DNA is a very bossy boss because he tells the rest of the cell just what to do and what not to do. But he is a good and wise boss that was passed on to you by your parents. Half of Mr. DNA in each of your cell came from your mother, and half came from your father. And the DNA in the cells of your mother and father came from your grandmothers and grandfathers. So you see, Mr. DNA has been around for a long time and has a great deal of wisdom. His wisdom or knowledge fills up 46 books that are kept right inside the cell.

Most books are written by putting the letters of the alphabet together in different ways to make words. But Mr. DNA has a very short alphabet made up of only four letters. These letters are A, T, C, and G. Thus, Mr. DNA's books are hard to read. Some of the words look like this: TA CG AT CG. Scientists haven't learned to read Mr. DNA's code yet, but they do know that the four letters in his alphabet stand for four chemicals. It is a very hard code to understand.

When scientists first saw Mr. DNA's books, they looked like tiny colored bodies. For lack of a better name, they were called colored bodies. But that was a long time ago, and the scientist of that day used the Greek language. So Mr. DNA's books were called chromosomes (kro´-mo-sohms), the Greek word for colored bodies. Today we know that they are like very tiny books that contain the knowledge that Mr. DNA needs to run his cell.

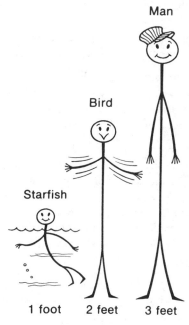

Figure 128   Mr. DNA's length.

Mr. DNA is really a curled-up string of chemicals. If he were taken out of the cell and uncurled, he would be about 3 feet long. Mr. DNA in a cell of a starfish is about 1 foot long, and in the cell of a bird he is about 2 feet long.

There are many DNA bosses in your body. They know when your body needs to grow and when it should stop growing. They know when to make new cells and when to replace old worn-out ones. And when new cells are made, the old Mr. DNA makes a new Mr. DNA for the new cell.

When you are born, your body is already made up of many cells, each with its own DNA boss. But all these cells developed because of orders sent out by the DNA boss in your very first cell.

Where do you think this first cell came from? Half of it came from your mother and half of it from your father. You see, it takes both a mother and a father to have a baby.

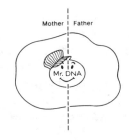

Figure 129   The two halves of Mr. DNA.

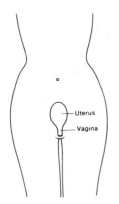

Figure 130   The mother's uterus.

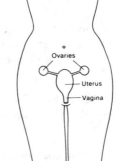

Figure 131   The mother's ovaries.

A mother has a place in her body where this first cell can grow and develop. This place is about the size of a pear and is called the uterus (yoo′ter-rus). And as this first cell grows into many cells, the uterus gets bigger and bigger until it can hold a full-size baby.

The mother's uterus is just below her navel (people sometimes call this the belly button). It is shaped like a bottle except that the bottle is turned upside down so that it opens between the mother's legs. When you were born, you came out of this opening, which is called the vagina (vuh-jy′-nuh).

The uterus, then, is the place where the first cell starts to grow and develop. And we know that half of the first cell comes from the mother and half from the father. But how do the two halves get together in the uterus?

Fortunately, the uterus has three body parts that lead into it. The body part that opens between the mother's legs we already know as the vagina. And at the top of the uterus there are two body parts that make eggs. They are called ovaries (o′-va-ries). There is a tube that leads from each ovary to the uterus. Each month an egg leaves an ovary and goes down one of the tubes toward the uterus. But eggs are only one half of the DNA boss. They must combine with another half from the father before a new baby can start to grow.

The father also has a body part to make his half of the first DNA boss. It is found in a small sack just behind his penis (pe′nis). When the mother and father decide to have a baby, the father puts his penis in the mother's vagina so that his half of Mr. DNA can get inside the mother's body. In just a few minutes, the father's DNA halves are swimming up the vagina to the uterus. These halves from the father are called sperms.

The sperms swim through the uterus and up to the tubes that lead to the ovaries. If an egg that has recently left the ovary happens to meet one of the father's sperm, the two halves of the DNA boss zip themselves together, and you have the first complete DNA boss. He now takes control and makes all future decisions about growth and development. He decides how tall you will be, what color your eyes will be, and even what size shoes you will wear. All this information is contained in Mr. DNA's chromosomes.

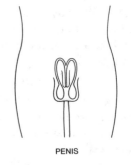

PENIS

Figure 132   The father's sperm factory.

Perhaps you have wondered why some babies are born girls and some boys. As you might expect, the answer is in Mr. DNA's 46 books. First, we should point out that 23 books come from the father and 23 books come from the mother. Thus, when the two halves of Mr. DNA are zipped together, he has a full new library of 46 books or, as scientists would say, 46 chromosomes. But not all new libraries are the same: Some contain the knowledge needed to form a boy, and others contain the knowledge needed to form a girl.

The 23 books or chromosomes that come from the mother never contain the information needed to form a boy. But some sperms carry a book of information about boys and some carry a book of information about girls. If a sperm with one of these books about boys is zipped together with the egg, a new baby boy will be born. If a sperm with a book of girl information combines with the egg, the baby will be a girl. Thus, it is the type of book carried by the sperm that determines whether the baby will be a boy or girl.

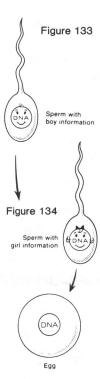

Figure 133

Sperm with boy information

Figure 134

Sperm with girl information

DNA

Egg

Figure 135

After the sperm and the egg combine in the tube between the uterus and the ovary, the new cell starts to grow and to move down the tunnel to the uterus. It plants itself in the side of the uterus and starts to grow rapidly. After about nine months, it is a full-grown baby. When the baby is ready to be born, the mother feels a slight pain and goes to the hospital. There the doctor helps the baby to come out of the tunnel between the mother's legs.

One day you may want to become a mother or a father, so you should know when and how to have babies.

First, you should know that girls don't produce eggs and boys don't produce sperms until about the time that they become teenagers. So young children couldn't become mothers or fathers even if they wanted to.

When you grow up, you may find a man or woman that you like very much. Then you decide to get married. When you get married, you promise to love and take care of each other. This is very important because unless a man and woman really love and take care of each other, they certainly will not be able to love and take care of children. That is why you should get married before you try to have children of your own.

P.S.

You may also be interested to know how fish have babies, since the mother and father fish never fall in love or get married. The mother just releases her eggs into the water and the father releases his sperms into the water. The two halves of the DNA boss zip themselves together and form the first cell of a fish. Unfortunately, there is no uterus to protect the first fish cell so many of them don't get to grow up. Humans are lucky that they develop in their mother's uterus where they are protected. Humans are also lucky that they have a mother and father who love each other and who love and care for their babies. If mothers and fathers didn't love each other enough to plan to take care of their children, babies wouldn't be much better off than fish. Poor fish.

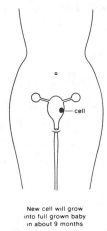

cell

New cell will grow into full grown baby in about 9 months

Figure 136   The fertilized cell implants itself.

Questions

1. The human body is made up of many tiny units. What are they called?

2. What do we call the cells that allow us to move?

3. How does a cell know how fast to grow or what job to do?

4. What is DNA?

5. What is the half of the DNA boss that comes from the mother called?

6. What is the half that comes from the father called?

7. Where do the sperm and egg come together to form the first DNA boss?

8. How does the father's sperm get inside the mother?

9. After the egg and sperm come together, how long is the time before a new baby is born?

10. Where in the mother's body does the baby develop?

11. Why are some babies born boys and some girls?

12. How does the new baby get out of the mother?

13. When should people have babies?

14. Why are human babies more fortunate than fish babies?

Unit 2:

Heredity

The following lesson on heredity is presented as a demonstration. Read through the lesson and assemble the entire kit before beginning.

To clarify the roles of the cell, DNA, and chromosomes, make your own model. You will need a tennis ball cut in half, a plastic golf ball cut in half, and strips of differently colored construction paper.

The tennis ball represents the cell. The golf ball represents the nucleus containing the DNA. Using fingernail polish, print DNA on the golfball. The strips of colored construction paper represent the chromosomes. Put the strips of colored paper inside the golf ball. Close the golf ball. Put the golf ball inside the tennis ball. You can use a rubber band to hold the tennis ball together.

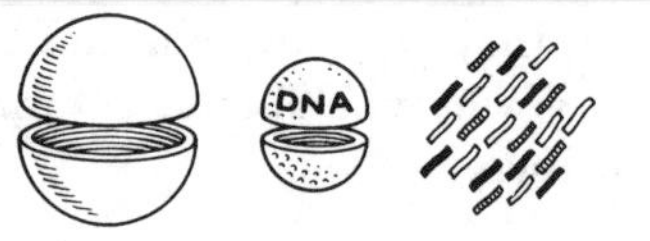

You are ready to demonstrate. Use your model and explain the following:

There are many, many cells that make up your body.

Demonstration Guidelines

The Cell Model

Cell Nucleus Chromosomes

Figure 137

The Cell Lesson

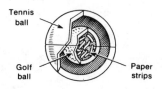

Figure 138

Figure 139

One scientist estimates that there are 26 trillion 500 billion.

There are many different kinds of cells.

Do you remember the many kinds of cells in the story?

Each cell in the body has a driver or an engineer. What is his name? (*Mr. DNA.*)

Here is where **Mr. DNA lives inside the cell.** (Open the tennis ball and show the children the golf ball with DNA painted on it.)

Mr. DNA is a very bossy boss. He tells us how fast to grow, what color eyes to have, and what size shoes to wear.

Where does Mr. DNA learn so much? (*Mr. DNA gets his wisdom from his 46 books or chromosomes.*) (Open the golf ball and pull out the strips of colored paper representing the chromosomes.)

To illustrate clearly where the first cell gets its DNA and chromosomes, assemble the following models. To construct your models you will need two soup dishes, manila paper, and construction paper.

The soup dishes can be placed together to represent the egg. Place the soup dishes together one on top of the other upside down so that they fit together. Now take 22 strips of colored paper and an x and place these inside the soup dishes.

Make four halves of sperms out of manila paper. Tape two halves together at the bottom, leaving the top open so that you can slide the 22 strips of colored paper plus an X inside the sperm. Thus, you have sperm to make a girl.

Tape the other two sperm halves together at the bottom, leaving the top open so that you can slide the 22 strips plus a Y inside the sperm. Thus, you have a sperm to make a boy.

Figure 140

The First Cell Model

Soup bowls — X — Colored paper strips (inside bowls)

Figure 141

Put colored paper strips inside sperm

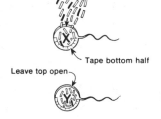

Tape bottom half

Leave top open

Figure 142

How did Mr. DNA gather so much information? Mr. DNA learned half of his knowledge from his mother and half of his knowledge from his father.

The knowledge Mr. DNA got from the mother was contained in the **egg.** (Show the children the egg and pull out the chromosomes or colored bodies of construction paper.)

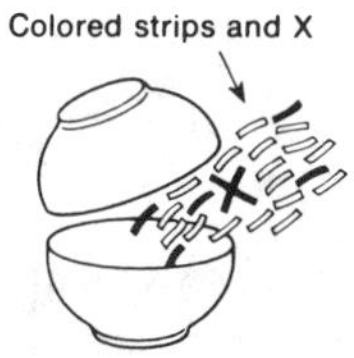

The mother's egg contains 23 books of knowledge called chromosomes.

The mother's books contain knowledge about the qualities of all her ancestors—her mother and father, grandmother and grandfather, and great grandmother and great grandfather.

The knowledge Mr. DNA got from the father was contained in the sperm. (Show the children the sperm and pull out the chromosomes or colored bodies of construction paper.)

The father's sperm contains 23 books of knowledge called **chromosomes.**

The First Cell Lesson

Colored strips and X

Figure 143

Pull out colored strips from untaped area

Figure 144

The father's books contain knowledge about the qualities of all his ancestors—his mother and father, grandmother and grandfather, and great grandmother and great grandfather.

We know that when a mother and father decide to have a baby, the father puts his penis in the mother's vagina so that his half of Mr. DNA can get inside the mother's body.

Once his sperms are inside the mother they swim about, looking for the egg.

If the egg happens to meet one of father's sperm, the two halves of the DNA boss zip themselves together and you have the first complete DNA boss. (Take one of the sperms and put it inside the egg.)

This new cell has a DNA driver with all the knowledge it needs; 23 books of wisdom from mother and 23 books of wisdom from father. (Open the soup dishes and show the children the 46 chromosomes.)

For this demonstration use the soup dishes with 22 chromosomes and the X chromosome inside. Also use the two sperm models. In one model put 22 chromosomes (colored strips) plus an X. In the other model put 22 chromosomes (colored strips) plus a Y.

One of mother's 23 books or chromosomes contains the information needed to make a girl.

Scientists call this book "X."

Let's look inside the egg and see if we can find this book or chromosome. (Open the soup dishes and pull out the 22 strips of colored paper. Pull out the X chromosome last.)

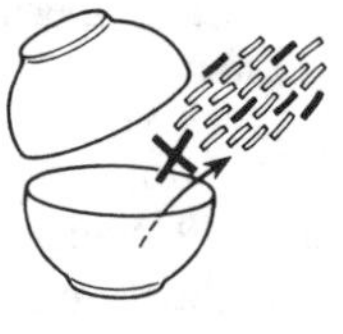

Father's 23 books or chromosomes sometimes have a book about girls and sometimes have a book about boys.

Here is one of father's sperms. Let's look inside it to see whether there is a book about boys or girls.

(Open up the sperm. Pull out the 22 strips of colored paper. Pull out the X chromosome last.)

Here is an X book. Who remembers what kind of knowledge is inside an X book? (*Girl knowledge.*)

If this sperm carrying an X book zips together with mother's egg, a new baby girl will be born.

(Take the sperm containing the X chromosome and put it inside the egg. Now show a picture of a baby girl.)

Here is another sperm from father. Let's look inside this sperm to see whether there is a book of information on boys or girls.

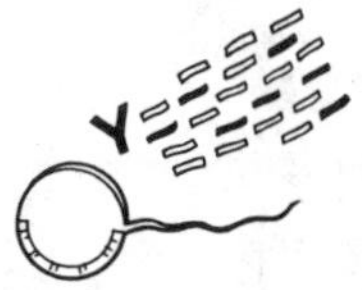

Fertilization

Figure 145

Sex Determination Model

Sex Determination Lesson

Figure 146

Figure 147

Figure 148

Figure 149

Figure 150

(Open up the sperm. Pull out the 22 strips of colored paper. Pull out the Y chromosome last.)

Here is a Y book. What kind of information do you suppose is inside the Y book? *(Boy knowledge.)*

If this sperm carrying the Y book zips together with mother's egg, a new baby boy will be born.

(Take the sperm containing the Y chromosome and put it inside the egg. Now show a picture of a baby boy.)

To illustrate clearly the relationship of the many genes to the chromosomes, construct the following book model. For your model you will need colored construction paper, tape, and cardboard.

Cover the cardboard with colored construction paper to make a book cover. Fill the book with pages of different colors of construction paper. Paste pictures on the different pages to represent inherited traits—curly hair, eye color, shoe size, etc.

The book can be used to represent one of the chromosomes. The pages can be used to represent the genes on the chromosomes.

The Gene Model

Figure 151

Figure 152

Mr. DNA's books have many pages containing information on many, many things.

Let's look at one of Mr. DNA's books or chromosomes.

(Take one of the chromosome books and open it to the different pages with the inherited traits pasted on them.)

This page contains the information needed to color the baby's eyes. (Show the picture on the page.)

This page contains the information needed to make the baby's hair curl. (Show the picture on the page.)

This page contains the information needed to make the hair red. (Show the picture on the page.)

You can see that every one of Mr. DNA's books or chromosomes contains pages of information on many topics.

These pages of information in Mr. DNA's books or chromosomes are called genes.

Each one of Mr. DNA's books or chromosomes contains thousands of pages or genes.

Every cell in the body contains Mr. DNA's books or chromosomes, and therefore every cell contains thousands of pages or genes.

These genes decide what color skin you will have, how tall you will be, what color eyes you will have, and if your hair will be curly.

The Gene Lesson

Figure 153

Figure 154

Figure 155

Using large sheets of manila construction paper, draw the head of a man and the head of a woman. These figures can be used later with the lesson as column headings to represent the genes inherited from the mother and the genes inherited from the father.

Do you remember how the cell got its library of 46 books or chromosomes? (Place the figure heads of the mother and the father on a board.)

Twenty-three books or chromosomes came from the mother's eggs and 23 books or chromosomes from the father's sperm.

(Place the soup bowl model of the egg containing 23 chromosomes under the mother. Place the construction paper model of the sperm containing 23 chromosomes under the father.)

This means that half the books or chromosomes in a fertilized egg contain pages or genes from your mother, and the other half contain pages or genes from your father.

(Place a fertilized egg between and below the model of the egg and the sperm. Place 46 chromosomes in the model.)

Make a large egg out of construction paper. Inside the egg match up 23 pairs of chromosomes. Make divisions on the chromosomes and make them different colors to represent the genes. Match the colors on both the chromosomes in a pair and in the same place. This illustrates the idea that a gene for a particular trait from the mother and the same gene from the father are located at the same point on matching chromosomes.

Now make a large model of a chromosome, pairing the traits from the father and the mother as illustrated in Figure 160. This illustrates the idea that one gene for each trait comes from the mother and one gene for each trait comes from the father.

Let's look more closely at the 46 books or chromosomes in a fertilized egg; these chromosomes seem to do something very strange.

They seem to line up inside the egg in two's.

One of father's books or chromosomes is always right beside one of mother's books or chromosomes. (Use Figure 161.)

These books or chromosomes have a very special reason for being beside each other.

They contain the same kind of information.

Here is one of the books or chromosomes from the father, and here is one of the books or chromosomes from the mother. (Use Figure 161.)

Look closely at them, and you will see that they contain the same kind of information.

We already know that the information on the chromosome or book is called a gene.

A scientist would say that the chromosomes contain similar genes.

If we lined the chromosomes up next to each other, we could see that there is a pair of genes for each trait.

(Point to the simple drawings on the chromosomes from the mother and father.)

Demonstration Guidelines

Figure 157

Figure 156

Figure 158

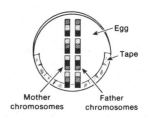

Figure 159

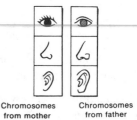

Chromosomes from mother   Chromosomes from father

Figure 160

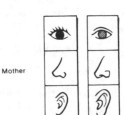

Chromosome pair

Figure 161

Here is some information on mother's chromosome about eyes.

We call this the eye gene.

Here is some eye information on the chromosome that came from the father.

What do we call this information *(Eye gene.)*

Here is some nose information on the chromosome that came from the mother.

What do we call this information? *(Nose gene.)*

Here is some information on the chromosome that came from the father.

What do we call this information? *(Nose gene.)*

You see, a human being has two genes or pages of information on every topic telling the body what to do.

These are two genes deciding how big your feet will be.

These are two genes deciding how tall you will be.

These are two genes deciding what color your eyes will be.

To illustrate dominant and recessive genes for eye color make two sets of eyes out of construction paper. Make one set of eyes brown and the other set of eyes blue.

Now turn the pair of brown eyes over and tape blue eyes on the back of them. This can be used to demonstrate that although a person has brown eyes (s)he can still be carrying a gene for blue eyes. Therefore, a brown-eyed parent and a blue-eyed parent can have a blue-eyed child.

Many times the two genes will agree. This might happen if the eye color gene you get from mother is brown and the eye color gene you get from father is brown.

In this case the two genes agree and your eyes will be brown.

Sometimes the genes do not agree. This might happen if the eye color gene you get from mother is brown and the eye color gene you get from father is blue.

One of the genes wants your eyes to be blue and the other gene wants your eyes to be brown.

What happens? Fortunately some genes are much more bossy than others, and they always get their own way.

A gene for brown skin always wins an argument with a gene for white skin.

A gene for being tall always wins an argument with a gene for being short.

A gene for curly hair always wins an argument with a gene for straight hair.

A gene for brown eyes always wins an argument with a gene for blue eyes.

When the eye color gene from the mother is brown and the eye color gene from the father is blue, the baby will always have brown eyes.

Dominant and Recessive Genes

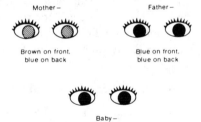

Mother –
Brown on front, blue on back

Father –
Blue on front, blue on back

Baby –
blue eyes

Figure 162

This is not the same as saying that if a mother's eyes are brown and a father's eyes are blue the baby's eyes will be brown.

Remember that everyone alive has two genes for everything.

If a mother has brown eyes, you know that one of her eye genes is brown but what about the other one? (Show the brown eyes that have blue on the back.)

This mother has brown eyes; she has one gene for brown eyes (turn over), **and her other gene is for blue eyes.**

You see, when her brown eye gene argued with her blue eye gene over what color eyes she should have, her brown eye gene won.

But she still has both the brown eye gene and the blue eye gene; this means that her baby could get a blue eye gene from her.

Here is a mother with brown eyes and a father with blue eyes. What color eyes will their baby have?

We know that the color of eyes the baby will have depends upon what genes the baby gets from its mother and father.

Let's suppose the baby gets a brown eye gene from the mother and a blue eye gene from the father. What color will the baby's eyes be? *(Brown eyes.)*

Let's suppose the baby gets a blue eye gene from mother and a blue eye gene from father. What color will the baby's eyes be? *(Blue eyes.)*

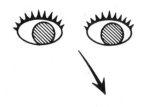

Turn over

Figure 163

To illustrate the dominant and recessive genes for curly hair make the following model. Cut out a drawing of a mother with straight hair shown on both sides of the construction paper. Cut out a drawing of a father with curly hair shown on both sides of the construction paper. By showing the children the front and back of both construction paper models you can illustrate that the mother carries two genes for straight hair and that the father carries two genes for curly hair. Curly hair is the dominant gene. Therefore, the child will have curly hair since the father does not carry the recessive gene for straight hair.

Here is a mother with straight hair and a father with curly hair.

(Turn the model of the mother over to show that she has two genes for straight hair.) **The mother has two genes for straight hair.**

(Turn the model of the father over to show that he has two genes for curly hair.) **The father has two genes for curly hair.**

The genes do not agree. One gene wants the baby to have curly hair, and the other gene wants the baby to have straight hair.

Do you know which gene will win the disagreement? *(The gene for curly hair.)*

A mother with two genes for straight hair and a father with two genes for curly hair can only have a baby with curly hair.

To illustrate how two tall parents can have a short child, construct two tall parents out of construction paper. Then construct two short parents out of construction paper.

Pin the short parents on the board. Pin the tall parents over the short parents so that the short parents cannot be seen. Now it appears that both parents

Demonstration Guidelines

Figure 164

Demonstration Guidelines

are tall so all of their children will be tall. Lift up the tall parents and show the class that the parents are each carrying a gene for being short. Because of this the parents have a short child. Pin the short child on the board.

Here are two tall parents. (Lift up the tall parents to show that they each carry a gene for being short.)

Although the mother is very tall, she has a short gene too.

The father also has two genes. He has one gene for being tall and one gene for being short.

The baby will get one gene from each parent. Let's see whether the baby will be tall or short.

Suppose that the baby gets a gene for being tall from the mother and a gene for being tall from the father.

Will the baby be tall or short? (*The baby will be tall.*)

Now suppose that the baby gets a gene for being tall from the mother and a gene for being short from the father.

The two genes disagree. One gene wants the baby to be tall. The other gene wants the baby to be short.

Do you remember who wins the argument between a tall gene and a short gene? (*The tall gene. The baby will be tall.*)

Now let us suppose that the baby gets a gene for being short from the mother and a gene for being short from the father.

Will the baby be tall or short? (*The baby will be short.*)

Now we can see why it is possible for two tall parents to have a short child.

The parents' genes are more important than what the parents look like.

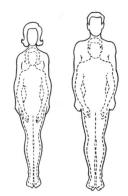

Figure 165

Ask the students to bring to class individual snapshots of themselves taken when they were five years of age in which their facial features are clearly visible. The teacher then could take small group pictures of students. Make a bulletin board display with the current pictures in the center and the childhood snapshots around the edge and let the students see if they can identify childhood snapshots of each other by comparing facial characteristics in the snapshots with those in the current pictures.

The study of heredity can be enhanced by having each student make a list of inherited characteristics such as eye and hair color, whether hair is curly or straight, etc., and then trace these characteristics as far back through the family as possible. This activity will afford the teacher an opportunity to help students distinguish between the characteristics that are inherited and those that are acquired.

Have the students discuss the statement, "What a person becomes is determined by heredity, the environment, and to some extent what he or she wants to be."

Unit Activities[1]

Inherited Characteristics

Heredity and Our Ancestors

Class Discussion

---

[1]These activities were taken from "Growth Patterns and Sex Education," *The Journal of School Health*, XXXVII (May 1967), published by the American School Health Association.

CHAPTER 19

Sex Education of the Fifth Grade Child

In the fifth grade, the student is in a flux of change—accelerated growth accompanied by anxieties, fears, and tensions. The objective of the fifth grade teachers is to help the students overcome these worries by giving them adequate knowledge about the new changes in their bodies and the reasons for these changes. The teacher must create a reciprocal, comfortable, accepting environment to maximize pupil learning. The unit suggested for the fifth grade is "Discovering Yourself." It is followed by a unit on "Making Responsible Decisions."

Discovering Yourself

An Overview of Unit One

One of the most rewarding objectives a fifth grade teacher can have is to help the students gain enough knowledge about their bodies and their body changes to become comfortable with themselves. The unit "Discovering Yourself" has been included at the fifth grade level to provide specific teaching in areas of concern to the student. The unit includes a discussion of the following information:

1. The parts of the body that are involved in producing offspring make up the reproductive system.

2. Puberty is the period when hormones cause secondary sex characteristics to develop in boys and girls.

3. The parts of the male reproductive system include the scrotum, testes, seminiferous tubules, epididymis, vas deferens, seminal vesicles, ejaculatory duct, prostate gland, Cowper's glands, urethra, and penis.

4. The organs in the male reproductive system are necessary for the production, movement, and nourishment of sperm.

5. Semen is a mixture of fluids and sperm.

6. Ejaculation is the discharge of semen from the male urethra.

7. If a male ejaculates while he is sleeping, it is called a wet dream or a nocturnal emission.

8. The parts of the female reproductive system include the ovaries, uterus, oviducts, vagina, mons veneris, labia, and clitoris.

9.   The hymen is a thin membrane that covers the vaginal opening.

10.   The menstrual cycle includes the maturing of an ovum, ovulation, thickening of the wall of the uterus, and menstruation.

11.   During the menstrual flow a girl has to wear some protection—tampon or feminine pads—to absorb the blood.

12.   Tampon use under some circumstances has been linked to a rare disease called toxic shock syndrome.

13.   Health habits such as a balanced diet and regular exercise are needed for a healthy menstrual cycle.

At the fifth grade level, students may be more comfortable if members of the opposite sex are not present. The decision whether or not to separate the sexes rests upon each individual teacher and depends entirely upon the structure and maturation of the class. The maturation of the boys in the class will also determine whether the section on menstrual protection can be included in the lesson on the female reproductive system. If the boys are mature enough to handle the discussion, it is a valuable addition to the fifth grade curriculum. It will satisfy the growing boy's curiosity about the sanitary vending machines in ladies' restrooms. However, the more detailed lesson on feminine hygiene is prepared for girls only. The girls are uncomfortable about discussing new changes in their femininity, and the hygiene unit covers their questions in depth. It is best handled by a qualified woman who can help the girls feel comfortable and be identified with as a feminine figure. It is especially important to adequately review the information in this unit. If any of the material in "Discovering Yourself" is not properly reviewed, misconceptions may result. The fifth grade teacher should make use of the review activities.

Making Responsible Decisions
An Overview of Unit Two[1]

In addition to accepting bodily changes, fifth grade students must accept responsibility for the decisions that they make. The unit "Making Responsible Decisions" examines decision-making skills. Students learn that:

1.   A decision is a choice that you make.

2.   For every decision, there are at least two choices.

3.   For every decision, there are results.

4.   For every decision, there are risks.

5.   Decision making is deciding which of two or more choices you will make.

6.   Facts, peer pressure, and your family are some of the things that influence our decisons.

7.   Making a decision requires that you consider the following steps: identifying the problem, listing the choices you could make, listing the risks for each choice, thinking about the results, and evaluating your choices.

---

[1]Concepts for this unit were adapted from *Health: Focus on You,* a K–8 health education textbook series (Westerville, Ohio: Charles E. Merrill, 1984; 936 Eastwind Drive, 43081).

8.   A responsible decision is one that respects yourself and others, is healthful and safe, respects the law, and follows your parents' guidelines.

Unit One:

Discovering Yourself

Lesson 1: Reproductive Cells

Have the class model living things out of clay—bird, horse, dog, human—or make models of living things from construction paper. Discuss with them the topic, "Living versus Nonliving Things."

Class Activity

We have been modeling and drawing examples of living things. Let us take one of our models (clay bird model) and compare it with a _____(bird) that is alive.

Living versus Nonliving

Using the blackboard list the differences between the clay bird model (or other model) and a living _____(bird):

1.   Living bird breathes.

2.   Living bird flies.

3.   Living bird sings.

4.   Living bird grows.

5.   Living bird dies.

We want to add to our list another difference between living and nonliving things.

Difference in Modeling

Remember when you began to model your living thing out of clay? You began with a hunk of clay and molded your (bird, cat, dog).

You knew that you were not really going to make something living at all—but a copy of something living.

Mother Nature copies living things too—only her copies will be living. So Mother Nature has to begin her model in a different way.

Mother Nature Copies Living Things

She begins with a tiny piece of living modeling clay called the cell. The cell is a very different type of modeling clay. It is smaller than the tiniest grain of sand.

The Cell—a Special Modeling Clay

But because the cell is living it can model a living thing all by itself.

The Cell is Living

You are probably wondering how such a tiny cell can model one of the elephants you see at the zoo.

You may also wonder how the tiny cell forms a human being.

The cell is a very special kind of modeling clay—so special that it can do very special tasks.

The Cell Can Do Special Tasks

One of its special duties is to divide and divide itself until there are millions of cells.

This is a very important task because each type of cell that models human beings has a special job to do.

These cells make up all parts of your body. They are called body cells. Body cells are concerned with keeping people alive.

Body Cells Keep Us Alive

Let's look at the work done by these very tiny body cells. Some of these cells make it possible for you to move; these are called muscle cells.

The Work of Cells

Other cells produce tears to wash your eyes. Some cells help you to fight disease and to get well when you are sick.

The cells that allow you to think are called brain cells. The food that you eat is taken to your muscles through tunnels that have walls made of cells.

To sum up the work of the cell, we could say that everything that keeps you alive—running, jumping, eating, sleeping, thinking—is a special job performed by one of the body cells.

Since the body cells can do everything that is necessary to keep us alive, we wouldn't think that a human being would need any other kind of cell.

But all human beings have two kinds of cells. And although body cells are very important because they keep us alive, the other kind of cells is important too.

Human Beings Have Two Kinds of Cells

These other cells are not concerned with us but with making more human beings.

These cells are called reproductive cells. All men and women have body cells to keep them alive and reproductive cells to make new human beings.

Reproductive Cells to Make New Human Beings

We all know that men and women are different. We also know that it takes both a mother and a father to have a baby.

Therefore, it probably won't seem strange to you that it takes two reproductive cells, one from the father and one from the mother, to make a new human being.

Two Kinds of Reproductive Cells

The reproductive cell that comes from the mother is called the egg cell.

The Egg Cell

All mothers have body cells to keep them alive and egg cells to make new human beings.

The reproductive cell that comes from the father is called the sperm cell.

The Sperm Cell

All fathers have body cells to keep them alive and sperm cells to make new human beings.

Lesson 2: Male Reproductive System

Use an overlay of the male reproductive system with this lesson. As the journey of the sperm is discussed, trace the route of the sperm on the overlay. You might also want to copy a line drawing of the male reproductive system for each student. Students can write in the terms as you discuss them.

Teacher's Notes

Reviewing Yesterday's Lesson

Yesterday we learned the difference between living and nonliving things. Who remembers the basic difference? (*The cell.*)

1. Living Versus Nonliving

We also learned that human beings have two kinds of cells. Can someone tell us the names of these two cells? (*Body cells and reproductive cells.*)

2. Two Kinds of Cells

What are body cells concerned with? (*Body cells are concerned with keeping us alive.*)

3. Body Cells

What are reproductive cells concerned with? (*Reproductive cells are concerned with making new human beings.*)

4. Reproductive Cells

We have all been very interested in our body cells as we have been growing up.

We are Interested in Our Body Cells

That is probably why we seem to know more about our body cells than about our reproductive cells. Let's see how much we know about our body cells.

Who knows what body cells make us able to swing a bat? (*Muscle cells.*)

Our Muscle Cells

Where are the muscle cells? (*They are in the muscle.*)

Who knows what cells cover the body? (*Skin cells.*)

Our Skin Cells

Show us some skin cells. Of course when we point to the skin we are pointing to many skin cells because we know that our eyes cannot see one cell.

For this unit the students should make a notebook entitled "Growing Up." One section of the notebook will be a sex education dictionary of terms. As this lesson is presented, have the students copy the terms in their notebooks and define them. Have them define the terms in their own words. Make sure that all the vocabulary words in this lesson appear in the notebook. You will find these words defined at the end of this lesson.

Unit Activity: "Growing Up" Notebook

Now who can tell us where the reproductive cells are made?

Where Reproductive Cells are Made

1.   Female reproductive cells or eggs are made in the ovaries, which cannot be seen because they are inside the body.

2.   Male reproductive cells or sperm are made in the testes, which are located in a little sac between the boy's legs.

A boy's body has a lot of growing to do before he can produce sperm. This growth period toward sexual maturity is called puberty.

During puberty, several changes occur in the boy's body:

1.   Deepening of the voice.

2.   Growth of body hair.

3.   More manly appearance.

4.   Growth of testes, penis, and scrotum.

5.   Muscle growth.

These changes, called the secondary sex characteristics, are necessary before a boy can produce sperm.

And of course a sperm must fertilize the egg for new life to start.

In order for a sperm and an egg to meet so that a new baby can begin to grow, the sperm cell must travel from the testes out of the penis and into the mother's body.

The Sperm Cell Must Meet the Egg Cell

You would think that this would be a short trip, since the testes and the penis are so close together.

A Long Journey for the Sperm Cell

But this isn't true. The sperm has to pass up into the body as it has many preparations to make before it can get to where it's going.

The sperm also has to wait until a boy is grown up to make this trip. No sperm makes this trip until a boy is about 11 or 12 years old.

Sperm's Journey and Growing Up

When a boy is about 11 or 12 years old, a tiny gland in his brain sends out a signal that tells the testes that it is time to prepare for the sperm's journey.

Pituitary Gland Alerts Testes

This tiny gland is called the pituitary gland, and the message it sends to the testes is called FSH. (*A hormone*).

FSH tells the testes to begin working to make many sperm. Sperm have to be made at just the right temperature. Do you remember the little sac between the boy's legs?

FSH Tells Testes to Make Sperms

The little sac that holds the boy's testes is called the scrotum. The scrotum helps the testes to make the sperm by keeping the testes at just the right temperature.

The Scrotum Regulates the Temperature of the Testes

After the sperm are made they do not stay in the testes long, for they have a long journey to make.

The Journey Begins

The very first stop on their trip is a little resting place right above the testes, called the epididymis.

First Stop: Epididymis

While the sperm is resting up for its long journey, it is growing up. A grown-up sperm looks like a tadpole.

The Sperm Grows Up to Look Like a Tadpole

Have you ever seen a tadpole? A sperm has a head and a tail just like a tadpole. A sperm moves like a tadpole too—it swims.

The Sperm Has a Head and a Tail

Now that the sperm is grown up it must wait its turn to be used.

It waits in a long tube that winds its way up into the body. This tube is called the vas deferens.

Vas Deferens: The Waiting Station

At last it is time for the trip; the sperm pass up into the body through the long vas deferens.

Energy is needed for the long journey ahead, and so the seminal vesicles empty some sugar into the vas deferens.

Energy Stop: Seminal Vesicle

The sperm are now going to travel along a very short path called the ejaculatory duct.

Ejaculatory Duct

As the sperm empty into the ejaculatory duct the prostate gland empties some milky water into the ejaculatory duct.

A Long Swim Ahead

Prostate Gland: Milky Water for the Swimming Sperm

Now the sperm is in a milky-sugary substance. This is called semen.

Semen: The Final Mixture

Let's stop for a minute to see if we can remember all the ingredients that are in semen.

The Ingredients in Semen

First, there was the sperm. Where did the sperm come from? (*Testes.*)

1. Sperms from Testes

Next, some sugar was added for the sperm to have energy. Where did the sugar come from? (*Seminal vesicle*).

2. Sugar from Seminal Vesicles

Last, some milky water was added to help the sperm swim easily. Where did the milky water come from? (*Prostate gland.*)

3. Milky Water from the Prostate Gland

So you see there are three ingredients in semen:

1. Sperm from the testes.

2. Sugar from the seminal vesicles.

3. Milky water from the prostate gland.

Now we are ready for the final stage of the trip. The ejaculatory duct connects with a long tube in the penis called the urethra.

The Urethra

We know that urine also leaves the body through the urethra. But the sperm and urine are never in the urethra at the same time.

Urethra and Urine

In fact, the semen with the sperm in it wants to make sure that there is no urine left in the urethra.

Right beside the urethra are two Cowper's glands.

The Cowper's glands squirt some cleansing fluid down the urethra to clean the urethra for the semen.

Now the urethra is clear for the semen. But wait: the semen must be deposited inside the mother so it can look for the egg.

Remember that we said the urethra was a long tube inside the penis. The father can use his penis to place the semen inside the mother.

The penis is usually very soft and hangs down between the boy's legs. But when semen is going to come out of the penis, the penis becomes very hard.

This makes it easier for the father to put his penis into the mother's vagina.

When the penis is inside the vagina, the semen comes out and the sperms begin to swim about looking for the egg.

It is very important that the teacher review the male reproductive system thoroughly before beginning the female reproductive system. Below are some review questions:

Reviewing the Male Reproductive System

1. Where are the male reproductive cells made?

2. Where are the female reproductive cells made?

3. How old is a boy when he begins to grow up and make sperm?

4. What is the name of the tiny gland in the brain?

5. Where does the FSH message come from?

6. What does FSH tell the testes to do?

7. How does the scrotum help the testes to make sperms?

8. Where do the sperm "grow up"?

9. How is a sperm like a tadpole?

10. Where does the sperm await its turn to be used?

11. What does the sperm use for energy?

12. What is the name of the short duct between the vas deferens and the urethra?

13. Where does the sperm get the milky water to help it swim?

14. What are the three ingredients in semen?

15. What is the name of the long tube inside the penis?

16. Do urine and semen every travel down the urethra at the same time?

Have the class go over the definitions they have written in their notebooks on the male reproductive system. You will find suitable fifth grade definitions at the end of this unit. As the students go over the definitions have them point out the anatomical structures on the model.	**Sex Educaton Dictionary**
Pass out to the students a diagram of the male reproductive system. Have the class members label the diagram together.	**Male Anatomical Drawing**
Have each student write a summary of the journey of sperm and put it in a notebook on growing up. The sex education dictionary should be in this notebook also.	**"Growing Up" Notebook**

Sex Education Dictionary

The place where the male reproductive cells, the sperm, are made. The testes look like two small balls and are located in a small sac between the boy's legs.	**Testes**
A small gland about the size of a marble in the brain that sends a message to the testes telling them to make sperm.	**Pituitary gland**
A message from the pituitary gland that tells the testes to begin working to make many, many sperm.	**FSH**
A small sac between the boy's legs and under his penis. The sac holds the two testes. It helps the testes to make sperm by keeping the testes at the right temperature.	**Scrotum**
There is a small tube on top of each testis. It is here that the sperm grow up to look like tadpoles.	**Epididymis**
The male reproductive cell, made in the testes. The sperm look like tadpoles—each has a head and a tail. They move by swimming in milky water. They use sugar for fuel.	**Sperm**
At first the vas deferens is a tube where the sperm wait their turn to be used. Then when it is time for the sperm to be used, they travel along the vas deferens, which goes up into the body. The vas deferens ends when it comes to a path called the ejaculatory duct.	**Vas Deferens**
The seminal vesicles provide the sperm with sugar energy. There are two seminal vesicles.	**Seminal Vesicle**
The ejaculatory duct connects the vas deferens and the urethra.	**Ejaculatory Duct**
The prostate gland dumps milky water into the ejaculatory duct to help the sperm swim more easily.	**Prostate gland**
A milky, sugary liquid containing the sperm. The semen contains the sperm from the testes, sugar from the seminal vesicles, and milky water from the prostate gland. The semen is a liquid, which finally leaves the male body through the urethra in the penis.	**Semen**
A tube inside the penis. The semen empties into the urethra by way of the ejaculatory duct. The semen travels down the urethra and out of the penis.	**Urethra**
There are two small glands beside the urethra. Cowper's glands squirt out a cleansing fluid to clear the urethra.	**Cowper's Glands**

Located between the boy's legs. It is soft and hangs down. The penis is used for intercourse and urination. When semen is going to come out of the penis, it becomes very hard. Then the penis is put inside the mother more easily.

Penis

Lesson 3: Female Reproductive System

Use an overlay of the female reproductive system with this lesson. Also, use an overlay showing the delivery of the baby. You might also want to copy a line drawing of the female reproductive system for each student. Students can write in the terms as you discuss them.

Teacher's Notes

If the primary secret of human happiness could be contained in two simple words they would be "Know Yourself." This is the basic principle of existence from which all good things flow. But knowing yourself is no easy assignment. It doesn't happen overnight.[2]

Discovering Yourself

You are continually changing, always growing, always having new feelings.

You are Always Changing

This means that to really know yourself you'll have to work at it over the whole of a lifetime.

Also, you'll have to work hard to know and understand others. This is an important part of knowing yourself.

Know and Understand Others

You can see why it is so important for a girl to know all about boys and how they grow to be men and fathers.

Girls Must Understand Boys

You can also see why it is so important for boys to know all about girls and how they grow to be women and mothers.

Boys Must Understand Girls

For this lesson the students will continue their notebook on "Growing Up." One section of the notebook will be a sex education dictionary of terms describing the female reproductive system. As this lesson is presented, have the students copy the terms in their notebooks, and define them in their own words. Make sure that all the words that are underlined in this lesson appear in the notebooks. You will find these words defined at the end of this unit.

Unit Activity: "Growing Up" Notebook

Boys and girls are both signaled to grow up by a tiny gland in the brain called the pituitary gland.

The Pituitary Gland

In boys we said that the pituitary gland secretes FSH at about the age of 11 or 12. In girls the pituitary gland secretes FSH as early as age 9 or 10.

The Age the Alarm Sounds

Girls begin to grow up one or two years earlier than boys.

Do you remember where the egg cells or reproductive cells of a female are made? (*In the ovary.*)

There are thousands of immature egg cells in each ovary until the pituitary gland sends out its FSH signal.

Drowsy Baby Eggs

The body of a girl makes some immediate changes after FSH is released:

   1.   **She begins to look more like her mother and other grownup girls she knows.**

---

[2]From *Your Years of Self Discovery* (Neenah, Wisconsin: The Life Cycle Center, Kimberly Clark Corporation).

2. Her hips become wider.

3. Her breasts become larger.

4. Hair begins to grow under her arms and where her legs come together.

These changes will make it easer for a girl's body to prepare for a baby each month.

This event is known as the menstrual cycle. The menstrual cycle is just another way to say that the girl's body prepares a nest for a baby to grow in each month.

Monthly Nest Preparation

Let me tell you how this nest is formed.

After the FSH is released and goes to the ovary, some of the eggs begin to grow. One of these eggs becomes mature.

The Grownup Egg

The girl's body is alerted that an egg is about to begin its journey looking for a sperm. A very comfortable nest must be prepared for the egg in case it meets the sperm.

Be on the Alert—Nest Needed

Does anyone know the name of the nest in the mother where the eggs grow? (*The uterus.*)

Uterus—A Comfortable Nest

So that the baby would have a comfortable nest in which to grow, a very soft lining of blood and food lines the uterus.

This lining looks something like red velvet. It makes a very safe, comfortable nest.

Now the mature egg will go looking for the sperm. The mature egg won't find any sperm in the ovary so it decides to leave.

Right outside the ovary is a long tube called the oviduct.

A Long Hallway

At the end of this tube and very close to the ovary are a lot of little fingers pointing to the egg saying, "Come this way into the oviduct."

Persuasive Little Fingers

So the egg travels into the oviduct and begins to journey down the tube toward the uterus.

If any sperm are in the oviduct they will begin to swim toward the egg. (You can stop here to review how the father puts his penis into the mother's vagina and how the sperm swims toward the egg.)

To review the demonstration of fertilization used previously at a lower grade level, make a sperm from construction paper and have two soup dishes. Place the soup dishes together. To show fertilization, open the two dishes and put the construction paper sperm inside.

Demonstration Guidelines

When one sperm meets the egg this is called fertilization.

Fertilization

The sperm cell and the egg cell are now joined together as one cell. This one cell contains everything from which a new baby will grow.

The Living Modeling Clay

The cell needs a very comfortable nest to do all this important modeling, so it journeys the rest of the way down the oviduct until it reaches the uterus.

The uterus is a very comfortable nest. Its walls have all the nourishment and comfort for a new baby to grow. The cell attaches to this wall.

Uterus—Growing Room

This cell is smaller than the tiniest grain of sand. You can see that it has a lot of growing to do in the nest.

A Very Small Cell

The uterus has to keep getting bigger to keep the nest big enough for the cell to grow into a baby.

The Cell and Nest Grow

You have probably seen a mother with a baby growing inside her. The word we use to describe her is "pregnant."

The Pregnant Mother

A mother with a baby growing inside her is pregnant. Some people look at a pregnant mother and think that the baby is growing in her stomach. It is not her stomach but her uterus that is getting bigger to hold the growing baby.

Not the Stomach!

While the baby is growing inside the mother, it needs extra food supplies.

Extra Food Supply Needed

A special cord connects the baby to the mother so that the baby can get all the supplies it needs.

A Special Attachment

This cord is called the umbilical cord. At one end it attaches to the baby at the navel; the other end attaches to a special place in the uterus called the placenta. The placenta is the place where food and waste are exchanged.

The Placenta

It brings all the things that the baby needs from its mother and takes away everything that the baby cannot use.

With all this comfort and care inside the mother, the baby will soon grow old enough to be born. This growth takes nine months.

Nine-Month Growing Period

When a baby is ready to be born, it usually comes head first through the vagina. The baby is born when it comes through the vagina.

The Birth Tunnel

After a baby is born it no longer needs to be connected to its mother's nest. The long cord comes out with the baby. The doctor ties the cord off and cuts it. The mark that is left on the baby from this cord is the belly button or navel.

A Cord Without a Job

A new life has begun. The mother and father will take care of this baby until it grows up.

Now we know a little bit more about ourselves. We know why our bodies are changing. We know why we have to know about both boys and girls and how they grow up . . . .

. . . Because the changes that are happening to you are natural and will be very important to you when you want to marry and have your own family.

Natural Changes Important to the Future

You probably aren't much interested in marrying and having a family now. There are many things you want to do and things you want to learn first.

You will be getting your ideas and education in tune before deciding to marry. Meanwhile, your body is growing and changing.

Mother Nature's Advance Preparations

Both boys' and girls' bodies are ready to have babies long before they marry. You will soon be noticing these changes.

Boys may notice an occasional discharge of clear, sticky fluid from the penis.

Noticeable Growing Changes in Boys

This is the semen, which is beginning to form during the early period when the boy is growing up.

Quite frequently the semen overflows at night, leaving a small spot on the sheets or pajamas.
Semen Overflows

Sometimes this overflowing of semen is accompanied by a dream about girls or a dream about growing up.
Semen May Be Accompanied by a Dream

This is why some people call this secretion a "wet dream." Scientifically a wet dream is called a seminal emission.
"Wet Dream"—Seminal Emission

A boy who does not understand this experience may be sleeping and awaken to find himself frightened and disturbed.

There is no reason for a boy to be upset. This is a normal part of growing up. It is a sign that semen is being made.
Wet Dreams Are a Normal Part of Growing Up

Girls' bodies are changing too. Remember when we talked about the menstrual cycle?
Girls' Bodies Prepare for Motherhood

We said that the menstrual cycle was just another way of saying that a girl's body prepares each month to have a baby.

Let's review what we already know about the menstrual cycle.

Each month one of the eggs matures. Where does this egg grow up? (*The ovary.*)
The Egg Matures

Then the egg leaves the ovary and enters the long tube. What is the tube called? (*The oviduct.*)
The Long Hallway

At the same time that the egg is traveling down the oviduct, a comfortable nest of blood is being made. Where is the nest? (*Uterus.*)
A Comfortable Nest of Blood

We know that if an egg is fertilized by a sperm in the oviduct a new life begins. This life will grow into a baby in the uterus.
Partnership Results in New Life

But what happens if the egg is not fertilized by a sperm?

Then the egg and the blood lining of the uterus are not needed.
Egg and Lining Not Needed

The egg and the blood leave the uterus and come down the vagina.
Together They Leave

A very thin piece of skin called the hymen covers the opening of the vagina.
A Thin Covering

In the middle of the hymen is an opening.

The egg and blood come through this opening to the outside of the body.

This is called the menstrual flow. It lasts about three to five days each month.

During the menstrual flow or menstruation a girl has to wear some protection to collect and absorb this blood.
Collecting the Unwanted Blood

(Both boys and girls should be familiar at this age with menstrual hygiene products. As you explain this simply and factually, show the class the feminine pad and tampon).
Demonstration Guideline

A feminine pad is a soft disposable pad used to absorb the menstrual flow. (Show one.)
Feminine Pads to Absorb Blood

A narrow elastic belt is used to keep the napkin firmly in place. (Show the belt.)
Feminine Belt to Hold Napkin

The belt is worn around the waist next to the skin. The pad is attached to the belt. (Attach a pad to the belt.) **Some pads have a strip of tape to hold them in place. They are worn without a belt.**

The tampon is another easy way of absorbing the menstrual flow. (Show a tampon.)

A Tampon for Internal Absorption

The tampon is worn inside the vagina. It is put into the same opening through which the menstrual fluid leaves the body.

A tampon works something like a blotter. It absorbs the blood as it flows from the uterus into the vagina.

Just Like a Blotter

A girl will only need to wear some type of sanitary protection for the three to five days in her menstrual cycle when the unneeded blood is trickling down the vagina.

When the menstrual flow is over, it is time to begin the monthly preparation of a nest all over again.

This preparation occurs over and over again, every month for years and years . . . and each month that no pregnancy occurs there is a menstrual flow.

The Cycle Repeats Itself

So you see the changes that will be happening to you are very natural and also very important.

These changes begin long before you are ready to have children, for a very good reason.

Why Early Changes?

We also know that it takes many years to adjust to these changes in our bodies and to understand them fully.

Many Years to Understand the Body

We also know that it takes many years to learn about ourselves.

Manys Years to Understand Self and Others

These years of learning and growing changes are important in having a good marriage and in becoming good parents in the future.

Marriage and Family

It is very important that the teacher review the female reproductive system thoroughly. The students should be familiar with the biology of sex at the end of the fifth grade. Below are some review questions:

Reviewing the Female Reproductive System

1. Why is it important to know yourself?

2. Is it important for boys to know about the growth changes in girls? Why?

3. Is it important for girls to know about the growth changes in boys? Why?

4. Who is signaled to grow up first, boys or girls?

5. What message does the pituitary gland send out in girls?

6. What is the menstrual cycle?

7. How many of the immature eggs in the ovary become mature each month?

8. Where is the nest that is prepared each month in the mother and what does it look like?

9. How does the egg get from the ovary to the uterus?

10. Where does the egg usually meet a sperm?

11. Where does the living modeling clay from which a baby is made come from?

12. Why does the uterus get bigger and bigger?

13. What do we mean when we say a woman is "pregnant"?

14. How does a baby get extra food supplies when it is growing inside the mother?

15. How long does a baby grow inside its mother?

16. How does a baby get out of the mother?

17. What is the navel?

18. How do boys know when they are growing up and beginning to make semen?

19. What happens to the comfortable nest of blood in the uterus if it is not needed?

20. How long does the menstrual flow last?

21. What does a girl wear to collect the menstrual blood?

After the class has reviewed the biological phases of growing up, begin a class discussion on the sociology of growing up. Below are a few questions you might use to stimulate class discussion: **Class Discussion**

1. Why do the many body changes in growing up begin years before we are ready to marry?

2. What are some of the other ways we need to grow up before we will be ready to marry?

3. What are some of the other ways we need to grow up before we will be ready to have children?

You might want to list the students' ideas on the blackboard and then have them add these ideas to a separate section of their "Growing Up" notebook.

Have the class go over the definitions they have written in their notebooks on   **Sex Education Dictionary**
the female reproductive system. (You will find suitable fifth grade definitions at the end of this unit.)

Pass out to the students a diagram of the female reproductive system. Have   **Female Anatomical Drawing**
the class members label the diagram together.

Each student should write a summary of the menstrual cycle and put it in   **"Growing Up" Notebook**
the notebook on growing up.

Sex Education Dictionary (Continued)

A gland in the brain that is about the size of a marble. The gland secrets   **Pituitary Gland**
FSH, which causes body changes.

There are two ovaries filled with thousands of immature eggs. Each month   **Ovary**
some of these eggs develop and one of them becomes mature. The ovaries look like ping pong balls.

A hormone from the pituitary gland, which makes the eggs in the ovary begin   **FSH**
to grow.

The preparation of a comfortable nest for a baby to grow in each month. The   **Menstrual Cycle** nest is made of blood. This nest is in the uterus, and if there is no pregnancy the blood trickles down the vagina as the menstrual flow.

A nest inside the girl about the size and shape of a pear. It has a rich red velvet lining and is comfortable for a baby to grow inside. The uterus can get bigger and bigger as the baby grows larger.

Uterus

A long tube with many fingers pointing near the end by the ovary. The fingers point to the grownup egg, telling it to come inside this tube and meet a sperm. If the egg is to be fertilized by a sperm this takes place within one of the oviducts.

Oviduct

The joining of a sperm and an egg. During fertilization, the egg and sperm each give part of what it knows to form a new baby.

Fertilization

A word used to describe a mother with a baby growing inside her uterus.

Pregnant

A food and waste exchange that connects a mother and her baby. It brings all the things that the baby needs from its mother and takes away everything that the baby cannot use.

Placenta

An opening between a girl's legs. This opening has three purposes:

Vagina

1. A man puts his penis in this opening to release his sperm.

2. A baby can be born through this opening when it is ready to leave the uterus.

3. The menstrual flow from the uterus can leave the body through this opening.

A mark that is left on the baby, showing where the baby was attached or connected to its mother. This mark is also called the belly button.

Navel

When a boy is growing up and beginning to make semen, occasionally this semen overflows at night. It may leave a small spot on his sheets or pajamas. Sometimes this overflowing of semen is accompanied by a dream about girls or a dream about growing up. This is why some people call this secretion a "wet dream." Scientifically a wet dream is called a seminal emission.

"Wet Dream," Seminal Emission

A thin piece of membrane that covers the opening from the vagina to the outside of the body. In the middle of the hymen is a small opening. The menstrual flow comes down the vagina and leaves the body through this opening.

Hymen

The unwanted egg, lining of the uterus, and blood, which leave the uterus each month if no baby is made. This blood trickles down the vagina for about three to five days. Some protection must be worn to absorb this blood.

Menstruation

A feminine pad is a soft disposable pad used to absorb the menstrual flow.

Feminine Pads

A narrow elastic belt used to keep the pad firmly in place. The belt is worn around the waist next to the skin. The pad is attached to the belt.

Feminine Belt

A tampon is used to absorb the menstrual flow inside the vagina. It is put into the same opening through which menstrual fluid leaves the body. A tampon works something like a blotter. It absorbs the blood as it flows from the uterus into the vagina.

Tampon

Lesson 4: Feminine Hygiene

Before presenting the following lesson, write a letter home to the girl's parents asking them to purchase a starter kit for their child to bring to school. This kit should include a tampon, a feminine pad, and a belt.

Preparing for this Lesson

The following lesson on feminine hygiene is a summary of five excellent pamphlets written for girls who are about to begin to menstruate. This summary will be most meaningful if the pamphlets are distributed to the girls for reading and for discussion with their mothers:

> · *Growing Up and Liking It* and *Strictly Feminine* (Director of Education, Personal Products Company, Box SS-6, Milltown, New Jersey 08850)
>
> · *It's Time You Knew* (Educational Director, Tampax Incorporated, 161 East 42nd Street, New York, New York, 10017)
>
> · *World of a Girl* (Scott Paper Company, International Airport, Philadelphia, Pennsylvania 19113)
>
> · *Your Years of Self Discovery* (The Life Cycle Center, Kimberly Clark Corporation, Box 551, Neenah, Wisconsin 54956)

About this Lesson

We learned in our previous lesson about growing up and the many changes that are made to equip boys to become fathers and girls to become mothers.

Equipped For Parenthood

One of the most important changes in your own body is the beginning of your menstrual cycle. This is something you have in common with all other girls.

All Girls Menstruate

All girls menstruate. That is why all of the girls in our class are here together today, to talk about menstruation.

You probably already have many questions about menstruation. This is quite natural as it is one more part of knowing yourself completely.

Knowing Yourself Completely

Menstruation is quite natural. It starts and stops each month.

Menstruation is Natural

Although menstruation is natural and happens in all girls, it is not the same for all girls, just as not all girls are the same height and the same weight.

Menstruation varies among Girls

Many girls, but not all girls, have some warning signs, which tell them that their menstrual flow is approaching.

Menstrual Warning Signals

Some girls feel tired or "down in the dumps."

Tiredness and the Blues

Others may have some back discomfort midway between their waist and buttocks.

Back Discomfort

Frequently girls feel a little fatter and have a few blemishes when their period is approaching.

Blemishes and Bulges

These signs of menstruation are not serious, though, and they quickly disappear.

Just as the advance signs of menstruation are not the same for all girls, neither is the menstrual flow itself.

The Menstrual Flow Varies

The menstrual flow usually changes in color and amount from the beginning to the end of menstruation.

At first the menstrual blood may be a pale rusty or brownish hue; then it turns red—the color you normally think of blood. Toward the end of the flow it is sometimes dark brown or black. Then it takes on a rusty color again at the very end of the flow.

Changes in Menstrual Blood Color

Only six to eight tablespoons of blood come through the vagina during menstruation. It may look like much more, but it really isn't.

Amount of Menstrual Flow

The amount of blood doesn't matter; neither does its color.

The important rule concerning menstruation is to be at ease.

Be At Ease

Normally we are more at ease in life when we are prepared. Each of you is prepared with a sanitary protection kit to absorb your menstrual flow when you begin to menstruate.

Be Prepared

Let's look at each product in this kit. Maybe you'll have some questions to ask me about these products.

Here is a feminine pad. It is a soft disposable pad worn outside the body to absorb the menstrual blood.

Feminine Pads to Absorb Flow

Some feminine pads have a strip of tape on one side of them. This tape helps the feminine pad stick to your underpants. This holds the pad in place.

A feminine pad may be attached to a belt to keep the pad firmly in place. Let's attach one of the napkins in our kit to the belt.

A Belt to Hold the Pad in Place

The following tips for attaching the feminine pad to the belt are found in the booklet "World of a Girl" (Scott Paper Company).[3]

Demonstration Guidelines

1. Place narrow end of the pad on the body at a position slightly beyond the rectum.

How to Use the Sanitary Belt

2. With the pad held firmly against the body, between the thighs fasten the wide tab to the front of the belt with pins or clasp.

3. Make certain the pad is snug against the body and fasten back tab firmly.

4. Now try walking, sitting, twisting. If your pad is correctly adjusted it will stay firmly in place.

If your pad is held firmly in place by a belt, it will be unnoticeable to you and to others.

You will want to take extra special care of the belt, since you will be wearing it next to your body just like underwear.

Caring for the Belt

It is a good idea to have at least two belts so that you can put a freshly cleaned belt on each day of your period.

1. Keep Two Belts.

To wash your belt use mild suds and rinse thoroughly.

2. Wash Carefully.

Then lay the belt on a flat surface to dry. Smooth out any wrinkles so it will dry flat.

3. Dry Carefully.

A belt will last through many washings if you care for it properly.

If washed and dried correctly, the belt will hold the pad firmly against your body without any telltale bulges.

You will want to change your pad often, though. Four times a day is a good rule—before breakfast, before lunch, before dinner, and before bedtime.

Change Napkin Four Times Daily

If you will be away from home for the day, perhaps at school, you will want to have extra pads with you.

Have a Spare

---

[3]Scott Paper Company, Internation Airport, Philadelphia, Pennsylvania 19113.

It's a good idea to wrap the pads you take from home in a tissue or put them in a cosmetic kit to keep them clean and fresh.

Spare Should be Clean and Fresh

You might want to keep a few extra sanitary pads or napkins in your locker at school.

A Spare for Your Locker

If you should be caught by surprise without a napkin or pad, there are machines that sell them in the girls' restroom.

A Spare in the Restroom

The tampon or sanitary protection that is worn inside the vagina is also sold in machines in the ladies' restroom. (Show the tampon.)

Tampons Are Available

The tampon is much smaller than the pad. It is put into the vagina through the small opening in the hymen.

Tampon Inserts Through Hymen

Although the opening in the hymen is small, the tampon is much smaller. A tampon will not break or tear the hymen.

Tampon Smaller Than Hymen

Let's learn how to insert the tampon.

For this demonstration use the tampon charts in the atlas (Figure 166). As you explain tampon insertion, point to the diagram. You can show the girls how to hold the tampon applicator. If they would like to practice insertion, tell the girls to do it at home. If they need any additional help, tell them to ask their mothers.

Demonstration Guidelines

The following explanation of tampon insertion is quoted from *Strictly Feminine,* published by the Personal Products Company.[4]

Holding the Applicator Correctly

> Be certain that you know how to hold the applicator in the proper way. Hold the plastic applicator toward your body. Place your thumb and your middle finger (or your fourth finger) on the finger grip. Place your index finger (or your middle finger) on the end of the plunger.

> Use whichever finger position is most comfortable for you. And don't worry if it takes a little practice to feel comfortable holding the applicator. Remember that these two recommended ways of holding the tampon are designed especially to help position it properly in your body.

---

[4]Milltown, New Jersey 08850.

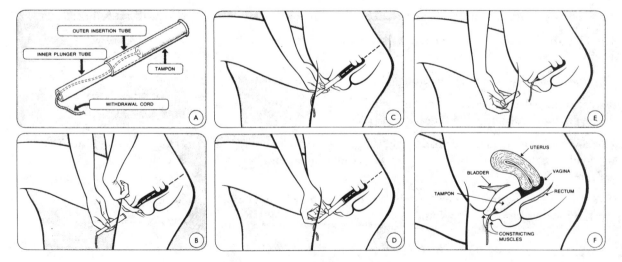

Figure 166   Inserting the tampon.

Remember that the most important rule for all tampon users, especially for first time users, is to relax.

Tampon Rule

Insert the tampon with a slight rotating motion. Remember that each girl and woman is a little different. Some girls slant the applicator toward the back of the waist, others toward the base of the spine and some even lower. Also you may have to slant the applicator differently depending on whether you are sitting, standing, or lying down. If you relax and insert the applicator gradually, you will soon find the method and direction of insertion which suits you best.

How to Use a Tampon

Insert the applicator until your fingers, on the finger grip, touch your body. When this is done, gently push the plunger with your fingers until the ends of the plunger and applicator tubes are even. Remove them from your body and dispose of them in the wastebasket.

Many girls like tampons better than pads because the flow is absorbed inside the body and there is no smell or odor.

No Odor from Tampon

Also, becasue no blood gets out of the body when you use the tampon, the tampon is safe for swimming.

Safe for Swimming

Tampons have been associated with a rare but serious disease called toxic shock syndrome (TSS). This disease can be fatal. It usually occurs in women and girls using tampons during their periods.

Toxic Shock Syndrome

There are some warning signs. There is a sudden fever, usually 102°F or more. There is vomiting or diarrhea. The blood pressure may drop. There may be dizziness and a rash that looks like sunburn. Someone with these signs needs a doctor right away.

How can a girl keep from getting TSS?

1.   You can be almost certain that you will not have TSS if you do not use tampons.

2.   You can lower your chances by using tampons and pads during the menstrual period. For example, you could use tampons during the day and napkins at night.

Girls can discuss tampon use with their mothers.

Girls must be careful in disposing of pads and tampons that have been used.

Disposing of the Tampon and Napkin

Soiled pads and tampons should be placed in a paper bag and thrown into a wastebasket or a restroom container.

They should never be flushed down the toilet. This usually will cause clogging.

No matter what type of sanitary protection you use—the tampon or napkin—you will be well protected.

Occasionally, though, you may find a spot of blood on your underpants, nightgown, or bedsheets.

Accidents Do Happen

Accidents occasionally happen, but they are no problem if you know how to quickly take care of them.

As soon as possible wash the blood stain with cold water and mild soap. Usually the stain will quickly disappear.

Washing a Blood Stain

Occasionally a girl may have cramps accompanying menstruation.

Occasional Discomfort

Cramps are the occasional pains a girl gets below her waist during menstruation.

Cramps During Menstruation

Sometimes discomfort can be caused by mistaken ideas a girl has heard about menstruation:

Mistaken Ideas About Menstruation

1. That a rainy day causes menstrual cramps.

2. That eating a lemon will start your menstrual flow ahead of time.

3. That taking a bath during menstruation will cause tuberculosis.

4. That a girl who is menstruating is possessed by an evil spirit.

5. That flowers will wilt if you touch them while menstruating.

You can see how a girl who believes any of these silly things can be frightened and feel sick inside during menstruation.

Other girls have menstrual cramps because they are constipated. Constipated is a word that describes a condition in which bowel movements are difficult.

Constipation—Unnecessary Menstrual Cramps

Constipation may cause menstrual pains. The best way to avoid this is to drink plenty of water and to eat lots of fruit.

The Water and Fruit Cure

Other girls have cramps because they have poor posture, which pushes all the important body parts together and makes menstruation more difficult.

The Poor Posture Villain

It's good to sit tall when you feel yourself slumping at your desk. Here is a good exercise that you can do:

Sit Tall—Feel Better

Sit in your chair with part of your back touching the back of your chair. Now put your arms straight down at your sides.

A Sit Tall Exercise

Take the palm of your hand and place it on the chair with your fingers pointing away from the chair.

Now push down on the palms of your hands as much as possible and count to five.

You should feel yourself sitting taller. This exercise is fun to do whenever you feel yourself slumping.

Incidentally, exercises are very good for a girl at the age at which she begins to menstruate.

Exercises—An Aid to Growing Up

They help a girl to feel better and get her body in good condition.

A girl who has a daily program of exercise rarely has menstrual cramps.

Rare Menstrual Discomfort

Familiarize your girls with exercises for painful menstruation. Have the girls dress in gym clothes and meet in the gym. Together the girls can learn the following exercises:

Demonstration Guidelines

Sit on the floor with your knees bent and your feet flat. Put one hand on the lower abdomen (below your waist) to feel muscle movement.

Abdominal Pumping Exercises[5]

---

[5]Adapted from *Exercises for Dysmenorrhea* (Toledo, Ohio: Department of Health, Physical Education, and Recreation, University of Toledo, 1969).

Figure 167   Figure 168

On count of "one" inhale deeply, pushing the abdomen out. On "two" pull the abdomen in holding your breath. On "three" exhale completely through the mouth. Repeat several times.

Lie on your back with your legs straight and your arms spread out straight from your shoulders. Raise your left leg, keeping your knee straight, and swing your leg over to touch the palm of your right hand with your toes. Return your leg by first bringing it straight up in the air and then returning it to its starting position. Repeat the exercise, using your right leg. Do this exercise several times with each leg.

Twisting Exercise[6]

Assume a crawling position with your hands and knees on the floor. Lower your chest to the floor and arch your back by pulling in your abdominal muscles (the muscles below your waist). Return to a resting position. Repeat several times.

Cat Exercise[6]

In addition to these exercises you will want to do at least one vigorous exercise each day.

Other Exercises

You might want to play your favorite record and solo dance for 15 minutes when you come home from school each day.

It's also fun to take a brisk 15-minute walk before or after your homework.

On some days, but not very often, menstrual cramps may need some special attention.

Sometimes lying in a special way seems to ease menstrual discomfort. Try these positions to find the one that makes you most comfortable.

Postures[6]

Lie on your back on the floor with your knees bent and your feet resting on a low chair or stool.

Lie on your back on the floor or on a firm bed with your head on a small pillow and your knees pulled up to your chest.

Figure 169   Figure 170

---

[6]Exercises for Dysmenorrhea, op. cit.

Kneel on the floor with your knees about 12 inches apart and lower your chest until it touches the floor. Turn your head to one side with one hand on each side of the head.

All the exercises and postures we have learned should help, but in addition you may want some extra tips on how to relieve menstrual discomfort:

Additional Tips to Relieve Discomfort

1. Place a hot water bottle or electric heating pad on your stomach.
2. Relax in a warm tub of water.

Now you know many facts and many of the things all women know about their menstrual periods.

The menstrual period is quite normal and natural if you are always at ease and always prepared.

Perhaps you have some questions to ask . . . .

Unit Activities

My Menstrual Cycle

Have the girls make a booklet of calendars for the next 12 months. Title the booklet "My Menstrual Cycle."

On the first page of the booklet have the girls copy the following paragraph, which explains how to keep a calendar of the menstrual cycle:

Circle the day you start to menstruate. Then count off 28 days into the next month and draw a box around the date. That is approximately when your menstrual flow is due again. Be sure to make another circle around the day you actually do begin menstruating the next month, and make a note of how long overdue you were. This will give you a due date for the next time.

Explain to the girls that a record of their menstrual periods will be helpful in understanding themselves completely. It will help them to know:

1. The length of each menstrual cycle (28 to 35 days).
2. The number of days that they have menstrual flow (3 to 5).
3. When their next menstrual flow will be.
4. If they have any menstrual irregularities.

The girls will want to carry a tampon or napkin in their purse when their period is nearing. An additional activity might be to make a carrying case. The girls can use yarn and leather or plastic and boondaggle. If class time does not permit, you might pass the materials out in class and have the girls make the carrying case with their Girl Scout troop or with their mothers. An outside-class activity such as this might promote discussion between the girls and other competent adults.

Tampon or Napkin Carrying Case

Have the children complete their "Growing Up" notebooks. Each notebook should include:

"Growing Up" Notebook

1. The journey of the sperm.
2. The menstrual cycle.
3. The sex education dictionary.

Collect the notebooks and check to see that the students have the correct information. Pass back the notebooks and allow the children to take them home to discuss with their parents.

At the close of the fifth grade the students should be familiar with the biological changes of growing up. As a review activity have each child write a letter to a fourth grade child explaining the process of growing up in detail. Tell your class that you plan to keep the letters and give them to the fourth grade children when they are in the fifth grade. Explain to your class the importance of being at ease with growing changes and the ease and assurance their letters will give to the other children if their explanations are clear. Put the letters in envelopes addressed to fourth graders.

First Letter of Information

After your sex education program has been instituted in your school system for more than one year you will have a set of letters to pass out to your fifth grade students. Pass out these letters to your class after you have covered and reviewed this unit. Have the children read the letters to themselves. Then have the children list on the blackboard some of the points made in the letters they read. After you are finished with this activity, erase the blackboard, collect the letters, and have the children begin writing their own letters to fourth graders.

Second Letter of Information

Unit Two:

Making Responsible Decisions

What do each of the following situations have in common?

Introduction

1. Mary's parents tell her to come home after school. Jill wants Mary to stop at Jill's house to see her new record player.

2. Bob and Jill walk home from school. Jill invites Bob in for lemonade. Her parents are not home. Bob's parents do not allow him in a friend's home when there are no parents home.

3. Karen, Jane, and Maria go for a bicycle ride. Karen and Jane want to cycle by the railroad tracks. Maria's parents have said that it is not safe to be near the tracks.

4. Mike and Tom are late for football practice. Mike suggests that they hitchhike. Tom read in the paper that boys have been molested when they have been picked up by hitchhikers.

In each of these situations, a young person like you had to make a decision. A decision is a choice that you make. For every decision (1) there are at least two choices; (2) there are results; and (3) there are risks. A *risk* is a chance that you take.

Making a Decision

Let's look at each of the situations again. I will make a chart on the blackboard. We will complete the chart together.

Situation	Choices	Results	Risks
1.			
2.			
3.			
4.			

Decision making is deciding which of two or more choices you will make. Many things influence the decisions you will make. For example, the possible results and risks were important in the situations we just discussed.

Facts also help us to make decisions. A friend may offer you a cigarette. You have learned facts about cigarette smoking. Cigarette smoking may cause lung cancer. You choose not to smoke because you want to be healthy. Facts are pieces of information that can influence your decision.

Let's look again at the decision Maria had to make. She could cycle by the railroad tracks with Karen and Jane. She could tell Karen and Jane that she was not allowed to cycle by the tracks. What things might influence her decision?

Maria might be influenced by her parents' guidelines. She knows that parents' guidelines are rules to keep her healthy and safe. Parents' guidelines may also be rules that help young people follow their family's religious beliefs. Parents' guidelines help young people choose responsible ways to act. What are some of your parents' guidelines?

Suppose Jane tried to influence Maria's choice. She might say, "No one will know that we were by the railroad tracks. We'll only stay for ten minutes." Maria feels pressure to make a certain choice. She chooses to cycle by the tracks with Jane and Karen.

When friends try to get you to make a certain choice, it is called peer pressure. Sometimes peer pressure is healthful. Your peers may pressure you to learn how to swim. You practice until you can swim well. You follow rules for health and safety. You feel good about yourself. Your peers helped you in a healthful way.

Sometimes peer pressure is harmful. Friends may try to talk you into doing things you should not do. How do you know when peer pressure is healthful and when it is harmful?

Here are some guidelines[7] for knowing the difference. Never allow peer pressure to influence you to make a choice that (1) does not follow your parents' guidelines; (2) does not show self-respect or respect for others; (3) is not healthful; (4) does not respect the law; or (5) is not safe. These choices would not be responsible.

Let's list the steps that you should take to make a responsible decision.[8] I'll write them on the blackboard and you write them on a sheet of paper.

1. Identify the problem.

2. List the choices you could make.

3. List the risks for each choice.

4. Think about the results.

5. Evaluate your choice.

Decision Making

1. Facts

2. Parents' Guidelines

3. Peer Pressure

Steps to Make a Responsible Decision

[7,8]Concepts adapted from *Health: Focus On You,* a K–12 textbook series (Westerville, Ohio: Charles E. Merrill, 936 Eastwind Drive, 43081).

When you evaluate your choice, ask yourself:

1. **Does my choice follow my parents' guidelines?**

2. **Does my choice show self-respect and respect for others?**

3. **Is my choice healthful?**

4. **Does my choice respect the law?**

5. **Is my choice safe?**

Review the four decision-making situations used to introduce the chapter. Use the five steps for decision making. Apply the five questions for evaluations. Which decision is the most responsible in each situation?

Decision-Making Review

Make copies of the Word Search given below for the students. There are ten words in the Word Search that can be used to complete the review sentences.

Vocabulary Review

```
D A Y C D M E H G L S O R
E C Y A Z R K P B S A F E
C H O I C E S A T H B N S
I N B R X S F R X E U A P
S Q Z O P U C E U A E P O
I D X I J L V N L L M T N
O P K L W T S T I T M V S
N E Q R I S K S R H V Q I
F F A C T S J U D Y S N B
W J K H T G G R O H W F L
I P E E R P R E S S U R E
```

1. A *decision* is a choice that you make.

2. A *risk* is a chance that you take.

3. *Results* are how things turn out after you make a choice.

4. For every decision there are at least two *choices*.

5. *Facts* are pieces of information that help you make wise decision.

6. Your *parents* have guidelines to help you make responsible choices.

7, 8. Your choices should always be *healthful* and *safe*.

9. *Peer Pressure* is the influence your friends have on your decisions.

10. The best decision is a *responsible* decision.

Complete the following sentence: A responsible decision (1) *follows my* *parents' guidelines,* **(2)** *shows self-respect and respect for others,* **(3)** *is healthful,* **(4)** *is safe,* **and (5)** *respects the law.*

Sentence Completion

Have students write anonymous letters to "Dear Helper" that describe difficult decisions that they must make. Discuss these decision-making situations with the class. Use the steps for making a responsible decision. Apply the five criteria for making a responsible decision.

Dear Helper

CHAPTER 20

Sex Education of the Sixth Grade Child

Throughout the elementary school years, sex education results in sequential learning experiences. Each new unit reinforces and expands upon previous learning experience. In the earlier elementary years the children have learned specific content appropriately chosen for their degree of maturation. By the sixth grade, the maturation of the child and the vast learning experiences the child retains have laid the foundation for the study of human sexuality in detail. The objective of the sixth grade teacher is to review and expand the child's understanding of the male and female sexual cycles, fertilization, pregnancy, and married and family love. A pretest to assess the knowledge of your class is followed by the fundamental sixth grade unit, "The Family as the Basic Unit of Society." This is accompanied by a unit called "Friendship, Dating, and Decision Making."

Pretest

The administration of a pretest serves as a valuable educational tool for evaluating the current status of your students. The pretest is designed to help the sixth grade teacher identify the subject matter that needs to be reviewed prior to beginning the unit. In addition, it allows the students to identify their own needs and limitations within the sequential learning process. The location of the concept by grade level accompanies each question to enable the teacher to quickly obtain the material for review.

The Family as the Basic Unit of Society

An Overview of Unit One

"We all belong to families that have experienced the joy of new life. In later years if we marry, we will belong to another family, and we will be concerned with the raising of another generation. For this reason we will want to learn about life from its earliest existence and trace through its development step by step." So begins the unit that culminates the elementary sex education program. The program has built upon concepts and subject matter each year to arrive at a unit in the sixth grade in which each concept can be interwoven into a coherent point of view—that sexual love and the upbringing of another generation are the basic functions of the family.

The sixth grade program "The Family as the Basic Unit of Society" includes a discussion of the following points:

1.   The pituitary gland secretes FSH, which causes other hormones to initiate puberty in the male and female.

2.   The secondary sex characteristics are the changes in the male and the female bodies that result from hormonal influences at puberty.

3.   The parts of the male reproductive system include the scrotum, testes, seminiferous tubules, epididymis, vas deferens, seminal vesicles, ejaculatory duct, prostate gland, Cowper's glands, urethra, and penis.

4.   The parts of the female reproductive system include the ovaries, uterus, oviducts, vagina, mons veneris, labia, and clitoris.

5.   Before fertilization or the coming together of the sperm and egg, there must be a coming together of the father and the mother.

6.   Intercourse is a special way that married husbands and wives express their love for one another.

7.   During intercourse, the man places his erect penis inside the woman's vagina and moves it back and forth, causing semen to be released into the vagina.

8.   The union of the sperm and egg is called fertilization.

9.   A design for a new baby is laid out when the chromosomes and genes from the sperm are joined with the chromosomes and genes from the egg.

10.   During the growth period in the uterus, the embryo uses the placenta to obtain food and oxygen and to remove wastes.

11.   The pregnant mother's health habits—nutrition, drug use, diseases—affect the health of the growing baby.

12.   At the eighth week of development, the embryo begins to resemble a human being and is called a fetus.

13.   Many changes occur in the month-by-month development of the fetus from fertilization to birth.

14.   There are three stages in the birth process—the baby's head appears in the birth canal, the baby is born, and the afterbirth is expelled.

15.   Each family has a responsibility to the helpless new being, to care for it and love it so that it may grow up happily and healthfully.

Friendship, Dating, and Decision Making

Three developmental tasks of this age group are (1) achieving new and more mature relationships with peers of both sexes; (2) desiring and achieving socially responsible behavior; and (3) acquiring a set of values and an ethical system as guides to behavior. This unit was developed to assist students as they work to meet these developmental tasks. During this unit students learn that

1.   Feeling good about yourself helps you to express love to others.

2.   Four skills that will help you become a loving person are labor or work, responsibility, respect, and understanding.

3. There are many kinds of loving relationships.

4. A friend is someone you know well and like.

5. Certain skills are helpful in forming and maintaining friendships.

6. Opposite-sex friends are important.

7. Dating is sharing social activities and time with someone of the opposite sex.

8. Parents help establish guidelines for dating behavior.

9. A value is a decison about how much people or things mean to you.

10. It is important to have the self-discipline to behave in ways that show others what you value.

Pretest: The Beginning of New Life

Part I. Human and Animal Beginnings

Below are listed ten statements about the beginning of human and animal life. If the statement is false place a (0) in the blank. If the statement is true place a (+) in the blank.

<u>+</u> 1. Human beings belong to the animal kingdom. (Kindergarten)
<u>+</u> 2. Every animal has a mother and a father in the beginning. (Kindergarten)
<u>0</u> 3. A fish egg grows to be a fish in its mother's uterus. (Grade 2)
<u>+</u> 4. A dog's egg is fertilized inside the mother dog's body. (Grade 2)
<u>+</u> 5. All life comes from the same kind of life. (Kindergarten)
<u>+</u> 6. All animal life begins when a sperm joins an egg. (Grade 2)
<u>0</u> 7. In human beings the egg is fertilized in the uterus. (Grade 4)
<u>0</u> 8. An animal baby (puppy, kitten) needs only a mother to begin new life. (Grade 2)
<u>0</u> 9. If an egg that is bought at a grocery store is placed in an incubator it will grow into a chick. (Grade 3)
<u>+</u> 10. A fertilized human egg grows in the mother's uterus. (Grade 4)

Part II. Animal Development

Below are listed eight steps necessary in the fertilization of an egg and growth from an egg to a chick. Arrange these sentences in order beginning with fertilization. (Grade 3)

<u>2</u> The rooster sends his sperm into the hen.
<u>7</u> The egg is kept warm.
<u>8</u> The egg begins to grow into a chick.
<u>1</u> The hen makes an egg.
<u>5</u> A shell covers the egg.
<u>3</u> A yolk covers the egg.
<u>6</u> The hen lays the egg.
<u>4</u> White covers the yolk of the egg.

Part III. Processes in New Life

Match the words in the left-hand column with the definitions in the right-hand column.

_D_	fertilization	A.	The joining together of the mother's and father's body in love. (Grade 5)
_C_	reproduction	B.	Contains the heredity information needed to make a girl. (Grade 4)
_B_	X chromosome	C.	The bringing about of the birth of a new plant or animal of the same kind. (Grade 2)
_E_	Y chromosome	D.	The joining together of a sperm and an egg. (Grade 2)
_A_	intercourse	E.	Contains the heredity information needed to make a boy. (Grade 4)

Part IV. Heredity

A baby receives two genes for every trait, one gene from the baby's mother and the other gene from the baby's father. A baby has received the following genes for different traits. Which gene is dominant? (Grade 4)

brown   A gene for brown skin or a gene for white skin.
tall   A gene for being tall or a gene for being short.
curly   A gene for curly hair or a gene for straight hair.
brown   A gene for brown eyes or a gene for blue eyes.

Part V. Male Reproductive System

Fill in the sentences describing the boy's body parts using the following words:

testes   vas deferens   epididymis   semen   penis
scrotum   seminal vesicle   prostate gland   urethra   Cowper's glands

scrotum	A small sac between the boy's legs that holds the testes.
epididymis	A tube on top of each testis where the sperm grow up to look like tadpoles.
testes	The place where the male reproductive cells, the sperm, are made.
seminal vesicle	Glands that provide the sperm with sugar energy.
vas deferens	A long tube that goes up into the body.
Cowper's glands	Two small glands that secrete cleansing fluid to clean the urethra.
semen	The milky sugary fluid that contains the sperm.
prostate gland	A gland that secretes milky water.
urethra	A tube inside the penis.
penis	Located between the boy's legs. It is soft and hangs down.

Part VI. Female Reproductive System

Fill in the sentences describing the girl's body parts and processes using the following words:

ovary   oviduct   vagina   hymen   feminine pad
Uterus   placenta   navel   menstruation   FSH

navel	A mark that is left on the baby showing where the baby was attached to its mother.

feminine pad	A soft disposable pad used to absorb the menstrual flow.
oviduct	A tube leading from the uterus to the ovary.
uterus	A nest in which a baby can grow inside a girl's body.
ovary	A storage room filled with thousands of eggs.
placenta	A food and waste exchange that connects a mother to her baby.
hymen	A thin piece of skin that covers the opening of the vagina to the outside of the body.
menstruation	The unwanted egg and blood that leave the uterus each month if no baby is made.
FSH	A hormone from the pituitary gland that tells the eggs in the ovary to mature and begin to grow.
vagina	A tunnel that leads from the uterus to the outside of the body.

Unit One:

The Family as the Basic Unit of Society

The family is the basic unit of society. One of its many responsibilities is to pass life on from generation to generation.

Introduction: The Origin of Life

During each minute of every day, every week, every hour, a new life begins. The new life brings much joy and happiness to each family.

The many hours waited and preparations made for the arrival of a new baby are soon forgotten. The family has learned a great deal about the origin of new life.

We all belong to families that have experienced the joy of new life. In later years, if we marry, we will belong to another family, and we will be concerned with the raising of another generation For this reason we will want to learn about life from its earliest existence and trace through its development step by step.

A baby begins life as a single cell, smaller than the tiniest grain of sand and barely visible to the naked eye.

Life Begins as a Single Cell

The first cell is created by the joining of two parent cells:

The First Cell

1. The egg or ovum from the mother.

2. The sperm from the father.

Let us trace back to the beginning of each of these parent cells. We will begin with the egg cell.

When a girl is born, each of her ovaries contains some 200,000 to 400,000 egg cells. These egg cells are sometimes called primary follicles.

Origin of the Egg Cell

These egg cells or primary follicles remain inactive until they receive a hormone message that tells them to begin to grow.

Between the ages of 11 and 14, these hormonal messengers begin acting under the direction of the pituitary gland in the brain.

Pituitary Messengers

This pea-sized gland sends out hormonal messengers that announce that it is time for the girl's body to undergo vast remodeling.

This remodeling period is known as puberty. During puberty, many changes take place in a girl's body as well as in the egg cells in her ovaries. All these changes are brought about by the hormone messengers we mentioned.

A Vast Remodeling Period

First, we will look at the changes in the girl's body at puberty. These changes are known as the secondary sex characteristics.

Secondary Sex Characteristics

During puberty the ovaries release a hormone messenger called estrogen. Estrogen causes each of the female reproductive organs to increase in size.

Estrogen Increases Organ Size

(Review the anatomy of the female reproductive organs with the class as you discuss the increase in organ size of each. As you identify each organ point to it on a diagram or overlay.)

Anatomy Review

A woman has two ovaries situated deep in the pelvis. They are slightly below and to each side of her navel.

1. Ovaries

Each ovary is oval: 1½ inches long, 1 inch wide, and ¾ inch thick.

At birth each ovary contains between 200,000 and 400,000 primary follicles or egg cells. These egg cells remain immature until puberty.

There are two oviducts. They extend from the ovary to the uterus. Each tube is 2 to 4 inches long and is lined with tiny hairs. The outer wall of the tube is composed of muscle that contracts in a slow rhythmic manner.

2. Oviducts

The uterus is a muscular organ extending from the oviducts to the vagina. It is about the size and shape of a pear. The stem end is at the vaginal end of the uterus. This part of the uterus is called the cervix. The upper part called the body connects with the oviducts.

3. Uterus

The uterine walls are divided into walls or layers. The inner wall lining is called the endometrium. This is a soft lining, which thickens each month to provide a nest for a growing baby. The outer uterine wall is quite muscular. It has the remarkable ability of being able to grow and expand enough to hold a 20-inch, 9-pound baby.

The vagina is a 4-inch-long muscular tube that extends from the cervix of the uterus to the outside of a woman's body. The vaginal opening is between a woman's legs. It is behind the urethra from which urine comes and in front of the rectum from which bowel movements pass.

4. Vagina

At rest, the vaginal walls are closed and touching each other. The walls are separated during menstrual flow, intercourse, and childbirth.

Just inside the vagina is a thin membrane called the hymen. This membrane has one or more openings through which the menstrual flow leaves the vagina. The size of this opening differs among girls, just as girls differ in size and height. The size of the hymen and its presence or absence mean little, if anything.

5. Hymen

The labia majora or outer lips are rounded folds of skin and fatty tissue that protect the structures lying between them and the vagina. The labia majora are covered by pubic hair. Inside the larger labia majora are two smaller and thinner folds of skin called the labia minora. They are the inner lips protecting the vagina.

6. Labia

Where the upper folds of the labia minora join together there is a

7. Clitoris

small organ the size and shape of a pea. This organ is called the clitoris. The clitoris is richly supplied with nerves and blood vessels. It is very sensitive to touch.

The mons veneris or mons pubis is a mountain of fatty tissue covering the pubic bone. This area is covered with curly hair and protects the inner female reproductive organs from a shock or blow.

8. Mons veneris (mons pubis)

Continuation of Lecture

In addition to increasing the size of the female reproductive organs, estrogen is responsible for the more streamlined appearance of the adult female.

The Streamlined Young Woman

Under estrogen influence, fat is deposited in the breasts and an elaborate duct system for the secretion of milk develops.

The Breasts Develop

Fat is also deposited in the buttocks and thighs, rounding out the female figure. The pelvis broadens and changes from a narrow funnel-like outlet to a broad, oval outlet.

Rounding the Figure

These bodily changes are only a part of the maturation of the female reproductive system at puberty.

During this vast remodeling period, the pituitary gland sends a message to the immature follicles or egg cells in the ovary via FSH.

A Message to the Egg Cells

FSH is short for follicle-stimulating hormone. FSH does just what its name says that it might—it stimulates the primary follicles or egg cells in the ovary to grow.

FSH's Important Message

Each month one of the egg cells that began to grow ripens and bursts out of the ovary—a process termed ovulation. This egg cell is guided by currents and by finger-like projections within the oviduct.

Ovulation

The ripened egg has a very brief life span and will soon disintegrate if a sperm cell does not meet it on the first, or at most, the second, day after its arrival in the oviduct.

The sperm cells are produced in the testes of the father. After their production in the testes, the sperm must pass through the penis and into the female vagina to fertilize the ovum.

Origin of Sperm Cells

During puberty, the testes release a hormone called testosterone. Testosterone makes the boy's body grow and mature.

Testosterone

After testosterone is released, some noticeable changes occur:

1. The voice becomes deeper.

2. The skin becomes thicker and tougher.

3. The bones become longer and the muscles larger.

4. Hair appears under the arms, on the pubic region, and on the chin and face.

5. The organs of the male reproductive system enlarge.

Accompanying these changes in a boy's body is the beginning of the production of sperms by the testes.

At puberty the pituitary gland in the brain sends a message alerting the testes to produce many sperm.

Alert Signal to Testes

The testes begin their work with the help of the scrotum, the small sac or pouch that holds the testes. The scrotum makes sperm production easier by maintaining the testes at an ideal temperature.

The Temperature of the Testes

On days when the weather is extremely cold the scrotum aids sperm production by pulling the testes close to the man's body.

Too Cold

On other days the weather is so warm that sperms cannot be produced. On these days the scrotum lowers the testes away from the body.

Too Warm

After the sperms have been produced by the testes they pass into a coiled tube located right above the testes. This tube is called the epididymis.

The Epididymis

The epididymis makes the sperm mature. The sperm take on a tadpole appearance with a large head and a tail, which beats back and forth.

A Tadpole With Head and Tail

Now that the sperm are mature, they are ready to make the journey up into the body. They wait in a long tube called the vas deferens. The vas deferens winds its way up into the body.

At last the sperm are ready to make the final preparations en route to the female vagina. The special term for the trip from the testes to the vagina is ejaculation.

Ejaculation

During ejaculation or the sperm trip, the sperm go up the vas deferens. Some fluids help.

Energy will be needed. The seminal vesicle, a comma-shaped structure, empties an abundant supply of sugar solution into the vas deferens.

After the sperm receive this extra nutrition, they journey into another tube called the ejaculatory duct. As the sperm empty into the ejaculatory duct, another fluid is added.

The Ejaculatory Duct

Once inside the female vagina, the sperm swim by beating their tails. A milky watery fluid helps them to swim. The ejaculatory duct is surrounded by the prostate gland. The prostate gland empties milky water into the ejaculatory duct. The sperm are in a fluid containing milky-water and sugar vital to their survival.

The Prostate Gland

This life-giving fluid is called semen. Semen contains three important ingredients:

Ingredients in Semen

1. Sperm from the testes
2. Sugar from the seminal vesicle.
3. Milky water from the prostate gland.

The ejaculatory duct empties the semen into a long tube inside the penis called the urethra.

The Urethra—the Last Tube

The urethra is the same tube through which urine passes to the outside of the body. But urine and semen never are in the urethra at the same time.

Urine Pathway

Between the bladder (where the urine is stored) and the urethra is a small valve. When semen is nearing the urethra, this valve closes, keeping urine inside the bladder.

To doublecheck to be extra sure that the urethra is free of urine, there are two Cowper's glands, one on either side of the urethra.

Two Cowper's Glands

Each of the Cowper's glands squirts cleansing fluid down the urethra to wash away any urine that might be left.

The final stage of ejaculation is the passage of semen down the urethra and out of the penis into the female vagina to fertilize the egg.

But before fertilization or the coming together of the sperm and the egg, there must be a coming together of the father and the mother.

Coming Together

This coming together is called sexual intercourse, which means an interchange, as one interchanges thought, feeling, friendship, or love with another.

Sexual Intercourse

Sexual intercourse is a special way that married husbands and wives express their love and their desire to share everything with one another.

Desire to Share

The father and the mother lie close to each other, sharing kind words, embraces, and kisses—interchanging the deep love they feel for one another.

Interchanging Love

The father's penis, which is usually soft, becomes hard and straight. This is called an erection.

The Penis Erects

The father places his erect penis into the mother's vagina and moves it back and forth, causing the semen to be released into the vagina.

Two Closely Fitting Passages

Married Love

Sexual intercourse is a very special part of married love, and the closeness brings much pleasure to the husband and wife. Because a husband and wife who love each other want to be close to each other, they will have sexual intercourse even when they do not intend to have a baby.

1. Sharing Each Other

When a married couple does want to have a baby, sexual intercourse provides another kind of sharing. It allows a married couple to share the joy of bringing new life into the world.

2. Sharing New Life

The sharing together in bringing about new life requires special timing. The short life span of the egg cell, 12 to 24 hours, limits the time period during each month in which a sperm and an egg can unite. This time period lasts about two days each month.

Timing in the Life-Bringing Process

The chance of a sperm and an egg joining together is greatly increased by the fact that the father produces millions of sperm when only one is needed.

Extra Sperm Cells

When the semen is released, millions of sperm swim up the vagina through the uterus and into the oviduct, but only a few reach the egg.

Few Reach Their Destination

When a sperm reaches the egg it becomes excited, and its tail beats more rapidly. The beating tail gives the sperm more force to push its head into the egg.

An Excited Sperm

The sperm cell cannot get into the egg cell by force alone. To help the sperm accomplish this task there is a special fluid inside the head of the sperm.

Attempted Breakthrough

This fluid is similar to the fluid that eats away at the food in your stomach. The sperm releases this substance as it nears the egg. This substance eats away at the covering of the egg cell and allows the sperm to enter.

The union of the sperm and egg is still not complete, however. The important directions for making a new baby are contained in the nucleus of the sperm and the nucleus of the egg. The nucleus of the sperm cell is in its head. The nucleus of the egg cell is in its center.

Not Yet Complete

Inside the nucleus of the sperm and inside the nucleus of the egg are genes. The genes contain all the instructions necessary for the design of every part of a new baby.

Gene Instructions

A design for a new baby is laid out when the sperm nucleus combines its information with the nucleus of the egg, or, to put it another way, when the genes from the sperm are joined with the genes from the egg.

Pooling of Information

This pooling of instructions or genes will result in such important decisions as:

Important Decisions

1. Whether the baby will be a boy or a girl.

2. What color of eyes the baby will have.

3. What color of hair the baby will have.

4. What color of skin the baby will have.

5. Whether the baby will be tall or short.

After the genes from the sperm cell join the genes from the egg cell, the fertilized egg begins to divide into many cells. These cells will be needed to carry out the instructions from the genes.

More Cells Needed

During the first three or four days after this union, the dividing cells drift down the oviduct toward the uterus.

Drifting to Destination

Meanwhile the uterus has been busily preparing a nest for the fertilized egg. The wall of the uterus is now extra thick and is filled with rich nourishing blood.

Preparations for a Comfortable Nest

When the group of dividing cells arrive at the uterus on the fourth day, they don't settle into the nest. Instead, they float around in the uterus for about four days.

Floating Cluster of Cells

Finally, in need of food and nourishment the group of cells burrow a nest in the uterine wall and settle inside. This is called "nesting."

Nesting for Nourishment

Comfortable in their new home, the dividing cells are carrying out the instructions from the genes. This group of dividing cells, called an embryo, will have a lot of growing to do before a baby is formed.

Carrying Out the Instructions

During this growth period inside the uterus the embryo will need a means of obtaining food, oxygen, and water and a means of removing waste products.

This food and waste service is provided by the placenta. The placenta is a depot in which the transport systems of mother and baby meet to exchange cargoes.

Food and Waste Service

The mother's transport system brings nutrition and oxygen to the placental depot while the baby's transport system brings waste products.

The placenta is connected to the growing embryo by the umbilical cord. When you are growing inside your mother, you had an umbilical cord attached to the placenta. But after you were born you didn't need the umbilical cord anymore, so the doctor tied and cut it. This left a scar, which you call your navel. So you see, the umbilical cord is attached to the baby at the location of the navel.

Link Between Mother and Baby

The growing baby needs this attachment. The baby is dependent upon the mother for everything.

Mother Shares Supplies

The mother takes care of the baby by taking care of herself. The baby can only receive as much food, oxygen, calcium, and vitamins as the mother has to share. In short, the baby has to depend on its mother's health for its own health.

This may be unfortunate for a baby who is growing inside a mother who does not take care of herself. The baby may receive some special supplies from its mother that it would rather not have.

Do you think that a baby needs these supplies to grow?

"Supplies Unwanted"

1. Alcohol, wine, or beer.

2. Ingredients from cigarette smoke.

3. Diseases such as flu, measles, or a cold.

4. Caffeine.

Because babies share all supplies, there is good reason for mothers to avoid smoking and drinking during pregnancy. Pregnant mothers should also avoid coming into contact with persons carrying disease.

Smoking, Drinking, Disease

Fortunately, many drugs to wipe out sickness (such as penicillin) can be supplied to the baby if needed. These supplies can be used to keep the baby healthy.

Lifesaving Supplies

The drug is given to the mother, and within an hour it arrives at the placenta depot to be shared with the baby.

A further health measure is the "bag of waters," which tightly surrounds the growing embryo in the uterus. This bag of waters is called the amnion.

Further Supplies

The amnion protects the growing embryo by cushioning it from blows. Also, the temperature of the amniotic water is ideal for the embryo's growth.

Comfortable Environment

With such ideal conditions in the uterus, the embryo's growth proceeds like clockwork. The time schedule for the growth of each body part is carefully planned.

Careful Clockwork

Divide the class into nine groups representing each month of intrauterine growth. Have a section of library books and materials available in your classroom. Each group will do research on the growth that takes place during its assigned month. Each group will also prepare a report to share with the class on what its members have learned. Large illustrations made by the group will be combined on one large bulletin board to show the nine-month developmental sequence.

Class Activity

Below is an outline, month by month, of the development of the baby. It is intended to help the teacher organize the nine groups and is not intended to be lecture material. The monthly facts were taken from *Pregnancy,* a booklet presented by the Carnation Company.[1]

End of First Month

1. About ⁹⁄₁₆ inch long.

2. Backbone and spinal canal forming.

3. Heart pulsating and pumping blood.

4. No eyes, nose, or external ears visible.

5. Digestive system beginning to form.

6. Small buds, which will eventually become arms and legs, are present.

End of Second Month

1. About 1⅛ inches long.

2. Weighs about ¹⁄₃₀ of an ounce.

3. Face and features forming: eyelids fused.

4. Limbs beginning to show distinct divisions into arms, elbows, fore-arm and hand, thigh, knee, lower leg, and foot.

5. Distinct umbilical cord formed.

6. Long bones and internal organs developing.

7. Tail-like process disappears.

End of Third Month

1. About 3 inches long.

2. Weighs about 1 ounce.

3. Arms, hands, fingers, legs, feet, and toes fully formed.

4. Nails on digits beginning to develop.

5. External ears are present.

6. Tooth sockets and buds forming in the jawbones.

7. Eyes almost fully developed but lids still fused.

8. Heartbeat can be detected with special instruments.

9. Baby's hands are fully formed with fingers and nails all distinctly present.

10. The uterus begins to enlarge with the growing fetus and can now be felt extending about halfway up to the umbilicus.

End of Fourth Month

1. The baby is now about 6½ to 7 inches long and weighs about 4 ounces.

2. It has a strong heartbeat, fair digestion, and active muscles.

3. Its skin is bright pink and transparent and is covered with a fine, down-like hair.

4. Most bones are distinctly visible throughout the body.

5. The head is disproportionately large at this stage.

---

[1]Address the Medical Department, Carnation Company, 5045 Wilshire Boulevard, Los Angeles, California 90036.

6. The eyes, ears, nose, and mouth approach typical appearance.

7. Eyebrows appear.

1. The baby measures about 10 to 12 inches long and weighs ½ to 1 pound.   **End of Fifth Month**

2. It is still bright red.

3. Its increased size now brings the dome of the uterus to the level of the umbilicus.

4. The internal organs are maturing at astonishing speed, but the lungs are insufficiently developed to cope with conditions outside the uterus.

5. The eyelids are still compeltely fused at the end of five months.

6. Some hair may be present on the head.

1. At the end of the sixth month the baby measures 11 to 14 inches and may weigh 1¼ to 1½ pounds.   **End of Sixth Month**

2. The skin is quite wrinkled and still somewhat red and is covered with a heavy protective, creamy coating.

3. The eyelids are finally separated, and eyelashes are formed.

4. Fingernails now extend to the ends of the fingers.

1. The baby's weight has almost doubled since last month, and it is about 3 inches longer.   **End of Seventh Month**

2. However, it still looks quite red and is covered with wrinkles, which will eventually be erased by fat.

3. At seven months the premature baby has a fair chance for survival in nurseries cared for by skilled physicians and nurses.

4. The seven-month baby is wrinkled and red.

1. In the absence of premature labor the growth and maturation of the baby in the last two months are extremely valuable.   **End of Eighth Month**

2. From the 2½ to 3 pounds at the beginning of the month, it will add 2 to 2½ more pounds and will lengthen to 16½ to 18 inches by the end of the eighth month.

3. The bones of the head are soft and flexible.

4. If born now its chances for survival are much greater than those of a seven-month fetus, although there is a popular misbelief to the contrary.

5. Ossificaton of all bones of the hand and wrist is not complete until the child is nearly 17 years old.

1. At birth or at full term the baby weighs, on an average, about 7 pounds if a girl and 7½ if a boy.   **End of Ninth Month**

2. Its length is about 20 inches.

3. The fine, downy hair has largely disappeared.

4. Fingernails may protrude beyond the ends of the fingers.

5. The size of the soft spot between the bones of the skull varies considerably from one child to another but generally will close within 12 to 18 months.

As birth nears, the uterus becomes narrow. This straightens the baby's body so that the head is pressed against the closed cervix.

Vigorous contractions by the muscles of the upper uterus begin the birth process by pushing the baby through the cervix and into the vagina.

These muscles contract and relax in periodic rhythm. They break the protective bag of waters or amnion.

The water from the amnionic sac spurts out into the vagina. This water lubricates the birth passage.

As the baby's head slips down through the cervix, the first stage of birth is completed.

The second stage of birth begins. This stage of birth is shorter but requires added force.

During this second stage, a great deal of effort is required by the mother. This is why the birth process is appropriately called labor.

Special muscles in the mother's body are geared to begin expelling the baby from the uterus through the vagina.

At the same time the muscles of the vagina stretch to allow the baby to pass through to the outside of the body.

At last the baby's head peeps through the opening. The birth of the baby's head is called crowning.

When the head appears the doctor gently assists in the removal of the baby from the birth canal.

After the baby is removed from the birth canal the doctor ties the umbilical cord and cuts it close to the body.

This cutting cannot be felt any more than you fell you hair being cut off at the beauty parlor or barbershop. This cutting of the cord leaves a scar that we call the belly button or navel.

The baby's birth is now complete. On the average, a baby will weigh 7 pounds at birth and be approximately 19 to 21 inches in length.

The baby may be covered with water, fluid, and downy hair from its stay in the uterus. The nurse or doctor will clean baby to remove these.

Meanwhile, the mother's job is not yet complete. The uterus is still contracting and expelling after the baby is born.

The remainder of the umbilical cord and the placenta are expelled through the vagina. Together they are called the afterbirth.

Three days after the mother and baby have completed the birth process, the baby turns to its mother again for food.

The mother will put the baby to her breast and the baby will suck on her nipples to get milk. This is what we know as breastfeeding the baby.

Some mothers prefer not to breastfeed their babies. Carefully prepared milk formulas are fed to the baby by bottle. Both breastfed and bottle-fed babies receive ample nourishment.

Side headings:

Birth Begins

Trickling Water

First Stage Over

The Mother Labors

Special Muscles

Stretching

Crowning

A Gentle Hand

Unneeded Cord

Baby is Through

Afterbirth

Food Again

Breast-Feeding

Bottle Feeding

Babies require a lot of care. They are born helpless and depend upon their family for survival. The family is indeed important.

Helpless Infant

Families must plan carefully for each baby. Each family has a responsibility to the helpless new being to care for it and love it so that it may grow up happily and healthfully. As long as there are families who share and love one another there will be more babies . . . more families . . . more babies.

The Family Plan

Unit Two:

Friendship, Dating, and Decision Making

Additional information for this unit can be found in the booklet *Family Living and Human Reproduction* by Linda Meeks and Phil Heit.[2]

Teacher Resource

Your relationships are the connections that you have with other people. You have many different kinds of relationships. You have relationships with family members. You have relationships with friends.

Relationships

As you grow older and more mature, you will have relationships with members of the opposite sex. You will have dating relationships.

(Have each student make a large four-leaf clover out of green construction paper.)

Ingredients in a Good Relationship

Each relationship that you will have is special. A good relationship is like a four-leaf clover. You have to look hard to find a four-leaf clover. There are many three-leaf clovers, but they are not as special. Special relationships take an effort on your part. There are four ingredients in a special relationship.[3] Write one of these ingredients on each of the four leaves of your four-leaf clover. The ingredients are:

1. *Respect:* to respect others means that you think they are worthwhile. You listen to their ideas even when they are different from yours. You care about their feelings as much as you care about your own.

2. *Responsibility:* to be responsible means that others can depend on you. If you have good relationships, others should be able to count on you and your wise behavior.

3. *Understanding:* to be understanding means that you care how others feel and how your behavior might affect them.

4. *Labor:* to labor means to work hard, to share work to demonstrate that you care.

When you have all four ingredients in a relationship, it is a loving relationship. So we could say that a loving relationship is one in which you share respect, responsibility, understanding, and labor with another person.

Loving Relationships

---

[2]The booklet can be obtained from Charles Merrill Publishing Co., 1300 Alum Creek Drive, Columbus, Ohio 43216.

[3]Erich Fromm, *The Art of Loving* (New York: Bantam Books, 1963).

If you are able to form loving relationships, you are a loving person. One of the most important things that you can be is a loving person.

A family is a group of people who are related and belong together. A family is the first place that you learn how to be a loving person. You learn many things about love from your parents:

Family Relationships

1. You learn to respect your parents and the guidelines they set for you.

2. You learn what it means to be responsible. You can count on your parents.

3. Your parents teach you understanding by caring about how you feel.

4. You learn that loving persons work hard or labor for those they love. You watch your parents earn a living to provide food, clothing, and shelter for you. They labor to keep your home nice.

The family is the first place that you practice love:

1. You respect your parents so you tell them where you are going and when you will return.

2. You are understanding when a younger brother or sister breaks one of your toys.

3. You are responsible so you always put your bicycle away at night.

4. You work or labor by cleaning your room, raking the leaves, and helping with dishes.

You learn that loving persons choose their actions. Some actions are loving and some are not. Which of these actions are loving and which are not?

1. Your sister wants to go to the movies. She cannot go until the dishes are done. You help her with the dishes.

2. Your parents ask you to come straight home from school. You stop at the store and buy a candy bar and then come home.

It often takes self-discipline to act in loving ways. Self-discipline is the effort that you make to behave in certain ways. For example, you may have wanted a candy bar. But you know that you should go straight home. You use self-discipline.

Self-Discipline

A friend is someone you know well and that you like. Friendship relationships are important to you. Again, friendships take labor or work. You have to work at making friends and at being a good friend. Here are some traits that are important in friendships:[4]

Friendship Relationships

· A friend is a good listener.

· A friend accepts the mistakes that I make.

---

[4]Linda Meeks and Phil Heit, *Health: Focus On You—Grade 7* (Columbus: Charles E. Merrill Co., 1984), p. 24.

- A friend avoids gossip.

- A friend is able to say, "I am sorry."

- A friend helps me feel good about myself.

- A friend shares with me.

- A friend praises me when I do something well.

- A friend tells me the truth.

- A friend keeps secrets.

- A friend has a sense of humor.

- A friend will help when I need assistance.

A loving person chooses actions with friends carefully. Which actions are loving and which are not?

Actions with Friends

1. Jill makes plans to eat dinner at Amy's house. Before Jill goes to Amy's house, another friend asks her to go to the movies. Jill wants to see the movie. She calls Amy and tells her she has a headache and cannot come over for dinner. She goes to the movie. (*Jill shows no understanding.*)

2. Ben goes over to Mike's house after school. Ben wants to smoke cigarettes. Mike's parents do not allow anyone to smoke in the house. Mike tells Ben he cannot smoke. (*Mike is responsible and shows respect for his parents' guidelines.*)

3. Ken and Todd are painting a model airplane. Ken knocks over the paint. It gets all over the basement floor. Ken and Todd clean up the paint together. (*Todd shows labor—he helps Ken clean up.*)

Friendships with members of the opposite sex are important too. When you have an opposite-sex friend, you learn about his or her thoughts and feelings. You become more comfortable with the opposite sex. You learn to share activities with one another.

Opposite-Sex Friendships

Have the students get into small groups. The groups should have both boys and girls in them. Each group can make a list of activities that opposite-sex friends can share together. (Example: bike riding.) Discuss the lists that the groups have made.

Activity List

Dating is spending time with someone of the opposite sex. Dating is an opportunity to participate in social activities. It is an opportunity to learn more about a member of the opposite sex. You learn more about yourself too.

Dating

When you begin to date, it is important to set up guidelines with your parents. Your parents will set an age that you are permitted to go out on dates. Your parents will want to meet your date. They will want to know how you met this person. They will want you to be home at a certain time. They will want to know where you are going. Parents are concerned about your health and safety.

Have students discuss dating guidelines with parents. Make a list of five guidelines.

Dating Guidelines

There are ways to act on a date and ways not to act. You have to use

Dating Behavior

self-discipline and act in ways that show (1) respect, (2) responsibility, (3) understanding, and (4) labor.

You have to act in ways that show others what you value. A value is a decision about how much people or things mean to you.

Which actions are loving and show healthy and safe values? Which ones do not?

1. Candy's parents do not like Mark. Mark is not polite. He sometimes drinks alcohol. Candy's parents want her to date boys who are polite and who do not use drugs. These boys would have values that Candy and her parents have. Candy tells her parents that she is going to her girlfriend's house. She really goes to a movie with Mark.

2. Jill calls David to go to the school play. David has not finished his history paper. David tells Jill that he wants to go with her but he has too much homework. He asks her to do something in a few days. Then David can get his paper written and still see Jill.

The Dating Game

(The following activity is taken from Robert Kaplan, Linda Meeks, and Jay Segal, *Group Strategies in Understanding Human Sexuality: Getting in Touch*.[5] This book contains 75 teaching strategies for human sexuality.)

This activity resembles the television show "The Dating Game." Three members of a group comprise a panel; one will be selected as a date. One group member is selected to ask the panel questions. At the culmination of a five-minute questioning period, this person writes down the name of one panel member as the first choice for a date. Group members who are observing the panel and acting as the audience also participate. Each person tries to guess who was selected from the panel. Members of the group explain who they think was chosen, and then the selector indicates who (s)he chose. Repeat the game several times:

·   What kinds of questions did the selector ask?

·   Do most people ask the same questions?

·   Were there any values held by group members that surprised you?

·   What traits or qualities do you look for in a date?

·   Are you a good date?

·   What kind of a person would you choose for a date?

Have each student make a list of "Qualities I Admire in a Date."

Dating Manners

Have students role-play these telephone conversations:

1. Boy calls girl to go roller-skating. She must say "No" because her parents think she is too young to date.

2. Girl calls boy to go to a birthday party. He asks his parents and accepts. He says his parents must meet her first.

[5]Robert Kaplan, Linda Meeks, and Jay Segal, *Group Strategies in Understanding Human Sexuality: Getting in Touch* (Dubuque, Iowa: Wm. C. Brown Co., 1978), p. 71.

3.   Boy calls girl to go to drive-in movie. His older friend will drive. She is not allowed to go to drive-in movie theaters.

4.   Girl calls boy to come to her house after school. Her parents will not be home. His parents do not approve.

5.   Boy asks girl to watch his soccer game and get an ice cream cone. Girl accepts. She must know what time to tell her parents that she will get home.

When young people like each other, they show their liking in different ways. They may smile at one another. They may tell one another that they like each other.

Dating and Sex

They may also show their liking by touching. Young people may hold hands. They may hug one another. They may kiss.

Sometimes young people begin petting one another. Petting is sexual touching without sexual intercourse. For example, a boy may touch a girl's breasts. Petting gets both boys and girls excited. During petting, boys and girls think more and more about sexual intercourse.

Petting

Most young people need to set limits on petting. This involves a great deal of self-discipline. Petting feels good and it is hard to set limits. But petting for long periods of time may get people so excited that they continue to sexual intercourse.

At your age, you are not ready to have sexual intercourse. You are not ready to love and be responsible for a baby. You are not ready for the responsibility of marriage. You are not ready to commit yourself to another person—to be responsible for their feelings and emotions. There is more to sexual intercourse than having a good feeling. This is why young people wait till they are mature to have sexual intercourse.

Sexual Intercourse

It is important to set limits on how far you will go sexually. Then your feelings will not lead you to do things that you do not want to do. You will control your actions.

Setting Limits

Here are some ways young people set limits:

1.   Many young people double date. They spend time with other couples to avoid too much sexual touching.

2.   Most parents ask their children not to be at someone's house when parents are not home. It is easier to stick to limits when parents are at home.

3.   Many young people choose activities that get them involved in other ways. They go bowling, bicycling, or roller-skating.

4.   All young people must learn to say "No" to actions they do not want to take. Learning to say "No" is part of being responsible. You like yourself better when you choose your actions.

CHAPTER 21

Sex Education in the Junior and Senior High School

Sex education in the elementary grades emphasizes the fact that sexuality exists and that it is the basis for all family life. Junior and senior high school sex education curricula emphasize the fact that sexuality exists and that it is good when responsible decisions are made.

Responsible sexuality is dependent upon a careful synthesis of information relative to the biological, psychological, and sociological aspects of human sexual behavior. But presenting this information is rendered difficult by the fact that junior and senior high school curricula in the United States do not demonstrate any consistent pattern of sex education. Thus, this chapter was planned around specific topics rather than by grade level.

Resource information for each of the units in this chapter is found in Sections One, Two, and Three of this book. The Atlas at the end of this book contains illustrations especially designed to accompany the various teaching units. The basic purpose of this chapter is to suggest methods whereby this resource information can be organized into a meaningful learning experience for junior and senior high school students.

The units are:

1. Education for Love, Chapter 1.

2. The Biological Male, Chapter 2.

3. The Biological Female, Chapter 3.

4. Human Sexual Response, Chapter 4.

5. Pregnancy, Childbirth, and Postpartum Period, Chapter 5.

6. Contraception, Chapter 6.

7. Abortion, Chapter 7.

8. Sexually Transmitted Diseases, Chapter 8.

9. Intelligent Choice of a Sexual Life-Style, Chapter 9.

10. Masturbation, Chapter 10.

11.   Homosexuality, Chapter 11.

12.   Intimacy, Marriage and Parenthood, Chapter 12.

The units included here are coordinated into a meaningful whole by the use of a notebook on human sexuality. The student records class notes and outside materials from each unit in this notebook. In addition, the student develops a vocabulary of terms through the use of unit vocabulary sheets. This compiling of information and vocabulary is an ongoing project throughout the program.

In addition to these methods, which provide for unity between topics, there are a variety of teaching techniques and procedures dealing with each topic individually. Open-ended questions are completed by the class and then discussed to measure attitudes. Parental interviews and questionnaires are completed to keep the line of communication open between parent and child. Classroom debates are employed to develop critical thinking. Diagrams are labeled to reinforce biological and anatomical knowledge. Models are constructed to clarify information. Research is examined and conducted by the class to distinguish fact from hearsay. Cartoons are used to depict the humor and ambiguity that attend sexuality. School and community campaigns are organized to develop responsibility and community concern. Patterns of living and problem-solving techniques are analyzed to give insight into a responsible code of ethics.

Unit 1

Education for Love

One of the outcomes of a successful sex education program is that the student will demonstrate concern for others.

Introduction

Practicing this concern in relationships with others can begin in the classroom. Thus, a series of activities "to get to know others" is probably the best way to begin a sex education class.

Several activities to promote learning about others are explained below.

As an opening lesson, hand out a copy of "The Person Next To You" to each student.

"The Person Next to You"

The Person Next to You[1]

Who is the person next to you?

You might say a name, and describe how tall he is, and the color of eyes and hair.

But none of these things are what the person is. A person is invisible activities.

The person nearest to you is an inexhaustible sort of existence. Nine-tenths of his possibility has not yet been touched off. There is all kinds of good that is struggling to be born from way within that person. There are also worries, fears, hates that are struggling to get themselves expressed. At the core of every man are these inexhaustible energies.

Deep within this person is a great toughness for his own integrity—a great

---

[1]Ross Snyder,"The Ministry of Meaning," Risk, 3:3 and 4(1965), pp. 171–173 (Geneva: World Council of Churches).

tenacity in the face of adversity. Human nature is the most indestructible thing that we know. It has almost unlimited ability to take whatever comes— to go on surviving in the midst of unbelievable difficulties and persecutions. A person is an overpowering will to survive, to arrive at destinations. To blossom and be—with all the spontaneity of a rose at seven o'clock on a June morning.

The person sitting next to you is an urge to become manifest. To become something in particular. . . .

He is at pain to be authentic. To experience a moment of truth. To have a story, and a song.

He is a need to be known even as he knows himself and at a level deeper than words.

The person sitting next to you is a unique world of experience. Within him is constantly going on a world premiere of experiences that no person has ever had, will ever have.

He is a cluster of memories of the past and expectations of the future.

He is a whole colony of persons, people met all during his life who have become inner inhabitants. Something of these people has entered into his person forever, so that the person sitting next to you is really a community. In that community live still the father and mother of this person, the boys and girls with whom he played most, the people with whom he went to school, the persons with whom he competed; the enemies he met; all the bad things of this world that came and interacted with him. They are still deep within. . . .

The person sitting next to you is a right to choose and decide, to run himself, to show responsibility in situations of life. He may greaten in the act of choice.

He has things he can do well. There are some things that he can do better than anybody else in the whole world. . . .

There is something his one life on earth means and cares for. But does he dare speak of it to you? . . .

The person sitting next to you is suffering.

He is working away at problems. He has fears. He wonders how he is doing. Often he doesn't feel too good about how he is doing; and finds that he can't respect or be a good friend of himself. When he feels that way about himself, he has a hard time loving others. When he doesn't feel good about himself and finds it hard to love others, he suffers.

He also suffers when two desires try to lead him in different directions. They clash against each other. He is indecision, he is disorganized. And in indecision and disorganization he is so close to chaos that pain becomes intense. For it is only when energy is in motion and in pattern that we are really happy.

The person sitting next to you is suffering partly because he keeps repeating patterns of solving problems and of relating himself to other people that never worked too well. But he learned them in a situation where he was very tense and somewhat fearful. Because of that he over-learned them; they tend to be the only ways which he can use. And so he goes on trying to solve his personal problems by using ways of feeling and attacking problems that don't work well, but were the means that he found when he was in a state of desperate need. . . .

In the fast darkness of the nonpersonal world, each of us is but a faint flow, hoping desperately to find light and warmth.

In the vastness of vibrant space which is galaxy beyond galaxy of continuous creation, we are an aliveness that savors its own existence . . . . and often finds it repellent.

Born of micro-patterned energy, we seek to be a link in the evolution of some stream of life, but suspect that we will be forgotten by the third generation.

Kin of the shrub and of the animal, alive only by the grace of our immersion in an ocean of air that so far is life-giving, we aspire to cover the earth with a network of thinking man's reverence for life, yet perhaps it will be of sick destruction.

Let us appear to each other before we are ended.

After the class has read the handout have them react to its contents. In particular, have them react to the end statement, "Let us appear to each other before we are ended."

Explain to the class that during the next few days the class members will be doing activities "to appear to each other."

Part of loving is self-love. To love others, a person must feel worthy and find the self lovable. What is it your students love about themselves?

Advertisement

Have the students bring to class several magazines, glue, and scissors. Give each student a sheet of poster board. Have each student make a poster to advertise himself/herself.

If you were going to advertise yourself, what things would you want someone else to know?

After the students have completed their posters, place them around the room. Have the class guess what poster belongs to whom.

Each student can explain his or her poster and can answer questions that the class might have.

The preceding activity was shared with the class. It would help the student to know each other better and it would also help you as the teacher to identify positive reinforcements in your pupils.

The following activity is aimed at examining the student's self-image. Why? Self-image is very much related to behavior, particularly sexual behavior.

Have your students examine self-image by writing a paper to answer the following questions.[2]

1. Have you recently looked at yourself through your mirror?
   a) What did or do you see?
   b) Do you like what you see?
   c) What changes would you make in your appearance?

2. What do you like best about yourself?
   a) What do you like least about yourself?

3. What "bugs" you the most about the way you behave?
   a) What do you consider are your good points?

4. Who could influence you the most to change?

5. Who would you most like to pattern yourself after?
   a) In what way?
   b) Why?

---

[2]The questions are from the Columbus YWCA *Youth Outreach Rap Session,* 1–10, 1973.

6. What do your friends like best or least about you?

7. Do you have any enemies?

   a) Why do some people dislike you?

8. Is it important to you for kids your age to like you?

   If yes, why?
   If no, why?

9. What about adults. Is it important that you be liked by them or be able to get along with them (parents, teachers, etc.)?

10. Is it difficult or easy for you to apologize or admit your mistakes?

11. Does change begin with you or someone else?
    Why?

12. How, when and where do you think that you can begin to make changes in yourself?

"Brown Bag"

In dealing with our sexual behavior, we test our values. The "brown bag" activity can be used at the onset of our sex education program to lead into a discussion of value formation.

Have each student select one personal belonging that is very meaningful. Have the student put the belonging in a paper bag and bring it to class.

Place all the bags in a pile. (Fragile might be written on bags with breakables.)

The teacher can open the bag and show the class the item. After looking at the item, the class can identify reasons why the item is valued by someone. For example, a necklace could be valued because a loved person gave it as a gift.

After each item is discussed, have the students claim their item and explain why they cherish it.

Learning About Others

Learning about others and sharing experiences is also a part of developing good personal relationships.

The following activity is designed to help students talk to others about their experiences.[3]

My Name _____

The object of this little exercise is to keep you busy and give the teacher a rest, as well as to help you get slightly acquainted with each other. The winner gets, well, maybe, a package of orange tapioca pudding mix. Find someone to fit each category below; the person who gets people for the greatest number of different categories wins. Use each person's name only twice, except that you can use the name of teacher only once, and your own name only once (besides the name at the top of the page so I can tell whose this is). Use only one name for each category; if you use two and one of them is wrong in any way you get no credit for that one. Get both the first and the last name—spelled right, please. Now, find someone who

1. has mixed up his own mint tea.

2. has a dog, a cat, and a bird, all at once.

3. is wearing a handmade article of clothing.

---

[3]This strategy is taken from Sidney B. Simon, et al., *Values Clarification* (New York: Hart Publishing Co., 1972). The directions are part of the handout.

4. has milked a goat.

5. has built a tree house.

6. is a surfer.

7. has drunk two brands of European beer.

8. has won a prize in a state or county fair.

9. has been out of the U.S. for six months at a time.

10. plays rugby.

11. plays pinochle.

12. plays chess.

13. plays guitar.

14. has climbed a 10,000 foot mountain.

15. is a radio ham.

16. has a frisbee at school.

17. has written a letter to a newspaper or a public official.

18. has made orange tapioca pudding in the last month.

19. has participated in a greased pig contest.

20. has been dunked in a carnival dunk tank.

To end the introductory activities, relate them all to love. That is, relate them to self-love as well as love of others.

Summary Activity

Discuss Erich Fromm's[4] statement:

> What does one person give to another? He gives of himself, of the most precious he has, he gives of his life. This does not mean that he sacrifices his life for the other—but that he gives him of that which is alive in him; he gives him of his joy, of his interest, of his humor, of his sadness—of all expressions and manifestations of that which is alive in him.

Unit 2

The Biological Male

Prior to this discussion, have the boys in the class make a list of things they don't understand about themselves.

Introduction

Then have the girls make a list of things that they don't understand about boys.

This activity provides a good introduction for the class.

Distribute the list of words pertaining to the biological male. This list is found at the end of this unit.

Vocabulary Sheet

The word list will be a valuable aid to the student in note taking.

It will also assist in the proper pronunciation and spelling of terms.

During the discussion of the biological male, students should be encouraged to compile interesting facts in their notebooks. Outside reading and materials should also be considered for the notebook.

Human Sexuality Notebook

---

[4]Eric Fromm, *The Art of Loving* (New York: Bantam Books, 1963), p. 20.

The teacher may wish to provide some class time to work on the notebooks.

The students may also develop a human sexuality dictionary to include the meaning of new words.

Dictionary of Terms

This dictionary may be included as a separate section in the human sexuality notebook.

An unlabeled diagram of the male anatomy may be distributed to the students prior to class. As the lesson is presented, the teacher may locate the male reproductive organs for the student, using the male anatomical drawing on the overhead projector (Fig. 15 in the Atlas). As each reproductive organ is located, the student should label the diagram.

Anatomical Diagram

For quick review have the students turn the diagram over to the blank side and list in chronological order the successive structures the sperms pass through during ejaculation.

Students can make illustrations for their notebooks or for the classroom bulletin board to visualize their understanding of male physiology.

Illustrations

An illustration can be used to depict the various glands involved in reproduction. Each gland can be carefully drawn on a silhouette drawing of a male. The glands should be carefully labeled. Arrows can be drawn from each gland to the side margin where the names of the hormones secreted by the glands should be listed.

An illustration can be prepared to depict the maturation and development of the male secondary sex characteristics at puberty. The secondary sex characteristics that are difficult to depict in an illustration are as follows:

1. Longer and heavier bones.

2. Larger muscles.

3. Thicker and tougher skin.

4. Deep voice.

5. Baldness in later life.

6. Characteristic distribution of body hair.

7. Increased metabolism.

It has been known for years that a castrated animal is less vigorous, aggressive, ambitious, impatient, exploitative, and violent. The following classroom activity can be used to demonstrate that in terms of energy, sex hormones must unquestionably be the most powerful substance known to man. Obtain a castrated rat and a normal rat and place each one in a separate cage with an exercise wheel. The normal rat will run 73 times the distance of the castrated rat on a daily basis.

Physiological Observations

Outside reports may be used in a variety of ways to enhance the learning experience. Topics may be assigned for group discussion, for outside reading, or for term papers.

Classroom Reports

An alternate method of using the outside report is to allow students to volunteer in advance to prepare a report to present to the class. The student's report can be used to enrich the classroom material when the teacher covers the appropriate subject matter.

The following topics can be dealt with in the variety of ways mentioned:

1. Cancer of the prostate.

2. Cryptorchidism.

3. Inguinal hernia.

4. Artificial insemination.

5. Biological evolution of the male.

6. Role of the endocrine glands.

7. Male aggression.

Classroom Debate

The teacher can organize a classroom debate to encourage the student to delve into the available literature on human sexuality. Critical analysis of a topic on human sexuality will help the student to develop the responsibility needed to make decisions regarding male sexuality.

For example, the students can explore the available pros and cons of circumcision. They should be careful to quote authorities and sources. This exercise will not only be valuable in learning to analyze a topic but will provide a classroom situation for discussion of the validity of medical arguments. What criteria can we use to distinguish fact from hearsay?

Other topics for debate might include:

1. Are males or females more healthy?

2. Are males or females more aggressive?

Words Pertaining to the Biological Male[5]

1. Abdomen (ab-do'men)

2. Acrosome (ak'ro-sōm)

3. Bulbourethral glands (bul-bo-u-re'thral)

4. Castration (kas-tra'shun)

5. Circumcision (ser-kum-sizh'un)

6. Climacteric (kli-mak-ter'ik)

7. Cowper's glands (kow'perz)

8. Cryptorchidism (krip-tor'ki-dizm)

9. Ejaculation (e-jak-u-la'shun)

10. Ejaculatory duct (e-jak'u-lah-to-re)

11. Epididymis (ep-i-did'i-mis)

12. Erection (e-rek'shun)

13. Eunuch (u'nuk)

14. Follicle-stimulation hormone (fol'li-k'l)

15. Foreskin (fōr'skin)

---

[5]Definitions of these terms can be found in the glossary at the end of this book.

16. Glans (glanz)

17. Gonad (gon'ad)

18. Hernia (her'ne-ah)

19. Hormone (hor'mōn)

20. Hyaluronidase (hi-ah-lu-ron'i-dās)

21. Hypothalamus (hi-po-thal'ah-mus)

22. Inguinal Hernia (ing'gwi-nal)

23. Interstitial cell stimulating hormone (in-ter-stish'al)

24. Luteinizing hormone (lu'tin-i-zing)

25. Milliliter (mil'li-leter)

36. Orgasm (or'gazm)

27. Penis (pe'nis)

28. Pituitary gland (pi-tu'itār'e)

29. Prepuce (pre'pūs)

30. Prostate gland (pros'tāt)

31. Retrograde ejaculation (ret'ro-grād)

32. Scrotum (skro'tum)

33. Semen (se'men)

34. Seminal vesicle (sem'i-nal ves'i-k'l)

35. Seminiferous tubules (se-mi-nif'er-us tu-būlz)

36. Silicone (sil'i-kōn)

37. Smegma (smeg'mah)

38. Spermatogenesis (sper-mah-to-jen'e-sis)

39. Spermatozoa (sper-mah-to-zo'ah)

40. Testes (tes'tez)

41. Testosterone (tes-tos'ter-ōn)

42. Uretha (u-re-thrah)

43. Vas deferens (vas def'er-enz)

44. Vasectomy (vas-ek'to-me)

Unit 3

The Biological Female

Prior to this discussion have the girls in the class make a list of things that they don't understand about themselves.

Then have the boys make a list of things that they don't understand about girls.

This activity provides a good introduction for the class discussion.

Introduction

Distribute the list of words pertaining to the biological female. This list can be found at the end of this unit.

Vocabulary Sheet

The word list will be a valuable asset to the student in notetaking.

It will also assist in the proper pronunciation and spelling of terms.

During the discussion of the biological female, students should be encouraged to compile interesting facts in their notebooks.

Human Sexuality Notebook

The teacher may wish to provide some class time to work on the notebooks.

Students may also develop a human sexuality dictionary to include the meanings of new words.

Dictionary of Terms

This dictionary may be included as a separate section in the human sexuality notebook.

An unlabeled diagram of the female anatomy may be distributed to the students prior to class. As the material is presented, the teacher may locate the female reproductive organs for the student using the female anatomical drawing on the overhead projector (Fig. 22 in the Atlas). As each reproductive organ is located, the students should label their diagrams.

Anatomical Diagram

For review have the students turn over the diagram to the blank side and list in chronological order the itinerary of the egg from ovulation to disintegration during the menses.

Students can make illustrations for their notebooks or for the classroom bulletin board to visualize the female physiology.

Illustrations

For example, an illustration can be used to show the secondary sex characteristics caused by the release of estrogen. These changes can be listed somewhere on the poster or bulletin board:

1. Deposition of fat in the breasts accompanied by development of an elaborate duct system.

2. Broadening of the pelvis, which changes from a narrow, funnel-like outlet to a broad, oval outlet.

3. Development of soft and smooth skin.

4. Deposition of fat in the buttocks and thighs.

5. Development of pubic hair with a flat upper border.

6. Early uniting of the growing end of long bones with the bone shaft.

Ask for girl volunteers to conduct a study in their physical education classes on physical performance during the menses. Have the girls decide upon certain skills to be measured in their physical education class. The girls should measure these same skills daily, comparing the level of performance from day to day. The study should reveal that there is no significant difference in performance during the menses.

Observations

Compare the results of your students' study with a study done at the Tokyo Olympics including 66 women athletes:

1. 70 per cent retained normal performance.

2. 15 per cent did better.

3. 15 per cent did worse.

Allow students to work in groups on classroom projects to clarify their understanding of the biology of femaleness. The following activities are suggested to supplement the learning experiences in this unit.

Projects

A group of students can construct a model of a primary follicle. Their model should clearly show the thin layer of follicular cells surrounding the immature ova. After the model has been constructed the group can explain to the class the process of ovulation.

A group of students can construct a model of the uterus. Different models can be used to depict the corpus or body, isthmus, cervix, myometrium, and endometrium. The group can explain through their models the changes in the endometrium throughout the menstrual cycle. They can also compare the sizes of the uterus at birth, at puberty, during pregnancy, and at menopause (see Fig. 23 in the Atlas).

Another group of students can supplement the uterine model project by constructing graphs to explain the menstrual cycle. These graphs should focus on the level of hormonal secretion during different phases of the menstrual cycle. These hormonal phases should be related graphically to the phases of the menstrual cycle: proliferative, secretory or progestational, and menstrual phases (see Fig. 26 in the Atlas).

Appoint two groups of students to discuss the safety of the sanitary tampon. One group can gather a list of common misconceptions and old wives' tales. The other group will gather available research articles on the topic. (This group can write to Tampax, Inc., for information.) Students can discuss toxic shock syndrome.

Reasearch

Present the foregoing material in a classroom discussion. The first group will represent lay persons. The second group will represent medical authorities. The first group will present one of the misconceptions listed in their findings. The second group, the medical authorities, will present medical research findings to clarify the point made.

Debate

Write Dear Helper letters for the students to answer. Ask for advice about lumps in the breast, vaginitis, toxic shock syndrome, and causes of painful menstruation.

Dear Helper

Words Pertaining to the Biological Female[6]

1. Amenorrhea (ah-men-o-re′ah)

2. Anemia (ah-ne′me-ah)

3. Bartholin's glands (bar′to-linz)

4. Cervix (ser′viks)

5. Cilia (sil′e-ah)

6. Climacteric (kli-mak-ter′ik)

7. Clitoris (kli′to-ris)

8. Corpus (kor′pus)

9. Corpus luteum (kor′pus lu′te-um)

10. Cumulus cells (ku′mu-lus)

---

[6]Definitions of these terms can be found in the glossary at the end of this book.

11.   Dysmenorrhea (dis-men-o-re'ah)

12.   Ectopic Pregnancy (ek-top'ik preg'nan-se)

13.   Endometrium (en-do-me'tre-um)

14.   Estrogen (es'tro-jen)

15.   Fallopian tube (fal-lo'pe-an)

16.   Fertilization (fer-ti-li-za'shun)

17.   Follicle stimulating hormone (fol'li-k'l)

18.   Follicular cells (fo-lik'u-lar)

19.   Genitalia (jen-i-ta'le-ah)

20.   Gonad (gon'ad)

21.   Graafian Follicle (graf'e-an fol'li-k'l)

22.   Hymen (hi'men)

23.   Isthmus (is-mus)

24.   Labia majora (la'be-ah)

25.   Labia minora (la'be-ah)

26.   Luteinizing hormone (lu'tin-i-zing)

27.   Menarche (me-nar'ke)

28.   Menopause (men'o-pawz)

29.   Menorrhagia (men-o-ra'je-ah)

30.   Menstruation (men-stroo-a'shun)

31.   Mittleschmerz (mit'el-shmarts)

32.   Mons veneris (monz ven'er-is)

33.   Myometrium (mi-o-me'tre-um)

34.   Ovary (o'vah-re)

35.   Oviducts (o've-dukts)

36.   Ovulation (ov-u-la'shun)

37.   Papanicolaou smear (pap-ah-nik-o-la'oo)

38.   Pelvis (pel'vis)

39.   Pituitary gland (pi-tu'i-ta-re)

40.   Placenta (plah-sen'tah)

41.   Primary follicle (fol'li-k'l)

42.   Progesterone (pro-jes'ter-on)

43.   Proliferation (pro-lif-er-a'shun)

44.   Puberty (pu'ber-te)

45.   Pudendum (pu-den'dum)

46.   Stigma (stig-mah)

47.   Stratum vascularis (stra'tum vas'ku-lar-is)

48. Tampon (tam'pon)

49. Toxic shock syndrome (TSS) (tok'sik shok sin'drom)

50. Uterus (u'ter-us)

51. Vagina (vah-ji'nah)

52. Vestibule (ves'ti-bul)

53. Vulva (vul'vah)

Unit 4

Human Sexual Response

Prior to the lecture on the human sexual response, pretest the students on the following questions:

Introduction

1. Are males or females more sexually aggressive?

2. Do males and females respond differently in the sexual situation?

3. For what purposes is the sex act performed? Rank in order these purposes.

4. Which factor is more important in affecting female sexual response: the amount of love the female has for her male sex partner or the sex technique the male uses to arouse the female?

The human sexual response vocabulary sheet should be distributed to the students prior to the lecture. This sheet will aid the student in note taking. It will also assist in the proper pronunciation and spelling of terms. (This sheet can be found at the end of the suggested methods and activities.)

Vocabulary Sheet

The discussion of the four phases of sexual response can be related to jumping off a diving board. To utilize this approach, draw a diving board on the chalkboard.

Discussion of the Four Phases of Sexual Response

There will be four phases of diving that you will discuss. Discuss the simple task of jumping off a diving board—do not relate this to sexual behavior at first.

Your discussion should include all the conditions that surround this activity. For example:

Phase I (Climbing the Board).

1. Excitement begins.

2. Person may be trying something new.

3. Person might be frightened if (s)he has never done this before.

4. Person may turn back out of fear.

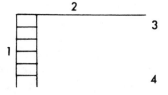

5. Person may be coaxed to try something when (s)he really would rather not.

Phase II (Walking Out on the Board).

1. The excitement is now building.

2. There is less chance that the person will turn back.

3. It is more difficult to turn back.

4. As the person reaches the end of the board, (s)he is very involved.

5. The person may fall off the board accidentally.

Phase III (Diving).

1. The dive may be very successful.

2. The dive most likely will be awkward, since it is a first attempt.

3. The person may hit the water very awkwardly and not enjoy the dive at all.

Phase IV (Getting Out of the Water).

1. The person has a new attitude about diving; (s)he has formed some feelings.

2. (S)He may decide from this one experience that (s)he does not like to dive.

3. (S)He may decide from this experience that (s)he enjoys diving.

4. If (s)he enjoys diving, it will become easier and easier to jump off the board.

After your class has discussed all possibilities for the initial experience of diving, relate this to human sexual response and sexual behavior.

Below are listed the phases of response, definitions, and possible discussion ideas.

Phase I—Excitement. The excitement phase begins with the initial sexual stimulation, ranges from a few minutes to as long as several hours, and ends by passage into the plateau phase.

> Discussion: relate the early part of excitement, kissing, petting, to climbing the diving board. Examine first apprehensions, new feelings that occur, and building tensions.

Phase II—Plateau. During the plateau phase tension builds up for the leap into orgasm.

> Discussion: relate building sexual tensions to the experience with the diving board. Once sexual tension builds up it is difficult to turn back. Also, a person may lose control (fall off the board) as (s)he becomes more involved. Self-discipline is important before this stage is reached.

Phase III—Orgasmic. The orgasmic phase in both male and female consists of rapid muscular contractions that release accumulating tensions.

> Discussion: the commitment to jump is made, and the person is involved in the peak of the activity. What will the first attempt be like? How will it affect the person?

Phase IV—Resolution. During the resolution phase, biological structures return to their pre-excitement state.

> Discussion: this can be related to the "cooling off" period in the water when talking biologically. Relating this to psychology or a person's real experience, we can consider his/her feelings after the activity. Have fears and anxieties increased because of a bad experience? Because of this experience will it be easier to jump again and again?

The purpose of discussing the diving board first was to get lots of students to talk. Many will explain their own thoughts about the first time they jumped into the water. Some very interesting comments will be made. Write these on the chalkboard and then when you shift the topic to sexual behavior emphasize the need to say "no" to heavy necking and petting. Intimate physical contact may lead to unwanted sexual intercourse.

The students should take notes on the discussion and carefully organize them into separate units to compile a notebook on human sexuality. Encourage outside reading and the inclusion of additional materials in the notebook. (The high school teacher may want to allow class time for the student to work on the notebook.)

Human Sexuality Notebook

The students should include the meanings of technical terms from the human sexual response lecture in the dictionary section of their notebooks on human sexuality.

Dictionary of Terms

List examples of pleasure seeking. Why is it important to make responsible choices about pleasure seeking? Why is it important to think about the consequences of your behavior?

Classroom Discussion

The students should diagram the brain and label the cerebral cortex and the hypothalamus. On the left side of the brain list the functions of the cerebral cortex. On the right side of the brain diagram list the functions of the hypothalamus.

Diagram of the Brain

A student or group of students can volunteer to do some research and report to the class on the differences between human sexuality and the sexuality of lower animals.

Report

Have the class analyze the following list, differentiating the effect of each on the sex drive of the male and of the female.

Classroom Discussion

Touch	Alcohol	Intelligence
Smell	Affection	Sense of humor
Sight	Love	Compatibility
Personality	Religious beliefs	Commitment to partner
Pornography	Physical attractiveness	Parental guidelines

The students can include in their notebook on human sexuality the following diagram summarizing the factors influencing the sex drive:[7]

Diagram of the Sex Drive

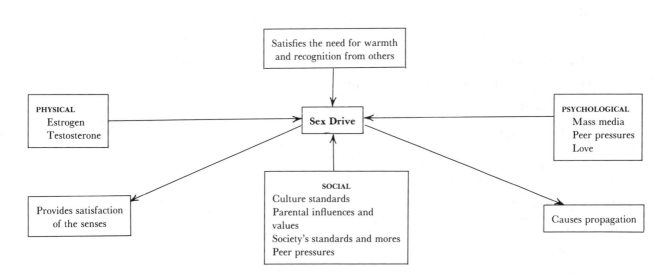

---

[7]Adapted from Florence Benell, *Behavioral Dynamics in Sex Education.*

Write Dear Helper letters for the students to answer. Ask for advice about sexual response in aging, premature ejaculation, impotence, and orgasmic dysfunction.

Dear Helper

Words Pertaining to the Human Sexual Response[8]

1.   Androgen (an'dro-jen)
2.   Bartholin's glands (bar'to-linz)
3.   Brain (brān)
4.   Castrate (kas'trat)
5.   Central nervous system (sen'tral ner'vus sis'tem)
6.   Cerebral cortex (ser-e'bral kor'teks)
7.   Cervix (ser'viks)
8.   Clitoris (kli'to-ris)
9.   Cowper's gland (kow'perz)
10. Ejaculation (e-jak-u-la'shun)
11. Erection (e-rek'shun)
12. Erectile tissue (e-rek'til)
13. Erogenous (e-ro'je-nus)
14. Excitement
15. Frigidity (fri-gi'di-tee)
16. Glans (glanz)
17. Hypogonadism (hi-po-go'nad-izm)
18. Hypothalamus (hi-po-thal'ah-mus)
19. Impotence (im'po-tens)
20. Masturbation (mas-tur-ba'shun)
21. Menopause (men'o-pawz)
22. Orgasm (or'gazm)
23. Orgasmic phase (or'gaz-mic)
24. Orgasmic dysfunction (or'gaz-mic dis-funk'shen)
25. Penis (pe'nis)
26. Plateau phase (plah-to')
27. Premature ejaculation (prē'ma-toor' e-jak-u-la'shun)
28. Resolution phase (rez-o-lu'shun)
29. Sexual dysfunction (seks'u-al dis-funk'shen)
30. Sexual response (seks'u-al)
31. Spinal cord (spi'nal)
32. Testicle (tes'ti-k'l)

---

[8]Definitions of these terms can be found in the glossary at the end of this book.

33. Uterus (u'ter-us)

34. Vagina (vah-ji'nah)

35. Vaginismus

Unit 5

Pregnancy, Childbirth, and Postpartum Period

Prior to the lecture on pregnancy, childbirth, and postpartum period, have the students write questions on 3 by 5 inch cards and place them in a question box.

Question Box

The pregnancy, childbirth, and postpartum period vocabulary sheet should be passed out to the students prior to the lecture. This sheet will be a valuable asset in helping the students to take notes. It will assist them in the proper pronunciation and spelling of terms.

Vocabulary sheet

The students should take notes on the pregnancy, childbirth, and lactation discussion and carefully organize them into a unit for their notebooks on human sexuality. Encourage the use of outside reading and materials in the organization and development of this unit.

Human Sexuality Notebook

The students should include meanings of the technical terms from the pregnancy, childbirth, and postpartum period lecture in the dictionary section of their notebooks of human sexuality.

Dictionary of Terms

Individually or in groups, students benefit from independent study, which expands beyond the classroom learning experience. The following report assignments supplement the learning sequence developed in this unit:

Reports

1. Preparation of a report on what constitutes a healthy diet for a mother during her nine-month pregnancy.

2. Development of a complete list of all the dominant and recessive genetic traits known to man.

3. Preparation of a report to be shared with the class on the fetal alcohol syndrome.

The teacher can allot class time for the development of projects to supplement the unit. Students may have many ideas for worthwhile activities. The following projects supplement this unit.

Projects

Students can study heredity by working out a family tree chart that encompasses the previous three generations. The students can use class time to write relatives for information. The information can be written with India ink on antiqued or smoked paper to indicate the historical content. Encourage the students to share the finished product with their families.

The students can develop a study of the development of the embryo during each of the nine intrauterine months. For this project the class can be divided into nine separate groups, each representing one of the months of pregnancy. Each group can report on the growth of the embryo during one month. Large illustrations can be made by each group to supplement its project.

An understanding of the Rh factor and of blood types is difficult to explain without a project to facilitate the learning experience. Obtain the help of the school nurse and the science teacher and take blood samples from the students to determine blood types and Rh factors. Chart the findings to show which blood types will mix and how the Rh factor will influence the blood of the baby.

Attend a Lamaze class in the community. Discuss it with the class.

Illustration, Charts, and Graphs

Illustrations, charts, and graphs are especially important in supplementing an organized sequential learning experience. The passage of time involved in the process of pregnancy can be depicted in a series of charts.

Develop charts that show the movement of the ovum beginning with ovulation and ending with implantation.

Develop charts that show the expansion of the mother's uterus during her nine-month pregnancy.

Make a graph that shows the life span of the egg and the life span of the sperm. Indicate on the graph when pregnancy can occur.

Make charts to illustrate the inheritance of hemophilia, color blindness, and other sex-linked diseases.

Draw a placenta on a large poster. On the left side of the poster, list the products that cannot be exchanged between the mother and the baby. On the right side of the poster, list the products that can be exchanged between the mother and the baby. On the poster show the specially constructed compartments within the placenta that store various products until they are needed. List the names of these stored products adjacent to the compartments.

Debates

The classroom debate is a valuable tool that can be used to bring additional material into the learning experience. The following debates can be used to highlight research information, although neither side of the debate teams should "win."

1. Environment vs. heredity.

2. Breast-feeding vs. bottle-feeding.

3. Lamaze vs. LeBoyer.

Models

Construct models of the cell, sperm, and ova, including the nucleus, chromosomes, genes, DNA, RNA, protein, and cellular enzymes.

Construct the following model of the DNA molecule:[9]

> Here are the directions for making your own DNA model to a scale that is about two hundred million times larger than the actual DNA coiled within each chromosome of a cell nucleus. The DNA in one chromosome would reach from New York to Rome, Italy, if it were enlarged to this scale!
>
> Materials: About 20 feet of clear soft wood that is a full inch square. (Many lumber yards carry a standard 1¹⁄₁₆ x 1¹⁄₁₆ inch clear pine called baluster that is excellent for this purpose.) Three feet of metal (preferably aluminum) rod ⅜ of an inch in diameter. Six feet of ¼ inch hardwood dowel rod. A 10 inch square of wood or metal heavy enough to support the metal rod in a vertical position.

[9]From Carleen M. Hutchins, *Life's key-DNA* (New York: Coward-McCann, Inc. 1961). Reprinted by permission of Coward-McCann, Inc. Copyright 1961 by the National Foundation.

The work of making the model can be done by hand with simple woodworking tools. However, it is advisable to use a drill press for drilling accurate holes in the blocks.

Cut 30 pieces of the baluster (1″x1″) exactly 7 inches long. Round the ends of each block slightly. Lay these blocks out in a row, turning them so that any variation in grain or size is in the same direction. Then mark the center line on the upper face of each block (3½ inches from either end if the cuts are accurate). On this center line locate a point one-third the width of the block from one side. Using this point as the center for the drill bore a ⅜ inch hole in each block so that it can be slipped over the metal rod. Fasten the rod into the 10 inch square support so that it will hold the blocks in a vertical pile.

With the blocks piled on the rod so that the same side of each is facing you, draw a line on the blocks where they will be cut later, as shown in the diagram: 12 blocks to represent the guanine-cytosine pairs and 18 blocks to represent the adenine-thymine pairs. This gives about the right proportion of the two types of base pairs in human DNA.

The position of the mark for the cut in both sets should be seven twelfths of the total length, or approximately 4 inches from the longer end. Take the blocks off the rod and cut them with a right angle cut on these lines as indicated.

Using a drill press and a proper jig, drill a ¼ inch hole into the exact center of the end of each piece where it has just been cut. Be careful not to go into the holes already in the longer pieces or they will have to be cleaned out to fit on the metal rod. In the long blocks drill to a depth of ⅜ of an inch; in the short blocks, 1 inch.

Glue a short length of the ¼ inch dowel rod into the end of each of the longer pieces, the ones with the vertical holes. The vertical rod will give trouble if you glue them into shorter ones by mistake. Leave about an inch of the dowel sticking out of the longer pieces so that they will fit snugly but easily into the opposite short pieces. If the holes are accurate, all of the straight-cut pieces will fit into each other, and all of the angle-cut pieces will be interchangeable. In this way the blocks can be used to illustrate the specific pairing of the nitrogen bases as well as the DNA code or key.

Put all of the pieces together, each with its proper opposite, and slip the blocks onto the vertical rod in any order. The more mixed up the better.

In this way the blocks represent a few of the types of paired chemical bases that lie with the coils of the double helix of a DNA molecule. The cut, where they are doweled together, represent the weak hydrogen bonds that are easily broken by chemical and physical changes in the surrounding medium.

For good demonstration purposes, each of the four bases can be labeled and painted a different color; for example, adenine-yellow; thymine-blue; guanine-orange; cytosine-green.

To represent one configuration of the bases within the double helix of DNA, each base pair is turned at an angle of 35 degrees to the next one. This means that there will be 10 pairs of blocks in one complete rotation (360°). Remember that the blocks can be placed in any order, as well as flipped end to end as they are piled on the vertical rod.

With this arrangement of base pairs, a long strip of clear plastic can be fastened to each end of the bottom block and wound upward so as to touch the ends of succeeding blocks in the form of a double helix. A white spot representing a sugar group can be painted on the plastic helix where it touches the end of each block. (The base pairs are joined to the sugar groups in the double helix.) In between the sugar groups can be painted a black spot to represent the phosphate groups alternating with the sugar along the two

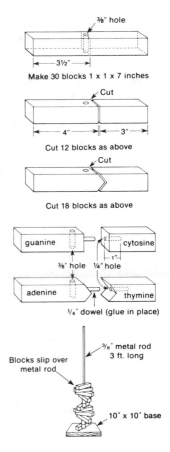

Figure 171

chains of the coiled helix. These sugar and phosphate groups make the backbone of the long chain polymer, the DNA molecule.

Words Pertaining to Pregnancy, Childbirth, and Postpartum Period[10]

1. Abortion (a-bor'shun)
2. Afterbirth (af'ter-berth)
3. Amniotic fluid (am-ne-ot'ik)
4. Birthplace alternatives
5. Breech birth
6. Bonding
7. Cervix (ser'viks)
8. Chorionic gonadotropin (ko-re-on'ik)
9. Chromosome (kro'mo-sōm)
10. Conception (kon-sep'shun)
11. Corpus luteum (kor'pus lu'teum)
12. Deoxyribonucleic acid (de-ok-se-ri-bo-nu-kle'ik)
13. Endocrine gland (en'do-krin)
14. Endometrium (en-do-me'tre-um)
15. Enzyme (en'zim)
16. Estrogen (es'tro-jen)
17. Fallopian tube (fal-lo'pe-an)
18. Fertilization (fer'ti-li-za-shun)
19. Fetal alcohol syndrome
20. Fetus (fe'tus)
21. Follicle-stimulating hormone (fol'li-k'l)
22. Genes (jēnz)
23. Gonadotropin (gon-ah-do-tro'pin)
24. Hormone (hor'mōn)
25. Implantation (im-plan-ta'shun)
26. Intrauterine (in-trah-u'ter-in)
27. Labor (la'bor)
28. Lactation (lak-ta'shun)
29. Lamaze technique (la-maz' tek-nēk')
30. LeBoyer technique

---

[10]Definitions of these terms can be found in the glossary at the end of this book.

31. Luteinizing hormone (lu′tin-i-zing)

32. Metabolism (me-tab′o-lizm)

33. Nucleus (nu′kle-us)

34. Obstetrician (ob-est-trish′un)

35. Oviducts (o′ve dukts)

36. Oxytocin (ok-se-to′sin)

37. Parturition (par-tu-rish′un)

38. Pituitary gland (pi-tu′i-tar-e)

39. Placenta (plah-sen′tah)

40. Pore (por)

41. Pospartum period (pōst-par′tem pir′ē ad)

42. Pregnancy (preg′nan-se)

43. Progesterone (pro-jes′ter-on)

44. Protein (pro′tēn)

45. Testosterone (tes-tos′ter-on)

46. Umbilical (um-bil′i-kal)

47. Uterus (u′ter-us)

Unit 6

Contraception

Most school districts have a policy on teaching about contraception. Check the policy before teaching this unit.	**Note to the Teacher**
The authors feel that contraception is an essential part of sex education. For many high school students this will provide the last opportunity to discuss contraception in a formal and meaningful way.	
Thus this unit is presented in a responsible manner. The teacher may wish to modify the approach or present the information as outlined by school policy.	
The contraception vocabulary sheet should be distributed to the students prior to the lecture. This sheet will aid the students in taking notes on the discussion. It will also assist in the proper pronunciation and spelling of terms.	**Vocabulary Sheet**
The students should take notes and carefully organize them into separate units to compile a notebook on human sexuality. Encourage outside reading and additional materials for inclusion in the notebook. (The high school teacher may want to allow class time for the student to work on the notebook.)	**Human Sexuality Notebook**
To enhance the presentation of the discussion of contraception, bring various contraceptive devices to class to show the students. If this is not possible, use the drawings of contraceptive devices provided in the Atlas.	**Classroom Presentation**
The following exercise is used to have the students identify factors that would perpetuate the human race. In addition to examining personal values, it will help the teacher to evaluate student perceptions about fertility and genetics.	**Values Clarification**

Fallout Shelter[11]

Your group is given the responsibility of selecting six persons from the list of candidates below who are to be placed in the fallout shelter in order to *perpetuate the human race*. In all probability there will be no other survivors, and you may not accompany the candidates. You have fifteen minutes to reach consensus on this matter. (No copping out by voting or drawing straws.)

The Candidates Are

1. High school dropout, sixteen, has a dubious I.Q., is pregnant.

2. Ex-policeman, twenty-eight; always wears a gun, thrown off the force for brutality. The gun goes with him.

3. Rabbi, or priest, seventy-five years old.

4. Female physician, thirty-six, has had hysterectomy.

5. Male violin player, forty-five, suspected of homosexual activity.

6. Male black militant, has no skills, has never worked.

7. Retired prostitute, thirty-nine.

8. Law student, twenty-six, and his wife twenty-nine; she has had a hereditary form of leukemia, and he won't go without her.

9. Male architect, thirty-six; ex-convict, convicted of pushing heroin.

   It would be helpful if there were more information available on each of the candidates, but you must remember that in the real world we are continually forced to make judgments based on incomplete data.

   After your committee has reached its decision, then it should discuss what four or five values you have been trying to protect.

Span Plan

One of the goals of family planning is to plan a family so that both parents can also meet individual goals other than those of producing offspring. The technique used to get students to look at long-range goal setting is called the "span plan." Give each student a copy of the span plan.

The task at hand is to (1) identify the age at which you expect to marry; (2) note offspring on the chart; and (3) block in the years planned for a career. In giving the directions, remember to explain to the students that marriage is not necessary for this activity, i.e., there can be one-parent families. Also, childless marriages are perfectly acceptable, and many women chose to have a career throughout marriage. The important message is that young people do some planning for the future and that this goal setting should be discussed with any future mate prior to marriage.

Charts, Illustrations, and Graphs

Have each student make a chart describing each of the following birth control methods and explaining (a) how it works, (b) instructions for effective use, (c) effectiveness, (d) benefits, (e) side effects, (f) contraindications, and (g) cost:

abstinence	spermicidal agents
oral contraceptives	rhythm
surgical sterilization	douche

---

[11]Reprinted by permission of Hart Publishing Co., Inc., from its copyrighted volume: Sidney B. Simon, Leland W. Howe, and Howard Kirschenbaum, *Values Clarification: A Handbook of Practical Strategies for Teachers and Students* (Hart Publishing Co., Inc.).

condom   withdrawal

IUD   sponge

diaphragm

Words Pertaining to Contraception[12]

1. Abortion (ah-bor′shun)

2. Asynchrony (ah-sin′kro-ne)

3. Basal body temperature (ba′sal)

4. Calendar

5. Cancer (kan′ser)

6. Carcinogenic (kar-si-no-jen′ik)

7. Cervical mucus (ser′vi-kal mu′kus)

8. Cervix (ser′viks)

9. Coitus interruptus (koi′tus in-ter-rup′tus)

10. Conception (kon-sep′shun)

11. Condom (kon′dum)

12. Contraception (kon-tra-sep′shun)

13. Contraindicated (kon-trah-in′di-ka-ted)

14. Corpus luteum (kor-pus lu′te-um)

15. Diaphragm (di′ah-fram)

16. Douche (doosh)

17. Ejaculation (e-jak-u-la′shun)

18. Endometrium (en-do-me′tre-um)

19. Enovid (e′no-vid)

20. Estrogen (es′tro-jen)

21. Fallopian tube (fal-lo′pe-an)

22. Fertile (fer′til)

23. Fertilization (fer-til-li-za′shun)

24. Gastrointestinal disturbance (gas-tro-in-tes′ti-nal)

25. Gynecology (gin-e-kol′o-je)

26. Implantation (im-plan-ta′shun)

27. Intercourse (in′ter-kors)

28. Intrauterine (in-trah-u′ter-in)

29. Metabolism (me-tab′o-li-zim)

30. Mucus method

---

[12]Definitions of these terms can be found in the glossary at the end of this book.

31. Nausea (naw'se-ah)

32. Obstetrics (ob-steh'triks)

33. Ossification (os-i-fi-ka'shun)

34. Oviducts (o've dukts)

35. Ovulation (ov-u-la'shun)

36. Population (pop-u-la'shun)

37. Pregnancy rate (preg'nan-se)

38. Progestogen (pro-jes'to-jen)

39. Progesterone (pro-jes'ter-on)

40. Promiscuity (pro-mis-cu'ity)

41. Prosthesis (pros-the'sis)

42. Rhythm (rith'm)

43. Sequential oral contraceptives

44. Sterilization (ster-i-li-za'shun)

45. Suppository (su-poz'i-to-re)

46. Surgical (sur'je-kal)

47. Thromboembolism (throm'bo-em'bo-lizm)

48. Tubular ligation (tu'bu-lar li-ga'shun)

49. Vaginal jelly (vaj'i-nal jel'e)

50. Vas deferens (vas def'erens)

51. Vasectomy (vas-ek'to-me)

Unit 7

Abortion

Introduce the unit on abortion by handing out a sheet with the following   **Introduction**
terms:

1. Spontaneous abortion.

2. Induced abortion.

3. Threatened abortion.

4. Imminent abortion.

5. Inevitable abortion.

6. Incomplete abortion.

7. Complete abortion.

8. Missed abortion.

9. Septic abortion.

10. Habitual abortion.

11. Therapeutic abortion.

12. Criminal abortion.

13. Embryonic abortion.

14. Fetal abortion.

Explain each term and then have the student put the sheet in the notebook.

Have the class divide into three groups to study and report to the class on the following:

Identifying Community Attitudes, Laws, and Services

1. Community Attitudes—what different attitudes prevail in the community regarding the abortion issue? What position do different religious groups take? Doctors? What abortion groups, such as Birthright, exist in the community? What positions are held among these various groups?

2. Laws—copy the Supreme Court ruling and all state rulings to put the issue into effect.

3. Services—examine the community's services for abortion counselling and for carrying out the abortion process. What psychological services are available? What is the cost of the different types of abortions in your locality?

For examination, have each student explain when the following method for abortion is used, how safe the method is, and what possible side effects may result:

Paper

1. Vacuum or suction curettage.

2. Dilation and curettage (D & C).

3. Saline injection.

4. Hysterotomy (abdominal surgery).

5. Menstrual extraction.

Words Pertaining to Abortion[13]

1. Abortion (a'bor-shun)

2. Amniotic sac (am-ne'ot-ik sac)

3. Aspiration (as-pi-ra'shun)

4. Cervix (ser'viks)

5. Curettage (kyur-e'tazh)

6. Fetus (fe'tus)

7. Forceps (for'seps).

8. Hysterotomy (his-ter-ot'o-me)

9. Miscarriage (mis-kar'ij)

10. Prostaglandin (pros-tah-glan'din)

11. Saline injection (sa'len)

---

[13]Definitions of these terms can be found in the glossary at the end of this book.

Unit 8

Sexually Transmitted Diseases

Introduce the unit on sexually transmitted diseases by emphasizing responsibility as an important component in living. Have the students react to this idea.

Introduction

The sexually transmitted diseases vocabulary sheet should be distributed to the students prior to the lecture. This sheet will be a valuable asset in students' note taking. It will also assist them in the proper pronunciation and spelling of terms.

Vocabulary Sheet

The students should take notes on the discussion and carefully organize them into separate units to compile a notebook on human sexuality. Encourage outside reading and the inclusion of additional literature on sexually transmitted diseases in the notebook.

Human Sexuality Notebook

The students should include meanings of the technical terms in the dictionary of terms section of their notebooks on human sexuality.

Dictionary of Terms

To enhance the presentation of the sexually transmitted diseases unit show pictures of the gonococcus and spirochete under the microscope (Fig. 63 and 67). The students can observe them carefully and draw them for their notebooks.

Classroom Presentation

Have the students write to someone in Congress to learn what legislation is being proposed for the control of sexually transmitted diseases in this country and in their specific locality.

Report

Invite a public health nurse or public health educator to discuss the control of sexually transmitted diseases in the immediate area. The resource person can be called upon to discuss the following topics:

Resource Person

1. What is the incidence of STD in our community?

2. Where do persons with STD in our community go for help?

3. Can teenagers in our community report that they may have contracted an STD and remain anonymous?

4. Will the public health authority tell their families?

5. How can STDs be controlled in our community?

6. How can parents be resource persons for education about STD?

The class members can work together on a campaign to educate the rest of the school or the community regarding the knowledge an informed citizen should have of STD. The students can collaborate on a pamphlet or on a series of articles for the school newspaper or perhaps for a school assembly.

Class Project

The students can plan the materials that should be included in their program. Suggested topics:

I. Information

1. What are sexually transmitted diseases?

2. Transmission of sexually transmitted diseases.

3. Signs and symptoms of sexually transmitted diseases.

4. Diagnosis of sexually transmitted diseases.

5. Treatment of sexually transmitted diseases.

II. Responsibility

1. The role of the schools in STD education.

2. The role of the public health department.

3. The role of the family doctor.

4. The role of the citizens.

Words Pertaining to Sexually Transmitted Diseases[14]

1. Abdomen (ab-do′men)

2. Acquired immune deficiency syndrome

3. Antibiotic (an-ti-bi-ot′ik)

4. Antibody (an′ti-bod-e)

5. Antiseptic (an-ti-sep′tik)

6. Anus (a′nus)

7. Arthritis (ar-thri′tis)

8. Bacteria (bak-te′re-ah)

9. Candidiasis (kan-di-di′ah-sis)

10. Cervix (ser′viks)

11. Chancre (shang′ker)

12. Chancroid (shang′kroid)

13. Chronic (kron′ik)

14. Conjunctivitis (kon-junk-ti-vi′tis)

15. Contagious (kon-ta′jus)

16. Diagnosis (di-ag-no′sis)

17. Erythromycin (e-rith-ro-mi′sin)

18. Fetus (fe′tus)

19. Genital organs (jen′i-tal)

20. Gonococcus (gon-o-kok′us)

21. Gonorrhea (gon-o-re′ah)

22. Granuloma inguinale (gran-u-lo′mah ing′gwi-nal-e)

23. Groin

24. Herpes genitalis (herpes simplex II)

25. Herpes Keratitis

---

[14]Definitions of these terms can be found in the glossary at the end of this book.

26. Homosexual (ho-mo-seks'u-al)
27. Incubation (in-ku-ba'shun)
28. Infectious (in-fek'shus)
29. Inoculate (in-ok'u-lat)
30. Immunity (i-mu'ni-te)
31. Latent (la'tent)
32. Lesion (le'zhun)
33. Lymph (limf)
34. Lymphogranuloma venereum (lim-fo-gran-u-lo'mah ve-ne're-um)
35. Moniliasis
36. Mucous membrane (mu'kus)
37. Nongonococcal urethritis (non-gon-o-kok'al u-re-thri'tis)
38. Organism (or'gan-izm)
39. Pelvic (pel'vik)
40. Penicillin (pen-i-sil'lin)
41. Placenta (pla-sen'tah)
42. Promiscuous (pro-mis'ku-us)
43. Rectum (rek'tum)
44. Residual (re-zid'u-al)
45. Silver nitrate (sil'ver ni'trat)
46. Sterility (ste-ril'i-te)
47. Streptomycin (strep-to-mi'sin)
48. Sulfanilamide (sul-fah-nil'ah-mid)
49. Syphilis (sif'i-lis)
50. Tetracycline (tet-rah-si'klen)
51. Treponema pallidum (trep-o-ne'mah pal'li-dum)
52. Trichomoniasis (trik'e-me-ni'e-sis)
53. Ulcer (ul'ser)
54. Urethra (u-re'thrah)
55. Urethritis (u-re-thri'tis)
56. Urination (u-ri-na'shun)

Unit 9

Intelligent Choice of a Sexual Life-Style

This is one of the most important units in the sex education curriculum.   **Introduction**

Thus, it should be very carefully planned prior to its introduction.

The authors have found that completion of a sexual behavior chart provides an excellent introduction to this topic.

This chart, which is found at the end of the unit, is introduced through an analogy to a basketball game.

Distribute copies of "The Rules of the Game" to the class.

Have the students read the introduction and the directions for completing the chart. The completed chart should not be collected. Student answers should be kept private to avoid invasion of privacy.

Before the students begin to fill out the chart, you may need to explain the following terms:

French kissing is a deep kiss accompanied by a close embrace and caressing. French kissing involves mutual exploration of tongue, mouth, and lips.

Necking is generally understood to include putting your arms around a person's neck or waist, holding hands, sitting close or cheek to cheek, and French kissing. It expresses your affection for that person, but it does not try to arouse him or her to readiness for intercourse.

Petting goes much further and involves caressing the most sensitive parts of the body, such as the breasts or genitals, and deep kissing. It is the kind of lovemaking that prepares a person for intercourse.

Sexual intercourse consists of inserting the erect penis into the vagina and a series of thrusting motions of the penis inside the vagina. Usually the act terminates after ejaculation.

The students can complete the chart, keeping their answers to themselves. Discuss the chart and the need for integrity, honesty, and responsibility.

The students should take notes on the discussion of an intelligent choice of a sexual code and carefully organize them into a unit for their notebooks on human sexuality. Encourage the use of original ideas and logical development of thought in this unit.

Human Sexuality Notebook

Have students copy on a sheet of paper the five criteria for making an Intelligent Choice of a Sexual Life-style that are identified in Chapter 10. Take these home to discuss with parents. What criteria might parents add to these five? Would parents change any of the five criteria?

Criteria for Making an Intelligent Choice

Distribute to the class a mimeographed sheet with the following open-ended questions written on it:

Responsible Sexuality Questionnaire

  1.   A responsible sexual decision is

  _____.

  2.   A decision that does not show responsibility is

  _____.

  3.   Self-discipline is

  _____.

The students will complete the sentences on the cards. Collect the cards. Divide the students into groups of five, giving each group five cards.

Each group reads and discusses the cards. Then the students make a list of items concerning responsible sexual behavior.

Have the students analyze the attitudes on dating, sex appeal, popularity, heterosexual relationships, and marriage that are advanced by mass media. Separate committees can be formed to report to the class on:

1. Television advertisements.

2. Family television shows.

3. Radio advertisements.

4. Newspaper articles.

5. Newspaper advertisements.

6. Magazine articles.

7. Magazine advertisements.

The Rules of the Game

Every basketball player learns early to abide by the rules of the game. (S)He knows that if (s)he does, the game will move along more smoothly, and (s)he'll get more chances to play. (S)He also knows that opponents have learned the same rules. Because basketball players are all committed to play by rules, each basketball player can predict and evaluate personal behavior and the behavior of others in the game. There is much value to be gained from abiding by the rules; it makes the game more meaningful and gives direction to its outcome.

Direction and meaning are essential to all human experience if the outcome is to be favorable. Rules or standards are essential to guide behavior according to the purpose of the game. Male-female dating is not meant to be a game, but it does possess some of the same ingredients. The first common ingredient is purpose. The purpose of male-female dating is to prepare oneself and one's companion for the deepest relationship known to man—married love. The depth of genuine married love is not reached haphazardly. It begins in much the same way that a coach approaches the team for the first time. First, the rules of the game are set for the players. In the preparation for love, first we set standards for ourselves. These standards are called commitments—commitment to what we believe is the appropriate type of sexual behavior for a particular human relationship. Neither the basketball game nor the human relationship should begin without commitment and a sense of direction.

After a commitment has been made to a given set of standards, the game can begin, the players always abiding by the rules. Of course at times it's most difficult to abide by the sexual standards to which one is committed. It's difficult to keep from fouling in a basketball game, too. But what happens when we break the rules? Let us suppose that a basketball player fouls an opponent, and the opponent is badly injured as a result of this infraction of the rules. Can the consequences of rule breaking be brushed off lightly? Certainly not. The player who was injured suffers unnecessary injury. And what about the player who committed the foul? If (s)he has compassion for others, (s)he aches inside from this mistake. This aching is a form of guilt—we have guilt feelings when we deviate from our standards. The effects of the mistake do not end with the two players involved; rarely does any mistake affect just the individual. There is what we call a "social mistake," a mistake that affects the members of society. In this case, the entire team of the injured player was hurt; friends and family were hurt. So you see one person's action can have quite an effect on society.

Sexual mistakes have the same consequences. When we deviate from a standard of behavior we have set for ourselves, and when we cause another person to deviate from standards, who is hurt? Both persons; each person has deviated from set standards and each person will suffer guilt feelings. Society, or the so-called social team, suffers too. The social team in this case is composed of your friends, your family, his or her friends, and his or her family.

How can a social mistake be avoided? Suppose that there is a basketball player standing under the basketball hoop. Another basketball player, not looking ahead, drives hard under the basket. (S)He sees the player (s)he is about to crash into, but it's too late to stop. BAM! Now we both know that the basketball player would like to have avoided the painful crash. If only (s)he had stopped to look and to think ahead. But it was just too late.

Sexual behavior works much in the same way. Teenagers can begin their dating years without looking and thinking ahead. Soon they become engaged in sexual activity that leads to full sexual activity quite different from what they had originally intended. For this reason it is necessary for young people to do some thinking and to adopt some personal standards, limits, or guidelines to assist them in disciplining their sexual activity.

The chart that follows has been designed to help you make some preparation for the future. (Look at the chart.) It will help you to set standards for yourself concerning your sexual behavior as it relates to another person. This relationship of yourself to another person is in the form of a commitment. When you make a commitment, you agree to take personal responsibility for your sexual behavior and for the rights and feelings of another individual.

In the center of the chart is an inverted triangle listing sexual behavior beginning with "light embracing or fond holding of hands" and ending with "sexual intercourse." It is represented by an inverted triangle to show that as we progress in sexual behavior, our relationship becomes more meaningful and we are more selective in choosing a partner. At the bottom of the chart is a code for indicating the depth of the relationship. "A" symbolizes casual attraction. "B" symbolizes good friends. "C" symbolizes going steady. "D" symbolizes tentative engagement (engagement that has not been formally announced). "E" symbolizes official or announced engagement. "F" symbolizes marriage.

On the left side of the triangle is a column entitled "Male Commitment"; males will fill in this column. On the right side of the triangle is a column entitled "Female Commitment"; females will fill in this column. You are ready to begin filling in your personal commitments. Begin on the line that says "light embracing or fond holding of hands." Decide what type of relationship is appropriate for this type of sexual behavior—this will be your commitment. Remember that whenever you decide upon this commitment it means that each time you engage in this behavior this is how you feel about the other person—you are committed to another person on the relationship level you indicate. Find the proper code (A, B, C, D, E, F) and mark it in the code box. There is a column to indicate any additional meaning this relationship might have to you. Now move down to the item "casual goodnight kissing." Find and record the proper code letter for the relationship and any additional criteria you feel are appropriate for the relationship. Continue these steps throughout the entire range of sexual behavior.

When you have completed half of the chart, you are ready to begin the other half. Males should now fill in the female half of the chart and females the male half. Begin again at "light embracing and fond holding of hands." This

CODE	Male Commitment ADDITIONAL CRITERIA	**Sexual Behavior Chart**	Female Commitment ADDITIONAL CRITERIA	CODE
		light embracing or fond holding of hands		
		casual good-night kissing		
		intense (French) kissing		
		horizontal embrace with some petting but not undressed		
		petting of female's breast from outside her clothing		
		petting of female's breast without clothes intervening		
		petting below the waist of the female under her clothing		
		petting below the waist of both male and female under clothing		
		nude embrace		
		sexual intercourse		

Personal Commitment	Code
casually attracted	A
good friends	B
going steady	C
tentatively engaged	D
officially engaged	E
married	F

time decide the commitment you would like the other person who is dating you to have. Think to yourself, if this boy or girl embraces me or holds my hand, how should he or she feel about me in our relationship? Look at the code and choose a relationship (A, B, C, D, E, F), and mark it in the code box. Add any additional criteria you want. Continue these steps throughout the entire triangle of sexual behavior.

After you have completed both sides, male commitment as well as female commitment, read through your commitments carefully. You may want to discuss these commitments with your friends, your parents, or your teacher. Although you discuss them with others, they are still personal. They are your personal standards of behavior, which have great meaning to you and will guide your sexual behavior. These personal standards should be in agreement with parental guidelines.

Unit 10

Masturbation

The basic material to be presented in this unit might include a discussion of Dr. Evans' article, "What Do You Tell Parents Who Are Concerned About Their Children's Masturbation?"

Introduction

The teacher may wish to begin with a general discussion, explaining what masturbation is and something about its frequency.

Then the teacher might outline the four philosophical positions on masturbation defined by the Sex Education Information and Educational Council of the United States:[15]

A. The traditional view, which regards masturbation as always gravely sinful and as harmful to health with some modification of its severity and rigidity in light of new scientific knowledge.

B. The view of many religionists, which sees masturbation often as an imperfect egocentric eroticism that deflects the individual from the Christian concept of sexuality as being ideally an essential relation with another.

C. An attitude of neutrality, which accepts maturbation [and] recognizes that further study of its various patterns is required, but is not prepared to encourage it among young people as an aid to more mature psychosexual growth.

D. And a more radical position, which views masturbation as not only harmless, but positively good and healthy, and therefore encourages it among young people as an aid to more mature psychosexual growth.

After you have outlined the preceding positions ask each student to discuss these four philosophical positions with their parents.

Words Pertaining to Masturbation[16]

1. Autoeroticism (aw-to-e-rot'i-sizm)
2. Cerebral cortex (ser-e'bral kor'teks)
3. Clitoridectomy (kli-to-rid-ek'to-me)
4. Clitoris (kli'to-ris)
5. Creative
6. Egocentric
7. Eroticism (e-rot'i-sizm)
8. Genitals (jen'i-tals)
9. Labia (la'be-ah)
10. Manipulation (ma-nip-u-la'shun)
11. Masturbation (mas-tur-ba'shun)
12. Mons pubus (monz pu'bis)
13. Penis (pe'nis)
14. Psychosexual (si-ko-seks'u-al)
15. Rectum (rek'tum)
16. Repression (re-presh'un)
17. Sanity (san'i-te)

---

[15]Warren R. Johnson, *Masturbation* (Study Guide No. 3), Sex Education Information and Education Council of the United States.

[16]Definitions of these terms can be found in the glossary at the end of this book.

18. Self-concept

19. Stimulus (stim'u-lus)

20. Transient psychosis

21. Tolerance (tol'er-ans)

Unit 11

Homosexuality

Prior to the discussion of homosexuality pretest the class on the following questions: **Pretest**

1. What is a homosexual?

2. How many homosexuals are there in the United States?

3. What causes homosexuality?

4. Can homosexuality be changed?

5. Can someone be a homosexual and a heterosexual at the same time?

The homosexuality vocabulary sheet should be distributed to the students prior to the discussion. This sheet will aid in note taking. It will assist the student in the proper pronunciation and spelling of terms.   **Vocabulary Sheet**

The students should take notes during class and carefully organize them into separate units to compile a notebook on human sexuality. Encourage students to do outside reading and gather outside materials for their unit on homosexuality.   **Human Sexuality Notebook**

The students should include the meanings of technical terms from the homosexuality lecture in the dictionary section of their notebooks on human sexuality.   **Dictionary of Terms**

Have the class examine the laws governing homosexuality in your state. Does the class support the legislation governing this behavior? If not, have the students discuss and adopt laws that they feel are adequate. A group of students can be appointed by the class to send a letter to their congressional representative expressing the views of the class.   **Legislation**

Have students research the following questions: **Research Questions**

1. Is homosexuality inherited?

2. Is homosexuality an illness?

3. What are the chances of a homosexual's being happy?

The class can write definitions distinguishing between the following terms: **Definitions**

· Masculinity vs. maleness

· Femininity vs. femaleness

(Maleness and femaleness refer to biological charateristics that are unique for each individual. Masculinity and femininity refer to patterns of behavior that are characteristic of males or of females in a particular culture.)

Invite a cultural anthropologist or sociologist to speak to the class on masculine and feminine roles.

Resource Speaker

After the speaker's visit, the discussion of masculine and feminine roles can be followed by a class project. The class can study the role changes of males and females throughout history with regard to:

Reports

1. Clothing fads.

2. Hair styles.

3. Dances.

4. Educational opportunities.

5. Family responsibilities.

6. Community responsibilities.

7. Sexual responsibilities.

After the class has identified changes in the masculine and feminine roles they can analyze each change:

Analysis and Evaluation

1. Has this change improved society?

2. Has this change resulted in any problems or complications in the functions of males and females in society?

3. Are the sexes becoming more alike?

4. Are "sameness" and "equality" in the sexes synonymous?

5. Differentiate between "sameness" and "equality."

Have the students make three lists to identify:

1. Patterns of behavior and traits that are characteristic of males in our culture.

2. Patterns of behavior and traits that are characteristic of females in our culture.

3. Patterns of behavior and traits that are characteristic of both males and females in our culture.

Have each student draw the chart shown below on a separate sheet of paper. Begin at the left-hand side of the chart, which represents patterns of behavior and traits exclusively characteristic of males in our culture. List characteristics exclusive to males in this area.

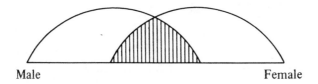

Male   Female

Begin at the right-hand side of the chart. This side represents patterns of behavior and traits exclusively characteristic of females in our culture. List characteristics exclusive to females in this area.

In the middle of the chart, the male and female characteristics overlap. List patterns of behavior and traits that are characteristic of both males and females in this area.

This chart can be used to show that although men are mostly masculine and girls are mostly feminine, no person is entirely masculine or feminine. There is some degree of femininity in all men and some degree of masculinity in all women.

Words Pertaining to Homosexuality[17]

1. Abortion (a-bor'shun)
2. Autosexual (au-to-sex'u-al)
3. Bestiality (bes-ti-al'i-ty)
4. Contrasexuality (con-tra-sex-u-al'i-ty)
5. Cunnilingus (cun-ni-ling'us)
6. Fellatio (fel-la'she-o)
7. Fetish (fe'tish)
8. Genetic (ge-net'ic)
9. Homosexual (ho-mo-sex'u-al)
10. Homosexuality (ho-mo-sex-u-al'i-ty)
11. Katasexual (kat-a-sex'u-al)
12. Lesbianism (les'bi-an-izm)
13. Narcissism (nar'sis-sizm)
14. Pederasty (ped'er-as-ty)
15. Prostitution (pros-ti-tu'tion)
16. Sapphism (saf'fizm)
17. Sodomy (sod'om-y)
18. Uranism (u'ran-izm)

Unit 12

Intimacy, Marriage, and Parenthood

On the chalkboard draw the continuum that depicts intimate relationships ranging from "destructive" through "satisfactory" to "high-quality." Ask students to give four characteristics for each of these three types of relationships. Then discuss the four types of intimate relationships—philosophical, psychological, creative, and physical.

Introduction

Behavior	I-Message Effect	Feeling
1.		
2.		
3.		

---

[17]Definitions of these terms can be found in the glossary at the end of this book.

Have students copy the following I-message chart on a sheet of paper:

Practicing Communication Skills

The students should write an I-message to complete the chart for each of the following situations:

1. You have expected an important phone call from a friend for a week. Your friend calls you and talks as if nothing has happened.

2. Your boyfriend or girlfriend asks you to go to a movie but your homework is not done.

3. Your parents ground you because you come home late.

Have students separate into four groups to make a list of projects and leisure time activities that can be shared by two opposite-sex friends in their age group. Discuss all four lists.

Group Project

Have students form groups and design their own checklists of questions to measure each of the nine factors in the relationship projection. Rank-order the nine factors from most important to least important for predicting a successful marriage.

Checklists

Have students develop research projects to learn about state laws regarding:

Research Projects

- divorce

- dissolution

- child custody

- joint custody

Peck and Granzig identified four major categories as motives for parenthood: egoistic, compensatory, conforming, and affectionate. They further delineated each motive:[18]

Analysis and Evaluation

Egoistic reasons focus on the self. They include:

- to have a child who will look like me

- to have a child who will carry on my admirable traits

- to have a child who will be successful

- to have someone who will carry on my name

- to have someone to inherit family money or property

- to have someone who will regard me as the greatest

- to do something I know I could do well

- to feel the pride of creation

- to keep me young at heart

- to help me feel fulfilled

---

[18]Ellen Peck, and William Granzig, *The Parent Test* (New York: G. P. Putnam's Sons, 1978).

Compensatory reasons involve having children to make up for something or to add to something. Such reasons may be:

- to make my marriage happier

- to make up for my own unhappy background

- to make up for a lack of satisfaction in my job

- to make up for social isolation, lack of friends

- to make me feel more secure about my masculinity or femininity

Conforming motives involve being like everyone else. These motives may include:

- to be like most other people

- to please my parents

- to forestall social criticism

Affectionate reasons involve caring and giving:

- to have a real opportunity to make someone happy

- to teach someone about all the beautiful things in life

- to have the satisfaction of giving myself to someone else

- to help someone grow and develop

Have students discuss these reasons for having children. Rank-order the four categories beginning with the category that describes reasons that are more likely to lead to successful, satisfied parenthood. (Affectionate reasons should rank first.)

Role Play

Give each of the students an index card. On the card, have each student write a situation in which a parent must discipline a child. Collect the cards. Select one. Read the situation. Have students describe an effective disciplinary technique—preventive discipline, behavior modification, logical consequences discipline, or physical punishment.

Guest Speaker

Invite someone from your local Child Abuse League to discuss reporting procedures for child abuse in your community.

Words Pertaining to Intimacy, Marriage, and Parenthood

1. Behavior modification

2. Child abuse

3. Creative intimacy

4. Discipline

5. Dissolution

6. Divorce

7. I-message

8. Intimate

9. Logical consequences discipline

10. Marriage

11. National Alliance for Optional Parenthood

12. Neglect

13. Philosophical intimacy

14. Physical intimacy

15. Preventive discipline

16. Psychological intimacy

17. Relationship projection

18. Sexual abuse

19. Total intimacy

CHAPTER 22

Suggested Bibliography and Films for Sex Education

The bibliography and films that are suggested for sex education in the classroom should be reviewed by the Sex Education Advisory Committee in a school district before either is used. When used with students, the teacher should be clear as to which concept (grades 7 through 12) the material will reinforce. All material should be adequately introduced and summarized.

As you examine the Student Bibliography you will notice that many of the books listed were written in the 70's. These books have become classics and still are found in most libraries. The information in these books is not outdated.

Suggested Student Bibliography for Sex Education

KINDERGARTEN TO GRADE THREE

Anders, Rebecca. *A Look at Death*. Minneapolis: Lerner Publication Co., 1978. The author describes many aspects of death. Parents and young children will find that the clear descriptions and photographs prompt discussion. This book is one of the titles in the Lerner Awareness Series, intended to present complex subjects to very young children. (4–7) Death

Berger, Terry. *A Friend Can Help*. Milwaukee: Raintree Publishers Ltd., 1974. The book tells how important it is for a child to have a peer with whom to discuss important problems. It is filled with excellent, attractive photos. (3–7) Friends

Berger, Terry. *How Does It Feel When Your Parents Get Divorced?* New York: Julian Messner, Inc., 1977. In this book a young girl describes the whole range of her feelings about her parents' divorce. The book reads easily but makes no attempt to gloss over hard times. It suggests, however, that in time the hurt will lessen. This candid story could stimulate discussion among children, especially those facing parental divorce. (5–8) Divorce

Bernstein, Joanne E., and Stephen V. Gullo. *When People Die*. New York: E. P. Dutton & Co. Inc., 1977. This book deals straightforwardly and objectively with the subject of death. Children are encouraged to ask questions and to discuss their feelings about death as well as the ceremonies, customs, and beliefs surrounding it. The book includes many photographs and illustrations to help clarify the topic. (5–8) Death

Blaine, Margery Kay. *The Terrible Thing That Happened at Our House*. New York: Parents' Magazine Press, 1978. The parents in this story fail to prepare their children for the changes that come about when the mother returns to work. It takes the anger and bewilderment of the young girl, who tells the story in the first person, to show the parents the difference between what they are doing and what the children have been used to. (4–7) Families

Buck, Pearl S. *Johnny Jack and His Beginnings*. New York: John Day Co., Inc., 1954. A beginning book written in story fashion for children who wonder about reproduction. (5–6) Reproduction

Bunin, Catherine, and Sherry Bunin. *Is That Your Sister? A True Story of Adoption*. New York: Pantheon Books, 1976. Written in the first person, in Catherine's own words, this book describes her feelings as an adopted child and the process of adoption. Catherine's mother, Sherry, says, "the fact that we are an interracial family presents some special situations, but does not keep our story from being a typical account of adoption." (4–8) Adoption

Caines, Jeanette Franklin. *Abby*. New York: Harper & Row, Publishers, Inc., 1973. This brief story depicts a loving, sensitive relationship between a mother and her two children, one of whom is adopted. The children are aware of the differences in their origins and accept that difference. (3–7) Adoption

Carrich, Carol. *The Accident*. New York: The Seabury Press, Inc., 1976. This quiet story with subdued illustrations sensitively and honestly expresses a boy's feelings of anger, guilt, and grief at the death of his pet. With his parents' support and understanding, Christopher is able to accept the death. (4–8) Death

Child Study Association of America. *Families are Like That! Stories to Read to Yourself*. New York: Thomas Y. Crowell Co., Publishers, 1975. This collection of ten short stories or exerpts from books by various authors, describes children and parents experiencing a wide variety of family feelings—disappointment, love, sorrow, contentment, and joy. (6–8) Family/Love

Clifton, Lucille. *Everett Anderson's Nine Month Long*. New York: Holt, Rinehart & Winston, 1978. It is sometimes difficult for a child to share a parent with a new stepparent or new sibling. This story, with its warm illustrations and gentle verse text, reassures the reader that a child can be loved as much after a parents' remarriage or the arrival of a new sibling as before. (4–7) Love/Remarriage

Darling, Louis. *Chickens and How To Raise Them*. New York: William Morrow & Co., Inc., 1955. A good source book for the classroom that explains in detail how to raise chicks. Presents a good overview of the life cycle of the chick. (5–6) Animals

Ets, Marie. *The Story of a Baby*. New York: The Viking Press, 1969. A well illustrated book containing information on fertilization and gestation. Intended to be read aloud to the young child. (5–6) Fertilization

Freeman, Don. *Corduroy*. New York: The Viking Press, 1968. The touching story of a teddy bear and a young girl. Illustrates the need to belong and feel wanted. (3–8) Friends

Girion, Barbara. *The Boy With the Special Face*. Nashville: Abingdon Press, 1978. A boy distains the face and unruly hair that others call "interesting" and wants instead to be conventionally good-looking. Older readers may question the role of the television as the arbiter of appearance or anything else, but youngsters—like Perry—may be impressed. (5–8) All About Me

Goldman, Susan. *Grandma Is Somebody Special*. Chicago: Albert Whitman & Co., 1976. This is a loving account of the special affection a grandparent can give a child. (4–7) Love

Grollman, Earl A. *Talking About Death: A Dialogue Between Parent and Child*. Boston: Beacon Press, 1976. This simple, honest explanation of death is accompanied by a parents' guide suggesting various ways to use the book. A section entitled "For Further Help" lists and describes people and agencies that may also help. (6–10) Death

Gruenberg, Sidonie M. *The Wonderful Story of How You Were Born*. New York: Doubleday & Co., Inc., 1970. A well illustrated story, told by a grandmother, about the beginning of life. Begins with an animal and plant analogy and ends with human reproduction.

Hazen, Barbara S. *Two Homes to Live In: A Child's Eye View of Divorce*. New York: Human Sciences Press, 1978. In this first-person narrative about his parents' divorce, a child struggles against taking sides, feeling walked out on, grief, and anger. The child's own anger is persuasive, as is the continuing love his parents show for him and his growing sense that they are three different but connected people. The illustrations show an appealing, tousled child in jeans who could be a boy or a girl, thus allowing easier identification by all children. (5–8) Divorce

Hess, Lio. *Easter In November*. New York: Thomas Y. Crowell Co., Publisher, 1964. On Gail's ninth birthday her father buys her a dozen chicks. The story also includes additional information on chickens that can be used to supplement the class project. (7–8) Chickens

Hutchins, Patricia. *The Best Train Set Ever*. New York: Greenwillow Books, 1978. Here are three stories showing how a family works—by cooperation, by encouragement, and by generating good cheer whenever possible. This book is for beginning readers to read to themselves. (5–8) Families

Isadora, Rachel. *Max*. New York: Macmillan Publishing Co., Inc., 1976. Young Max is protrayed as an energetic youngster, who discovers that ballet is not only fun but an excellent way to warm up for baseball. He includes it in his regular baseball training. The all-girl dancing class accepts Max; no sex discrimination is shown by Max or the class. (4–7) All About Me

Jordan, Helen J. *How a Seed Grows*. New York: Thomas Y. Crowell Co., Publisher, 1960. By explaining a simple experiment the book illustrates the growth of seeds. The children could do the experiment after hearing the story, and the class could discuss the results. (5–6) Seed

LaFarge, Phyllis. *Joanna Runs Away*. New York: Holt, Rinehart & Winston, 1973. Joanna loves animals, and she wants to find a better life for them and a less lonely life for herself. She runs away one day on impulse, hoping to find a happier existence. She finally realizes that her loneliness is related to the fact that she is interested in animals to the exclusion of any interest in other children. (7–8) Animals–Friends

Lapsley, Susan. *I Am Adopted*. Scarsdale: Bradbury Press, Inc., 1974. This book treats the subject of adoption from a child's perspective, showing what it means to the child. Boys may relate to this book more than girls, since it is written from Charlie's point of view. (3–7) Adoption

Lisker, Sonia Olson, and Leigh Dean. *Two Special Cards*. New York: Harcourt Brace Jovanovich, Inc., 1976. Grieved at her parents' divorce, a little girl finds she can love each parent individually—and that both still love her. (6–8) Divorce

May, Julian, *Living Things and Their Young*. Chicago: Follett Publishing Co., 1969. Describes different methods of reproduction and development of family life from the lower animals to humans.

Meeks, Esther, and Elizabeth Bagwell. *The World of Living Things*. Chicago: Follett Publishing Co., 1969. Discusses the different forms of reproduction with a build-up to human reproduction. Emphasizes the difference between maleness and femaleness and the importance of the family. (5–6) Reproduction

Meeks, Esther and Elizabeth Bagwell. *Families Live Together*. Chicago: Follett Publishing Co., 1969. A photographic explanation of the family situation and of warm, loving family relationships. (5–6) Family

Meeks, Esther and Elizabeth Bagwell. *How New Life Begins*. Chicago: Follett Publishing Co., 1969. Explains the different life cycles on earth and the life cycle and generations of humans. Emphasizes the baby's need for the protection and care of the parents. (5–6) Life Cycle

Miles, Betty. *Around and Around—Love*. New York: Alfred A. Knopf, Inc., 1975. This photographic picture book suggests how many different ways people express love for each other every day and how love changes yet endures as people grow. (3–8) Love

Miles, Miska (pseud.). *Aaron's Door*. Boston: Atlantic Monthly Press, 1977. Aaron's encompassing fear, loneliness, and shame are all too real: he is afraid to love or be loved after his adoption and transforms all possibilities into threats. The reader senses that Aaron needs an active physical proof of love. (5–8) Adoption

Nolan, Madeena Spray. *My Daddy Don't Go To Work*. Minneapolis: Carolrhoda Books, Inc., 1978. The little girl tells this story of a strong, loving family tested both personally and financially by the father's unemployment. In the end the father agrees for now to shoulder family domestic duties and be content with his wife's income so as to keep the family intact. (4–7) Family

Podendorf, Illa. *The True Book of Plant Experiments*. Chicago: Children's Press, 1960. An interesting book of facts that David learns from doing plant experiments. The children can listen to the story and then repeat David's experiments. The experiments demonstrate the growth of a seed. (7–8) Plants

Pursell, Margaret S. *A Look At Divorce*. Minneapolis: Lerner Publications Co., 1976. This short, simple book sees divorce as a solution to unhappiness, leading in most cases to happiness. This view may seem superficial or oversimplified and is best suited to starting a discussion. (4–7) Divorce

Pursell, Margaret, S. *A Look At Adoption*. Minneapolis: Lerner Publications Co., 1978. This is a clear, reassuring presentation of a complicated, often confusing subject, a book young children will listen to and may want to discuss. It is one of the titles in the Lerner Awareness Series, intended to present complex subjects to very young children. (3–7) Adoption

Rice, Eve. *Ebbie*. New York: Greenwillow Books, 1975. In this story a young child shows great ingenuity in teaching his family to call him by the name he prefers. The story illustrates that little things (such as names) can matter a great deal to children and that a child needs to be heard and respected. (4–7) All About Me

Rogers, Helen Spelman. *Morris and His Brave Lion*. New York: McGraw-Hill Book Co., 1975. This is a tender story of a little boy's sorrow over his parents' divorce. His fathers' gift of a lion helps Morris to find his own courage. His mothers' explanations of divorce and people's emotional changes are clear enough for children to understand. (5–7) Divorce

Schlein, Marian. *The Girl Who Would Rather Climb Trees*. New York: Harcourt Brace Jovanovich, Inc., 1975. A girl's imaginative, if deceiving, maneuver can gently outwit grownups' misguided assumptions. Although oversimplified, the point that not all little girls like dolls is made clear. The illustrations of a scruffy, busy little girl are delightful. (4–8) All About Me

Selsam, Millicent E. *Seeds and More Seeds*. New York: Harper & Row, Publishers,

Inc., 1959. A story about a little boy who grows different kinds of seeds. Illustrates the concept that life comes from the same kind of life. (7–8) Seed

Selsam, Millicent. E. *Egg to Chick.* New York: International Publishers Co., Inc., 1964. An excellent book for the children to read on the changes in the egg as it grows into a chicken. The book is well illustrated and a good supplement to the class project. (8–9) Egg

Simon, Norma. *All Kinds of Families.* Chicago: Albert Whitman & Co., 1976. This story discusses the differences and similarities in families. Through illustrations and text the reader learns that families vary but are to be found everywhere. We also learn that the family unit is steady and fertile, nurturing the emotional and physical growth of the child. (5–8) Families

Simon, Norma. *Why Am I Different?* Chicago: Albert Whitman & Co., 1976. This book encourages young children to recognize and accept differences in themselves and others. The author's introductory note speaks of helping "children feel pride in the specialness of 'being one!'" Questions scattered throughout the text encourage thought and promote discussion. (4–8) All About Me

Skorpen, Liesel Moak. *Bird.* Harper & Row Publishers, Inc., 1976. A withdrawn boy tries to conceal his attachment to a bird by calling it "dumb," but his sorrow at its disappearance and joy at its return show his true feelings. This story shows how responsibility for the bird enlivens the boy. He applies what he learns to his relationships with people. (6–8) Friends/Animals

Skorpen, Liesel Moak. *Michael.* New York: Harper & Row Publishers, Inc., 1975. Michael is deeply afraid of thunderstorms, but his affection for the rabbit overcomes his fear in this warm, believable story. The rabbit also brings him closer to his father because his father understands Michael's affection for it by remembering the pet rabbit he had when he was young. (4–8) Friends/Animals

Tobias, Tobi. *Jane Wishing.* New York: The Viking Press, 1977. A little girl's wishes regularly evade the mundane realism of her family's comments upon them. Under the assault of jibes, common sense, and some sympathy, Jane decides to be happy with what she has. Most of this text is dialogue, with an ironic counterpoint that may be lost on some young readers. (6–8) All About Me

Wasson, Valentina P. *The Chosen Baby,* 3rd ed. rev. New York: J. B. Lippincott Co., 1977. This edition of a 1939 classic is revised in both text and illustrations to appeal to today's children and to reflect today's practices. The text is smoother and the dialogue more natural than in its first edition. The soft, warm colored illustrations compliment a story whose clarity should reassure adopted children and impart understanding to those who are not adopted. (3–8) Adoption

GRADE FOUR TO GRADE SIX

Adler, Irving and Ruth Adler. *Evolution.* New York: The John Day Co., 1965. An excellent book to explain in detail the DNA molecule, chromosomes, and genetic information. The book explains the division of cells and the process by which DNA replicates itself.

Alton, Lee H. *Seven Feet Four and Growing.* Philadelphia: The Westminster Press, 1978. Despite the basketball theme, this book describes little actual play; both the situation and resolution are presented in conversations. These make clear Bill's view of things, the drawbacks of tallness, and the decisions that need to be made in his life. (9–11) Decision Making/Discovering Yourself

Andry, Andrew and Steven Schepp. *How Babies are Made.* New York: Time-Life Books, 1968. The story of plants, animals, and humans in detail. Photographs help to make the explanations clear and simple. (9–10) Human Growth

Baldwin, Anne Norris. *A Little Time.* New York: The Viking Press, 1978. This simply told first-person story dramatizes the love, anger, jealousy, and tenderness a retarded child's family can feel. It will arouse empathy in readers who have known people with Down's syndrome and increase awareness and understanding in others. (9–11) Family

Branscum, Robbie. *Johnny May*. New York: Doubleday & Co., Inc., 1975. The first-person narrative takes its spunky heroine well into puberty in a remote setting and a less complicated time than our own. The dialogue is colorful and the humor earthy. Although Johnny May seems a bit naive for her age, this novel might elicit many questions from the class. (9–11) Puberty/ Menstruation

Bunting, Anne Evelyn. *Skateboard Four*. Chicago: Albert Whitman & Co., 1976. Nobody rides the park trails on skateboards more skillfully than the members of the Skateboard Four, Morgan, Big John, Tim, and Paco—until Albert moves into the neighborhood. Morgan soon learns that the price of leadership can be setting a sensible example and rising above petty jealousy. (8–10) Decision Making/Discovering Yourself

Butler, Beverly K. *Gift of Gold*. New York: Dodd, Mead & Co., 1972. This story portrays a blind girl who surmounts her handicap and gains increased self-understanding at the same time. Cathy's dating and the relationships her girlfriends have with young men help her develop a mature attitude toward love and marriage. (11) Relationships

Chicago Museum of Science and The University of Illinois. *The Miracle of Growth*. Champaign, IL: University of Illinois Press, 1967. A detailed discussion of conception, birth, and development from infancy to adolescence, giving special consideration to heredity. (9–10) Growth

Cohen, Barbara Nash. *Benny*. New York: Lothrop, Lee & Shepard Co., 1977. Ability at baseball and a special understanding of a refugee's character are the touchstones by which this boy gains self-confidence. The narrative shows how the expectations of a family, especially when an older child has made a mark, can handicap a child from realizing his worth. (9–11)

Comfort, Alex and Jane Comfort. *The Facts of Love*. New York: Crown Publishers, Inc., 1979. Exceptionally clear, factual and responsive, *Facts of Love* offers parents and teachers a vehicle for conveying information children need and a means of expanding and enriching dialogue between parent/teacher and child. (11– up) Responsibility

Cosgrove, Margaret. *Eggs—and What Happens Inside Them*. New York: Dodd, Mead & Co., 1966. An explanation of the embryology of new life—tadpoles, chicks, reptiles, elephants, and humans. Reviews concepts about the egg learned in the second grade and the chick material of the third grade. Explains human embryology, a fourth grade topic. (9–10) Embryology

Fife, Dale. *Who'll Vote For Lincoln?* New York: Coward, McCann & Geoghegan, Inc., 1977. The point is made through a school class election that promises that cannot be kept should not be made. Responsible decision-making practice becomes a key issue between two candidates in their campaigns. (9–10) Decision Making

Greene, Constance C. *Leo the Lioness*. New York: The Viking Press, 1970. This candid first-person narrative deals with a teens' image of herself and examines the results of her critical attitude toward other people. The author deals with boy/girl relationships and attitude change. (11) Relationships

Greene, Constance Clarke. *I Know You, Al*. New York: The Viking Press, 1975. At twelve-and-a-half, the narrator is a year younger than her best friend, Al, short for Alexandra. The narrator's level-headedness and common sense help her friend through some trying events, including her amenorrhea and numerous family concerns. (11) Menstruation/Discovering Yourself

Herman, Charlotte. *The Difference of Ari Stein*. New York: Harper & Row Publishers, Inc., 1976. Most readers will find Ari's tangle with mixed feelings familiar. Learning to stand up for one's own beliefs is an important part of growing up. Ari's dilemma is shown with quiet seriousness and told in his own voice. (9–12) Discovering Yourself

Hooks, William Harris. *Doug Meets The Nutcracker*. New York: Frederick Warne & Co., Inc., 1971. To nine-year old Doug, ballet is "girl stuff." But after seeing a performance of "The Nutcracker" he decides he would like to take up dancing. The boy's parents, although divorced, are supportive and the various other interesting situations in the book stimulate discussion. (9–10) Discovering Yourself

Hurwitz, Johanna. *The Law of Gravity*. New York: William Morrow & Co., Inc., 1978. In this story a girl comes to appreciate the attractions of the city where she lives and the importance of accepting people as they are, not as she would have them be. (9–10) Family

Ingelman-Sundberg, Axel and Claes Wirsen. *A Child is Born, The Drama of Life Before Birth*. New York: Delacorte Press, 1966. A photographic depiction of the processes involved in human reproduction. Includes the first photograph taken of a live child within a womb. (11) Reproduction

Limbacher, Walter. *I'm Not Alone*. George A. Pflaum, 1969. Explains "being human" and its implications for adults and little children. Can be included in a unit on self-discovery. (10–11) Being Human

Levine, Milton and Jean H. Seligman. *Human Reproduction*. New York: Harper & Row Publishers, Inc., 1967. A discussion of the structure and function of the reproductive systems, the development of the fetus, and the fertilization of twins. Includes a detailed discussion of the bodily and emotional changes accompanying adolescence. (11) Reproduction

Levy, Elizabeth. *Lizzie Lies a Lot*. New York: Delacorte Press, 1976. A little girl becomes a compulsive liar—to impress people, to get out of trouble, but usually for no reason at all. Not until her best friend accuses her of lying does she see the trouble she is making for herself and decide to try telling the truth. (9–11) Responsible Decision Making

May, Julian. *How We Are Born*. Chicago: Follet Publishing Co., 1969. The story of human reproduction from conception to the birth of the baby. Discusses fetal development and care of the baby by the parents after birth.

May, Julian. *Man and Woman*. Chicago: Follett Publishing Co., 1969. A discussion of the changes that take place during adolescence and the implications of being a man or a woman.

Melton, David. *A Boy Called Hopeless*. Independence, MO: Independence Press, 1976. A journal kept by a infant's older sister tells this simple yet dramatic story of brain injury, it's possible causes, and a detailed, concrete method of treating it. The book portrays candidly the emotional strain on the family and the love that holds the family together. (9–11) Family

Perl, Lila, *The Telltale Summer of Tina C*. New York: The Seabury Press, Inc., 1975. This story helps us explore a twelve-year-old's intense self-concern. Tina exaggerates her least attractive features, is swift to disapprove of her parents, and thinks little of others' feelings. Only when she must concern herself with the welfare of another does she accept unquestioningly and see what is important. (10–13) Discovering Yourself

Pevsner, Stella. *And You Give Me A Pain, Elaine*. New York: The Seabury Press, Inc., 1978. This book shows the effects of a girl's maturing in her relations with a troublesome sister. Numerous subplots contribute to the realism of the story and show the experiences that form Andrea's growing awareness of herself and others. (9–12) Relationships

Power, Jules. *How Life Begins*. New York: Simon & Schuster, Inc., 1965. Where babies come from and how they develop are creatively expressed in text, photographs, and drawings. An excellent supplement for use in the fourth grade classroom. (9–10) Birth and Development

Rock, Gail. *Addie and the King of Hearts*. New York: Alfred A. Knopf, Inc., 1976. This story shares a high-spirited, uncompromising girl's discovery that the movie portrayal of love and marriage is not necessarily true to life. Addie matures throughout the story and discovers some wonderful feelings with which a class of young boys and girls could relate. (9–11) Relationships

Scheinfeld, Amram. *Why You Are You*. New York: Abelard-Schuman, Ltd., 1958. An excellent book for the fourth grade unit on heredity, dealing with such topics as the wonders of genes and chromosomes and how they work in heredity; what makes boys and girls; the way children get their looks; how twins are produced; and how different races developed. An understanding of the environment accompanies the heredity material. (9–10) Heredity

Shura, Mary Frances Craig. *The Season of Silence*. New York: Atheneum Publishers, 1976. Susie grows up during a spring full of sadness, violence, and discovery. At the end of this book, she is satisfied that she has renewed her relationship with her sister and has salvaged a friendship with a young boy. She is happily aware that her body is maturing and she knows she has learned something about life, love, and death. (10–12) Discovering Yourself/Relationships

Smith, Doris Buchanan. *Kick a Stone Home*. New York: Thomas Y. Crowell Co., Publishers, Inc., 1974. Sara is struggling to sort out her confused feelings about her parent's divorce, the death of her dog, and her growing interest in boys. She discovers quite a bit about herself, as a person, through these events. (10–11) Relationships

Strain, Frances B. *Being Born*. New York: Hawthorn Books, Inc., 1972. An excellent discussion of where babies come from, with carefully drawn analogies. The book is also well illustrated and contains a good discussion of mating and marrying. (10–11) Babies

Van Leeuwen, Jean. *I Was a 98-Pound Duckling*. New York: The Dial Press, 1972. The importance of personal appearance to individuals who consider themselves "unattractive" is shared by the author in this humorous book. This thirteen-year-old girl soon realizes, however, that boys will accept her as she is. (10–11) Relationships

JUNIOR AND SENIOR HIGH SCHOOL

Albrecht, Margaret. *Parents and Teen-agers: Getting Through to Each Other*. New York: Parent's Magazine Press, 1972. Straight talk about parents and teens communicating. Family Relations

Albrecht, Ruth E., and E. Wilbur Boch (eds.). *Encounter: Love, Marriage, and Family*. Boston: Holbrook Press, 1972. This is a collection of articles covering change, dating, sexual behavior, marriage, marriage laws, marital adjustments, and parenthood. Marriage

American Friends Service Committee. *Who Shall Live?* New York: Hill & Wang, 1970. This book addresses the topic of abortion—ethical, legal, and population aspects. Abortion

Avers, Charlotte J. *The Biology of Sex*. New York: John Wiley & Sons, Inc., 1974. This textbook entry emphasizes the biological aspects of sex, including heredity and population. Biology

Axline, Virginia. *Dibs: In Search of Self*. New York: Ballantine Books, Inc., 1967. A wonderful book that shares with the reader a small boy's search for identity. Self-concept

Bach, Alice, *Molly Make-Believe*. New York: Harper & Row Publishers, Inc., 1974. The story describes Molly's search for her own identity. The author sensitively chronicles the painful experience of a teenager's struggle to accept the illness and face the impending death of a beloved grandparent. Family

Baer, Jean. *The Second Wife*. New York: Doubleday & Co., Inc., 1972. The author explores the relationships with stepmother and first wife. Relationships

Beck, Lester F. *Human Growth*. New York: Harcourt, Brace & World, 1969. The wonders of human growth and development are presented in this text especially designed for junior high school age students. Physiology

Bell, Robert R. *Social Deviance*. Homewood, IL: Dorsey Press, 1971. Highlighted in this book are the subjects of pornography, drugs, homosexuality, and prostitution. Deviance from Norm

Bell, Robert R. (ed.). *Studies in Marriage and the Family*. New York: Thomas Y. Crowell Co., Publishers, 1973. A number of different studies are shared in this topical text. Among the many subjects are lower class families, women who work, and the formally married. Marriage

Bennett, Jay. *Masks: A Love Story*. New York: Franklin Watts, Inc., 1971. This story illustrates the types of love people may experience—love for parents and family, love for the opposite sex—and the ways in which love varies from person to person. Relationships

Bernard, Jessie. *The Future of Motherhood*. New York: The Dial Press, 1974. A potentially injurious experience for both mother and child can be improved upon. This book looks at some alternatives for consideration. Motherhood

Bernstein, Rose. *Helping Unmarried Mothers*. New York: Association Press, 1971. This book was designed for counselors but can be helpful for all. Unmarried Mothers

Biller, Henry B. *Father, Child and Sex Role*. Lexington, MA: Heath Lexington Books, 1971. This book discusses how sex roles develop. Sex Roles

Blaine, Graham B. *Are Parents Bad for Children?* New York: Coward, McCann & Geoghegan, 1973. Author Blaine shares a conservative view of parents and value transmittance or lack thereof. Family

Blood, Robert O., Jr. *Marriage*. New York: Free Press, 1969. Aspects of marriage are discussed in this textbook. Marriage

Boston Children's Medical Center. *Pregnancy, Birth and the Newborn Baby*. New York: Delacorte Press, 1972. This is a nontechnical book discussing the development and birth of a child. Infertility, abortion, miscarriage, and genetics also are discussed. Birth

Bradbury, Bianca. *Those Traver Kids*. New York: Houghton Mifflin Co., 1972. This is a vivid, realistic account of family disintegration. The children's struggle for stability and self-respect is highlighted, and child abuse is a theme in the story. Child Abuse

Bradbury, Bianca. *In Her Father's Footsteps*. New York: Houghton Mifflin Co., 1976. Working with her father's new woman friend to save some animals and feeling her own blossoming romance with Hokie both help Jenny to like and respect this woman who in fact will be her stepmother. Family/Relationships

Brill, Mordecai L., et al. *Write Your Own Wedding*. New York: Association Press, 1974. This is a do-it-yourself manual for preparing a wedding. Wedding

Brooks, Jerome. *The Testing of Charlie Hammelman*. New York: E. P. Dutton & Co., Inc., 1977. In this story a shy young man describes how he realizes the courage to carry out promises he has made to a deceased teacher. By his own determination and the help of a girl who encourages him, he becomes a success to himself. Self-concept/Dating

Cain, Arthur. *Young People and Sex*. New York: The John Day Co., 1967. Young people today are bombarded with sex, whether it be in movies, discussion, or current literature. This has left today's generation in a state of confusion. Dr. Cain's book has a dual purpose: clarification and control. The book is written to help them to know what they are doing, when they are doing it, and why. Sex

Calderone, Mary S. (ed.). *Sexuality and Human Values*. New York: Association Press, 1974. The author shares the personal dimensions of the sexual experience. Sexual Experience

Casler, Lawrence. *Is Marriage Necessary?* New York: Human Services Press, 1974. The inadequacies of marriage are discussed in this book. Marriage

Charney, Israel. *Marital Love and Hate*. New York: Macmillan, Inc., 1972. The range of emotions in marriage are shared in this text, including love, hate, honor, dishonor, obeying, and disobeying. Relationships

Clinebell, Charlotte Holt. *Meet Me in the Middle*. New York: Harper & Row, Publishers, Inc., 1973. The text looks at sex role liberation and how this affects the marriage experience. Sex Roles

Cox, Frank D. *Youth, Marriage and the Seductive Society,* 2nd ed. Dubuque, IA: Wm. C. Brown, Co., Publishers, 1974. As the title suggests, this book focuses in on dating, premarital sex, youthful marriage, and alternative life-styles. Relationships

Crawley, Lawrence Q., Malfetti, James L., et al. *Reproduction, Sex, and Preparation for Marriage*. 2nd ed. Englewood Cliffs, NJ: Prentice-Hall, Inc., 1973. This book presents an anatomical treatise on sexuality. Physiology

D'Ambrosio, Richard. *No Language But a Cry*. New York: Doubleday & Co., Inc., 1970. Laura Meyers is a badly burned victim of child abuse. Because of this atrocity she is also rendered mute. This is a poignant account of a defeated human being who, through the love and help of others, becomes a capable, worthwhile person. Child Abuse

Doppler, George F. *America Needs Total Divorce Reform—Now!* New York: Vantage Press, 1973. Various types of reformations and solutions in divorce are discussed. Divorce

Duberman, Lucile. *Marriage and Its Alternatives*. New York: Praeger Publishers, 1974. Duberman takes a look at today's society and makes predictions on the family, marriage, and sex for the year 2000. Marriage

Dyer, William G. *Creating Closer Families*. Provo, UT: Brigham Young University Press, 1975. The need to improve family communication and relationships are addressed. Family Relationships

Farber, Seymour M., and Roger H. Wilson. *Teenage Marriage and Divorce*. Berkeley: Diablo Press, 1967. The title topics are discussed in this late 1960's symposium. Teen Marriage

Fasteau, Marc Feigen. *The Male Machine*. New York: McGraw-Hill, Inc., 1974. Many of men's sexual attitudes and fears are disclosed in this book. The central theme concerns the male's fearful attitude toward women. Male Attitudes

Fletcher, Joseph. *The Ethics of Genetic Control*. Garden City, NJ: Anchor Press, 1974. Concerns regarding genetic engineering are shared by the author. Genetics

Fromm, Erich. *The Art of Loving*. New York: Harper & Row, Publishers, Inc., 1967. Learning to love, like other arts, demands practice and concentration. More than any other art, it demands genuine insight and understanding. In this startling book, Dr. Fromm discusses love in all aspects, not only romantic love, so surrounded by false conceptions, but also love of parents for children, brotherly love, erotic love, self-love, and love of God. Love

Gold, Don. *Letters to Tracy.* New York: Popular Library, 1972. Author Gold presents a book of letters from a father to his daughter dealing with many sensitive questions. Relationships

Greenblat, Cathy, et al. *The Marriage Game.* New York: Random House, 1973. This is an actual simulation game about marital decisions. Marriage

Handman, Heidi, and Peter Brennan. *The Sex Handbook.* New York: G. P. Putnam's Sons, 1974. This handbook contains information on birth control, sexual patterns, pregnancy, clinics, and hotline information numbers. Pregnancy

Hettlinger, Richard F. *Growing Up With Sex.* New York: The Seabury Press, Inc., 1971. The view that the author shares is one especially geared toward the junior or senior high school age groups. Maturing

Humphreys, Laud. *Out of the Closets.* Englewood Cliffs, NJ: Prentice-Hall Inc., 1972. This book presents an account of the gay-liberation movement. Homosexuality

Jensen, Gordon D. *Youth and Sex.* Chicago: Nelson-Hall, 1973. Various forms of youth behavior toward sex are presented in this book designed especially for teens. Maturing

Johnson, Eric W. *Sex: Telling It Straight.* New York: Bantam Books, Inc., 1971. A book of high school slang vocabulary in the area of sexuality. Maturing

Jones, Kenneth L., et al. *Marriage and Reproduction.* San Francisco: Canfield Press, 1970. A short but factual presentation of both marriage and reproduction. An accurate supplemental resource. Reproduction

Kasirsky, Gilbert. *Vasectomy, Manhood and Sex.* New York: Springer Publishing Co. Inc., 1972. Aspects of the surgical procedure and rehabilitation are discussed in this short book. Birth Control

Kerr, M. E. *If I Love You, Am I Trapped Forever?* New York: Harper & Row Publishers, Inc., 1973. This narrative looks at love from a young man's point of view. Having accepted the idea that love is something that grows stale and soon disappears, Alan becomes bitter and isolates himself to protect himself against further hurt. Relationships

Landers, Ann, *Ann Landers Talks to Teenagers About Sex.* Greenwich, CT: Fawcett Publications, Inc., 1968. Straight talk about love and sex with answers to questions every teenager asks. Included in the list of topics are premarital sex, venereal disease, and homosexuality. Love and Sex

Leboyer, Frederick. *Birth Without Violence.* New York: Alfred A. Knopf, Inc., 1975. Leboyer suggests ways of easing the trauma in the birth process. Birth

LeMasters, E. E. *Parents in Modern America,* 2nd ed. Homewood, IL: Dorsey Press, 1974. A thought-provoking book for students on what it means to be a parent. Parenting

LeShan, Eda. *What Makes Me Feel This Way?* New York: Macmillan, Inc., 1972. This is a book about feelings, written especially for teens. Feelings

Lieberman, E. James, and Ellen Peck. *Sex and Birth Control—A Guide for the Young.* New York: Thomas Y. Crowell Co., Publishers, 1973. The authors provide traditional choices in birth control for young couples. Birth Control

Lifton, Betty Jean. *Twice Born.* New York: McGraw-Hill, Inc., 1975. This book chronicles an adopted child's search for her biological parents. Adoption

Madison, Winifred. *Growing Up in a Hurry.* Boston: Little, Brown & Co., 1973. Karen feels unloved by her parents and unaccepted by those outside her family.

A boyfriend fills her need for love but abandons her when she becomes pregnant. The question of abortion is treated without moral overtones. Relationships

Martin, Del and Phyllis Lyon. *Lesbian/Woman*. San Francisco: Glide, 1972. This autobiography shares the life of a lesbian couple. Homosexuality

McGrady, Mike. *The Kitchen Sink Papers: My Life as a Househusband*. New York: Doubleday & Co., Inc., 1975. This humorous satire presents a very thought provoking look at the switch in sex roles. Sex Roles

McKillip, Patricia A. *The Night Gift*. New York: Atheneum Publishers, 1976. Joslyn's story might be anyone's story. In this first-person narrative, she tells about her fairly small circle of friends and her unrequited first love. The author has captured the complexity of ordinary human relations—in friendship, in families, and especially in love—throughout her novel. Relationships

Peters, Donald L. *For Thinking Teens*. New York: Richard Rosen Press, 1967. The problems of adolescence present interesting reading for the thinking teens. Maturity

Purson, Elaine C., and William V. D'Antonio. *Female and Male*. Philadelphia: J. B. Lippincott Co., 1974. The two authors describe the anatomical and physiological processes of intercourse. Physiology

Rimmer, Robert H. *The Harrad Experiment*. Los Angeles: Sherbourne Press, 1966. Rimmer provides a look at male-female roommates in college in his 1960 classic book. Relationships

Toffler, Alvin. *Future Shock*. New York: Random House, 1970. Toffler provides a unique look into the future, especially in regard to traditional personal relationships. Relationships

Witt, Elmer. *Life Can Be Sexual*. St. Louis, Concordia Publishing House, 1967. This is a book on how to think about sex and sexuality, written from a Christian perspective. An excellent book to assist the student in the formation of values and attitudes. Attitudes

Suggested Teacher Bibliography—Texts

Anthony, E. James, and Cyrille Koupernik (eds.). *The Child In The Family*. New York: John Wiley & Sons, Inc., 1970.

Bardis, Panos D. *Studies in Marriage and the Family*. Lexington, MO: Xerox, 1975.

Batchelor, Edward (ed.). *Homosexuality and Ethics*. New York: Pilgram Press, 1980.

Boston Women's Health Book Collective. *Our Bodies, Ourselves*. New York: Simon & Schuster, Inc., 1979.

Boswell, John. *Christianity, Social Tolerance and Homosexuality*. Chicago: The University of Chicago Press, 1980.

Bryant, Clifton D. *Sexual Deviancy in Social Context*. New York: Watts, Franklin, Inc., 1980.

Bullough, Vern L. *Sexual Variance in Society and History*. Chicago: University of Chicago Press, 1980.

Comfort, Alex. *The Joy of Sex*. New York: Simon & Schuster, Inc., 1972.

Conger, J. J. *Adolescence and Youth*. New York: Harper & Row, Publishers, Inc., 1973.

Crooks, Robert, and Karla Baur. *Our Sexuality*. Menlo Park: CA: The Benjamin/Cummings Publishing Co., Inc., 1980.

Fast, Julius, and Hal Walls. *Bisexual Living*. New York: M. Evans & Co., 1975.

Francke, Linda. *The Ambivalence of Abortion*. New York: Random House, 1978.

Gaylen, Willard. *Feelings, Our Vital Signs*. New York: Ballantine Books, Inc., 1979.

Goldberg, Herb. *The New Male From Macho to Sensitive But Still All Male*. New York: The New American Library, Inc., 1979.

Grantly, Dick-Read. *Childbirth Without Fear,* 4th ed. New York: Harper & Row, Publishers, Inc., 1972.

Heinonen, D. Slone, and S. Shapiro. *Birth Defects and Drugs in Pregnancy*. Littleton, MA: Publishing Services Group, 1977.

Kaplan, Helen. *The Illustrated Manual of Sex Therapy*. New York: Quadrangle/ New York Times, 1975.

Katz, Jonathan. *Gay American History*. New York: Avon Books, 1976.

LoPiccolo, Joseph, and Leslie LoPiccolo (eds.). *Handbook of Sex Therapy*. New York: Plenum Publishing Corp., 1978.

Masters, William, and Virginia Masters. *Pleasure Bond*. Boston: Little, Brown, & Co., 1974.

Meeks, Linda B., and Philip Heit. *Human Sexuality: Making Responsible Decisions*. New York: Saunders College Publishing, 1982.

Money, John. *Love and Sickness: The Science of Sex Gender Difference and Pair Bonding*. Baltimore: The Johns Hopkins University Press, 1980.

Peck, Ellen, and William Granzig. *The Parent Test: How to Measure and Develop Your Talent for Parenthood*. New York: G. P. Putnam's Sons, 1978.

Powell, John. *Fully Human, Fully Alive*. Niles, IL: Argus Communication, 1976.

Public Health Service, Center for Disease Control. *STD Fact Sheet,* 34th ed. Washington, DC: US Government Printing Office, 1979.

Rubin, Isadore. *Sexual Life After Sixty*. New York: Basic Books, 1965.

Seligson, Marsha. *Options*. New York: Charter, 1978.

Shain, Merle. *When Lovers Are Friends*. New York: Bantam, Books, Inc., 1978.

Shapiro, Howard. *The Birth Control Book*. New York: Avon Books, 1978.

Shecky, Gail. *Hustling & Prostitution in Our Wide Open Society*. New York: Delacorte Press, 1971.

Shecky, Gail. *Passages: Predictable Crises in Adult Life*. New York: E. P. Dutton, Inc., 1974.

Singer, June. *Androgeny*. New York: Anchor Books, 1977.

Talese, Gay. *Thy Neighbor's Wife*. New York: Doubleday & Co., Inc., 1980.

Weinberg, George. *Society and the Healthy Homosexual*. New York: Anchor Books, 1973.

Willison, Marilyn Murray. *Diary of a Divorced Mother*. New York: Weyden, 1980.

Wydro, Kenneth. *Flying Solo*. New York: Berkley Publishing Corp., 1978.

Suggested Teacher Bibliography—Articles

Bauman, J. E., R. C. Kolodny, and S. K. Webster. "Vaginal Organic Acids and Hormonal Changes in the Menstrual Cycle." Fertility and Sterility, 38 (1982), pp. 572–579.

Brooks-Gunn, J., and D. N. Ruble. "The Development of Menstrual-Related Beliefs and Behaviors During Early Adolescence." *Child Development,* 53 (1982), pp. 1567–1577.

Dembo, M. H., and B. Lundell. "Factors Affecting Adolescent Contraception Practices—Implications for Sex Education." *Adolescence,* 56 (1979), pp. 657–664.

Doty, R. L., M. Ford, G. Preti, and G. R. Huggins. "Changes in the Intensity and Pleasantness of Human Vaginal Odors During the Menstrual Cycle." *Science,* 190 (1975), pp. 1316–1317.

Falk, R., M. Gispert, and D. H. Baucom. "Personality Factors Related to Black Teenage Pregnancy and Abortion." *Psychology of Women Quarterly,* 5 (1981), pp. 737–746.

Gispert, M., and R. Falk. "Sexual Experimentation and Pregnancy in Young Black Adolescents." *American Journal of Obstetrics and Gyneclogy,* 126 (1976), pp. 459–466.

Graham, C. A., and W. C. McGraw. "Menstrual Synchrony in Female Undergraduates Living on a Coeducational Campus." *Psychoneurodocrinology,* 5 (1980), pp. 245–252.

Grief, E. B., and K. J. Ulman. "The Psychological Impact of Menarche on Early Adolescent Females—A Review of the Literature." *Child Development,* 53 (1982), pp. 1413–1430.

Hazard, W. R., and V. Einstein. "Legal Aspects of Sex Education: Implications for School Administrators." *Journal of Research and Development in Education,* 16 (1983), pp. 34–40.

Hendricks, L. E. "Unmarried Black Adolescent Fathers' Attitudes Toward Abortion, Contraception, and Sexuality—A Preliminary Report." *Journal of Adolescent Health Care,* 2 (1982), pp. 199–203.

Johnson, S. M., and L. F. Snow. "Assessment of Reproductive Knowledge in an Inner-City Clinic." *Social Science and Medicine,* 16 (1982), pp. 1657–1662.

Jones, J. B., and S. Philliber. "Sexually Active But Not Pregnant—A Comparison of Teens Who Risk and Teens Who Plan." *Journal of Youth and Adolescence,* 12 (1983), pp. 235–251.

Kilmann, P. R., et al. "Sex Education—A Review of Its Effects." *Archives of Sexual Behavior,* 10 (1981), pp. 177–205.

Kirk-Smith, M. *Research in Communication, Psychology, Psychiatry, and Behavior,* 3 (1978), p. 379.

Koblinsky, S., and J. Atkinson. "Parental Plans for Children's Sex Education." *Family Relations,* 31 (1982), pp. 29–35.

Koff, E., J. Rierdan, and S. Jacobson. "The Personal and Interpersonal Significance of Menarche." *Journal of Child Psychiatry,* 20 (1981), pp. 148–158.

Koff, E., J. Rierdan, and K. Sheingold. "Memories of Menarche—Age, Preparation, and Prior Knowledge as Determinants of Initial Menstrual Experience." *Journal of Youth and Adolescence,* 11 (1982), pp. 1–9.

Marcy, S. A., J. S. Brown, and R. Danielson. "Contraceptive Use by Adolescent Females in Relation to Knowledge, and to Time and Method of Contraceptive Counseling." *Research in Nursing and Health,* 6 (1983), pp. 175–182.

McClintock, M. K. "Social Control of the Ovarian Cycle and the Function of Estrous Synchrony." *American Zoologist,* 21 (Feb. 1981).

Michael, R. P., R. W. Gonsall, and P. Warner. "Human Vaginal Secretions—Volatile Fatty Acid Content." *Science,* 186 (1974), pp. 1217–1219.

Morris, N. M., and J. R. Udry. "Pheromonal Influences on Human Sexual Behavior—An Experimental Search." *Journal of Biosocial Science,* 10 (1978), pp. 147–157.

Philliber, S. G., and M. L. Tatum. "Sex Education and the Double Standard in High School." *Adolescence,* 17 (1982), pp. 273–283.

Roebuck, J., and M. G. McGee. "Attitudes Toward Premarital Sex and Sexual Behavior Among Black High School Girls." *Journal of Sex Research,* 13 (1977), pp. 104–114.

Rogel, M. J., et al. "Contraceptive Behavior in Adolescence—A Decision-Making Perspective." *Journal of Youth and Adolescence,* 9 (1980), pp. 491–506.

Rogers, V., et al. "Sex Education—Curriculum Issues." *Journal of Research and Development in Education,* 16 (1983), pp. 45–52.

Rothenberg, P. B. "Communication About Sex and Birth Control Between Mothers and Their Adolescent Children." *Population and Environment,* 3 (1980), pp. 35–50.

Scott, E. C., and F. E. Johnston. "Critical Fat, Menarche, and the Maintenance of Menstrual Cycles—A Critical Review." *Journal of Adolescent Health Care,* 2 (1982), pp. 249–260.

Shah, F., and M. Zelnick. "Parent and Peer Influence on Sexual Behavior, Contraceptive Use, and Pregnancy Experience of Young Women." *Journal of Marriage and the Family,* 43 (1981), pp. 339–348.

Whisnant, C., E. Brett, and L. Fegans. "Implicit Messages Concerning Menstruation in Commercial Educational Materials Prepared for Young Adolescent Girls." *American Journal of Psychiatry,* 132 (1975), pp. 815–820.

Zelnick, M., and J. F. Kanter. "Sexual Activity, Contraceptive Use and Pregnancy Among Metropolitan-Area Teenagers: 1971–1979." *Family Planning Perspectives,* 12 (1980), pp. 230–237.

Suggested Audiovisuals for Sex Education

KINDERGARTEN TO GRADE THREE

All Kinds of Babies. Carousel Films, 1501 Broadway, New York, NY 10036. 16 mm, color, 10 min. 1969. A perusal of life generally, and humans in particular, as an answer to the age-old question, "Where did I come from?" A starting place for sex education.

Animal Babies Grow Up. Coronet Instructional Media, 65 East South Water Street, Chicago, IL 60614. 16 mm, color, 10 min., 1967. Illustrates how animals are born and the stages of their growth and development.

Animal Mothers and Babies. SVE Instructional Materials, 1345 Diversey Parkway, Chicago, IL 60614. A filmstrip and record combination or a filmstrip and audiocassette combination, in color, 1977. Could be used as an introduction to the topic of reproduction. Shows a variety of habitats and settings while the sound track plays appropriate songs. Animals included are lions, zebras, elephants, kangaroos, bears, birds, insects, familiar domestic animals, and others. Script included.

Animals Hatched from Eggs. Coronet Instructional Media, 65 East South Water Street, Chicago, IL 60614. 16 mm, color, 10 min., 1970. As a means of introducing the topic of reproduction, the film shows how certain animals are hatched from eggs. The instructor should "bridge the gap" between oviparous (hatched from eggs) reproduction, as shown here, and viviparous (born alive) reproduction of humans.

Baby Chicks. Imperial Educational Resources, 19 Marble Avenue, Pleasantville, NY 10570. A filmstrip and audiocassette combination, in color. The biological aspects of reproduction, human growth, and development. Teacher's guide included.

Baby Plants. Imperial Educational Resources, 19 Marble Avenue, Pleasantville, NY 10570. A filmstrip and audiocassette combination, in color. The biological aspects of reproduction, human growth, and development. Teacher's guide included.

Being Me. Audio-Visual Services, The Pennsylvania State University, University Park, PA 16802. 16 mm, black and white, 13 min., 1969. Preteen girls in a creative dance class conducted by Hilda Mullin use body movement to develop self-awareness.

An Egg Becomes a Chick. Coronet Instructional Media, 65 East South Water Street, Chicago, IL 60601. 16 mm, in color, 10 min., 1968. Questions, ideas, and information about chicken eggs from fertilization to hatching are covered. This material is related to the birth process.

Families. Perennial Education, 477 Rodger Williams, P.O. Box 855 Ravinia, Highland Park, IL 60035. 16 mm/slides 8 mm, in color, 9 min., 1970. Designed to initiate discussion among young students about the nature of families. Uses animation and children's drawings for basic concepts. Study guide included.

The Family in the Purple House. BFA Educational Media, 2211 Michigan Avenue, P.O. Box 1795, Santa Monica, CA 90406. 16 mm, in color, 13 min., 1970. Documentary on a family without a father attempts to help children understand and appreciate different lifestyles and family units.

Family Life and Sex Education—Early Elementary Grades. Denoyer Gippert, Times Mirror, 5235 Ravenswood Avenue, Chicago, IL 60640. Slides, in color, 1965. From the announcement of pregnancy, a family is traced through the hospital visit, the birth of the baby, and the return home. Teacher's guide included.

A Family Talks About Sex. Perennial Education, 477 Rodger Williams, P.O. Box 855 Ravinia, Highland Park, IL 60035. 16 mm/slides 8 mm/videocassette, in color, 29 min., 1977. A number of family situations are shown for the purpose of enabling communication between parents and children of all ages. Ages of children involved are from toddlers to college-age students. A variety of topics are discussed according to the questions asked and ages involved. Study guide included.

Farmyard Babies. Coronet Instructional Media, 65 East South Water Street, Chicago, IL 60601. 16 mm, in color, 10 min., 1952. Questions about babies of the farmyard are answered, such as "What do they eat, sound like, and look like?" Potentially useful as an introduction to a unit on reproduction.

Fertilization and Birth. Perennial Education, 477 Rodger Williams, P. O. Box 855 Ravinia, Highland Park, IL 60035. 16 mm/slides 8 mm, in color, 10 min., 1967. The reproductive system of a fish is explained, followed by a simple presentation of the human reproductive system and its functions. The film concludes with birth scenes and suckling of the young of both humans and animals. Study guide included.

Happy Little Hamsters. Perennial Education, 477 Rodger Williams P.O. Box 855 Ravinia, Highland Park, IL 60035. 16 mm/videocassette/slides 8 mm, in color, 13 min. A story about two hamsters and their litter of eight babies. The life cycle of the hamster is shown. A potential introduction to the subject of reproduction.

How Come I Am? Professional Arts Incorporated, P.O. Box 80003, Stanford, CA 94305. 16 mm, in color, 12 min., 1968. Intended for young audiences but useful for teacher's or teacher training programs. A classroom setting is used to discuss children's questions about babies, birth, reproduction, and other "mysteries."

How You Came To Be Here. Multi-Media Resource Center, 1525 Franklin Street,

San Francisco, CA 94109. 16 mm/unspecified videotape, in color, 6 min., 1977. Explains in animation how babies are born, drawing analogies from the birth of cats and the sprouting of seeds.

Human and Animal Beginnings. Perennial Education, 477 Rodger Williams, P.O. Box 855 Ravinia, Highland Park, IL 60035. 16 mm/slides 8 mm, in color, 13 mins., 1966. Concepts of the family and basic information about human reproduction are covered. Study guide included.

Kittens Are Born. McGraw-Hill Films, 1221 Avenue of the Americas, New York, NY 10020. 16 mm/videocassette, in color, 12 min., 1971. A female cat is followed through pregnancy, labor, and the birth of three kittens. Potentially informative and appealing to all ages.

A Lady Fireman? SVE Instructional Materials, 1345 Diversey Parkway, Chicago, IL 60614. Filmstrip and record combination or filmstrip and audiocassette combination, in color, 9 min., 1976. Emphasis is on service to community but useful to introduce discussion of gender roles and gender-related careers. Guide included.

Life Before Birth. Association Films, 6644 Sierra Lane, Dublin, CA 94566. 16 mm, black and white, 26 min., 1960. Development of the chick embryo.

Mammals and Milk. Aims Instructional Media, 626 Justice Avenue, Glendale, CA 91201. 16 mm, in color, 14 min., 1977. Explains and illistrates that mammals have mammary glands that produce milk for the young.

Meeting Strangers: Red Light, Green Light. BFA Educational Media, 2211 Michigan Avenue, P.O. Box 1795, Santa Monica, CA 90406. 16 mm, in color, 20 min., 1969. Guidelines for the child to effectively identify potential child molesters and hints for children to protect themselves against the advances of strangers.

The Newborn Calf. Indiana University, Audio Visual Center, Bloomington, IN 47405. 16 mm, in color, 11 min., 1970. The birth and early development of a calf are shown. Shows the calf and cow together and the weaning of the calf. Suitable for an introduction to birth and reproduction.

The Prince and the Princess. Eye Gate Media, 146-01 Archer Avenue, Jamaica, NY 11435. Filmstrip audiocassette combination, in color, 1973. One in a series of titles using fables to teach self-acceptance in relation to contemporary issues. This title deals principally with roles for women and men.

Sex Education for Young Children. Time-Life Multimedia, Time Life Building, Rockefeller Center, New York, NY 10020. 16 mm, black and white, 20 min., 1971. Request information about special order purchase. Three titles in this series are (1) Beginning, (2) Birth, and (3) Full Circle.

The Story of Birth. BFA Educational Media, 2211 Michigan Avenue, P.O. Box 1795, Santa Monica, CA 90406. A filmstrip and record combination or filmstrip and audiocassette combination, in color. Paper sculpture figures are used to present facts about the birth process. Begins with a chick in the "special place" in the mother hen and then shows hatching. Proceeds to show the baby in a "special place" in the mother and goes on to the father's and the physician's roles in arranging the mother's stay at the hospital. Study guide included.

The Story of Human Life, No. 1. Educational Activities, P.O. Box 392, Freeport, NY 11520. A filmstrip and record combination or filmstrip and audiocassette combination, in color, 12 min., 1969. The life cycle and human growth, including individual and gender differences, the basics of reproduction, and how babies are born. Teacher's guide included.

The Story of Our New Baby. Coronet Instructional Media, 65 East South Water Street, Chicago, IL 60601. 16 mm, in color, 11 min., 1946. Parents share with their child the progression of their expected child from a "tiny cell" into a person.

It Takes a Lot of Growing. Carousel Films, 1501 Broadway, New York, NY 10036. 16 mm, in color, 9 min., 1969. Film emphasizes the place of the child in the family. Special attention is placed on gender roles: boys vs. girls, mothers vs. fathers.

Whom Do You Look Like? Imperial Educational Resources, 19 Marble Avenue, Pleasantville, NY 10570. A filmstrip and audiocassette combination, in color. The biological aspects of reproduction, human growth, and development. Teacher's guide included.

The Zoo Trip "Show and Tell." Eye Gate Media, 146-01 Archer Avenue, Jamaica, NY 11435. A filmstrip and record combination or filmstrip and audiocassette combination, in color, 1967. Covers basic facts about reproduction, including human reproduction. Study charts included.

GRADES FOUR TO SIX

About Sex and Growing Up. Family Life Productions, 219 Henderson Street, Box 427, Saluda, NC 29773. A filmstrip and record combination or filmstrip and audiocassette combination, in color, 7 to 10 min., 1968. Each of the four filmstrips is described separately. The titles are (1) Maturing Boys and Girls, (2) Becoming a Woman, (3) Becoming a Man, and (4) Where Babies Come From.

Adam's Rib. Audio-Visual Services, The Pennsylvania State University, University Park, PA 16802. 16 mm/videocassette, black and white, 30 min. Addresses the question of the relative influences of inheritance and environment in determining traditional gender roles among women. A children's group dramatizes women's roles, and a discussion follows of their ideas about those roles and how they may be varied.

Adolescence, Love and Maturity. Sterling Educational Films, 241 East 34th Street, New York, NY 10016. 16 mm, in color, 10 min., 1968. An introduction to values regarding reproduction. Humans are compared with animals with respect to instinctive vs. affectionate sexual behavior and reproduction. Topics covered include the female cycle, fertilization, and infant care, among others.

Are We Still Going to the Movies? Audio-Visual Services, The Pennsylvania State University, University Park, PA 16802. 16 mm, in color, 14 min., 1974. A young couple having a platonic relationship at a picnic face the question, "Should we?" as he persists and she resists. Following the situational presentation, questions are asked to initiate class discussion. Instructor's guide included. Also known as "Adolescent Sexual Conflict: Are We Still Going to the Movies?"

The Beginining of Pregnancy. Association Films, 6644 Sierra Lane, Dublin, CA 94566. 16 mm, black and white, 30 min., 1956. Explains events in early pregnancy, inheritance, and development of twins.

Being Boys—Being Girls. Sterling Educational Films, 241 East 34th Street, New York, NY 10016. 16 mm, in color, 10 min., 1968. Little specific sexual content, but emphasizes aspects of physical characteristics of boys and girls and their differences. Also relates aspects of developing social responsibilities.

Boy to Man (Revised). Churchill Films, 662 North Robertson Boulevard, Los Angeles, CA 90069. 16 mm, in color, 15 min., 1975. Uses animation and a conceptual framework to illustrate the physiological changes that take place in maturing males.

Changing from Boy to Man. Imperial Educational Resources, 19 Marble Avenue, Pleasantville, NY 10570. A filmstrip and audiocassette combination, in color. The biological aspects of reproduction, human growth, and development. Teacher's guide included.

Changing from Girl to Woman. Imperial Education Resources, 19 Marble Avenue, Pleasantville, NY 10570. A filmstrip audiocassette combination, in color. The biological aspects of reproduction, human growth, and development. Teacher's guide included.

Clorae and Albie. Education Development Center, 39 Chapel Street, Newton, MA 02160. 16 mm, in color, 36 min., 1976. Emphasizes the need for women to consider carefully and prepare for the responsibilities of life in or out of marriage with or without children. The lives of Clorae and Albie, two women in their 20's who met in secondary school, are followed. One got married; the other went to work. Both consider their development, education, and independence to be important.

The Day Life Begins. Association Films, 6644 Sierra Lane, Dublin, CA 94566. 16 mm, black and white, 23 min., 1964. Produced for television. Covers reproduction of animals from ameba to man in a step-by-step fashion, including some material on human embryology.

Different Folks. Agency For Instructional Television, Box A, Bloomington, IN 47401. 16 mm/videocassette combination, in color, 15 min., 1975. A program designed to initiate classroom discussions among 11- to 13-year-olds. An extensive teacher's guide and list of activities augment the dramatic presentation of "appropriate" gender roles in marriage. A boy is confused by his parent's choice of household duties—the father does most of the housework, and the mother earns the living. After a family crisis, the boy learns that apparent sex roles can be deceiving and that masculinity and femininity can have broader definitions than those provided by his more traditional friends. Teacher's guide included.

Dolphins and Men. Time-Life Multi-media, Time Life Building, Rockefeller Center, New York, NY 10020. 16 mm, unspecified videotape, in color, 25 min., 1973. Although principally a study of dolphin behavior, the film presents an interesting finding, namely that dolphin's play is sexual, making the dolphin the only animal aside from man to engage in sex purely for pleasure. Originally presented on television.

Egg and Sperm. Sterling Educational Films, 241 East 34th Street, New York, NY 10016. 16 mm, in color, 10 min., 1968. Three diverse vertebrate species illustrate the process of fertilization, sperm and egg development, and fetal development. These examples are compared with human development.

Especially for You. Perennial Education, 477 Rodger Williams, P.O. Box 855 Ravinia, Highland Park, IL 60035. A filmstrip and audiocassette combination, in color, 1975. Aids boys and girls in the understanding of attitudes about human growth and reproduction. Discussion of pubertal changes, the union of sperm and egg, and the development of the human being are included. The female reproductive system is related to growth and maturity, and the development of a boy into a man is described. Teacher's guide included. Available in Spanish.

The Fable of He and She. Extension Media Center, University of California, Berkeley, CA 94720. 16 mm, in color, 11 min., 1974. Animated film lampoons sexrole stereotyping. "Hardibars" (males) and "Mushimels" (females) are separated by an earthquake. Confusion reigns, then members of each group discover they can function in opposite gender roles. When the two groups are reunited, men rejoice at the possibility of returning to "normal," but the women have different plans!

A Family Talks About Sex. Perennial Education, 477 Rodger Williams, P.O. Box 855 Ravinia, Highland Park, IL 60035. 16 mm/slides 8 mm/videocassette, in color, 29 min., 1977. A number of family situations are shown for the purpose of enabling communication between parents and children of all ages. Ages of children involved range from toddlers to college-age students. A variety of topics are discussed according to the questions asked and ages involved. Study guide included.

Female of the Species. Eye Gate Media, 146-01 Archer Avenue, Jamaica, NY 11435. A filmstrip and record combination or filmstrip and audiocassette combination, in color, 1972. Designed to bring awareness to the student about physical and psychological "drives" and how they are best handled. General coverage of a variety of topics.

Getting Closer. Agency For Instructional Television, Box A, Bloomington, IN 47401. 16 mm/videocassette, in color, 15 min., 1975. A program designed to initiate classroom discussions among 11- to 13-year-olds. A shy and self-conscious boy cannot find the courage to ask a girl to dance. Use of an extensive teacher's guide following this dramatic presentation can assist the discussion leader in bringing out typical adolescent anxieties and concerns, especially those related to interactions with the members of the opposite sex. Teacher's guide included.

Girl to Woman (Revision). Churchill Films, 662 North Robertson Boulevard, Los Angeles, CA 90069. 16 mm, in color, 17 min., 1975. Uses animation in depicting the turbulent change in growth and development young girls experience during puberty.

Glands and Hormones. Sterling Educational Films, 241 East 34th Street, New York. NY 10016. 16 mm, in color, 10 min. Facts and new responsibilities related to development at puberty. Internal and external changes described as well as socialization and hygiene.

The Great Cover-Up. Extension Media Center, University of California, Berkeley, CA 94720. 16 mm, in color, 12 min., 1977. Vignettes and animation are used to show how society's choice of clothing expresses its attitudes in areas such as sexuality, politics, and esthetic appreciation. A historical approach is taken.

Growing Up (Boy's Version). Association Films, 6644 Sierra Lane, Dublin, CA 94566. 16 mm, in color, 10 min. Animation and live action are used to show glandular development and childbirth, emphasizing family relations for 9- to 11-year-olds. (Like the girl's version but without discussion of menstruation.)

Growing Up (Girl's Version). Association Films, 6644 Sierra Lane, Dublin, CA 94566. 16 mm, in color, 11 min. Animation and live action are used to show glandular development, menstruation, and childbirth, emphasizing family relations for 9- to 11-year-olds. (Like the boy's version but with discussion menstruation).

Human Growth. Indiana University, Audio-Visual Center, Bloomington, IN 47405. 16 mm, in color, 21 min., 1976. Using animation and discussions with students from fifth grade to high school, sexual development is presented. Includes the biology of puberty, the basics of reproduction, and a live birth scene.

Human Sexuality Series. Eye Gate Media, 146-01 Archer Avenue, Jamaica, NY 11435. Six filmstrip-record combination or six filmstrip-audiocassette combination, in color, 1972. Designed to bring awareness to the student about physical and psychological "drives" and how they are best handled. Coverage includes a variety of topics.

I Wonder, I Wonder. Family Life Publications, 219 Henderson Street, Box 427, Saluda, NC 29773. Filmstrip-record combination, in color. Sex education through the use of an illustrated story for children in which a mother gives birth to twins. Part of a filmstrip series including many topics for young children.

Inheriting Your Physical Traits. Coronet Instructional Media, 65 East South Water Street, Chicago, IL 60601. 16 mm, in color, 11 min., 1970. Shows the role of chromosomes and genes in determining traits such as sex, eye color, height, and weight.

It Has Nothing To Do with You. Audio Visual Services, The Pennsylvania State University, University Park, PA 16802. 16 mm, in color, 14 min., 1974. A young man discovers that his parents have argued and separated. He is forced to choose between them. Having thus presented the situation, questions are asked of the viewers with the goal of initiating class discussions. Instructor's guide included.

Male and Female Plants and Animals. Coronet Instructional Media, 65 East South Water Street, Chicago, IL 60601. 16 mm, in color, 10 min. 1974. Covers the reproductive system in plants and animals while showing the similarities to the human reproductive systems.

Menstruation—Linda's Film. Phoenix Films, 470 Park Avenue South, New York, NY 10016. 16 mm, in color, 18 min., 1974. Animation explains the process. Myths and "old wives' tales" are dispelled.

Miracle of Life. Pyramid Films, P.O. Box 1048, Santa Monica, CA 90406. 16 mm, in color, 15 min., 1977. The miracle of life is brought to the screen through the development of endoscopic lenses. The actual process of fertilization, cell division, growth and development, and other events of reproduction and embryology are documented in vivo. Technically advanced yet fascinating treatment and photography make this film suitable for any age level.

The New Baby. Sterling Educational Films, 241 East 34th Street, New York, NY 10016. 16 mm, in color, 20 min., 1962. A visit to a home where a third child is expected shows the family preparing for baby's arrival. Includes prenatal and early postnatal care and sibling reactions and adjustments.

Peer Groups: Ages 6–13. *The American Journal of Nursing,* Educational Services Division, 10 Columbus Circle, New York, NY 10019. 16 mm/videotape, black and white, 44 min., 1967. Behavioral changes and development discussed include gender-related behavioral and maturational differences.

The People Problem. Films Incorporated, 1144 Wilmette Avenue, Wilmette, IL 60091. 16 mm, in color, 17 min., 1972. A major television network presentation explores the overpopulation problem, the effects it has on human life, and the accelerated use of limited resources. Birth control is introduced but not emphasized more than other general considerations about overpopulation in the world. Study guide included.

A Place for Aunt Lois. Wombat Productions, Little Lake, Glendale Road, P.O. Box 70, Ossining, NY 10562. 16 mm, in color, 17 min., 1974. Two young girls are rather firmly entrenched in familiar, traditional gender role attitudes and behavior—their time being spent discussing their futures as wives and mothers and playing with dolls. But when recently divorced Aunt Lois arrives, their thoughts expand to consider alternatives. Study guide included.

Rookie of the Year. Time-Life Multimedia, Time-Life Building, Rockefeller Center, New York, NY 10020. 16 mm/videocassette, in color, 47 min., 1975. Originally a major television network special, this film dramatizes aspects of learned gender role stereotypes, especially those relating to the "proper place" for girls and women. Discussion guide available.

Then One Year. Churchill Films, 662 North Robertson Boulevard, Los Angeles, CA 90069. 16 mm, in color, 19 min., 1972. Primary and secondary changes at adolescence in boys and girls are presented.

We. Modern Talking Picture Service, 2323 New Hyde Park Road, New Hyde Park, NY 11040. 16 mm, in color, 28 min., 1973. Findings from the 1970 census are presented by an actor-narrator and by graphic illustration. Suburban growth, movement of people from rural to urban areas, and movement toward coasts are related. Offers background for an introduction of the topic of birth control.

What are Values? BFA Educational Media, 2211 Michigan Avenue, P.O. Box 1795, Santa Monica, CA 90406. 16 mm, in color, 9 min., 1977. An explanation of what values are, how they are learned, what actions tell us about values, and the importance for individuals to recognize their own values and to live by them.

You Irresistible You. Benchmark Films, 145 Scarborough Road, Briarcliff Manor, NY 10510. 16 mm, in color, 11 min., 1975. Sex attraction gimmicks for males are humorously examined. The central character uses most of these before calling for a date, only to learn that she still has a headache.

Your Body During Adolescence. Audio Visual Services, The Pennsylvania State University, University Park, PA 16802. 16 mm, black and white, 10 min., 1955. Through the use of animation and narration, explanations are given for reproduction, puberty, and the roles of the glands involved in these processes.

JUNIOR AND SENIOR HIGH SCHOOL

Abortion. CTV Television Network, 42 Charles Street East, Toronto, Canada, M4Y 1T5. 16 mm/videocassette, in color, 13 min., 1973. Discusses the pros and cons of abortion and shows an abortion performed in a Montreal clinic.

About Conception and Contraception. 855 Perennial Education, 477 Rodger Williams, P.O. Box 855 Ravina, Highland Park, IL 60035. 16 mm/8 mm /videocassette, in color, 11 min., 1973. Animation illustrates how conception occurs and how the various birth control devices, surgical methods, and the pill function in preventing conception. There is no narration on the sound track. Study guide available.

About Puberty and Reproduction. Perennial Education, 477 Rodger Williams, P.O. Box 855 Ravinia, Highland Park, IL 60035. 16 mm/8 mm/videocassette, in color, 12 min., 1975. Deals with pubertal changes in boys and girls. Menstruation is explained in detail, and brief coverage is given to pregnancy and childbirth. Study guide available.

About V.D. Perennial Education, 477 Rodger Williams, P.O. Box 855 Ravinia, Highland Park, IL 60035. 16 mm/8 mm/videocassette, in color, 14 min., 1975. Utilizes animation to explain transmission, symptoms, and the effects of syphilis and gonorrhea. Study guides available.

Adjusting. Sunburst Communications, 39 Washington Avenue, Room 5, Pleasantville, NY 10570. Filmstrip-record combination or filmstrip-audiocassette, in color, 9 min., 1976. Discusses the changes in family life after a separation and how teenagers can cope with their feelings of loneliness, anger, and rejection. Teacher's guide included.

Am I Wife, Mother . . . or Me? Learning Corporation of America, 1350 Avenue of the Americas, New York, NY 10019. 16 mm, in color, 31 min., 1975. Hope Lange and Earl Holliman dramatize a modern marital dilemma. A 36-year-old wife and mother, while dedicated to her responsibilities for running the family, begins to question whether there is anything in her day-to-day activities "just for me." Compelled to pursue her "destiny," she drives away from the home to enter a new world—one with a career, potential romance, and personal accomplishment.

Anatomy and Physiology of the Human Reproductive Organs. Aldine Publishing, 529 South Wabash Avenue, Glendale, CA 91201. Videocassette, in color, 34 min., 1974. An introduction to the human reproductive system, male and female. Covers germ cell (gamete) production and hormone influences, menstruation, pregnancy, and other functions related to reproduction and the reproductive systems. Study guide included.

Anatomy of a Teenage Engagement. Coronet Instructional Media, 65 East South Water Street, Chicago, IL 60601. 16 mm, in color, 26 min., 1969. A young couple has second thoughts as each becomes more aware of his/her partner's personality, emotions, habits, and physical drives.

Are You Ready for Sex? Perennial Education, 477 Rodger Williams, P.O. Box 855 Ravinia, Highland Park, IL 60035. 16 mm/8 mm/videocassette, in color, 24 min., 1976. Students dramatize and discuss questions concerning sexual responsibility, interpersonal communications, peer group pressures, sexual maturity, personal values, sexual intercourse, the use of contraceptives, and sexual abstinence. Study guide available.

Attaining Sexual Maturity. Sunburst Communications, 39 Washington Avenue,

Room 5, Pleasantville, NY 10570. Filmstrip-record combination or filmstrip-audiocassette, in color, 11 min., 1977. Part one of a three-part program explores how there is a lag between the biological force of sexuality and the development of the understanding needed to fit sexuality into one's life. Discusses maturbation, homosexual experimentation, denial of sexual feelings, the desire for emotional and physical contact, and the fascination of adolescents with their own bodies. Teacher's guide included.

A Baby is Born. Perennial Education, 477 Rodger Williams, P.O. Box 855 Ravinia, Highland Park, IL 60035. 16 mm/8 mm/videocassette, in color, 23 min. 1973. Describes birth in the context of general reproduction. Problems common in first births become apparent: (1) extended pregnancy; (2) lengthy labor; (3) parental anxiety; (4) episiotomy; (5) emotions accompanying birth. A physician explains how to space the birth of babies by using proper birth control methods. Study guide available.

Birth Control—Five Effective Methods. Sterling Educational Films, 241 East 34th Street, New York, NY 10016. 16 mm, in color, 10 min., 1975. Compares the use, the advantages and disadvantages, and the availability of pills, IUD, diaphragm and jelly, condom, and foam. Rhythm and coitus-interruptus are not recommended. Brief review of the male and female reproductive systems is included.

Celebration in Fresh Powder. Association Films, 6644 Sierra Lane, Dublin, CA 94566. 16 mm, in color or black and white, 28 min., 1973. Explores moral issues for abortion as four high school girls discuss the alternatives for one of them who is pregnant: should she marry her boyfriend, have an abortion, or have the baby alone? She reveals her decision to her parents in the end.

Changes. Agency for Instructional Television, Box A, Bloomington, IN. 47405. 16 mm/videocassette, in color, 15 min., 1975. A program designed to initiate classroom discussions among 11- to 13-year-olds. An extensive teacher's guide and list of activities augment the dramatic presentation. The purpose is to help adolescents understand and cope with the emotions and physiological changes they confront.

The Circle Called Man. Aims Instructional Media, 626 Justin Avenue, Glendale, CA 91201. 16 mm, in color, 22 min., 1976. Graphic animation without dramatics or scare tactics presents the facts about syphilis and gonorrhea. A 135-page illustrated student booklet is included. A book for parents is available.

The Day Before Tommorrow. Sterling Educational Films, 241 East 34th Street, New York, NY 10016. 16 mm, in color, 28 min. or 52 min., 1971. Documents population pressures around the world by offering statistics and comments from world leaders and population authorities. Discusses unwanted pregnancies and their effect on the individual and society. Family planning programs are mentioned. Edited (28 min.) or full-length (52 min.) versions are available.

Does Anyone Need Me Anymore? Learning Corporation of America, 1350 Avenue of the Americas, New York, NY 10019. 16 mm, in color, 29 min., 1975. Maureen Stapleton and Paul Sorvino portray a couple who are hard-working, love each other, yet are confronted with considerations about growth and personal identity that are new and frightening. The wife begins to question her life-style and values and the dream of new possibilities.

Family. Films Incorporated, 1144 Wilmette Avenue, Wilmette, IL 60091. 16 mm, in color, 21 min., 1973. Examines the effects of Western society's history and industrialization on the family and explores alternatives such as a return to the nuclear family, communal living, shaping neighborhoods differently, and the extended family.

Far Cry from Yesterday. Perennial Education, 477 Rodger Williams, P.O. Box 855 Ravinia, Highland Park, IL 60035. 16 mm/super 8 mm/videocassette, in color, 20 min., 1973. An unmarried teenage couple acccepts unplanned pregnancy because they are "in love." Deals with insights into responsibility, care, and planning. Study guide included.

Female Sexual Response. Family Life Publications, 219 Henderson Street, Box 427, Saluda, NC 29773. Filmstrip-record combination or filmstrip-audiocassette, in color, 19 min., 1974. Views regarding the woman's role in the sexual union and her physical and emotional reactions.

Gays and Role Playing. KUT-FM, Box 7158, University of Texas, Austin, TX 78712. Audiocassette, 25 min., 1976. Two members of gay organizations explain gender roles as related to dress, sexual and social behavior, and expectations, especially as these have been "role played" in the gay community.

Growing Pains. Pyramid Films, P.O. Box 1048. Santa Monica, CA 90406. 16 mm, in color, 13 min., 1973. Familiar television personality establishes the atmosphere for a question and answer session on sexuality, masturbation, dating, and love, placing emphasis on patience and responsibility. A doctor discusses the physiology of puberty.

How Life Begins. Indiana University, Audio-Visual Center, Bloomington, IN 47405. 16 mm, in color, 46 min., 1968. Originally a television special narrated by a celebrity. Relates how life begins from union of egg and sperm to embryonic development and live birth sequence, first in animals, then in humans. Guide included.

Human Body: Reproductive System. Coronet Instructional Media, 65 East South Water Street, Chicago, IL 60601. 16 mm, in color, 13 min., 1959. Through animation and photomicrography, differences in male and female, the physiology and anatomy of reproductive systems, and the functions of organs in the creation of new life are covered.

It Couldn't Happen to Me. Perennial Education, 477 Rodger Williams, P.O. Box 855 Ravinia, Highland Park, IL 60035. 16 mm/8 mm/videocassette, in color, 28 min., 1973. Young people and professionals discuss the topics of premarital sex, birth control, and pregnancy. Attitudes and morals are incorporated in the discussion. Study guide included.

It Happens. Pyramid Films, P.O. Box 1048, Santa Monica, CA 90406. 16 mm, in color, 23 min., 1972. Portrait of a pregnant 15-year-old faced with decisions for which she is unprepared. Alternatives are presented throughout the story, but the final decision is not revealed. The open-ended presentation can lead to discussion.

A Lonely Way Back. Cine-image Films, 3931 Maquoketa Drive, Des Moines, IA 50311. 16 mm, in color, 22 min., 1974. Dramatizes the psychological problems associated with venereal disease in teenagers.

Male Sexual Response. Family Life Publications, 219 Henderson Street, Box 427, Saluda, NC 29773. Filmstrip-record combination or filmstrip-audiocassette, in color, 21 min., 1974. Describes the role of the man in the sexual union and discusses his physical reactions and attitudes.

Margaret Sanger. Audio Visual Services, The Pennsylvania State University, University Park, PA 16802. 16 mm, black and white, 30 min., 1960. Historical documentation of Sanger's attempts to introduce family planning in America. Includes presentation of women's struggles for equality in that time period. Narrated by Katherine Hepburn. Guide included.

Masturbatory Story. Perennial Education, 477 Rodger Williams, P.O. Box 855 Ravinia, Highland Park, IL 60035. 16 mm/videocassette/super 8 mm, in color, 15 min., 1978. An appraisal and explanation of the needs and desires involved with masturbation, particularly in males. Presented in a light manner, the goal is to expose and destroy myths about masturbation.

More Common Than Measles or Mumps. Films Incorporated, 1144 Wilmette Avenue, Wilmette, IL 60091. 16 mm, in color, 10 min., 1974. Animated cartoon presents facts about venereal disease—contraction, cures, prevention, and common misconceptions.

Mother and Child. Walter J. Klein Co., 6301 Carmel Road, Box 220766. Charlotte, NC 28222. 16 mm, in color, 15 min., 1975. The La Leche League and two celebrities, Susan St. James and the late Natalie Wood, are featured in this presentation about breast feeding. Information and "inside tips" are offered.

My Mom's Having a Baby. Time-Life Multimedia, Time-Life Building, Rockefeller Center, New York, NY 10020. 16 mm/videocassette, in color, 47 min., 1977. Major network television special that received top ratings. Presents the "facts of life" to a 9-year-old boy who is somewhat confused, anxious, and jealous about the impending arrival of a sibling. He and friends discuss their ideas about where babies come from, then decide to ask parents and a pediatrician, who uses narration and animation to explain the events leading to birth. The film closes with a live birth sequence.

Naturally . . . a Girl. Association Films, 6644 Sierra Lane, Dublin, CA 94566. 16 mm, in color, 14 min., Explains why menstruation happens and its relationship to womanhood.

Our Instincts and Why We Have Them. Eye Gate Media, 146-01 Archer Avenue, Jamaica, NY 11435. Filmstrip-record combination or filmstrip-audiocassette, in color, 1972. Designed to bring awareness to the student about physical and psychological drives and how they are best handled. Many topics are included in this series.

Phoebe—Story of Premarital Pregnancy. Audio Visual Services, The Pennsylvania State University, University Park, PA 16802. 16 mm, in color or black and white, 30 min., 1969. Presents the feelings, concerns, shame, and abject fear a high school student experiences on the day she finds herself pregnant. Other individuals can be helped to clarify their own values and personal goals through the evaluation of her situation.

Physical Aspects of Puberty. University of Southern California, Division of Cinema-Television, Film Distribution Center, University Park, Los Angeles, CA 90007. 16 mm, black and white, 19 min., 1953. An explanation in animation of the changes occurring in boys and girls during puberty and the sometimes painful social consequences of those changes.

The Price of Life. Association Films, 6644 Sierra Lane, Dublin, CA 94566. 16 mm, in color, 12 min., 1973. Touches on abortion as three vignettes pursue questions concerning the value of life.

Psychological Differences Between the Sexes. McGraw-Hill Films, 1221 Avenue of the Americas, New York., NY 10020. 16 mm, in color, 13 min., 1965. Offers explanations for the "basic differences" in the reactions of boys and girls to given situations. "Primary" personality differences between men and women are explored, and ways to promote better understanding between the genders are offered.

Puberty in Boys. Films Incorporated, 1144 Wilmette Avenue, Wilmette, IL 60091. 16 mm, in color, 10 min., 1969. Animation and illustration explain changes in boys, including sperm formation, secondary sex characteristics, and hormones, among others.

Pupae. Extension Media Center, University of California, Berkeley, CA 94720. 16 mm, black and white, 30 min., 1974. Dramatic presentation of two teenage boys and their attitudes toward females. One of the boys is boastful and lacking in sensitivity; the other is sensitive and inhibited. Indicates the origin of some sexual attitudes, especially hang-ups that remain to plague adults. Includes a scene in which a boy appears to be masturbating.

Rollin' with Love. Focus International, 1 East 53rd Street, New York, NY 10022. 16 mm/super 8 mm/videotape, in color, 5 min., 1977. Tennis balls come "out of the closet" in this light-hearted, informative presentation of homosexuality. Tennis balls are used and set into motion to enact roles of parents, gays, and others in situations designed to inform the public and dispel myths about homosexuality. Instructor's guide included.

Sexual Response. University of Washington Press, Seattle, WA 98105. Videocassette, in color, 30 min., 1975. This series covers a very wide range of topics, with each topic on a different tape. Some of these include: Sex Ethics; Love and Romance; Marriage; Homosexuality; and Rape/Venereal Disease.

Sexuality and the Teenager Series. Perennial Education, 477 Rodger Williams, P.O. Box 855, Ravinia, Highland Park, IL 60035. 16 mm, in color, 19 to 28 min., 1968 (3 parts). After examining physical, emotional, and social factors about teenage sex in parts I and II, a roundtable discussion considers human need for successful social relationships in part III.

Sexuality: The Human Heritage. Audio Visual Services, The Pennsylvania State University, University Park, PA 16802. 16 mm, in color, 59 min., 1975. Discusses the development of human sexuality from prenatal hormone influences to influences from family and society after birth. Examines gender acquisition in childhood, homosexuality, marital roles, menopause, teenage peer pressures to "do it" or "not to do it," sex for the elderly, and other topics.

Teen Sexuality: What's Right for You? Perennial Education, 477 Rodger Williams, P.O. Box 855, Ravinia, Highland Park, IL 60035. 16 mm/8 mm/videocassette, in color, 29 min., 1976–1977. Boys and girls in groups candidly discuss such topics as masturbation, pornography, homosexuality, and venereal disease in light of their own experiences and backgrounds. Study guide available.

Teenage Mother: A Broken Dream. Carousel Films, 1501 Broadway, New York, NY 10036. 16 mm, in color, 14 min., 1977. An unwed 15-year-old mother explains why she wanted a baby and expresses her hopes for the future, a future affected by the fact that she is in a detention home and her baby is in an orphanage.

Teenagers. Time-Life Multimedia, Time-Life Building, Rockefeller Center, New York, NY 10020. 16 mm/videotape, in color, 32 min., 1971. Deals with the ubiquitous teenage questions by comparing approaches around the world, including such topics as promiscuity, dating patterns, and adolescence.

Then One Year. Churchill Films, 662 North Robertson Boulevard, Los Angeles, CA 90069. 16 mm, in color, 19 min., 1972. Primary and secondary changes at adolescence in boys and girls.

VD: A New(er) Focus. American Educational Films, 132 Lasky Drive, Beverly Hills, CA 90212. 16 mm/videocassette/8 mm, in color, 20 min., 1976. An update of the film "VD: A New Focus," including new material on gonorrhea, nongonoccocal urethritis, herpes, and syphilis.

What About McBride? Audio Visual Service, The Pennsylvania State University, University Park, PA 16802. 16 mm, in color, 10 min., 1974. Two boys air their views regarding a mutual friend they believe is homosexual. Questions follow designed to initiate class discussion. Instructor's guide included.

When Life Begins. McGraw-Hill Films, 1221 Avenue of the Americas, New York, NY 10020. 16 mm, in color, 12 min., 1971. Shows and explains development of the fetus in vivo, including an outline of the stages and organ development from fertilization to the live birth sequence. Guide included.

When Love Needs Care. Perennial Education, 477 Rodger Williams, P.O. Box 855 Ravinia, Highland Park, IL 60035. 16 mm/8 mm/videocassette, in color, 13 min., 1972. Shows the examination of two teenagers being treated for venereal disease. The importance of detecting VD early and of contacting potentially infected sex partners is presented.

Word Is Out. New Yorker Films, 16 West 61st Street, New York, NY 10023. 16 mm, in color, 2 hours, 1978. Described in a SIECUS review as a "perfectly beautiful film about some people I wish I could have as friends." Twenty-six interviews of homosexual persons are included in the film. A great variety of people is shown, making it obvious that stereotypes are inappropriate.

Young, Single and Pregnant. Perennial Education, 477 Rodger Williams, P.O. Box 855 Ravinia, Highland Park, IL 60035. 16 mm/8 mm/super 8 mm/videocassette, in color, 18 min., 1973. Experts and teenagers explore reasons for becoming pregnant, parental reactions, alternative solutions, and prevention. Discussion guide included.

Other Reference Sources For Education For Sexuality

There are a myriad of resources available throughout the community to the educator in the area of sexuality. These can often be obtained at little or no cost by contacting the appropriate individual, organization, or agency. The following reference sources may provide useful information in planning sexuality curricula.

American Association of Retired Persons, 1909 K. Street NW, Washington, DC 20049. Aging

Association for the Advancement of Health Education, AAHPERD, 1900 Association Drive, Reston, VA 22091. Teaching Sexuality

American Association of Sex Educators and Counselors, 5010 Wisconsin Avenue NW, Suite 304, Washington, DC 20016. In-service Information on Sexuality

American Institute of Family Relations, 5287 Sunset Boulevard, Los Angeles, CA 90027. Sex and Marriage

American Medical Association, 535 N. Dearborn Street, Chicago, IL 60610. Pre/post Partum Child Care

American School Health Association, Kent, OH 44240. Health of School-age Children

American Social Health Association, 1740 Broadway, New York, NY 10019. Family Relations, Sex Education, and Marriage

Association for Childhood Education International, 3615 Wisconsin Avenue, NW, Washington, DC 20016. Parenting and Child Development

Association for the Study of Abortion, 120 W. 57th Street, New York, NY 10019. Abortion

Child Study Association of America/Wel-Met Inc., 50 Madison Avenue. New York, NY 10010. Parenting and Child Development

Committee for Single Adoptive Parents, P.O. Box 4074, Washington, DC 20015. Adoption

Family Life Publications, Inc., P.O. Box 427, Saluda, NC 28773. Teaching Materials

Homosexual Community Counseling Center, 30 E. 60th. New York, NY 10022. Homosexuality

Institute for Family Research and Education, 760 Ostrom Avenue, Syracuse, NY. 13210. Family Planning, Sex Education

Kimberly-Clark Corporation, The Life Cycle Center, P.O. Box 2001, Neenah, WI 54956. Family Life/Menstruation

National Center for Health Statistics, Scientific and Technical Information Branch,

Health Resources Administration, 5600 Fishers Lane, Rockville, MD 20852. Statistics: Birth, Marriage, Divorce, and Mortality

National Congress of Parents and Teachers, 700 N. Rush Street, Chicago, IL 60611. Sex Education

National Council of Churches, Commission on Marriage and Family, 475 Riverside Drive, New York, NY 10027. Sex Education

National Gay Task Force, 80 Fifth Avenue, Room 506, New York, NY 10011. Homosexuality

National Genetics Foundation, 250 W. 57th Street, New York, NY 10019. Genetics

National Organization for Women, Task Force on Marriage, Divorce, and Family Relations, 5S Wabash, Suite 1615, Chicago, IL 60603. Family

Negative Population Growth, Inc., 103 Park Avenue, New York, NY 10017. Population Control

Parents Without Partners, 7910 Woodmont Avenue, Washington, DC 20014. Single Parenting

Personal Products Co., Consumer Information Center, Box 6, Milltown, NJ 08850. Menstruation

Planetary Citizens, 777 United Nations Plaza, New York, NY 10017. Population Control

Planned Parenthood Federation of Canada, 88 Eglinton Avenue E, Suite 404, Toronto, Ontario 10019. Contraception/Family Planning

Searle Laboratories, P.O. Box 5110, Chicago, IL 60680. Family Planning, Fertility, Menstruation

SIECUS, 122 E. 42nd Street, Suite 922, New York, NY 10017. Sex Education

United States Department of Commerce, Bureau of the Census, Social, and Economic Statistics Administration, 14th Street. Between Constitution and E. Street. NW, Washington, DC 20230. Statistics: Birth, Population, Fertility, and Mortality

A list of local reference sources in the community is helpful to the educator. You may want to list these sources in your area in the space provided below:

A Speech to Introduce Sex Education to the Community

A successful sex education program requires the support of the community. Thus an early step in introducing sex education should be open communication with parents. Parent-teacher meetings are excellent opportunities for such a discussion. In planning a presentation for parents, a review of the speech that follows may be of some value. This speech was given by one of the authors in presenting a modern view of sex education to a Maryland community. It includes many of the basic concepts presented in this book. A suggested program format follows:

1. Have a speaker outline the problems that attend human sexuality at the current time.

2. Disseminate a brief statement of the philosophy of your sex education program and some specific objectives for each grade level. This is very important because the parent will have no idea of what might be included in a sex education curriculum.

3. Provide a panel to discuss the curriculum in the local school district: an elementary teacher, a junior high school teacher, a high school teacher, and a school administrator.

A Modern View of Education for Sexuality (Text of a Speech)

It is a very great pleasure to be invited to speak on the topic: a modern view of education for sexuality. I should tell you that for the past 25 years I have been speaking to audiences who seemed more interested in "the ancient view!" So your invitation comes as a great joy. It permits me to attempt a speech that I would not otherwise dare to give—a speech that brings forth ideas that have been with me for many years, but which have remained unspoken until your invitation awakened my courage.

Ten years back, there were people who really thought, or who had been led to believe, that sex education was a communist plot. Back then, there were people who really thought, or who had been led to believe, that sex education would ultimately be responsible for the decline and fall of American civilization. At that time, the main argument for sex education was that it might be a way of preventing unwanted pregnancies—a task that somehow was to be accomplished not by teaching about contraception, but by instilling fear of sexually transmitted diseases.

Such was the ancient view of education for sexuality, a view that seems somewhat absurd now as we look back. But before we attempt a discussion of what might constitute a modern view, perhaps it would be wise to pause and see what we can learn from a distillation of past experiences.

Looking back over the stormy history of education related to sexuality, one question looms larger than all the others: Why were so many parents, all wanting the very best for their children, so divided over the issue of sex education? It is against the background of this question that modern sex education comes into view.

My personal struggle with this question has led me to three rather startling conclusions:

1. Through the years and to the present, both the support for and the opposition to sex education can be traced to a common philosophical viewpoint.

2. This common view, past and present, stems from a belief about human reality that not only complicates our thinking about sexuality, but which also has enormous consequences for happiness in general.

3. Although this belief has permeated all human history, it is probably invalid.

If I am right in these assumptions, we are standing at the transition between two epochs in sex education that are so dissimilar in character that they appear to represent a discontinuity in human experience, rather like going from the belief that the earth is flat to the modern view. All of this is to say that when I speak of the modern view of sex education I am not just speaking of some new ideas. Rather, I am talking about a new epoch—one that breaks from all recorded history.

For as long as anyone can remember, we humans have made an assumption about pleasure, often without being fully aware of it, that has dominated much of our thinking and behaving. Full-blown, this assumption states: The nature of human reality is such that pleasure is ordinarily associated with a snare. First comes the pleasure, then the snag or pain. We learn, for example, that the pleasure of eating may be followed by clogged arteries, obesity, or diabetes. Drinking may be followed by hangovers, cirrhosis, or loss of brain cells. Smoking may be followed by lung cancer or emphysema; sweets, by tooth decay; gambling, by bankruptcy; the thrill of speed, by accident; love, by disappointment; youth, by aging; life, by death. We walk down the road of life observing hundreds of side roads marked pleasure, but we have come to feel that they all lead to trouble, rather like the baited trap used to catch wild animals.

We are dealing here, as I am sure you realize, with a very tricky assumption. On the one hand, we do not really believe that pleasure is ordinarily followed by a snare. We say that we can think of many exceptions. And yet we each hold on to a little bit of the early Greek myth that really intense pleasures are reserved for the gods alone; that we must not tempt fate with too much pleasure seeking; and even when our lives are filled with joy we should not expect it to last.

As you know, sex is no exception. Indeed, it is the most lingering part of the myth. Human participation in the pleasures of sex is and always has been, so we believe, one of the quickest ways to anger the gods. We don't, of course, talk like that today, but throughout history parents have exhibited more concern over the possibility of sexual pleasures disrupting their children's lives than any other factor.

And so it came to pass in the history of education that the snags associated with the pleasure of sex (unwanted pregnancies, sexually-transmitted diseases, pressures for and against abortion, loss of self-esteem, prostitution, and sexual molestation) led people to support sex education—meaning the dissemination of knowledge useful in avoiding snags. And so it also came to pass that some people opposed sex education—opposed it out of the belief that knowledge of how to avoid snags would only encourage young people to move further down the road to pleasure, steps that would probably anger the gods and bring even more serious snags.

I trust that you begin to understand the implications of what's being said: If there were no snags associated with the pleasure of sex, no ill consequences, no developmental or personality problems, nothing whatsoever that was negatively associated with sex, even then we would not want our children having sex-just-for-the-fun-of-it. Right? Of course I am right. Even if it were scientifically demonstrated that having sex were good for children, or senior citizens for that matter, we would not approve of sex-just-for-the-fun-of-it. Why? Because we believe that there will always be a snag associated with sex-just-for-the-fun-of-it. Even if there were no snags, you and I would not believe it. Deep in our hearts we feel that there will always be something wrong with sex-just-for-the-fun-of-it. Maybe we even believe that there ought to be a snare associated with the pleasure of sex. At any rate, we have taught our children to feel guilty when they stumble on the snags. Just as the children of all generations before them, they feel that the snags with which they collided represent punishments, punishments for ill-advised pleasure seeking. We have never invited our children to entertain the view that "bad things really do happen to good people"—that we trip on snags not so much because we are evil but because we failed to beat the odds. Rather, we promulgate, perhaps unintentionally, the notion that the snags that mark the road to pleasure are placed there as punishments; which is to say, we personify life's odds—giving them the power "to make losers" of people who behave in certain ways.

In the real world, of course, there are many snags associated with sex. And as good parents we want our children to avoid as many of them as possible. Yet we should resist the temptation to describe unwanted pregnancies and sexually transmitted diseases as traps strategically placed to discourage certain types of sexual behavior. We want our children to be fully aware that certain actions taken by them increase the odds of pregnancy or disease or rape, but these problems do not come as punishments, not any more than influenza or cancer or heart disease. We want our children to understand the difference between risk factors and punishment factors. We want them to understand that an unwanted pregnancy may render them losers against certain biological odds, but it does not make them into diminished human beings—diminished because they angered the gods by seeking pleasure.

I think that one of our greatest failures as parents has been our inability to help our children deal effectively and safely with pleasure. Most of us, at least in our roles as parents, believe in the self-actualization ethic: It is the end of all our efforts as parents to create a climate suitable for the best possible development of our children. We want good schools, good teachers, good coaches, good clubs, good friends, and good health for our children. But sometimes we miss the larger view. It is nice to be educated and talented and healthy. However, there is something many times more important, something on which to expend one's health, something on which to expend one's talent, something to do with one's education. And all of these "somethings" are pleasure related. I am afraid that we tend to overlook the connection between the problems that our children encounter and pleasure.

So for at least one brief evening, I would like to have you seriously consider the possibility that teenage suicide and drug abuse and unwanted pregnancies and sexually transmitted disease and a long list of snags on which our children regularly trip and fall have less to do with health and education and talent and more to do with ignorance of pleasure options. Hence, no matter how forbidding it might seem, I would like to talk with you about the role of pleasure in sex education.

Let me see if I can render this role more lively. Close your eyes for a few moments. Imagine, if you can, that you have passed into another world. In this world, sex and pleasure have been totally disassociated. It is still possible to have children, but it is rather like donating blood: a very good thing to do, but there is little pleasure associated with the physical process.

What do you see in this new world?

- There are no unwanted pregnancies here; sex is only for reproduction.

- There is no prostitution here. Who would pay to give blood?

- Women's magazines no longer carry articles on the side effects of various contraceptives. In fact, there is no need for contraception at all.

- Rape has been replaced by other acts of violence, now primarily directed at men. Women can move about at night as freely as men.

- There is no longer any distinction between heterosexuality and homosexuality, no such thing as sexual orientation. No stigma attached to the fact that many men seem to prefer the company of other men; many women, the company of other women.

- As you ponder this imaginary world in your mental skies, what's happened to the marriage rate? Has it changed? If not to have children, why do people get married in this new world?

- What has happened to the divorce rate?

- How has the separation of sex and pleasure affected advertising? What new themes have advertisers picked up?

- How has the change affected motion pictures? T.V.?

- Do people still dress the same?

- Has music changed?

- Finally, what's the general attitude toward sex education in this imaginary world we have concocted? Now that pleasure and sex are separated, does anyone care whether sex education goes on in their schools?

If so, are the attitudes any different from those toward the teaching of digestion? Or respiration? Or circulation?

Open your eyes. Let's get out of that world. None of you want to get stuck there! But I hope that the experience gives you a better understanding of the central role that pleasure plays in our ways of thinking about our sexuality. I hope you understand how ridiculous it would be to teach about sexuality and not to discuss pleasure—even if the very thought frightens us. And it really does. To come here tonight and tell you that when we discuss sexuality with our children we must not leave pleasure out, to come and suggest what needs to be said about pleasure, to do this is one of my most frightening experiences. I dare to do it because if there is one thing of which I am sure it is this: With or without our help, our children are going to travel the roads of pleasure, and perhaps the best thing that you and I could ever do for them would be to assist them to find noncontradictory pleasures—pleasures without snags.

We say that our schools and universities are committed to truth, but could it be that the truths of greatest consequence are those that permit us to separate contradictory and noncontradictory pleasures? We say that our churches are committed to spiritual health, but could it be that their primary functions are to describe the differences between contradictory and noncontradictory pleasures? Could it be that that's what hell and heaven have always been about? Could it be that mental illness is nothing more than ill preparedness to distinguish between contradictory and noncontradictory pleasure? Could it be that depression is the feeling that noncontradictory pleasure is not an option for us? Or that it is no longer an option? All of this is to say—to say again— we can't exclude a discussion of pleasure from the education of our children.

Now I have my courage up! Let's talk about pleasure. Pleasure is a feeling, a good feeling, a positive biofeedback signal. It is a message that at least for the moment we are doing something that is pleasing. And suppose that I suggested to you that the ultimate test of education is whether people can achieve high level pleasure without destroying themselves, achieve joy without contradiction. I suspect that a number of you might agree. The problem is how to accomplish this kind of education.

Tonight I dare to suggest that the purpose of modern sex education, sex education in Epoch Two, will be to teach people how to promote sexual pleasure to a noncontradictory pleasure. Perhaps this idea frightens you. It does me. Like you, I grew up thinking that there would always be something wrong with pleasure seeking, that it would always be followed by a snag. If not now, then soon. You and I grew up in a kind of pleasure bondage, a world that did not seem to know or admit the existence of noncontradictory pleasure. But perhaps we can create a better climate for our children. At least we can try.

So here is what I think we should teach in Epoch Two, when and if it arrives. The central theme, in my view, should be noncontradictory pleasure. It might be approached this way.

Pleasure is a feeling, a signal to our consciousness that our thinking and behaving is in harmony with the way that we have been programmed—a signal that our way of living corresponds with the software that has been created for us or that we have created for ourselves. Actually, we are each possessed with two types of programming: a genetic package and a value program.

First the genetic program. At time of conception, we each receive one of the most complex biological programs known to humankind. This program makes its directions known to us primarily through pleasure and pain. When we are hungry this program sends us a discomfort message, and when we eat we find it pleasurable. When we are thirsty, it is pleasurable to drink. When we are tired, it is pleasurable to rest. When we are too hot or too cold, it is pleasurable to return to a more moderate temperature. Such is the nature of our biological programming.

Secondly, we each have a program related to values. Sometimes these are our very own values, in which case we have programmed ourselves. Sometimes these are hand-me-down values, in which case we live by the script of another. In either case, pleasure is a signal that our behavior accords our values; pain, the opposite. Most of us do not feel pleasure when we lie or cheat or steal or exploit others. Most of us are not programmed that way. We feel more pleasure when we are loving and helpful and co-operative and creative. We feel pleasure when we move toward our values.

An understanding of these two types of pleasure programming, genetic and value, is essential to the happiness of all of us. For example, our genetic and value programming sometimes complement each other and bring us to the peak of human experience. At other times, genetic and value pleasures clash violently to bring us to the depth of despair. Clearly then, to know one's self is to understand the nature of both of these types of human software and how they relate to each other. Thus sex education, good sex education, must focus on both genetic and value programming.

Modern education for sexuality, perhaps more than any other part of the curriculum, has the power to really help students understand noncontradictory pleasure. Let me give you a little of the flavor of what this new approach might be like. For the moment you are my class, a class in modern sex education, and the topic for discussion is how to get to high order noncontradictory pleasure. In a previous class you learned about genetic and value programming for pleasure. So you know about human software. The problem is to break the code that will allow us to access these programs and get a printout from our feelings that reads: NONCONTRADICTORY JOY. Conceptually, this is an easy lesson: You take your highest order value pleasure and you supplement it with the highest order genetic pleasure with which it is compatible. Presto! You have noncontradictory pleasure. But despite its apparent simplicity, it is one of the most difficult of all human tasks.

Let us say that after some careful self-examination you conclude that your highest order value pleasure is love. How many in this class have really loved someone? How many found this to be a value pleasure? Well, that was easy. We now have a value pleasure. Let's combine it, if we can, with a compatible biological pleasure. Most of you find it very pleasurable to go out to dinner with people that you love, right? Some of you find eating so pleasurable that you could do it with people you hate! In fact, hating drives some people to eating. But it's not the same as loving and eating. I think that you will agree that loving-eating is a higher order pleasure. The same could be said for drinking or exercising or creating, perhaps even working. It's more fun, I think you will agree, to drink or exercise or compete or create or work with people you love. And certainly this is true for sex. Some people find this biological pleasure so intense that they can engage in it with people they hate or paid partners or even animals. But, with morality aside and pleasure as the only consideration, the fact remains that there are very few pleasures known to humans that exceed sex with someone you really love. Indeed, I think that love is the desire on the part of two or more people to create together a climate in which all parties can experience more noncontradictory pleasure than either could alone. That's what we work at, that's why we sacrifice short term pleasures in our interpersonal relationship: to create a climate in which we can find more noncontradictory pleasure. That's what we have to teach our children. Not just what pleasures they must forego. Not just what they must not do. Not just how to be healthy. We must help them to find something to be healthy for. Something to work for. Something to sacrifice for. We must help them to find the way to noncontradictory pleasure.

I am sorry. I am talking to you as though you were parents, but we are supposed to be in a class in modern sex education. We were discussing the formula for high order pleasure: You take the highest value pleasure and match it with the highest genetic pleasure with which it is compatible. Given this formula, it is not surprising that for as long as anyone can remember humans have been eating and drinking and exercising and creating and sleeping with people they love. Interesting. Interesting that with all of our preoccupation with pleasure through the years, we have not been able to improve on the formula.

That's the good news. But match a genetic pleasure with an incompatible value pleasure and you have disaster: self-hate, guilt, insomnia, anorexia, sexual dysfunction, suicide.

Matching value pleasures with genetic pleasures—that's the most difficult task that any of us face. We can't just go out and do what feels good. We must square our values with our biology. That is what it means to know thyself. That is what education, education at its best, is about. That is what modern education for sexuality must be about.

Back to being parents. Our children need our help to find the road to noncontradictory pleasure. They need their teacher's help. They need the help of authentic spiritual leaders. They need all the coaching they can get. Even then, many will fail. And in many of these same places that you and I failed. The road to noncontradictory pleasure is a difficult climb marked by confusing detours. But hopefully our children will come to realize that such a road does exist, that it is not fated that all pleasure must be followed by a snag. And to the extent that we are good parents, our children will understand— understand because we have told them—that we really do sympathize with their pleasure struggles, that we have tripped on many of the same snags, that no matter how hard or where they fall we will do our best to help, that we love them and that love means trying to create a climate in which those we love can not only be healthy and knowledgeable and creative and capable of standing on their own, but more importantly, can find noncontradictory pleasure in living.

Glossary of Terms

Abortion	The termination of pregnancy prior to the 28th week of gestation.
Induced abortion	Expulsion or removal of an embryo resulting from an intentional act by the mother or another person.
"AC-DC"	A person who has sexual realtions with members of either sex.
Adopt	To take a child of other parents into the family.
Adultery	Sexual intercourse wherein at least one partner is married to another person.
Afterbirth	The placenta that is discharged at the third stage of labor. All nonhuman mammals eat the afterbirth.
AIDS	A disease, called Acquired Immune Deficiency Syndrome, which diminishes the body's immunity against invading agents.
Amenorrhea	The absence of menstruation.
Amniocentesis	A medical procedure to determine genetic defects in the unborn child by removal of a small amount of amniotic fluid.
Amniotic sac	A fluid-filled sac that serves to protect the embryo.
Androgen	Hormonal substances that produce masculine characteristics.
Androphobia	An abnormal fear of men.
Annulment	A legal proceeding that renders a marriage void.
Aphrodisiac	A drug or other substance that increases sexual drive.
Autoeroticism	Another term for masturbation or self-stimulation.
Bartholin's glands	Two secreting glands found at either side of the vaginal entrance.
Bestiality	Having sexual intercourse with animals.
Bisexual	*Anatomy:* having sexual organs of both sexes. *Behavior:* having sexual relations with both sexes.
Breech birth	Childbirth in which the baby is presented buttocks first.
Bulbourethral (Cowper's) glands	Tubular glands that secrete into the male urethra.
"Butch"	A very masculine appearing female homosexual.
Behavior Modification	A discipline technique in which parents use positive rewards to encourage children to repeat desirable behaviors, and negative rewards to stop undesirable behaviors.

Cantharides	A dangerous substance (obtained from a South European beetle) that irritates the bladder, urethra, and digestive system; also called "Spanish fly."
Castration	Removal of the gonads.
Celibacy	A way of life in which the individual abstains from any sexual activity.
Cervix	The neck of the uterus.
Cesarean birth	A method of childbirth in which a surgical incision is made through the abdominal wall and uterus. The names comes from Julius Caesar, who was thought to have been born in this manner.
Chancre	An ulcer or sore caused by the syphilis bacterium. It usually is the first sign of syphilis.
Chancroid	An infection of the genitalia, usually venereal. Painful lesions develop and local lymph nodes are generally enlarged.
Child abuse	Maltreatment of children that may include physical abuse, neglect, emotional maltreatment, and/or sexual abuse.
Chorionic Villi Biopsy (CVB)	A procedure to screen for genetic defects in the unborn child by removal of cells from the chorionic villi.
Circumcision	A surgical procedure in which the foreskin of the penis is removed.
"Clap"	A slang expression for gonorrhea.
Clitoris	The female organ devoted entirely to increasing sexual tension, located just above the urinary opening.
Coitus	Another term for sexual intercourse.
Coitus interruptus	Withdrawal of the penis prior to ejaculation in an attempt to avoid pregnancy.
Colostrum	The portion of milk first secreted following pregnancy.
Conception	The physiological uniting of sperm and egg.
Condom	Rubber sheath worn over male penis to prevent pregnancy or veneral disease.
Congenital	Being present at birth but not hereditary.
Continence	Refraining from sexual activity.
Contraceptive	Something used to prevent pregnancy.
Copulation	Sexual intercourse.
Colpotomy	A technique of tying the oviducts through an incision in the vagina rather than the abdomen.
Corpus luteum	Temporary endocrine gland formed in the ovary after ovulation; its secretes estrogen and progesterone.
Couvade	Sympathetic pregnancy among husbands. A psychological reaction in which men experience many of the symptoms of pregnancy.
"Crabs"	Pubic lice.
Creative Intimacy	A sharing in the work or development of a project, task, or creation of something new.
Cryptorchidism	Undescended testes. In this condition the male is sterile until the testes descend or are surgically relocated.
Cul-de-sac	A closed pouch located between the anterior surface of the rectum and the posterior surface of the uterus.

Cunnilingus	Oral stimulation of the female genitals.
Dating	A sharing of social activities and time with a person of the opposite sex.
Decision	The act of making up your mind.
Decision-making	Deciding which of two or more choices you will make.
Detumescence	Loss of male erection secondary to a loss of blood from erectile tissue.
Diaphragm	A dome-shaped device worn over the cervix to prevent pregnancy.
Discipline	Training that develops self-control and self-discipline.
Dissolution	The legal end to a marriage in which partners mutually agree to stated terms, fulfill a waiting period, and receive court approval.
Divorce	The legal end to a marriage where the court determines the conditions for the termination of the marriage contract including the division of property and custody and visitation arrangements for children.
Douche	Cleansing the vagina with a liquid.
Dysmenorrhea	Painful menstruation.
Dyspareunia	Painful intercourse; may be caused by physical or psychological factors.
Ectopic pregnancy	Extrauterine pregnancy; pregnancy that occurs outside the uterus (e.g., in the oviduct).
Ejaculation	Male discharge of semen.
Ejaculatory duct	Anatomical junction of the vas deferens and the duct of the seminal vesicle with the male urethra. It is embedded in the prostate gland.
Emasculate	To deprive of manliness; to castrate.
Endometrium	The lining of the uterus.
Epididymis	Anatomical structure connecting the testis with the vas deferens.
Estrogen	Female sex hormone produced by the ovaries.
Eugenics	The science concerned with improving genetic constitution.
Eunuch	A term for the castrated male.
Facts	Pieces of information that are used to influence the decisions that you make.
Family	A group of people who are related by blood or by marriage.
Fallopian (uterine) tubes	A tube-like extension of the uterus whereby eggs from the ovaries may pass to the uterus.
Father	A man who has a child.
Fecundity	The power of producing offspring.
Fellatio	Oral stimulation of the penis.
"Femme"	Feminine appearing lesbian.
Fetish	An inanimate object that arouses erotic feelings.
Follicle stimulating hormone (FSH)	A hormonal substance released by the pituitary gland to stimulate the gonads.
Foreplay	Any form of sexual behavior preliminary to sexual intercourse.
Foreskin	A retractable fold of skin found over the head of an uncircumcised penis; also termed the prepuce.

Fornication	A term used to describe sexual intercourse outside marriage, in many states fornication is illegal.
Frattuier	One who gains sexual satisfaction by rubbing against women in crowds.
French kiss	Kiss that includes tongue contact.
Frenulum	Anatomical attachment of the penis to the foreskin.
Friend	Someone you know well and like.
Frigidity	A general term for female sexual unresponsiveness.
Gamete	Sperm or ovum; a reproductive cell.
"Gay"	Another term for homosexual.
Genital Herpes	A viral infection that produces painful blisters in the genital area.
Genitalia	External sexual organs.
Gestation	That period of time extending from conception to childbirth; pregnancy.
Gonadotropic hormones	Pituitary secretions that stimulate the sex glands.
Gonads	Testes or ovaries; sex glands.
Gonococcus	The bacterium that causes gonorrhea.
Gonorrhea	A veneral disease caused by the gonococcus.
Gravid	The state of being pregnant.
Gynecology	The medical science that deals with the treatment of disorders of the female reproductive system.
Handicap	A limit that results when someone has a disability.
Hermaphrodite	A person possessing both testes and ovaries.
Herpes Keratitis	The leading cause of infectious blindness caused by touching an active herpes sore and then rubbing the eye.
Heterosexual	One whose sexual interests are directed toward a member of the opposite sex.
Hirsutism	A condition in which an unusual growth of hair is exhibited.
Home	A place where a family lives.
Homosexual	One whose sexual interests are directed toward a member of the same sex.
"Honeymoon" cystitis	Irritation of the female bladder wall from sexual intercourse.
Human Chorionic Gonadotropin (HCG)	A hormonal substance produced by the placenta which serves as a basis for pregnancy detection.
Hustler	A male homosexual prostitute or a female prostitute.
Hyaluronidase	An enzyme found in the head of the sperm that is thought to aid in penetration of the egg.
Hydrocele	A condition in which fluid accumulates in the scrotum.
Hymen	A membrane that partially guards the entrance to the vagina.
Hysterectomy	The surgical removal of the uterus.
I-Messages	Statements about the self, revelations of inner feelings and needs, information not processed by others; a message which contains a behavior, an effect, and a feeling.

Impotence	Inability of the male to have an erection.
Incest	Sexual relations that occur between closely related individuals; incest is universally taboo.
Inguinal hernia	Hernia is an abnormal protrusion of the contents of some anatomical cavity. In inguinal hernia the protrusion is through the inguinal canal, that is, the canal through which the testes normally descend.
Insemination	Artificial or natural deposition of semen into the vagina.
Interstitial cells	Cells in the testicles that produce male sex hormones.
Intimate	Belonging to one's deepest nature; informal warmth or privacy; a very private or personal nature.
Intromission	Insertion of the penis into the vagina.
IUD (intrauterine contraceptive device)	A small plastic device inserted into the uterus to prevent pregnancy.
Katasexual	Sexual behavior with a nonhuman partner.
Lamaze Technique	A method of childbirth involving relaxation and controlled breathing as ways of preventing tension and fear during delivery.
Laparoscopy	A method of female sterilization in which a small instrument called a laparoscope is utilized to visualize and block the oviducts.
LeBoyer Technique	A technique that focuses on preventing traumatic experiences for the baby at birth, including placement of the baby in a tube of water at body temperature.
Lecherous	Being very lustful.
Lesbian	A female homosexual.
Leukorrhea	A whitish vaginal discharge containing mucus and pus.
Luteinizing hormone (LH)	Pituitary hormone that stimulates the gonads.
Libido	Sex drive.
Life Principle	A generalized accepted intention of purpose that is applied to specific choices and circumstances.
Logical Consequences Discipline	A discipline technique in which a child is allowed to experience the results of undesirable behaviors so that (s)he will want to change the behaviors.
Loving Relationship	A relationship in which you share respect, responsibility, understanding and labor.
Lymphogranuloma venereum	A venereal disease of viral nature. Lesions develop on the genitalia and are usually followed by enlargement of the lymph nodes.
Maidenhead	Another term for hymen.
Masochism	A condition in which pain or humiliation is necessary for sexual satisfaction. The word comes from the name, Leopold von Sacher-Masoch, author of the nineteenth century masochistic novel "Venus in Furs."
Mastectomy	Removal of a breast.
Mastitis	Inflammation of the breast.
Menarche	The first menstrual flow; usually occurs between 12 and 14 years of age.
Menopause	The last menstrual flow; usually occurs between 45 and 50 years of age.
Menorrhagia	Excessive bleeding at the time of menstrual flow.

Mini-laparotomy	A small 2- to 3-centimeter abdominal incision made to accomplish female sterilization.
Miscarriage	An occurrence in which the fetus is expelled for reasons beyond the control of the mother.
Miscegenation	Marriage or sexual intercourse between persons of different races.
Mons veneris	Mound covered with hair and found in the female pubic region.
Mother	A woman who has a child.
Myometrium	Muscles of the uterus.
Narcissism	Excessive love of one's self.
National Alliance for Optional Parenthood (NAOP)	A group whose purpose is to make persons aware that parenthood is optional.
Nocturnal emission	Involuntary ejaculation occurring during sleep.
Nulliparous (Nonparous)	Describes a woman who has never borne a child.
Nymphomania	A condition in which the female physiologically or psychologically has an insatiable sexual desire.
Obstetrician	A physician specializing in the care of pregnant women and in the delivery of babies.
Onanism	Ejaculation of semen outside the vagina. The term applies only to the situation in which the penis is withdrawn from the vagina during intercourse. It is not a synonym for masturbation.
Oral Contraceptive	Hormonal substances taken to prevent pregnancy; in most cases estrogen and progesterone are taken to prevent ovulation.
Oral Herpes	A viral infection producing blisters of the lips, mouth, and oral cavity.
Orchitis	Inflammation of the testes; frequently following mumps.
Orgasm	A series of muscular contractions that occur at the peak of sexual activity. In the male, these contractions are responsible for ejaculation. In the female, they promote relief of congestion in the pelvic area.
Ovary	The female reproductive gland. It releases eggs and produces estrogen and progesterone.
Panhysterectomy	Removal of uterus, ovaries, and oviducts.
Parents' Guidelines	Rules parents make to keep their children healthy and safe and to teach them responsible ways to act.
Parthenogenesis	Reproduction without male fertilization.
Parturition	The act of giving birth.
Pederasty	Sexual intercourse by means of the anal canal; also refers to male sexual relations with a young boy.
Pedophilia	An abnormal interest in a child on the part of an adult.
Peer Pressure	The influence that friends exert to affect the decisions that you will make.
Pelvic Inflammatory Disease (PID)	Infections of internal reproductive organs or other pelvic areas.
Petting	Sexual touching without having sexual intercourse.
Philosophical Intimacy	A sharing of your philosophy of life and your life principle.

Penis	Male organ for copulation and urination.
Penis captivus	A condition in which the penis becomes trapped in the vagina, as occurs in copulation among dogs. It does not occur with humans.
Pervert	One who departs from accepted standards of sexual conduct; often used to describe the homosexual.
Phallus	The penis.
Phimosis	In this condition the foreskin is too narrow to allow it to be retracted over the head of the penis.
Physical Intimacy	A sharing of physical expressions and affection.
Physical Punishment	A form of discipline in which an act such as spanking is used to teach a child not to repeat undesirable behavior.
Pimp	A person who solicits for a prostitute.
Polyandry	Having more than one husband.
Polygamy	Having more than one wife.
Pornography	Literature or art serving only for the purpose of sexual arousal in the beholder.
Potent	Able to perform sexual intercourse; able to have an erection.
Preventive Discipline	Discipline that involves discussing behaviors with children, helping them to repeat desirable behaviors and change undesirable behaviors.
Primigravida	One who is pregnant for the first time.
Progesterone	A hormonal substance produced by the corpus luteum; it prepares the uterus for implantation and maintains pregnancy.
Prostate gland	Anatomical structure that surrounds the neck of the urinary bladder and the beginning of the male urethra.
Prostatectomy	Surgical removal of part or all of the prostate gland.
Psychological Intimacy	A sharing of your needs, drives, weaknesses, strengths, intentions, emotions, and deepest problems.
Psychosexual	Refers to the psychological or emotional aspects of sexuality.
Responsible Decision	A decision which is healthful, safe, legal, respects you and others, and follows parental guidelines. (Meeks, Linda and Phil Heit, *Health: Focus On You K–8*, Columbus: Charles E. Merrill, 1984).
Rhythm method	A method of contraception in which the partners attempt to schedule sexual intercourse in such a way that no sperms are present during the short life span of the egg.
Ridgling	A term describing a male with one testicle.
Risk	A chance that you take.
Rule	Something that tells you how to act.
Sadism	A condition in which a person is sexually stimulated by inflicting pain upon another.
Salpingectomy	A surgical procedure in which the oviducts are removed.
Sapphism	Female homosexuality or lesbianism; the term comes from the name of the Greek poetess, Sappho.

Satyriasis	An insatiable sex desire in men.
Scrotum	Sac-like container that encloses the testicles. A major function of the scrotum is temperature regulation.
Self-discipline	The effort that you make to behave in certain ways.
Semen	Fluid ejaculated at male orgasm.
Seminal vesicles	Glands that connect with the ejaculatory duct and secrete, among other substances, fructose.
Seminiferous tubules	Tubules in the testes that produce sperm.
Sexology	The science of sex.
Sexuality	A term that includes all aspects of maleness and femaleness: sociological, philosophical, psychological as well as biological aspects.
Sexually Transmitted Diseases (STDs)	Any of a wide range of diseases that may be transmitted by sexual contact.
SIECUS	Sex Information and Education Council of the United States. Publishes study guides on sex education. (Address: 1855 Broadway, New York, NY 10023.)
"Sixty-nine"	A slang term describing mutual oral–genital relations.
Smegma	A wax-like secretion that accumulates under the foreskin.
Sodomy	Illegal sexual behavior; most often anal intercourse.
"Soixante-neuf"	French for 69; used to described two sexual partners, both of whom are providing oral–genital stimulation.
Spanish fly	See Cantharides.
Spermatogenesis	The physiological process whereby sperms are produced.
Spermicide	Chemical substance that kills sperms.
Statutory rape	Sexual intercourse with a girl under the age of statutory consent.
Stepbrother	The son of a person's stepmother or stepfather.
Stepfather	A man who marries a person's mother.
Stepmother	A woman who marries a person's father.
Stepsister	The daughter of a person's stepmother or stepfather.
Sterility	The inability to have children.
"Straight"	Another term for heterosexual.
Stranger	Someone you do not know well.
Syphilis	A bacteria-caused venereal disease; the disease may cripple or kill.
Tampon	Absorbent type material that is inserted into the vagina to absorb the menstrual flow.
Teat	The nipple of the breast.
Testes	Male gonads; testicles.
Testicular Self-Examination (TSE)	Male self-examination of the testes for signs of cancer.
Testosterone	Male sex hormone produced by the testes.
T Lymphocytes	A group of white cells that protect the body against foreign agents but which may be rendered ineffective by AIDS.

Total Intimacy	A sharing of philosophical, psychological, creative, and physical intimacy.
Toxic Shock Syndrome	A serious disease associated with use of tampons and thought to be caused by a bacteria called staphylococcus aureus.
Transsexual	A person who thinks that he was "meant" to be a member of the sex other than the one indicated by his sexual organs.
Transvestite	A person with a compulsive desire to wear the clothes of the opposite sex.
Treponema pallidum	The bacterium that causes syphilis.
Tubal pregnancy	Implantation of a fertilized egg in the oviduct.
Tumescence	Increased size of the penis or other anatomical structures secondary to the accumulation of blood.
Umbilical cord	An anatomical connection between the unborn baby and the placenta.
Urethra	A canal extending from the bladder to the external urethral orifice. In the male it extends approximately 9 inches; the female length is about 1½ inches. In the male the canal serves as a passageway for urine and ejaculate.
Urethritis	An inflammation of the urethra.
Uterus	The womb; the organ that receives the fertilized ovum, supports it during pregnancy, and contracts to aid in expulsion at the time of childbirth.
Vagina	The female's birth canal and organ for sexual intercourse.
Vaginismus	A condition in which the muscles of the vagina involuntarily contract and prevent entry of the penis.
Vaginitis	An inflammation of the vagina.
Vasectomy	Male sterilization in which the sperm duct is cut and tied off.
Vas (ductus) deferens	Anatomical structure connecting the epididymis with the ejaculatory duct.
Venereal Warts	Genital warts caused by an infectious virus.
Virginity	A term to describe the state of never having participated in sexual intercourse.
Virilism	Masculinization of the female.
Voyeur	A "Peeping Tom," a person who obtains pleasure from observing the reproductive anatomy or behavior of others.
Vulva	External female anatomy; includes the labia majora, labia minora, and clitoris.
Whore	A prostitute or a disparaging term for a promiscuous woman.
Widow's and Widower's Syndromes	A sexual disfunction following a long period of sexual abstinence associated with the death of a spouse.
Womb	Another term for uterus.
X chromosome	Female sex chromosome.
Y chromosome	Male sex chromosome.
Yohimbine	Substance obtained from the yohimbe tree; some think yohimbine has aphrodisiac properties.
You-Message	A shaming and blaming message that blocks psychological intimacy.
Zooerastia	Bestiality; sexual intercourse with nonhuman partners.

Atlas of Teaching Illustrations

[This Atlas is made up of the more important illustrations used in the body of the text. It is our thought that teachers may wish to remove these for overhead projection or for other kinds of reproduction to facilitate discussion of the material with their students.]

Figure 1

Descent of Testes

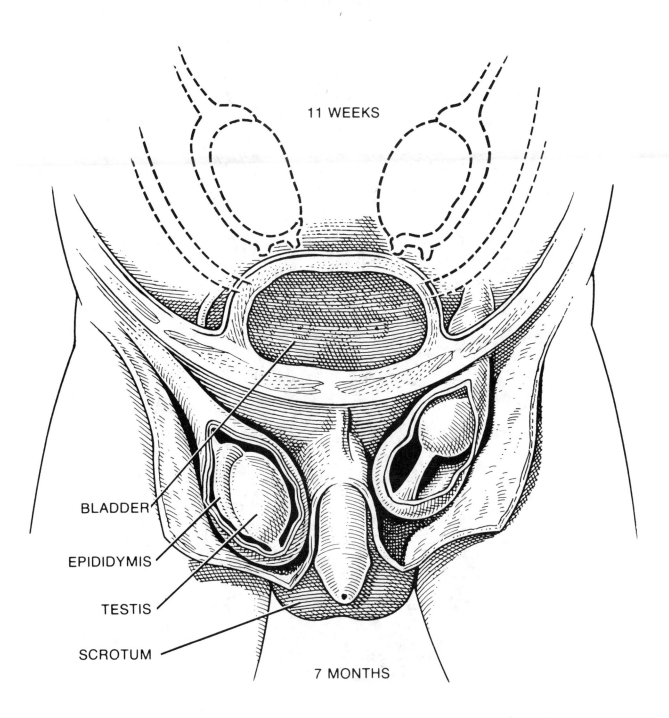

11 WEEKS

BLADDER

EPIDIDYMIS

TESTIS

SCROTUM

7 MONTHS

Figure 2

Hernia

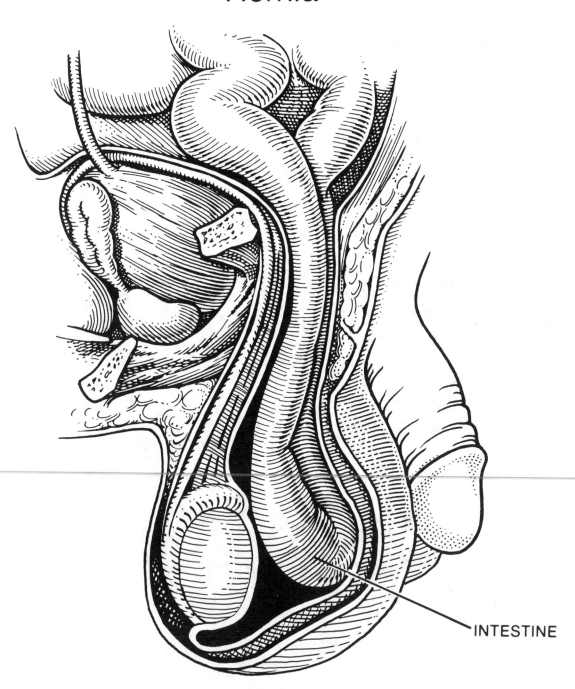

INTESTINE

Figure 3

Cremasteric Muscles

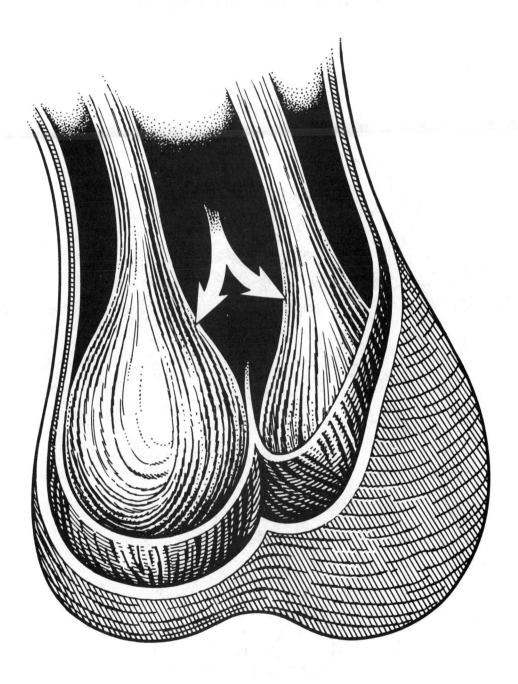

Figure 4

Seminiferous Tubules
and Interstitial Cells

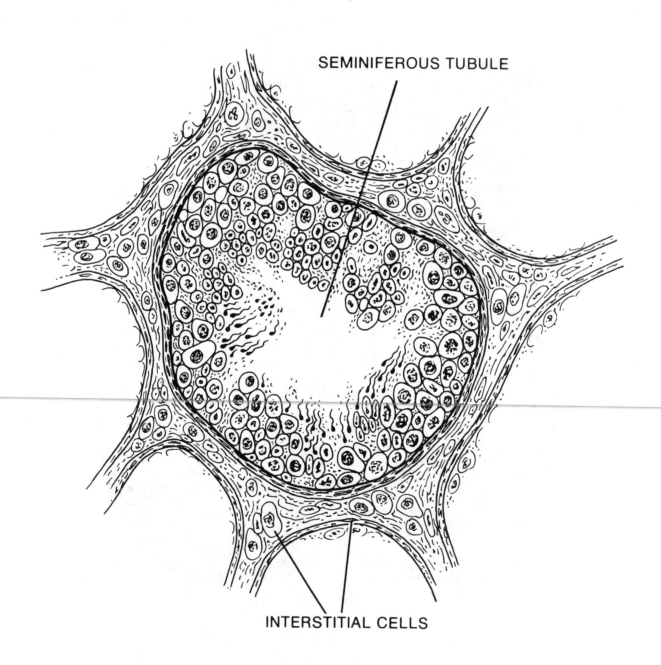

SEMINIFEROUS TUBULE

INTERSTITIAL CELLS

Figure 5

Male Secondary Sex Characteristics

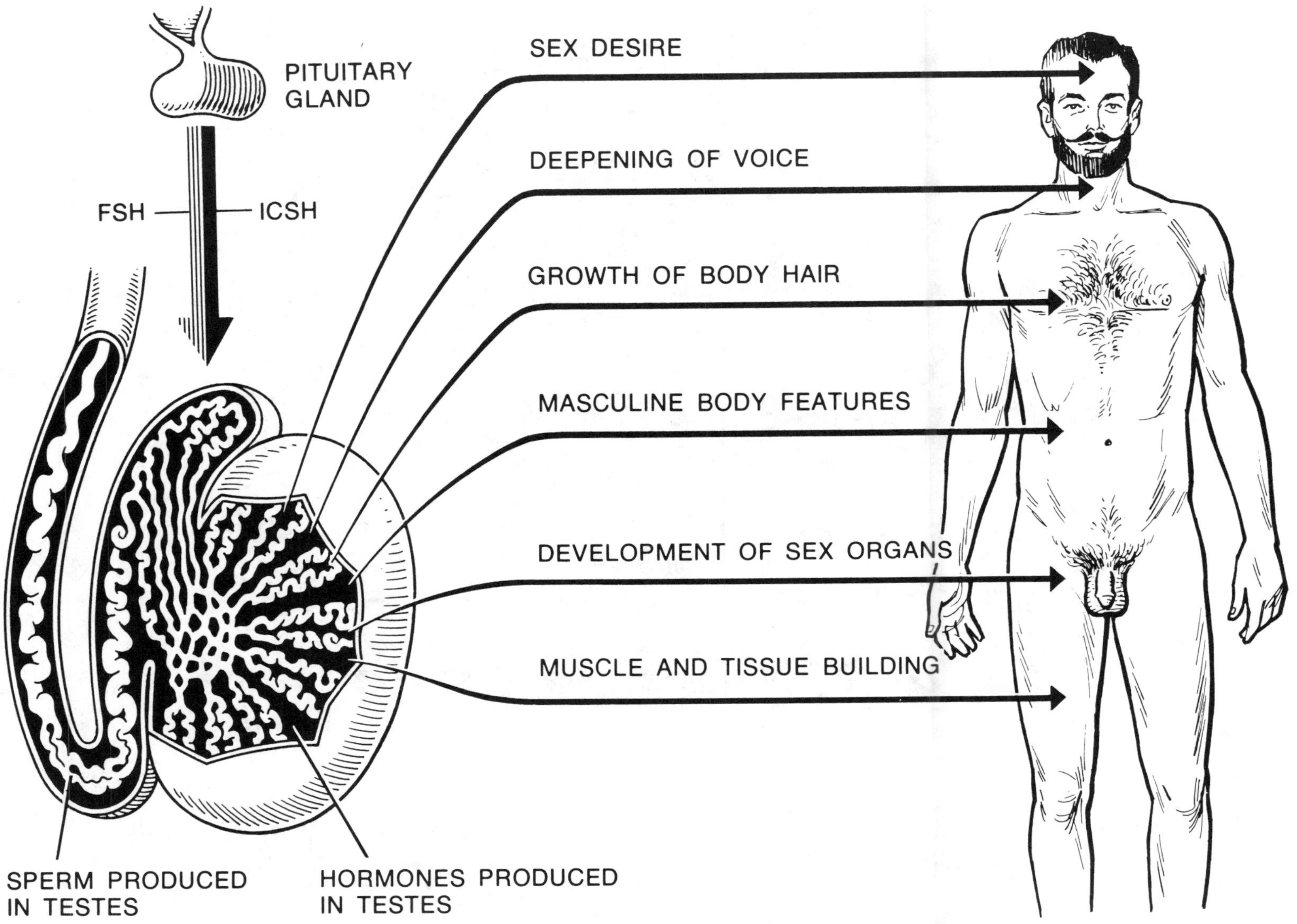

SEX DESIRE

DEEPENING OF VOICE

GROWTH OF BODY HAIR

MASCULINE BODY FEATURES

DEVELOPMENT OF SEX ORGANS

MUSCLE AND TISSUE BUILDING

PITUITARY GLAND

ICSH

FSH

HORMONES PRODUCED IN TESTES

SPERM PRODUCED IN TESTES

Figure 6

The Testis, Epididymis, and Vas Deferens

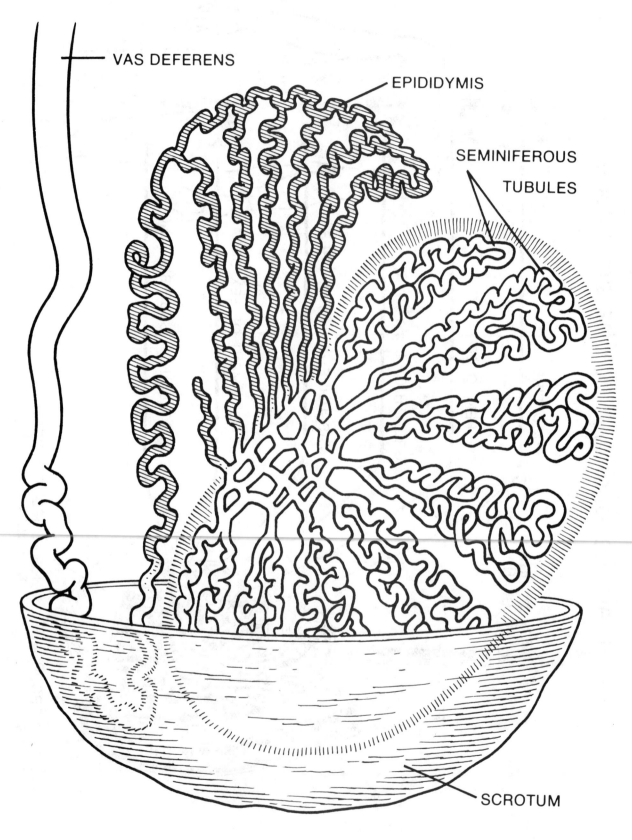

VAS DEFERENS

EPIDIDYMIS

SEMINIFEROUS

TUBULES

SCROTUM

Figure 7

Sperm Development

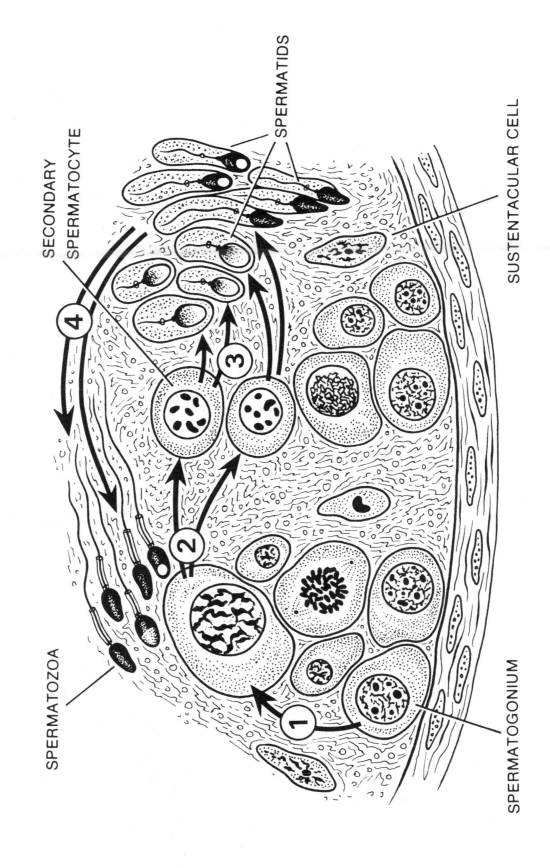

SPERMATOZOA

SECONDARY
SPERMATOCYTE

SPERMATIDS

SUSTENTACULAR CELL

SPERMATOGONIUM

Figure 8

Seminal Vesicle

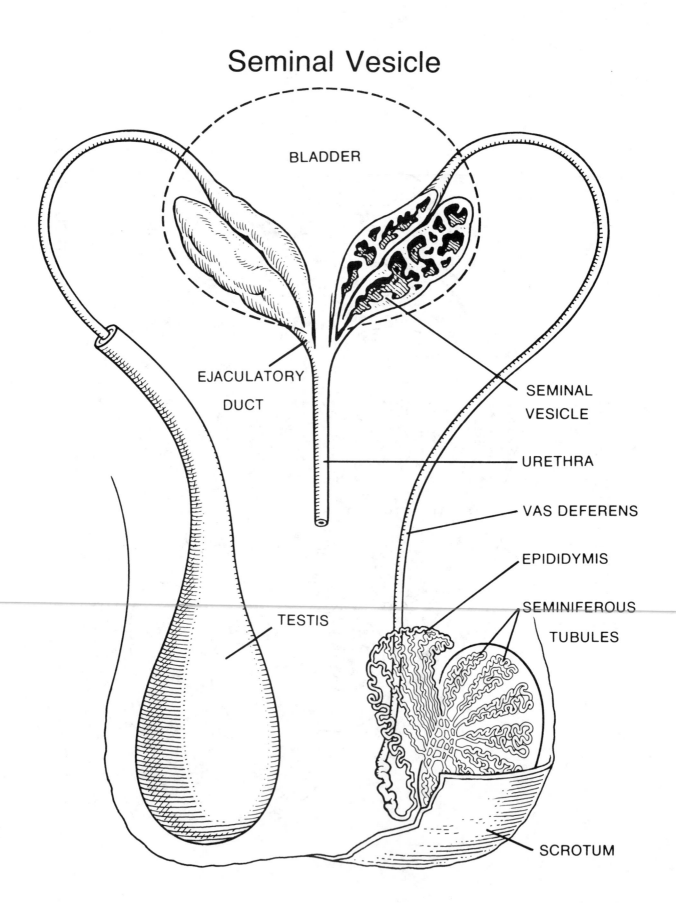

BLADDER

EJACULATORY

DUCT

SEMINAL

VESICLE

URETHRA

VAS DEFERENS

EPIDIDYMIS

SEMINIFEROUS

TUBULES

TESTIS

SCROTUM

Figure 9

Prostate and Bulbourethral Glands

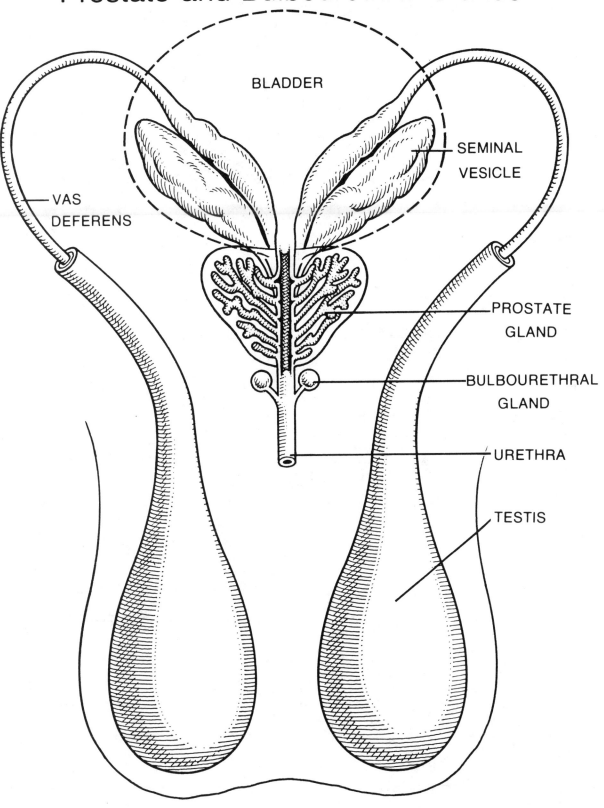

BLADDER

SEMINAL VESICLE

VAS DEFERENS

PROSTATE GLAND

BULBOURETHRAL GLAND

URETHRA

TESTIS

Figure 10

Prostatic Hypertrophy

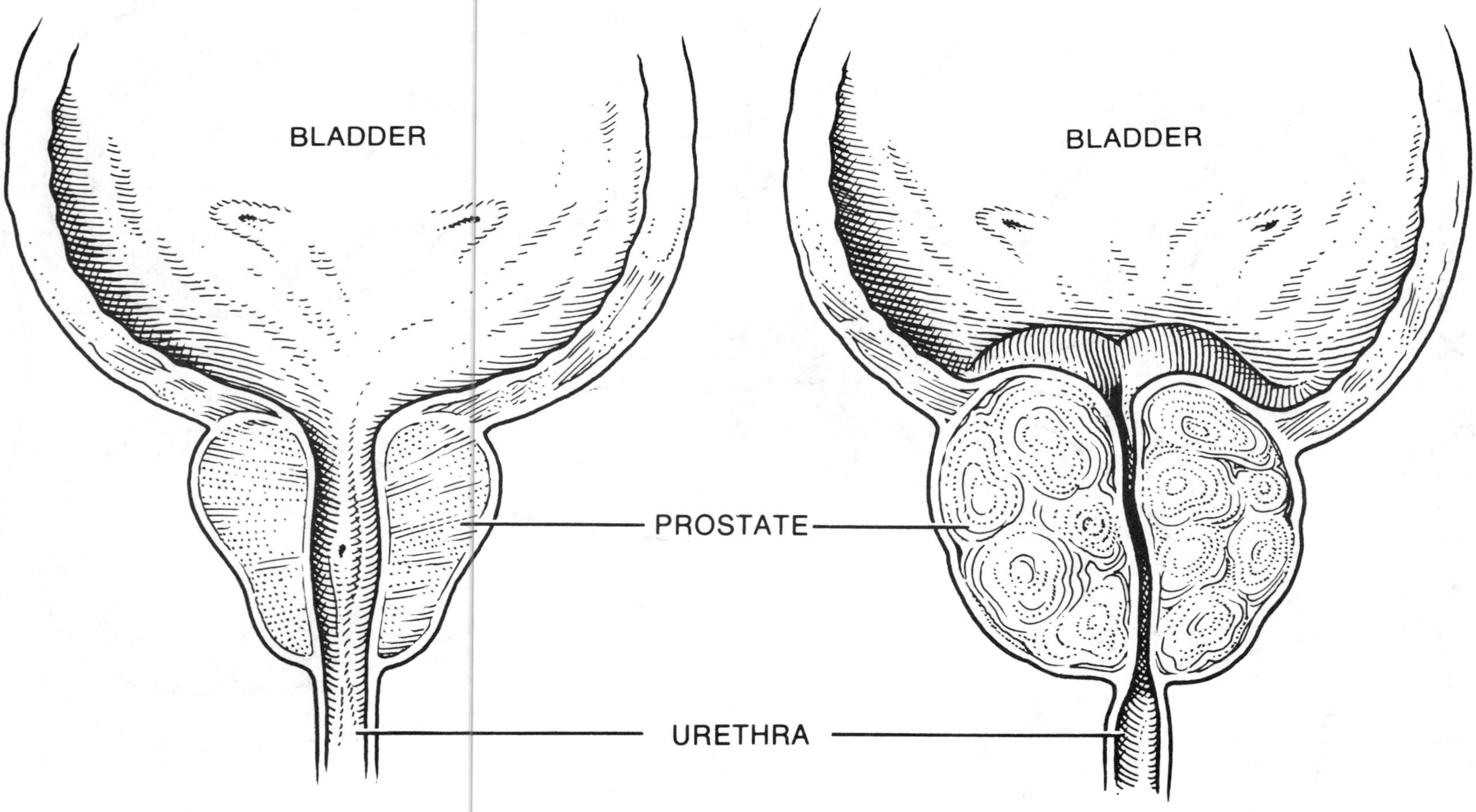

BLADDER

BLADDER

ENLARGED PROSTATE

NORMAL PROSTATE

PROSTATE

URETHRA

Figure 11

Rectal Examination of the Prostate

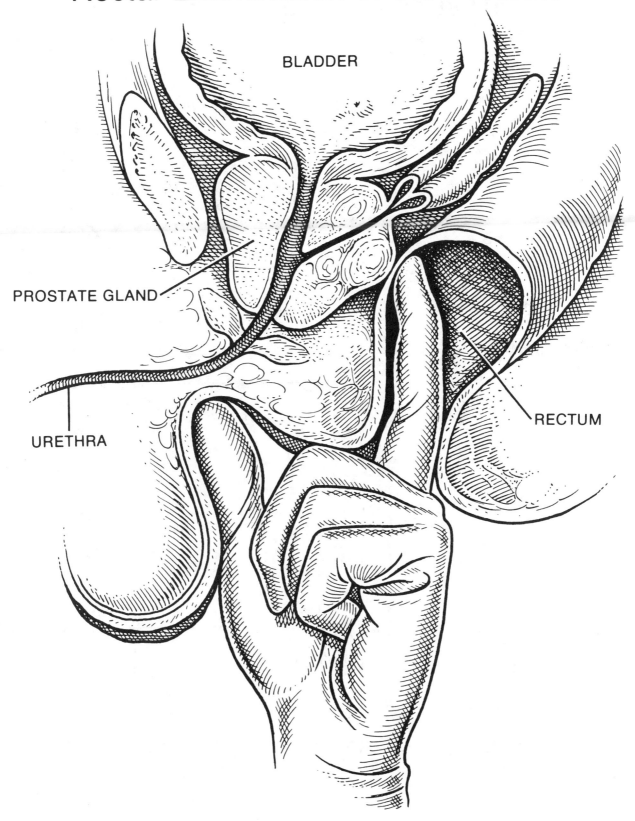

Figure 12

Bulbourethral Glands and Penis

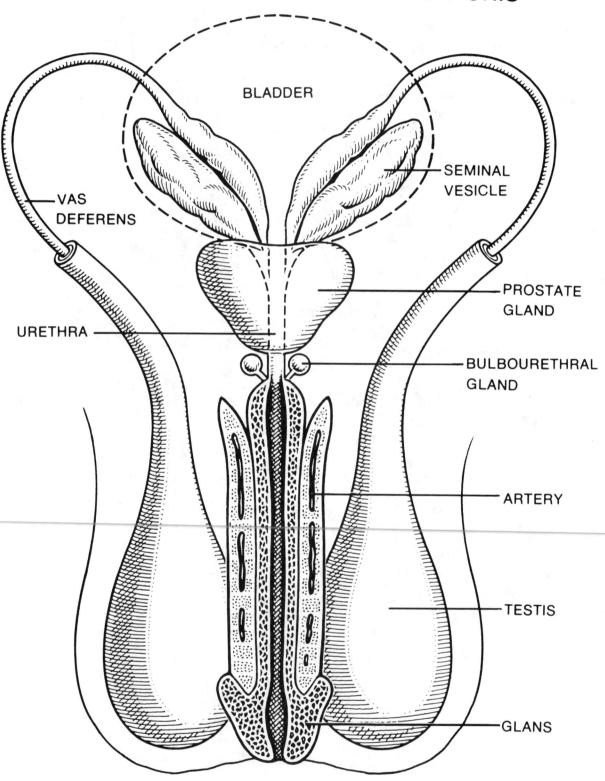

BLADDER

SEMINAL VESICLE

VAS DEFERENS

PROSTATE GLAND

URETHRA

BULBOURETHRAL GLAND

ARTERY

TESTIS

GLANS

Figure 13

Smegma Secretion

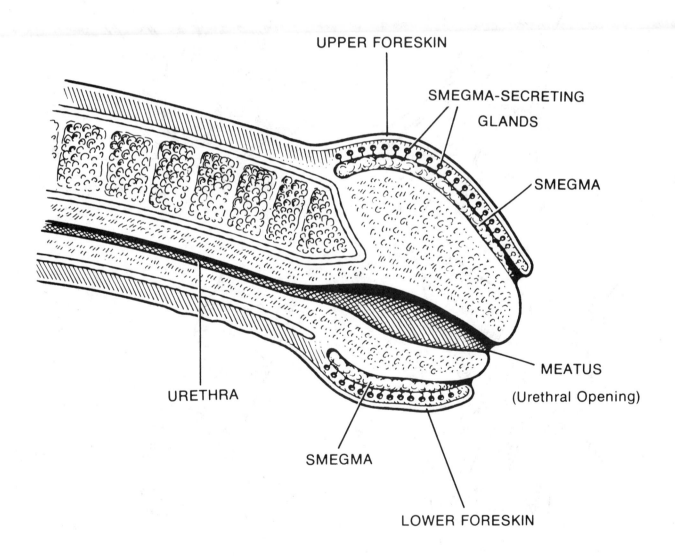

UPPER FORESKIN

SMEGMA-SECRETING

GLANDS

SMEGMA

MEATUS

(Urethral Opening)

URETHRA

SMEGMA

LOWER FORESKIN

Figure 14

Circumcision

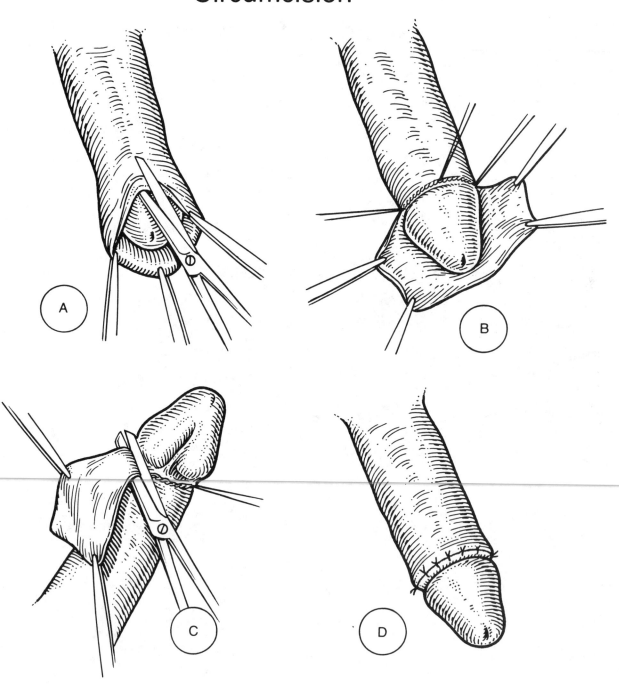

Figure 15

Male Reproductive System (Side View)

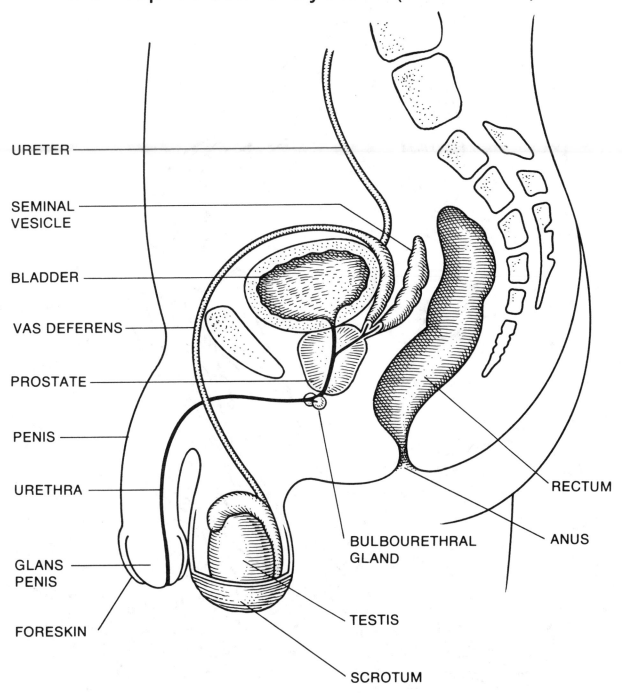

URETER

SEMINAL
VESICLE

BLADDER

VAS DEFERENS

PROSTATE

PENIS

URETHRA

GLANS
PENIS

FORESKIN

BULBOURETHRAL
GLAND

TESTIS

SCROTUM

RECTUM

ANUS

Figure 16

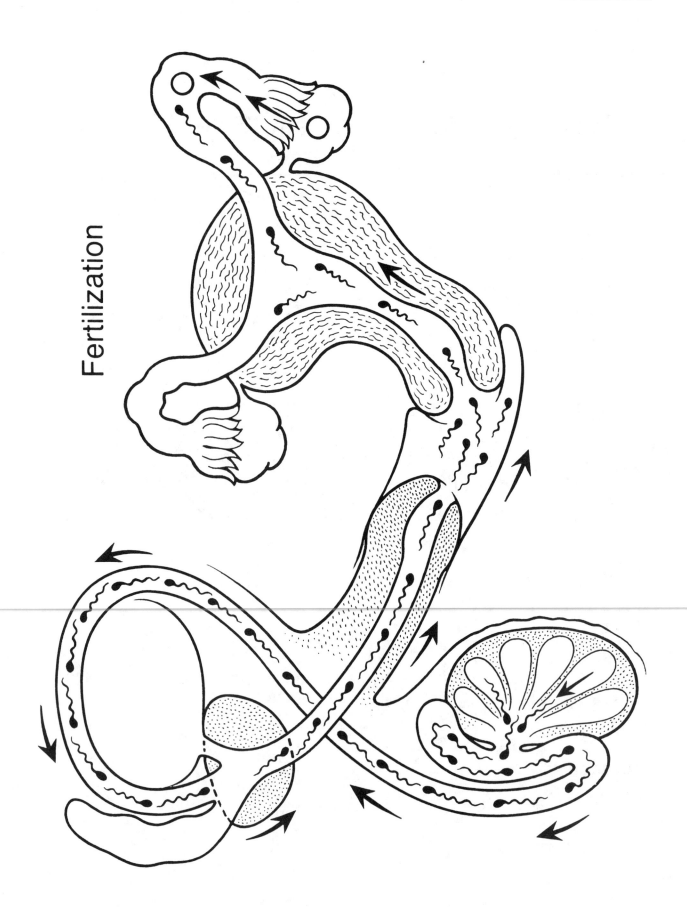

Fertilization

Figure 17

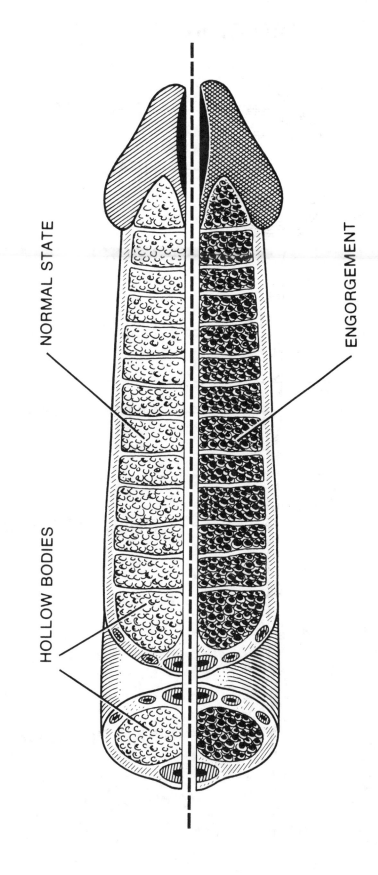

Erectile Tissue

NORMAL STATE

ENGORGEMENT

HOLLOW BODIES

Figure 18

Structure of a Sperm

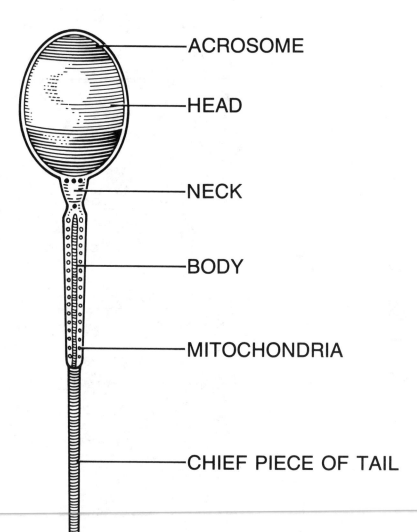

ACROSOME

HEAD

NECK

BODY

MITOCHONDRIA

CHIEF PIECE OF TAIL

END PIECE OF TAIL

Figure 19

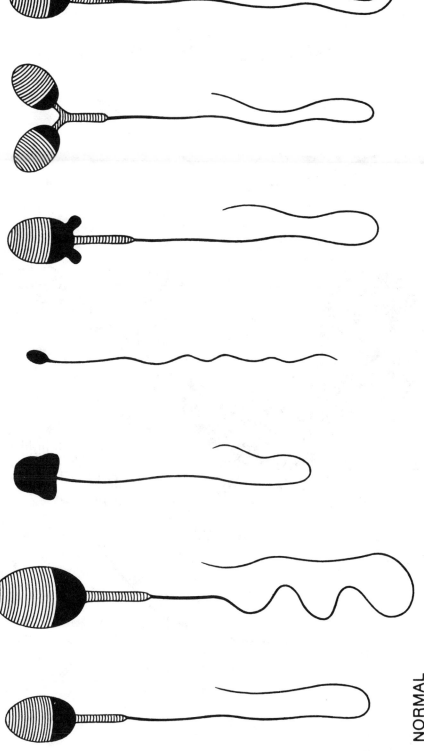

Abnormal Sperm

NORMAL
SPERM

Figure 20

Artificial Insemination

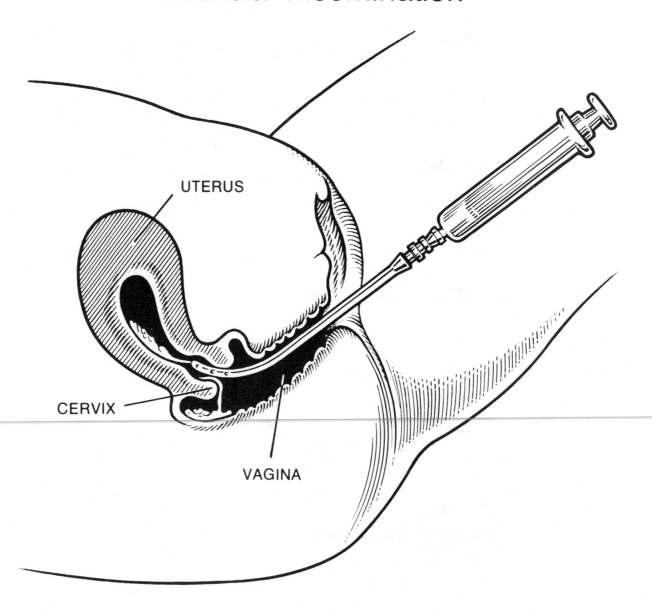

UTERUS

CERVIX

VAGINA

Figure 21

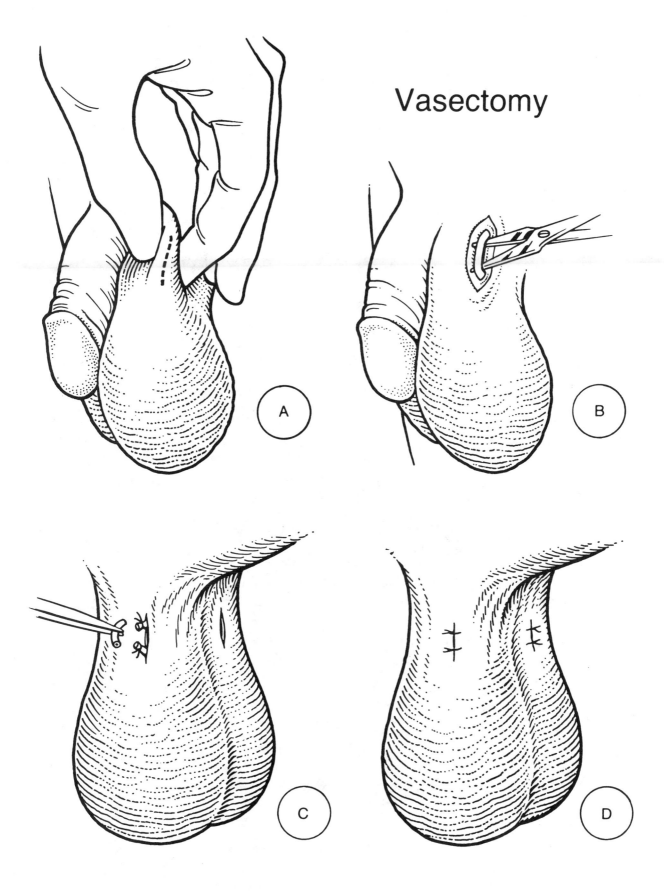

Vasectomy

Figure 22

Female Reproductive System
Side View

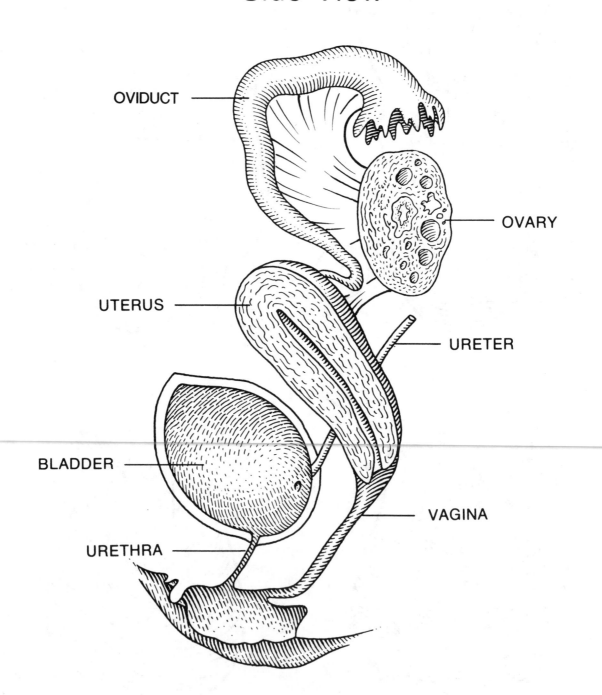

OVIDUCT

OVARY

UTERUS

URETER

BLADDER

VAGINA

URETHRA

Figure 23

Growth of the
Female Reproductive System

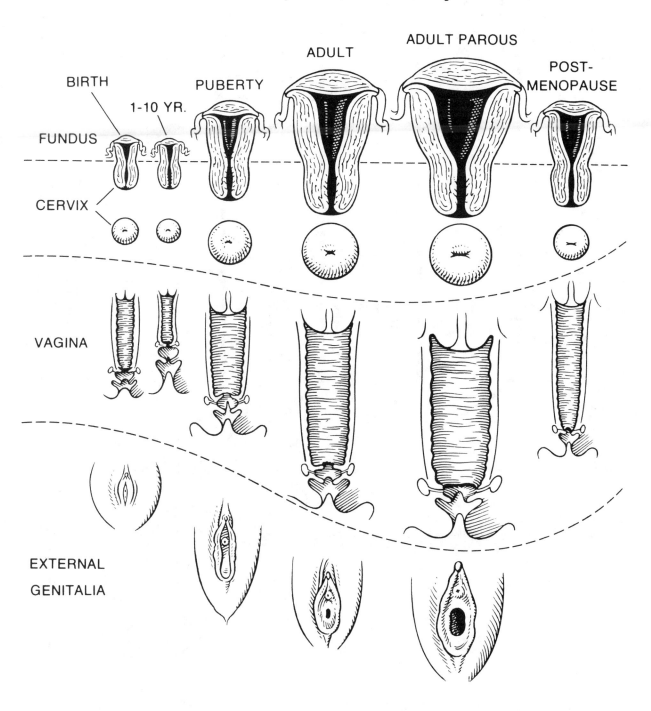

Figure 24

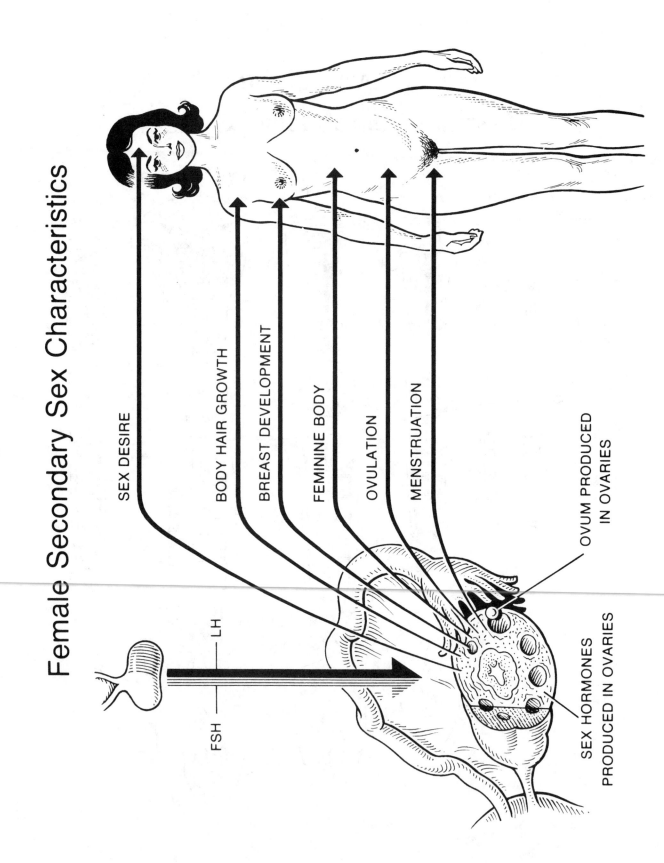

Female Secondary Sex Characteristics

SEX DESIRE

BODY HAIR GROWTH

BREAST DEVELOPMENT

FEMININE BODY

OVULATION

MENSTRUATION

OVUM PRODUCED IN OVARIES

SEX HORMONES PRODUCED IN OVARIES

LH

FSH

Figure 25

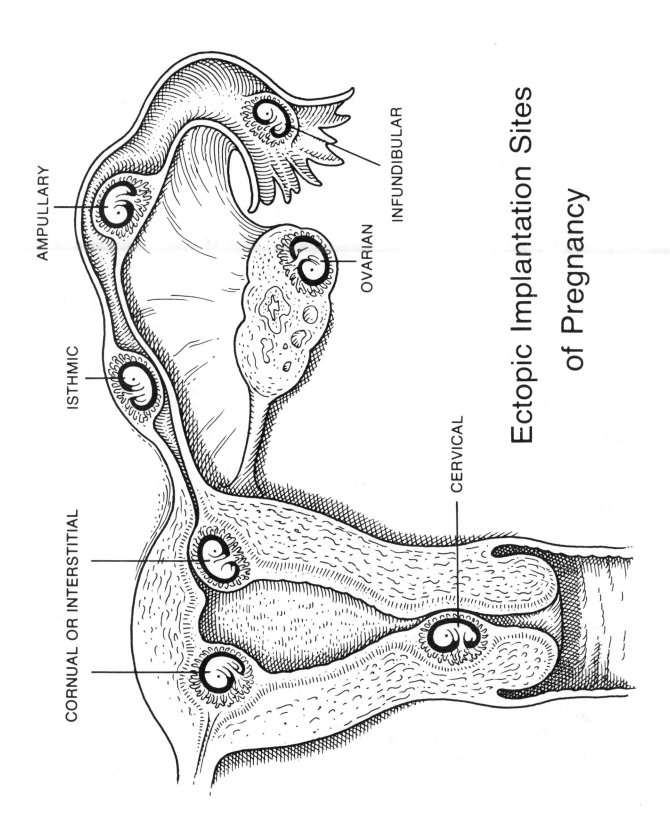

AMPULLARY

ISTHMIC

CORNUAL OR INTERSTITIAL

INFUNDIBULAR

OVARIAN

CERVICAL

Ectopic Implantation Sites
of Pregnancy

Figure 26

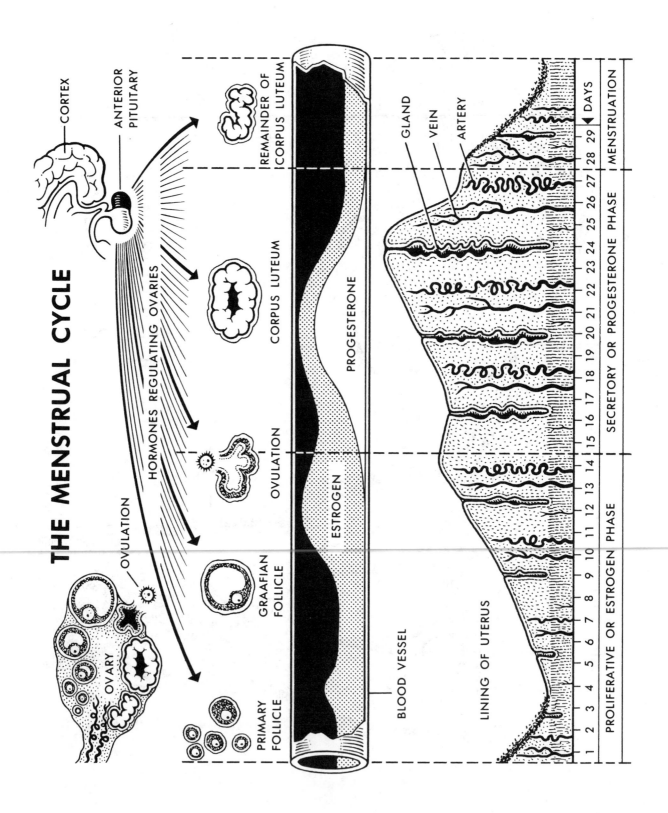

THE MENSTRUAL CYCLE

Figure 27

Lining of the Uterus in Three Stages

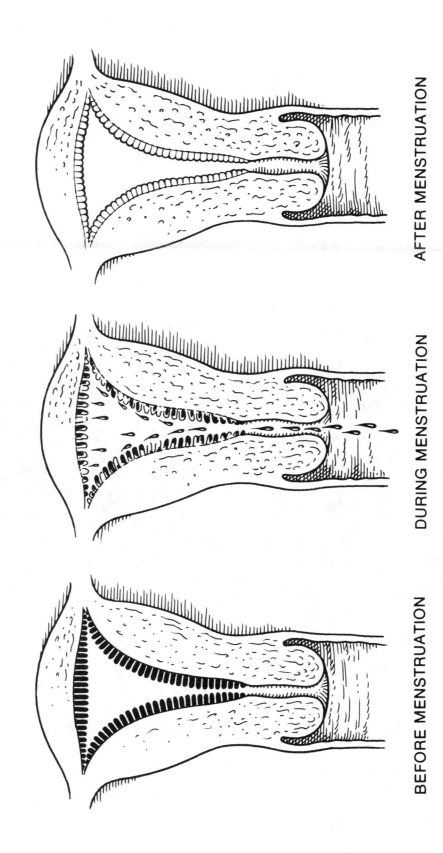

BEFORE MENSTRUATION

DURING MENSTRUATION

AFTER MENSTRUATION

Figure 28

Vaginal Muscles

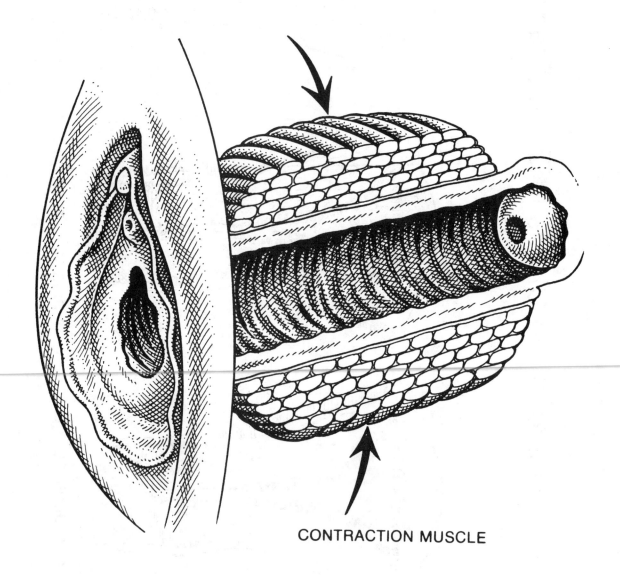

CONTRACTION MUSCLE

Figure 29

The Hymen

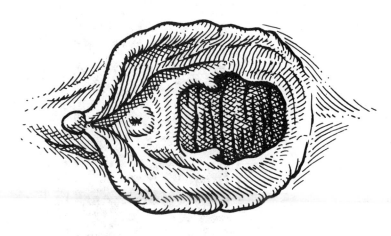

PAROUS
INTROITUS

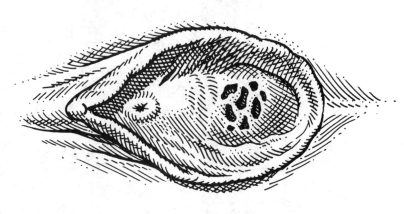

CRIBRIFORM
HYMEN

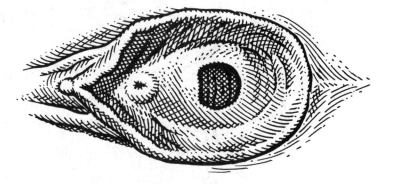

ANNULAR
HYMEN

Figure 30

Virginal Pregnancy

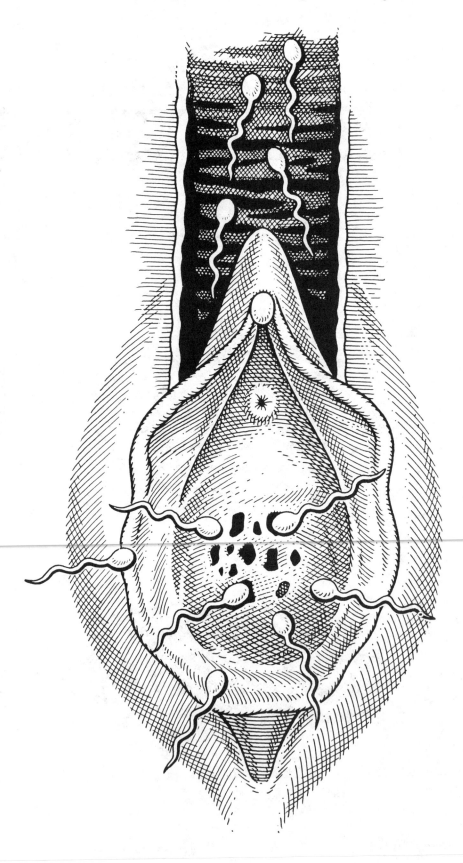

Figure 31

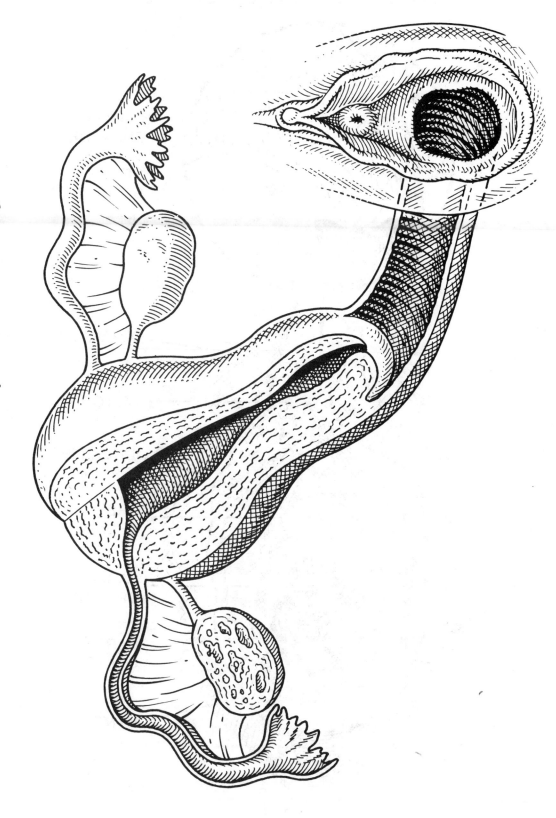

The Female Reproductive System

Figure 32

Female External Genitalia

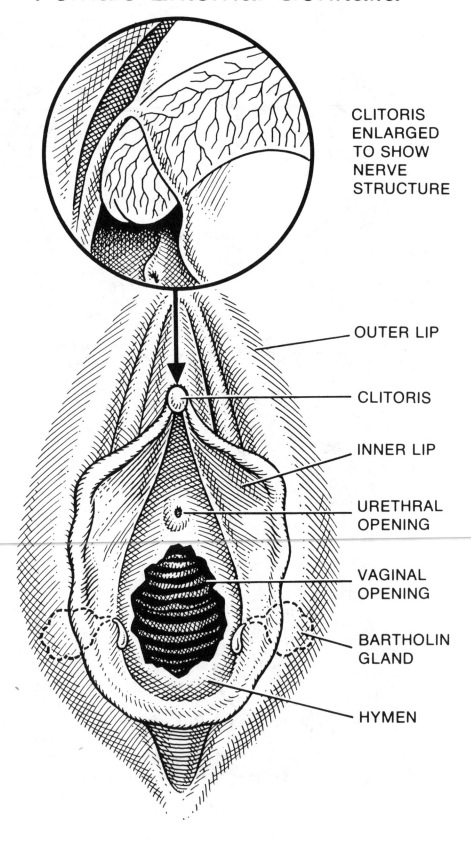

CLITORIS
ENLARGED
TO SHOW
NERVE
STRUCTURE

OUTER LIP

CLITORIS

INNER LIP

URETHRAL
OPENING

VAGINAL
OPENING

BARTHOLIN
GLAND

HYMEN

Figure 33

Orgasmic Platform, Seminal Pool

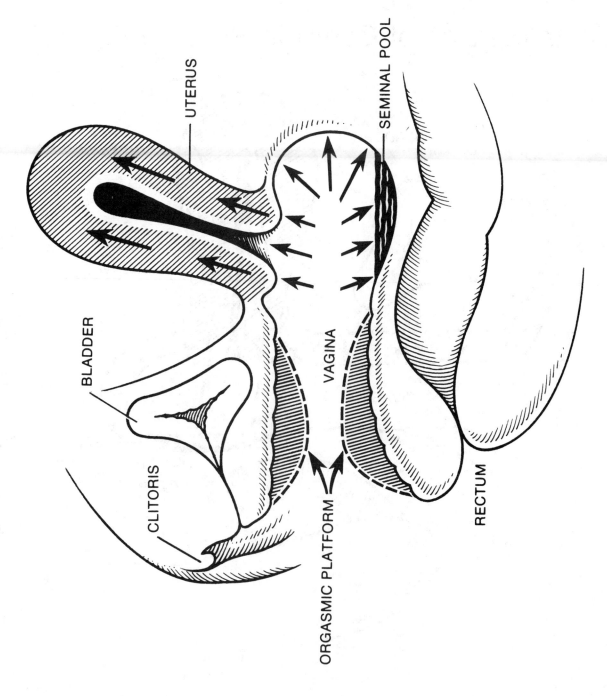

Figure 34

Immersion of Cervix in Seminal Pool

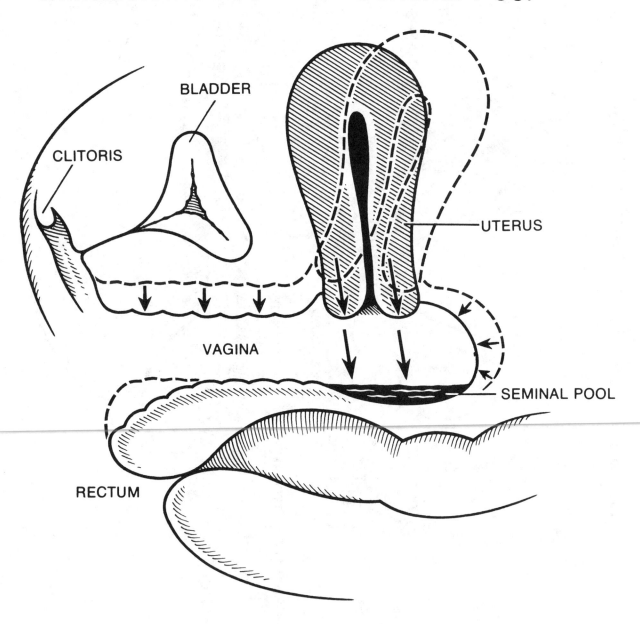

BLADDER

CLITORIS

UTERUS

VAGINA

SEMINAL POOL

RECTUM

Figure 35

Nerve Endings Sensitive to Sexual Stimulation

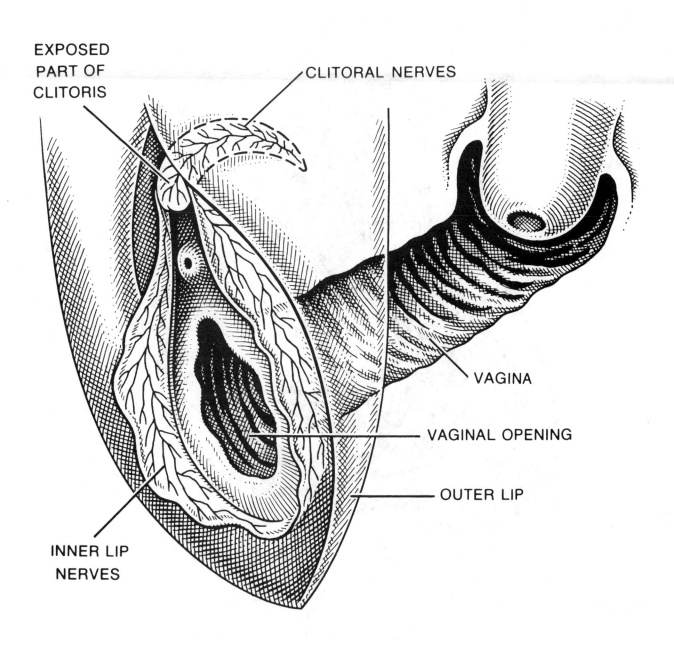

EXPOSED
PART OF
CLITORIS

CLITORAL NERVES

VAGINA

VAGINAL OPENING

OUTER LIP

INNER LIP
NERVES

Figure 36

Amniotic Sac

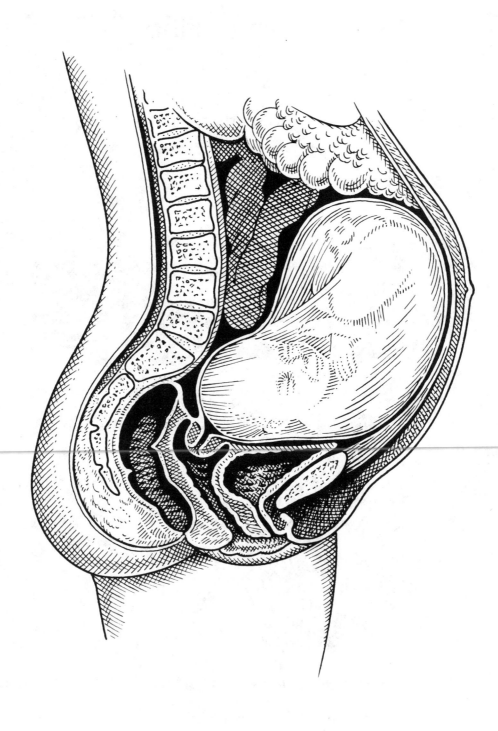

Figure 37

Childbirth Sequence I

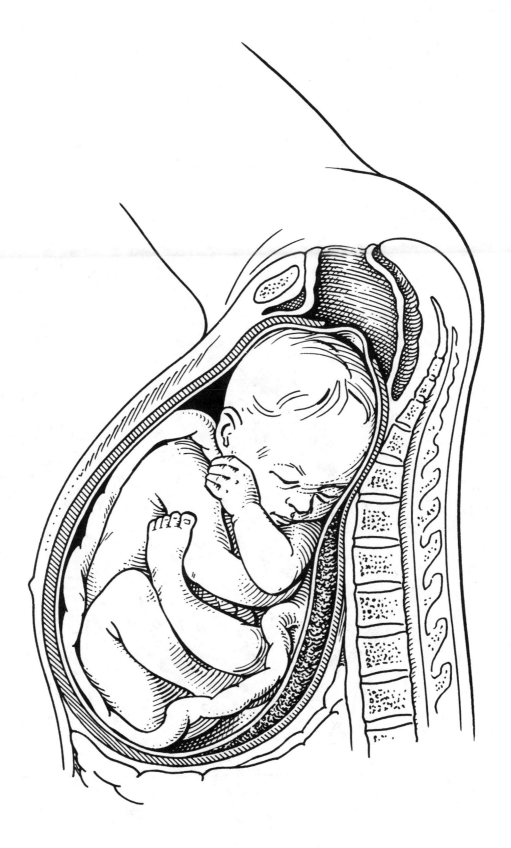

Figure 38

Childbirth Sequence II

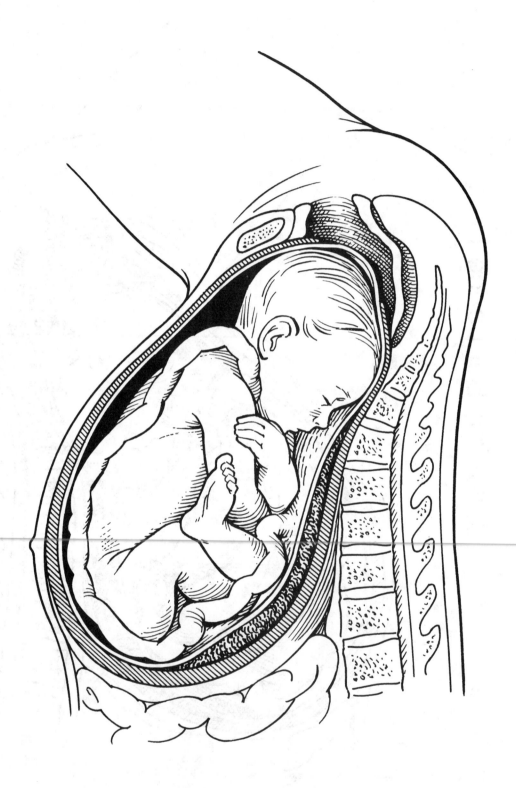

Figure 39

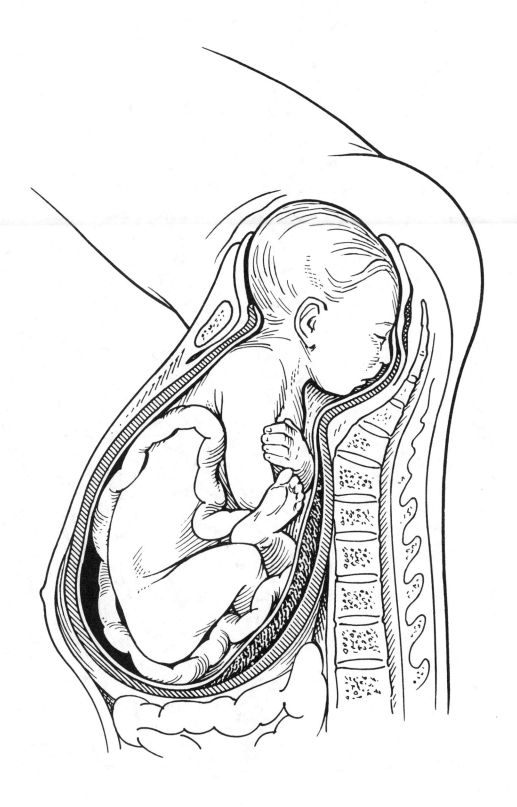

Childbirth Sequence III

Figure 40

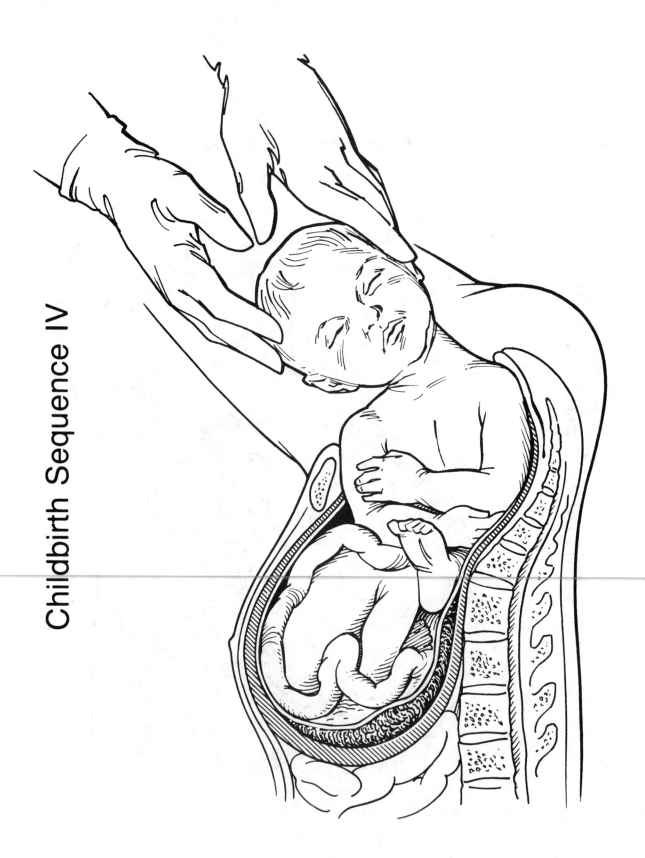

Childbirth Sequence IV

Figure 41

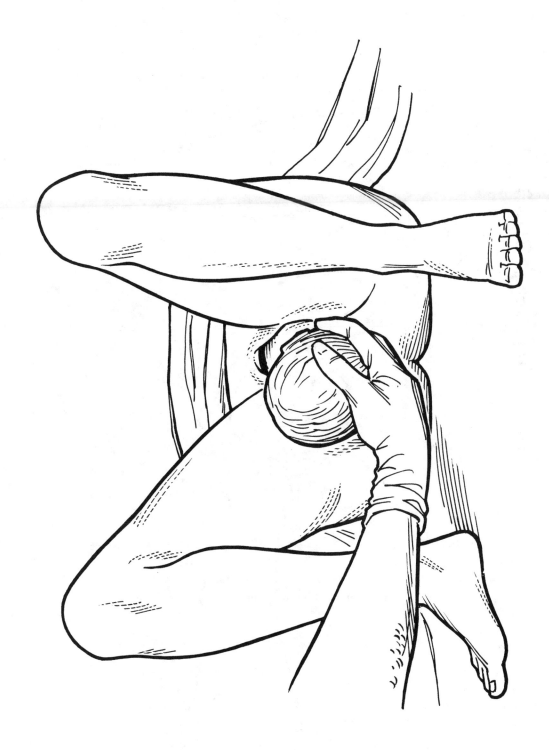

Childbirth Sequence V

Figure 42

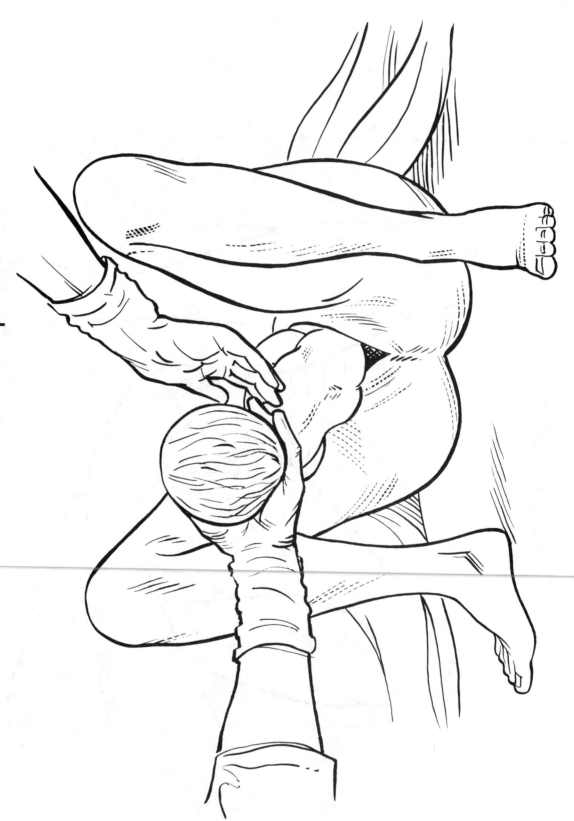

Childbirth Sequence VI

Figure 43

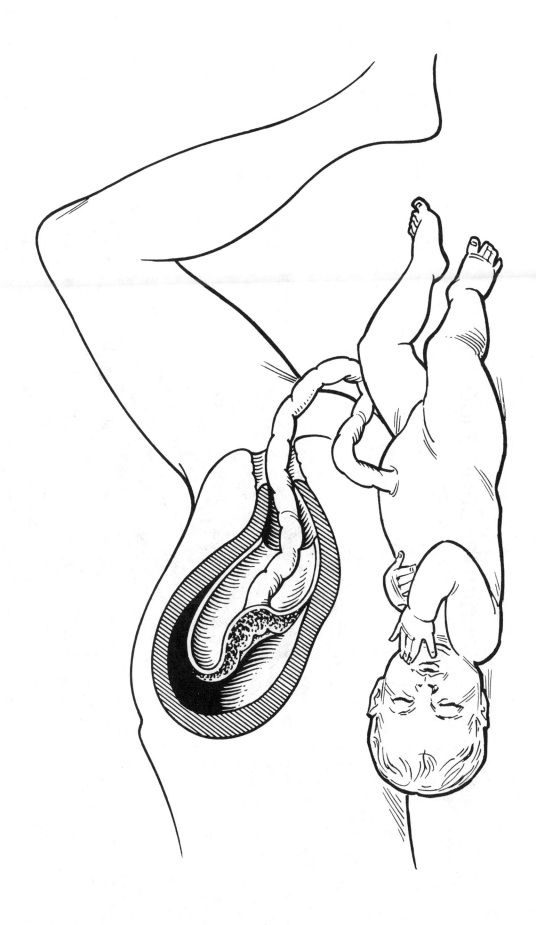

Childbirth Sequence VII

Figure 44

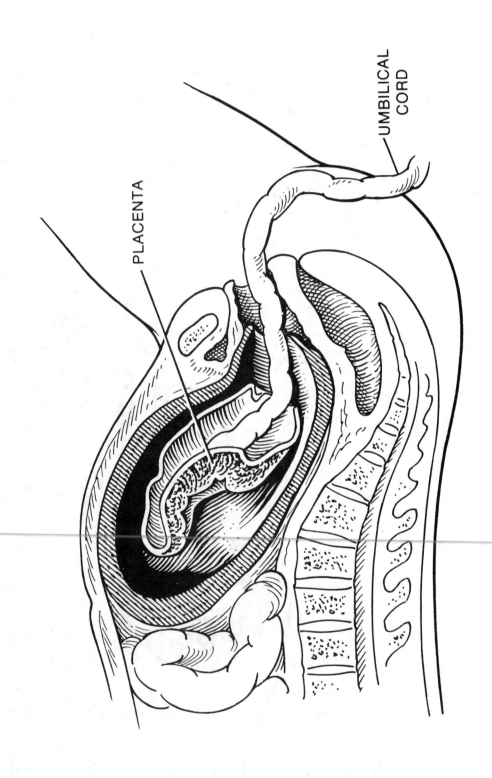

Childbirth Sequence VIII

UMBILICAL CORD

PLACENTA

Figure 45

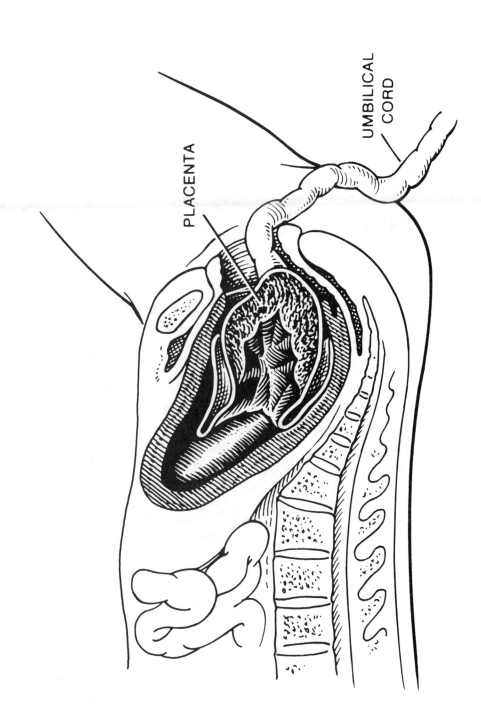

Childbirth Sequence IX

PLACENTA

UMBILICAL CORD

Figure 46

Vaginal Ring for Progestin Administration

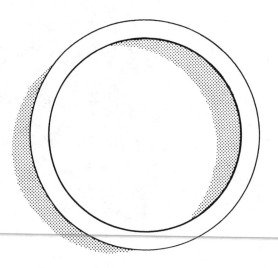

Figure 47

Progestin Implant

Figure 48

Female Sterilization

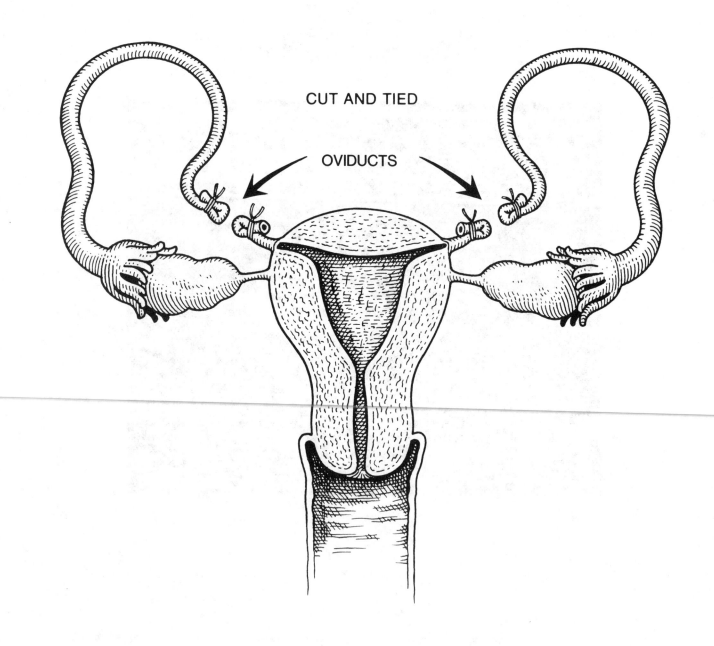

CUT AND TIED

OVIDUCTS

Figure 49

Mechanical Contraception

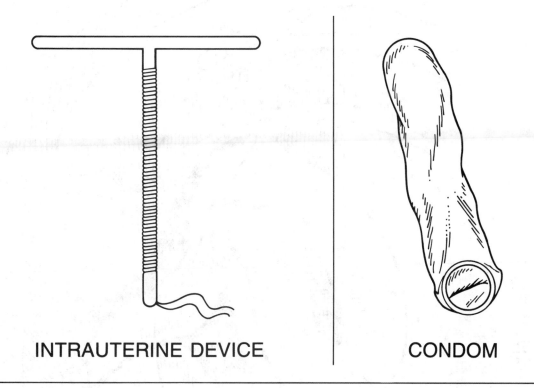

INTRAUTERINE DEVICE

CONDOM

CERVICAL CAP

DIAPHRAGM AND INSERTION
DEVICE

Figure 50

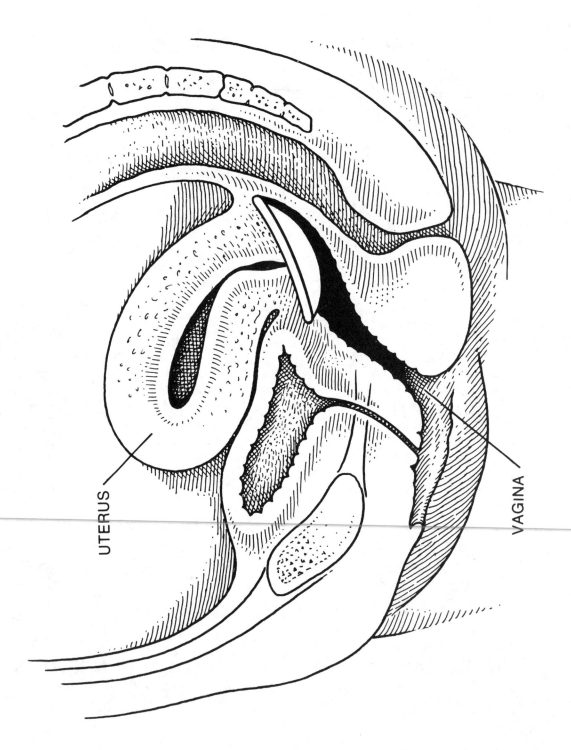

Diaphragm

UTERUS

VAGINA

Figure 51

Intrauterine Devices (IUD's)

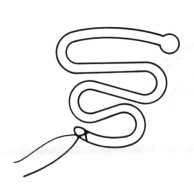

LIPPES LOOP
1964

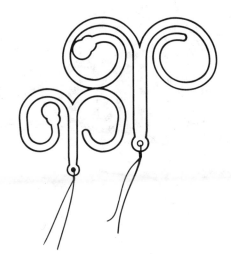

SAF-T-COIL
1967

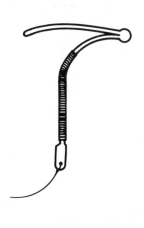

COPPER 7
1973

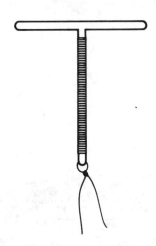

COPPER T
1976

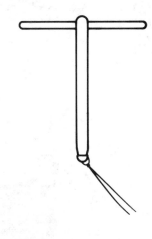

PROGESTASERT
1976

Figure 52

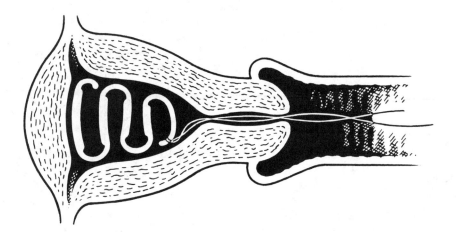

Insertion of IUD

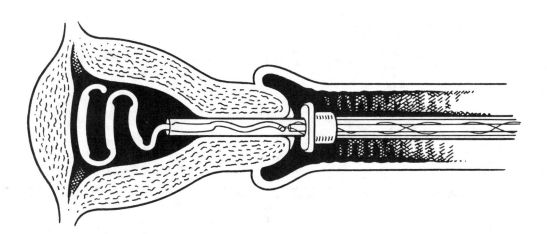

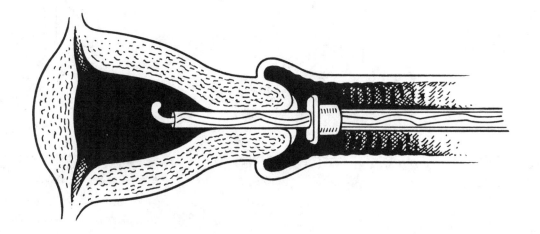

Figure 53

Rhythm Method by Basal Body Temperature

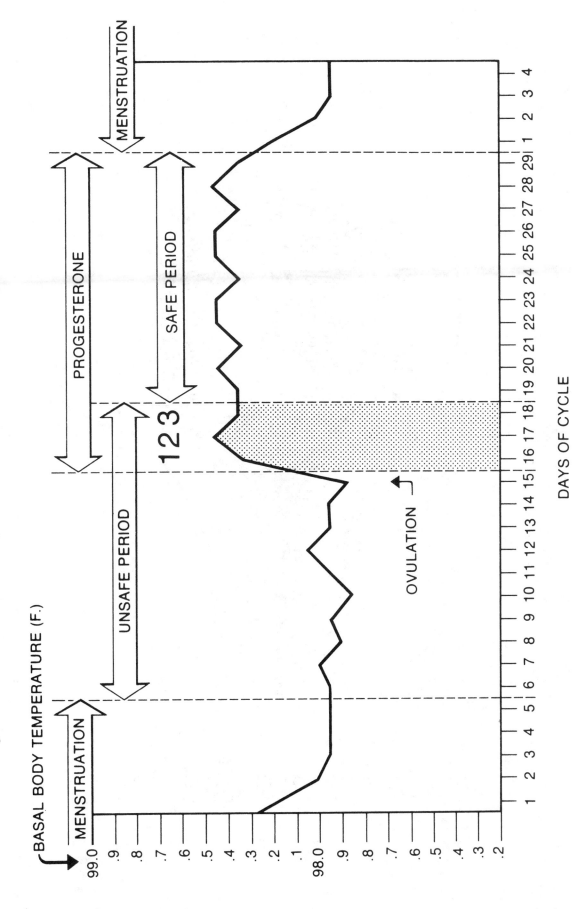

Figure 54

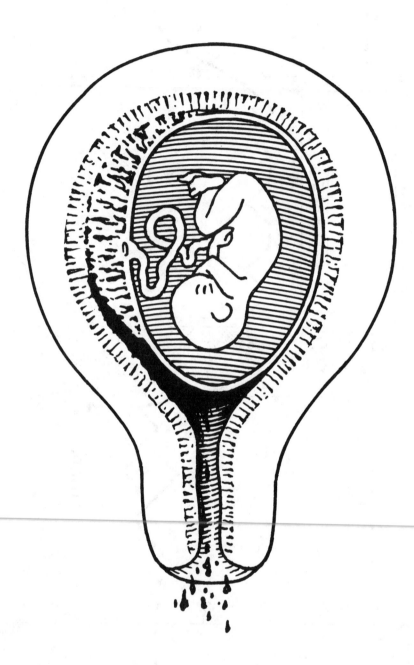

Threatened Abortion

Figure 55

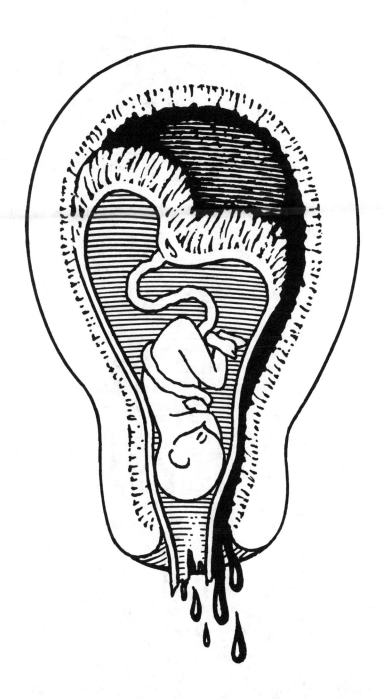

Inevitable Abortion

Figure 56

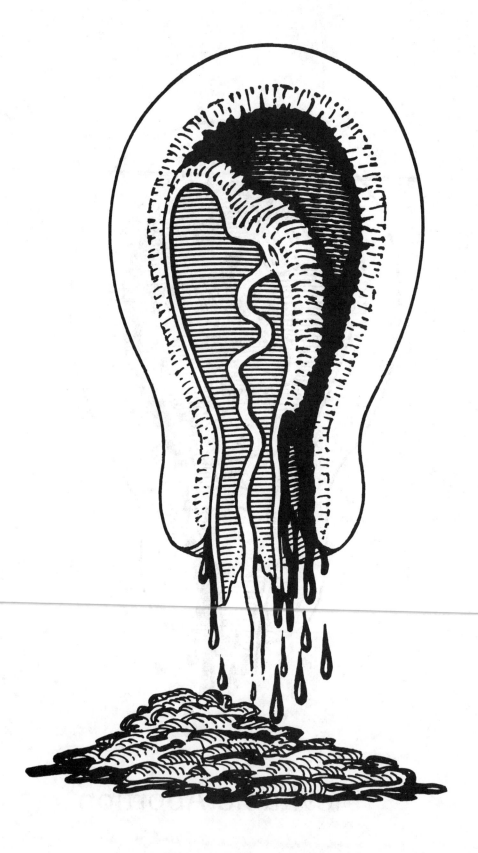

Incomplete Abortion

Figure 57

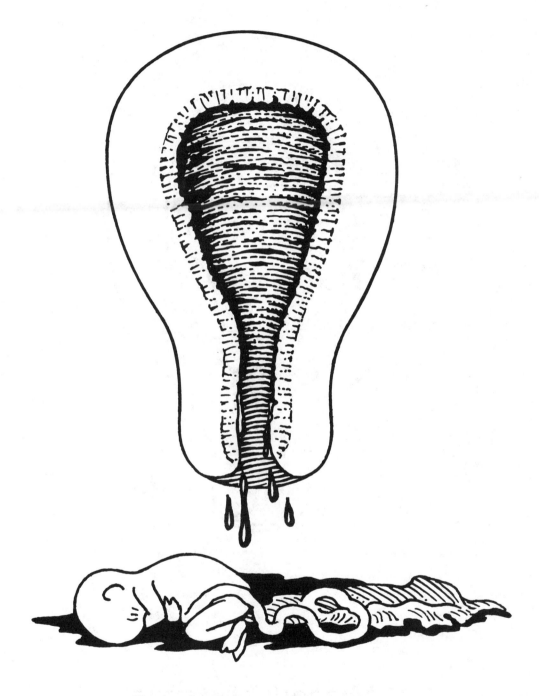

Complete Abortion

Figure 58

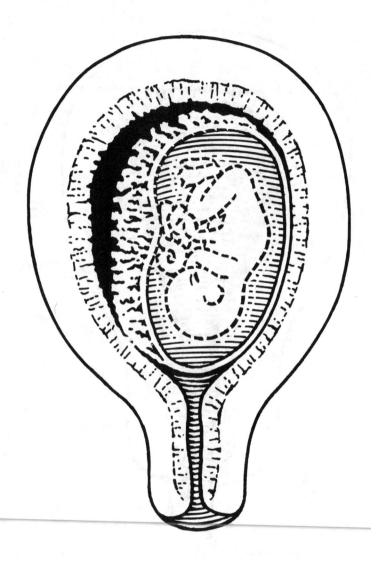

Missed Abortion

Figure 59

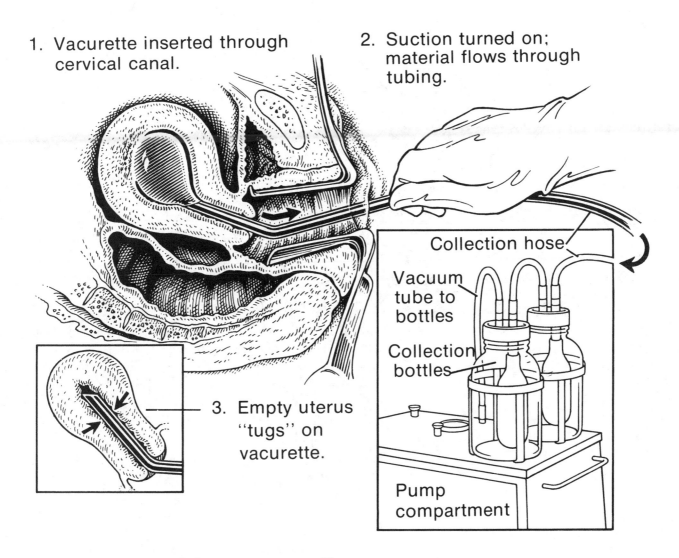

1. Vacurette inserted through cervical canal.

2. Suction turned on; material flows through tubing.

3. Empty uterus "tugs" on vacurette.

Collection hose

Vacuum tube to bottles

Collection bottles

Pump compartment

Vacuum Curettage

Figure 60

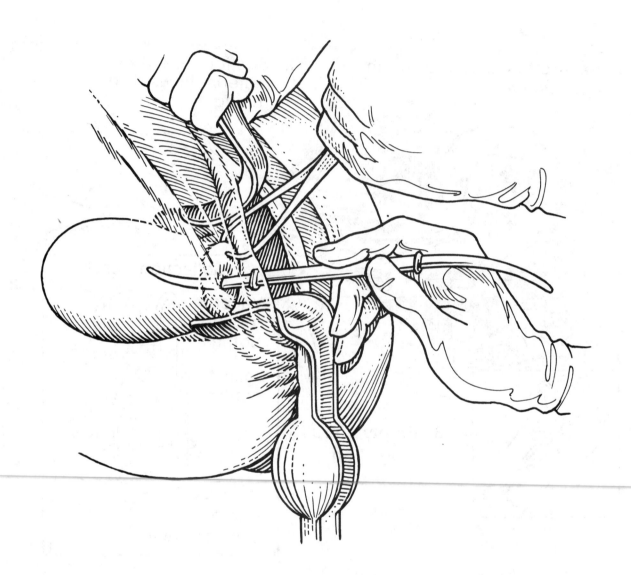

Dilatation of Cervix

Figure 61

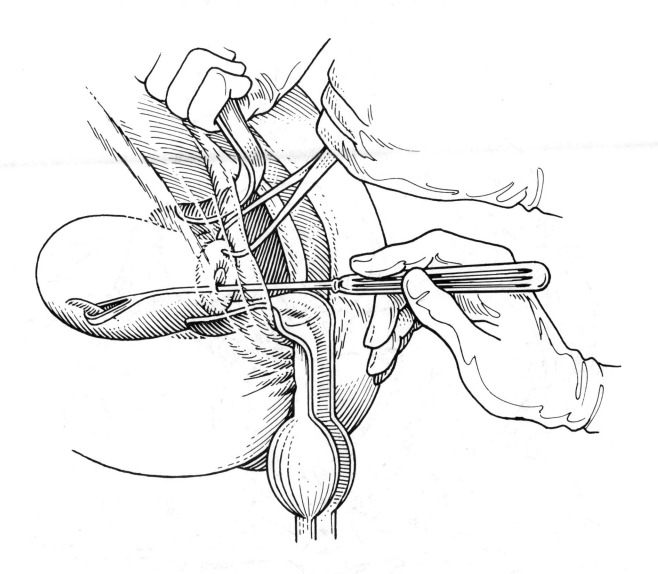

Curettage

Figure 62

Application of Silver Nitrate
at Birth

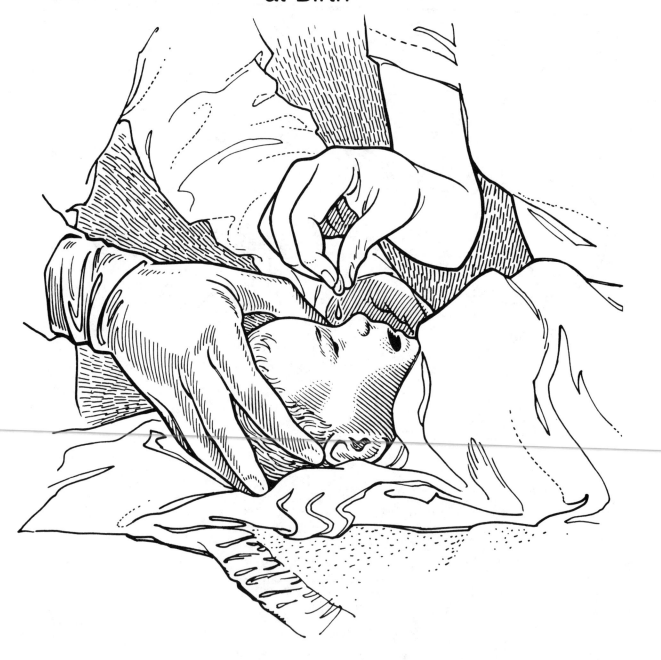

Figure 63

Gonorrhea

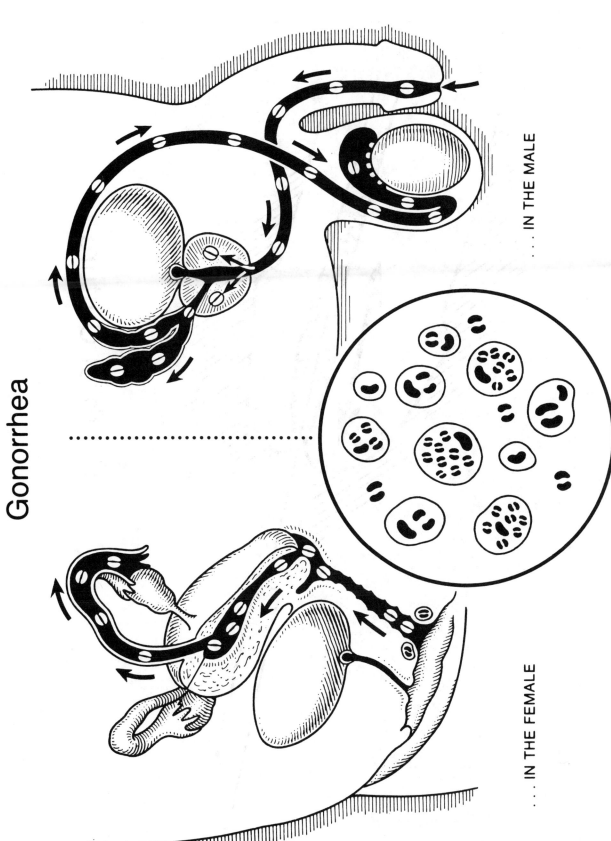

. . . IN THE MALE

. . . IN THE FEMALE

Figure 64

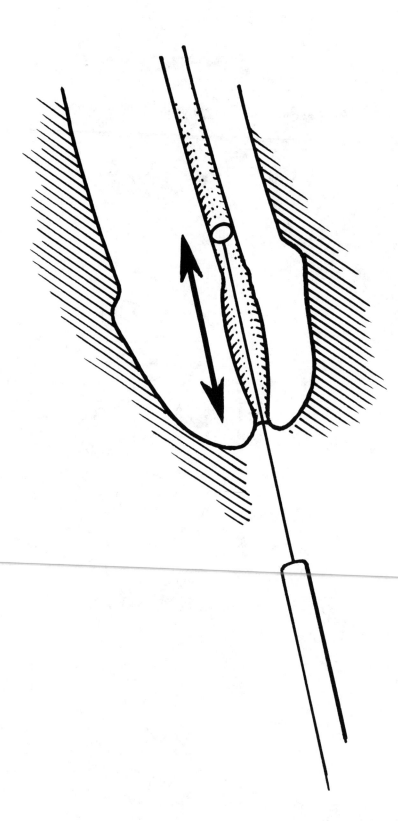

Urethral Culture

Figure 65

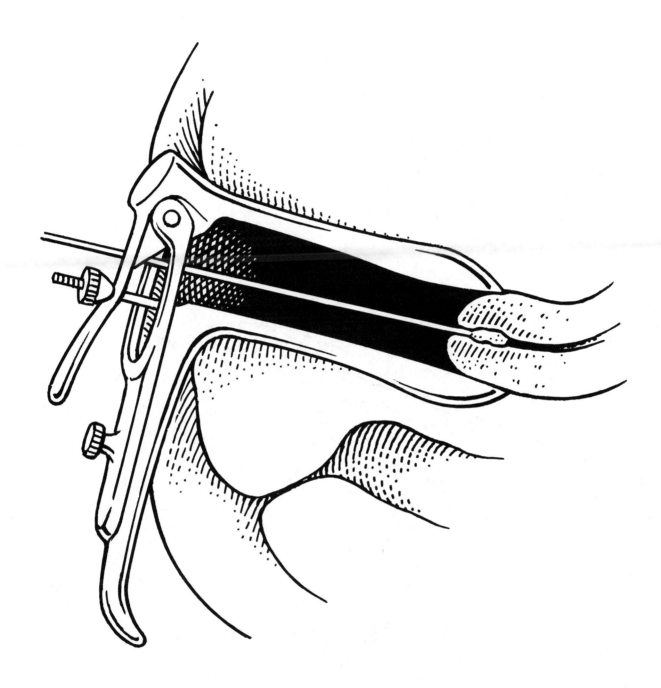

Endocervical Culture

Figure 66

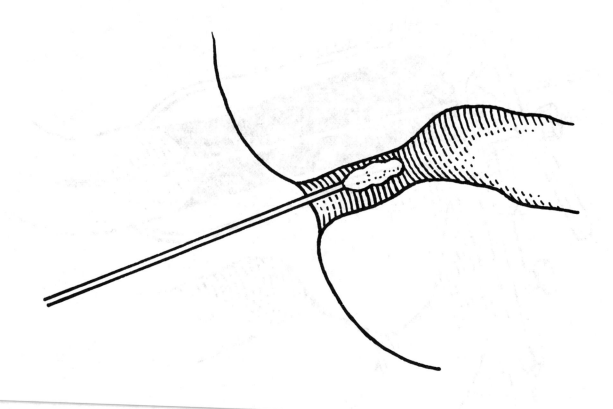

Anal Culture

Figure 67

The Stages of Syphilis

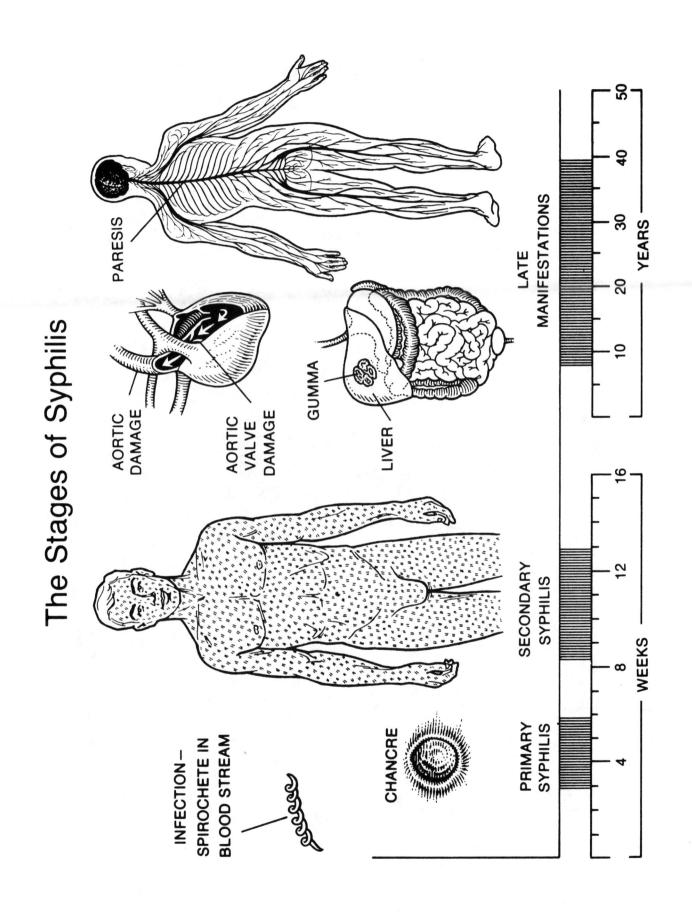

INFECTION—
SPIROCHETE IN
BLOOD STREAM

CHANCRE

PARESIS

AORTIC
DAMAGE

AORTIC
VALVE
DAMAGE

GUMMA

LIVER

LATE
MANIFESTATIONS

PRIMARY
SYPHILIS

SECONDARY
SYPHILIS

4   8   12   16
WEEKS

10   20   30   40   50
YEARS

Figure 68

Chancroid

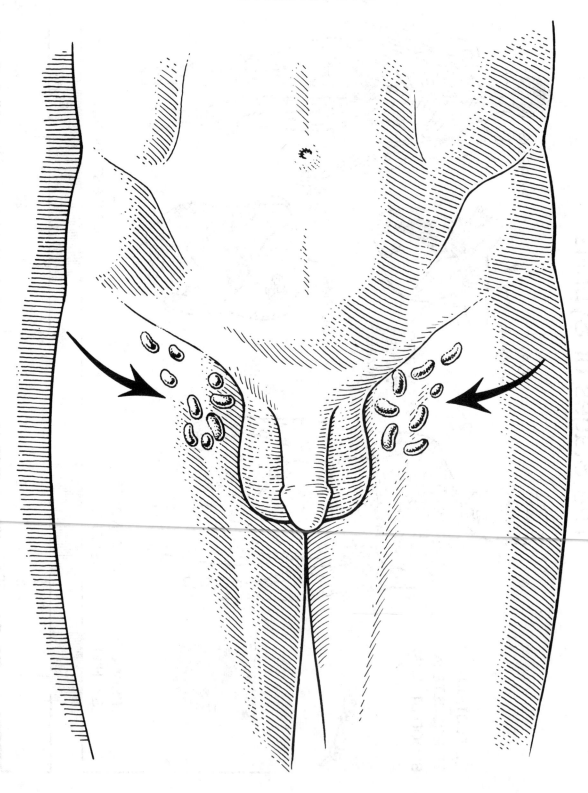

Figure 69

Comparison of the size of some agents

restrained by a condom

1. WATER AND AIR
MOLECULES (0.0001 MICRON)

2. HERPES SIMPLEX
(0.1 MICRON)

3. NEISSERIA GONORRHOEAE
(0.8 MICRON)

4. TREPONEMA PALLIDUM
(SYPHILIS) (0.2 MICRON)

5. SPERM
(3 MICRONS)

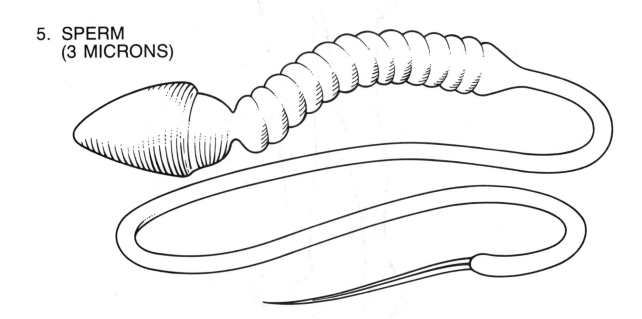

Figure 73

Male Child

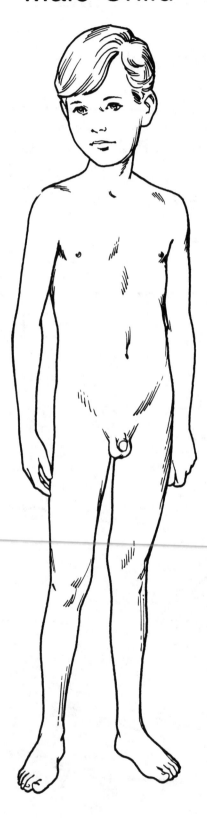

Figure 74

Female Child

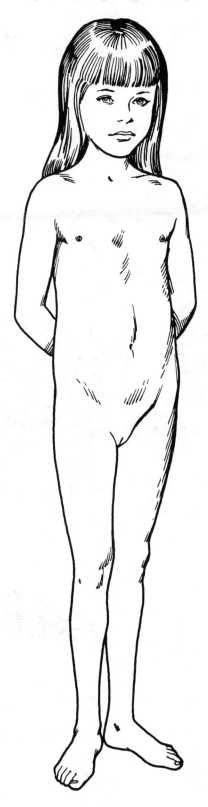

Figure 90

Let's Look at a Flower

OVARY

SEEDS

Figure 91

Model Fish

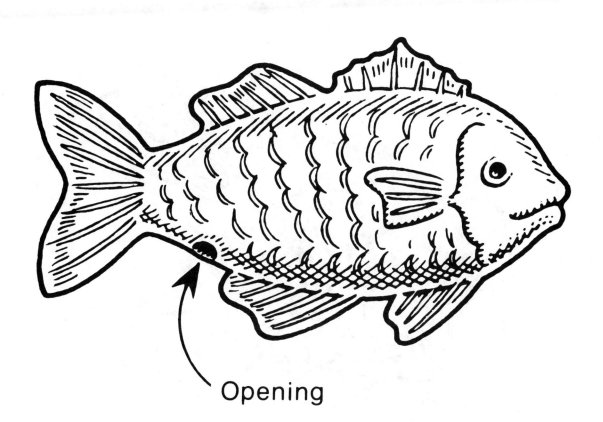

Opening

Figure 92

Frog

Figure 93

Fertilized Frog Eggs

Figure 96

Male Dog

Figure 97

Female Dog

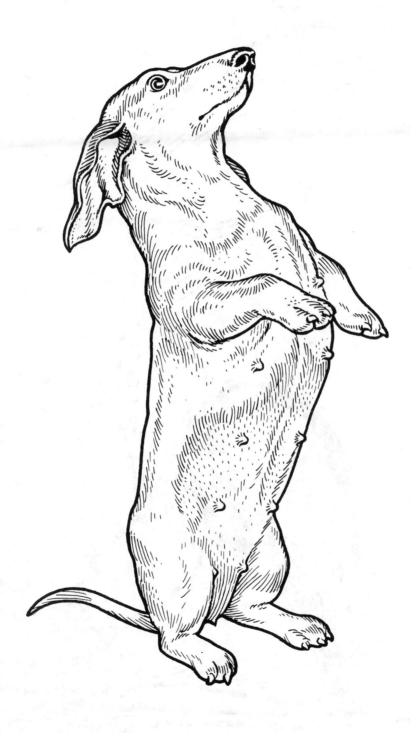

Figure 99

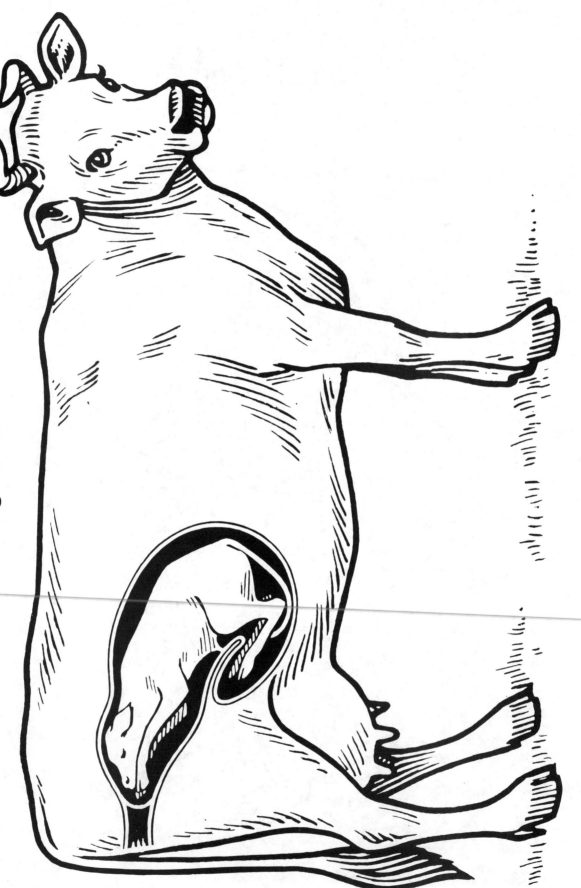

Pregnant Cow

Figure 106

The Chicken's Egg-laying System

Figure 107

How Fertilization Begins

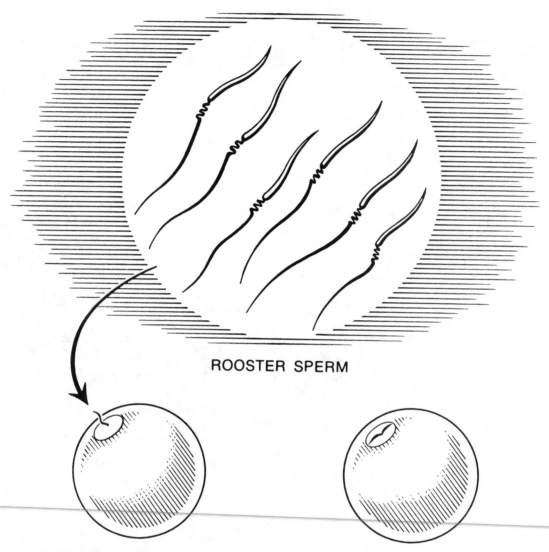

ROOSTER SPERM

A SPERM ENTERS THE
OVA FERTILIZING IT...

THE CELL DIVIDES—
FIRST SPLITTING INTO TWO...

THEN INTO FOUR...

THEN EIGHT...

AND ON AND ON

Figure 108

Development of an Egg

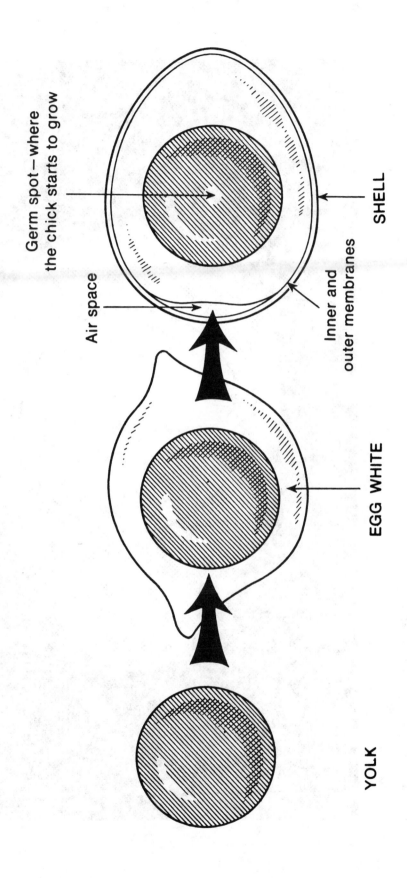

Germ spot—where the chick starts to grow

Air space

SHELL

Inner and outer membranes

EGG WHITE

YOLK

Figure 110

Growth of a Chick

Day 1

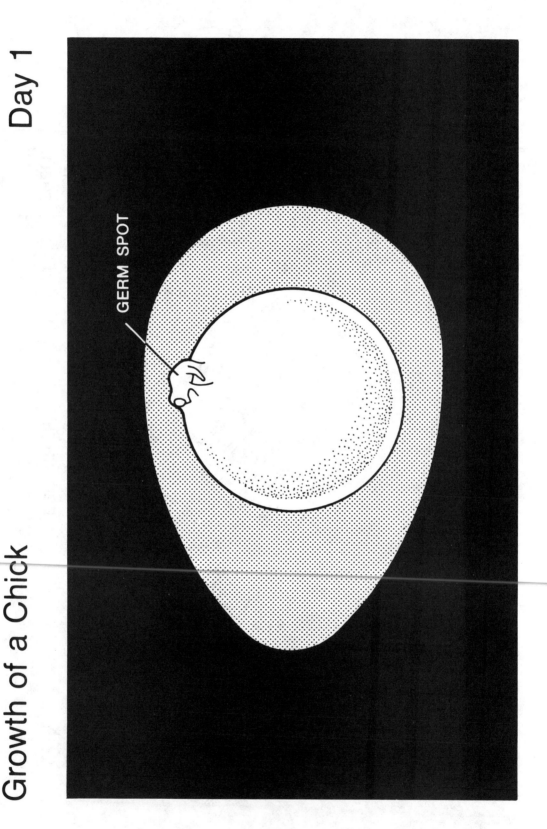

GERM SPOT

Figure 111

Growth of a Chick

Day 2

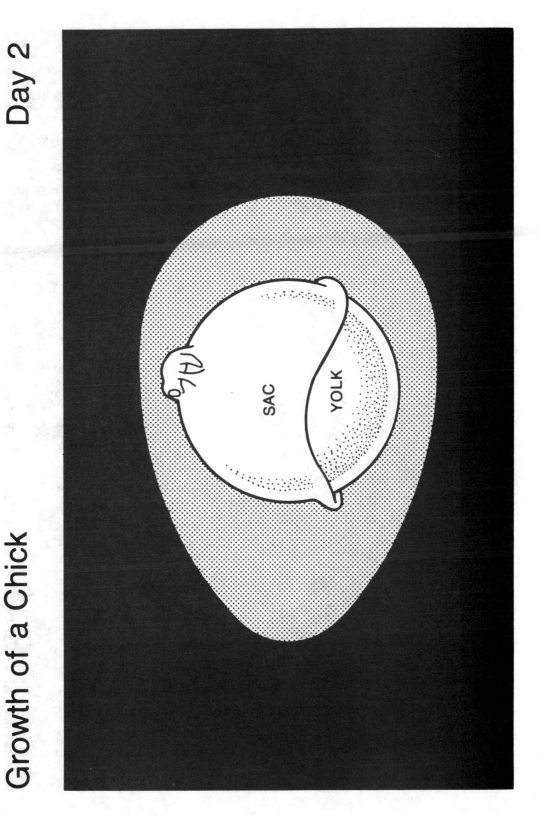

Figure 112

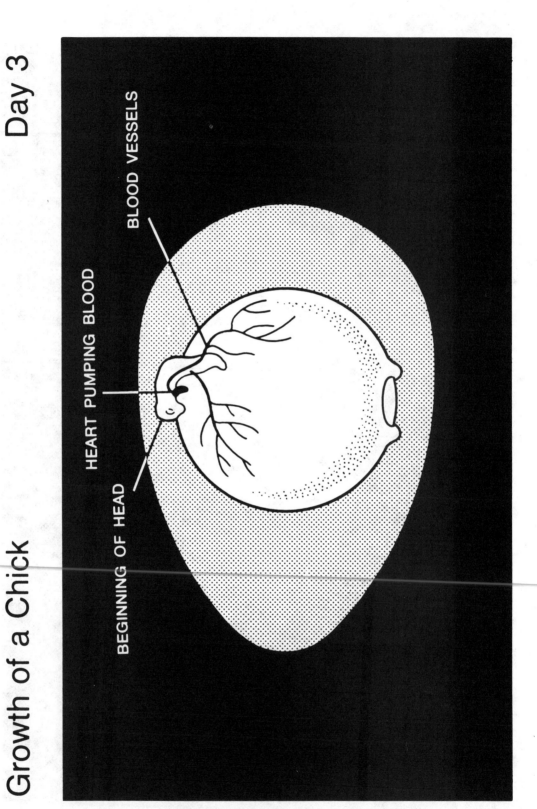

Growth of a Chick   Day 3

BLOOD VESSELS

HEART PUMPING BLOOD

BEGINNING OF HEAD

Figure 113

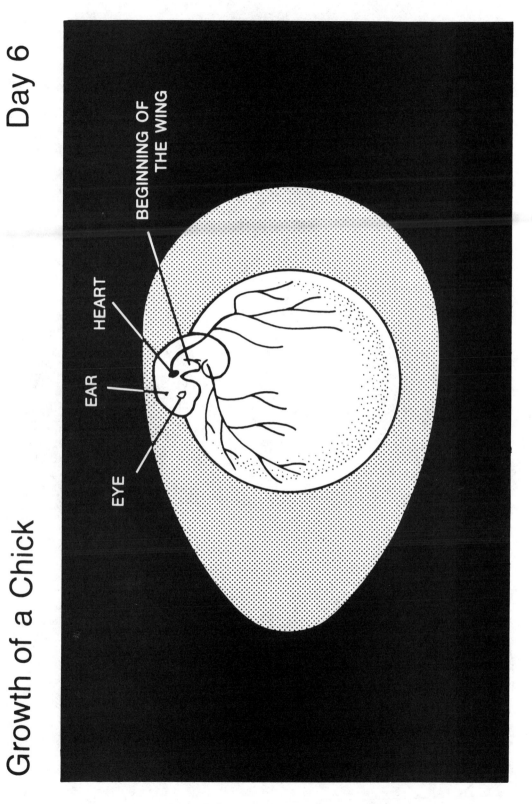

Growth of a Chick   Day 6

BEGINNING OF THE WING

HEART

EAR

EYE

Figure 114

Candling an Egg

6 DAYS

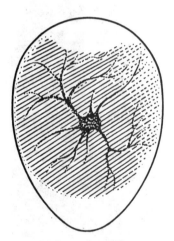

GOOD EGG

20-21 DAYS

GOOD EGG

BAD EGG

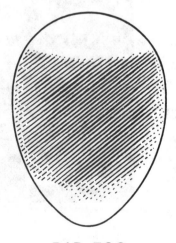

BAD EGG

Figure 115

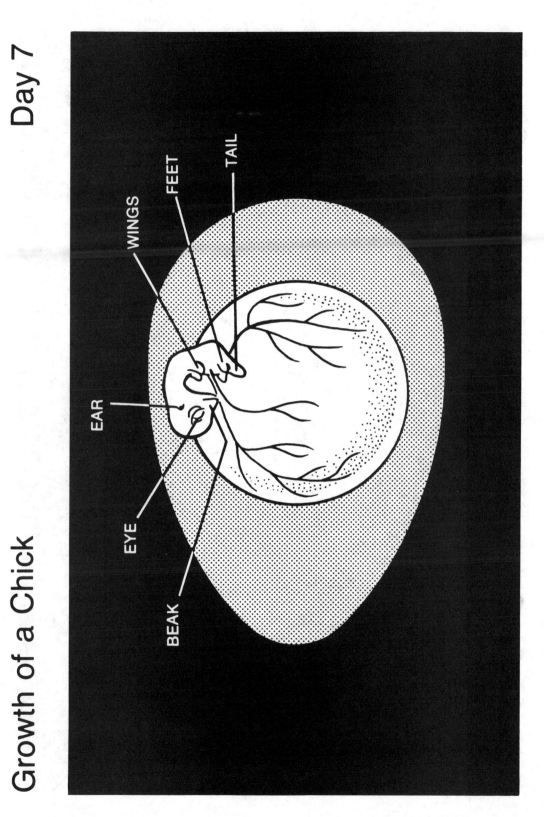

Growth of a Chick   Day 7

WINGS

FEET

TAIL

EAR

EYE

BEAK

Figure 116

Day 13

Growth of a Chick

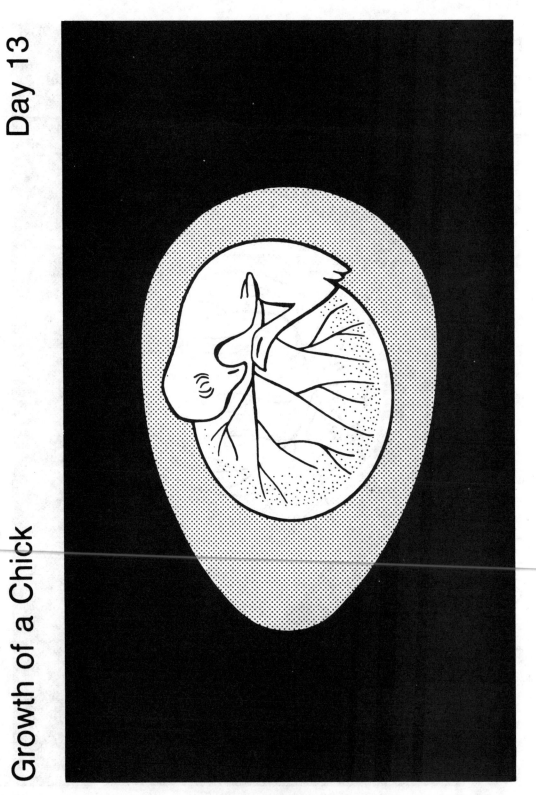

Figure 120

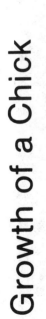

Growth of a Chick   Day 16

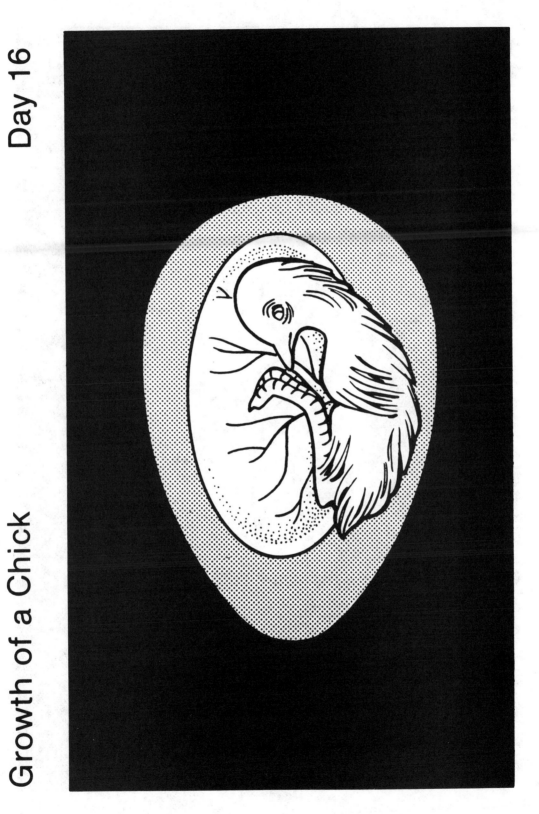

Figure 121

Day 19

Growth of a Chick

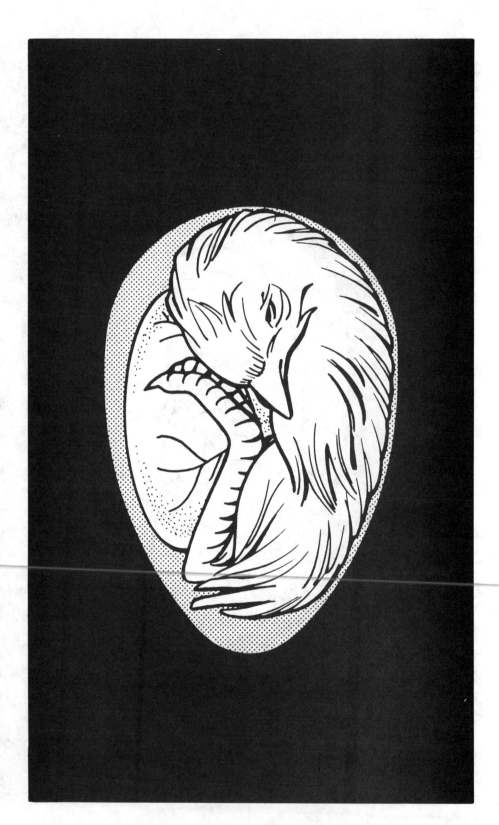

Figure 122

Day 20

Growth of a Chick

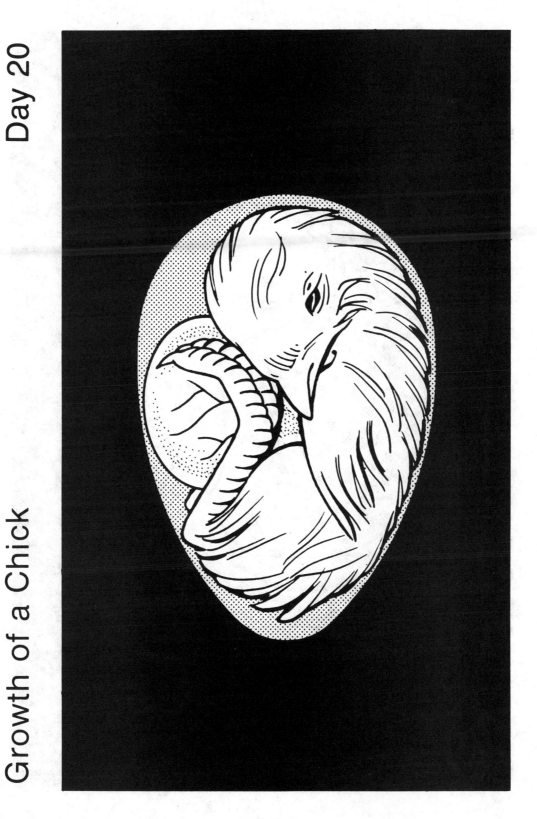

Figure 123

Day 21

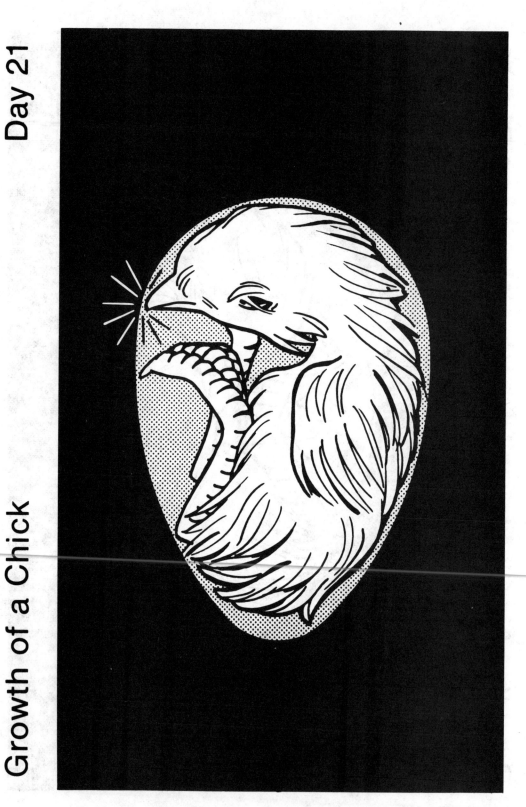

Growth of a Chick

Figure 124

The Parts of a House

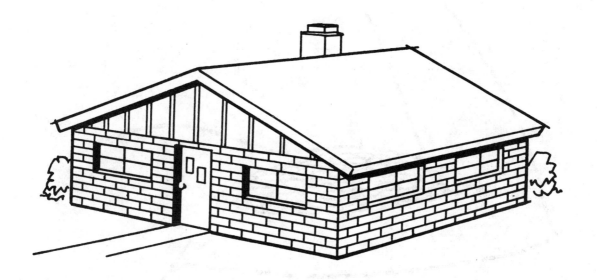

Figure 125

The Parts of a Muscle

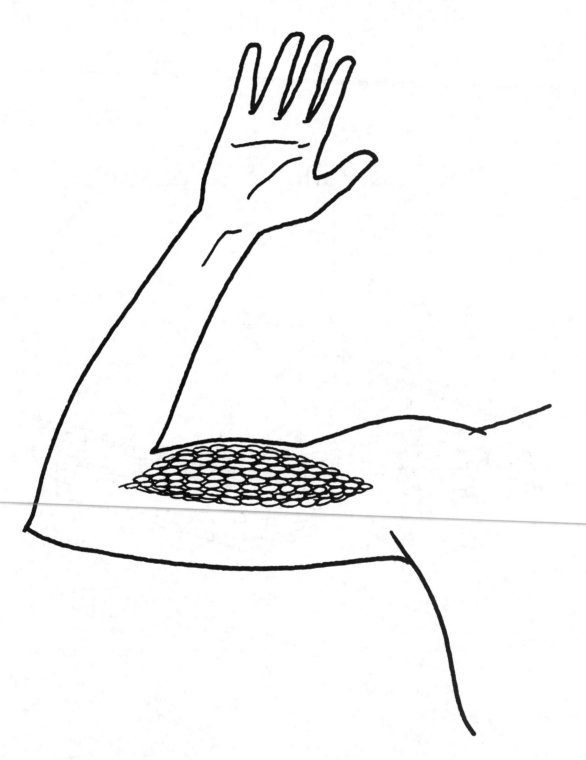

Figure 126

The Parts of a Car

Figure 127

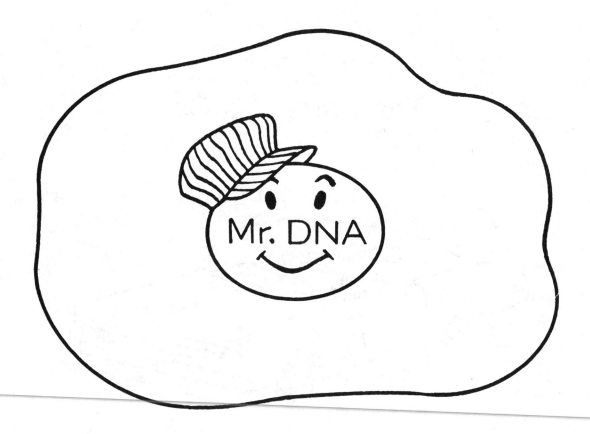

Cell

Figure 128

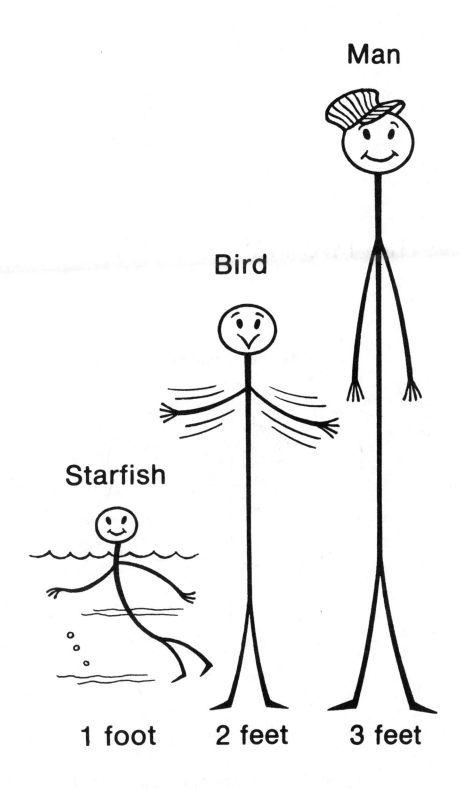

Man

Bird

Starfish

1 foot

2 feet

3 feet

Mr. DNA's length

Figure 129

The Two Halves of Mr. DNA

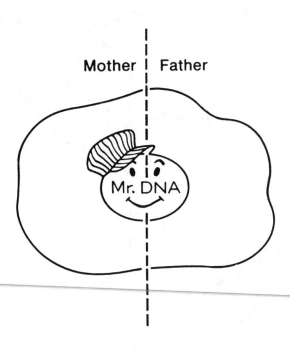

Figure 130

The Mother's Uterus

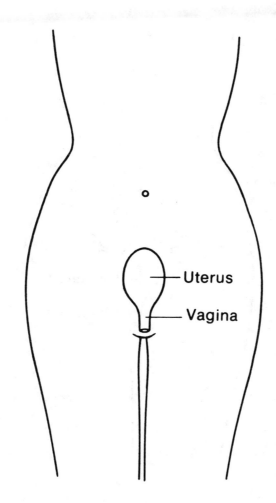

Figure 131

The Mother's Ovaries

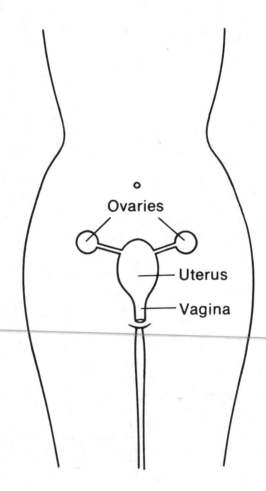